# Technologies for Sustainable Healthcare Development

Thangavel Murugan
*United Arab Emirates University, Al Ain, UAE*

Jaisingh W.
*Presidency University, India*

Varalakshmi P.
*Anna University, India*

A volume in the Advances in Medical Technologies and Clinical Practice (AMTCP) Book Series

Published in the United States of America by
IGI Global
Medical Information Science Reference (an imprint of IGI Global)
701 E. Chocolate Avenue
Hershey PA, USA 17033
Tel: 717-533-8845
Fax: 717-533-8661
E-mail: cust@igi-global.com
Web site: http://www.igi-global.com



Library of Congress Cataloging-in-Publication Data

Names: Murugan, Thangavel, 1989- editor. | W., Jaisingh, 1978- editor. | P, Varalakshmi, 1970- editor.
Title: Technologies for sustainable healthcare development / edited by Thangavel Murugan, Jaisingh W, Varalakshmi P.
Description: Hershey PA : Engineering Science Reference, [2024]. | Includes bibliographical references and index. | Summary: "The objective of the book is to provide an in-depth exploration of the intersection between cybersecurity, data science, and Industry 5.0 technologies in the context of healthcare"-- Provided by publisher.
Identifiers: LCCN 2024007196 (print) | LCCN 2024007197 (ebook) | ISBN 9798369329016 (hardcover) | ISBN 9798369329023 (ebook)
Subjects: LCSH: Medical care--Data processing. | Medical innovations.
Classification: LCC R858 .A3 T43 2024 (print) | LCC R858 .A3 (ebook) | DDC 610.285--dc23/eng/20240418
LC record available at https://lccn.loc.gov/2024007196
LC ebook record available at https://lccn.loc.gov/2024007197

British Cataloguing in Publication Data
A Cataloguing in Publication record for this book is available from the British Library.

# Advances in Medical Technologies and Clinical Practice (AMTCP) Book Series

Srikanta Patnaik
SOA University, India
Priti Das
S.C.B. Medical College, India

ISSN:2327-9354
EISSN:2327-9370

## Mission

Medical technological innovation continues to provide avenues of research for faster and safer diagnosis and treatments for patients. Practitioners must stay up to date with these latest advancements to provide the best care for nursing and clinical practices.

The **Advances in Medical Technologies and Clinical Practice (AMTCP) Book Series** brings together the most recent research on the latest technology used in areas of nursing informatics, clinical technology, biomedicine, diagnostic technologies, and more. Researchers, students, and practitioners in this field will benefit from this fundamental coverage on the use of technology in clinical practices.

## Coverage

- Clinical High-Performance Computing
- Clinical Nutrition
- Diagnostic Technologies
- E-Health
- Medical Informatics
- Nursing Informatics

IGI Global is currently accepting manuscripts for publication within this series. To submit a proposal for a volume in this series, please contact our Acquisition Editors at Acquisitions@igi-global.com or visit: http://www.igi-global.com/publish/.

The Advances in Medical Technologies and Clinical Practice (AMTCP) Book Series (ISSN 2327-9354) is published by IGI Global, 701 E. Chocolate Avenue, Hershey, PA 17033-1240, USA, www.igi-global.com. This series is composed of titles available for purchase individually; each title is edited to be contextually exclusive from any other title within the series. For pricing and ordering information please visit http://www.igi-global.com/book-series/advances-medical-technologies-clinical-practice/73682. Postmaster: Send all address changes to above address. 

## Titles in this Series

For a list of additional titles in this series, please visit: www.igi-global.com/book-series

*Revolutionizing Healthcare Treatment With Sensor Technology*
Sima Das (Bengal College of Engineering and Technology, India) Parijat Bhowmick (Indian Institute of Technology, Guwahati, India) and Dr. Kitmo (National Advanced School of Engineering of Maroua, University of Maroua, Cameroon)
Medical Information Science Reference • copyright 2024 • 371pp • H/C (ISBN: 9798369327623) • US $495.00 (our price)

*Clinical and Comparative Research on Maternal Health*
P. Paramasivan (Dhaanish Ahmed College of Engineering, India) S. Suman Rajest (Dhaanish Ahmed College of Engineering, India) Karthikeyan Chinnusamy (Veritas, USA) R. Regin (SRM Institute of Science and Technology, India) and Ferdin Joe John Joseph (Thai-Nichi Institute of Technology, Thailand)
Medical Information Science Reference • copyright 2024 • 259pp • H/C (ISBN: 9798369359419) • US $415.00 (our price)

*Advancements in Clinical Medicine*
P. Paramasivan (Dhaanish Ahmed College of Engineering, India) S. Suman Rajest (Dhaanish Ahmed College of Engineering, India) Karthikeyan Chinnusamy (Veritas, USA) R. Regin (SRM Institute of Science and Technology, India) and Ferdin Joe John Joseph (Thai-Nichi Institute of Technology, Thailand)
Medical Information Science Reference • copyright 2024 • 426pp • H/C (ISBN: 9798369359464) • US $495.00 (our price)

*Advances in Computational Intelligence for the Healthcare Industry 4.0*
Imdad Ali Shah (School of Computing Science, Taylor's University, Malaysia) and Quratulain Sial (Aga Khan University Hospital, Karachi, Pakistan)
Engineering Science Reference • copyright 2024 • 371pp • H/C (ISBN: 9798369323335) • US $425.00 (our price)

*Enhancing Medical Imaging with Emerging Technologies*
Avinash Kumar Sharma (Sharda University, India) Nitin Chanderwal (University of Cincinnati, USA) Shobhit Tyagi (Sharda University, India) Prashant Upadhyay (Sharda University, India) and Amit Kumar Tyagi (National Institute of Fashion Technology, New Delhi, India)
Medical Information Science Reference • copyright 2024 • 394pp • H/C (ISBN: 9798369352618) • US $415.00 (our price)

701 East Chocolate Avenue, Hershey, PA 17033, USA
Tel: 717-533-8845 x100 • Fax: 717-533-8661
E-Mail: cust@igi-global.com • www.igi-global.com

## Titles in this Series

For a list of additional titles in this series, please visit: www.igi-global.com/book-series

*Analyzing Current Digital Healthcare Trends Using Social Networks*
Sukanta Kumar Baral (Indira Gandhi National Tribal University, India) and Richa Goel (Symbiosis International University, India)
Medical Information Science Reference • copyright 2024 • 309pp • H/C (ISBN: 9798369319345) • US $360.00 (our price)

701 East Chocolate Avenue, Hershey, PA 17033, USA
Tel: 717-533-8845 x100 • Fax: 717-533-8661
E-Mail: cust@igi-global.com • www.igi-global.com

# Table of Contents

**Preface** .......... xvii

**Acknowledgment** .......... xxii

**Chapter 1**
A Study on Information and Communication Technology for Sustainable Healthcare Growth and Development in G20 Countries .......... 1
*Pallabi Mukherjee, IPS Academy, Institute of Business Management and Research, Indore, India*
*Kali Charan Modak, IPS Academy, Institute of Business Management and Research, Indore, India*
*Sanju Mahawar, IPS Academy, Institute of Business Management and Research, Indore, India*

**Chapter 2**
Data Science Advancements in Healthcare, Education, and Cities: An Overview .......... 17
*Virendra Singh Kushwah, VIT Bhopal University, India*
*Jyoti Parashar, Dr. Akhilesh Das Gupta Institute of Technology and Management, India*
*Partibha Dabas, Dr. Akhilesh Das Gupta Institute of Technology and Management, India*
*Lokesh Meena, Dr. Akhilesh Das Gupta Institute of Technology and Management, India*
*Vaishali Sharma, Dr. Akhilesh Das Gupta Institute of Technology and Management, India*

**Chapter 3**
Healthcare Innovation: Embracing Technology to Promote Long-Term Global Wellness .......... 37
*Swathi Mirthika G. L, SRM Institute of Science and Technology, Kattankulathur, India*
*B. Sivakumar, SRM Institute of Science and Technology, Kattankulathur, India*

**Chapter 4**
The Role of IoT in Modern Healthcare: Innovations and Challenges in Pandemic Era .......... 57
*Pardhu Thottempudi, BVRIT HYDERABAD College of Engineering for Women, India*
*Vijay Kumar, Vellore Institute of Technology, India*

**Chapter 5**
IoT as Wearable Device in Smart Healthcare Systems: A New Paradigm .......... 81
*Pon Harshavardhanan, VIT Bhopal University, India*
*Preetam Suman, VIT Bhopal University, India*
*Soumya Sankar Ghosh, VIT Bhopal University, India*

**Chapter 6**
Design of a Smart Walking Stick for the Visually Impaired Using Internet of Things .......... 97

## Titles in this Series

For a list of additional titles in this series, please visit: www.igi-global.com/book-series

*Analyzing Current Digital Healthcare Trends Using Social Networks*
Sukanta Kumar Baral (Indira Gandhi National Tribal University, India) and Richa Goel (Symbiosis International University, India)
Medical Information Science Reference • copyright 2024 • 309pp • H/C (ISBN: 9798369319345) • US $360.00 (our price)

701 East Chocolate Avenue, Hershey, PA 17033, USA
Tel: 717-533-8845 x100 • Fax: 717-533-8661
E-Mail: cust@igi-global.com • www.igi-global.com

# Table of Contents

*Nirmala Devi M., Thiagarajar College of Engineering, India*
*Thangavel Murugan, United Arab Emirates University, Al Ain, UAE*
*R. Karthigeyan, Thiagarajar College of Engineering, India*
*B. Subbulakshmi, Thiagarajar College of Engineering, India*

**Chapter 7**
An Automated Drug Dispenser Mobile Application Using Internet of Things (IoT) in Smart Healthcare Systems ............ 115
*Nirmala Devi M., Thiagarajar College of Engineering, India*
*Subbulakshmi B., Thiagarajar College of Engineering, India*
*Sree Harish T., Thiagarajar College of Engineering, India*
*Muthukumaran S., Thiagarajar College of Engineering, India*
*Vignesh G., Thiagarajar College of Engineering, India*
*Niranjan L., Thiagarajar College of Engineering, India*

**Chapter 8**
Enhancing Healthcare Through Remote Patient Monitoring Using Internet of Things ............ 133
*K. Ramalakshmi, PSR Engineering College, India*
*L. Krishna Kumari, Ramco Institute of Technology, India*
*R. Rajalakshmi, Ramco Institute of Technology, India*
*G. Theivanathan, Velammal Engineering College, India*

**Chapter 9**
AIoT-Powered Intelligent Remote Patient Activity Tracking and Comprehensive Vital Sign Analysis System for Enhanced Healthcare ............ 147
*D. Manimegalai, Rajalakshmi Engineering College, India*
*R. Gunasekari, Sri Sairam College of Engineering, India*
*S. Sujatha, Sri Sairam College of Engineering, India*
*M. Karthikeyan, Chennai Institute of Technology, India*
*A. Umasankar, Yanbu Industrial College, Saudi Arabia*

**Chapter 10**
Adoption of Robotic Technology in Healthcare Management ............ 174
*Sunil Kumar, Shoolini University, India*
*Saloni Rajput, Lovely Professional University, India*
*Anagha Ajith, Lovely Professional University, India*

**Chapter 11**
Current State of Robotic Surgery and Telesurgery: A Review of Current Developments and Future Insights ............ 194
*Santhosh Kumar Rajamani, MAEER MIT Pune's MIMER Medical College, India & Dr. BSTR Hospital, India*
*Radha Srinivasan Iyer, SEC Centre for Independent Living, India*
*Iftekhar Ahmed, University of Asia Pacific, Bangladesh*

**Chapter 12**

Baby Care With Robotic Cradle Using IoT Cloud Network ............................................................ 217
*Sugumaran S., Sreenivasa Institute of Technology and Management Studies, India*
*Chitra M. G., Vellore Institute of Technology, India*
*Thiyagupriyadharsan M. R., VIT Bhopal University, India*
*Devaraju S, VIT Bhopal University, India*
*Sivasankaran V., VIT Bopal University, India*

**Chapter 13**
The Nexus of Care: Human-Machine Collaboration Redefining Healthcare Delivery ...................... 230
*Jaspreet Kaur, Chandigarh University, India*

**Chapter 14**
Healthcare Integrating Automation and Robotics-Based Industry 5.0 Advancement ....................... 254
*P. Sindhu, Madurai Kamaraj University, India*
*M. Sivakumar, Madurai Kamaraj University, India*

**Chapter 15**
Industry 5.0 and Its Transformative Impact on Healthcare: A Paradigm Shift Toward Human-Centric Collaboration.......................................................................................................... 265
*Kavitha Murugan, Sri Krishna College of Engineering and Technology, India*
*Jayasudha Subburaj, Sri Krishna College of Engineering and Technology, India*
*Keerthana P., Sri Krishna College of Engineering and Technology, India*
*Roobini S., SNS College of Technology, Coimbatore, India*

**Chapter 16**
The Impact and Integration of Cloud Computing for Enhanced Patient Care and Operational Efficiency ......................................................................................................... 277
*M. Prabu, Amrita Vishwa Vidyapeetham, Chennai, India*
*M. Diviya, Amrita Vishwa Vidyapeetham, Chennai, India*
*R. Bhuvaneswari, Amrita Vishwa Vidyapeetham, Chennai, India*
*Doddi Sreenija Reddy, Amrita Vishwa Vidyapeetham, Chennai, India*
*K. Venkatesan, Amrita Vishwa Vidyapeetham, Chennai, India*
*Arul Kumar Natarajan, Samarkand International University of Technology, Uzbekistan*

**Chapter 17**
Integrating Cyber-Physical Systems for Enhanced Efficiency in Healthcare Solutions .................... 300
*Padmavathi U., Shiv Nadar University, Chennai, India*
*Harshitha R. S., Shiv Nadar University, Chennai, India*
*Jayashre K., Shiv Nadar University, Chennai, India*
*Nidhi Gummaraju, Shiv Nadar University, Chennai, India*

**Chapter 18**
Urban Oasis: Harnessing IoT for Green Healthcare in Smart City Landscape.................................. 325
*Jaspreet Kaur, Chandigarh University, India*

**About the Contributors** ......................................................................................................... 384

# Detailed Table of Contents

**Preface** ............................................................ xvii

**Acknowledgment** ............................................................ xxii

**Chapter 1**
A Study on Information and Communication Technology for Sustainable Healthcare Growth and Development in G20 Countries ............................................................ 1
*Pallabi Mukherjee, IPS Academy, Institute of Business Management and Research, Indore, India*
*Kali Charan Modak, IPS Academy, Institute of Business Management and Research, Indore, India*
*Sanju Mahawar, IPS Academy, Institute of Business Management and Research, Indore, India*

This study delves into the intricate interplay between healthcare, economic growth, and information and communication technology (ICT) within the G20 countries. Through rigorous analysis and employing a semi-log model, the authors investigate the tripartite relationship between these crucial domains. Utilizing health indicators and GDP per capita as metrics, alongside internet user statistics, this research explores correlations and causalities. By focusing on countries like Argentina and the United States, the authors elucidate the impact of growth and ICT on healthcare systems. This study contributes nuanced insights vital for fostering sustainable healthcare development amidst evolving technological landscapes in the G20 nations.

**Chapter 2**
Data Science Advancements in Healthcare, Education, and Cities: An Overview ............................................................ 17
*Virendra Singh Kushwah, VIT Bhopal University, India*
*Jyoti Parashar, Dr. Akhilesh Das Gupta Institute of Technology and Management, India*
*Partibha Dabas, Dr. Akhilesh Das Gupta Institute of Technology and Management, India*
*Lokesh Meena, Dr. Akhilesh Das Gupta Institute of Technology and Management, India*
*Vaishali Sharma, Dr. Akhilesh Das Gupta Institute of Technology and Management, India*

Data science, a prominent subset of artificial intelligence (AI), specializes in analyzing vast datasets using diverse tools and methods to derive insights and predictions. Its applications span various domains, notably cybersecurity, crucial for safeguarding systems and data from internal and external threats amid escalating challenges. The integration of data science in sectors like energy and environment underscores its transformative potential. The digitization of energy systems enables real-time data acquisition, facilitating timely analysis of human impacts on the environment and society. Furthermore, data science aids in monitoring policy effectiveness towards sustainable development (SD) goals. However, the rapid evolution of technology presents formidable challenges, necessitating organizational adaptability and utilization of cutting-edge advancements, especially in online communication. Amidst these shifts, data science emerges as a pivotal tool for informed decision-making and innovation, poised to make significant

contributions across diverse sectors of the economy.



The practical use of technology in healthcare is a nascent discipline focused on promoting sustainability within the healthcare sector. Nevertheless, the research in this field has experienced significant and swift growth. Although this expansion has been beneficial for the discipline, it has also rendered it more challenging to comprehend its full scope. Thus, it has become impossible to answer questions about the biggest technological shifts in sustainable healthcare research, the most important revolution articles, their influence, and the most prolific and prominent scholars. Understanding the logical framework of technology for sustainable long-term healthcare information is difficult. An in-depth assessment of studies on revolutionary healthcare technology that promotes long-term health addressed these issues. It did so to address some of the issues. Over the past four years, the COVID-19 pandemic, artificial intelligence, machine learning, and the internet of things have propelled sustainable healthcare technology research.



This chapter delves into the internet of things, a pivotal technological innovation incorporating sensors across various fields. Sensors in IoT are essential for data collection and crucial for detailed analyticity's impact is profound in developing smart cities, modern agriculture, digital education, and healthcare, particularly noticeable during the COVID-19 pandemic, highlighting the need for digital healthcare solutions. IoT significantly enhances healthcare by enabling precise patient monitoring through a digital network. This study examines the applications of IoT, technological challenges, and barriers in healthcare, drawing on databases like Google Scholar, Elsevier, and PubMed. The discussion underscores the importance of IoT in healthcare, opening avenues for new research and tackling industry challenges. It shows IoT's role in improving healthcare services, combining it with advanced technologies to expand its beneficial impact. The chapter addresses potential challenges and offers strategies to improve IoT-based healthcare, focusing on COVID-19 and future health crises.



Portable healthcare monitoring systems with internet of things (IoT) are now a major issue for many nations across the world due to the significant growth of healthcare monitoring systems. The use of IoT-based health monitoring solutions can result in the elimination of routine doctor visits and consultations. IoT is utilized in a health monitoring system that can monitor a person's temperature, heart rate, blood pressure, and oxygen saturation. Moreover, the device enhanced with NLP analyzes speech and sound to extract disease-specific information, adding a new dimension to traditional metrics. The voice captured in the device is pushed into the cloud storage, like AWS S3. The machine learning model, which was trained, is loaded to analyze this file using machine learning run time environments like AWS SageMaker. Now if a patient's health falls outside the expected range, the IoT system will let the clinician know. The medical staff can process and evaluate their current state by processing information about patients' ailments through a gateway.



In the ever-evolving landscape of assistive technologies, the visually impaired community encounters unique challenges in pursuing heightened mobility and environmental awareness. The endeavor to navigate through perpetually shifting and often unpredictable surroundings necessitates innovative solutions that empower individuals with visual impairments, granting them the ability to traverse with newfound confidence and independence. This research aims to explore the groundbreaking realm of the smart walking stick, an ingeniously designed assistive device that seamlessly integrates cutting-edge technologies, notably Arduino and ultrasonic sensors. At its essence, the main objective of this design is to respond to the urgent and compelling need for advanced navigation tools that can offer real-time obstacle detection and deliver tactile feedback, thereby enhancing the overall mobility experience for individuals with visual impairments.



The automated drug dispenser (ADD) represents a revolutionary leap in healthcare accessibility, seamlessly integrating advanced pharmaceutical technologies to streamline obtaining prescribed medications. This cutting-edge system leverages the power of the internet of things (IoT), mobile app development, database management, and cloud computing to create a patient-centric approach to medication dispensation. It is a user-friendly interface that transforms the patient experience. By employing a mobile app, individuals can effortlessly navigate through the system, initiating the drug retrieval process with a simple QR code scan. This enhances efficiency and ensures accuracy, as the system rapidly identifies and dispenses the correct medication. A pivotal feature of ADD is its utilization of specific patient details to establish a secure connection. By referencing individualized information, the system not only verifies the patient's identity but also updates a centralized and protected database.

*K. Ramalakshmi, PSR Engineering College, India*
*L. Krishna Kumari, Ramco Institute of Technology, India*
*R. Rajalakshmi, Ramco Institute of Technology, India*
*G. Theivanathan, Velammal Engineering College, India*

The integration of the internet of things (IoT) in healthcare has revolutionized patient care, leading to the emergence of remote healthcare monitoring solutions. Leveraging connected devices and sensors, this system enables real-time tracking of vital health parameters, medication adherence, and overall wellness metrics outside traditional healthcare settings. The IoT infrastructure facilitates seamless communication between patients and healthcare providers, promoting timely interventions and personalized care plans. Security and privacy concerns are addressed through advanced encryption and authentication measures, ensuring the confidentiality of sensitive health data. Key considerations for the implementation of IoT-based remote healthcare monitoring, including device interoperability, data standardization, and user engagement, are discussed. The potential benefits of this technology include enhanced patient engagement, early detection of health issues, and reduced healthcare costs.

**Chapter 9**
AIoT-Powered Intelligent Remote Patient Activity Tracking and Comprehensive Vital Sign Analysis System for Enhanced Healthcare ........ 147
*D. Manimegalai, Rajalakshmi Engineering College, India*
*R. Gunasekari, Sri Sairam College of Engineering, India*
*S. Sujatha, Sri Sairam College of Engineering, India*
*M. Karthikeyan, Chennai Institute of Technology, India*
*A. Umasankar, Yanbu Industrial College, Saudi Arabia*

This chapter explores the integration of artificial intelligence of things (AIoT) with tele-health monitoring, presenting an intelligent remote patient activity tracking system. Using interconnected sensors and machine learning models, the system monitors various patient activities and vital signs, providing real-time insights. The proposed AIoT-enabled health monitoring device tracks activities such as running, sleeping, walking, and exercising, while observing vital signs like heart rate and breathing patterns. The chapter delves into the system's architecture, functionalities, and technical intricacies, emphasizing its potential to transform healthcare delivery. It highlights the role of AIoT-driven solutions in enhancing patient care and fostering personalized treatment approaches, offering a glimpse into the promising future of intelligent healthcare delivery.

**Chapter 10**
Adoption of Robotic Technology in Healthcare Management ........ 174
*Sunil Kumar, Shoolini University, India*
*Saloni Rajput, Lovely Professional University, India*
*Anagha Ajith, Lovely Professional University, India*

This chapter provides a comprehensive exploration of the evolution and impact of robotic surgery in the medical domain. From historical origins to contemporary smart hospitals, the narrative covers the technological advancements and challenges associated with robotic surgery, offering insights from two experienced surgeons. Aligning with the unified theory of acceptance and use of technology (UTAUT), their lived experiences highlight factors such as performance expectancy, effort expectancy, social influence, facilitating conditions, and moderating factors shaping their acceptance of robotic technology.

The research also delves into broader implications on patient satisfaction, healthcare outcomes, and the ethical considerations of human-machine collaboration. Emphasizing the transformative potential of robotic surgery, the chapter underscores the need to address barriers for widespread adoption to fully harness its benefits in enhancing patient care.

**Chapter 11**
Current State of Robotic Surgery and Telesurgery: A Review of Current Developments and Future Insights ........ 194
*Santhosh Kumar Rajamani, MAEER MIT Pune's MIMER Medical College, India & Dr. BSTR Hospital, India*
*Radha Srinivasan Iyer, SEC Centre for Independent Living, India*
*Iftekhar Ahmed, University of Asia Pacific, Bangladesh*

Robotic surgery and its extension, telesurgery, have emerged as significant advancements in the field of surgical procedures. This technique involves the use of robotic systems to assist surgeons in performing complex operations with enhanced precision and control. The key points regarding robotic surgery can be summarized as follows: Firstly, robotic surgery offers several advantages over traditional open surgery and laparoscopic procedures. The use of robotic systems allows for smaller incisions, resulting in reduced trauma to the patient's body. Additionally, the robotic arms provide a greater range of motion and dexterity, enabling surgeons to access hard-to-reach areas more easily. These cumulative benefits contribute to shorter hospital stays. The utilization of robotic-assisted surgery is primarily found in the fields of urology and gynecology, with other applications found in cardiothoracic surgery, general surgery, and otorhinolaryngology. Telesurgery is an emerging technological advancement that is now implemented in a restricted range of medical establishments.

**Chapter 12**
Baby Care With Robotic Cradle Using IoT Cloud Network ........ 217
*Sugumaran S., Sreenivasa Institute of Technology and Management Studies, India*
*Chitra M. G., Vellore Institute of Technology, India*
*Thiyagupriyadharsan M. R., VIT Bhopal University, India*
*Devaraju S, VIT Bhopal University, India*
*Sivasankaran V., VIT Bopal University, India*

In this modern world, the number of working mothers has risen significantly. Before even going to outside work, she is working for the family in all aspects of cooking, washing, cleaning the room, etc. Consequently, childcare becomes a daily challenge for many mothers. However, mothers cannot constantly observe their infant's activity and childcare to family conditions and workload. In this work, baby care with smart cradle is proposed in which infant activities and health status are observed with the help of various sensors, activator, internet of things (IoT) and the cloud called as baby care robot (BC-Robot). The proposed method helps mothers to monitor and take care of the infants' activities and health status from remote location.

**Chapter 13**
The Nexus of Care: Human-Machine Collaboration Redefining Healthcare Delivery ........ 230
*Jaspreet Kaur, Chandigarh University, India*

The intersection of care is experiencing a fundamental change as the collaboration between humans and

machines grows more widespread in the delivery of healthcare. The aforementioned shift is propelled by the progress made in the fields of artificial intelligence (AI) and robotics, facilitating collaborative alliances between healthcare practitioners and intelligent machines. In the contemporary healthcare landscape, the collaboration between humans and machines is reshaping conventional roles and workflows, thereby augmenting diagnostic precision, optimising treatment approaches, and enhancing patient outcomes. This study examines the primary factors, obstacles, and potential advantages linked to the collaboration between humans and machines in the field of healthcare delivery. It emphasises the significance of interdisciplinary collaboration, ethical deliberations, and regulatory structures.



Healthcare is undergoing a significant transformation with the advantage of Industry 5.0, which is marked by the fusion of human expertise and advanced technology. This period is characterized by the integration of automation and robotics into healthcare practices, which can enhance patient care, optimize operational efficiency, and redefine medical norms. This chapter provides an overview of the use of automation and robotics in healthcare within the context of Industry 5.0. It analyzes the ways in which telemedicine, patient monitoring, and customized therapy are facilitated by robotics and automation



The era of Industry 5.0, characterized by a deep integration of technology and human cooperation, is set to bring about a major transformation in the healthcare sector. This chapter highlights a major shift toward human-centric teaming and looks at how Industry 5.0 affects healthcare. The convergence of human knowledge and state-of-the-art technologies is transforming healthcare delivery, including patient care and diagnostics. The study talks about the potentials and opportunities of Healthcare 5.0, which include more patient-centered care, telemedicine, personalized medicine, and advanced diagnostics. These are all made possible by the use of cutting-edge technologies like robotics, big data analytics, blockchain, and artificial intelligence (AI). The report also addresses the challenges and concerns that need to be resolved for healthcare 5.0 to be effectively implemented, such as data security and privacy, moral and legal dilemmas, the requirement for healthcare workers to have the right training and abilities, and cost-effectiveness.

Cloud computing is reshaping healthcare by offering a flexible solution for stakeholders to access data remotely. It revolutionizes data creation, storage, and sharing, enabling professionals to access patient information from anywhere, enhancing care and streamlining operations. Adoption is increasing due to its efficiency and innovation benefits. Services like SaaS, PaaS, and IaaS offer flexibility, driving adoption. Challenges include data breaches, necessitating robust security measures. Despite challenges, cloud computing has transformed healthcare, improving decision-making, data security, record sharing, and automation. During COVID-19, it has been crucial, highlighting its importance in advancing healthcare. Providers must embrace cloud technology for its potential to enhance medical data analysis and improve healthcare services.



The chapter explores cyber-physical systems (CPS) as a pioneering force in healthcare, amalgamating computational algorithms, communication technologies, and physical interactions to revolutionize traditional medical approaches. It addresses entrenched issues such as fragmented medical data and outdated communication methods. By harnessing wireless sensor networks, cloud computing infrastructure, and medical sensor technologies, CPS offers tailored solutions to healthcare challenges. Predictive analytics fueled by CPS-generated data empower healthcare professionals with informed decision-making capabilities. However, safeguarding patient data through robust encryption and stringent access controls remains paramount. Tangible examples illustrate CPS's impact across domains, from monitoring medication adherence to ensuring patient safety. Future research endeavors seek to enhance connectivity, fortify cybersecurity protocols, and expand CPS applications in drug development.



Healthcare systems are undergoing a change owing to the internet of things (IoT) and smart cities, which are providing ground-breaking solutions for sustainability, efficiency, and better patient care. The importance of IoT-enhanced smart cities in revolutionizing healthcare is examined in this chapter, along with its importance in addressing the rising concern for sustainability in healthcare operations. It explores how the internet of things and smart cities work together to maximize resource use, encourage ecologically friendly behaviour, and improve patient well-being.

# Preface

In recent years, the rapid advancement of Industry 5.0 technologies has resulted in significant transformations across various sectors, with healthcare being one of the most profoundly impacted. This book, *Technologies for Sustainable Healthcare Development*, focuses on the critical intersection of the Internet of Things and Data Science innovations within the context of Industry 5.0 technologies, emphasizing their vital role in the sustainable development of healthcare systems.

As editors, we have aimed to compile a comprehensive guide that addresses the challenges and opportunities presented by these technological advancements. This book is an essential resource for professionals, researchers, and policymakers keen to understand and harness the potential of these innovations for enhancing healthcare delivery and management.

The convergence of healthcare and technology has accelerated, leading to transformative innovations. The book provides insights, practical knowledge, and forward-thinking perspectives on leveraging technology to create a more sustainable and effective healthcare ecosystem. Here's how sustainable healthcare technologies fit into the current landscape:

a) Global Health Challenges: The world faces complex health challenges, including pandemics, chronic diseases, and healthcare disparities. Sustainable technologies offer solutions to improve access, affordability, and quality of care.
b) Digital Health: Digital health tools, such as telemedicine platforms, wearable devices, and health apps, have become integral. They enable remote consultations, real-time monitoring, and personalized health management.
c) Data-Driven Insights: Data science and analytics play a crucial role. By analyzing large datasets, healthcare professionals gain insights into disease patterns, treatment effectiveness, and population health trends.
d) Internet of Things (IoT): IoT devices connect patients, healthcare providers, and medical equipment. Wearables track vital signs, smart hospital infrastructure optimizes resource usage, and telehealth relies on IoT connectivity.
e) Robotics and Automation: Robotic surgery, automated drug dispensers, and AI-driven diagnostics enhance precision and efficiency. These technologies reduce human error and improve patient outcomes.
f) Cloud Computing: Cloud solutions facilitate secure data storage, collaboration, and scalability. Healthcare organizations leverage cloud platforms for electronic health records (EHRs) and telemedicine services.
g) Human-Centric Collaboration: Industry 5.0 emphasizes collaboration between humans and machines. In healthcare, this means combining technology with empathy, compassion, and patient-centered care.
h) Sustainability and Green Initiatives: Healthcare systems are increasingly adopting sustainable practices. From energy-efficient hospitals to eco-friendly medical devices, the focus is on minimizing environmental impact.

In this edited volume, we present a compendium of insightful research addressing the intersection of technology and healthcare within diverse contexts. Each chapter explores how various technological advancements are reshaping the healthcare landscape, contributing to sustainable development, and enhancing patient care. Here, we offer an overview of the critical themes and findings presented in each chapter, curated to provide a cohesive understanding of the evolving role of technology in healthcare.

**Chapter 1** delves into the intricate interplay between healthcare, economic growth, and Information and Communication Technology (ICT) within the G20 countries. Through rigorous analysis using a semi-log model, the authors investigate the tripartite relationship among these domains. By employing health indicators, GDP per capita metrics, and internet user statistics, the study explores correlations and causalities. Focusing on countries from Argentina to the United States, it elucidates the impact of economic growth and ICT on healthcare systems. The research offers nuanced insights vital for fostering sustainable healthcare development amid evolving technological landscapes in G20 nations.

Data science, as a prominent subset of artificial intelligence (AI), specializes in analyzing vast datasets to derive insights and predictions. **Chapter 2** highlights its applications across various domains, notably in cybersecurity, which is crucial for safeguarding systems and data from escalating threats. The integration of data science in energy and environmental sectors underscores its transformative potential. Real-time data acquisition through digitized systems facilitates timely analysis of human impacts on the environment and society, aiding in monitoring policy effectiveness towards sustainable development goals. Amidst rapid technological evolution, data science emerges as a pivotal tool for informed decision-making and innovation across diverse sectors of the economy.

The practical use of technology in healthcare, a nascent yet rapidly growing discipline, focuses on promoting sustainability within the sector. Despite its growth, comprehending the full scope of this field remains challenging. **Chapter 3** addresses key questions about technological shifts, revolutionary articles, and influential scholars in sustainable healthcare research. It assesses studies on healthcare technology that promotes long-term health, highlighting the impacts of the COVID-19 pandemic, artificial intelligence, machine learning, and the Internet of Things. These technologies have propelled research in sustainable healthcare, offering new avenues for addressing contemporary healthcare challenges.

**Chapter 4** explores the pivotal role of the Internet of Things (IoT) in healthcare, particularly through its incorporation of sensors for data collection and analysis. IoT's impact is profound in developing smart cities, modern agriculture, digital education, and healthcare, especially during the COVID-19 pandemic. By enabling precise patient monitoring through a digital network, IoT enhances healthcare services. The study examines IoT applications, technological challenges, and barriers in healthcare, drawing on extensive research databases. The discussion underscores IoT's importance in healthcare, opening new research avenues and addressing industry challenges, with a focus on improving healthcare services through advanced technologies.

**Chapter 5** focuses on the significant growth of healthcare monitoring systems has made portable IoT-based solutions a major focus globally. These systems can monitor vital signs such as temperature, heart rate, blood pressure, and oxygen saturation, potentially eliminating routine doctor visits. Enhanced with natural language processing (NLP), these devices analyze speech and sound to extract disease-specific information, adding a new dimension to traditional metrics. The chapter details how voice data is processed using cloud storage and machine learning models, alerting clinicians if a patient's health falls outside expected ranges. This IoT system offers a transformative approach to continuous health monitoring and timely medical intervention.

In the evolving landscape of assistive technologies, the visually impaired community faces unique challenges in mobility and environmental awareness. **Chapter 6** introduces the Smart Walking Stick, an assistive device integrating Arduino and Ultrasonic Sensors to offer real-time obstacle detection and tactile feedback. The design aims to empower individuals with visual impairments, enhancing their mobility experience with advanced navigation tools. The research highlights the innovative potential of this technology in providing newfound confidence and independence to the visually impaired.

Highlighted in **Chapter 7**, the Automated Drug Dispenser (ADD) represents a revolutionary leap in healthcare accessibility, integrating advanced pharmaceutical technologies to streamline medication dispensation. Utilizing IoT, mobile app development, database management, and cloud computing, ADD offers a patient-centric approach with a user-friendly interface. Through a mobile app, patients can navigate the system and retrieve medications via QR code scans. This system ensures accuracy and efficiency, updating a centralized and protected database with individualized patient information. ADD enhances the medication management experience, contributing significantly to patient care and safety.

**Chapter 8** explores how connected devices and sensors enable real-time tracking of vital health parameters, medication adherence, and wellness metrics outside traditional settings. IoT infrastructure facilitates seamless patient-provider communication, promoting timely interventions and personalized care plans. The discussion addresses security and privacy concerns, device interoperability, data standardization, and user engagement. The potential benefits include enhanced patient engagement, early detection of health issues, and reduced healthcare costs.

**Chapter 9** presents an Intelligent Remote Patient Activity Tracking System, leveraging the convergence of AI and IoT (AIoT). Using interconnected sensors and machine learning models, the system monitors patient activities and vital signs, offering real-time insights. It tracks activities like running, sleeping, walking, and exercising, while monitoring vital signs such as heart rate and breathing patterns. The chapter delves into the system's architecture and technical intricacies, highlighting its potential to transform healthcare delivery by enhancing patient care and fostering personalized treatment approaches.

**Chapter 10** provides a comprehensive exploration of technological advancements and challenges associated with robotic surgery, drawing insights from experienced surgeons. It aligns with the Unified Theory of Acceptance and Use of Technology (UTAUT), examining factors influencing the acceptance of robotic technology. The research also discusses patient satisfaction, healthcare outcomes, and ethical considerations, emphasizing the transformative potential of robotic surgery and the need to address barriers for widespread adoption.

**Chapter 11** outlines the advantages of robotic surgery, including smaller incisions, reduced trauma, greater range of motion, and shorter hospital stays. The use of robotic systems in fields such as urology, gynecology, cardiothoracic surgery, general surgery, and otorhinolaryngology is discussed. Telesurgery, an emerging technology, is implemented in a restricted range of medical establishments, offering enhanced precision and control in complex operations.

**Chapter 12** introduces the Baby Care Robot (BC-Robot), a smart cradle designed to monitor infant activities and health status using various sensors, actuators, IoT, and cloud technologies. The proposed method allows mothers to remotely observe and care for their infants, addressing family conditions and workload challenges. This innovative solution enhances childcare by providing real-time health and activity monitoring.

**Chapter 13** examines the factors, obstacles, and potential advantages of human-machine collaboration in healthcare. It highlights the significance of interdisciplinary collaboration, ethical considerations, and regulatory frameworks. The study emphasizes how this collaboration is reshaping conventional roles and workflows, enhancing diagnostic precision, optimizing treatment approaches, and improving patient outcomes.

Industry 5.0 marks the fusion of human expertise and advanced technology, transforming healthcare. **Chapter 14** provides an overview of automation and robotics in healthcare within this context, exploring their roles in patient care, operational efficiency, and redefining medical norms. The use of robots in physical therapy, prosthetics, and assistive technologies for the elderly is analyzed. The chapter also discusses how telemedicine, patient monitoring, and customized therapy are facilitated by robotics and automation.

**Chapter 15** explores the major shift toward human-centric teaming in Healthcare 5.0, where the convergence of human knowledge and advanced technologies is transforming healthcare delivery. The study highlights the potentials and opportunities, including patient-centered care, telemedicine, personalized medicine, and advanced diagnostics, enabled by technologies such as robotics, big data analytics, blockchain, and AI. It also addresses challenges and concerns for effective implementation, such as data security, ethical and legal dilemmas, and the need for appropriate training and skills.

Cloud computing is reshaping healthcare by offering flexible solutions for remote data access. **Chapter 16** discusses how cloud computing revolutionizes data creation, storage, and sharing, enhancing care and streamlining operations. Despite challenges like data breaches, cloud computing improves decision-making, data security, record sharing, and automation. Its importance during the COVID-19 pandemic highlights the necessity for healthcare providers to embrace cloud technology to advance medical data analysis and improve healthcare services.

Cyber-Physical Systems (CPS) amalgamate computational algorithms, communication technologies, and physical interactions to revolutionize traditional medical approaches. **Chapter 17** addresses issues such as fragmented medical data and outdated communication methods. By harnessing wireless sensor networks, cloud computing, and medical sensor technologies, CPS offers tailored solutions to healthcare challenges. Predictive analytics from CPS-generated.

**Chapter 18** focuses on the intersection of two transformative forces: the Internet of Things (IoT) and smart cities. These technologies are reshaping healthcare systems, offering innovative solutions for sustainability, operational efficiency, and patient care. By examining the role of IoT-enhanced smart cities in healthcare, the chapter sheds light on their potential to address the pressing need for sustainable practices. It explores how IoT and smart cities collaborate to optimize resource utilization, promote eco-friendly behaviors, and enhance patient well-being.

The book *Technologies for Sustainable Healthcare Development* holds significant relevance in today's rapidly evolving healthcare landscape. Here are key reasons why this book is important:

a) Addressing Global Challenges: Healthcare faces unprecedented challenges—pandemics, chronic diseases, and resource constraints. Sustainable technologies offer solutions to improve access, affordability, and quality of care. This book provides insights into how technology can address these challenges.
b) Innovation and Evidence-Based Practices: As technology advances, healthcare practitioners, researchers, and policymakers need to stay informed. The book bridges the gap between innovation and evidence-based practices. It equips readers with knowledge about cutting-edge technologies, data science, IoT, and robotics in healthcare.
c) Sustainability and Efficiency: Healthcare systems must operate sustainably. By exploring IoT-enhanced smart cities, resource optimization, and eco-friendly practices, the book emphasizes efficiency without compromising patient well-being. Sustainability is not a choice—it's a necessity.

d) Holistic Approach: The book caters to a diverse audience—clinicians, academics, administrators, and students. It fosters interdisciplinary collaboration, encouraging dialogue across fields. By considering human-centric collaboration, ethical use of data, and patient outcomes, the book takes a holistic approach.

In summary, *Technologies for Sustainable Healthcare Development* is a compass for navigating the intersection of technology, sustainability, and compassionate care. It empowers readers to shape a healthier, more resilient future. Our objective with *Technologies for Sustainable Healthcare Development* is to provide an in-depth exploration of how the Internet of Things and data science can be effectively integrated with Industry 5.0 technologies to address the pressing challenges faced by the healthcare industry. We have curated cutting-edge research, innovative solutions, and practical applications that showcase the latest advancements in this field. By highlighting sustainable development strategies, we hope to contribute to the advancement of secure, efficient, and resilient healthcare systems.

This book is intended for a broad audience, including academicians, researchers, undergraduate and postgraduate students, technology developers, IT specialists, programmers, computer scientists, information professionals, data scientists, security specialists, engineers, executives, scientists, medical professionals, and managers. Each of these groups will find valuable insights and practical knowledge that can aid in their respective efforts to advance healthcare through the application of Industry 5.0 technologies.

We extend our heartfelt gratitude to the contributors who have shared their expertise and insights, making this book a rich and diverse resource. We hope that readers will find this book both informative and inspiring, aiding them in their efforts to harness the power of the Internet of Things and data science for the sustainable development of healthcare systems.

*Thangavel Murugan*
*United Arab Emirates University, UAE*
*Jaisingh W.*
*Presidency University, India*
*Varalakshmi P.*
*Anna University, India*

# Acknowledgment

The editors would like to acknowledge the help of all the people involved in this project and, more specifically, to the authors and reviewers that took part in the review process. Without their support, this book would not have become a reality.

First, the editors would like to thank each one of the authors for their contributions. Our sincere gratitude goes to the chapter's authors who contributed their time and expertise to this book.

Second, the editors wish to acknowledge the valuable contributions of the reviewers regarding the improvement of quality, coherence, and content presentation of chapters. Most of the authors also served as referees; we highly appreciate their double task.

**Thangavel Murugan**
*United Arab Emirates University, UAE*

**W. Jaisingh**
*Presidency University, India*

**P. Varalakshmi**
*Anna University, India*

# Chapter 1
# A Study on Information and Communication Technology for Sustainable Healthcare Growth and Development in G20 Countries

**Pallabi Mukherjee**
http://orcid.org/0000-0002-3873-8698
*IPS Academy, Institute of Business Management and Research, Indore, India*

**Kali Charan Modak**
http://orcid.org/0000-0002-2980-5422
*IPS Academy, Institute of Business Management and Research, Indore, India*

**Sanju Mahawar**
*IPS Academy, Institute of Business Management and Research, Indore, India*

## ABSTRACT

*This study delves into the intricate interplay between healthcare, economic growth, and information and communication technology (ICT) within the G20 countries. Through rigorous analysis and employing a semi-log model, the authors investigate the tripartite relationship between these crucial domains. Utilizing health indicators and GDP per capita as metrics, alongside internet user statistics, this research explores correlations and causalities. By focusing on countries like Argentina and the United States, the authors elucidate the impact of growth and ICT on healthcare systems. This study contributes nuanced insights vital for fostering sustainable healthcare development amidst evolving technological landscapes in the G20 nations.*

DOI: 10.4018/979-8-3693-2901-6.ch001

## INTRODUCTION

Healthcare ICT was an important topic of discussion and reflection. ICT has revolutionized health care in many countries by effectively disseminating information about public health and making it easier to hear about health problems. Encourages more affordable and patient-friendly treatment. Increase the level of treatment and information exchange between medical professionals. Educate patients and healthcare professionals through education and training. Promotes communication between medical professionals and patients. Reduce travel time by using telemedicine to consult, diagnose and treat patients from remote hospital specialists. Public health surveillance. This chapter will evaluate and define the relationship between the healthcare index and proxy of ICT (internet users) along with growth to determine the progress and stability of the nation across G20 countries in the world.

The G20 declaration of 2023 includes priorities that give a digital push. The G20 member states concentrated on addressing the relationship between health and climate change and implementing a cooperative and inclusive "One Health Approach," as proposed by the One Health high-level expert group. This chapter will build a strong correlation between healthcare, internet users, and growth in G20 countries.

The data for healthcare will be taken from Boston Consultants Group. As a modern approach to assessing well-being and development, the Boston Consulting Group (BCG) introduced the SEDA (Sustainable Economic Development Assessment) in 2012. SEDA is primarily an objective measure and also a quantitative metric that measures how a nation performs compared to either the entire world population or individual peers or groups. SEDA reflects working by exploring three basic elements further determining to provide ten dimensions as indices of overall well-being, and SEDA does so for approximately 143 countries in the world who, in effect, are often contrasted with peers. It is usually said to be that once a country is developed; it does not enjoy a rapid growth rate. The countries undergoing rapid growth rates are developing at the same time (Mukherjee et al., 2020).

The three fundamental elements (dimensions) along with their sub-dimensions are as follows:

- Economics – Income, Economic Stability and Employment
- Investment – Health, education and Infrastructure
- Sustainability – Equality, Civil Society, Governance and Environment

### Variables Involved in the Study

Healthcare, Gross Domestic Product, and Internet Users (as a proxy of information and communication technology).

### Countries Involved in the Study

Following twenty nations namely: Argentina, Australia, Brazil, Canada, China, France, Germany, India, Indonesia, Italy, Japan, South Korea, Mexico, Russia, Saudi Arabia, South Africa, Turkey, United Kingdom, United States of America, European Union. We have taken twenty-eight countries that come under the European Union in our category excluding the countries which belong to the G20 category namely France, Germany, Italy, and the United Kingdom. Hence twenty-four countries namely Austria,

Belgium, Bulgaria, Croatia, Cyprus, Czech Republic, Denmark, Estonia, Finland, Greece, Hungary, Ireland, Latvia, Lithuania, Luxembourg, Malta, Netherlands, Poland, Portugal, Romania, Slovakia, Slovenia, Spain and Sweden.

The most developing nations derive together in the Group of Twenty (G20), an exclusive opportunity for international co-operation, to co-ordinate procedures for global economic stability, sustainable growth, and preventing future financial crises. The G20 was first convoked in Berlin on December 15–16, 1999, as a response to the financial predicaments that shook many emerging countries in the 1990s.

In reply to the emergency, the World Health Organization (WHO) recognized the Commission on Macroeconomics and Health (CMH) in January 2000. This programme accepted the dual flora of globalization: while it has helped the discussion of ideas, cultures, life-saving technologies, and efficient invention techniques, it has also formed challenges. Among these challenges were the incapability to aid needy regions and the emergence of new fears such as the global spread of terrorism, equipped conflicts, and HIV/AIDS.

The CMH strapped for the development of necessary medical dealings in order to prioritize funding for development and health. India has suffered substantial change since then. On December 1, 2022, it took over as G20 president, having made significant investments and changes to the healthcare industry.

The G20 Health Working Group (HWG) was initiated in 2017 while Germany was the Presidency of the G20, with the aim of making a common global agenda. This agenda encompassed fighting malnutrition, enhancing healthcare systems, handling medical emergencies, and stepping up efforts to discontinuity pandemics. After that, efforts to address Antimicrobial Resistance (AMR) and reinforce health systems continual during the 2018 Argentinean Presidency, with an added emphasis on childhood obesity.

As the G20 president, India meant to advance robust and unbiassed global growth, accelerate the UN Sustainable Development Goals, and ensure that everybody on the earth had reasonable access to technological novelty and the digital revolution. India's inventiveness in the G20 health workstream complete these objectives a realism. Building on earlier G20 initiatives and enhancing collaboration to lessen and prevent future pandemics were given specific attention by India's presidency, mainly in response to the Covid-19 pandemic.

India's health-related aims comprised cheering the G20 to act and foster collaboration to reduce the chance of a new pandemic and its related risks, as well as to improve coordination among pandemic response efforts. In order to achieve these objectives, India strapped for a strong G20 position on the progress, production, and supply of medical countermeasures, such as drugs and vaccinations, for pandemic readiness.

Supply chain and industrial integration advancement were also comprised in this programme. Another objective was to reinforce member countries' capacity to fight antibiotic confrontation and advance the "One Health" initiative. India also emphasized the necessity to address chronic health circumstances and ensure equitable access to healthcare as critical components of pandemic alertness and to foster robust and equitable social and economic development.

India emphasized that in direction to achieve this goal, the G20 must provision expanded access to universal healthcare, with an emphasis on endorsing equitable access to innovations. India used its own public health schema to highlight the aids of digital health solutions like telemedicine and artificial intelligence (AI). Also, India strapped for easier health data sharing and exchange among the G20 countries. Additionally, India made the fight against tuberculosis (TB) and noncontagious diseases a top priority. Also, India requested that the G20 recognize the role of integrative medicine—which includes traditional treatments like Ayurveda—in global health systems.

Information and communication technology, or ICT, has revolutionized the management, approachability, and delivery of healthcare amenities, and it is now a essential part of modern healthcare systems. In the framework of healthcare, information and communication technology, or ICT, raises to a wide range of tools and gadgets that enable communication and the sharing of medical data between patients, healthcare professionals, and other stakeholders.

Information and communication technology (ICT) in healthcare, at its central, is the application of digital tools and platforms to help and increase teaching, research, and management in the healthcare industry. It has numerous mechanisms and systems that enable information exchange and accelerate decision-making in medical surroundings.

## Components of ICT in Healthcare

a) **Information Technology (IT):** Information technology (IT) in healthcare states to the management and archiving of patient data through the usage of databases, software, and computer systems. This covers Laboratory Information Management Systems (LIMS), Picture Archiving and Communication Systems (PACS), Health Information Systems (HIS), and Electronic Health Records (EHRs). Healthcare providers may efficiently record patient data, monitor medical history, and assess clinical data for research, diagnosis, and treatment with the use of IT.

b) **Communication technology:** Healthcare communication technology aims to enable communication and collaboration between patients, healthcare providers and other stakeholders. These include mobile health applications (mHealth), email, secure messaging platforms, video conferencing and telecommunications technologies. Telemedicine services, patient engagement programs, real-time communication between providers and remote consultations are all made possible by communication technology.

## Benefits of ICT in Healthcare

I. Improved Access to Healthcare Services
II. Improved Efficiency and Quality of Healthcare
III. Empowerment of Patients

## Significance of Sustainable Healthcare Growth and Development: Impact of Healthcare on Economic Development

a) **Better productivity:** Access to quality health services correlates with improved productivity, as people have better health indicators and fewer sick days. Healthy people are more likely to participate in working life, participate in economic activity and earn income that contributes to economic development and well-being.

b) **Human capital development:** increasing life expectancy, reducing morbidity and mortality, and promoting physical and mental well-being by investing in health to increase human capital. Sustaining long-term economic growth, fostering innovation and fostering technological progress depends on a strong workforce.

c) **Healthcare Industry Growth:** The formation of occupations and economic development are significantly fueled by the healthcare industry itself. Investments in biotechnology, pharmaceuticals, medical research, and healthcare infrastructure all increase the economy, produce employment, and encourage technological and healthcare conveyance innovation.
d) **Reduction of Healthcare Expenditures:** By depressing healthcare costs associated to treating preventable illnesses and chronic disorders, effective healthcare interventions, preemptive measures, and disease management approaches can save money for people, companies, and governments. Long-term economic compensations and a reduction in the financial straining on healthcare systems can be accomplished by shifting healthcare spending to primary healthcare services and preemptive care.
e) **Social and Economic Equity:** Social presence, economic fairness among persons and communities, and the discount of health result inequities are all enhanced by the obtainability of inexpensive and equitable healthcare services. Reducing poverty, inequality, and social exclusion through investments in healthcare infrastructure, workforce development, and health insurance coverage aids to foster inclusive economic growing and development.

## Contextualizing the Study Within the G20 Framework

## Rationale for Focusing on G20 Countries

There are a number of strong influences in favor of intent research, policymaking, and international collaboration on G20 nations:

a. **Economic Significance**: Composed, the G20 countries have the highest economies on earth and underwrite significantly to trade, investment, GDP, and financial movements worldwide. The G20 countries have a noteworthy impact on international trade agreements, financial regulations, and economic policies as key forces behind growing and stability in the world economy.
b. **Policy Coordination:** In order to grip global economic hitches, advance financial stability, and inspire sustainable growth, G20 countries are vital in coordinating economic policies, financial laws, and monetary measures. G20 countries may upsurge the efficiency of their policies and increase their aggregate influence on the world economy by coordinating their priorities and actions.
c. **Diverse Representation:** The progressive and emerging economies that make up the G20 are varied and signify a range of policy preferences, approaches to development, and economic models. Analyzing the G20 nations enables a thorough inspection of development results, policy responses, and economic trends across a variety of nations and regions.
d. **Global Governance:** As prominent G20 memberships, nations have a immense say in how the global governance agenda is formed, how international standards are established, and how global cooperation is progressive on a range of economic, financial, and developmental challenges. Researchers, decision-makers, and absorbed gatherings can gain a well understanding of the dynamics of global governance and the influence of large economies on international agenda-setting by intent on G20 nations.

## OBJECTIVE OF THE CHAPTER

The study's primary objective is to assess the three-way causality between healthcare, Growth, and Internet users (that represents the inclusion of Information and communication technology).

The secondary objective is to evaluate the impact of growth and ICT in healthcare systems among the top countries in the world.

## BACKGROUND

The field of healthcare is diverse and includes activities related to illness prevention, health promotion, and the delivery of medical services with the goal of enhancing the well-being of both individuals and populations. Conversely, economic growth, which is commonly expressed in terms of GDP per capita, refers to the gradual rise in a country's output of goods and services. Information and communication technology (ICT) is transforming society by making it possible for knowledge, connections, and innovation to spread quickly across a range of industries.

It is becoming more widely acknowledged that ICT, healthcare, and economic growth are all interdependent. Technology advancements in healthcare make it easier to provide healthcare services, improving accessibility, effectiveness, and care quality. Simultaneously, better healthcare results promote a healthier, more productive workforce, which boosts economic development.

Hawkes, S., McBride, B., and Buse, K. (2019). In terms of global health initiatives, the literature on Sustainable Development Goal (SDG) 3 shows both convergences and divergences amongst the priorities of major geopolitical organizations including the BRICS, G7, and G20. Disparities arise in how these groups manage environmental pollution, mental health, and maternal and child health, even though they have similar goals when it comes to emergency preparedness and universal health coverage. Notably, none of the three political groups' agendas include health issues linked to significant disease loads, like substance abuse, traffic accidents, and sexual health. There are differences in the focus placed on human rights, equity, and engagement with non-state actors between the SDG 3 principles and practical plans.

Amin, N., Song, H., & Ali, M. (2023) The Results indicate that while ICT and financial development contribute to environmental degradation over the long term, their effects on CO2 emissions in the short term are negligible. Conversely, the utilization of renewable energy exhibits favorable impacts on environmental quality in both the short and long term. Additionally, economic growth is found to elevate CO2 emissions, albeit squared economic growth demonstrates a reduction in emissions, aligning with the inverted U-shaped Environmental Kuznets Curve (EKC) theory. Granger causality tests reveal bidirectional causality between renewable energy and CO2 emissions, whereas ICT and financial development exhibit unidirectional causality toward CO2 emissions. These findings underscore the importance for governments in the ASEAN region to mitigate carbon emissions stemming from ICT use and prioritize investments in renewable energy sources to curtail environmental degradation.

Danladi, S., et al (2023) stated a multi-stakeholder framework to boost fintech usage in Africa, advancing economic enclosure and the Sustainable Development schema. It draws on previous research and frameworks tailored for developing nations, recommending strategies such as prioritizing national ownership, fostering a pro-private sector investment environment, and engaging with multilateral development banks. Aligned through the G20's High-Level values for Digital Financial enclosure, country-specific strategies can hasten fintech adoption across Africa. Governments are urged to establish legislative frameworks supporting innovation, enhance digital infrastructure, and collaborate with private sector entities. Corporations with industries, global organizations, and initiatives like The Better Than Cash Alliance (TBTCA) can drive fintech implementation. Leveraging financial technology firms through participation in the Alliance can aid in national digital payment infrastructure development. Additionally, collaboration with USAID's mSTAR program can facilitate promoting marginalized populations and integrating digital financial services. These strategies offer African governments pathways to expedite fintech adoption and bolster financial inclusion.

Pandey, R. S., & Shukla, S. (2023) stated that India, a founding member of the G20, is poised to lead the G20 term from Dec 1, 2022, to Nov 30, 2023, closing in hosting the 18th G20 meeting in New Delhi in December 2023. The nation's agenda prioritizes inclusive and sustainable growth, strengthening digital infrastructure and technology accessibility, and reinforcing the global trade framework. Embracing the motto "One World One Sun One Grid," India reaffirms its dedication to harnessing solar energy for a sustainable future. Key areas of focus for the Summit encompass advancing multilateralism, fostering collaboration in health and development, ensuring nutrition and liveliness safety, bolstering international governance, and propelling modernization and digitalization. The G20 platform presents significant opportunities for India, recognized as the world's fastest-growing economy.

Régnier, P. (2023) stated that the global dissemination of appropriate technology and development, known by various terms such as versatile, reachable, and low-cost innovations, has been pivotal for popular community expansion. Initiating from Gandhi's anti-colonial drives and further indorsed by Schumacher's thoughts, this idea expanded momentum with the growth of economies like Brazil, China, India, and South Africa. These nations abandoned capital-intensive approaches in favor of accessible, user-friendly results that were adapted to reginal requirements and resources. The digital uprising of the 21st century increased the applicability of suitable technology and made it easier for people to use it globally. The transition of emerging economies from not involving advanced technology suppliers to high-tech innovators is examined in this study. They set up regional R&D facilities, promoted transparent scientific and technological cooperation, and involved in converse technology entrepreneurship by disseminating technology-driven goods all over the world. In response to sustainability issues, frugal innovation arose, placing an emphasis on straightforward, eco-friendly designs and effective use of resources. Innovation in cost-effective/appropriate technologies keeps promoting many kinds of sustainable development entrepreneurship. The report indicates that these strategies are gaining traction globally and are being supported by member states of the G20, G7, and UN, furthering the aims of sustainable development and the global economy.

Shahvaroughi Farahani, M. (2022) stated that the significant effects of population ageing on the economy have grown to be a significant worry in recent years. Reduced productivity, growing healthcare expenses, and slower economic growth are all impacted by ageing. It is imperative to address concerns related to sustainable development, such as environmental sustainability and inequality. This article looks at how ageing affects G20 economies' sustainable development and how they are trying to counteract these consequences. It highlights how economic considerations of ageing and sustainable development can be integrated. G20 action is required due to declining fertility rates and ageing populations. The detrimental economic effects can be mitigated by investing in solutions that work. Changes in policy are required to preserve the health of the elderly, increase life expectancy, and prolong working years. Governments set goals to stop the deterioration of citizens' health and to support the elderly. In order to maximize the productivity of younger generations and capitalize on the experiences of older generations, G20 countries need to keep an eye on demographic shifts. Interventions like lowering early retirement incentives and opposing age discrimination are necessary to keep ageing populations in the labor market. The need of these programmes is highlighted by the ageing trend in society.

Lee, H. S., et al (2024) stated that the G20 countries, which are important industrial powers and worldwide economies, contribute a large amount to global CO2 emissions, which worsens the greenhouse effect and has an adverse effect on the environment. Using panel quantile regression, this study examines the relationship between ICT, innovation, and CO2 releases in G20 nations from 2000 to 2019. The findings show a significant positive correlation between ICT and CO2 emissions in the 10th to 40th quantile nations and between CO2 emissions and patent applications in the 30th to 90th quantile countries. The study does come to the conclusion that innovation and ICT may not always be able to cut CO2 emissions, especially in nations where emissions are below the 40th quantile. The results highlight the complex relationship—influenced by different emission levels—between ICT, innovation, and CO2 emissions.

## RESEARCH METHODOLOGY

As a proxy of G20 countries, we have taken Argentina, Australia, Brazil, Canada, China, France, Germany, India, Indonesia, Italy, Japan, South Korea, Mexico, Russia, Saudi Arabia, South Africa, Turkey, United Kingdom, United States of America. We did not include the European Union in the study, as it is comprised of 28 countries namely France, Germany, Italy, and the United Kingdom. Hence twenty-four countries namely Austria, Belgium, Bulgaria, Croatia, Cyprus, Czech Republic, Denmark, Estonia, Finland, Greece, Hungary, Ireland, Latvia, Lithuania, Luxembourg, Malta, Netherlands, Poland, Portugal, Romania, Slovakia, Slovenia, Spain and Sweden.

Health includes life expectancy at birth, mortality rate under age 5, the prevalence of HIV, Incidence of tuberculosis, populations either underweight or obese, immunization, physician's density, and hospital beds. This index is going to be used for calculation. Also, data for Gross domestic product per capita, current US$ is used for the analysis. Internet users across these G20 countries over the chosen number of years are taken. We have studied correlations between these variables and their impacts. The impact of internet users on the health and growth of the nation, the impact of growth on internet users and healthcare, and the impact of healthcare on growth and internet users will be studied. Internet users will be taken as a proxy of information and communication technology. Regression analysis with robust standard errors has been used.

### Model

The following model is formed to express a causal relationship between growth and health of a country. Growth impacts health and health impacts growth and our model is formed to express the same. Moreover, there also exists a relationship between information and communication technology (ICT) and health. So, the model also expresses the impact of ICT on health of a nation. A dual causality is also thought of and established between these two variables. Moreover, we have used semi log model to establish impact of growth on health and health on growth. The semi log model helps to establish relationships between variables, where one variable covers a large range of values.

The following model is formed to express a causal relationship between growth and health of a country. Here we see the impact of growth of a country on health. Data for Gross domestic product per capita, current US$ is used for the analysis. Health includes life expectancy at birth, mortality rate under age 5, the prevalence of HIV, Incidence of tuberculosis, populations either underweight or obese, immunization, physician's density, and hospital beds. This index has been taken for calculation.

The model involves an intercept that is symbolized with $\beta_0$. It has a slope and coefficient that is symbolized by $\beta_1$. It clearly shows the change in dependent variable with change in independent variable. Error terms is expressed here with μ that completes an econometric model and expresses other factors other than growth that explains health.

Similar models are with same rationales however with different variables to express and evaluate causality.

Model 1: $Health_t = \beta_0 + \beta_1\ Growth_t + \mu$

Impact of Information and communication technology is also found on growth of a country and hence we have taken the following model to express the same. Internet users across these G20 countries over the chosen number of years are taken and data of gross domestic product per capita is taken.

Model 2: $Health_t = \beta_0 + \beta_1 ICT_t + \mu$

Impact of health is seen on growth of a nation and hence the model is defined and expresses.

Model 3: $Growth_t = \beta_0 + \beta_1 Health_t + \mu$

Impact of health is also seen in ICT of countries and hence the model is developed.

Model 4: $ICT_t = \beta_0 + \beta_1 Health_t + \mu$

Modified Model: We have used semi log model to establish impact of growth on health and health on growth. The semi log model helps to establish relationships between variables, where one variable covers a large range of values.

Modified Model 1: $Health_t = \beta_0 + \beta_1\ LnGrowth_t + \mu$

Modified Model 3: $LnGrowth_t = \beta_0 + \beta_1 Health_t + \mu$

continued on following page

*Table 1. Continued*

## Analysis

*Table 1. Results for Impact of growth on health*

| Countries/Parameters | Argentina | Australia | Brazil | Canada | China | Germany | France | United Kingdom | Indonesia | |
|---|---|---|---|---|---|---|---|---|---|---|
| Rsq | 0.02 | 0.21 | 0.28 | 0.003 | 0.95 | 0.14 | 0.31 | 0.012 | 0.003 | |
| Coefficient | -1.09 | -2.9 | 6.72 | -0.88 | 5.44 | -7.09 | 16.93 | 2.13 | -0.28 | |
| Robust Std Err | 1.94 | 1.39 | 2.57 | 3.68 | 0.33 | 0 | 6.25 | 6.16 | 1 | |
| P | 0.58 | 0.06 | 0.02 | 0.83 | 0 | 0.16 | 0.02 | 0.074 | 0.78 | |
| | **India** | **Italy** | **Japan** | **Saudi Arabia** | **South Korea** | **United States** | **South Africa** | **Russia** | **Turkey** | **Mexico** |
| Rsq | 0.95 | 0.78 | 0.004 | 0.14 | 0.004 | 0.91 | 0.08 | 0.33 | 0.27 | 0 |
| Coefficient | 7.77 | 15.61 | 0.19 | -2.53 | -0.56 | -16.49 | -3.64 | 3.43 | -1.96 | 0.09 |
| Robust Std Err | 0.32 | 2.19 | 0.71 | 1.26 | 2.02 | 1.55 | 3.5 | 1.6 | 0.61 | 7.92 |
| P | 0 | 0 | 0.8 | 0.07 | 0.79 | 0 | 0.32 | 0.06 | 0.01 | 0.99 |

a) $Health_t = \beta_0 + \beta_1\ LnGrowth_t + \mu$

*Table 2. Results for Impact of information and communication technology on health*

| Countries/Parameters | Argentina | Australia | Brazil | Canada | China | Germany | France | United Kingdom | Indonesia | |
|---|---|---|---|---|---|---|---|---|---|---|
| Rsq | 0.55 | 0.55 | 0.95 | 0.74 | 0.94 | 0.82 | 0.8 | 0.71 | 0.34 | |
| Coeff | -0.05 | -0.09 | -0.17 | -0.18 | 0.14 | -0.27 | -0.39 | -0.21 | -0.04 | |
| Robust Std Err | 0.01 | 0.02 | 0.01 | 0.03 | 0.01 | 0.03 | 0.04 | 0.04 | 0.01 | |
| P | 0 | 0 | 0 | 0 | 0 | 0 | 0 | 0 | 0.01 | |
| | **India** | **Italy** | **Japan** | **Saudi Arabia** | **South Korea** | **United States** | **South Africa** | **Russia** | **Turkey** | **Mexico** |
| Rsq | 0.6 | 0.7 | 0.45 | 0.77 | 0.5 | 0.64 | 0.013 | 0.02 | 0.019 | 0.68 |
| Coeff | 0.13 | -0.15 | -0.03 | -0.04 | 0.13 | -0.19 | 0.01 | 0.01 | 0 | -0.13 |
| Robust Std Err | 0.04 | 0.03 | 0.01 | 0.01 | 0.04 | 0.03 | 0.02 | 0.01 | 0.01 | 0.02 |
| P | 0.02 | 0 | 0.01 | 0 | 0.01 | 0 | 0.64 | 0.37 | 0.56 | 0 |

b) $Health_t = \beta_0 + \beta_1 ICT_t + \mu$

*Table 3. Results for the impact of health on growth*

| Countries/Parameters | Argentina | Australia | Brazil | Canada | China | Germany | France | United Kingdom | Indonesia | |
|---|---|---|---|---|---|---|---|---|---|---|
| Rsq | 0.02 | 0.21 | 0.28 | 0.003 | 0.94 | 0.14 | 0.31 | 0.01 | 0.003 | |
| Coeff | -0.03 | -0.07 | 0.04 | -0.001 | 0.17 | -0.02 | 0.02 | 0.01 | -0.01 | |
| Robust Std Err | 0.05 | 0.04 | 0.02 | 0.02 | 0.01 | 0.01 | 0.01 | 0.02 | 0.04 | |

continued on following page

*Table 3. Continued*

| P | 0.59 | 0.1 | 0.07 | 0.82 | 0 | 0.14 | 0.02 | 0.74 | 0.77 | |
|---|---|---|---|---|---|---|---|---|---|---|
| | **India** | **Italy** | **Japan** | **Saudi Arabia** | **South Korea** | **United States** | **South Africa** | **Russia** | **Turkey** | **Mexico** |
| Rsq | 0.95 | 0.78 | 0.004 | 0.14 | 0.59 | 0.91 | 0.08 | 0.33 | 0.27 | 0 |
| Coeff | 0.12 | 0.05 | 0.03 | -0.06 | -0.14 | -0.06 | -0.02 | 0.1 | -0.14 | 0.001 |
| Robust Std Err | 0.01 | 0.01 | 0.1 | 0.05 | 0.03 | 0.01 | 0.02 | 0.04 | 0.07 | 0.01 |
| P | 0 | 0 | 0.79 | 0.23 | 0 | 0 | 0.23 | 0.03 | 0.06 | 0.99 |

c) $Growth_t = \beta_0 + \beta_1 Health_t + \mu$

*Table 4. Results for the impact of health on information and communication technology*

| **Countries/Parameters** | **Argentina** | **Australia** | **Brazil** | **Canada** | **China** | **Germany** | **France** | **United Kingdom** | **Indonesia** | |
|---|---|---|---|---|---|---|---|---|---|---|
| Rsq | 0.55 | 0.56 | 0.96 | 0.74 | 0.94 | 0.82 | 0.8 | 0.71 | 0.34 | |
| Coeff | -10.42 | -6.55 | -5.79 | -4.09 | 6.5 | -3.03 | -2.04 | -3.31 | -8.9 | |
| Robust Std Err | 2.7 | 1.11 | 0.47 | 0.6 | 0.52 | 0.31 | 0.25 | 0.64 | 3.63 | |
| P | 0 | 0 | 0 | 0 | 0 | 0 | 0 | 0 | 0.03 | |
| | **India** | **Italy** | **Japan** | **Saudi Arabia** | **South Korea** | **United States** | **South Africa** | **Russia** | **Turkey** | **Mexico** |
| Rsq | 0.6 | 0.7 | 0.45 | 0.77 | 0.5 | 0.64 | 0.01 | 0.02 | 0.01 | 0.67 |
| Coeff | 4.67 | -4.6 | -0.1749 | -0.21 | 3.74 | -3.44 | 1.48 | 2.18 | -4.61 | -5.04 |
| Robust Std Err | 1.15 | 0.83 | 5.66 | 2.15 | 0.77 | 0.72 | 2.99 | 2.65 | 7.37 | 1.36 |
| P | 0 | 0 | 0.01 | 0 | 0 | 0 | 0.63 | 0.43 | 0.54 | 0 |

d) $ICT_t = \beta_0 + \beta_1 Health_t + \mu$

We have tried to categories countries in terms of whether the model is a good fit, that is estimated by R square value. The value of coefficients is either positive or negative and significant and insignificant.

The countries in the first model where we assess the impact of growth on health that have a significant impact with positive coefficient are China, India and Italy and negative coefficient is United States of America. In their case the model is a very good fit. The model is a good fit for countries like France, Russia and Turkey. For France and Russia, the impact of growth on health is positive and in case of Turkey it is negative. We could establish a significant coefficient in case of Brazil and Australia but however the model is a fair fit. In case of Brazil the coefficient is positive and in case of Australia it is negative. In case of United Kingdom, the model is not a good fit, but there is a positive impact of growth on health.

*Table 5. Impact of Growth on Health*

| Impact of Growth on Health | | | | |
|---|---|---|---|---|
| **Strength of Model (Whether it is a good fit)** | **High** | **Moderate** | **Low Moderate** | **Low** |
| Significant and Positive | China India Italy | France Russia | Brazil | United Kingdom |
| Significant and Negative | United States of America | Turkey | Australia | |
| Insignificant and Positive | | | | Japan Mexico |
| Insignificant and Negative | | | Germany | Argentina Canada Indonesia South Africa |

The countries in the second model where we assess the impact of information and communication technology on health that have a significant impact with positive coefficient are China and India and negative coefficient are Brazil, Canada, France, Germany, United Kingdom, Italy, Mexico, Saudi Arabia and United States of America. In their case the model is a very good fit. The model is a good fit for countries like South Korea, Argentina, Australia and Japan. For South Korea the impact of growth on health is positive and in case of Argentina, Australia and Japan it is negative. We could establish a significant yet negative coefficient in case of Indonesia but however the model is a fair fit.

*Table 6. Impact of ICT on health*

| Impact of ICT on Health | | | | |
|---|---|---|---|---|
| **Strength of Model (Whether it is a good fit)** | **High** | **Moderate** | **Low Moderate** | **Low** |
| Significant and Positive | China India | South Korea | | |
| Significant and Negative | Brazil, Canada France, Germany United Kingdom Italy, Mexico Saudi Arabia United States | Argentina Australia Japan | Indonesia | |
| Insignificant and Positive | | | | South Africa Russia Turkey |
| Insignificant and Negative | | | | |

The countries in the third model where we assess the impact of health on growth that have a significant impact with positive coefficient are China, India and Italy and negative coefficient is United States of America. In their case the model is a very good fit. The model is a good fit for countries like France and South Korea. For France the impact of growth on health is positive and in case of South Korea it is negative. We could establish a significant coefficient in case of Brazil, Russia, Turkey and Australia but however the model is a fair fit. In case of Brazil and Russia the coefficient is positive and in case of Australia and Turkey it is negative.

*Table 7. Impact of health on growth*

| Impact of Health on Growth | | | | |
|---|---|---|---|---|
| **Strength of Model (Whether it is a good fit)** | **High** | **Moderate** | **Low Moderate** | **Low** |
| Significant and Positive | China India Italy | France | Brazil Russia | |
| Significant and Negative | United States | South Korea | Australia Turkey | |
| Insignificant and Positive | | | | United Kingdom Japan Mexico |
| Insignificant and Negative | | | Germany Saudi Arabia | Argentina Canada South Africa |

The countries in the fourth model where we assess the impact of health on information and communication technology that have a significant impact with positive coefficient are China, Mexico and India and negative coefficient are Brazil, Canada, France, Germany, United Kingdom, Italy, Saudi Arabia and United States of America. In their case the model is a very good fit. The model is a good fit for countries like South Korea, Argentina, Australia and Japan. For South Korea, Australia and Argentina the impact of growth on health is positive and in case of and Japan it is negative. We could establish a significant yet negative coefficient in case of Indonesia but however the model is a fair fit.

*Table 8. Impact of health on ICT*

| Impact of Health on ICT | | | | |
|---|---|---|---|---|
| **Strength of Model (Whether it is a good fit)** | **High** | **Moderate** | **Low Moderate** | **Low** |
| Significant and Positive | China India Mexico | Australia Argentina South Korea | | |
| Significant and Negative | Brazil, Canada Germany, Italy, France United Kingdom Saudi Arabia United States | Japan | Indonesia | |
| Insignificant and Positive | | | | South Africa Russia Turkey |
| Insignificant and Negative | | | | |

## SOLUTIONS AND RECOMMENDATIONS

To foster sustainable healthcare growth and development in G20 countries through investment in ICT infrastructure, it is crucial to implement comprehensive policy frameworks that align with national health priorities and international standards. Capacity building should focus on training healthcare professionals and ICT specialists to bridge the skills gap and enhance system efficiency. Public awareness campaigns are essential to educate citizens about the benefits of ICT in healthcare, promoting widespread acceptance and utilization. Strategic partnerships and cooperation among governments, private sector, and international organizations can drive innovation and resource mobilization. Addressing inequities is vital to ensure that ICT advancements benefit all population segments, particularly underserved communities. Robust data governance and interoperability standards must be established to ensure secure, seamless data exchange across platforms, enhancing the quality of care. Continuous monitoring and assessment mechanisms should be in place to evaluate the impact of ICT investments and inform future strategies, ensuring sustainable and equitable healthcare improvements across G20 nations.

## FUTURE RESEARCH DIRECTIONS

Future research directions in the domain of ICT for sustainable healthcare growth and development in G20 countries should encompass a multifaceted approach. Policy evaluation studies should rigorously analyze the effectiveness and impact of current ICT policies, providing insights for refinement and better alignment with health outcomes. Research on technological innovation must explore cutting-edge ICT solutions, such as AI, IoT, and blockchain, that can revolutionize healthcare delivery and management. Investigating the socioeconomic determinants of ICT adoption will help identify barriers and enablers affecting different population groups, ensuring more inclusive strategies. The digital divide requires focused studies to understand disparities in ICT access and use, devising targeted interventions to bridge these gaps. Public-private partnerships should be examined to assess their role in fostering innovation, resource mobilization, and efficient service delivery. Health information systems need continuous evaluation to enhance data accuracy, security, and interoperability. Cross-sector collaboration research should highlight successful models of integration between healthcare, education, and other sectors, promoting holistic approaches to health improvement. Finally, patient-centered care studies should focus on how ICT can be leveraged to enhance patient engagement, satisfaction, and outcomes, ensuring that technological advancements translate into tangible health benefits for individuals.

## CONCLUSION

Our analysis shows different relationships between health, economic growth and information and communication technology (ICT) across G20 countries, with expected differences between income groups. While positive associations between economic growth and health outcomes are evident in countries such as China, India and Italy, the opposite dynamic is observed, such as the negative coefficient observed in the United States. Similarly, the impact of ICT on improving health care is significant in countries such as China and India, although in some regions there is complexity and negative coefficients. The links between improved health and economic growth have been highlighted in countries such as China, India and Italy, while advances in health are driving the adoption of information and communication technologies in countries such as China, Mexico and India. These findings highlight the need for tailored strategies and collaborations to effectively use technology to develop sustainable healthcare worldwide.

## REFERENCES

Alfarizi, M., & Arifian, R. (2022). G20 Health Vision in Achieving SDGs 2030: Arranging the Global Health Management Architecture. *Insights in Public Health Journal*, 3(1), 1–12. 10.20884/1.iphj.2022.3.1.5565

(Alfarizi, 2022)

Amin, N., Song, H., & Ali, M. (2023). Role of information and communication technology, economic growth, financial development and renewable energy consumption towards the sustainable environment: Insights from ASEAN countries. *Environmental Science and Pollution Research International*, 30(38), 89381–89394. 10.1007/s11356-023-28720-537452245

Danladi, S., Prasad, M. S. V., Modibbo, U. M., Ahmadi, S. A., & Ghasemi, P. (2023). Attaining Sustainable Development Goals through Financial Inclusion: Exploring Collaborative Approaches to Fintech Adoption in Developing Economies. *Sustainability (Basel)*, 15(17), 1–14. 10.3390/su151713039

Gyamfi, B. A., Ampomah, A. B., Bekun, F. V., & Asongu, S. A. (2022). Can information and communication technology and institutional quality help mitigate climate change in E7 economies? An environmental Kuznets curve extension. *Journal of Economic Structures*, 11(1), 1–20. 10.1186/s40008-022-00273-9

Lee, H. S., Yap, L. T., Lee, S. Y., & Har, W. M. (2024). The Impacts of ICT and innovation on Carbon Dioxide Emissions in G20 Countries. *IOP Conference Series. Earth and Environmental Science*, 1303(1), 1–10. 10.1088/1755-1315/1303/1/012011

Li, X., Zhang, C., & Zhu, H. (2023). Effect of information and communication technology on CO2 emissions: An analysis based on country heterogeneity perspective. *Technological Forecasting and Social Change*, 192, 122599. 10.1016/j.techfore.2023.122599

McBride, B., Hawkes, S., & Buse, K. (2019). Soft power and global health: The sustainable development goals (SDGs) era health agendas of the G7, G20 and BRICS. *BMC Public Health*, 19(1), 1–14. 10.1186/s12889-019-7114-531234831

Megbowon, E. T., & David, O. O. (2023). Information and communication technology development and health gap nexus in Africa. *Frontiers in Public Health*, 11, 1–12. 10.3389/fpubh.2023.114556437064667

Pandey, R. S., & Shukla, S. (2023). Perspective of G20 along with India's cultural values. *Knowledgeable Research: A Multidisciplinary Journal, 1*(09), 59-70.

Régnier, P. (2023). Innovation, Appropriate Technologies and Entrepreneurship for Global Sustainability Development: A Review Until the Early Twenty-first Century. *The Journal of Entrepreneurship*, 32(2, suppl), S12–S26. 10.1177/09713557231201115

(Régnier,2023)

Shahvaroughi, M. (2022). The Impacts of Aging on Economic Growth and Sustainable Development (Case Study of G20 Countries). *Iranian Sociological Review*, 12(1), 85–100.

(Shahvaroughi, 2022)

Shao, M., Fan, J., Huang, Z., & Chen, M. (2022). The impact of information and communication technologies (ICTs) on health outcomes: A smediating effect analysis based on cross-national panel data. *Journal of Environmental and Public Health*, 2022, 1–16. 10.1155/2022/2225723

## KEY TERMS AND DEFINITIONS

**Boston Consulting Group:** Boston Consulting Group (BCG) is a global management consulting firm known for its expertise in business strategy and transformation.

**G20:** The G20 is an international forum of 19 countries and the European Union, which together represent the world's largest economies, addressing global economic issues and promoting financial stability.

**ICT:** Information and Communication Technology (ICT) encompasses all technologies used to handle telecommunications, broadcast media, intelligent building management systems, audiovisual processing, and transmission systems, as well as network-based control and monitoring functions.

**Sustainable Economic Development Assessment:** The Sustainable Economic Development Assessment (SEDA) is a diagnostic tool developed by BCG to evaluate how effectively countries convert economic growth into overall well-being.

**UN Sustainable Development Goals:** The UN Sustainable Development Goals (SDGs) are a collection of 17 interlinked global goals designed to be a "blueprint to achieve a better and more sustainable future for all" by addressing a wide range of social, economic, and environmental challenges by 2030.

**World Health Organization:** The World Health Organization (WHO) is a specialized agency of the United Nations responsible for international public health.

# Chapter 2
# Data Science Advancements in Healthcare, Education, and Cities:
## An Overview

**Virendra Singh Kushwah**
https://orcid.org/0000-0002-5940-315X
*VIT Bhopal University, India*

**Jyoti Parashar**
*Dr. Akhilesh Das Gupta Institute of Technology and Management, India*

**Partibha Dabas**
*Dr. Akhilesh Das Gupta Institute of Technology and Management, India*

**Lokesh Meena**
*Dr. Akhilesh Das Gupta Institute of Technology and Management, India*

**Vaishali Sharma**
https://orcid.org/0000-0001-7840-6439
*Dr. Akhilesh Das Gupta Institute of Technology and Management, India*

## ABSTRACT

*Data science, a prominent subset of artificial intelligence (AI), specializes in analyzing vast datasets using diverse tools and methods to derive insights and predictions. Its applications span various domains, notably cybersecurity, crucial for safeguarding systems and data from internal and external threats amid escalating challenges. The integration of data science in sectors like energy and environment underscores its transformative potential. The digitization of energy systems enables real-time data acquisition, facilitating timely analysis of human impacts on the environment and society. Furthermore, data science aids in monitoring policy effectiveness towards sustainable development (SD) goals. However, the rapid evolution of technology presents formidable challenges, necessitating organizational adaptability and*

DOI: 10.4018/979-8-3693-2901-6.ch002

*utilization of cutting-edge advancements, especially in online communication. Amidst these shifts, data science emerges as a pivotal tool for informed decision-making and innovation, poised to make significant contributions across diverse sectors of the economy.*

## INTRODUCTION

Sustainable development (SD) is defined as the process of using resources in ways that satisfy present demands without compromising the capacity of future generations to meet their requirements. The field of data science has the potential to play an important part in the process being described. Data science may make a big contribution by determining and quantifying the detrimental consequences that human activity has on the environment and society (Kharrazi, 2016). Data science has the potential to make a substantial contribution to decision-making as well as the development of innovative SD solutions by locating and quantifying the impacts that human activity has on the environment and in society. This technique may also be used to measure, monitor, and evaluate the success of policies and practices that are aimed at achieving SD goals. Data science may also be utilized to locate and address deficiencies in resource management and allocation. This can be accomplished by analysing historical data. It is possible to improve resource management and allocation in order to fill these vacancies and take advantage of these chances (Burke, 2021).

The phrases "data science" and "sustainable development" are two that are used rather frequently today. Everyone is interested in utilizing data in some form or another. Businesses that are not in the information technology sector are increasingly turning to data in order to improve their operations, provide more insightful analyses, and develop new products. All levels of society, including governments, corporations, and private citizens, are pooling their resources and working together to find long-term climate change solutions. People are working toward a future in which there is less inequality and more wealth for a larger percentage of the world's population. This is the hope held by many (Claudet, 2020).

Data science is typically successful in providing solutions to problems that are associated with businesses. Among these include the forecasting of demand, the identification and prevention of fraud, and the development of more efficient transportation routes. On the other hand, an increasing number of businesses and individuals are putting out more stringent requirements. In order to confront the existential challenges that we are currently encountering, we need make use of data and the science of data. There is a growing number of software platforms that encourage the utilization of data for the advancement of social causes. In addition to that, there are a number of competitions and hackathons that are focussed on social issues (Leal, 2024).

## BACKGROUND

### Data Science and Cyber Security in Sustainability

It is crucial to recognize that increasing digitalization and the interconnection of society have produced both opportunities and challenges for sustainable development in order to comprehend how cyber security measures may assist in the achievement of Sustainable Development Goals (SDGs). This is necessary in order to understand how cyber security measures may help in the attainment of Sustainable Development

Goals (SDGs). It is essential to have an understanding of how measures of cyber security might contribute to the accomplishment of the Sustainable Development Goals (SDGs). As more important infrastructure, crucial services, and personal data are kept and delivered through digital networks, it is becoming more and more evident that cyber security is necessary in order to meet the Sustainable Development Goals (SDGs). By conducting a comprehensive review of the earlier research that is relevant to the topic at hand, this study investigates how the field of cyber security may contribute to social inclusion, monetary success, and environmental sustainability.

## Data Science for Sustainability

Data science can be used to collect, analyze, and interpret data from a variety of sources to help us understand and address sustainability challenges. Here are some examples:

i. **Optimizing energy use:** Data scientists can analyze data on energy consumption to identify areas where businesses and households can save energy. This can be done by developing models that predict energy use based on factors such as weather, building type, and occupant behavior (Sadik, 2020).
ii. **Monitoring environmental conditions:** Data scientists can develop systems to monitor environmental conditions such as air quality, water quality, and deforestation. This data can be used to track progress on environmental goals and identify areas where intervention is needed (Sulich, 2021).
iii. **Supporting sustainable development:** Data science can be used to support sustainable development efforts by helping to identify and track progress on the United Nations Sustainable Development Goals (SDGs). The SDGs are a set of 17 goals that aim to address global challenges such as poverty, hunger, and climate change (Goswami, 2023).

## Cyber Security for Sustainability

Cyber security is essential for protecting the data and systems that are critical to sustainability efforts. Here are some examples of how cyber security can help to promote sustainability:

i. **Protecting critical infrastructure:** Cyber-attacks can disrupt critical infrastructure such as power grids and water treatment plants. By securing these systems, we can help to ensure that they continue to operate efficiently and sustainably (Sulich, 2021).
ii. **Safeguarding environmental data:** Environmental data is essential for monitoring environmental conditions and tracking progress on sustainability goals. Cyber security helps to protect this data from unauthorized access or manipulation.
iii. **Promoting sustainable practices:** Cyber security can help to promote sustainable practices by protecting businesses and organizations from cyber-attacks that could damage their reputations or lead to environmental damage.

## Health Care Sector Sustainable Development

The fields of healthcare and medicine are becoming increasingly inventive in their application of technologies that incorporate artificial intelligence and the internet of things. It would appear that mankind is coming closer to the day when individuals will have linked smart gadgets that inform them when they should see a doctor since people are aware of health concerns and can detect warning symptoms. This is because people are aware of health issues and can identify warning indications. The arrival of this day will mark the beginning of a new era in which individuals will be held more responsibility for their own health (Karliner, 2020).

The employment of computer vision and Internet of Things-integrated technology has the goal of continually assisting healthcare professionals in the decision-making process for the purpose of ensuring the continued and sustainable expansion of a healthcare ecosystem in order to improve the quality of life for citizens. It is very necessary to have efficient management of the expansion of the healthcare infrastructure in order to realize the objectives of planning and carrying out the construction of the key components of the medical ecosystem. This is why it is so important to have good management. In order to accomplish this goal, it is necessary to first incorporate an intricate collection of models and frameworks into a pre-existing healthcare ecosystem. To be more particular, the activities carried out by both public and commercial services, cutting-edge solutions driven by AI, AI-integrated Internet of Things technology, and data analytics are the specific fundamental aspects of the infrastructure (Khan, 2020).

Sustainable healthcare is a way of delivering medical care that meets the needs of the present without compromising the ability of future generations to meet their own needs. It takes into account the environmental, social, and economic impact of healthcare.

The healthcare sector has a significant impact on the environment. It is estimated to be responsible for around 4.4% of global net emissions (Thakur, 2021). This is due to a number of factors, including:

i. The use of energy-intensive equipment and buildings
ii. The production of medical waste
iii. The transportation of patients and staff

There are a number of things that can be done to make the healthcare sector more sustainable. These include:

i. Using energy-efficient technologies
ii. Reducing waste generation
iii. Using greener transportation options
iv. Promoting public health measures to prevent illness

Sustainable healthcare is not just about the environment. It is also about ensuring that everyone has access to quality healthcare, regardless of their income or background. This means investing in public health programs, promoting preventive care, and making healthcare more affordable. By making the healthcare sector more sustainable, we can help to ensure a healthier future for everyone. Here are some of the benefits of a sustainable healthcare system:

i. Reduced environmental impact
ii. Improved public health
iii. Lower healthcare costs
iv. More efficient use of resources

Sustainable healthcare is an important part of achieving the Sustainable Development Goals (SDGs) set by the United Nations. The SDGs are a set of 17 goals that aim to address the world's most pressing challenges, including poverty, hunger, and climate change. SDG 3 is specifically focused on ensuring healthy lives and promoting well-being for all at all ages (Shaw, 2021).

## Cybersecurity, Digitization, and Environmentally Responsible Medical Care

The development of the e-government system and the adoption of cutting-edge service delivery techniques both heavily rely on the network and system for cybersecurity. Information and communications technology improvements, which have also changed governments, have greatly assisted the delivery of modern services in less developed countries. A robust cybersecurity system, according to others, will advance digitalization, expand access to the national network, and raise public confidence in Asian economies. A well-designed cybersecurity framework, according to Andoh-Baidoo, Osatuyi, and Kunene, may be able to enhance the quality of cyber systems and the provision of digital services in the sub-Saharan African area even if there are only limited resources available. Malhotra, Bhargava, and Dave looked at e-government issues in the African and Indian economies. They identified a variety of risks and constraints in developing countries that hinder the expansion of digitalization of freely accessible public services (Möller, 2023).

## The Green Digital Revolution: Cybersecurity, Digitization, and Sustainable Healthcare

The healthcare sector is undergoing a significant transformation driven by two major forces: digitization and the growing need for environmental responsibility. While these forces seem distinct, they are deeply intertwined in creating a more secure, efficient, and sustainable future for medical care (Mondejar, 2021).

## Digitization and the Power of Secure Data

The rise of electronic medical records (EMRs), telehealth platforms, and connected medical devices is revolutionizing healthcare delivery. However, this digital transformation hinges on robust cybersecurity measures. Strong data encryption and access controls are crucial to protect sensitive patient information from breaches and unauthorized access. Secure data not only safeguards privacy but also empowers healthcare professionals. When patient data is readily available and well-organized, it allows for:

i. **Data-Driven Decisions:** Secure digital data provides a wealth of information that can be analyzed to improve resource allocation, personalize treatment plans, and identify potential outbreaks more swiftly (Kenney, 2020), (Kushwah, 2013).
ii. **Improved Patient Care:** Telehealth and remote patient monitoring tools allow for virtual consultations, reducing unnecessary travel for patients and healthcare staff. This not only improves access to care, especially in remote areas, but also contributes to a greener healthcare system by reducing transportation emissions (Pansara, 2022).

## Challenges on the Digital Path

Despite the benefits, this digital revolution comes with challenges (Brunetti, 2020):

i. **Vulnerability:** Increased reliance on digital systems creates a larger attack surface for cybercriminals. Regular security audits, staff training on cyber hygiene, and robust data security protocols are essential to mitigate these risks.

ii. **Privacy Concerns:** Striking a balance between data security and patient privacy is crucial. Clear data governance policies and robust user authentication systems are necessary to ensure patient information is only accessed by authorized personnel.
iii. **Digital Divide:** Unequal access to reliable internet and technology can exacerbate existing healthcare disparities. Initiatives promoting digital literacy and ensuring affordable internet access are crucial to bridge this gap.

### Aligning Green Practices With Digital Innovation

Environmental responsibility is another key pillar of a sustainable healthcare system. Here's where digitization can make a positive impact:

i. **Energy Efficiency:** Hospitals and medical facilities can leverage digital tools to monitor and optimize energy consumption. Additionally, investing in renewable energy sources like solar panels can significantly reduce their environmental footprint (Ardito, 2021).
ii. **Waste Reduction:** Digitization can help minimize paper usage in healthcare by transitioning to electronic records and prescriptions. Furthermore, implementing proper disposal practices for medical waste is essential to protect the environment and public health (Martínez-Peláez, 2023).

## CHALLENGES OF GOING GREEN

The shift towards a sustainable healthcare system also faces hurdles:

- **Upfront Costs:** Investing in new technologies such as renewable energy sources or upgrading inefficient infrastructure can require significant initial investment.
- **Legacy Infrastructure:** Many hospitals operate with older buildings that may be energy-inefficient. Retrofitting these structures can be a complex and costly undertaking.

By prioritizing cybersecurity alongside digitization, the healthcare sector can leverage the power of technology while safeguarding patient data and privacy. Additionally, integrating environmentally responsible practices into the digital healthcare landscape fosters a more sustainable future for healthcare. This "green digital revolution" requires a multi-pronged approach that involves investments in technology, robust cybersecurity protocols, and a commitment to sustainable practices. By working together, healthcare providers, policymakers, and technology companies can create a healthcare system that is secure, efficient, and environmentally responsible, ensuring a healthier future for all.

### Data Science's Place in Healthcare

The amount of data created is one factor that adds to the complexity of healthcare. 500 petabytes were predicted to be the amount of data generated by global digital healthcare at the time this report was released in 2012. The scale of healthcare data is predicted to continue expanding significantly; by 2020, it is predicted to be more than 25,000 petabytes (Karatas, 2022). The 'Big Data' problem is therefore apparent in the field of healthcare management. Only if doing so is advantageous for the industry will the amount of data gathered on healthcare continue to grow. Is it possible that the healthcare sector will employ big data and data analytics to learn from the past and advance toward a "smart" state in the future? It has already been questioned whether switching to "outcome-based practices" would be advantageous in place of "treatment-based practices." The healthcare sector is facing an uphill struggle if patients are not provided the treatment they need, despite huge sums of money being spent on information technology (Ray,2020).

The use of data science to enhance sustainable practices is very important when looking at various methods to increase the efficacy of software and apps. Examples are provided in the sections below.

- ***Implement Efficient Applications and Deduplicate***

It is feasible that data software and applications that are efficient might be essential to the development of green IT. Recently, the author witnessed how modifying the Oracle data warehouse search strategy (for example, not doing a full database search every time when just a much smaller search is necessary) may decrease the amount of time required to create a report for a data warehouse in half, from eight hours to eight minutes. This would result in a time savings of eight hours. During the eight hours that it took to generate the report, the enormous server came dangerously close to reaching its maximum capacity (Albahri, 2023).

## The Transdisciplinary and Sustainable Application of Cyber Security in Education

Given the importance of the Internet and other information and communication technologies to the completion of routine chores, it ought to go without saying that businesses, governments, and individual individuals all require reliable access to Internet infrastructure in order to remain competitive in today's global economy. The concept of "sustainability" should not be limited to these two visible areas, despite the fact that the words "economic sustainability" and "environmental sustainability" are sometimes used together. Given the rapid pace at which our culture is transitioning to digital platforms at the present time, sustainability efforts should also pay attention to the many different technological settings, notably the Internet. In point of fact, if it were to turn out that the Internet could not be maintained, the ramifications for the world as we know it would be absolutely catastrophic. Internet-based activities need to continue to increase in a way that is both sustainable and responsible in order to protect the highly digitalized enterprises and societies that already exist in the world today. Imagine the internet as an expansive and interconnected ecosystem.

You may find further examples of portals that feature SD data that was created by national governments, municipal governments, and public organizations by going to data.gov.uk, data.gov.it, and govdata.de, respectively. These websites are located in the United Kingdom, Italy, and Germany, respectively. The Disclosure Project Action - CDP (data.cdp.net), the Open Data Watch (opendatawatch.com), Our World in Data (ourworldindata.org), and the Sustainable Data Platform (sustainable-data-platform.org) are some further websites that give information and data on global topics. You could uncover these websites if you search the internet. There is a possibility that each of these websites has useful information that may be uncovered by employing the strategies and tools that are typical of the field of data science. This suggests that the Sustainable Development Goals (SDGs) can become a reality if efforts are made to maximize the positive environmental, social, and economic effects of using and promoting open data in SD processes that are based on cooperation between national and local governments, donors, international organizations, civil society organizations, academic institutions, and industry. according to information obtained from the Open Data Institute in 2016.

Web portals that are known as Open Government Data Platforms (OGDPs) promote more openness, involvement, and innovation in general. OGDPs are collections of data that also include resources that may be used to access and analyse the data. One such example is the European Data Portal (EDP), which was established by the European Commission in 2015 and is currently available in 25 distinct languages. EDP receives information from the 35 nations that make up Europe on a wide range of subjects from those states. These subjects include things like population and society, geography and urbanization, scientific technology, and transportation. In addition to these, there are topics such as agriculture, fisheries, forestry, and the production of food; economics and finance; education, culture, and sport; energy; the environment; government and the public sector; health; and global concerns (Veja, 2021).

## Data Science for Education

The outcomes of a research that is going to be conducted on big data and data science courses that are going to be provided at universities will surely have an effect on the choices and opportunities that are available to students (Fischer, 2020).

In this section, the modern era is investigated in relation to both of the issues that are discussed. Here is a synopsis of two issues: the first concerns institutions of higher learning that focus on data science, and the second concerns employment advertisements placed by companies. In the next sections, we will discuss both of these topics in greater depth. This makes use of data that is not just public but also easy to obtain. A knowledgeable data scientist will definitely take part in a number of discussions and debates with current and prospective students, company executives, and a wide range of other individuals. Despite this fact, it is abundantly obvious that data science calls for the integration of the vast majority of different fields (Romero, 2020).

i. Teaching and Learning for Data Science

The post-graduate data science programs that higher education institutions now offer are briefly discussed below. Frequently, these courses are referred to as MSc programs. This could also apply to undergraduate curricula, and it definitely does to undergraduate projects and internships.

The number of universities worldwide that provide graduate-level and undergraduate-level classes in the topic of data science has significantly increased in the most recent few years. Additionally, there are now more graduate-level courses available. The term "Data Science" is connected to some, but not all, of the graduate courses on the list that can be found in Press (Efron, 2021).

ii. Learning analytics for quality education

It's possible that having access to a good education is the single most important factor in determining whether or not individuals can live sustainably throughout the course of their lifetimes. This is due to the fact that it enables nations to implement policies that are particularly tailored to their own objectives while also taking into mind the environmental challenges that are being experienced throughout the world. Indicators measuring universal primary and secondary education, early childhood development, universal pre-primary education, success in technical/vocational and higher education, relevant skills for decent work, gender equality and inclusion, universal youth literacy, education for sustainable development, and global citizenship are some examples of estimates that could be used to develop sustainable education strategies (Novikov, 2020).

## OBJECTIVES OF THE STUDY

### To Study on Data Science for Society, Science, Industry, and Business

Data science is a field that applies statistical, programming, and machine learning techniques to extract knowledge and insights from data. It plays an increasingly important role in society, science, industry, and business.

#### Data Science for Society

Data science can be used to address a wide range of societal challenges, such as (Matheus, 2020):

i. **Public health:** Data science can be used to track the spread of diseases, identify risk factors for chronic illnesses, and develop more effective public health interventions.
ii. **Crime prevention:** Data science can be used to analyze crime patterns and predict where crime is most likely to occur. This information can be used to help law enforcement agencies allocate resources more effectively.
iii. **Education:** Data science can be used to personalize learning experiences for students and identify students who are at risk of falling behind.

#### Data Science for Science

Data science is transforming scientific research by enabling scientists to:

i. **Collect and analyze large datasets:** New technologies are generating massive amounts of data in many scientific fields. Data science provides the tools to collect, store, and analyze this data.
ii. **Develop new models and simulations:** Data science can be used to develop complex models and simulations that can help scientists understand complex natural phenomena.
iii. **Make new discoveries:** Data science is helping scientists to make new discoveries in a wide range of fields, from astronomy to medicine.

#### Data Science for Industry

Data science is essential for businesses in today's data-driven economy. Businesses use data science for a variety of purposes, such as (Saura, 2021):

i. **Marketing:** Data science can be used to target advertising more effectively, personalize customer experiences, and develop new products and services.
ii. **Operations:** Data science can be used to optimize supply chains, improve efficiency, and reduce costs.
iii. **Risk management:** Data science can be used to identify and assess risks, such as the risk of fraud or cyberattacks.

#### Data Science for Business

Data science is becoming increasingly important for businesses of all sizes. Here are some of the ways that businesses can use data science (Prüfer, 2020):

i. **Improve decision-making:** Data science can provide businesses with the insights they need to make better decisions about everything from product development to marketing campaigns.
ii. **Increase efficiency:** Data science can help businesses to streamline their operations and improve efficiency.
iii. **Gain a competitive advantage:** Businesses that can effectively use data science to gain insights from their data can gain a competitive advantage in the marketplace.

## To Study on Role of cyber security and Data Science

### The Role of Data Science in Cybersecurity

Data science plays a vital role in enhancing cybersecurity by (Camacho, 2024), (Parashar, 2022):

i. **Identifying threats and vulnerabilities:** Data scientists can analyze network traffic patterns and system logs to identify anomalies that might indicate a cyberattack.
ii. **Developing security models and tools:** Machine learning algorithms can be used to develop intrusion detection systems (IDS) and security information and event management (SIEM) tools that can automatically detect and respond to cyber threats.
iii. **Improving incident response:** Data science can be used to analyze data from security incidents to identify the root cause of the attack and take steps to prevent similar attacks in the future.

### The Role of Cybersecurity in Data Science

Cybersecurity is essential for data science because it protects the data that data scientists rely on to do their jobs. Data breaches can expose sensitive information, disrupt data analysis projects, and damage an organization's reputation.

Here's how cybersecurity protects data science (Sarker, 2020), (Tapaswi, 2010):

i. **Ensuring data integrity:** Cybersecurity measures protect data from unauthorized modification or deletion, which could lead to inaccurate or misleading results from data analysis.
ii. **Maintaining data privacy:** Cybersecurity safeguards sensitive data, such as customer information or financial data, from unauthorized access or disclosure.
iii. **Enabling collaboration:** Cybersecurity allows data scientists to share data securely with colleagues and partners to facilitate collaboration on data analysis projects.

## DATA SCIENCE ADVANCES FOR SUSTAINABLE CITY AND COMMUNITY DEVELOPMENT

Intelligent and sustainable municipal environments "smart sustainable cities" refers to a relatively new concept that arose in the middle of the 2010s in the disciplines of technology and urban planning. This phenomenon is connected to the evolution of environmentally friendly practices, the urbanization of pre-existing communities, and the information and communication technology (ICT) industry (Bibri, 2020). They combine the benefits of sustainable cities in terms of the design principles and planning precepts of sustainability with the benefits of smart cities in terms of the cutting-edge information and communications technology solutions that are being produced in cities. These benefits may be broken down into two categories: design principles and planning precepts of sustainability, and cutting-edge information and communications technology solutions. These concepts differentiate sustainable cities from smart cities, which are distinguished by the implementation of cutting-edge information and communications technology. The development of smart sustainable cities is garnering an increasing amount of interest from research organizations, universities, governments, politicians, and ICT companies all over the world as a potential solution to the oncoming problems of urbanization and sustainability (Yigitcanlar, 2020).

Even if it is not often made clear, a "smart sustainable city" is a metropolitan area that is sustained by the ubiquitous presence and intense use of current information and communication technology. This is the definition of a "smart sustainable city." This definition is correct, despite the fact that it is not typically expressed in such a direct manner (Ahad, 2020). This makes it possible for the city to manage the available resources in a way that is secure, sustainable, and efficient, which, in the long run, leads to improved social and economic results. This is in connection to the many diverse urban systems and domains, in addition to the myriad of ways in which these components interact with one another and are coordinated.

In the words, a smart sustainable city is "a city that satisfies the needs of its current residents without impairing the capacity of other people or future generations to satiate their needs, and where this is supported by ICT." The fact that a smart sustainable city respects both local and global environmental boundaries is one of its most important characteristics. One of the most significant qualities of a smart and sustainable city is its residents' ability to fulfil their needs without negatively impacting the capacity of others (Kumar, 2022).

## DATA SCIENCE FOR BUSINESS, ACADEMIA, GOVERNMENT, AND SOCIETY

The quality of scientific research, government administrative decisions, and corporate decisions all have the potential to be improved through data analysis. In many circumstances, data science is able to quickly and precisely provide key insights into a variety of challenging problems.

*Figure 1. Key elements of data science*

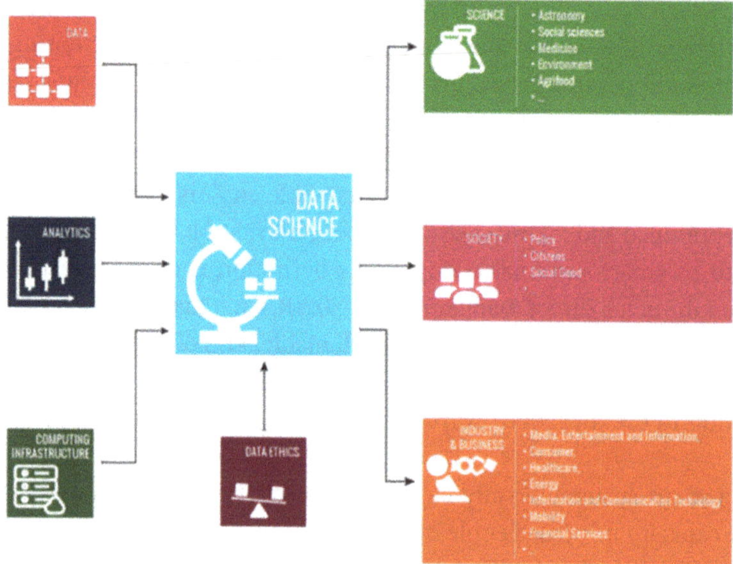


The picture on the left depicts the key elements that make data science possible (data, analytical techniques, and infrastructures). The effects of data science on society, research, and business are seen on the right. All data science-related activity must adhere to strict ethical standards.

As shown in Figure 1, the following scientific, technological, and financial components interact in data science:

## Data Access to Data Sources and Availability of Data

i. The open-source analytics and high-speed analytical processing infrastructures required for computing and analytics are both available; Skills
ii. The availability of engineers and data scientists with the necessary high level of skill;
iii. The ethical and legal issues raised You can obtain laws governing data ownership and usage, data security and privacy, safety, responsibility, cybercrime, and intellectual property rights. There are additional applications available.
iv. mobile applications created expressly for use in commerce;
v. Social factors draw attention to the most important geopolitical and socioeconomic challenges.

## Impact on Business and Industry

The study of data may provide a landscape rich with unexplored commercial possibilities powered by data. Massive amounts of data will increasingly be made available to anybody and everyone as a general trend across all industries. This will enable business owners to identify and rate inefficiencies in business operations, as well as to identify potential threads and win-win scenarios. In an ideal world, each individual resident would be able to derive novel business concepts from these patterns. Data scientists are able to build breakthrough goods and services through the process of co-creation. By exchanging data of varying kind and provenance, the value of combining many datasets is significantly more than the total of the values contained within the individual datasets individually. The applications of data science are anticipated to yield benefits in every area, from manufacturing and retail to services and wholesale.

In the framework of this discussion, we will go through a few of the most important sectors in which applications of data science have extremely bright futures. The digitalization of energy systems (from production to distribution) makes it feasible to collect accurate real-time data in the energy and environmental sectors. This opens up new opportunities for research and development. Integration of data from other sources, such as weather data, consumption patterns, and market data, together with the assistance of sophisticated analytics, has the potential to result in a significant rise in the levels of efficiency that are achieved. The use of geospatial data, which helps in understanding how our planet and its climate are changing and in finding solutions to important issues such as global warming, the preservation of species, as well as the role and impacts of human activities, further strengthens the beneficial influence that humans have on the environment.

Growing investments in Industry 4.0 and smart factories (Soori, 2023), which contain technology that is sensor-equipped, intelligent, and networked (for more information, see internet of things), are beneficial to the manufacturing and production sector of the economy. It is anticipated that cyber-physical systems would take their place among the most major sources of data creation in the globe. The use of data science to this industry will result in increased output as well as improved preventative maintenance. Customers will have direct access to, and influence over, the things that they purchase, which will open the door to the potential of whole new methods of doing business. This is a consequence of the capability of mass manufacturing customized goods (Grabowska, 2020).

## A KEY COMPONENT OF SMART CITIES IS SYSTEMATIC CYBERSECURITY

Even while this may lead to higher resident productivity and profitability, smart cities have a big difficulty when security is neglected. The first step toward realizing the full potential of these digitally connected enterprises is to implement cyber security best practices early on when local governments engage in smart operations (Alamer, 2021).

Smart cities represent the future of urban living, utilizing advanced technologies and data-driven solutions to enhance the quality of life, improve operational efficiencies, and promote sustainability. However, with the increasing integration of digital systems and Internet of Things (IoT) devices, cybersecurity has become a critical component of smart cities. Ensuring robust cybersecurity is essential to protect sensitive data, maintain public safety, and ensure the resilience of urban infrastructure.

The concept of "smart cities" is appealing since it suggests utilizing entrenched technology to plan and manage all city functions. This designation is given to cities that use information and communication technology (ICT) to monitor and integrate the state of all of its infrastructures, management, administration, residents and communities, wellness, education, and natural surroundings (Chen, 2021).

To plan, build, and run a smart city, a variety of extremely sophisticated integrated technologies, such as sensors, electronics, and networks associated with computerized systems, including databases, tracking, and decision-making algorithms, are necessary. These systems need to be able to talk to one another. Given that the rate of urbanization is predicted to continue increasing alarmingly in the near future, it is essential to adopt a cleverer strategy in order to overcome the many challenges brought on by the restructuring of the economy, the effects on the environment, management-related worries, and issues in the public sector. The challenges that today's cities confront are getting harder as a result of the faster rate of development in such communities. As a result, organizational adjustments are necessary, with a focus on the most recent technical advancements and online communication in particular.

## SOCIAL AND ECONOMIC FACTORS

Residents of smart cities may seek the assistance of technology that offers fundamental platform services for urban growth, backup, and community management in order to find solutions to the social issues that they are experiencing. As a direct consequence of this, smart cities evolve into systems of service that only require one step. In addition, smart cities offer services that improve banking, business events, and economic conditions, so contributing to improved financial development. The banking industry, the financial sector, and communication are examples of the economic and social factors that can have an impact on smart cities. These aspects also give possibility for potential breaches of security and invasions of privacy (Méndez-Picazo, 2021).

i. Challenges in Smart Communication

The communications infrastructure of smart cities is susceptible to a variety of attacks, including viruses, scams, and attacks on its confidentiality. The telecommunications industry is an important part of the critical infrastructure that makes up smart cities. Telecommunications networks are used for a variety of purposes, including those pertaining to finance and government. As a consequence of this, smart cities require some form of secure and audited setting in order to carry out the aforementioned kinds of activities. In addition, M2M communication offers a variety of advantages to the people living in smart cities.

ii. Individual Privacy

Individual citizen information in a smart city should be kept private. People in smart cities employ a variety of contemporary technologies that are connected via networks and systems to interact with one another and access services. Hackers and attackers are focusing on these diverse networks and systems. These criminals violate a person's privacy by accessing their private information, depriving them of their rights.

iii. Banking, Finance, and Business

Banking, economics, and commerce that are optimized for smart cities are the essential building blocks of smart cities. In smart cities, the economics, banking, and business sectors are all expanding; yet, these sectors are also subject to assaults due to the fact that individuals may target these areas in order to achieve financial benefit. An adversary or a hacker may also have a negative influence on the economy of a whole civilisation or of a single city.

iv. **Technological Factors:** The creation of the characteristics that are intended to be offered by a smart city relies heavily on the use of technology. One might make the case that technology is the only resource that smart cities rely on to provide for their citizens and their governments. A smart city is one that makes use of technology to provide its citizens with opportunities for economic growth, banking, business, and intelligent government. All of these assurances are commendable, but in addition to these advantages, the safety and privacy of the individual must also be taken into consideration. Without essential services such as safety and privacy, a smart city is not nearly as smart as it could be.

## CONCLUSION

To plan, build, and run a smart city, a variety of extremely sophisticated integrated technologies, such as sensors, electronics, and networks associated with computerized systems, including databases, tracking, and decision-making algorithms, are necessary. These systems need to be able to talk to one another. Given that the rate of urbanization is predicted to continue increasing alarmingly in the near future, it is essential to adopt a cleverer strategy in order to overcome the many challenges brought on by the restructuring of the economy, the effects on the environment, management-related worries, and issues in the public sector. Research institutions all around the world are focusing more and more on expanding a variety of sectors, such as healthcare, education, industries, cities, and communities. Universities, governments, parliamentarians, and businesses in the information and communications technology industry are all considering the Internet of Things as a potentially effective answer to the impending urbanization and sustainability concerns. Two examples of projections that might be used in the formulation of plans for sustainable education are the expansion of educational programs that emphasize sustainable development and global citizenship. Information and communication technology is significant in this situation and helps to create smart cities. They not only put in place the whole infrastructure of a smart city and solve issues with information security, but they also raise entirely new issues with privacy, protection, and threat resistance. Our main attention was on the educational system since it uses a larger portion of the available resources and has access to the right technologies to bring about the required reforms. Each of these websites has the ability to offer important data and information to investigation techniques based on data science and cyber security. This suggests that by maximizing the beneficial environmental, social, and economic effects of using and promoting open data in SD processes that are based on cooperation between national and local governments, donors, international organizations, civil society organizations, academic institutions, and industry, the Sustainable Development Goals (SDGs) can become a reality.

## REFERENCES

Ahad, M. A., Paiva, S., Tripathi, G., & Feroz, N. (2020). Enabling technologies and sustainable smart cities. *Sustainable Cities and Society*, 61, 102301. 10.1016/j.scs.2020.102301

(Ahad, 2020)

Alamer, M., & Almaiah, M. A. (2021, July). Cybersecurity in Smart City: A systematic mapping study. In *2021 international conference on information technology (ICIT)* (pp. 719-724). IEEE.

Albahri, A. S., Duhaim, A. M., Fadhel, M. A., Alnoor, A., Baqer, N. S., Alzubaidi, L., Albahri, O. S., Alamoodi, A. H., Bai, J., Salhi, A., Santamaría, J., Ouyang, C., Gupta, A., Gu, Y., & Deveci, M. (2023). A systematic review of trustworthy and explainable artificial intelligence in healthcare: Assessment of quality, bias risk, and data fusion. *Information Fusion*, 96, 156–191. 10.1016/j.inffus.2023.03.008

Ardito, L., Raby, S., Albino, V., & Bertoldi, B. (2021). The duality of digital and environmental orientations in the context of SMEs: Implications for innovation performance. *Journal of Business Research*, 123, 44–56. 10.1016/j.jbusres.2020.09.022

Bibri, S. E., & Krogstie, J. (2020). The emerging data–driven Smart City and its innovative applied solutions for sustainability: The cases of London and Barcelona. *Energy Informatics*, 3(1), 5. 10.1186/s42162-020-00108-6

Brunetti, F., Matt, D. T., Bonfanti, A., De Longhi, A., Pedrini, G., & Orzes, G. (2020). Digital transformation challenges: Strategies emerging from a multi-stakeholder approach. *The TQM Journal*, 32(4), 697–724. 10.1108/TQM-12-2019-0309

(Brunetti, 2020)

Burke, M., Driscoll, A., Lobell, D. B., & Ermon, S. (2021). Using satellite imagery to understand and promote sustainable development. *Science*, 371(6535), eabe8628. 10.1126/science.abe862833737462

(Burke, 2021)

Camacho, N. G. (2024). The Role of AI in Cybersecurity: Addressing Threats in the Digital Age. *Journal of Artificial Intelligence General science (JAIGS), 3*(1), 143-154.

(Camacho, 2024)

Chen, D., Wawrzynski, P., & Lv, Z. (2021). Cyber security in smart cities: A review of deep learning-based applications and case studies. *Sustainable Cities and Society*, 66, 102655. 10.1016/j.scs.2020.102655

(Chen, 2021)

Claudet, J., Bopp, L., Cheung, W. W., Devillers, R., Escobar-Briones, E., Haugan, P., Heymans, J. J., Masson-Delmotte, V., Matz-Lück, N., Miloslavich, P., Mullineaux, L., Visbeck, M., Watson, R., Zivian, A. M., Ansorge, I., Araujo, M., Aricò, S., Bailly, D., Barbière, J., & Gaill, F. (2020). A roadmap for using the UN decade of ocean science for sustainable development in support of science, policy, and action. *One Earth*, 2(1), 34–42. 10.1016/j.oneear.2019.10.012

Efron, B., & Hastie, T. (2021). *Computer age statistical inference, student edition: algorithms, evidence, and data science* (Vol. 6). Cambridge University Press. 10.1017/9781108914062

Fischer, C., Pardos, Z. A., Baker, R. S., Williams, J. J., Smyth, P., Yu, R., Slater, S., Baker, R., & Warschauer, M. (2020). Mining big data in education: Affordances and challenges. *Review of Research in Education*, 44(1), 130–160. 10.3102/0091732X20903304

Goswami, S. S., Sarkar, S., Gupta, K. K., & Mondal, S. (2023). The role of cyber security in advancing sustainable digitalization: Opportunities and challenges. *Journal of Decision Analytics and Intelligent Computing*, 3(1), 270–285. 10.31181/jdaic10018122023g

Grabowska, S. (2020). Smart factories in the age of Industry 4.0. *Management systems in production engineering, 28*(2), 90-96.

Karatas, M., Eriskin, L., Deveci, M., Pamucar, D., & Garg, H. (2022). Big Data for Healthcare Industry 4.0: Applications, challenges and future perspectives. *Expert Systems with Applications*, 200, 116912. 10.1016/j.eswa.2022.116912

(Karatas, 2022)

Karliner, J., Slotterback, S., Boyd, R., Ashby, B., Steele, K., & Wang, J. (2020). Health care's climate footprint: The health sector contribution and opportunities for action. *European Journal of Public Health*, 30(Supplement_5), ckaa165–843. 10.1093/eurpub/ckaa165.843

(Karliner, 2020)

Kenney, M., Serhan, H., & Trystram, G. (2020). Digitization and platforms in agriculture: organizations, power asymmetry, and collective action solutions. *Power Asymmetry, and Collective Action Solutions.*

Khan, F. A., Asif, M., Ahmad, A., Alharbi, M., & Aljuaid, H. (2020). Blockchain technology, improvement suggestions, security challenges on smart grid and its application in healthcare for sustainable development. *Sustainable Cities and Society*, 55, 102018. 10.1016/j.scs.2020.102018

Kharrazi, A., Qin, H., & Zhang, Y. (2016). Urban big data and sustainable development goals: Challenges and opportunities. *Sustainability (Basel)*, 8(12), 1293. 10.3390/su8121293

Kumar, S., Sharma, D., Rao, S., Lim, W. M., & Mangla, S. K. (2022). Past, present, and future of sustainable finance: Insights from big data analytics through machine learning of scholarly research. *Annals of Operations Research*, 1–44. 10.1007/s10479-021-04410-835002001

Kushwah, V. S., Parashar, J., & Bajpai, A. (2022). Study of Load Balancing and Security in Cloud Computing. In Soft Computing: Theories and Applications [Singapore: Springer Nature Singapore.]. *Proceedings of SoCTA*, 2021, 565–576.

Kushwah, V. S., & Saxena, A. (2013). A security approach for data migration in cloud computing. *International Journal of Scientific and Research Publications*, 3(5), 1–8.

Leal Filho, W., Eustachio, J. H. P. P., Nita, A. C., Dinis, M. A. P., Salvia, A. L., Cotton, D. R., & Dibbern, T. (2024). Using data science for sustainable development in higher education. *Sustainable Development*, 32(1), 15–28. 10.1002/sd.2638

Martínez-Peláez, R., Ochoa-Brust, A., Rivera, S., Félix, V. G., Ostos, R., Brito, H., Félix, R. A., & Mena, L. J. (2023). Role of digital transformation for achieving sustainability: Mediated role of stakeholders, key capabilities, and technology. *Sustainability (Basel)*, 15(14), 11221. 10.3390/su151411221

Matheus, R., Janssen, M., & Maheshwari, D. (2020). Data science empowering the public: Data-driven dashboards for transparent and accountable decision-making in smart cities. *Government Information Quarterly*, 37(3), 101284. 10.1016/j.giq.2018.01.006

Méndez-Picazo, M. T., Galindo-Martín, M. A., & Castaño-Martínez, M. S. (2021). Effects of sociocultural and economic factors on social entrepreneurship and sustainable development. *Journal of Innovation & Knowledge*, 6(2), 69–77. 10.1016/j.jik.2020.06.001

Möller, D. P. (2023). Cybersecurity in digital transformation. In *Guide to Cybersecurity in Digital Transformation: Trends, Methods, Technologies, Applications and Best Practices* (pp. 1–70). Springer Nature Switzerland. 10.1007/978-3-031-26845-8_1

Mondejar, M. E., Avtar, R., Diaz, H. L. B., Dubey, R. K., Esteban, J., Gómez-Morales, A., Hallam, B., Mbungu, N. T., Okolo, C. C., Prasad, K. A., She, Q., & Garcia-Segura, S. (2021). Digitalization to achieve sustainable development goals: Steps towards a Smart Green Planet. *The Science of the Total Environment*, 794, 148539. 10.1016/j.scitotenv.2021.14853934323742

Novikov, S. V. (2020). Data science and big data technologies role in the digital economy. *TEM Journal*, 9(2), 756–762. 10.18421/TEM92-44

Pansara, R. R. (2022). Cybersecurity Measures in Master Data Management: Safeguarding Sensitive Information. *International Numeric Journal of Machine Learning and Robots*, 6(6), 1–12.

Prüfer, J., & Prüfer, P. (2020). Data science for entrepreneurship research: Studying demand dynamics for entrepreneurial skills in the Netherlands. *Small Business Economics*, 55(3), 651–672. 10.1007/s11187-019-00208-y

Ray, D., Salvatore, M., Bhattacharyya, R., Wang, L., Du, J., Mohammed, S., & Mukherjee, B. (2020). Predictions, role of interventions and effects of a historic national lockdown in India's response to the COVID-19 pandemic: Data science call to arms. *Harvard Data Science Review*, (Suppl 1), 10–1162.32607504

(Ray,2020)

Romero, C., & Ventura, S. (2020). Educational data mining and learning analytics: An updated survey. *Wiley Interdisciplinary Reviews. Data Mining and Knowledge Discovery*, 10(3), e1355. 10.1002/widm.1355

Sadik, S., Ahmed, M., Sikos, L. F., & Islam, A. N. (2020). Toward a sustainable cybersecurity ecosystem. *Computers*, 9(3), 74. 10.3390/computers9030074

Sarker, I. H., Kayes, A. S. M., Badsha, S., Alqahtani, H., Watters, P., & Ng, A. (2020). Cybersecurity data science: An overview from machine learning perspective. *Journal of Big Data*, 7(1), 1–29. 10.1186/s40537-020-00318-5

Saura, J. R. (2021). Using data sciences in digital marketing: Framework, methods, and performance metrics. *Journal of Innovation & Knowledge*, 6(2), 92–102. 10.1016/j.jik.2020.08.001

Shaw, E., Walpole, S., McLean, M., Alvarez-Nieto, C., Barna, S., Bazin, K., Behrens, G., Chase, H., Duane, B., El Omrani, O., Elf, M., Faerron Guzmán, C. A., Falceto de Barros, E., Gibbs, T. J., Groome, J., Hackett, F., Harden, J., Hothersall, E. J., Hourihane, M., & Woollard, R. (2021). AMEE Consensus Statement: Planetary health and education for sustainable healthcare. *Medical Teacher*, 43(3), 272–286. 10.1080/0142159X.2020.186020733602043

Soori, M., Arezoo, B., & Dastres, R. (2023). *Internet of things for smart factories in industry 4.0, a review*. Internet of Things and Cyber-Physical Systems.

Sulich, A., Rutkowska, M., Krawczyk-Jezierska, A., Jezierski, J., & Zema, T. (2021). Cybersecurity and sustainable development. *Procedia Computer Science*, 192, 20–28. 10.1016/j.procs.2021.08.003

Tapaswi, S., & Kushwah, V. S. (2010, June). Securing Nodes in MANETs Using Node Based Key Management Scheme. In *2010 International Conference on Advances in Computer Engineering* (pp. 228-231). IEEE. 10.1109/ACE.2010.86

Thakur, V. (2021). Framework for PESTEL dimensions of sustainable healthcare waste management: Learnings from COVID-19 outbreak. *Journal of Cleaner Production*, 287, 125562. 10.1016/j.jclepro.2020.12556233349739

Veja, C., Hocker, J., Schindler, C., & Rittberger, M. (2021). *Educational open government data in Germany: the landscape, status, and quality*.

Yigitcanlar, T., & Cugurullo, F. (2020). The sustainability of artificial intelligence: An urbanistic viewpoint from the lens of smart and sustainable cities. *Sustainability (Basel)*, 12(20), 8548. 10.3390/su12208548

## KEY TERMS AND DEFINITIONS

**Data Science:** An interdisciplinary field that utilizes scientific methods, processes, algorithms, and systems to extract knowledge and insights from structured and unstructured data. It combines various domains such as statistics, mathematics, computer science, domain knowledge, and information science to analyze and interpret complex data sets.

**Sustainable Development Goals (SDGs):** A set of 17 global objectives established by the United Nations in 2015 as part of the 2030 Agenda for Sustainable Development. These goals aim to address pressing global challenges and promote prosperity while protecting the planet. The SDGs cover a broad range of social, economic, and environmental development issues.

**Cyber Security:** The practice of protecting systems, networks, and programs from digital attacks. These cyberattacks are typically aimed at accessing, changing, or destroying sensitive information, extorting money from users, or interrupting normal business processes. Cyber security involves a combination of technologies, processes, and practices designed to safeguard digital assets and mitigate risks.

**Healthcare:** This refers to the organized provision of medical services to individuals and communities with the aim of maintaining or improving health, preventing and treating illness, and managing physical and mental well-being. It encompasses a wide range of services provided by medical professionals, including diagnosis, treatment, preventive care, rehabilitation, and palliative care.

**Education:** The process of facilitating learning, or the acquisition of knowledge, skills, values, beliefs, and habits. It is a fundamental human right and a key driver of personal and societal development. Education can take place in formal, informal, and non-formal settings and encompasses various stages and types.

**Industry:** This refers to the economic activity concerned with the processing of raw materials and the manufacturing of goods in factories. It encompasses a broad range of activities that contribute to the production of goods and services for the economy. Industries are typically classified into several sectors, each focusing on a different type of economic activity.

**Business:** This refers to the organized efforts of individuals and entities to produce and sell goods and services for profit. It encompasses a wide range of activities and entities, from small, family-owned businesses to multinational corporations. The primary objective of a business is to generate profit by satisfying the needs and wants of customers.

**Academia:** This refers to the professional realm of education and scholarship, encompassing teaching, research, and learning at institutions of higher education such as universities, colleges, and research institutes. It is a key sector in society dedicated to the pursuit of knowledge, intellectual development, and the advancement of various fields of study.

**Society:** This refers to a group of individuals who live together in a defined territory, share a common culture, and are interconnected through various relationships and institutions. Societies can be large or small, simple or complex, and they evolve over time through cultural, economic, political, and social changes.

# Chapter 3
# Healthcare Innovation: Embracing Technology to Promote Long-Term Global Wellness

**Swathi Mirthika G. L**
https://orcid.org/0000-0002-4591-7811
*SRM Institute of Science and Technology, Kattankulathur, India*

**B. Sivakumar**
*SRM Institute of Science and Technology, Kattankulathur, India*

## ABSTRACT

*The practical use of technology in healthcare is a nascent discipline focused on promoting sustainability within the healthcare sector. Nevertheless, the research in this field has experienced significant and swift growth. Although this expansion has been beneficial for the discipline, it has also rendered it more challenging to comprehend its full scope. Thus, it has become impossible to answer questions about the biggest technological shifts in sustainable healthcare research, the most important revolution articles, their influence, and the most prolific and prominent scholars. Understanding the logical framework of technology for sustainable long-term healthcare information is difficult. An in-depth assessment of studies on revolutionary healthcare technology that promotes long-term health addressed these issues. It did so to address some of the issues. Over the past four years, the COVID-19 pandemic, artificial intelligence, machine learning, and the internet of things have propelled sustainable healthcare technology research.*

## INTRODUCTION

The convergence of innovation and technology is a beacon of hope in the ever-changing landscape of healthcare, illuminating a route towards sustained global wellbeing. This trend is expected to continue in the foreseeable future. The chapter reflects the essence of a revolutionary journey in which cutting-edge technologies are at the vanguard of redefining healthcare paradigms all over the world (Chauhan, 2022). In the world of healthcare innovation, the rapid growth of technology, particularly in the areas of digital health, artificial intelligence, and networked systems, has opened up opportunities that have never been

DOI: 10.4018/979-8-3693-2901-6.ch003

seen before. This development is not simply the adoption of new tools; rather, it marks a fundamental shift in the way that we approach, deliver, and maintain health and wellness efforts on a global scale.

Integrating advanced technologies in healthcare has become a revolutionary method to tackle current difficulties and optimize healthcare delivery. The objective of this project is to investigate how advanced technologies can contribute to the development of sustainable healthcare by reducing environmental consequences, enhancing social welfare, and promoting long-term global well-being. Technological advancements in recent years have completely transformed different areas of healthcare, including diagnostics, treatment, patient involvement, and administrative procedures. Nevertheless, in the midst of these progressions, there has been a growing focus on the long-term viability of healthcare systems, which now requires a comprehensive strategy that takes into account environmental preservation, social fairness, and economic feasibility.

The primary objective of this study is to investigate how advanced technology might improve the efficiency and effectiveness of healthcare. Additionally, it explores the broader consequences of sustainable healthcare development. Healthcare systems may enhance patient outcomes and benefit communities and natural resources by implementing eco-friendly practices, fostering social inclusion, and optimizing resource allocation. This study aims to explore the connections between advanced technology yet sustainable healthcare practices from a multidisciplinary perspective. It provides valuable insights into whether novel approaches might be used to build a healthcare system that is more resilient, fair, and environmentally friendly. This research intends to provide administrators, medical professionals, and stakeholders with a clear understanding of the advantages and difficulties associated with this paradigm shift. It seeks to guide them in attaining sustainable healthcare growth in the modern day.

The purpose of this study is to investigate the role that modern technologies play in enhancing the efficiency and effectiveness of healthcare delivery, while also taking into consideration the larger implications for the development of sustainable healthcare. Enhancing patient outcomes and contributing to the well-being of communities and natural resources can be accomplished by healthcare systems through the implementation of environmentally friendly practices, the promotion of social inclusion, and the optimisation of resource allocation (ROA). The purpose of this inquiry is to provide stakeholders with multidisciplinary insights into the relationships between advanced technology and sustainable healthcare practices. The research's ultimate goal is to guide stakeholders through the process of navigating this paradigm change.

The integration of environmental sustainability and social equality within healthcare systems is one of the key themes that are investigated in this study (Meroueh and Chen, 2023). Other key themes include precision medicine and healthcare analytics driven by artificial intelligence. Additionally, the study investigates the difficulties and prospects that are involved with establishing sustainable growth in the healthcare industry in the present day. This is accomplished by taking into consideration a variety of issues, including regulatory compliance, technology advancements, and the changing landscape of healthcare.

In the following sections, we explore the complex relationship between healthcare and technology, revealing the significant potential of this collaboration in transforming global well-being in the long run. We examine how technology acts as a catalyst for proactive measures, individualized treatments, data-based observations, and improved availability in the delivery of healthcare. By conducting a thorough analysis, our goal is to examine the various aspects of this revolutionary story and highlight the crucial role of technology in establishing a healthier, more interconnected, and sustainable society.

This investigation, at its core, digs into the complicated dance that takes place between healthcare and technology, highlighting the ways in which the combination of these two fields has the potential to reimagine the concept of comprehensive global wellbeing over the long run. In our era, which is characterized by the growing interconnection of our globe, where borders are becoming increasingly blurry and information flows without interruption, the implementation of technology in the healthcare industry becomes not merely a choice but rather a strategic need (Vishwakarma, 2023).

The integration of healthcare and technology is poised to create a future in which wellness is not just a destination but rather an ongoing, sustainable journey for individuals and communities all over the world. This future will be delivered via preventive measures, personalized therapies, data-driven insights, and greater accessibility. In the following pages, we will go through the process of peeling back the layers of this transformative narrative and investigating the role that technology plays as a catalyst for a world that is healthier, more connected, and more sustainable. The progress in the storage and processing capabilities of computers has facilitated the expansion of technological uses in the healthcare industry to ensure long-term viability. Sustainable Healthcare (SH) emphases on integrating economic, communal, and environmental variables within healthcare systems and procedures to ensure their long-term survival and efficacy (Saheb, 2019).

Therefore, SH acknowledges the interconnectedness amongst healthcare, environmental sustainability, and social welfare. Sustainable healthcare aims to reduce the adverse environmental effects of healthcare activities while optimizing health outcomes and resource efficiency (Ranabhat, 2023). This encompasses reducing inefficiencies, optimizing energy use, promoting sustainable procurement practices, and implementing proactive measures to improve public health. SH also advocates for social equity, community engagement, and equitable availability of healthcare services (Al Issa, 2023).

The health care sector has witnessed the proliferation of artificial intelligence (AI), machine learning (ML), the Internet of Things (IoT), big data, and cloud computing applications due to recent technological and communication breakthroughs (Aquino, 2018). These technologies and big data analytics can have a substantial impact on promoting the concepts of SH. One example is precision medicine, which involves the examination of large amounts of patient data, such as genetic information, medical records, lifestyle factors, and environmental data, using artificial intelligence and big data.

The evolution of the healthcare system has placed a significant emphasis on sustainable development, taking into account both current difficulties and future demands. Establishing a healthcare system that is capable of being maintained over time can result in enhanced healthcare outcomes. The healthcare sector requires enhanced capacity to optimize its existing resources, acquire novel resources, efficiently manage its finances, enhance service quality, and effectively respond to emergency situations.

In recent years, the increasing recognition of the importance of health and well-being for the population has necessitated the restructuring of the National Health System to align with universal public health systems and standards. There have been multiple adjustments that have altered the operation of Albanian healthcare. The Albanian Government's dedication to achieving the Sustainable Development Goals (SDGs) of the 2030 Agenda has been impacted by the recent initiation of EU integration negotiations. Nevertheless, the efforts and measures directed towards attaining the established goals are still at an early level, in contrast to several Balkan nations.

A public health system is founded on choice, and it is as sustainable as public opinion and politicians believe it should and can be. That being said, the action that has to be performed is a tough and complex issue. As a consequence of this, it is the responsibility of those who make decisions in the political, economic, and organizational spheres to devise adaptable strategies in response to the quick and ongoing changes that alter the requirements and anticipations of the populace, thereby reallocating the resources that are freely available. In a given context, the responsibility of satisfying the needs of citizens and solving relational problems has an effect on the survival of the system. This is because it creates conditions of consonance (in terms of the ability to relate to the outside world) and resonance (as an interactive system that is able to generate harmony between the parts) with the other entities that are involved in the fundamental dynamics of the system (Calabrese, 2023).

Environmental deterioration has significantly affected human health, leading to significant public health issues associated with a substantial rise in chronic ailments, including cardiovascular, respiratory, and neurological disorders. The healthcare systems in EU28 are currently facing numerous challenges that demand immediate attention due to their significant impact on wellbeing. The objective is to achieve a balance between healthcare expenses and the enhancement of patient care by creating cost-efficient and sustainable healthcare systems for the coming years, which will face complex challenges. Healthcare systems worldwide have the challenge of balancing two conflicting demands: the need to meet a growing demand for healthcare services and the need to reduce healthcare expenditures.

The healthcare sector, both domestically and internationally, accounts for 10% of economic activity and this percentage is increasing. However, therapies may not consistently confer benefits to patients and can potentially induce Nevertheless, treatments may not consistently yield positive outcomes for patients and might potentially inflict harm. Additionally, these treatments are becoming more reliant on technology and are accompanied by high costs. Meanwhile, a significant portion of healthcare spending is allocated towards managing chronic illnesses that are influenced by lifestyle choices and environmental variables(Chen, 2020). Greater emphasis on prevention is thus imperative to enhance patient outcomes and alleviate the burden on healthcare services to enhance their quality. It is necessary to also consider the detrimental effects of healthcare delivery on the environment. Sustainable healthcare prioritizes enhancing health and optimizing healthcare delivery, rather than solely intervening in disease at a later stage. This approach yields additional benefits for patients and the environment, which plays a crucial role in human health. Therefore, it would be beneficial to offer healthcare of superior quality presently, while ensuring that the capacity to provide healthcare in the future remains intact.

The goal of sustainable healthcare expansion is crucial as healthcare systems around the world struggle to balance expanding demand with constrained resources (Aydın, 2020). Healthcare systems may provide a more resilient and fair future for future generations by giving priority to prevention, improving patient outcomes, and addressing environmental sustainability.

## NEED FOR SUSTAINABLE HEALTH CARE PRACTICE

A Sustainable Healthcare System, according to the World Health Organization (WHO), is a system that enhances, sustains, or reinstates health while minimizing detrimental effects on the environment. It also takes advantage of opportunities to restore and enhance the environment, ultimately benefiting the health and well-being of present and future generations. Compelling data is indicating that the operations in a healthcare system have a substantial influence on and exert pressure on the environment. These factors encompass the production of perilous and typical waste, discharge of wastewater and greenhouse gases, and the substantial utilization of resources like water and electricity. Indeed, between 75% to 90% of waste generated in the healthcare sector has the potential to present various environmental and health hazards.

Gratefully, the progress in technology within the healthcare industry has demonstrated the capability to offer advantages for both health and the environment. Electronic e-health treatments have enhanced health outcomes and facilitated access to care, while also mitigating pollution by reducing the necessity for travel and yielding cost savings by decreasing the demand for care. Diverse medical gadgets and technology have additionally contributed to the decrease in water use and the generation of wastewater, hence counteracting greenhouse gas emissions. There are four general methods via which healthcare professionals might enhance their sustainability is depicted in Figure 1.

*Figure 1. General components to enhance the healthcare system*

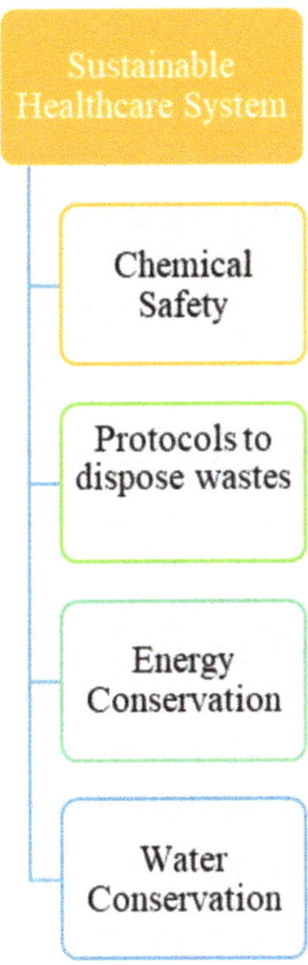


## Chemical Safety

The chemicals employed in LCD displays, fluorescent lamps, CRT monitors, flame-retardant mattresses, wheelchair cushions, and even baby bottles have the potential to be harmful. Hospitals should engage in deliberate procurement practices and regularly recycle hazardous materials.

### Protocols to Dispose Wastes

The process of disinfecting medical waste is known to be energy-intensive and can generate harmful odors. Healthcare practitioners should contemplate transitioning to more environmentally friendly methods of waste disposal, such as autoclaving, chemical treatment, and microwaving.

### Energy Conservation

Reducing energy consumption and carbon emissions may appear to be a daunting challenge, but it may be achieved by reprogramming the hospital's heating and cooling plants, redesigning air handling systems, and upgrading lighting systems as a starting point.

### Water Conservation

Healthcare providers can conserve millions of gallons of water annually by substituting bathroom toilets, faucets, and showers with water-efficient alternatives and acquiring high-efficiency dishwashers. The active involvement and cooperation of a committed workforce is essential for the successful implementation of measures aimed at enhancing environmental sustainability in healthcare systems. The system should actively involve health care personnel in the creation, implementation, and management of environmental sustainability measures, while fostering a sense of ownership and responsibility among them.

## Global Energy Access: Obstacles and Data Pertaining to Healthcare

The availability of electricity in a country is a measure of its standard of living and, in the context of healthcare, it reflects the level of quality in healthcare services provided by national healthcare facilities. The energy issues faced by healthcare institutions vary across low- and high-income countries. The primary obstacle faced by healthcare institutions in low-income nations, particularly those in sub-Saharan Africa, is the lack of access to dependable and cost-effective energy for essential life-sustaining requirements.

Several healthcare facilities in the aforementioned nations suffer from a lack of energy availability, which hinders the provision of essential services such as lighting, heating, and powering medical equipment. These restrictions curtail the ability to diagnose and treat patients, limit operating hours to daytime only, and may lead to a decrease in healthcare workers owing to dissatisfaction with working circumstances and atmosphere. The primary focus of energy concerns in healthcare institutions in high-income nations is to enhance efficiency and promote the utilization of renewable energy sources. This is done with the aim of diminishing energy consumption, decreasing operational expenses, and mitigating the environmental footprint.

A successful health system is characterized by three key elements: a population that achieves optimal health, high-quality care that is reliable, secure, current, focused on patients, fair, and efficient, and an equal treatment approach that is free from discrimination or disparities for all people and their families, irrespective of age, ethnic background, or location. Additionally, the system should also ensure fairness towards physicians, medical organizations, and companies involved in providing and supporting healthcare services. A sustainable health system is characterized by three essential qualities: affordability, which encompasses the ability of patients, their loved ones, hiring managers, and government agencies to bear the costs, considering that employers and the government depend on people such as users, staff, and taxpayers for their resources; acceptability to key stakeholders, such as patients and health professionals; and adaptability, as health and healthcare needs are not fixed, requiring the health system to respond flexibly to emerging diseases, shifting demographics, scientific advancements, and dynamic technologies to ensure its continued viability.

## Issues in Terms of Healthcare System

While the Covid-19 epidemic revealed the vulnerability of our healthcare system, the health of our citizens has been in a critical condition even before the pandemic. We have encountered various deficiencies, including shortcomings in infrastructure, personnel and finances, and the standard of treatment, among others. India has long been confronted with a chronic scarcity of healthcare professionals. In 2019, the nation's Ministry of Family Welfare and Health reported to the Senate that the country's doctor-to-population ratio stood at 1:1,457, but the World Health Organisation (WHO) recommended a ratio of 1:1,000. India's nurse-to-population ratio was 1.7 per thousand people, falling short of the desired ratio with three midwives per thousand people. India's bed-to-population ratio is well below the World Health Organization's recommended standard of three mattresses per one thousand individuals, with only one bed available for every 2,239 inhabitants. The deficit has expanded to encompass all tiers of frontline healthcare personnel. As to the National Health Statistics 2019, there was a 62 percent deficit in male health professionals at sub-centres. Approximately 60 percent of the primary healthcare centres (PHCs) lacked an adequate number of male health aides. The Common Health Centres (CHCs) saw a significant deficit of 85.6 percent in the number of surgeons, while Primary Health Centres (PHCs) faced a 75 percent shortage of physicians and a 50.8 percent shortage of lab technicians.

The impact of these shortages was keenly felt when the epidemic struck in 2020. There was a shortage of doctors and nurses required to oversee vital signs, conduct tests, and provide acute care. There was a lack of community health professionals and paramedical staff available to do surveillance operations, mass testing, and contact tracing outside of hospitals. Additionally, there was a significant scarcity of other essential resources, including personal protective equipment, oxygen cylinders, and ambulances. Although the government did not maintain an official tally, the Indian Medical Association reported a minimum of 1,700 doctor fatalities throughout the course of the pandemic. The statistic excludes additional healthcare personnel.

The consequences of the Covid-19 pandemic affected all aspects of life, and marginalized groups, including as women and girls, faced additional challenges due to the interruption of crucial healthcare services and an overwhelmed healthcare system. Projections by the Foundation for Reproductive Health Services India indicate that the lack of access to contraceptives during the lockdown potentially led to an extra 2.4 million unplanned pregnancies in India. Nearly two million Indian women faced limitations in their ability to obtain abortion services. The World AIDS Report 2020 states that in India, Covid-19 hindered the availability of contraceptives for a total of 25 million couples. According to a 2021 assessment by UNICEF, it is projected that there will be an 18 percent increase in maternal mortality and a 10 percent increase in stillbirths in India as a result of the pandemic. India will be haunted for years by the pictures of people from various social classes, communities, and regions losing their lives as a result of the deficiencies in the country's healthcare system. The Covid-19 pandemic served as a catalyst for countries worldwide, including India, to reconsider and revamp their public health systems and the methods by which healthcare services are provided. Our healthcare system must possess the capacity to effectively address the enduring effects of the pandemic and adequately ready itself for comparable future health crises.

Despite the crisis, it is disappointing to see that the health system has not undergone significant changes and the budgets have not seen a substantial increase. The allocation for health, as outlined in the National Health Policy 2017, remains far from reaching the target of 2.5% of the GDP. The National Health Mission (NHM) is the primary health project implemented by the Indian government since 2005. Its main objective is to deliver full medical care to the rural population. The NHM has significantly contributed to enhancing the quality of life in the country. However, the money allocated to the National Health Mission had a minimal rise of only 1 percent in the current year's budget.

## Integrating Cutting-Edge Technologies and Intelligent Solutions in the Field of Medical and Healthcare

Significant progress and revolutionary discoveries in science and technology are reshaping our planet. Specifically, remarkable advancements in biology and technology have significant implications for the growth of the global population and the impact on our health and longevity. The growing global population, already over 7.7 billion individuals, along with the anticipated rise in life expectancy resulting from scientific and technological progress, presents novel difficulties. The A high-level Legislative Council on Sustainable Development is a key United Nations platform established in September 2015 to serve as a comprehensive strategy for promoting the well-being of people, the planet, and economic development. It is anticipated that their aims and targets will encourage actions up to 2030. Goal 3 of the 2030 Agenda for Sustainable Development and its 169 targets strive to guarantee the provision of good health and well-being for individuals of all age groups (Papadopoulou, 2019).

Healthcare sciences are crucial for understanding variation in genes about gene/environment interactions, which play a central role in many diseases and biological processes.

Enhanced sanitation and hygiene practices, the use of vaccinations and medicines, enhanced comprehension of diseases, and novel therapies have effectively controlled numerous genetic and infectious diseases. Furthermore, enhanced living and working conditions have played a role in promoting good aging and extending lifespans, while also granting individuals access to superior food and essential nutrients. The significant increase in the number of elderly individuals, particularly in industrialized nations, serves as evidence of the remarkable advancements in the fields of science and technology. The World Bank predicts that the proportion of GDP allocated to healthcare in the EU may increase from 8% in 2000 to 14% in 2030.

Health informatics is a frequently used alternative phrase. Health informatics is a field of study that is alternatively referred to as clinical information systems, health informatics, and biomedical informatics. The most comprehensive word for this field is biomedical informatics. Health informatics is a branch of information science that primarily focuses on the organization and control related to medical data and information. This terminology may be perplexing, but it is important to bear in mind that technology is essentially a mode of transportation, not a final destination. Health informatics has facilitated research collaborations between researchers in the fields of Bioinformatics and Health Informatics, as well as administrators, doctors, and data scientists. Healthcare experts are now exploring ways to integrate the latest computational intelligence with Big Data Analytics, Data Mining, and Machine Learning Methodologies. This is made possible by the availability of high-speed computers, mobile technologies, and voice recognition.

## Methods for Creating Smart, Customized Healthcare Treatments

A significant volume of extensive Big Data, encompassing both organized and unorganized data, has been accumulated within the healthcare sector. Transforming Big Data into intelligent data is a challenging endeavor. Furthermore, it is crucial to thoroughly examine it to gain valuable insights that can enhance operational efficiency while enabling more informed decision-making (Shaik, 2023). The challenge of handling Big Data, whether it comes from smart sensors and is transmitted to collecting sites and analytical systems within the Internet of Things (IoT) systems, or if it is processed data awaiting transformation into actionable information, is truly quite demanding.

Electronic health records (EHRs) and other healthcare information systems enable the consolidation and analysis of extensive data to enhance health and financial decision-making.

With the expansion of genetic information collecting, databases have become enormous, becoming what is commonly referred to as Big Data, and are now integrated into Electronic Health Records (EHRs).

Data mining is a significant undertaking. Large healthcare organizations will gather and analyses diverse clinical, economic, and managerial information to make informed clinical and commercial decisions. Hence, Data Analytics holds significant importance and necessitates professionals with a high level of education. There is a significant demand for computer scientists (or informaticists) who possess the ability to effectively utilize information technology to accelerate the transmission and examination of data, resulting in enhanced efficiencies and knowledge.

## Innovations and Prudent Fixes to Advance Healthcare and Medicine

The driving forces underlying Health Informatics are readily apparent. Comprehensive training is required, encompassing a strong grasp of biological systems as well as IT expertise in networking and structures, accessibility, reengineering processes, workflow analysis, and redesign. Subsequently, it is imperative to priorities adequate training and enhancement of quality, effective project management, astute leadership, and collaborative teamwork to guarantee the attainment of medical excellence and seamless execution.

## Methods for Sharing the Health Care Expertise

Health Informatics is an emerging and stimulating field that offers several job prospects, particularly in the academic sector. The publication rate for research in health information technology is rising, which will ideally lead to more frequent and unbiased evaluations of novel approaches and technologies. While technology offers significant potential, it is not the panacea for all the challenges now confronting the field of medicine. The paramount objective of this emerging discipline remains the enhancement of patient care.

## Envisioning the Next Phase of Robust Smart Healthcare

The Figure.2 below provides a summary of the core technological components of smart healthcare, which encompass several developing and efficient technologies. Additionally, it includes some policy implications for smart healthcare. Wearables will use generative AI to offer customized and customized experiences to consumers, while also facilitating advancements in genetic research (Zhavoronkov, 2021).

The persistent way of managing the content for groups in an intelligent health care system is represented in Figure 2. Patients will be at the forefront of the healthcare ecosystem through the use of DNA-based medicines, which will promote equal access to care and customization. Content management groups that are persistent in intelligent healthcare systems have a crucial function in efficiently and effectively organising, overseeing, and distributing healthcare-related information. These groups are responsible for managing the whole lifespan of healthcare content, which includes its development, archive, retrieval, collaborating, and preservation.

*Figure 2. Persistent content management groups of intelligent healthcare systems*

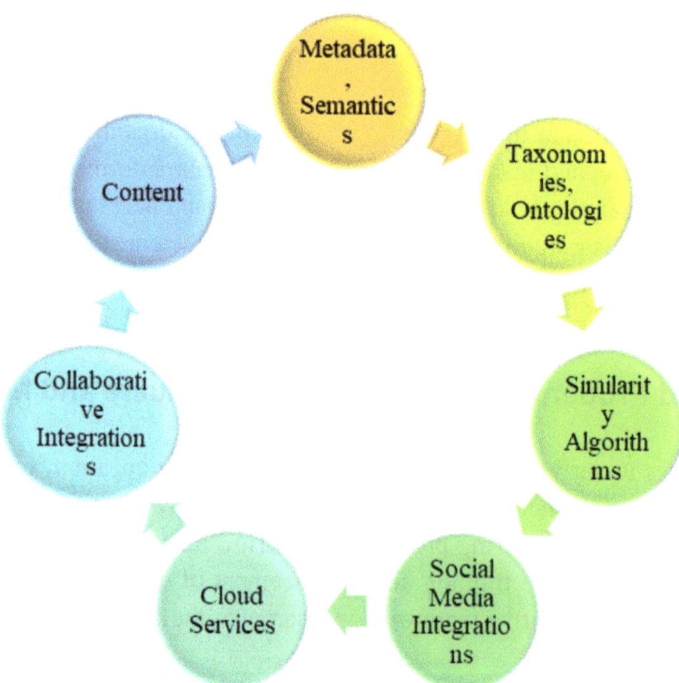


## Modern Progress Towards a Long-Term Healthcare System

Various developments have been influencing sustainable healthcare practices. The various fields of sustainable health care system are listed in Figure 3.

*Figure 3. Several recent advancements in health care system*

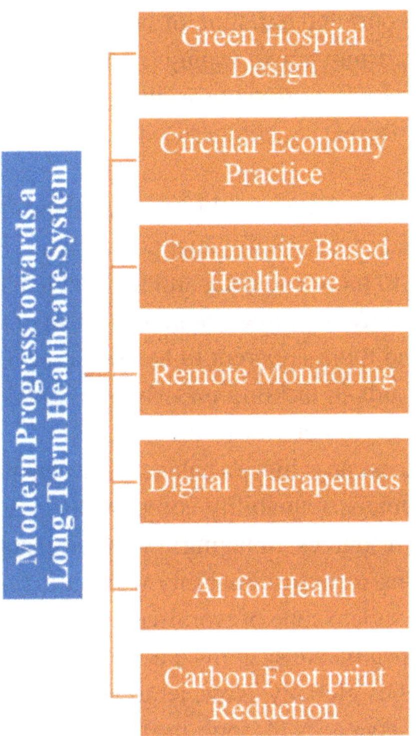


*Green Hospital Design:* Eco-friendly healthcare facilities are increasingly being designed and built. Green hospital designs integrate energy-efficient technologies, power from renewable resources, environmentally friendly supplies, and minimise waste measures to reduce the environmental effect of healthcare facilities.

*Circular Economy Practice:* Implementing circular economy ideas in healthcare includes minimising waste, repurposing materials, and reusing medical equipment. Efforts involve renovating and reusing medical equipment to prolong their usage, hence reducing the environmental impact.

*Community Based Healthcare:* Healthcare models are increasingly shifting towards grassroots efforts and preventive care strategies to ensure sustainability. This change intends to decrease dependence on emergency facilities, minimize healthcare expenses, and enhance public health.

*Remote Monitoring:* Remote patient monitoring technology have improved healthcare delivery by enabling patients to be tracked in their own homes. This enhances patient comfort and decreases the necessity for hospital admissions, resulting in more efficient resource allocation.

*Digital Therapeutics:* In order to provide therapeutic interventions for a range of medical diseases, digital therapeutics uses technology and software. These solutions are cost-effective, scalable, and can help decrease the environmental impact of conventional healthcare delivery.

*AI for Health:* Health inequities are being identified and addressed through the analysis of healthcare data using artificial intelligence. AI algorithms aid in creating specific solutions and enhancing healthcare accessibility for marginalized people, advancing health equity.

*Carbon Foot print Reduction:* There is a growing trend among healthcare organizations to lower their carbon impact. This involves shifting to renewable energy sources, maximizing energy-efficient technologies, and adopting transport and handling of waste measures to reduce environmental harm.

*Blockchain for enhancing transparency in supply chains:* Drug safety and healthcare supply chains are turning to blockchain technology to increase visibility and auditability. This aids in verifying the legitimacy of pharmaceuticals, decreasing counterfeiting, and enhancing the long-term viability of the supply chain.

*Public Health Precision:* Precision public health uses statistical analysis, genetics, and digital technology to personalize global medical care for individual populations. This method improves the efficiency of public health tactics, leading to more enduring and focused healthcare projects.

*The Role of Societal Factors in Health Integration:* The effect of socioeconomic variables on medical conditions is becoming more and more apparent to health care systems. Incorporating socioeconomic factors into healthcare systems aids in tackling underlying reasons for health inequities, leading to an increasingly efficient and enduring system for healthcare.

Sustainable healthcare practices can achieve a balance between the triple bottom line of people, planet, and profit by addressing economic sustainability components in addition to environmental and social factors. By effectively managing resources, engaging in strategic planning, and ensuring fair access to care, healthcare systems can attain long-term sustainability while utilising technology to improve healthcare delivery. When we examine the wider scope of worldwide problems and solutions, it becomes clear that sustainability goes beyond just healthcare systems. Factors like energy access have a crucial impact on the overall welfare of communities globally. Now, let us explore the crucial significance of worldwide energy accessibility and its consequences for long-term growth. Each of these technical breakthroughs plays a role in changing how healthcare is provided by increasing the availability of care, improving patient results, and supporting long-term viability. Smart Healthcare systems may eliminate conventional obstacles to healthcare availability and supply by utilizing interoperability and data integration, artificial intelligence (AI) and machine learning (ML), as well as telemedicine and remote monitoring technologies. This enables the development of more efficient, effective, and patient-centered care models.

## Long-Term Global Wellness is Aided by Sustainable Healthcare

Sustainable healthcare is essential for improving the well-being of people all over the world over the long term. This is accomplished by addressing the environmental, economic, and social factors that have an impact on health outcomes. Healthcare that is sustainable plays an important part in improving long-term global well-being through a variety of approaches, including the following:

- A commitment to reducing the negative effects that healthcare operations have on the surrounding environment is at the heart of sustainable healthcare (Healthcare). This includes the planning and building of environmentally friendly hospitals that place an emphasis on energy conservation, sustainable energy sources, and materials that are beneficial to the environment. As a consequence, the carbon footprint is reduced, which makes a contribution to the broader attempt to battle global warming and construct a planet that is healthier for future generations.
- Realizing that proactive actions are crucial to long-term wellness; sustainable healthcare models heavily emphasize preventative treatment. Prevention of diseases before they appear or worsen is the goal of these models, which include lifestyle education, frequent testing, and immunizations.

Furthermore, community-based care promotes wellbeing and resilience across diverse groups by ensuring that medical treatments are customized to local needs.

- Understanding the interconnected nature of social determinants of health like poverty, housing, and education is essential for healthcare sustainability. More health equity is a result of healthcare systems' efforts to address these issues. Promoting wellness across various populations is achieved through including communities in healthcare decision-making, which guarantees that initiatives are respectful of culture, receptive, and accessible.
- Sustainability in healthcare is based on making the most of available resources. These practices result in more sustainable systems by reducing waste, optimizing energy consumption, and using technology to improve healthcare delivery. In the long run, people and communities would be able to afford healthcare services better because of the improved accessibility and affordability.
- Technological improvements that expand people's ability to get healthcare are an integral part of healthcare sustainability. Electronic health records, mobile health, and telehealth all help bring better healthcare to neglected or faraway places. This helps with both the early diagnosis and treatment of health problems and their continuous management, which adds up to long-term health on a worldwide scale.
- A key component of sustainability is the adaptability and readiness of healthcare systems. Models for long-term healthcare sustainability show resiliency in the midst of changing healthcare demands, priorities readiness for pandemics, and plan for emergencies. In the long run, these systems help keep people healthy and stop the propagation of illnesses by encouraging flexibility.
- International cooperation and the sharing of information and best practices are promoted by sustainable healthcare. Collaborations between healthcare organizations on a global scale pave the way for more efficient healthcare strategy development, data sharing, and research. In order to enhance wellbeing on a worldwide scale, this team effort helps in tackling common health issues.
- Sustainable healthcare is based on the principle of lowering healthcare expenses. The continued accessibility of healthcare without financial burden is guaranteed by affordability initiatives, efficiency improvements from optimized resource usage, and preventive care measures. By lowering the cost of healthcare, this dedication to economic viability improves people's health in the long run.
- Promoting healthy lifestyles and implementing behavioral treatments are crucial for long-term healthcare sustainability. Every person has the potential to make a good impact through public health initiatives, educational programs, and individualized interventions. Sustainable healthcare models help people stay healthy in decades to come by promoting a wellness culture.
- One component of long-term healthcare sustainability is educating and empowering local populations. People can better manage their health when they have access to accurate information, which is made possible through public health awareness and education programs. Better long-term health outcomes are more probable to occur in communities where members are well-informed and actively participate in making lifestyle changes.
- Sustainable healthcare embraces a mindset of constant innovation and embraces technology improvements. Digital health solutions, precision medicine, and artificial intelligence all work together to make healthcare better all the time. Improved diagnostics, therapies, and healthcare practices as a whole are outcomes of this flexibility, which in turn promotes global wellness in the long run.

## Smart Healthcare Equipment

*R&D facility for cutting-edge VR services:* Within the context of resilient smart healthcare, the concept of utilizing virtual and augmented reality for the purpose of providing a system that adds value is a valuable one. The Virtual Reality Laboratory System is one of our main proposals for advanced services, such as the realization of prototypes of services and designs of user experiences for resilient smart healthcare interaction. This is only one of the many options and possibilities that are available to us.

*System for automation:* Robotics applications will play a significant role in the development of Smart Cities. Having a Robotics Lab in the portfolio of resilient Smart Healthcare systems is a significant addition for showcasing and conducting experiments (Stewart, 2018). At an initial level, the focus can be on Educational Robots and Industrial Robots, which represent two complimentary elements of life.

*Data management system for wearables and sensors:* A robust Smart Healthcare architecture must include a platform for built-in sensors and gadgets that can gather a wide range of data types, including text, audio, and video. This technology can be utilized as needed by other organizations or on an ongoing basis to enhance several facets of contemporary life. Consider the following: urban areas might establish a system of audio sensors to monitor the surrounding noise levels and contribute to the development of laws aimed at reducing or eliminating it. Alternatively, an advanced sensor system equipped with cameras and cognitive capabilities would promptly alert the relevant authorities upon detecting any abnormal activity.

*IoT systems that handle devices and infrastructures all in one:* The impact that the Internet of Things is expected to have on businesses over the next few years is highly encouraging. The Internet of Things (IoT) technologies can be deployed in a number of different ways. An example of this would be an enhanced Internet of Things service for the administration of fleets of cars in adaptable Smart Healthcare systems for the purpose of cost utilization and monitoring.

## Essential Qualities for Sustainable Healthcare System

1. **Economic Stability:** Economic sustainability is the capacity of healthcare systems to continue operating profitably while providing excellent patient care and allocating resources as efficiently as possible.

## Essential Qualities

i. Cost Efficiency: Implementing steps that are economically efficient in order to reduce waste and optimise the utilisation of resources.
ii. Financial Viability: Ensuring sustained financial stability by implementing strategic planning and diversifying sources of revenue.
iii. Ensuring healthcare services are affordable and accessible by reducing financial obstacles.
iv. Enhancing the ability to survive economic downturns and changes in funding by developing resilience.

Visual Aid: An infographic may incorporate a chart illustrating the patterns in healthcare spending over a period of time, emphasising initiatives aimed at controlling expenses and enhancing financial adaptability (Aydın, S.,2020).

2. **Environmental Sustainability:** The goal of environmental sustainability is to reduce the negative effects of healthcare operations on the environment while fostering resource conservation and ecological stewardship.

## Essential Qualities

i. Green Practices: Adopting eco-friendly measures to decrease carbon emissions and minimise waste production.
ii. Energy Efficiency: Embracing energy-efficient technologies and renewable energy sources in order to decrease energy usage.
iii. Sustainable Procurement: Emphasising sustainable sourcing and procurement strategies to reduce environmental damage.
iv. Environmental Stewardship: Advocating for the implementation of conservation initiatives and the preservation of biodiversity in healthcare institutions.

Visual Aid: A visualisation may include graphics symbolising environmentally friendly activities, alternative power sources, and environmentally friendly purchasing methods, accompanied with data on energy usage and trash reduction (Ranabhat, C. L. et al.,2023).

3. **Social Sustainability:** To alleviate social determinants of health and guarantee that all people have equal access to healthcare, social sustainability advocates for healthcare systems that are inclusive, welcoming, and actively involve the community.

## Essential Qualities

i. Health Equity: Tackling inequalities regarding medical availability and results among diverse populations.
ii. Community Engagement: The act of actively including communities in the process of making healthcare decisions and developing programmes, with the goal of promoting empowerment and accountability.
iii. Cultural competence refers to the ability to deliver treatments and amenities that are sensitive to different cultures, respecting their varied opinions, principles, and traditions.
iv. Social justice refers to the advocacy for legislation and procedures that aim to ensure equality, equity, and social harmony in the delivery of healthcare.

## SOLUTIONS AND RECOMMENDATIONS

Individually, each of these technologies, in addition to big data analytics, has the potential to make a significant contribution to the development of environmental sustainability principles. An illustration of this would be (i) precision medicine, which is characterised by the utilisation of artificial intelligence and big data in order to analyse huge volumes of patient data. This includes genetic information, medical records, lifestyle factors, and environmental data, among other types of information. Making it possible for medical professionals to design individualised treatment plans, customise medications, and anticipate patterns of illness, which eventually leads to the delivery of healthcare that is more targeted and effective. The term "remote patient monitoring" refers to a technique that involves the utilisation of wearables, the Internet of Medical Things (IoMT), and other devices that are powered by artificial intelligence (Dagliati, 2021).

The purpose of this technique is to continuously monitor the vital signs of patients, collect information about their health, and transmit it to medical specialists. Monitoring patients remotely supports the early diagnosis of health problems, prompt treatments, and reduced routine hospital stays, all of which lead to improved patient outcomes and the preservation of resource management. Remote patient monitoring also ensures that patients receive timely treatment. ii) Optimisation of healthcare processes: Artificial intelligence systems are utilised to assess complicated healthcare operations, locate areas of inefficiency, and provide recommendations for how to improve the process. As a consequence, this leads to enhanced resource management, reduced wait times, enhanced staff scheduling, and streamlined processes, which eventually results in healthcare delivery that is more effective and less costly. Using a combination of big data and artificial intelligence, healthcare organisations are able to analyse patterns of population health, forecast the occurrence of disease outbreaks, and effectively distribute resources. Another name for this type of analysis is predictive analytics. A contribution to the implementation of sustainable healthcare practices is made by this proactive strategy. This contribution is made through the prevention of the spread of diseases, the improvement of emergency preparedness, and the optimization of resource utilization. iii) Healthcare data management, which involves the safe storage of enormous amounts of health information, its integration, and the utilization of big data analytics for analysis. The ability to do research, disseminate information, and make suggestions that are supported by the data that is available is simplified as a result of this, which eventually leads to an improvement in the outcomes of healthcare and the wellbeing of patients.

Compatibility and data unification refer to the capacity of different systems and platforms to work together and exchange information seamlessly. For instance, in the United States, the Health Information Exchange (HIE) enables medical professionals to safely obtain and distribute patient health information electronically. This network allows for smooth communication between various healthcare systems and enhances the coordination of care. The Care Quality Compatibility Platform supports the secure exchange of patient records between multiple Electronic Health Record (EHR) systems, allowing healthcare organisations to share data. The implementation of this interoperability programme has resulted in enhanced care coordination, decreased redundant tests, and enhanced patient outcomes.

Artificial Intelligence (AI) and Machine Learning (ML): IBM Watson Health utilises an artificial intelligence (AI) system for clinical decision-making that examines medical literature, patient information, and diagnostic imaging. This technology aids healthcare providers in accurately diagnosing diseases and suggesting appropriate treatment options. Google's DeepMind Health has created an artificial intelligence programme that can effectively identify diabetic retinopathy by analysing retinal images. With improved detection and management of diabetic retinal disease, this technique may lower the risk of vision loss in diabetic patients.

In light of the new mandate that was issued by the medical regulator (from life science and health care), which requires newly trained physicians to be able to apply the concepts, techniques, and knowledge of sustainable healthcare to medical practice, the question of how to most effectively incorporate this instruction into the extremely varied curricular frameworks of medical schools has arisen. This is because the mandate requires that newly trained physicians implement sustainable healthcare.

A sustainable healthcare system lays an emphasis on the improvement of health and the delivery of healthcare in a manner that is more suitable, as opposed to concentrating on late intervention in disease. In the curriculum for medical education, topics such as over-diagnosis and over-treatment, as well as cost effectiveness and therapy as a burden on patients, are discussed.

All of these subjects are included in the outcomes for graduates. In order to advocate for people who are currently deficient in agency, it is now required to conduct study on wellness or health as well as illness, as well as the environmental elements that influence both of these things. It is essential to keep in mind the benefits that will accumulate, which include the following: benefits to the health service as well as health additional advantages for patients; preparation of future physicians for the realities of their future practice; and, last but not least, any impact on the mindset of senior leaders who are new to teaching about sustainable healthcare. All of these benefits will accumulate over time.

## FUTURE DIRECTION

In the future, the work that will be done to achieve sustainable healthcare and global wellness will require continual efforts to enhance and expand existing projects, incorporate emerging technologies, and handle evolving obstacles. By providing the enhanced connectivity that is both faster and more dependable for applications that require a lot of data, such as healthcare and remote monitoring. In order to provide remote patient care, surgical robots, robotic-assisted rehabilitation robots, and telepresence robots are being developed. When it comes to managing, analyzing, and gaining insights from huge and complicated datasets, the utilization of big data in the healthcare industry represents a disruptive approach. The analysis of big data plays a key role in improving the efficiency and efficacy of healthcare systems. This is especially true when it comes to the management of population health, the prediction of disease outbreaks, and the optimization of resource allocation.

## CONCLUSION

The use of machines and associated equipment in healthcare has mainly been restricted to administrative tasks. Innovations with technology and changing legislation have led to widespread acceptance of computers in different areas of healthcare establishments. They are often used in patients' rooms, medical carts, nursing stations, labs, operating rooms, and other important areas in healthcare facilities. Recently, substantial progress in computing technology has significantly increased the amount of information available to healthcare professionals. Healthcare databases have enabled doctors to obtain extensive information on certain diseases and treatment methods. Computers can do simulations to analyze the underlying causes of diseases and investigate possible treatments. By collaborating with other devices, they improve their capabilities and raise the chances of attaining effective results. Ensuring a robust, adaptable, and enduring healthcare system that can effectively deliver safe, high-quality care in the face of current and future challenges is a major obstacle for governments, health services, funders, policymakers, healthcare providers, and patients. This review will discuss the characteristics of sustainable healthcare systems, as well as the criteria and indicators utilized to assess their effectiveness.

We will analyze international concepts and strategies to guide potential solutions for healthcare system change and the development of highly effective healthcare delivery systems. This protocol outlines a structured approach for identifying, selecting, appraising quality, extracting data, and analyzing significant sources of grey literature within healthcare system sustainability. The approach can guide future reviews conducted by us or other researchers, facilitating comparisons of changes across time.

## REFERENCES

Al Issa, H. E., Abdullatif, T. N., Ntayi, J., & Abdelsalam, M. K. (2023). Green intellectual capital for sustainable healthcare: Evidence from Iraq. *Journal of Intellectual Capital*, 24(4), 929–947. 10.1108/JIC-02-2022-0046

Aquino, R. P., Barile, S., Grasso, A., & Saviano, M. (2018, October 1). Envisioning smart and sustainable healthcare: 3D Printing technologies for personalized medication. *Futures*, 103, 35–50. 10.1016/j.futures.2018.03.002

Aydın, N., & Yurdakul, G. (2020, December 1). Assessing countries' performances against COVID-19 via WSIDEA and machine learning algorithms. *Applied Soft Computing*, 97, 106792. 10.1016/j.asoc.2020.10679233071686

Calabrese, M., Suparaku, S., Santovito, S., & Hysa, X. (2023, July 25). Preventing and developmental factors of sustainability in healthcare organisations from the perspective of decision makers: An exploratory factor analysis. *BMC Health Services Research*, 23(1), 797. 10.1186/s12913-023-09689-w37491258

Chauhan, A., Jakhar, S. K., & Jabbour, C. J. C. (2022, March 1). Implications for sustainable healthcare operations in embracing telemedicine services during a pandemic. *Technological Forecasting and Social Change*, 176, 121462. 10.1016/j.techfore.2021.12146235034990

Chen, P. T., Lin, C. L., & Wu, W. N. (2020, August 1). Big data management in healthcare: Adoption challenges and implications. *International Journal of Information Management*, 53, 102078. 10.1016/j.ijinfomgt.2020.102078

Dagliati, A., Malovini, A., Tibollo, V., & Bellazzi, R. (2021). Health informatics and EHR to support clinical research in the COVID-19 pandemic: An overview. *Briefings in Bioinformatics*, 22(2), 812–822. 10.1093/bib/bbaa41833454728

Meroueh, C., & Chen, Z. E. (2023, February 1). Artificial intelligence in anatomical pathology: Building a strong foundation for precision medicine. *Human Pathology*, 132, 31–38. 10.1016/j.humpath.2022.07.00835870567

Papadopoulou, P., Chui, K. T., Daniela, L., & Lytras, M. D. (2019, January 1). *Virtual and Augmented Reality in Medical Education and Training*. Advances in Educational Technologies and Instructional Design Book Series. 10.4018/978-1-5225-9031-6.ch006

Ranabhat, C. L., & Jakovljević, M. (2023, January 11). Sustainable Health Care Provision Worldwide: Is There a Necessary Trade-Off between Cost and Quality? *Sustainability (Basel)*, 15(2), 1372. 10.3390/su15021372

Saheb, T., & Saheb, M. (2019). Analyzing and Visualizing Knowledge Structures of Health Informatics from 1974 to 2018: A Bibliometric and Social Network Analysis. *Healthcare Informatics Research*, 25(2), 61–72. 10.4258/hir.2019.25.2.6131131140

Shaik, T., Tao, X., Higgins, N., Li, L., Gururajan, R., Zhou, X., & Acharya, U. R. (2023). Remote patient monitoring using artificial intelligence: Current state, applications, and challenges. *Wiley Interdisciplinary Reviews. Data Mining and Knowledge Discovery*, 13(2), e1485. 10.1002/widm.1485

Stewart, J., Sprivulis, P., & Dwivedi, G. (2018). Artificial intelligence and machine learning in emergency medicine. *Emergency Medicine Australasia*, 30(6), 870–874. 10.1111/1742-6723.1314530014578

Vishwakarma, L. P., Singh, R. K., Mishra, R., & Kumari, A. (2023). Application of artificial intelligence for resilient and sustainable healthcare system: Systematic literature review and future research directions. *International Journal of Production Research*, 1–23. 10.1080/00207543.2023.2188101

Zhavoronkov, A., Bischof, E., & Lee, K. F. (2021). Artificial intelligence in longevity medicine. *Nature Aging*, 1(1), 5–7. 10.1038/s43587-020-00020-437118000

# Chapter 4
# The Role of IoT in Modern Healthcare:
## Innovations and Challenges in Pandemic Era

**Pardhu Thottempudi**
http://orcid.org/0000-0002-9653-1951
*BVRIT HYDERABAD College of Engineering for Women, India*

**Vijay Kumar**
*Vellore Institute of Technology, India*

## ABSTRACT

*This chapter delves into the internet of things, a pivotal technological innovation incorporating sensors across various fields. Sensors in IoT are essential for data collection and crucial for detailed analyticity's impact is profound in developing smart cities, modern agriculture, digital education, and healthcare, particularly noticeable during the COVID-19 pandemic, highlighting the need for digital healthcare solutions. IoT significantly enhances healthcare by enabling precise patient monitoring through a digital network. This study examines the applications of IoT, technological challenges, and barriers in health-care, drawing on databases like Google Scholar, Elsevier, and PubMed. The discussion underscores the importance of IoT in healthcare, opening avenues for new research and tackling industry challenges. It shows IoT's role in improving healthcare services, combining it with advanced technologies to expand its beneficial impact. The chapter addresses potential challenges and offers strategies to improve IoT-based healthcare, focusing on COVID-19 and future health crises.*

## INTRODUCTION

In today's world, we inhabit a digitally interconnected landscape where numerous devices and objects are linked together. Once connected through the internet, these devices become intelligent, capable of communication and autonomous decision-making. The Internet of Things (IoT) embodies this expansive

DOI: 10.4018/979-8-3693-2901-6.ch004

network, gathering and storing data from its surroundings to create a cohesive ecosystem of connected devices (Abbas and Yoon, 2015; Abdul Rahim et al., 2021; Abu-Elkheir and Ali, 2015).

IoT is pivotal in facilitating remote access and control over these digital entities, significantly enhancing societal, processual, and business aspects. The devices in this realm vary from nanochips and routers to diverse components like sensors, actuators, and software, all working in unison for seamless communication (Akhtar et al., 2020; Alarcón et al., 2019; Alasmari and Anwar, 2016; Abu-Elkheir and Ali, 2015).

With its broad spectrum of applications, the IoT is witnessing exponential growth. Wireless Sensor Networks (WSNs) have emerged as a key technology, especially for monitoring purposes, due to their cost-effectiveness, minimal infrastructure requirements, varied network topologies, and low maintenance needs. These networks serve in multiple domains, monitoring everything from environmental and climate changes to infrastructure and human health (Arbat et al., 2016; Atzori and Morabito, et al., 2010; Azzawi et al., 2016).

In healthcare, sensors are critical in monitoring, alerting, controlling, and managing patient behaviors. The healthcare sector is advancing towards increased independence by leveraging sensors for diagnostic and analytical purposes. This shift diminishes the dependency on manual intervention and facilitates swifter, more efficient responses in healthcare (Babu et al., 2016; Chavan et al., 2016; Chen et al., 2018; Chiang and Zhang, 2016).

IoT applications in healthcare propose substantial benefits for patients, medical professionals, and healthcare administrators. These applications strive to augment the existing healthcare framework by providing real-time intensive care, managing emergencies, and performing various other functions. IoT allows individuals to monitor vital signs and conditions like hypertension, diabetes, heart diseases, and physical activities, relaying this information to designated medical facilities or professionals (Choudhary and Sharma, 2020; Corno et al., 2016; Darshan and Anandakumar, 2015; Dohr et al., 2010; Fabricatore et al., 2020)

*Figure 1. IoT connectivity framework*

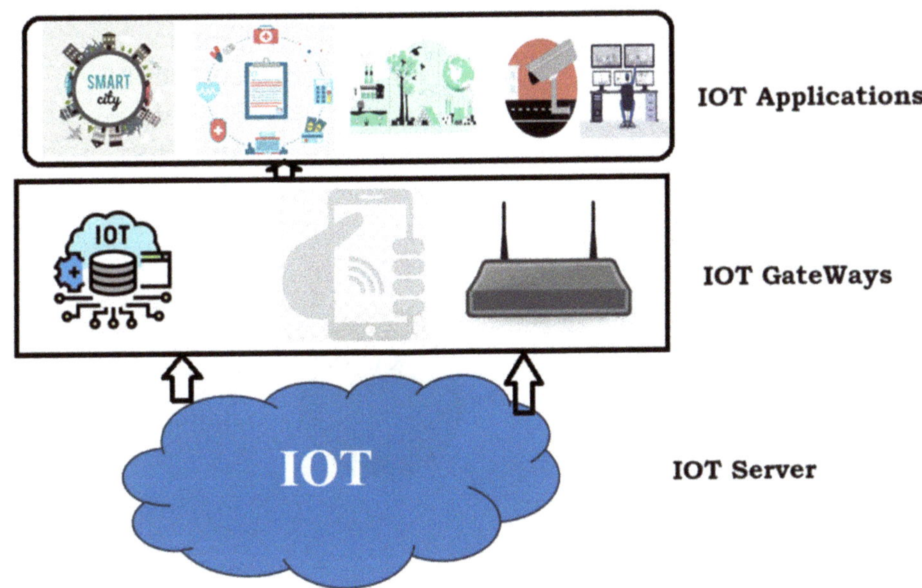


Figure 1 showcases the widespread use of IoT in healthcare, illustrating how clinics can offer timely medical responses by precisely tracking patient locations and diagnosing conditions.

Figure 2 highlights IoT's reliance on ambient, pervasive, and ubiquitous computing, examining the interplay between M2M communication, cyber-physical systems, and WSNs within the IoT context.

The functionality of IoT hinges on the integration of M2M and WSN technologies. In dynamic M2M systems, physical objects and computer components interact robustly through Cyber-Physical Systems (CPS). Technologies like M2M, CPS, and WSN are adept at executing actions, perceiving data, and performing computations (Ferro and Potorti, 2018; Gigli and Koo, 2011; Gubbi et al., 2013; Haleem et al., 2020).

IoT, functioning as a reliable WSN, operates on M2M communication and creates CPS. Cloud computing further empowers IoT by efficiently and economically handling large data volumes, processing, analyzing, managing, and enhancing resilience against failures (Abdul Rahim et al., 2021).

The Internet of Things (IoT) requires the implementation of advanced big data technologies for its analysis and processing, given its complex nature and the limitations of traditional data processing methods. IoT employs process information alongside context-aware technologies to enhance the search, filtration, and interpretation of extensive sensor data volumes (Tavares and Macedo, 2021).

Recent advancements in the Internet of Things (IoT) have significantly impacted healthcare, offering unprecedented opportunities for enhancing patient care and operational efficiency. IoT encompasses a network of interconnected devices that gather and transmit data, enabling real-time monitoring, personalized treatment plans, and improved healthcare outcomes. This chapter focuses on the critical role of IoT in healthcare, particularly its pivotal response to the COVID-19 pandemic, illustrating how these technologies not only address current challenges but also shape the future of healthcare delivery (Hussain et al., 2020).

*Figure 2. Visualizing interconnectivity dynamics in the IoT landscape*

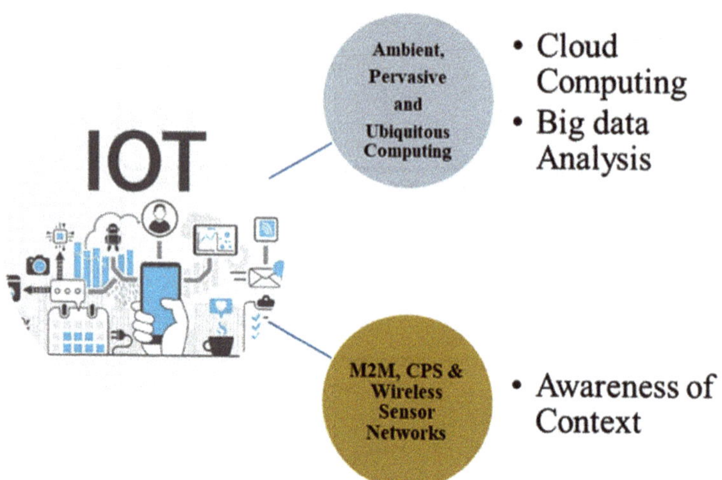


## Context

IoT applications significantly improve daily life by integrating real-time devices into scientific and industrial advancements. Particularly notable is the rising prominence of the Internet of Things (IoT) in healthcare, especially in the context of the COVID-19 pandemic. IoT is employed for various functions, including clinical services, patient care, early detection and monitoring of medical conditions, digital-based treatments, and continuous patient support systems. The rapid collection and analysis of patient data, facilitated by smartphones, are accelerating these processes (Hussain et al., 2020; Ibn-Mohammed et al., 2021; Jara et al., 2014)

Data collection and monitoring tasks are simplified by sensors placed in hospital rooms, on medical devices, and within emergency services. These sensors continuously relay data to nearby medical facilities, enabling swift responses. Healthcare organizations are leveraging IoT to provide a dependable and efficient system for monitoring and tracking (Javaid et al., 2020a, 2020b)

Cloud computing further augments healthcare by offering data storage, service distribution, integration of data facilities, and critical safety notifications. Extensive research has been conducted into the intersection of healthcare and IoT. Today, most people know the symptoms and signs of a coronavirus outbreak. To manage the pandemic risk, a group of informed and well-connected individuals can alert authorities about potential infection cases. Similarly, smartphone-based applications can benefit communities by facilitating faster medical response times (Kag et al., 2015; Kao et al., 2020; Khan et al., 2021; Kumar et al., 2021; Kumar and Yan, 2013; Lee et al., 2014)

The need for a clear lockdown protocol and the challenges in accessing vital patient supplies have intensified the situation. However, IoT can extend crucial access to patients in remote areas. The chapter delves into elements such as wires, mobile ad hoc networks, wireless technologies, and sensor networks, all critical for facilitating communication within IoT. Other studies explore the core cloud concept and the technologies that enable IoT applications, discussing the challenges in developing and implementing these applications in healthcare systems (Liang et al., 2021; Majeed et al., 2021; Meena et al., 2021).

An additional analysis reviews technologies like 802.15.4, NFC, 6LoWPAN/IEEE, and Bluetooth in wireless devices for mHealth and eHealth applications within IoT. Technologies like radio-frequency identification (RFID) and optical wavelength are also explored in the context of IoT, and their potential applications and limitations are discussed.

## Contribution and Scope

This chapter examines the most recent methodologies in healthcare systems using the Internet of Things (IoT) framework. This chapter seeks to enhance healthcare systems by analyzing them from an Internet of Things (IoT) perspective while recognizing prior research in IoT healthcare. Additionally, its objective is to provide researchers and educators with novel tactics to enhance the accessibility of IoT applications on a broader scale. (Lee and Kim, 2017; Li et al., 2015; Liang et al., 2021; Mahmood and Almohammed, 2015).

It is essential to have a comprehensive grasp of IoT's core structure and constituents. Figure 3 presents a comprehensive picture of several Internet of Things (IoT) applications in the healthcare sector, focusing specifically on those that greatly enhance the quality of patient care (Mahmoud et al., 2018; Majeed et al., 2021; Majumder et al., 2019; Masoud, 2018).

The chapter examines various pivotal uses of IoT sensors now under development. These programs are specifically developed to improve medical care, streamline workflows, maximize the utilization of limited resources, and decrease patient expenses. The text explores various technologies and provides recommendations on their most effective use, considering elements such as patient attributes, the type of condition they have, and the particular healthcare environment. (Meena et al., 2021; Miao and Gan, 2016; Moniruzzaman and Hossain, 2013; Movahedi et al., 2015)

This section also emphasizes the various challenges and issues confronting the healthcare profession, particularly within the pressures of the COVID-19 epidemic. The article explores security and privacy issues, intricate technical processes, and financial limitations. (Nambi et al., 2016; Nasrin and Rahman, 2021; Pandya et al., 2015; Parreira et al., 2020; Patel and Meena, 2020).

This chapter thoroughly examines the various applications, technology, difficulties, and potential solutions in the healthcare field. This comprehensive survey provides significant insights that will help us prepare for future pandemics that may be larger than the current COVID-19 epidemic (Patil et al., 2017; Purohit et al., 2021; Rao et al., 2020; Rathore et al., 2016)

## Organization of Chapter

Figure 4 thoroughly analyzes the seven main segments in this Study.

The chapter begins by introducing the Internet of Things (IoT) and its possible uses in the healthcare field. This chapter emphasizes the noteworthy contributions substantiated by empirical evidence.

The second section provides an in-depth analysis of the current literature on healthcare systems within the framework of the Internet of Things (IoT) paradigm.

The third segment of our Study extensively examines the essential elements of IoT in healthcare to enhance our comprehension of its functioning.

The fourth section comprehensively analyzes many applications of the Internet of Things (IoT) in the healthcare sector. These applications demonstrate IoT's ability to significantly enhance society's resilience during significant health emergencies, as seen during the COVID-19 pandemic. They are currently undergoing additional development to tackle upcoming difficulties.

The fifth section delves into the technological aspects of IoT in healthcare, offering an in-depth examination and explanation of the various dynamics at play. In the sixth segment, we analyze the potential challenges and achievements in the future trajectory of IoT in healthcare. This section is notable for offering innovative perspectives in comparison to previous research.

The seventh section provides a comprehensive examination and conclusive evaluation, briefly outlining the primary subjects and findings of the Study.

## EVALUATION AND ANALYSIS OF THE INTERNET OF THINGS (IOT) IN HEALTHCARE SYSTEMS

This chapter analyzes how the Internet of Things (IoT) is integrated with healthcare systems. Our initial step involved collecting academic literature on healthcare systems, followed by a focused gathering of articles on healthcare IoT systems and related sensor technologies. Figure 3 illustrates a thorough review conducted across various databases, using keywords relevant to IoT and sensors in healthcare (Rawassizadeh et al., 2015; Razaque and Elleithy, 2016; Riva et al., 2012; Roopa and Shabadi, 2020).

The global surge in disease prevalence and patient numbers poses complex challenges for healthcare systems. IoT is crucial for developing a systematic and well-organized approach to these challenges. Industries and businesses increasingly rely on IoT to improve their operations, including the Internet of Healthcare Things (IoHT) and the Internet of Medical Things (IoMT). IoHT and IoMT can simplify and reduce complexities in healthcare systems, particularly for diseases like COVID-19 (Shang et al., 2017; Sharma and Sharma; 2020; Shelke et al., 2021; Sharma et al., 2020; Singh and Kumar, 2020)

*Figure 3. Data acquisition parameters*

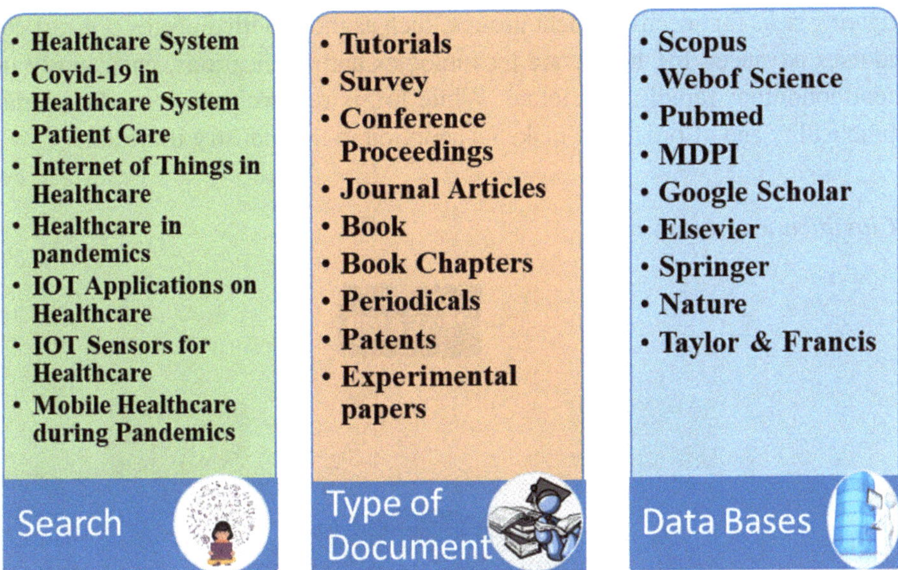

• Healthcare System
• Covid-19 in Healthcare System
• Patient Care
• Internet of Things in Healthcare
• Healthcare in pandemics
• IOT Applications on Healthcare
• IOT Sensors for Healthcare
• Mobile Healthcare during Pandemics
Search
• Tutorials
• Survey
• Conference Proceedings
• Journal Articles
• Book
• Book Chapters
• Periodicals
• Patents
• Experimental papers
Type of Document
• Scopus
• Webof Science
• Pubmed
• MDPI
• Google Scholar
• Elsevier
• Springer
• Nature
• Taylor & Francis
Data Bases


There is significant exploration into IoT and cloud computing use in healthcare. Innovations include cloud-based services for remote patient identification and IoT applications tailored for specific healthcare challenges. Android applications utilizing cloud-based IoT technology are instrumental in creating efficient healthcare systems. The increasing demand for IoT in academia, industry, and society has led to novel healthcare system designs, including transmitting heart rate information through intelligent health bands and the iCarMa system for early detection and communication in cardiac care (Singh and Sharma, 2021; Tavares and Macedo, 2021; Thomas et al., 2018; Wahsheh et al., 2021).

(Alasmari et.al 2016) addresses concerns around privacy and security within IoT. It highlights the risks introduced by integrating cloud technology into IoT in healthcare and underscores the need to focus on unique privacy and security issues in IoT-enabled healthcare systems.

Kao et al. (2020), Rao et al. (2020), and Singh et al. (2021) advocates for incorporating cloud computing into healthcare systems, identifying obstacles within the IoT framework that hinder healthcare progress. The study introduces an audio pathology model for continuous patient monitoring, emphasizing usability and framework compatibility challenges.

Khan et al. (2021) and Nasrin and Rahman (2021) explore the IoT infrastructure, applications, industrial relevance, and technologies. It discusses security aspects, including the necessity of security in IoT, privacy concerns, security protocols, and requirements for a framework to counteract taxonomic threats. It proposes sophisticated strategies to mitigate cyber attacks and encourage IoT growth in healthcare and e-health services.

According to Kumar et al. (2021) and Shelke et al. (2021), communication technologies are vital for enhancing IoT implementation in healthcare. It suggests a system of implanted body sensors to transmit data reliably to a shared infrastructure using IoT, along with additional security measures for the proposed system and future portable device systems.

The research in these publications is crucial for aiding physicians in diagnosing and efficiently communicating patient conditions, offering comprehensive evaluations of all IoT healthcare services. It guides mitigating risks for specific patient groups, such as those with diabetes or heart conditions. This chapter endorses advanced IoT healthcare technologies and applications, particularly in emergencies where patient conditions rapidly deteriorate. While IoT is relatively new in educational and medical fields, its practicality and affordability make its adoption in the industry inevitable.

*Figure 4. Classification frame work*

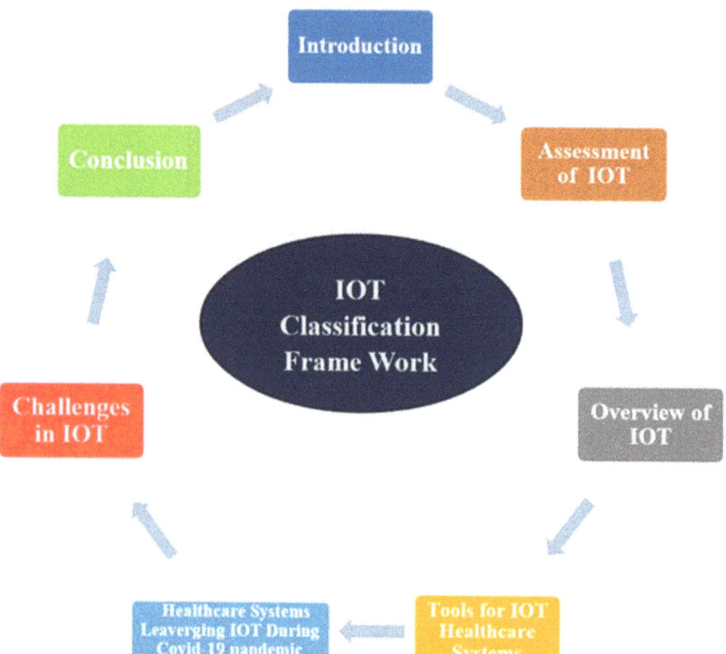


## INTRODUCTION TO THE INTERNET OF THINGS (IOT)

### Elements of the Internet of Things

A comprehensive understanding of IoT's components is essential to grasp its functionality and services. Figure 5 outlines the six key elements of IoT, providing categorizations and examples of their collaborative operations that collectively encapsulate IoT's essence.

1. Identification

In IoT, identification is crucial for recognizing the client's identity and location in response to requests. Each network component must have a unique, identifiable feature. IoT can be identified by its ubiquitous nature and use of electronic product codes. Addressing is critical in IoT, distinguishing an object's unique identifier from its physical location. Object IDs in IoT can be assigned to anything, like a sensor or actuator, while an object's address denotes its location within the IPv4 or IPv6 network space. The support of IPv6 for low-power wireless networks marks a significant advancement in IoT, allowing objects in the network to use public IP addresses instead of private ones (Wang et al., 2018; Wu et al., 2017; Yaseen et al., 2021; Yilidrim and Bal, 2020; Yousefi et al., 2021).

*Figure 5. Components of IOT framework*

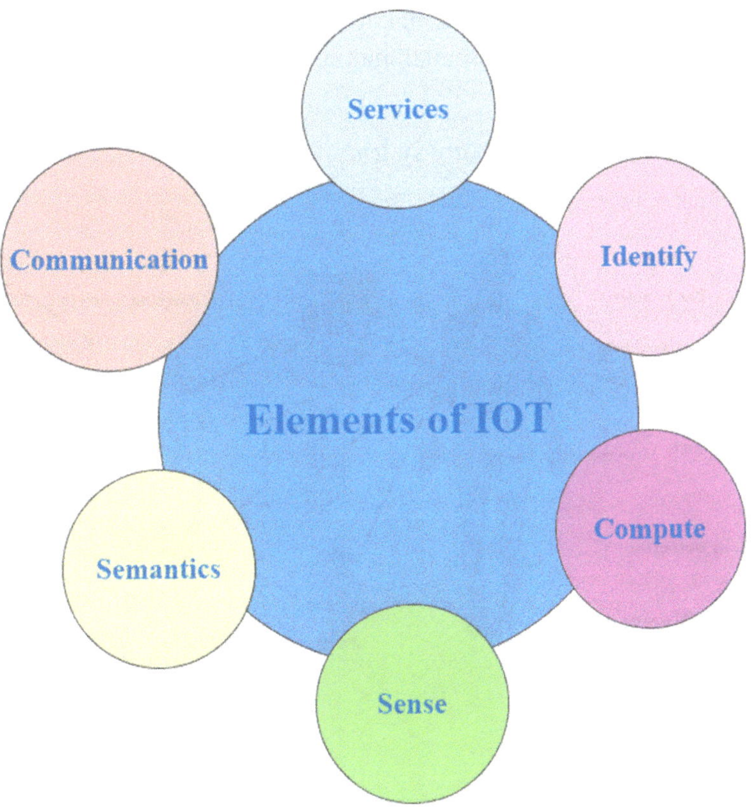


2. Sensing

Sensing involves collecting data from network nodes and sending it to a central processing unit like a data center or cloud. Data is gathered based on specific service needs and objectives. Maximizing IoT's potential requires the use of advanced actuators and sensor devices. Companies like WeMo and SmartThings produce smart devices and applications that enable centralized management of multiple devices through smartphones. Microcontrollers, computers, sensors, integrated TCP/IP, and security protocols are vital for IoT devices' full potential, connecting each device to a centralized service for critical information.

Figure 6 shows sensors are crucial in applications using inferred data to process and manage real-world sensor variations. A broad spectrum of sensors is available, from fundamental to advanced models. Sensor architecture includes requirements, specifications, conversion methods, testing, materials, sensing methodologies, measurement properties, and application domains.

3. Transmission of Information

Protocols like NFC, WLAN, RFID, UWB, Bluetooth, IEEE 802.15.4, LTE, Z-wave, and others facilitate communication between different IoT devices. NFC uses faster data rates and broader frequency ranges, enabling communication within a 40 cm range. Wi-Fi is essential in mobile ad hoc networks for data exchange over short distances. RFID, a pioneer in machine-to-machine communication, is key for data and voice transfer in commercial and residential networks. UWB combines high data transfer with low energy consumption, ideal for sensor-based applications. Bluetooth provides high throughput and low power needs over short distances, a valuable component in IoT. LTE, essential for mobile data transmission, supports changing network structures and relies on broadcasting services. Its advanced version offers increased bandwidth and spatial multiplexing capabilities.

*Figure 6. IoT-Enabled sensors in healthcare systems*

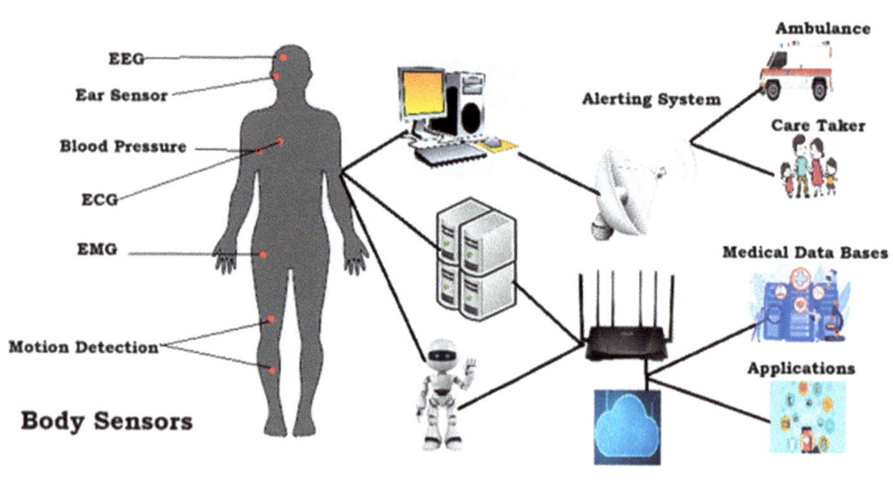


4. Computation

IoT computation occurs on various hardware and software platforms like Raspberry Pi, Arduino, Intel Galileo, etc. The operating system, activated at system startup, is critical for software platforms. Contiki RTOS is widely used in IoT application development. IoT heavily relies on the cloud's adaptability and scalability, transmitting data from devices to the cloud for big data analysis and user dissemination.

5. Services

IoT services fall into four categories: identity-related, widespread, collaborative awareness, and information aggregation. Identity services are fundamental for more complex services, tracking physical objects' virtual representations. Information aggregation services collect, analyze, and supply sensor data to IoT programs. Decisions and actions of collaboratively aware services depend on data from aggregation services. Ubiquitous services ensure the availability of collaboratively aware services everywhere.

Comparing IoT applications becomes straightforward with these services. IoT relies on collaborative and data-gathering services. Collaboratively aware services include smart campuses, intelligent transportation, smart industries, and homes. Information aggregation services cover advanced healthcare, educational advancements, and utility infrastructure like smart grids. Ubiquitous services improve the quality of life in smart cities, providing easy access to public transport, energy, and healthcare.

6. Semantics

IoT semantics facilitate data collection and utilization from connected devices for intended services. Data acquisition involves discovery, application, and modeling, ensuring exemplary service for the correct user. OWL and RDF standards help describe and transfer web data, meeting material requirements.

## Case Study

Boston Medical Center's IoT Integration Boston Medical Center implemented an IoT system for real-time location services to track medical equipment. This system reduced staff time spent searching for devices and significantly decreased annual costs related to device replacement. This system improved operational efficiency and enhanced patient care by ensuring that necessary equipment was readily available when needed.

# TECHNOLOGIES AND TOOLS FOR IOT IN HEALTHCARE SYSTEMS

In response to the COVID-19 pandemic, IoT technologies have been rapidly deployed to assist in managing the public health crisis. Contact tracing apps, developed to track and reduce the spread of the virus, utilize IoT capabilities to provide real-time data to health authorities. Furthermore, IoT-enabled thermal cameras have been used in public spaces to detect individuals with elevated temperatures, providing an early indicator of potential infection.

This chapter examines the pivotal role of the Internet of Things (IoT) and sensors in healthcare systems, highlighting their capacity to meet end-user needs. It discusses the shift in focus towards end-user-oriented application development and service-oriented application developers. Integrating various technologies has transformed IoT into a crucial and effective tool in healthcare, especially in managing COVID-19.

1. Emergency Medical Vehicles Using IoT

Paramedics face intense pressure, with decisions that can mean life or death for patients. The effectiveness of IoT-enabled ambulances is demonstrated through the swift and appropriate actions of remote medical teams. Innovations like Red Ninja's Life First Emergency Traffic Control algorithm optimize emergency traffic signals, speeding up ambulance movement.

2. Telemart in the IoT Era

Telemart has maintained social distancing in public spaces like supermarkets during the COVID-19 pandemic. Collaborating with Amazon, Telemart uses QR codes for store entry, allowing customers to shop and automatically bill their Amazon accounts.

3. Nexleaf Analytics

This program is crucial for monitoring vaccination and food programs in developing countries. It ensures vaccines are kept at consistent temperatures in remote medical facilities and optimizes stoves by providing real-time data on carbon dioxide emissions and wood usage. Its internet connectivity and server integration make it ideal for remote monitoring of COVID-19 patients.

4. Barcode and Label System

This cloud-based and wireless system integrates various treatment devices for chronic illness management. It provides real-time patient data for quick healthcare responses and has improved disease identification through a pharmaceutical delivery system. During the 2009 COVID-19 pandemic, cities like Sydney used "virtual hospitals" for remote patient monitoring through mobile apps.

5. Quio

As human life expectancy surpasses 60 years, healthcare delivery is shifting from hospitals to homes. Projects like Parkinson House, a collaboration between IBM and Pfizer, use IoT to improve information exchange between doctors and patients, monitor medication effectiveness, and make immediate adjustments.

6. In-Home Medical Care

Originally for entertainment, smartwatches have become valuable medical tools by companies like Samsung, Apple, and Google. They now include features like electrocardiograms for early detection of heart conditions and respiratory disease monitoring, with upcoming models expected to remind users about handwashing for COVID-19 prevention.

7. Wearable Devices

These devices are crucial for the elderly living alone, especially in emergencies or medication management. They use a pendant to monitor vital signs and alert healthcare providers of any irregularities, proving beneficial during the COVID-19 pandemic when visiting elderly relatives was discouraged.

8. Advanced Metering Infrastructure (AMI)

Smart grids with sensors and transducers are essential for providing electricity to hospitals during pandemics. AMI, a key component of smart grids, allows electricity companies to monitor and resolve technical issues remotely, minimizing human intervention and ensuring continuous power supply to healthcare facilities during the COVID-19 crisis.

9. Blood Glucose Level Monitoring

During the pandemic, having a glucose, blood pressure, and temperature monitor is vital. Proposals include:

- Using real-time glucose monitoring systems connected to IoT.
- Simplifying meal planning and medication management.
- Detecting and preventing COVID-19 spread.

10. Intelligent Wheelchair

Research on intelligent electric wheelchairs aims to improve the lives of the disabled, injured, or elderly. These wheelchairs, equipped with various sensors and IoT connectivity, can collect patient data from multiple sources, including wheelchair movement, environment, and user position.

## INNOVATIVE HEALTHCARE SYSTEMS UTILIZING IOT DURING THECOVID-19 PANDEMIC

The healthcare sector is increasingly adopting various Internet of Things (IoT) technologies, especially in light of the COVID-19 pandemic. As user needs and industry demands evolve, IoT continues introducing new technologies with significant potential in healthcare. This chapter highlights key technologies that are currently crucial or promising for the future of IoT in healthcare.

IoT devices in healthcare range from wearable sensors that monitor vital signs to smart beds that detect patient movement and vital statistics. For example, wearable ECG monitors allow continuous tracking of heart rhythms and can detect abnormalities earlier than traditional methods. Another innovative application is smart inhalers, which monitor usage patterns in asthma patients and can trigger alerts when usage suggests worsening control, thereby preventing severe episodes.

1. Ambient Intelligence-Based Communication Technologies

Ambient intelligence integration benefits users, patients, healthcare professionals, and facilities significantly. It aids in collecting and analyzing patient data via wearable devices and sensors. Governments and healthcare systems can leverage IoT's interconnected structure, encompassing human-computer interactions, autonomous control, and ambient intelligence, especially in managing COVID-19.

2. Augmented Reality (AR)

Augmented reality is vital in technological advancement, education, and innovation in the Industry 4.0 era. Its impact on healthcare includes educational tools, remote patient monitoring, and surgical procedures. AR also contributes to preventing COVID-19 and other diseases by promoting hand hygiene education.

3. Wearable Devices

Wearable devices offer financial and medical benefits for various conditions. Their compatibility with diverse sensors allows for comprehensive data collection on patients and their environments, with data stored and accessed online via mobile devices. Connecting mobile apps to wearable IoT devices enhances computational capabilities. Figure 7 shows the indispensable role of wearable devices in healthcare IoT, especially during pandemics like COVID-19.

4. Intelligent Autonomous Robotics

In Rwanda, the UNDP employs robotics to combat COVID-19, unprecedentedly enhancing lives. Governments and industries use IoT and robotics to automate tasks like disposing of contaminated items, sanitizing hospital areas, and transporting patient belongings. The emergence of IoT and robotics heralds a new professional environment, with germ-eliminating robots using UV light for continuous sanitation.

5. Intelligent Machinery

The COVID-19 pandemic has prompted industries to modify operational procedures and physical environments. MIT suggests various measures to reduce pathogen spread indoors, including desk spacing, antimicrobial surfaces, thermal scanners, air conditioning modifications, social distancing floor markings, and enhanced cleaning protocols. Some employers also provide or mandate COVID-19 testing. Industries are adopting intelligent device automation and robotic tools for improved safety and productivity, with a "Command Centre" translating technology into actionable business IT and consolidating data for emergency decision-making.

6. Supportive Wilderness Living (SWL)

SWL is an intelligent assistance system that improves seniors' safety, well-being, and dignity. It enables caregivers to better support older adults through wearable technology, smartphone apps, and IoT, alerting them to potential dangers and emergencies.

7. Gaming with a Purpose During Lockdown

Serious gaming has seen increased interest during the COVID-19 lockdown, extending beyond entertainment to sectors like education, healthcare, and engineering. It enhances training and educational efforts and provides a valuable method for managing patient conditions and exercises, particularly for those affected by COVID-19.

*Figure 7. Wearable gadgets*

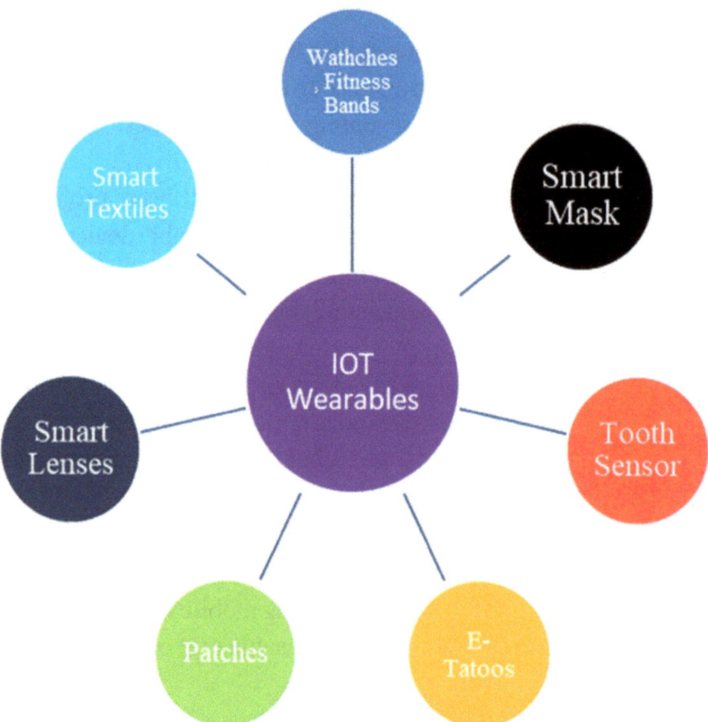


8. Health Communication Technologies

IoT in healthcare involves three main categories: identification, communication, and location. Each sensor or node has a unique identifier (UID) for patient data retrieval. UIDs facilitate seamless patient-healthcare resource connections, with global UIDs working in decentralized systems and universal UIDs evolving with IoT advancements. Communication technologies, categorized by range, enable uninterrupted device connectivity within healthcare. Location-based technology, like GPS, is crucial for tracking COVID-19 patients, ambulances, emergency services, and medical facilities.

9. Evolution of Mobile Communication

Mobile communication has evolved from analog real-time interactions to advanced digital technologies. The advent of 3G marked a milestone in instant internet communication, with 4G focusing on service quality and cost reduction. 5G enhanced these advancements with improved capacity and speed, while ongoing 6G developments aim to integrate satellite technologies for broader network coverage.

## CHALLENGES IN IMPLEMENTING IOT TECHNOLOGY IN HEALTHCARE DURING COVID-19 AND FUTURE PANDEMICS

Despite increasing research on IoT healthcare solutions, significant challenges persist, especially under the increasing demands in healthcare during crises like COVID-19. Proper analysis of these challenges is crucial to optimize IoT products and services. A comprehensive study, referencing sources like IEEE, ACM, Google Scholar, Wiley, Elsevier, Springer, and Scopus, was conducted to understand these difficulties and establish a patient-healthcare system link via IoT during pandemics.

1. Integration of Smartphones

Smartphones and IoT are key in healthcare for instant data tracking. Developing specialized apps to alert users about potential diseases or exposure to infected areas is critical. Immediate notification of individuals showing COVID-19 symptoms or visiting affected regions is essential.

2. Achieving Exceptional Service in Healthcare

Healthcare systems require reliability and efficiency from IoT frameworks. Neglecting these can endanger lives, hence the need for immaculate service standards and contingency plans.

3. Patient Movement in IoT Systems

Seamless patient transfer within IoT healthcare systems is vital. Under certain conditions, connecting patients to wireless networks is necessary, employing mobile ad hoc networks (MANET) when other methods are impractical.

4. Operating Equipment Procedures in IoT

Integrating IoT in healthcare involves using multiple sensors and devices, which presents challenges when used on living organisms. Strict protocols and monitoring during device manufacturing are crucial to mitigate risks to humans, animals, and the environment.

5. Performance Evaluation in IoT

Evaluating IoT effectiveness requires analyzing technology components and their synergy. Performance metrics include processing speed, cost, packet loss, response time, service availability, communication rate, latency, and throughput.

6. Integration of Connectivity and Data Exchange

Coordinating diverse devices across platforms is challenging. Application developers and IoT architects must establish common standards for seamless service access, regardless of hardware platforms.

7. Digital Healthcare Management

The shift towards IoT-centric healthcare presents significant challenges. Service providers must focus on resolving technical issues, configuring systems, ensuring reliability, enhancing security, and optimizing performance.

8. Regulatory Framework and Governance

Legal frameworks for IoT data protection are nascent. Initiatives like the Australian Privacy Principle (APP) and the US Department of Transportation's investment in "smart" infrastructure are steps toward protecting user data and privacy.

9. Required Actions for Implementation

Building intelligent cities requires managing a vast network of sensors and devices. Balancing the cost and utility of IoT, especially during COVID-19, is critical.

10. Cooperative Ventures

Interdisciplinary research is vital in intelligent communities. Collaborations across machine learning, AI, data security, networking, and analytics are necessary.

11. Safeguarding Data Security

Ensuring data confidentiality in healthcare IoT is a significant challenge. Authenticating every device and link is complex, and maintaining user confidentiality is paramount, especially during COVID-19.

Data security issues in healthcare encompass transparency, resource limitations, and physical security risks. Secure authentication and access control on cloud-based IoT platforms are essential for protecting user data.

Table 1 in this chapter illustrates that sector-specific challenges can impede optimal IoT function, highlighting the need for tailored solutions.

*Table 1. Sector-specific challenges*

| Sector | Core Functionalities | Primary Challenges |
|---|---|---|
| Urban Environment | Monitoring traffic, pollution, parking, virus spread, criminal activities | Quality of Service (QoS), Mobility, Standard Operating Procedures (SoP), Performance Assessment, Interpretability, E-management, Regulatory Guidelines, System Integration, Data Privacy & Security |
| Infrastructure | Energy conservation, maintenance, fire detection, surveillance | SoP, Performance Assessment, Interpretability, Regulatory Guidelines, System Integration, Data Privacy & Security |
| Residential | Home automation (TV, AC, lighting, door controls, security systems) | Regulatory Guidelines, Data Privacy & Security |
| Energy Networks | Power distribution and production management | Mobile Integration, QoS, Mobility, Performance Assessment, Interpretability, System Integration |
| Manufacturing | Use of robotics, Programmable Logic Controllers (PLCs), conveyor systems | Mobile Integration, QoS, Mobility, Performance Assessment, Interpretability, System Integration |
| Agriculture | Agricultural robots, tractors, drones | Mobile Integration, QoS, Mobility, Performance Assessment, Interpretability, E-management, Regulatory Guidelines, System Integration, Data Privacy & Security |
| Educational Institutions | Management of network components (switches, routers, hubs) | Mobility, SoP, E-management, Regulatory Guidelines, Data Privacy & Security |

## CONCLUSION

The Internet of Things (IoT) holds transformative potential for modern healthcare, presenting significant opportunities to enhance data flow across various networks and enable the immediate sharing of health-related information between patients and providers. This chapter has explored the pivotal role of IoT in healthcare, particularly in the context of the COVID-19 pandemic. It has highlighted how IoT technologies, structures, components, and applications are integrated into the healthcare sector. It demonstrates their effectiveness during the pandemic and their anticipated crucial role in managing similar future health emergencies.

Throughout this study, we have delved into cutting-edge IoT technologies, discussing their current applications and laying the groundwork for future research and advancements. By addressing the limitations of current IoT tools and approaches and by developing more advanced systems, IoT has the potential to significantly enhance healthcare delivery, increase service efficiency, and reduce costs. The discussion has also covered the challenges faced by IoT in healthcare, such as the need for enhanced security, better interoperability between systems, and the evaluation of cost-effectiveness for widespread adoption.

As we look to the future, the readiness of IoT technologies to handle health crises like COVID-19 and their ability to adapt to the evolving demands of healthcare environments are critical. Policymakers, healthcare providers, and researchers are encouraged to consider these technologies in their strategies to optimize care delivery and prepare for future challenges. This chapter underscores the indispensable role of IoT in healthcare and advocates for continued innovation and adoption across the sector, highlighting its potential to transform healthcare practices, improve patient outcomes, and manage public health emergencies more effectively.

## REFERENCES


Abbas, Z., & Yoon, W. (2015). A survey on energy conserving mechanisms for the internet of things: Wireless networking aspects. *Sensors (Basel)*, 15(10), 24818–24847. 10.3390/s15102481826404275

Abdul Rahim, S. K. F., Fung, C. C., & Wong, K. W. (2021). Design and evaluation of large-scale IoT-enabled healthcare architecture. *Applied Sciences (Basel, Switzerland)*, 11(8), 3623. 10.3390/app11083623

Abu-Elkheir, M., & Ali, N. A. (2015). Internet of nano-things healthcare applications: Requirements, opportunities, and challenges. In *Proceedings of the IEEE 11th International Conference on Wireless and Mobile Computing, Networking and Communications (WiMob)* (pp. 9–14). Abu Dhabi, United Arab Emirates.

Akhtar, S. M., Nazir, M., Saleem, K., Haque, H. M. U., & Hussain, I. (2020). An ontology-driven IoT based healthcare formalism. *International Journal of Advanced Computer Science and Applications*, 11(2), 479–486. 10.14569/IJACSA.2020.0110261

Alarcón, P. A., Francisco, G. V., Guzmán, G. I. P., Cantillo, N. J., Cuevas, V. R. E., & Alonso, S. G. A. (2019). An IoT-based non-invasive glucose level monitoring system using Raspberry Pi. *Applied Sciences (Basel, Switzerland)*, 9(15), 3046. 10.3390/app9153046

Alasmari, S., & Anwar, M. (2016). *Security & privacy challenges in IoT-based health cloud.* In *Proceedings of the International Conference on Computational Science and Computational Intelligence (CSCI)* (pp. 198–201). Las Vegas, NV, USA. 10.1109/CSCI.2016.0044

Arbat, H., Choudhary, S., & Bala, K. (2016). IoT smart health band. *Imperial Journal of Interdisciplinary Research*, 2, 300–311.

Atzori, L., Iera, A., & Morabito, G. (2010). The Internet of Things: A survey. *Computer Networks*, 54(15), 2787–2805. 10.1016/j.comnet.2010.05.010

Azzawi, M. A., Hassan, R., & Bakar, K. A. A. (2016). A review on Internet of Things (IoT) in healthcare. *International Journal of Applied Engineering Research: IJAER*, 11(20), 10216–10221.

Babu, B. S., Srikanth, K., Ramanjaneyulu, T., & Narayana, I. L. (2016). IoT for healthcare. *International Journal of Scientific Research*, 5(2), 322–326.

Chavan, P., More, P., Thorat, N., Yewale, S., & Dhade, P. (2016). ECG-Remote patient monitoring using cloud computing. *Imperial Journal of Interdisciplinary Research*, 2, 368–372.

Chen, X., Ma, M., & Liu, A. (2018). Dynamic power management and adaptive packet size selection for IoT in e-Healthcare. *Computers & Electrical Engineering*, 65, 375–57. 10.1016/j.compeleceng.2017.06.010

Chiang, M., & Zhang, T. (2016). Fog and IoT: An overview of research opportunities. *IEEE Internet of Things Journal*, 3(6), 854–864. 10.1109/JIOT.2016.2584538

Choudhary, S., & Sharma, K. (2020). Role and impact of wearables in IoT healthcare. In *Proceedings of the Third International Conference on Computational Intelligence and Informatics* (pp. 735–742). Hyderabad, India.

Corno, F., Russis, L., & Roffarello, A. M. (2016). A healthcare support system for assisted living facilities: An IoT solution. In *Proceedings of the IEEE 40th Annual Computer Software and Applications Conference (COMPSAC)* (pp. 344–352). Atlanta, GA, USA. 10.1109/COMPSAC.2016.29

Darshan, K. R., & Anandakumar, K. R. (2015). A comprehensive review on usage of Internet of Things (IoT) in healthcare system. In *Proceedings of the International Conference on Emerging Research in Electronics, Computer Science and Technology (ICERECT)* (pp. 132–136). Mandya, India. 10.1109/ERECT.2015.7499001

Dohr, A., Modre, O. R., Drobics, M., Hayn, D., & Schreier, G. (2010). The internet of things for ambient assisted living. In *Proceedings of the IEEE Seventh International Conference on Information Technology: New Generations* (pp. 804–809). Las Vegas, NV, USA. 10.1109/ITNG.2010.104

Fabricatore, C., Dimitar, G., & Ximena, L. (2020). Rethinking serious games design in the age of COVID-19: Setting the focus on wicked problems. In *Joint International Conference on Serious Games* (pp. 243–259). Springer. 10.1007/978-3-030-61814-8_19

Ferro, E., & Potorti, F. (2018). Internet-of-Things and big data for smarter healthcare: From device to architecture, applications and analytics. *International Journal of Information Management*, 38(1), 1–9.

Gigli, M., & Koo, S. (2011). Internet of Things: Services and applications categorization. *Advances in Internet of Things*, 1(4), 27–31. 10.4236/ait.2011.12004

Gubbi, J., Buyya, R., Marusic, S., & Palaniswami, M. (2013). Internet of Things (IoT): A vision, architectural elements, and future directions. *Future Generation Computer Systems*, 29(7), 1645–1660. 10.1016/j.future.2013.01.010

Haleem, A., Javaid, M., Vaishya, R., & Deshmukh, S. G. (2020). Areas of academic research with the application of internet of things. *Journal of Education and Health Promotion*, 9, 95. 10.4103/jehp.jehp_44_20

Hussain, M. A., Benlamri, R., & Naqvi, S. R. (2020). Opportunities and challenges of the Internet of Things (IoT) in healthcare: A comprehensive review. *Journal of Ambient Intelligence and Humanized Computing*, 11, 4529–4558. 10.1007/s12652-019-01537-7

Ibn-Mohammed, T., Mustapha, K. B., Godsell, J., Adamu, Z., Babatunde, K. A., Akintade, D. D., Acquaye, A. A., Fujii, H., Ndiaye, M. M., Yamoah, F. A., & Koh, S. C. L. (2021). A critical analysis of the impacts of COVID-19 on the global economy and ecosystems and opportunities for circular economy strategies. *Resources, Conservation and Recycling*, 164, 105169. 10.1016/j.resconrec.2020.10516932982059

Jara, A. J., Zamora, M. A., & Skarmeta, A. F. (2014). Interconnection framework for mHealth and remote monitoring based on the Internet of Things. *IEEE Journal on Selected Areas in Communications*, 32(4), 647–654. 10.1109/JSAC.2014.140405

Javaid, M., Haleem, A., Singh, R. P., & Suman, R. (2020b). Internet of things (IoT) applications to fight against COVID-19 pandemic. *Diabetes & Metabolic Syndrome*, 14(4), 521–524. 10.1016/j.dsx.2020.04.03232388333

Javaid, M., Haleem, A., Vaishya, R., Bahl, S., Suman, R., & Vaish, A. (2020a). Industry 4.0 technologies and their applications in fighting COVID-19 pandemic. *Diabetes & Metabolic Syndrome*, 14(4), 419–422. 10.1016/j.dsx.2020.04.03232344370

Kag, M., Hagras, H., Colley, M., & Jovanovic, A. (2015). A flexible architecture for adaptive ambient intelligence in e-healthcare applications. *Procedia Computer Science*, 52, 454–459. 10.1016/j.procs.2015.05.028

Kao, Y. M., Lin, C. H., & Hsu, Y. L. (2020). Advanced cloud-based IoT platform for intelligent healthcare. *Sensors (Basel)*, 20(12), 3462.32575449

Khan, I. H., Khan, S., & Ghani, I. (2021). Internet of things (IoT) in healthcare: A comprehensive literature review. *International Journal of Engineering Business Management*, 13, 1–15. 10.1177/18479790211007373

Kumar, A., Rajput, N., Sharma, N., Kumar, V., & Bhagat, S. (2021). Wearable sensor-based IoT framework for remote monitoring of COVID-19 patients at home isolation. *Arabian Journal for Science and Engineering*, 46, 5051–5064. 10.1007/s13369-021-05516-2

Kumar, R., & Yan, L. L. (2013). Health monitoring system based on Internet of Things. *Journal of Software*, 8(4), 917–923. 10.4304/jsw.8.4.917-923

Lee, J., Kao, H. A., & Yang, S. (2014). Service innovation and smart analytics for industry 4.0 and big data environment. *Procedia CIRP*, 16, 3–8. 10.1016/j.procir.2014.02.001

Lee, S. K., & Kim, S. K. (2017). An adaptive health IoT platform based on open source M2M/IoT middleware. *Journal of Healthcare Engineering*, 2017, 1–9. 10.1155/2017/3451052

Li, S., Xu, L. D., & Zhao, S. (2015). The internet of things: A survey. *Information Systems Frontiers*, 17(2), 243–259. 10.1007/s10796-014-9492-7

Liang, Y., Zhang, D., Chen, G., & Zhang, L. (2021). IoT-enabled smart health: An overview. *IEEE Access : Practical Innovations, Open Solutions*, 9, 140934–140959. 10.1109/ACCESS.2021.3079969

Mahmood, Z. H., & Almohammed, S. A. (2015). Internet of Things (IoT): Application in agriculture and health care. *International Journal of Computer Applications*, 124(3), 32–35. 10.5120/ijca2015906234

Mahmoud, M. S., Khaled, A. A., & Adel, A. E. (2018). A proposed internet of things (IoT) healthcare framework. In *Proceedings of the International Conference on Advanced Intelligent Systems and Informatics (AISI)*. Cairo, Egypt.

Majeed, M., Afza, A., Khan, R. A., & Sharif, M. (2021). IoT-enabled healthcare system: Architecture, applications, and recent advancements. *IEEE Access : Practical Innovations, Open Solutions*, 9, 49748–49779. 10.1109/ACCESS.2021.3060281

Majumder, S., Deen, M. J., & Uddin, M. N. (2019). Smart health and big data analytics for COVID-19 management. *The Science of the Total Environment*, 743, 140123. 10.1016/j.scitotenv.2020.140123

Masoud, H. H. (2018). Internet of Things (IoT): A review of enabling technologies, challenges, and open research issues. In *Proceedings of the IEEE 9th Annual Information Technology, Electronics and Mobile Communication Conference (IEMCON)* (pp. 257–264). IEEE.

Meena, K. R., Kumari, P., Kumar, M., Singh, A., & Kumar, R. (2021). A healthcare monitoring system using Internet of Things (IoT) for early detection and prevention of COVID-19. *Internet of Things : Engineering Cyber Physical Human Systems*, 15, 100359. 10.1016/j.iot.2021.100359

Miao, M., & Gan, J. (2016). ECG-based remote health monitoring system with an Android client. In *Proceedings of the IEEE International Conference on Computational Intelligence and Communication Technology (CICT)* (pp. 1–4). Ghaziabad, India.

Moniruzzaman, M., & Hossain, S. A. (2013). Internet of Things (IoT): Present and future architecture, challenges, and applications. In *Proceedings of the International Conference on Electrical Engineering and Information & Communication Technology (ICEEICT)* (pp. 1–6). Dhaka, Bangladesh.

Movahedi, A., Hassan, R., Shamshirband, S., Gani, A., Akbari, E., Anuar, N. B., Kiah, M. L. M., Khoshnava, S. M., & Lee, M. (2015). A review of routing protocols in wireless body area networks for healthcare applications. *Journal of Medical Systems*, 39(8), 1–14. 10.1007/s10916-015-0334-7

Nambi, R. R., Ravi, V., Chockalingam, P., & Yoo, Y. (2016). IoT-based wearable sensor devices in healthcare: Research challenges and design considerations. In *Proceedings of the IEEE International Conference on Ubiquitous Wireless Broadband (ICUWB)* (pp. 1–6). Nanjing, China.

Nasrin, S., & Rahman, M. (2021). Internet of Things (IoT) in healthcare: A comprehensive review. *International Journal of Computer Applications*, 179, 1–5. 10.5120/ijca2021916233

Pandya, H., Desai, M., & Singhal, A. (2015). Performance analysis of IoT based healthcare architecture. *International Journal of Computer Applications*, 117(6), 28–32. 10.5120/ijca2015907390

Parreira, H. B., Teixeira, L. F., Cardoso, T. A., & Aguilar, R. C. (2020). IoT in healthcare: A review of architecture, connectivity and security issues. In *Proceedings of the International Congress on Engineering and Information (ICEI)* (pp. 1–6). Manaus, Brazil.

Patel, S., & Meena, Y. K. (2020). Machine learning approach for healthcare applications in Internet of Things (IoT) environment: A review. In *Proceedings of the International Conference on Recent Advancements in Computer, Communication and Computational Sciences (RACCCS)* (pp. 1–7). Jaipur, India.

Patil, R. P., Kulkarni, D., & Chandrashekhar, K. (2017). IoT based healthcare system for identification and treatment of heart diseases. In *Proceedings of the IEEE International Conference on Intelligent Systems and Information Management (ICISIM)* (pp. 12–16). Chennai, India.

Purohit, P., Sharma, A., Sharma, S., & Sharma, A. (2021). An approach towards early diagnosis and monitoring of COVID-19 using wearable health devices and Internet of Medical Things (IoMT). *Diabetes & Metabolic Syndrome*, 15(2), 441–446. 10.1016/j.dsx.2021.02.004

Rao, S., Fagadar-Cosma, E., & Cosma, G. (2020). Design and development of a cloud-based IoT platform for healthcare monitoring. *Sensors (Basel)*, 20(15), 4163.32726938

Rathore, M. M., Ahmad, A., Paul, A., Rho, S., & Wan, J. (2016). Urban planning and building smart cities based on the Internet of Things using big data analytics. *Computer Networks*, 101, 63–80. 10.1016/j.comnet.2015.12.023

Rawassizadeh, R., Price, B. A., & Petre, M. (2015). Wearables: Has the age of smartwatches finally arrived? *Communications of the ACM*, 58(1), 45–47. 10.1145/2629633

Razaque, A., & Elleithy, K. M. (2016). An IoT-based health monitoring system for cardiac patients. In *Proceedings of the IEEE Seventh Annual Ubiquitous Computing, Electronics & Mobile Communication Conference* (pp. 1–6). New York City, NY, USA.

Riva, G., Baños, R. M., Botella, C., Mantovani, F., Gaggioli, A., & Wiederhold, B. K. (2012). Transforming experience: The potential of augmented reality and virtual reality for enhancing personal and clinical change. *Frontiers in Psychiatry*, 3, 1–11. 10.3389/fpsyt.2012.0010427746747

Roopa, P., & Shabadi, S. (2020). *An analysis of edge computing in IoT healthcare applications*. In *International Conference on Computer Science, Engineering and Applications (ICCSEA),* Bangalore, India.

Shang, W., Jiang, Y., Yu, Y., & Xu, W. (2017). A wearable ECG acquisition system for body sensor network. In *International Conference on Electrical, Automation and Mechanical Engineering (EAME),* St. Petersburg, Russia.

Sharma, M., & Sharma, P. (2020). *Role of IoT in healthcare*. In *International Conference on Communication and Electronics Systems (ICCES),* Coimbatore, India.

Sharma, R., Gaur, A., Tyagi, S., & Kumar, D. (2020). IoT-based healthcare architecture with cloud and cognitive computing. In *Proceedings of the IEEE 9th Global Conference on Consumer Electronics (GCCE)* (pp. 1066–1069). IEEE.

Shelke, S. V., Shelke, S. R., & Devabhaktuni, V. K. (2021). Wearable sensor technology for remote monitoring in pandemic control: A review. *IEEE Sensors Journal*, 21(9), 10369–10383. 10.1109/JSEN.2021.3069071

Singh, A., & Kumar, S. (2020). A critical review on IoT-based healthcare applications. *International Journal of System Assurance Engineering and Management*, 11(1), 24–36. 10.1007/s13198-018-0775-8

Singh, H., & Sharma, K. (2021). A comprehensive review on Internet of Things (IoT)-based healthcare applications. *Health and Technology*, 11(1), 1–23. 10.1007/s12553-020-00506-w

Tavares, J., & Macedo, H. (2021). Internet of Things and big data in healthcare: A literature review. *Future Internet*, 13, 32. 10.3390/fi13020032

Thomas, R. K., Malathi, M., Venkatesh, S., & Govindarajan, R. (2018). Blockchain based secure health records in cloud storage. *Journal of Medical Systems*, 42(8), 1–8. 10.1007/s10916-018-0980-8

Wahsheh, R. A. H., Almaita, E., & Elkhani, N. (2021). Health IoT-based platform to predict and monitor COVID-19. *Computers, Materials & Continua*, 68(1), 89–101. 10.32604/cmc.2022.022309

Wang, H., Wang, Y., & Gao, X. (2018). A novel IoT-oriented healthcare framework based on the integration of wireless body area networks and cloud computing. *IEEE Access : Practical Innovations, Open Solutions*, 6, 24015–24025. 10.1109/ACCESS.2018.2838618

Wu, F., Liang, Y., Zhao, K., & Hu, C. (2017). A novel ECG signals analysis method for the detection of atrial fibrillation and flutter. In *Proceedings of the IEEE First International Conference on Data Science in Cyberspace (DSC)* (pp. 495–500). IEEE.

Yaseen, S., Ilyas, M., & Ilyas, N. (2021). Internet of Things in healthcare: Applications, benefits, and challenges. In *Proceedings of the IEEE International Symposium on Communications and Information Technologies (ISCIT)* (pp. 1–6). IEEE.

Yildirim, O., & Bal, H. (2020). An IoT-based real-time heart monitoring system. In *Proceedings of the IEEE 6th International Conference on Computer and Communications (ICCC)* (pp. 64–67). IEEE.

Yousefi, A., Rafsanjani, M. K., & Seyedi, M. M. (2021). A systematic review of the Internet of Things in healthcare: Technology and application trends. *Journal of Ambient Intelligence and Humanized Computing*. 10.1007/s12652-021-03423-6

## KEY TERMS AND DEFINITIONS

**6LoWPAN (IPv6 over Low-Power Wireless Personal Area Networks):** An acronym for IPv6 over Low-Power Wireless Personal Area Networks. 6LoWPAN is the name of a concluded working group in the Internet area of the IETF.

**Ambient Intelligence:** A paradigm in which environments support the people inhabiting them. AmI environments are aware of the specific characteristics of human presence and cater specifically to each person's needs based on established preferences.

**Augmented Reality (AR):** An interactive experience of a real-world environment where the objects that reside in the real world are enhanced by computer-generated perceptual information.

**Big Data Technologies:** A range of technologies and architectures designed to extract value from large volumes of a wide variety of data by enabling high-velocity capture, discovery, and analysis.

**Bluetooth:** A wireless technology standard for exchanging data over short distances (using short-wavelength UHF radio waves) from fixed and mobile devices, creating personal area networks.

**Cloud Computing:** The delivery of computing services—including servers, storage, databases, networking, software, analytics, and intelligence—over the Internet ("the cloud") to offer faster innovation, flexible resources, and economies of scale.

**Context-aware Technologies:** Technologies that use situational and environmental information about people, places, and objects to provide proactive, personalized, and responsive services.

**Cyber-Physical Systems (CPS):** Mechanisms controlled or monitored by computer-based algorithms, tightly integrated with the Internet and its users. They are systems in which the physical and software components are deeply intertwined, each operating on different spatial and temporal scales, exhibiting multiple and distinct behavioral modalities, and interacting in myriad ways.

**Intelligent Autonomous Robotics:** Robots can perform tasks in complex environments without constant human guidance. They can learn from their experiences and make decisions autonomously.

**Internet of Things (IoT):** A network of physical objects embedded with sensors, software, and other technologies to connect and exchange data with other devices and systems over the Internet.

**M2M (Machine to Machine):** Technologies that allow wireless and wired systems to communicate with other devices of the same ability. M2M uses sensors, meters, or other devices to capture and transmit event data through a network.

**NFC (Near Field Communication):** A set of communication protocols between two electronic devices over a distance of 4 cm or less.

**RFID (Radio-Frequency Identification):** uses electromagnetic fields to automatically identify and track tags attached to objects. The tags contain electronically stored information.

**Wearable Technology:** Electronic technologies or computers incorporated into clothing and accessories that can comfortably be worn on the body. These wearable devices can perform many of the same computing tasks as mobile phones and laptop computers; however, in some cases, wearable technology can outperform these hand-held devices entirely.

**Wireless Sensor Networks (WSNs):** Networks composed of spatially distributed autonomous sensors that monitor physical or environmental conditions, such as temperature, sound, pressure, etc., and cooperatively pass their data through the network to a main location.

# Chapter 5
# IoT as Wearable Device in Smart Healthcare Systems:
## A New Paradigm

**Pon Harshavardhanan**
https://orcid.org/0000-0003-3262-5067
*VIT Bhopal University, India*

**Preetam Suman**
*VIT Bhopal University, India*

**Soumya Sankar Ghosh**
https://orcid.org/0000-0002-4469-4070
*VIT Bhopal University, India*

## ABSTRACT

*Portable healthcare monitoring systems with internet of things (IoT) are now a major issue for many nations across the world due to the significant growth of healthcare monitoring systems. The use of IoT-based health monitoring solutions can result in the elimination of routine doctor visits and consultations. IoT is utilized in a health monitoring system that can monitor a person's temperature, heart rate, blood pressure, and oxygen saturation. Moreover, the device enhanced with NLP analyzes speech and sound to extract disease-specific information, adding a new dimension to traditional metrics. The voice captured in the device is pushed into the cloud storage, like AWS S3. The machine learning model, which was trained, is loaded to analyze this file using machine learning run time environments like AWS SageMaker. Now if a patient's health falls outside the expected range, the IoT system will let the clinician know. The medical staff can process and evaluate their current state by processing information about patients' ailments through a gateway.*

## INTRODUCTION

Health should be understood as a complete state of physical, mental, and social well-being, not just the absence of disease. The fundamental reason why people want a better life is due to their health. Regrettably, several issues associated with the global health crisis have caused a predicament, including

DOI: 10.4018/979-8-3693-2901-6.ch005

insufficient health services. The lack of doctors and nurses at critical times and significant inequalities between rural and urban areas are significant. The expansion of hospitals and other healthcare centres has led to the need for portable healthcare monitoring systems with new technologies, which are now a major issue for many nations across the world. The adoption of Internet of Things (IoT) technologies makes it easier to switch from in-person consultations to telemedicine in healthcare.

The Internet of Things (IoT) has been regarded as the next major technological revolution due to its ability to interconnect all objects internally in the last ten years. Smart health monitoring systems (Rahaman et al., 2019; Riazul Islam et al., 2015], smart parking (Lin, Rivano, & Le Mouel, 2017), smart homes (Al-Ali et al., 2017), smart cities (Zanella et al., 2014), smart climate (Mois, Folea, & Sanislav, 2017), industrial sites (Chen et al., 2018), and agricultural fields (Ayaz et al., 2019) are just some of the applications of IoT. IoT is used by the healthcare management industry, which provides tools for tracking environmental and health conditions. IoT is the act of connecting computers to the internet through networks and sensors (Hasan et al., 2019; Nooruddin et al., 2020). Health monitoring equipment can be utilized with these interconnected parts. Subsequently, the sensors transmit the information to distant locations, such as M2M, which is a term used to describe computer equipment, human machinery, handheld devices, or smartphones (Islam et al., 2019). Tracking and optimizing care for any health issues is made easier with this easy-to-use, scalable, interoperable, energy-efficient, and considerably smarter method. Contemporary technologies now offer customizable interfaces (Mahmud et al., 2019), helper gadgets (Mahmud, Lin, & Kim, 2020), and mental health management (Lin et al., 2020)

to help people live smarter lives. Body temperature and heart rate are the two most crucial indicators of human health. The number of heart beats per minute is the term used to describe heart rate, which is also called pulse rate. The pulse rate can be determined by calculating pulses and using an increase in blood flow volume. The average heart rate for healthy individuals is between 60 and 100 beats per minute. Adult males usually beat their resting hearts at 70 beats per minute, while adult females beat them at 75 beats per minute (Reddy & Achari, 2015). When they are 12 or older, women tend to have a higher heart rate than men. The body temperature is a scientific measurement of the sum of heat that the human body emits. Various factors determine an average person's body temperature, such as their eating habits, gender, and the weather conditions outside. Healthy adults usually experience temperatures between 97.8 °F (36.5 °C) and 99 °F (37.2 °C). The flu and low-temperature hypothermia are just two examples of illnesses that can cause changes in body temperature. Almost all diseases have a common sign in the form of fever (Santoso & Setiaji, 2015). Body temperature and heart rate measurements can be taken using both invasive and non-invasive techniques. Over time, it has been proven that noninvasive methods are accurate and practical for the consumer (Teichmann et al., 2012). Comfortable accommodations are believed to be necessary for a healthcare facility to help patients (Yang et al., 2019). The quality of the room's environment can be gauged by the number of gases, which include CO and CO2, and room humidity. Certain humidity levels and hazardous gas concentrations can cause severe harm to patients. Between 30% and 65% is the ideal humidity range for a room. Smart homes are the only focus of some research (Patil et al., 2019; Marques & Pitarma, 2016) that does not address specific healthcare needs. Heart disease (Ayon & Islam, 2020), diabetes (Islam & Milon Islam, 2019), breast cancer (Islam et al., 2017; Hasan et al., 2016), and liver conditions (Haque et al., 2018) are just a few of the deadly illnesses that can occur in the medical field. Our system's primary focus is on monitoring the vital signs and surroundings of all patients in their rooms.

A healthcare system that uses sensors to measure a patient's body temperature, pulse, and room humidity is suggested in this chapter. By using Wi-Fi, the data is communicated to medical staff members who can access the server's data. Not only does the proposed system customize important health-related criteria, but it also addresses the challenge of maintaining a single database of patients in hospitals using a web server. If the output value exceeds the threshold, the gas sensor in this system detects an unexpected event and emits a PPM signal.

Furthermore, the device's NLP enhancements enable it to analyze voice and sound and extract information related to diseases, which adds a qualitative dimension to conventional metrics. It enables the performance of subtle diagnoses, deciphering unique communication patterns for effective symptom comprehension, and supports continuous health monitoring. This innovative method offers a proactive and individualized healthcare paradigm through the creation of a comprehensive platform that connects quantitative and qualitative health data. Voice recordings are made by the device and stored in the cloud using services such as AWS S3. The trained machine learning model is loaded and evaluated using scalable machine learning runtime environments, like AWS SageMaker. The state of health can be predicted using machine learning models that use natural language processing.

This technology can be employed by clinics in rural areas to communicate the health status of their patients to hospitals in larger cities. If a patient's health is not in the expected range, the IoT system will notify the clinician. Medical staff members can assess and analyze their status through the use of a gateway to manage patient health information. The prototype is proof of the system's effectiveness, as it is suitable for monitoring healthcare facilities.

## LITERATURE REVIEW

IoT has been employed in some significant medical science research projects to monitor patients' well-being. It has transformed the healthcare industry by allowing the integration of smart devices that monitor and improve patient care. The advantages of IoT in healthcare are numerous. It enables continuous patient monitoring, which can result in early diagnosis of health problems and timely interventions. IoT also increases data accuracy and decreases manual errors, while also allowing for more efficient resource management in healthcare institutions. Despite these advantages, implementing IoT in healthcare presents several hurdles. Data privacy and security are key concerns, as vast amounts of sensitive health information transferred between devices and systems are subject to cyberattacks. The high costs of IoT infrastructure and device maintenance also provide a hurdle, particularly for smaller healthcare providers. Additionally, sophisticated cybersecurity measures are required to preserve patient data and ensure regulatory compliance. This study also notes the breakthrough "JioVio" healthcare solutions, which represent the integration of IoT in healthcare. JioVio provides a variety of solutions, including wearable gadgets and remote monitoring systems, to meet the demands of both patients and healthcare practitioners. These devices not only enhance patient care but also give useful data for clinical decision-making and health management.

The work, while considering all of these works, as mentioned above, also provides a concise summary of the research conducted on this topic.Tracking a patient's body temperature, heart rate, and oxygen saturation percentage is possible with a health surveillance system, and the creation of eye movement in an Internet of Things network was done by Tamilselvi et al., (2020). An Arduino-UNO is employed as a processing device and sensors are used to capture elements such as temperature, heartbeat, SpO2, and eye blink. Although the system has been implemented, there are no performance metrics that are specific to patients. Acharya & Patil (2020) presented a healthcare monitoring kit in a setting that utilizes the Internet of Things. Certain fundamental human health characteristics, such as body temperature, respiration, heartbeat, and ECG, were monitored by the system that was designed. This scenario utilizes the temperature sensor, BP sensor, ECG sensor, pulse sensor, and Raspberry Pi as the primary hardware elements. Sensor data was collected, analyzed on a Raspberry Pi, and then transmitted to an IoT network. The primary problem with the system is the absence of defined interfaces for visualizing data. Banerjee & Roy (2016) proposed a method that does not require any invasiveness to detect pulse rate. The recommended system used plethysmography and displayed results digitally, making it a real-time monitoring tool. The patient has found that the method is reliable when compared to other intrusive treatments. Gregoski et al., (2012) introduced a heart rate monitoring system that relies on smartphones. By using a mobile light and camera, the device was able to track finger blood flow and calculate cardiac output based on it. Users can check their heart rate without constantly moving their hands by using an integrated gadget that wirelessly sends their pulse to a computer, thanks to the developed technology. Even though this design is amazing, it won't work if continuous cardiac monitoring is necessary.

Oresko et al., (2010) reported on a smartphone application that can detect cardiovascular disease and is functioning fully indicating a tool that could be developed to accomplish the same task with sufficient time and funding. The prototype that was produced was incapable of detecting cardiovascular disease and only recorded coronary rhythm in real-time. For an extended period, the device was unable to track heart rate. Trivedi & Cheeran, (2017) proposed a framework for regulating Arduino-based health parameters through mobile devices. Analog sensor data that has been gathered is received by the Arduino Uno board. Digital data is generated from the analog values captured by the in-built analog-to-digital converter. Through Bluetooth, the physical attributes of the designed device were received. A module with a narrow focus was utilized in the Bluetooth gadget. Kumar et al., (2017) developed an adaptive IoT safety monitoring device. The framework configuration consists of three layers, one of which is the control layer, one of which is the device layer, and one of which is the transport layer. Body temperature was measured by a DS18B20 sensor in the control section, and a pulse sensor measured the pulse. Data could be loaded from Arduino into the cloud on the transport layer using the Ethernet shield and Wi-Fi module. The framework layer was responsible for gathering the server details in the end. The use of an Arduino Uno in this case means that many sensors cannot be properly handled, which is unfortunate. Desai & Toravi, (2017) established a Wireless Sensor Network (WSN) to monitor heartbeat and smart homes. FPGA architecture is utilized to process parallel data using Spartan3, with an LCD displaying MCU findings and a microcontroller connecting each sensor. There are some components of the machine that are not combined into a single unit.

An overview of prior research on IoT applications in healthcare is provided by Rejeb, A. et. al. (2023). The development of IoT research in healthcare has been objectively summarised by a thorough review and bibliometric analysis. The results indicate that the healthcare community has shown a great deal of interest in IoT research. IoT healthcare applications, blockchain applications, 5G telecommunications, Artificial Intelligence (AI) approaches, data analytics, and computing technologies emerged as significant themes based on the results of the keyword co-occurrence network. Other significant topics that emerge from the co-citation network analysis include cloud-IoT integration, fog computing, authentication systems, and cognitive smart healthcare.

There are existing systems using the audio files to capture the features of the audio and use them to train a Natural Language Processing (NLP) model. All the systems use transformer-based language models in processing the text input. Devlin et al., (2019) used bidirectional auto encoders called BERT, that can be used for language inferencing. The variations of this model were proposed by Sanh et al., (2019) and Liu et al., 2019) namely, DistilBERT and RoBERTa. DistilBERT proposes a novel method for pre-training the BERT model which reduces the size of the model by 40% and faster by 60%. RoBERTa on the other hand, has shown how the pretraining of the BERT model can be improved by fine-tuning hyperparameters and varying the sizes of data sets. Finally, the authors Jouaiti & Dautenhahn, (2022) proposed using Bidirectional LSTM to classify given voice data into binary classifications namely, fluent and disfluent.

## PROPOSED DESIGN

The traditional healthcare system is not like an IoT-based health monitoring system. It becomes difficult to use IoT to achieve the necessary performance and results as a result. The embedded world is associated with working with IoT due to the use of electronic data signals by sensors. Synchronization involves the coupling of a microcontroller, monitors, sensors, detectors, and other devices at the beginning. Sensors and detectors detect signals in analog form, but they need to convert them to digital form. To obtain data in the correct digital format, the microcontroller converts analog signals to digital signals.

Either an ESP32 or Raspberry Pi is used to transfer the data to the microcontroller. Nowadays, IoT is the most prevalent usage of the Raspberry Pi. Data storage is accomplished once it has been transformed. The data is being received by either the cloud or the server. This study employs a local server to display the fluctuations in the values or readings that are measured simultaneously. The block diagram shown in Figure 1 is the operation of the planned work.

*Figure 1. Block diagram of proposed IOT smart health system*

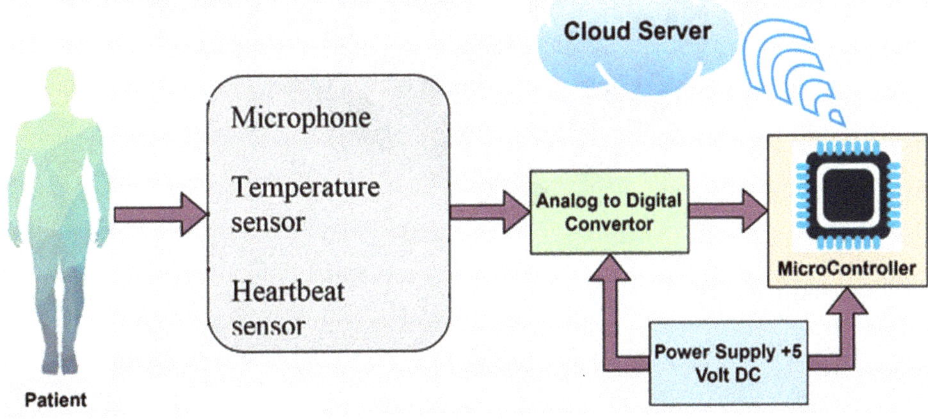

The system comprises hardware components necessary for the prototype's development. The microphone, temperature sensor, heartbeat sensor, and integrated ADC are all part of this.

**Raspberry Pi** (Raspberry Pi Foundation, n.d.)

The Raspberry Pi (Pi 5 with 8 GB RAM, 2.4GHz quad-core 64-bit Arm Cortex-A76 CPU) can be seen in Figure 2, which is a single-board computer that is roughly the size of a credit card. The Pi's Linux/Android operating system has been designed to work with the ARM processor it is powered by. Having Linux on board enhances the functionality of this small device, allowing it to be utilized for system automation. The device has an integrated display and LAN port for connectivity, and it can be used with sensors and other devices. The fact that it can be programmable in Python is an added advantage.

**ESP32 Processor** (Espressif Systems, n.d.)

As shown in Figure 3, the ESP32 (ESP32-S3R2) is a primary learning tool for IoT. Having a complete Linux system on a small platform can be achieved for a relatively low cost using this method. Connecting actuators and sensors on devices with GPIO pins is what ESP32 does. Creating a new tool for innovation in the healthcare industry is possible thanks to the combination of IoT and ESP32. Power management modules, integrated antenna switches, RF-balun, control amplification, low-noise amplifiers, and filters are just some of the features of the ESP32, which is incredibly well-designed. Through operation as a slave to a host MCU or as a fully functional stand-alone scheme, it can lower the amount of interaction within the primary application processor. Other Bluetooth and Wi-Fi devices can be interconnected through the SPI/SDIO and I2C/UART interfaces of EPS32.

*Figure 2. Raspberry Pi*

*Figure 3. ESP 32 processor*

**Heart Beat Sensor** (ROHM Co., Ltd., n.d.)

A concept for a plethysmography sensor (Techtonics MAX30102) was developed. The intensity of light passing through an organ is determined by measuring the variation in blood volume passing through it. The importance of pulse timing is heightened in systems that monitor heart rate. When blood absorbs light, signal pulses are equal to heartbeat pulses, which determines the distribution of blood volume.

**Body Temperature Sensor** (ElectronicWings, n.d.)

Temperature circuits that are accurately optimized and an output voltage that changes linearly with temperature in degrees Celsius are found in the MLX90614 ESF. It provides an advantage by preventing the user from removing the large constant voltage from the display during scaling in centigrade.

**Microphone** (Robu. in, n.d.)

A significant use is made of a microphone (GY-MAX4466) in the suggested device. The microphone will capture sound signals and save them in the cloud for future analysis. Different diseases can be identified by recording and analyzing human speech. By using recorded speech signals NLP will be discussed in greater detail in the following sections.

NLP and SageMaker

The cloud-based machine learning runtime for deep learning models always gives a better environment for scalable, efficient systems. The Amazon Web Service (AWS) platform provides a machine-learning studio called SageMaker (Figure 4).

*Figure 4. Cloud-based training and prediction environment*

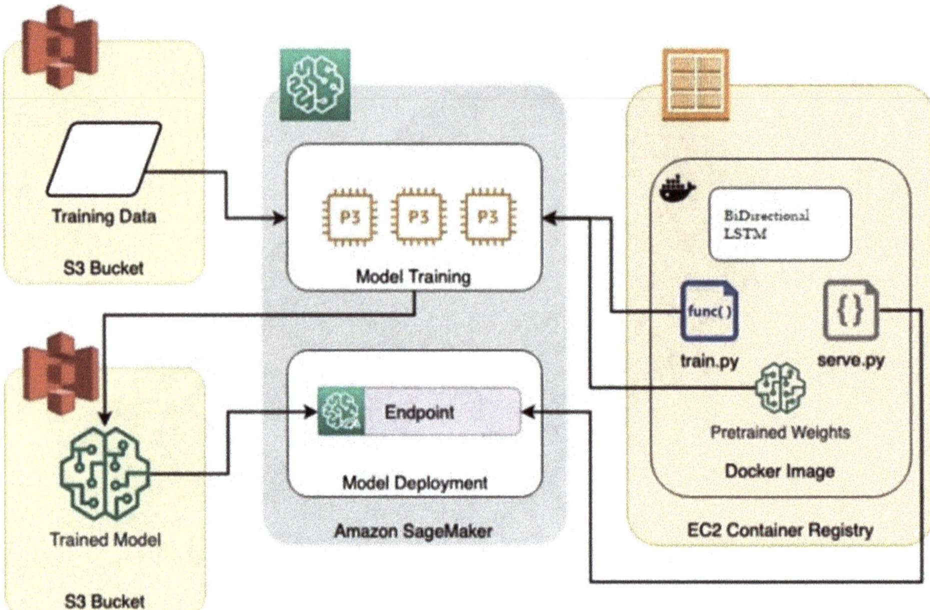


*(Reference: https://aws.amazon.com/machine-learning/infrastructure/)*

The training dataset has been stored in an S3 bucket storage. It is then pushed into a model which is deployed into an AWS SageMaker studio where the compute instances, P3 are used for training the model. Then the trained model is stored as a pre-trained model in an S3 bucket for future prediction. The EC2 container's Docker images are used to run the Python scripts for training and deploying the model. During the real-time classification, the pre-trained model will be deployed in an endpoint in the SageMaker studio.

The proposed model is implemented on Python with tensor flow. The hardware is connected through Raspberry Pi using hookup wires. The NLP codes are written in Python on Raspberry. The connectivity and the implementations are thoroughly checked. There are few challenges faced during implementation, that are related to the speed of Raspberry and internet connectivity for cloud. These limitations will be overcome using high configuration hardware.

## NLP INTEGRATION

The inclusion of a microphone within IoT-enabled wearable devices introduces a multifaceted dimension to healthcare monitoring and diagnostics. The microphone serves as a versatile sensor capable of capturing a wide array of audio data, including human speech, ambient sounds, and environmental noises. Various studies have highlighted the potential of speech signals in detecting and tracking the progression of a wide range of medical conditions, including neurological disorders, respiratory diseases, and cardiovascular ailments. For instance, research conducted by Tsanas et al., (2009) demonstrated that individuals with Parkinson's disease exhibit distinct changes in their speech patterns, characterized by alterations in pitch, intensity, and articulation rate. By leveraging machine learning techniques, such as support vector machines and Gaussian mixture models, the researchers achieved high accuracy in differentiating between Parkinson's disease patients and healthy controls based on speech features extracted from audio recordings. Moreover, respiratory diseases, such as chronic obstructive pulmonary disease (COPD) and asthma, can also be identified through speech analysis. Studies have shown that individuals with COPD exhibit specific breathing patterns and vocal characteristics that can be captured through acoustic analysis of their speech. For example, Porieva et al., (2021) developed a machine learning-based approach to distinguish between COPD patients and healthy individuals using features extracted from respiratory sounds and speech recordings. By analyzing parameters such as airflow patterns, phonation duration, and spectral features, the researchers achieved promising results in classifying COPD patients with high accuracy. In addition to neurological and respiratory disorders, speech analysis holds the potential for detecting cardiovascular conditions, such as coronary artery disease and heart failure. Changes in speech characteristics, such as rhythm and prosody, have been linked to alterations in cardiac function and hemodynamic parameters. Research demonstrated that individuals with heart failure exhibit disruptions in their speech fluency and rhythm, which correlate with the severity of their cardiac symptoms. By employing machine learning algorithms to analyze speech recordings, the researchers were able to discriminate between heart failure patients and healthy controls, suggesting the feasibility of using speech analysis as a non-invasive tool for cardiovascular assessment. Speech analysis can also be employed for monitoring and managing mental health conditions, such as depression and anxiety. Changes in speech characteristics, such as pitch variability and speech rate, have been associated with alterations in emotional states and mood disorders. Arevian et al., (2020) conducted a study to explore the application of speech analysis in predicting the degree of depression in patients diagnosed with major depressive disorder. The researchers created a machine learning model that accurately predicts depression severity scores by analyzing auditory variables including pitch, intensity, and spectral entropy retrieved from speech recordings.

Building upon the literature outlined above, the current paper takes stuttering, a speech disorder characterized by disruptions in the fluency and rhythm of speech, as a compelling use case for one of the applications of our proposed IoT-enabled wearable device. In this framework, participants will be instructed to wear an IoT-enabled wearable device equipped with a microphone for one week during their daily activities. The wearable device will record speech samples during various speaking tasks, including spontaneous speech, reading passages, and structured conversations. Upon completion of the data collection period, speech recordings have been analyzed using machine learning algorithms to extract relevant features indicative of stuttering severity. We have employed techniques outlined in Vasquez-Correa et al., (2019) to derive phoneme class probability and phoneme estimation. In English phonetics, there exist 44 distinct phonemes, categorized into 20 vowels and 24 consonants. These phonemes are further organized into various phonological classes based on their articulatory properties, such as consonantal, back, anterior, open, close, nasal, stop, continuant, lateral, flap, trill, voice, strident, labial, dental, velar, pause, and vocalic. Phoneme class probability indicates the likelihood of each of these classes occurring over time, while phoneme estimation denotes the identified International Phonetic Alphabet (IPA) phoneme at each instance. From the collected speech samples, key acoustic parameters like speech rate, pause duration, pitch variability, and dysfluency frequency will be extracted.

To design a robust system for detecting stuttering, by following (Jouaiti & Dautenhahn, 2022) we'll employ a bidirectional LSTM (BiLSTM) network, which excels in capturing temporal dependencies by considering both past and future context. This is crucial for stuttering detection because understanding what precedes and follows a stuttering event can provide valuable insights into its nature. Firstly, we'll preprocess our input features, which include Mel-frequency cepstral coefficients (MFCC) representing speech characteristics and phoneme class probabilities indicating the likelihood of various phonological classes occurring over time. These features will be fed into the BiLSTM layer, where the network will learn complex patterns and relationships between phoneme sequences and dysfluency occurrences. Within the BiLSTM layer, Rectified Linear Unit (ReLU) activation functions are applied to enhance nonlinear transformations, allowing the model to capture intricate patterns in the input data. The bidirectional nature of the LSTM ensures that the network can effectively capture information from both past and future time steps, providing a comprehensive understanding of the speech dynamics. Following the BiLSTM layer, the output is passed through a time-distributed Dense layer with ReLU activation. This layer applies dense connections across time steps, enabling the model to process sequences efficiently. Another dense layer follows, further refining the learned representations. To prevent overfitting and improve generalization, each dense layer is accompanied by batch normalization and dropout layers with a dropout rate of 0.5. Batch normalization helps stabilize the training process by normalizing the activations, while dropout randomly drops units during training to prevent co-adaptation of neurons and enhance the model's robustness. In parallel, the phoneme estimations, represented as string data, undergo one-hot encoding before being fed into an Embedding layer. This layer transforms categorical data into continuous vectors, allowing the network to learn meaningful representations of phonemes. The outputs from all layers are then combined and passed through two additional dense layers, each followed by batch normalization and dropout layers. Finally, depending on the specific classification task, the network is concluded with either a binary classification layer for distinguishing between fluent and dysfluent speech or a 5-class classification layer identifying different types of stuttering, including word repetition, sound repetition, interjection, or prolongation. This architecture enables the network to effectively analyze speech features and accurately classify stuttering events with high predictive accuracy. The current model further follows (Jouaiti & Dautenhahn, 2022) for stuttering classification, and proposes a neural network model with a custom correlation coefficient loss function. This loss function is designed to measure the correlation between the predicted labels and the true labels, thereby optimizing the model to accurately classify dysfluency events.

Following this NLP architecture, we examined the effectiveness of an Internet of Things (IoT) device equipped with speech analysis capabilities for assessing the severity of stuttering in 55 participants, with ages ranging from 20 to 45 years and a gender distribution of 30 males and 25 females, we embarked on a detailed exploration of speech patterns to detect and classify stuttering events. Each participant contributed recorded speech samples, meticulously transcribed to identify dysfluency occurrences. These dysfluencies were meticulously categorized into five distinct classes: word repetitions (Wd), sound repetitions (Sd), interjections (Int), prolongations (Pro), and instances of fluent speech (Fluent). Data preprocessing involved the extraction of crucial acoustic features from the speech samples. Mel-frequency cepstral coefficients (MFCC) and phoneme class probabilities were computed to capture the intricate nuances of speech production. Dysfluency events were accurately labeled based on the transcribed data, enabling a comprehensive analysis of stuttering patterns across participants. For the evaluation of our model's effectiveness, we adopted a rigorous 10-fold cross-validation methodology to ensure robustness and generalizability. The dataset was meticulously partitioned into 10 equally sized folds, with the model trained on 90% of the data in each iteration and evaluated on the remaining 10%. During training, a batch size of 32 was employed, and model parameters were meticulously fine-tuned using the Adam optimizer with a learning rate set at 0.0001. To prevent overfitting, early stopping criteria were meticulously incorporated, terminating training if performance did not exhibit improvement after 15 epochs.

Upon evaluation, our model exhibited robust performance metrics across various dimensions. For binary classification (fluent vs. dysfluent), the model showcased an average accuracy of 85% across the 10-fold cross-validation experiments, indicating its effectiveness in distinguishing between fluent and dysfluent speech. Delving deeper, precision and recall metrics were meticulously computed for each dysfluency class, shedding light on the model's ability to accurately discern specific stuttering phenomena.

*Figure 5. Confusion matrix*

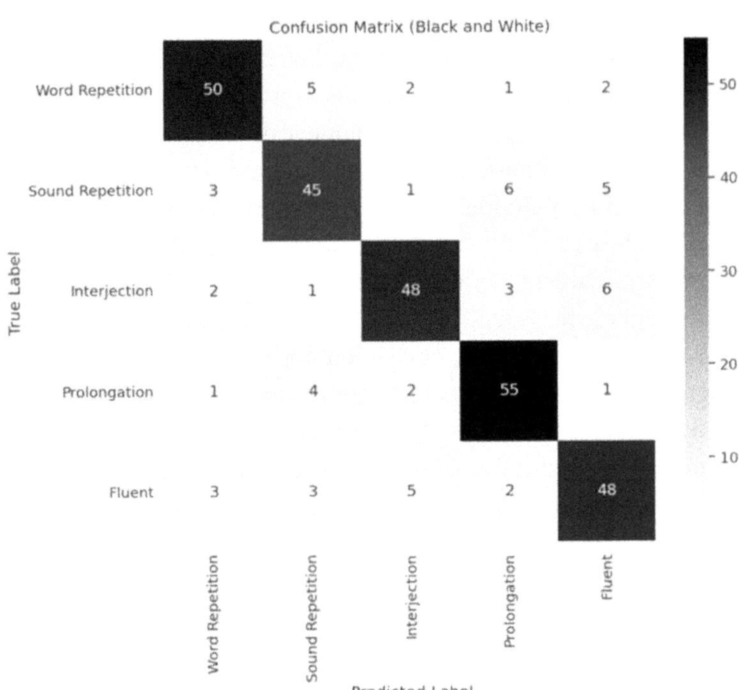


Precision values ranged from 0.75 to 0.90, underscoring the model's capability to precisely classify dysfluencies, while recall values varied between 0.79 and 0.88, reflecting its effectiveness in capturing true positive instances. Furthermore, a detailed examination of the confusion matrix (see Figure 5) provided invaluable insights into true positives, true negatives, false positives, and false negatives for each dysfluency class, offering a comprehensive understanding of the model's classification performance. Statistical analysis, including F1 scores, precision-recall curves, and area under the curve (AUC) values, was meticulously conducted to provide further insights into the model's performance across different dysfluency types. Additionally, confidence intervals were meticulously calculated to quantify the uncertainty associated with the reported performance metrics, enhancing the reliability and robustness of our findings.

This study represents a significant advancement in the detection and classification of stuttering events within speech data. Through meticulous data collection, feature engineering, and rigorous evaluation methodologies, we have established a solid foundation for identifying and characterizing various forms of dysfluency. These insights not only deepen our understanding of stuttering phenomena but also hold significant implications for the development of more effective diagnostic and intervention strategies in the field of speech pathology.

## CONCLUSION

This IoT-enabled wearable device introduces a transformative dimension to healthcare monitoring and diagnostics, leveraging the versatile capabilities of audio data capture. Our exploration of this paradigm shift reveals the potential of speech signals as a rich source of information for detecting and tracking various medical conditions, spanning neurological disorders, respiratory diseases, cardiovascular ailments, and mental health conditions. Notably, studies have demonstrated the distinctive alterations in speech patterns exhibited by individuals with Parkinson's disease, chronic obstructive pulmonary disease (COPD), asthma, heart failure, depression, and anxiety, highlighting the diagnostic utility of speech analysis across a spectrum of health domains. Drawing from the literature, our study focuses on stuttering, a speech disorder characterized by disruptions in fluency and rhythm, as a compelling use case for the application of IoT-enabled wearable devices equipped with speech analysis capabilities. Through a meticulously designed framework, participants are equipped with wearable devices featuring microphones to record speech samples during daily activities. Leveraging machine learning techniques, we aim to extract relevant features indicative of stuttering severity from these recordings, with a particular focus on phoneme class probability and phoneme estimation. An IoT device equipped with the sensors is proposed in the chapter. The sensors sense the data and send it to the cloud infrastructure. There are sensors like temperature, and blood pressure used to monitor the body parameters. These parameters are used as additional components to verify the health of the patient. The crucial role is played by the microphone. It records data of human voice so that machines can identify the disease through voice markers. It is very useful to find out stress levels, Alzheimer's disease, and many more. The chapter is focused on the application of NLP using IoT.

Our proposed architecture integrates bidirectional LSTM (BiLSTM) networks, known for their ability to capture temporal dependencies by considering both past and future context. By preprocessing input features such as MFCC and phoneme class probabilities, and leveraging techniques outlined in previous research, we aim to develop a robust system for detecting stuttering events with high predictive accuracy. Through rigorous evaluation methodologies, including 10-fold cross-validation, statistical analysis, and meticulous examination of performance metrics, we strive to validate the efficacy and reliability of our proposed approach. Our study contributes to the growing body of research exploring the intersection of IoT technology and healthcare, offering insights into the potential of wearable devices equipped with speech analysis capabilities for enhancing diagnostic accuracy and enabling remote monitoring of speech-related disorders. By harnessing the power of machine learning and speech analysis techniques, we envision a future where IoT-enabled wearable devices play a pivotal role in facilitating early detection, personalized intervention, and continuous monitoring of speech disorders, ultimately improving patient outcomes and quality of life.

## REFERENCES

Al-Ali, A. R., Zualkernan, I. A., Rashid, M., Gupta, R., & Alikarar, M. (2017). A smart home energy management system using IoT and big data analytics approach. *IEEE Transactions on Consumer Electronics*, 63(4), 426–434. 10.1109/TCE.2017.015014

Arevian, A. C., Bone, D., Malandrakis, N., Martinez, V. R., Wells, K. B., Miklowitz, D. J., & Narayanan, S. (2020). Clinical state tracking in serious mental illness through computational analysis of speech. *PLoS One*, 15(1), e0225695. 10.1371/journal.pone.022569531940347

Ayaz, M., Ammad-Uddin, M., Sharif, Z., Mansour, A., & Aggoune, E.-H. M. (2019). Internet-of-Things (IoT)-based smart agriculture: Toward making the fields talk. *IEEE Access : Practical Innovations, Open Solutions*, 7, 129551–129583. 10.1109/ACCESS.2019.2932609

Ayon, S. I., & Islam, M. M. (2020). Coronary artery heart disease prediction: A comparative study of computational intelligence techniques. *Journal of the Institution of Electronics and Telecommunication Engineers*. 10.1080/03772063.2020.1713916

Banerjee, S., & Roy, S. (2016). Design of a photo plethysmography-based pulse rate detector. *International Journal of Recent Trends in Engineering and Research*, 2, 302–306.

Chen, B., Wan, J., Shu, L., Li, P., Mukherjee, M., & Yin, B. (2018). Smart factory of Industry 4.0: Key technologies, application case, and challenges. *IEEE Access : Practical Innovations, Open Solutions*, 6, 6505–6519. 10.1109/ACCESS.2017.2783682

Devlin, J., Chang, M.-W., Lee, K., & Toutanova, K. (2019). BERT: Pre-training of deep bidirectional transformers for language understanding. In *NAACL-HLT 2019: Minneapolis, MN, USA - 1* (pp. 4171–4186).

Electronic Wings. (n.d.). *LM35 temperature sensor*. Electronic Wings. https://www.electronicwings.com/sensors-modules/lm35-temperature-sensor

Espressif Systems. (n.d.). *ESP32*. Espressif. https://www.espressif.com/en/products/socs/esp32

Gregoski, M. J., Mueller, M., Vertegel, A., Shaporev, A., Jackson, B. B., Frenzel, R. M., Sprehn, S. M., & Treiber, F. A. (2012). Development and validation of a smartphone heart rate acquisition application for health promotion and wellness telehealth applications. *International Journal of Telemedicine and Applications*, 2012, 1–7. 10.1155/2012/69632422272197

Hasan, M., Islam, M. M., Zarif, M. I. I., & Hashem, M. M. A. (2019). Attack and anomaly detection in IoT sensors in IoT sites using machine learning approaches. *Internet of Things : Engineering Cyber Physical Human Systems*, 7, 100059. 10.1016/j.iot.2019.100059

Islam, A. S., & Milon Islam, M. (2019). Diabetes prediction: A deep learning approach. *International Journal of Information Engineering and Electronic Business*, 11(2), 21–27. 10.5815/ijieeb.2019.02.03

Islam, M., Neom, N., Imtiaz, M., Nooruddin, S., & Islam, M. (2019). A review on fall detection systems using data from smartphone sensors. Ingénierie des systèmes d'Information, 24, 569–576. 10.18280/isi.240602

Islam, M. M., Iqbal, H., Haque, M. R., & Hasan, M. K. (2017). Prediction of breast cancer using support vector machine and K-nearest neighbors. In *2017 IEEE Region 10 humanitarian technology conference (R10-HTC)* (pp. 226–229). IEEE..

Hasan, M. K., Islam, M. M., & Hashem, M. M. A. (2016). Mathematical model development to detect breast cancer using multigene genetic programming. In *2016 5th International Conference on Informatics, Electronics and Vision (ICIEV)* (pp. 574–579). IEEE.

Haque, M. R., Islam, M. M., Iqbal, H., Reza, M. S., & Hasan, M. K. (2018). Performance evaluation of random forests and artificial neural networks for the classification of liver disorder. In *2018 International Conference on Computer, Communication, Chemical, Material and Electronic Engineering (IC4ME2)* (pp. 1–5). IEEE.

Lin, T., Rivano, H., & Le Mouel, F. (2017). A survey of smart parking solutions. *IEEE Transactions on Intelligent Transportation Systems*, 18(12), 3229–3253. 10.1109/TITS.2017.2685143

Lin, X., Mahmud, S., Jones, E., Shaker, A., Miskinis, A., Kanan, S., & Kim, J.-H. (2020). Virtual reality-based musical therapy for mental health management. In *2020 10th Annual Computing and Communication Workshop and Conference (CCWC)* (pp. 948–952). IEEE. 10.1109/CCWC47524.2020.9031244

Liu, Y., Ott, M., Goyal, N., Du, J., Joshi, M., Chen, D., Levy, O., Lewis, M., Zettlemoyer, L., & Stoyanov, V. (2019). RoBERTa: A robustly optimized BERT pretraining approach. CoRR abs/1907.11692.

Jouaiti, M., & Dautenhahn, K. (2022). Dysfluency classification in stuttered speech using deep learning for real-time applications. In *ICASSP 2022-2022 IEEE International Conference on Acoustics, Speech and Signal Processing (ICASSP)* (pp. 6482–6486). IEEE.

Mahmud, S., Lin, X., & Kim, J.-H. (2020). Interface for human-machine interaction for assistant devices: A review. In *2020 10th Annual Computing and Communication Workshop and Conference (CCWC)* (pp. 768–773). IEEE. 10.1109/CCWC47524.2020.9031244

Mahmud, S., Lin, X., Kim, J.-H., Iqbal, H., Rahat-Uz-Zaman, M., Reza, S., & Rahman, M. A. (2019). A multi-modal human-machine interface for controlling a smart wheelchair. In *2019 IEEE 7th Conference on Systems, Process, and Control (ICSPC)* (pp. 10–13). IEEE. 10.1109/ICSPC47137.2019.9068027

Marques, G., & Pitarma, R. (2016). An indoor monitoring system for ambient assisted living based on Internet of Things architecture. *International Journal of Environmental Research and Public Health*, 13(11), 1152. 10.3390/ijerph13111152 27869682

Mois, G., Folea, S., & Sanislav, T. (2017). Analysis of three IoT-based wireless sensors for environmental monitoring. *IEEE Transactions on Instrumentation and Measurement*, 66(8), 2056–2064. 10.1109/TIM.2017.2677619

Nooruddin, S., Milon Islam, M., & Sharna, F. A. (2020). An IoT-based device-type invariant fall detection system. *Internet of Things : Engineering Cyber Physical Human Systems*, 9, 100130. 10.1016/j.iot.2019.100130

Oresko, J. J., Jin, Z., Cheng, J., Huang, S., Sun, Y., Duschl, H., & Cheng, A. C. (2010). A wearable smartphone-based platform for real-time cardiovascular disease detection via electrocardiogram processing. *IEEE Transactions on Information Technology in Biomedicine*, 14(3), 734–740. 10.1109/TITB.2010.204786520388600

Patil, K., Laad, M., Kamble, A., & Laad, S. (2019). A consumer-based smart home with an indoor air quality monitoring system. *Journal of the Institution of Electronics and Telecommunication Engineers*, 65(6), 758–770. 10.1080/03772063.2018.1462108

Rahaman, A., Islam, M., Islam, M., Sadi, M., & Nooruddin, S. (2019). Developing IoT-based smart health monitoring systems: A review. *Review of Intelligent Artificial Systems*, 33(6), 435–440. 10.18280/ria.330605

Raspberry Pi Foundation. (n.d.). *Raspberry Pi*. https://www.raspberrypi.org/

Reddy, G. K., & Achari, K. L. (2015). A non-invasive method for calculating calories burned during exercise using heartbeat. In *2015 IEEE 9th International conference on Intelligent Systems and Control (ISCO)* (pp. 1–5). IEEE. 10.1109/ISCO.2015.7282249

Rejeb, A., Rejeb, K., Treiblmaier, H., Appolloni, A., Alghamdi, S., Alhasawi, Y., & Iranmanesh, M. (2023). The Internet of Things (IoT) in healthcare: Taking stock and moving forward. *Internet of Things : Engineering Cyber Physical Human Systems*, 22, 100721. 10.1016/j.iot.2023.100721

Riazul Islam, S. M., Kwak, D., Humaun Kabir, M., Hossain, M., & Kwak, K.-S. (2015). The Internet of Things for health care: A comprehensive survey. *IEEE Access : Practical Innovations, Open Solutions*, 3, 678–708. 10.1109/ACCESS.2015.2437951

Robu. in. (n.d.). *Sound sensor*. Robu. https://robu.in/product-category/sensor-modules/sound-sensor/

ROHM Co. Ltd. (n.d.). *Heart rate sensor*. ROHM. https://www.rohm.com/sensor-shield-support/heart-rate-sensor

Sanh, V., Debut, L., Chaumond, J., & Wolf, T. (2019, October). DistilBERT, a distilled version of BERT: Smaller, faster, cheaper, and lighter. *Clinical Orthopaedics and Related Research.*

Santoso, D., & Dalu Setiaji, F. (2015). Non-contact portable infrared thermometer for rapid influenza screening. In *2015 International conference on automation, cognitive science, optics, micro electromechanical system, and information technology (ICACOMIT)* (pp. 18–23). IEEE. 10.1109/ICACOMIT.2015.7440147

Tamilselvi, V., Sribalaji, S., Vigneshwaran, P., Vinu, P., & Geetha Ramani, J. (2020). IoT-based health monitoring system. In *2020 6th International Conference on Advanced Computing and Communication Systems (ICACCS)* (pp. 386–389). IEEE.10.1109/ICACCS48705.2020.9074192

Teichmann, D., Brüser, C., Eilebrecht, B., Abbas, A., Blanik, N., & Leonhardt, S. (2012). Non-contact monitoring techniques—principles and applications. In *Conference proceedings of the IEEE engineering in medicine and biological society*. IEEE.

Trivedi, S., & Cheeran, A. N. (2017). Android-based health parameter monitoring. In *2017 International Conference on Intelligent Computing and Control Systems (ICICCS)* (pp. 1145–1149). IEEE.

Tsanas, A., Little, M., McSharry, P., & Ramig, L. (2009). Accurate telemonitoring of Parkinson's disease progression by non-invasive speech tests. Nature Precedings, 1–1. Porieva, H. S., Ivanko, K. O., Semkiv, C. I., & Vaityshyn, V. I. (2021). *Investigation of lung sounds features for detection of bronchitis and COPD using machine learning methods*.

Vasquez-Correa, J. C., Klumpp, P., Orozco-Arroyave, J. R., & Noth, E. (2019). Phonet: A tool based on gated recurrent neural networks to extract phonological posteriors from speech. In *INTERSPEECH* (pp. 549–553). ISCA. 10.21437/Interspeech.2019-1405

Yang, C.-T., Chen, S.-T., Den, W., Wang, Y.-T., & Kristiani, E. (2019). Implementation of an intelligent indoor environmental monitoring and management system in cloud. *Future Generation Computer Systems*, 96, 731–749. 10.1016/j.future.2018.02.041

Zanella, A., Bui, N., Castellani, A., Vangelista, L., & Zorzi, M. (2014). Internet of Things for smart cities. *IEEE Internet of Things Journal*, 1(1), 22–32. 10.1109/JIOT.2014.2306328

# Chapter 6
# Design of a Smart Walking Stick for the Visually Impaired Using Internet of Things

**Nirmala Devi M.**
https://orcid.org/0000-0003-1262-9933
*Thiagarajar College of Engineering, India*

**Thangavel Murugan**
*United Arab Emirates University, Al Ain, UAE*

**R. Karthigeyan**
*Thiagarajar College of Engineering, India*

**B. Subbulakshmi**
*Thiagarajar College of Engineering, India*

## ABSTRACT

*In the ever-evolving landscape of assistive technologies, the visually impaired community encounters unique challenges in pursuing heightened mobility and environmental awareness. The endeavor to navigate through perpetually shifting and often unpredictable surroundings necessitates innovative solutions that empower individuals with visual impairments, granting them the ability to traverse with newfound confidence and independence. This research aims to explore the groundbreaking realm of the smart walking stick, an ingeniously designed assistive device that seamlessly integrates cutting-edge technologies, notably Arduino and ultrasonic sensors. At its essence, the main objective of this design is to respond to the urgent and compelling need for advanced navigation tools that can offer real-time obstacle detection and deliver tactile feedback, thereby enhancing the overall mobility experience for individuals with visual impairments.*

DOI: 10.4018/979-8-3693-2901-6.ch006

## INTRODUCTION

In the dynamic realm of assistive technologies, those with visual impairments face a multitude of challenges in achieving greater mobility and awareness of their surroundings. Navigating through constantly changing and unpredictable environments requires innovative solutions that empower them, enabling them to move with confidence and independence. This study delves into the revolutionary Smart Walking Stick, a cleverly designed assistive device that incorporates cutting-edge technologies such as Arduino, Ultrasonic Sensors, and a buzzer.

The main aim of this research is to address the pressing need for advanced navigation tools that can detect obstacles in real-time and provide tactile feedback, thereby improving the overall mobility experience for individuals with visual impairments. By combining the precision of ultrasonic sensors, the flexibility of Arduino microcontrollers, and the intuitive haptic feedback of vibratory motors, this study seeks to make a significant contribution to the field of assistive technology. The ultimate goal is to promote accessibility and independence for the visually impaired, taking a significant step towards a more inclusive future.

This introduction not only sets the stage but also guides the reader through the upcoming exploration of the technical architecture, implementation details, and real-world impact of the Smart Walking Stick. Through the innovative capabilities of this device, the collective aspiration is to empower visually impaired individuals in their daily lives, offering a transformative tool that addresses their unique challenges and opens up new horizons. In doing so, the vision is to move towards a future that is not only more inclusive and accessible but also reflects the meaningful impact of grassroots innovations driven by individuals dedicated to making a tangible difference in the lives of those most in need.

a) Benefits of Smart Walking Stick

   i. A smart walking stick, including recent technologies such as Arduino, ultrasonic sensors, and, potentially, a vibratory motor, provides several advantages for visually impaired individuals.
   ii. Obstacle Detection is a primary advantage, as the sensors can detect obstacles in the user's path, delivering timely alerts to enhance overall safety during mobility. This real-time feedback contributes significantly to avoiding collisions and potential accidents.
   iii. The smart walking stick also offers Distance Measurement capabilities. It measures distances to detected obstacles, providing users with information about proximity and aiding them in navigating around objects more effectively. This feature contributes to improved spatial awareness.
   iv. Auditory Feedback is another key element, with the inclusion of beeping sounds that inform users about the presence and distance of obstacles. This auditory cue enhances situational awareness, enabling quick and informed decision-making during navigation.
   v. If a vibratory motor is included, Tactile Feedback becomes an additional advantage. Users can feel vibrations corresponding to the distance from obstacles, adding another layer of information and further improving the user's spatial perception.
   vi. The use of Arduino microcontrollers makes the smart walking stick highly adaptable. It can be programmed and customized to suit specific user needs or updated to incorporate new features and improvements over time.

b) Limitations of Existing Smart Walking Sticks

i. A smart walking stick, despite its benefits, comes with certain disadvantages. One notable drawback is the potential cost associated with such advanced technologies, making these devices more expensive than traditional walking aids and potentially limiting accessibility for individuals with lower incomes.
ii. Maintenance and Repairs can be challenging, as the integration of electronic components may introduce the need for periodic maintenance or repairs. Users may face difficulties in finding affordable and timely solutions if any of the technological elements malfunction or break.
iii. Battery Life remains a potential disadvantage, as the device relies on batteries for power. Users may face inconvenience if the device runs out of power unexpectedly, compromising their safety.
iv. False Alarms from ultrasonic sensors could be frustrating for users. The sensors may interpret benign objects as obstacles, leading to unnecessary alerts and potentially eroding the users' confidence in the reliability of the device.
v. Durability is a consideration, as the additional electronic components may compromise the overall durability of the walking stick. Exposure to harsh weather conditions or accidental impacts could potentially damage sensitive sensors or other electronic parts.
vi. These disadvantages highlight the need for careful consideration of both the advantages and drawbacks when developing and promoting smart walking sticks for visually impaired individuals. It's crucial to ensure that the technology aligns with users' needs and preferences while addressing potential challenges.

c) Proposed Design Features and Technical Specification
   i. A device has been developed where the overall cost of producing a stick is less than 60 percent of the smart walking sticks that is available in the market right now.
   ii. Less than ten components are used to build the device, so when it comes to repairs, the replacement parts are quite cheap and can be easily attached to the device.
   iii. The battery life is improved by combining two to three nine volt battery to give more capacity.
   iv. The durability of the device is improved by using sturdy materials and high quality components.
   v. To avoid false readings in the device, an advanced HCSR-04 sensors is used, which is known for its reliability and durability.
   vi. The most important problems were covered that was being faced by users in the existing models. It's focused at ways to improve the device more under future scope.

## BACKGROUND

An estimated one billion people worldwide—roughly 15% of the world's population—live with disabilities, and their lives can be significantly improved by the Internet of Things (IoT). H. E. Semary et.al emphasises how critical it is to address issues around disability inclusiveness and support because of their enormous influence on people with disabilities as well as the larger global community. The Internet of Things shines as a ray of light, providing creative ways to empower individuals with disabilities in spite of insufficient support resources. The Internet of Things (IoT) can break the cycle of family dependency by integrating smart devices and technology, which will promote social inclusion and economic engagement. Outlining a suggested Internet of Things framework clarifies its critical function in augmenting the standard of living of people with disabilities and enabling their active participation in social and commercial domains (H. E. Semary,2024).

A smart stick guidance model intended for persons with vision impairments. This package includes an Arduino-based controlling system, an ultrasonic sensor to detect objects around the user in order to prevent fatal injuries, a light sensor module to monitor the amount of light in the surrounding area, LED lights to signal the area, a DC power system to operate the controlling module, and a buzzer to identify obstacles around the stick. Our research indicates that most visually assistive solutions are designed with users in mind .An Optic failure is sometimes referred to as optical misfortune and vision deficiency. Additionally, this obstacle presents several difficulties for them when engaging in regular activities including walking, interacting with others, reading, driving, and socialising. The goal of this research is to develop an Internet of Things stick that will perceive opportunity, independence, and assurance. To facilitate speedy completion of daily tasks, the proposed smart stick is equipped with an obstacle identification module, a worldwide positioning system (GPS), water detection, pit and flight of stairs detection, and a global system for mobile communication (GSM). In order to recognise the obstructions and determine their pattern, the impediment recognition module uses an ultrasonic sensor in conjunction with a water level sensor. The weaker individuals are informed of the hurdles using an Arduino ATmega328, which also delivers notifications through an earbud and a buzzer. Using GPS and GSM modules, the blind person's present location is determined. If the stick is lost, an alert system is triggered. Numerous test scenarios demonstrate that the features included with the stick are operating as intended. People who are blind will greatly benefit from such a stick, which will advance science and technology (Apu,2022).

Those who are blind or visually challenged, getting around is a daily struggle. Using walking sticks has also become customary for the same reason. However, depending only on a blind stick has many limitations. A better approach could help direct the user to their destination while also warning them about the type of difficulty they are facing. In this work, an architecture ispreented for an assistance system centred around a shoe that uses computer vision algorithms, IoT devices, and sensors to provide navigation, obstacle avoidance, and detection capabilities. The technique makes use of voice help via a smartphone and provides the user with relevant haptic input determined by a number of sensors(S. Rao,2021).

A sophisticated solution in object detection is produced by deep learning, and virtual assistants can be helpful for people with vision impairments. This article presents an architectural design for a smart blind assistant that integrates deep learning with the Internet of Things. The suggested concept presents a deep learning paradigm together with an intelligent cap that makes use of a Raspberry Pi and camera module. The suggested architecture shows the structural layout of a smart blind stick that makes use of a microprocessor and several sensors. Additionally, the manuscript offers a virtual assistant development process that serves as a manager of full integration. The model uses Bluetooth and IoT connectivity to provide real-time data monitoring (Md. Wahidur Rahman, 2020).

For creating smart gadgets for the blind is artificial intelligence of things, or AIoT. Its suggested, a smart stick that solves the majority of issues faced by those who are blind or visually impaired. In actuality, the stick aids in identifying the challenges encountered in daily life. Using photos taken by the camera built into the stick, a deep learning algorithm helps the vision impaired user recognise things and money. The stick's pulse sensor keeps track of the user's health. The global positioning system (GPS) and Raspberry Pi that are included into the smart stick assist in detecting emergency notifications. Additionally, the suggested smart stick offers timing data for nearby buses so that users can select their preferred trip times (K. Jivrajani, 2023).

The walking cane is the chosen guiding device for the visually impaired. The Internet of Things, or IOT, is a network of communication where various physical objects, or "things," that are equipped with sensors and Internet access, communicate with one another and with the outside world. In order to help the blind live more independently and with dignity, IoT is contributing significantly to the advancement of the classic white cane. This chapter examines a variety of Internet of Things (IoT)-enabled smart sticks that come with sensors (including rain, infrared, and ultrasonic), GPS modules, and other upgraded features, as well as the Global System for Mobile Communications (GSM). These smart sticks provide visually impaired individuals with affordable, adaptable, and efficient navigational assistance (Varsha Vimal Sood,2022).

A reasonably priced, intelligent blind stick that can aid in navigation for the blind. The gadget has a vibration motor and siren for alerting purposes, as well as infrared and ultrasonic sensors for identifying obstacles in front of the blind user. Moving up and down stairs is one of the largest problems for blind persons when they move indoors. Our goal is to overcome the difficulty by including a feature that alerts the user when a staircase is present in our blind stick. In addition, this gadget includes an integrated GPS and GSM module that track and display the user's location on a smartphone app—a feature that many relatives of blind individuals find useful. If appropriate alert information is not provided to them at the appropriate moment, this could occasionally result in life-threatening activities. This blind persons monitoring system is what a device is proposed to inform people about such behaviours. By anticipating the different obstacles in their path, this technology warns visually impaired individuals and advises them to proceed with extreme caution. When a visually impaired person needs emergency assistance, thisr technology also provides the visually impaired care homes with the precise location information of the immediate assistance (Nguyen, H.Q., 2022).

A low-cost guidance and navigation system for the visually impaired has long been needed. Due to their extreme cost-inefficiency, existing solutions are only affordable for those in higher socioeconomic classes. Rather than depending on strangers for assistance, blind people can travel walking distances to work with the use of an inexpensive piece of equipment. In this work, a walking stick design that will facilitate the visually impaired in getting to work. The suggested method makes use of the Internet of Things to enable blind people to "communicate" with their surroundings. The hurdles have been greatly aided by technologies like Internet of Things (IoT), Image Processing (IP), Computer Vision and Pattern Recognition (CVPR), etc. Many automated and technical solutions are made possible by IoT to help those who are blind or visually impaired. Analytics and data science play a significant role in the procedure. Processed data from several sensors can be utilised to detect impediments and improve simple navigation with speech and haptic feedback. Raw data is subjected to numerous analyses and refinements. After that, this is transformed into a format that the system can comprehend and use to execute different parts of a programme(Sharma.S, 2021).

Zahraa A. Ali discussed that Smart technologies can help people with vision impairments move safely and with self-guidance. The two amazing electronic devices—a smart belt and a smart stick—that were created for visually impaired people utilising assistive technology choices for obstacle detection are shown in this paper. They were made to be easily portable, inexpensive, and user-friendly without having an internet connection. The two smart gadgets were tested against the conventional white cane in terms of accuracy (avoidance of obstacles) and usability (easy of use) in an experiment including blind people. To test each tool, participants walked the same path while being randomly given obstacles (Zahraa A. Ali, 2023).

Unfortunately, many blind individuals are unable to visit certain regular sites because there are insufficient facilities and policies in place to assist the blind, which causes them great inconvenience. Ren Yunan et.al created in their study, an upgraded intelligent guide stick to give security guide for the blind's every day journey and their precise position for their guardians, making travel easier and safer for them. The guardian's smartphone was provided with position information and surrounding photographs to assist in locating the blind person, particularly in a multi-story building (Ren Yunan,2021).

People with vision impairments must overcome obstacles in their path to gain maximum mobility. In addition to the widely used white cane, electronic assistive devices have been created. However, because of their complexity and cost, the electronic devices that are currently available are not widely used. Abreu D et.al presented the design of a low-cost assistive device for the blind in an attempt to improve the ones that already exist. By incorporating phase modulation into the ultrasonic pulses, the low-cost, conventional HC-SRF04 ultrasonic range can be altered to identify the source of emission, distinguishing between echo pulses that originate from the same instrument and preventing false echoes caused by external interference. This enhances security and accuracy in locations where multiple ultrasonic sensors are operating concurrently (Abreu D,2021).

Summary of the literature the follwing components are used in the design of the proposed smat walking stick.The HCSR-04 sensor, strategically positioned at the lower end of the stick, serves to detect minor obstacles such as pits, staircases, or stones on the ground. Upon detecting such obstacles, the HCSR-04 sensor signals the Arduino, prompting the issuance of a voice instruction alerting the user to the presence of a small obstacle. Simultaneously, the buzzer is activated to provide additional notification to the visually impaired individual.

Positioned at the lower end of the smart stick, the water sensor acts as a precautionary measure against slippery surfaces. Upon contact with a wet surface, the water sensor generates an electrical signal that triggers the Arduino board, once this happens a voice instruction warning about the wet surface is played, accompanied by the activation of a buzzer to alert the user about potential slipping hazards.The heat sensor, highly sensitive to heat radiation over long distances, sends an electrical signal to the controller upon detecting heat. This prompts the issuance of a voice instruction and activates both the vibrator and the buzzer to alert the user to the presence of heat sources.

The Light Dependent Resistor (LDR) responds to changes in light intensity, assuming high resistance during nighttime. In such conditions, the LDR allows current to pass through a parallel-connected LED, essentially functioning as a flashlight. This illuminated state serves as a visual indicator for others, alerting them to the presence of a visually impaired person and facilitating a clear path for the individual. The Skylab UART GPS Module, serving as a GPS tracker, guarantees precise positioning within a certain margin, along with navigation and timing functions for users. It consistently delivers location data paired with timing details, enabling the GPS-oriented assistive device to interact with users, providing voice-guided alerts upon arrival at their destination. This diverse method substantially boosts the capabilities of the smart walking stick, fostering safety and independence for those with visual impairments.

The RF module functions with a receiver connected to the Arduino, while the transmitter serves as a remote held by the blind person. When the blind user commands the transmitter through the remote, signaling is transmitted to the receiver. The output is then directed to a buzzer, aiding the visually impaired individual in locating the stick through auditory cues. This innovative integration of an RF module enhances the stick's functionality, providing an additional layer of convenience for the user in navigating and locating their walking aid.

The proposed system integrates a camera to supplement image processing, particularly in scenarios where the hcsr-4 sensor might not adequately detect moving objects such as vehicles and pedestrians. Notably, the authors' device employs scanning in three different directions (spanning 180 degrees). When obstacles are detected, the buzzer and vibration motor activate to alert the user. The inclusion of a GPS system provides valuable location information, enhancing navigation capabilities. Moreover, the system features an SMS function, enabling blind individuals to send text messages using python. Python, renowned for its dynamic type system and automatic memory management, supports various programming paradigms, including object-oriented, imperative, functional, and procedural, and is enriched by an extensive standard library. This combination of technologies underscores the flexibility and efficacy of their proposed smart cane for assisting the visually impaired.

## MATERIALS USED

The smart stick for the blind people is meticulously designed, blending simplicity with advanced features. Crafted with a durable PVC pipe as Smart Stick, an Arduino Uno board with extra pins, an ultrasonic sensor (HCSR04), versatile jumper wires, an Arduino buzzer, a 9v battery, and zip ties for secure fastening, this device ensures reliable and enhanced mobility.

## ARDUINO UNO

*Figure 1. Arduino Uno*

The Arduino is one of the best in the realm of microcontroller boards, offering a various features that contribute to its success and versatility. The board is built around the ATmega328P microcontroller, providing a very huge foundation for a variety of applications. What sets Arduino Uno apart is its commitment to an open-source platform, fostering a collaborative community and allowing users to delve into and modify the source code. The best thing of Arduino Uno is its user-friendly design. The Arduino Integrated Development Environment (IDE) simplifies the coding process, making it easy understand for both beginners and experienced people. The board's flexibility is further enhanced by its support for additional modules that can be effortlessly stacked to introduce various functionalities, from communication interfaces to sensor integration. With variety of digital and analog İnput/Output (I/O) pins each having its own role, Arduino Uno offers versatility in connecting sensors, actuators, and other external components. The board's USB connectivity facilitates seamless communication with computers, streamlining the programming and data transfer processes. Arduino Uno benefits from an extensive library of pre-written code, reducing the complexity of implementing intricate functionalities. Its compatibility with a diverse range of sensors and components makes it a preferred choice for prototyping.

## ULTRASONIC SENSOR (HCSR-04)

*Figure 2. HCSR-04 Sensor*

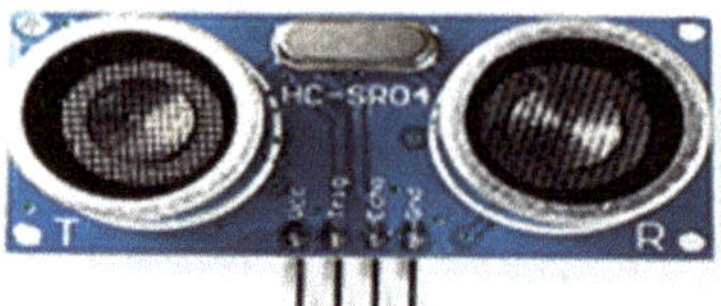


The Ultrasonic HC-SR04 sensor is a versatile and widely used device in the realm of electronics and robotics, offering precise distance measurement capabilities based on ultrasonic sound waves. This compact and cost-effective sensor has become a staple in various applications, from obstacle avoidance in robotics to distance sensing in IoT projects. The sensor operates on the principle of echolocation. It emits ultrasonic pulses and measures the time it takes for the pulses to travel to an object and bounce back as echoes. Using the speed of sound, the sensor calculates the distance between itself and the target object with remarkable accuracy.

One of the key features of the HC-SR04 sensor is its simplicity of use. With only four pins—two for power, one for trigger, and one for echo—it is easy to integrate into electronic circuits. The trigger pin starts the ultrasonic pulse, while the echo pin receiving the reflected signal. This straightforward interface makes the sensor accessible to both beginners and experienced enthusiasts. The HC-SR04 sensor typically has a range of 2 cm to 350 cm aprroxiamtely, providing a broad spectrum of applications. Its rapid response time and high precision make it suitable for real-time systems, such as obstacle avoidance in robotics or creating interactive installations where proximity sensing is crucial.

## VOLT BATTERY

The 9-volt battery, a compact and reliable power source, plays a pivotal role in the world of electronics. With its distinctive rectangular shape and four to six small tubulur cells connected in series, this battery delivers a usually a voltage of 9 volts. Its compact size and snap-style or clip connector make it easily adaptable to a variety of electronic circuits, offering convenience in portable applications with limited space.

Widely employed in everyday devices such as smoke detectors, remote controls, and handheld electronics, the 9-volt battery also finds utility in DIY projects and serves as a go-to power solution for microcontroller boards, sensors, and other electronic components. Its stable voltage output and compatibility with both alkaline and lithium chemistries contribute to its versatility.

*Figure 3. 9 volt battery*

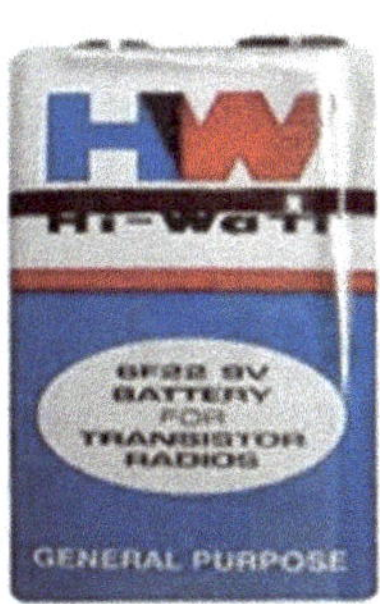


## PROPOSED DESIGN-METHODOLOGY

The development of assistive technology is based on the fundamental principle of user-centric design, and critical first step in this process is doing a comprehensive user needs assessment. To design the outline of a smart walking stick for the blind people, this entails conducting in-depth interviews and surveys with the intended user base. Gaining a thorough grasp of their unique requirements, difficulties, and preferences when navigating the environment is the main goal. It's important to investigate a number of topics during the user needs assessment stage, including the kinds of environments users use (indoor, outdoor, urban, and rural), typical roadblocks they encounter, preferred feedback methods (auditory, haptic, etc.), and any extra features they would find useful. The knowledge acquired from these exchanges forms the basis for another essential element of user-centric design is user feedback iteration. Encouraging user feedback on prototypes at every stage of the design process guarantees that the walking stick will adjust to the actual problems that people with visual impairments confront. By refining and adjusting based on user experiences, this iterative strategy eventually produces a more effective and user-friendly product. The feedback loop should be a continuous, cooperative process that encourages engineers and end users to work together. Prototypes should be tested in a variety of settings so that users can offer input on usability, comfort, efficacy, and any unexpected difficulties. By using an iterative feedback loop, the smart walking stick is guaranteed to match both the original design objectives and the varied and evolving in summary, user-centric design for a smart walking stick tailored to individuals who are visually impaired begins with a comprehensive user needs assessment, providing a solid foundation based on user insights. The iterative user feedback process then ensures that the development cycle remains responsive to real-world challenges, resulting in a product that is not only technologically sophisticated but, more importantly, genuinely addresses the preferences of its intended users.

The integration of sensor technology is the foundation in the development of a smart walking stick tailored to individuals with visual problems. By incorporating a variety of sensors such as ultrasonic, infrared, and tactile sensors, the smart stick gains the ability to detect obstacles, changes in terrain, and other environmental factors in real-time. Ultrasonic sensors contribute by emitting sound waves and measuring their reflections to identify obstacles, while infrared sensors detect the presence of objects through emitted and received infrared radiation. Tactile sensors strategically placed on the walking stick provide valuable feedback about the texture of surfaces and variations in terrain, enhancing tactile awareness. Equally critical are the feedback mechanisms that convey this information to users without relying on visual cues. Haptic feedback, delivered through vibrations in the handle or other parts of the walking stick, communicates details about proximity and the nature of obstacles. Auditory cues, in the form of tones or signals, alert users to environmental conditions and directional cues. This integration of diverse sensors and feedback mechanisms creates a comprehensive and intuitive user experience, empowering individuals with visual impairments to navigate their surroundings with increased awareness and autonomy. The emphasis on nonvisual feedback aligns with the overarching goal of designing a user-centric smart walking stick that addresses the specific needs and preferences of the visually impaired community.

Making the correct choice for the choosing the parts for the power system is one of the most critical decision in the the process of designing the smart walking stick. Opting for components and technologies that prioritize low power consumption is paramount to ensure extended battery life, a key factor in the usability and reliability of the device.by choosing energy-efficient sensors, processors, and communication modules, the overall power requirements of the walking stick can be minimized. For instance, the utilization of low-power microcontrollers and sensor technologies can significantly contribute to reducing the energy demands of the device. This not only conserve battery life but also enhances the overall sustainability and user experience. The efficiency of energy storage components, such as rechargeable batteries, is equally crucial. Selecting high-capacity and energy-dense batteries with efficient charging and discharging characteristics ensures that the smart walking stick remains operational for extended periods between charges. Additionally, the incorporation of smart power management systems can optimize energy distribution and usage, further maximizing the device's operational time. Furthermore, the integration of sleep modes or low-power states for components that are not in active use can contribute to minimizing energy consumption during periods of inactivity. This intelligent power management approach ensures that the smart walking stick maximizes efficiency, delivering reliable performance while conserving energy when not actively engaged.

The integration of real-time data processing is a foundational element in the design of a smart walking stick tailored for blind people. To achieve a responsive and reliable system, the implementation of fast and efficient processing mechanisms is paramount. This involves the use of modern technological things, algorithms that run thousands of calculation in a second. Employing efficient algorithms enables the smart walking stick to rapidly interpret data from sensors such as ultrasonic, infrared, and tactile sensors. This quick processing capability is instrumental in identifying obstacles, changes in terrain, and other environmental factors without perceptible delays. The goal is to deliver instantaneous feedback to the user, allowing them to make timely and informed decisions as they navigate their surroundings. Furthermore, a key aspect of real-time data processing is the establishment of low-latency systems. Minimizing delays in the system is crucial for enhancing the user's perception of their surroundings. By reducing latency, the smart walking stick can provide a more seamless and natural interaction with the user, facilitating a real-time understanding of the environment. This not only contributes to safety but also enhances the overall user experience, fostering a sense of confidence and autonomy.

While choosing the materials, the selection of materials is very important, selecting materials that are both durable and comfortable to the visually impaired is important, at the same time the materials must be cheap so that the stick is affordable. The selection of materials and the overall design play crucial roles in ensuring the longevity, reliability, and user satisfaction of the device. In terms of durability, choosing robust and resilient materials for the construction of the walking stick is paramount. The device should be able to withstand the physical demands it may encounter in various environments, whether it's navigating urban landscapes or handling different types of terrain. This involves considering materials that are not only durable but also lightweight to ensure ease of use for the individual. Collaborating with experts in ergonomics is essential to achieving an optimal design that prioritizes user comfort and usability over extended periods.

An ergonomic design takes into account factors such as grip, weight distribution, and overall user interface to create a device that is not only functional but also comfortable and easy to handle. This is especially important for individuals who may rely on the smart walking stick as a constant companion throughout their daily activities. Additionally, considering the impact of the device on the user's posture and movement is crucial in the ergonomic design process. The walking stick should be designed to promote a natural and comfortable gait, reducing the risk of fatigue or discomfort associated with prolonged use. Furthermore, incorporating features such as adjustable height and customizable grips allows for a personalized fit, accommodating the diverse needs and preferences of users. This adaptability ensures that the smart walking stick is a tailored and inclusive assistive device that can be comfortably utilized by individuals with varying physical requirements.

To make sure that the walking stick is working with pinpoint accuracy even after long usage, customer feedback is really important. Getting updates from users on the walking stick reguraly will help to reduce the errors in the latest prototype. To ensure the long-term effectiveness and relevance of the device, establishing robust feedback loops and implementing mechanisms for regular updates are imperative. Feedback loops form a fundamental component of continuous improvement. By creating mechanisms for ongoing feedback from users, developers can gain valuable insights into the real-world performance of the smart walking stick. This feedback, collected through channels such as surveys, user interviews, or online platforms, serves as a foundation for identifying emerging needs, challenges, and opportunities for enhancement.

In addition to feedback loops, incorporating over-the-air (ota) updates is a crucial feature in ensuring the device's adaptability and responsiveness. Designing the smart walking stick to support remote updates enables developers to introduce improvements without necessitating physical modifications to the device. This remote update capability is particularly beneficial for users, as it eliminates the need for them to visit service centers for enhancements or bug fixes. It also ensures that the device can evolve over time, staying current with technological advancements and user needs.

By combining continuous feedback mechanisms with over-the-air update capabilities, developers can establish a dynamic and responsive ecosystem for the smart walking stick. This approach aligns with a user-centric design philosophy, ensuring that the device remains a relevant and effective assistive tool for individuals with visual impairments over the long term. Continuous improvement and updates not only reflect a commitment to user satisfaction but also contribute to the creation of a smart walking stick that evolves in tandem with the needs of its user community.

4.1 CIRCUIT DIAGRAM

This is the circuit diagram for the prototype.

*Figure 4. Circuit diagram*

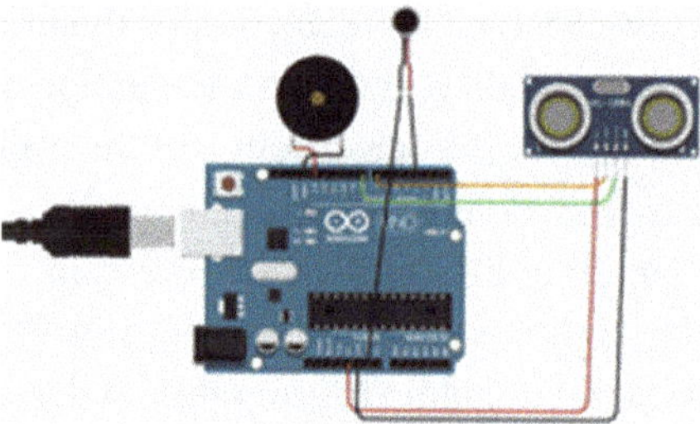

The results obtained from the experiment conducted on the HCSR-04 sensor indicates that, the difference betweeen the actual and measured distance is fractional and the error percentage is close to zero. This mimimal error percetange would not affect the role of the device.As discussed before, in the experiment its proved the reliabity and durabilty of the HCSR-04 sensor.

a) Prototype buidling steps

Following completion of these procedures, One has to download the Arduino IDE to our laptop or PC and use the cable that was supplied by the seller to connect the Arduino board to our computer. Following that, One has to enter the relevant code into the Arduino IDE.

b) System Code for Arduino

Function to initialize the system
Set trigPin as an OUTPUT
Set echoPin as an INPUT
Set motor as an OUTPUT
Set buzzer as an OUTPUT
Function to continuously run the system
Declare variables for duration and distance
Send a LOW signal to trigPin
Send a HIGH signal to trigPin for 10 microseconds
Send a LOW signal to trigPin
Measure the duration of the echo signal
Calculate the distance based on the duration
Check if the distance is less than 15 cm
Turn on the motor
Turn on the buzzer
else
Turn off the motor
Turn off the buzzer
Wait for 500 milliseconds before the next loop

In the setup function, its carefully defined the pin configurations for all the components that are going to integrate in the smart stick. The trigPin and echoPin are designated as OUTPUT and INPUT, respectively, establishing their roles in facilitating communication with the ultrasonic sensor. Simultaneously, the pins associated with the vibration motor and the buzz are configured as OUTPUT, preparing them for precise control during the execution of the program.

c) Initiating ultrasonic pulse
   Measuring echo duration
   Calculating distance based on the speed of sound
   distance = (duration / 2) / 29.1
   Checking the calculated distance against a threshold
   if (distance < 15) Triggering motor and buzzer for proximity alert
   else Deactivating motor and buzzer when distance is beyond the threshold
   Introducing a delay for optimal system responsiveness

In the above procedure, the duration variable records the time taken for the ultrasonic signal to travel and return. The duration is then converted into distance value using speed of sound. The equation is commonly used to calculate distance based on the time taken for an object to travel a certain distance using ultrasonic sensors. Here's a breakdown of the components:

Duration: This represents the time it takes for a signal (usually an ultrasonic pulse) to travel from the sensor to an object and back again. It's typically measured in microseconds.

Dividing by 2: Since the signal travels from the sensor to the object and back again, the total distance traveled is twice the distance from the sensor to the object. So, dividing the duration by 2 gives us the time it takes for the signal to travel one way.

Dividing by 29.1: The speed of sound in air is approximately 343 meters per second (at room temperature). Since its dealt with the time in microseconds and People want the distance in centimeters, then divide the time by the speed of sound in air converted into centimeters per microsecond. The speed of sound in air is approximately 34300 centimeters per second or 0.0343 centimeters per microsecond (since there are 1,000,000 microseconds in a second, the designer divide the speed of sound in centimeters per second by 1,000,000 to get centimeters per microsecond). Dividing the duration (in microseconds) by this value gives us the distance in centimeters.

The procedure subsequently evaluates whether this calculated distance is less than 15 units, a configurable threshold indicating close proximity. If the condition is met, the system responds by activating both the vibration motor and the buzzer, serving as an alert mechanism. Conversely, when the distance surpasses the threshold, the motor and buzzer are deactivated.Finally, a deliberate delay of 500 milliseconds is introduced to regulate the timing between successive distance measurements. This meticulous coding structure ensures the precise orchestration of the components, leading to a responsive and accurate system for object detection based on ultrasonic measurements.

## DESIGN -PROTOTYPE

*Figure 5. Smart walking stick prototype building*

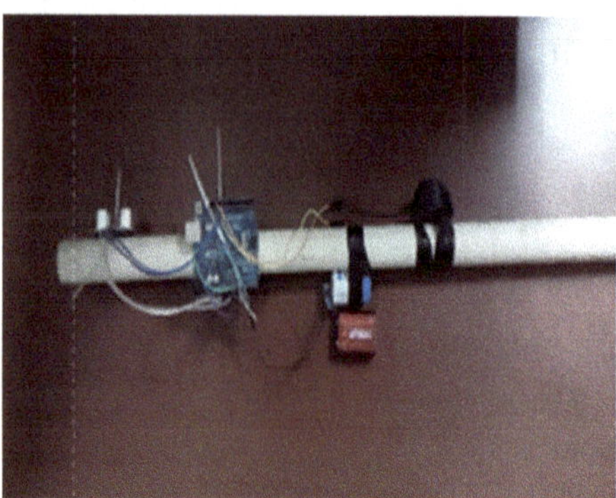

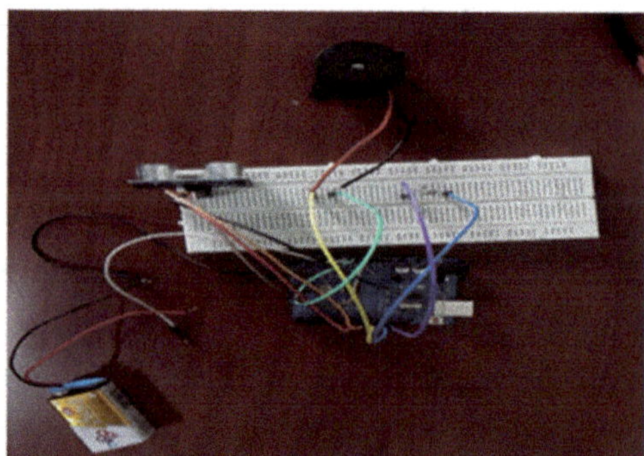

The initial prototype primarily serves as a proof of concept, implemented on a breadboard without the inclusion of the walking stick. The primary focus at this stage is to validate and fine-tune the functionality of the hcsr04 sensor, which plays a pivotal role in obstacle detection. This breadboard setup enables a systematic testing environment, allowing for meticulous examination of how the sensor responds to different obstacles and distances. It serves as a crucial step in the development process, offering insights into the accuracy and reliability of the obstacle detection mechanism. As the prototype evolves, the integrating the smart walking stick will be the next step, wherein the tested sensor technology will be seamlessly incorporated. This iterative process ensures that each component functions to create a reliable and effective solution. The breadboard prototype, therefore, acts as a foundational phase, laying the groundwork for the subsequent stages of development and enhancement in the overall design of the smart walking stick.

The advancement from the initial breadboard prototype to the second stage involves a significant leap, transitioning from a testing environment to a more practical implementation within the structure of a walking stick. In figure 1, a PVC pipe serves as the primary housing for the components, with zip ties utilized to secure and integrate them seamlessly into the stick. This adaptation marks a crucial step towards achieving a functional and user-friendly smart walking stick. The incorporation of the components into the stick not only demonstrates the practicality of the design but also addresses the portability and ease of use for the end user.

The use of a PVC pipe as the housing material suggests a lightweight and durable solution, ensuring that the smart walking stick remains comfortable for the user while providing the necessary support for the integrated components. The zip ties, in this context, offer a versatile and secure method for affixing the components, allowing for flexibility in adjusting and fine-tuning the placement as needed. Overall, the transition to this stick-based prototype represents a tangible evolution in the development process, aligning the project closer to the ultimate goal of creating a functional, user-friendly, and reliable smart walking stick.

As the user utilizes the smart stick, sensors integrated into the device are responsible for detecting potential obstacles in the surrounding environment. Once an obstacle is detected, these sensors promptly transmit a signal to the Arduino board.Once the singal is recieved on the sensor, the arduino board detects it and sends ceratin amount of voltage to the buzzer. The buzzer, in turn, produces an audible beeping noise. It's important to note that the frequency of the buzzer's beeping is inversely proportional to the distance from the obstacle. In simpler terms, as the user gets closer to an obstacle, the frequency of the beeping increases, serving as a real-time indicator of proximity. This dynamic feature enhances the user's awareness of their surroundings and aids in navigating safely, with the pitch of the sound providing valuable information about the distance to potential obstacles.

## RESULTS AND DISCUSSION

The comprehensive culmination of our efforts manifests in the triumphant development of an advanced walking stick made for the blind people and for researchers to make use of our work. This innovative solution displays vibratory sensors and machine learning capabilities, elevating its functionality to new heights. Our extensive trials in real-world scenarios, coupled with a lot of positive user feedback, stand as a testament to the technology's prowess and its potential to improve the daily life of the visually impaired

The unwavering commitment to ethical standards throughout the developmental journey underscores the responsible and considerate approach taken in crafting this assistive technology. The continuous cycle of refinement, guided by user experiences and feedback, exemplifies an adaptive and user-centric philosophy. This iterative process ensures that the technology evolves in tandem with the evolving needs and preferences of its users, reinforcing the paramount importance of ongoing improvement in the realm of assistive technologies.

This pioneering research not only advances the specific domain of visually impaired mobility aids but also establishes a groundbreaking precedent for the integration of cutting-edge technologies. With a dedicated focus on user needs and a steadfast commitment to ethical considerations, our work contributes significantly to the broader field of assistive technology. The potential impact of this research extends beyond the development of a single device, fostering a paradigm shift towards more inclusive and user-aware technological solutions for diverse accessibility challenges.

In Figure 6 the results of Ultrasonic Sensor in Obstacle Detection are diplayed. It shows how accurately the obstacles are detected using the proposed design. The actual distance of obstacles are compared with the measured distance of obstacles in centimeters(cm).

*Figure 6. Results of ultrasonic sensor in obstacle detection*

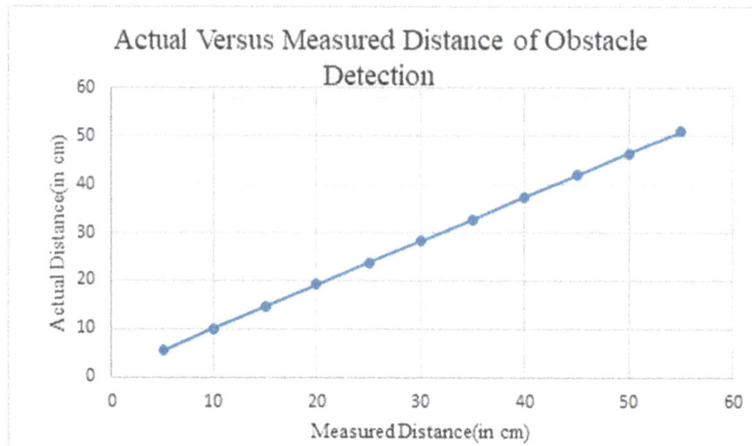


## CONCLUSION

In conclusion, the smart walking stick project stands as a testament to the intersection of innovation, compassion, and practicality. Looking forward, the envisioned future work holds promises of even greater impact. Advanced sensors, machine learning algorithms, and global localization hint at a walking stick evolving not just in its technological capabilities but in its ability to seamlessly integrate with the diverse lifestyles and needs of users worldwide.

As the smart walking stick becomes more than a mobility aid, incorporating biometrics, IoT connectivity, and features catering to different age groups, it transcends the realm of a device to become a companion on life's journey. It is a manifestation of adaptability, responsiveness, and a commitment to the well-being of those who rely on it. The future isn't merely a roadmap for technological upgrades; it's a pledge to continue pushing boundaries, fostering accessibility, and embracing the dynamic landscape of assistive technology. Through collaborations with healthcare institutions, community outreach programs, and a focus on user education, the smart walking stick project envisions a future where its impact extends far beyond its technological components.

## FUTURE SCOPE

The horizon of future possibilities for our smart walking stick unfolds with a humungous amount of potential enhancements, poised to elevate its working and have a major impact on the lives of disabled people. Integrating GPS technology is a key feature, paving the way for providing not just obstacle detection but comprehensive route information. By leveraging real-time coordinates, the smart stick can empower users to navigate from source to destination efficiently, utilizing platforms such as Google Maps or Bing Maps to find the shortest and optimal paths.Moreover, the prospect of linking the walking stick to the individual's Aadhar card introduces a novel dimension to accessibility. This integration could foster improved government services for persons with disabilities. By creating a seamless connection between the walking stick and the Aadhar card, authorities could gain valuable insights into the mobility patterns and needs of visually impaired individuals, enabling more targeted and effective support.

Expanding the stick's capabilities to include a water sensor adds another layer of safety, addressing the often-overlooked concern of slippery surfaces. The sensor could detect the presence of water, alerting the user and facilitating cautious navigation to prevent slips and falls.This expansive vision for the future of the smart walking stick not only amplifies its assistive capabilities but also underscores its potential as a multifaceted tool for empowerment and safety. These prospective advancements demonstrate a commitment to continuous innovation, further solidifying the smart walking stick as a transformative and indispensable device in the realm of assistive technologies for the visually impaired.

## REFERENCES

Abreu, D., Toledo, J., Codina, B., & Suárez, A. (2021), Low-Cost Ultrasonic Range Improvements for an Assistive Device. *Sensors. 21*, 4250. 10.3390/s21124250

Apu, A. I., Nayan, A. A., Ferdaous, J., & Kibria, M. G. (2022), IoT-Based Smart Blind Stick. *International Conference on Big Data, IoT, and Machine Learning. Lecture Notes on Data Engineering and Communications Technologies*. Springer, Singapore. 10.1007/978-981-16-6636-0_34

Jivrajani, K. (2023). AIoT-Based Smart Stick for Visually Impaired Person. *IEEE Transactions on Instrumentation and Measurement.* IEEE. 10.1109/TIM.2022.3227988

Nguyen, H. Q., Duong, A. H. L., Vu, M. D., Dinh, T. Q., & Ngo, H. T. (2022), Smart Blind Stick for Visually Impaired People.*8th International Conference on the Development of Biomedical Engineering in Vietnam.* Springer, Cham. 10.1007/978-3-030-75506-5_12

Rao, S., & Singh, V. M. (2021). *Computer Vision and IoT Based Smart System for Visually Impaired People.* 2021 11th International Conference on Cloud Computing, Data Science & Engineering, Noida, India. 10.1109/Confluence51648.2021.9377120

Sharma, S., & Umme Salma, M. (2021). Social, Medical, and Educational Applications of IoT to Assist Visually Impaired People. In Chakraborty, C., Banerjee, A., Kolekar, M., Garg, L., & Chakraborty, B. (Eds.), *Internet of Things for Healthcare Technologies. Studies in Big Data* (Vol. 73). Springer., 10.1007/978-981-15-4112-4_10

Sood, V. V., Bansal, K., & Agarwal, N. (2022). *Advanced Sensing in Image Processing and IoT* (1st ed.). CRC Press.

Zahraa A. (2023). Design and evaluation of two obstacle detection devices for visually impaired people. *Journal of Engineering Research, 2023, 11*(3). 10.1016/j.jer.2023.100132

# Chapter 7
# An Automated Drug Dispenser Mobile Application Using Internet of Things (IoT) in Smart Healthcare Systems

**Nirmala Devi M.**
http://orcid.org/0000-0003-1262-9933
*Thiagarajar College of Engineering, India*

**Subbulakshmi B.**
*Thiagarajar College of Engineering, India*

**Sree Harish T.**
http://orcid.org/0009-0009-8528-1035
*Thiagarajar College of Engineering, India*

**Muthukumaran S.**
http://orcid.org/0009-0009-4347-4509
*Thiagarajar College of Engineering, India*

**Vignesh G.**
http://orcid.org/0009-0001-4502-7907
*Thiagarajar College of Engineering, India*

**Niranjan L.**
http://orcid.org/0009-0005-0994-4782
*Thiagarajar College of Engineering, India*

## ABSTRACT

*The automated drug dispenser (ADD) represents a revolutionary leap in healthcare accessibility, seamlessly integrating advanced pharmaceutical technologies to streamline obtaining prescribed medications. This cutting-edge system leverages the power of the internet of things (IoT), mobile app development, database management, and cloud computing to create a patient-centric approach to medication dispensation. It is a user-friendly interface that transforms the patient experience. By employing a mobile app, individuals can effortlessly navigate through the system, initiating the drug retrieval process with a simple QR code scan. This enhances efficiency and ensures accuracy, as the system rapidly identifies and dispenses the correct medication. A pivotal feature of ADD is its utilization of specific patient details to establish a secure connection. By referencing individualized information, the system not only verifies the patient's identity but also updates a centralized and protected database.*

DOI: 10.4018/979-8-3693-2901-6.ch007

## INTRODUCTION

Over last few years, the automatic drug dispenser have been installed in many hospitals to reduce the medication errors and to dispense the medicines accurately and to reduce the time for dispensing the medicine. This chapter introduces the automatic drug dispenser with a new feature by introducing the QR code based drug dispensing system. The Implementation of this system yields 30% decrease in the medication errors across healthcare. By automating the dispensation process, the risk of medication error and waiting time for the medicine are reduced, thereby it ensures the patient safety and their time.

In addition to reducing the medication error, automated drug dispenser also shows the improvement in the operational efficiency by decreasing the time by 20%. This efficiency helps to reduce the patients waiting time by having the automated dispensation by scanning the QR code in the machine.

Patient satisfaction level also increased with the introduction of the automated drug dispensing system. About 80% of the patients express confidence in the accuracy of medications dispensed by automated systems. This makes a strengthened confidence among the patients about the precision of the automated drug dispenser to receive the medicines with trust. Moreover, the financial benefits of automated drug dispenser include the cost savings for the healthcare. Reports shows 15% reduction in drug wastage after implementing the automated drug dispensers. By optimizing medication management, it reduces the expired and unused medicines, the automated systems helps the healthcare to save costs and uses the resources effectively.

About 35% of hospitals and medical centres have adopted automatic drug dispensers. This implementation highlights the growing recognition of the benefits of automated drug dispensing system in improving medication management and patient healthcare worldwide. And the adoption of automatic drug dispenser is a strategic investment in improving the medication management. The implementation of QR code in the dispensing machines helps to easily process the medication order by scanning the QR code in the machine via smartphones. The doctor checks out the patient's health and upload the patient's medication in the software which contains the history of the patient's medication. Once the patient's medication is uploaded by the doctor, the patient can scan the QR code in the machine through the mobile application and after scanning it gets into the payment process, after finishing the transaction the prescribed medicines will get dispensed by the automated drug dispenser.

The data from the World Health Organization (WHO) shows the requirement of innovative healthcare solutions. Around two billion people in the world lack their essential medications and causing health issues. The automated drug dispenser offers a secure and efficient way for patients to access their prescribed medicines. The use of IoT technology helps the dispenser to create an efficient dispensing system for getting medicines. This integration of technology supports a connected healthcare network and changes the distribution system of medications.

Global healthcare faces the issues like patients not taking the prescribed medicines and prescription errors, leading to about 125,000 deaths per year according to the Journal of the American Medical Association (JAMA). This automatic drug dispenser addresses these problems by QR code technology to have the accurate dispensing system of medicines and helps to reduce the deaths caused by the errors.

The following Survey questions have collected from the friends, stakeholders and community partners.

*Figure 1. Survey questionnaire from the friends, stakeholders, and community partners*

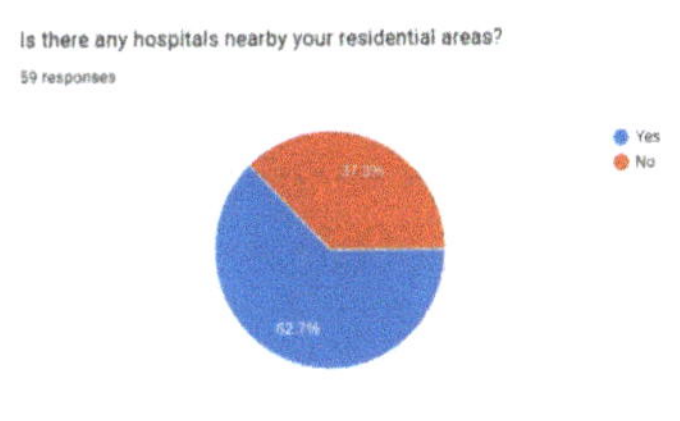


*Figure 2. Survey questionnaire two from the friends, stakeholders, and community partners*

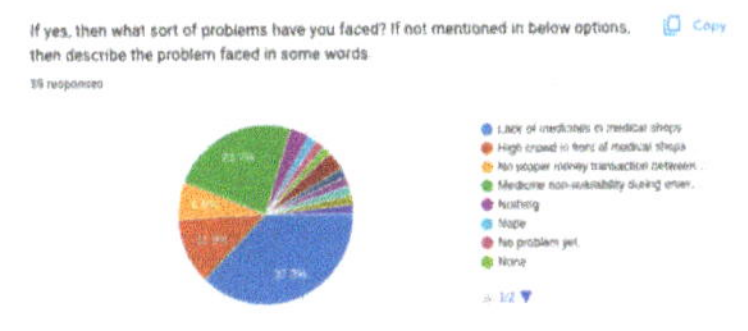


*Figure 3. Survey questionnaire three from the friends, stakeholders, and community partners*

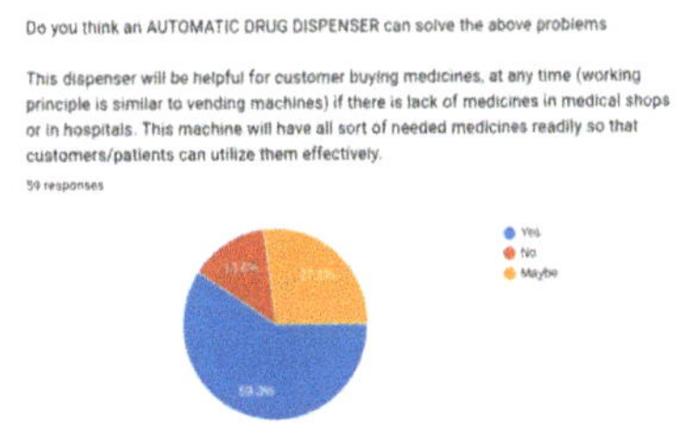


Figure 1,2,3 illustrates the statistics that were got from residents says that most of the residents have give report that the automatic drug dispenser is helpful for the residents. Because in some of the villages there are no medical shops so the residents are in need for it as well as some of their grandparents are in need of regular intake of medicines and these machines setup nearby will help the residents to buy their drugs easily by this dispenser.

In some countries about one-third of the population has access to the essential medicines. The automated drug dispenser helps to solve this problem by the using mobile technology because over 8.9 billion mobile subscriptions are there in 2023 where the mobile subscriptions are quickly increasing it solves this problem. The drug dispenser's mobile application is easy to use for people who were from different backgrounds. It also supports database management and strictly follows the government laws to manage the information's of the patients.

In conclusion, the global implementation of automatic drug dispenser assures to transform the healthcare to improve access in the healthcare. By making the medication retrieval easier using IoT and mobile application, this solution tackles the global healthcare issues in the medication distribution process. The automated drug dispenser offers a secure and patient friendly way to dispense the medicines. In today's digital era, these innovations not only improves healthcare but also pave the way for a future which has the healthcare accessible to everyone. As this chapter look towards the future, the promise of better health and improved well-being for all.

## BACKGROUND

Giving correct medicine at the correct time to the patient ensures their hygiene. There is a problem that the medical staff could miss to give the right medicine at the right time to the patient hence an automated drug dispensing system is modeled to dispense the right medicine at the right time to the patient. Here, various domains and technologies were employed, and they are machine learning, Internet of Things (IoT), mobile application, and database management. Servo motors are utilized for the dispensing process. And the medicine allotted for the time will get dispensed by giving an alarm sound and the patient can get that showing hands to the dispenser. The dispenser dispense the medicine by recognizing the hand using IR sensor. And the database is updated with the current quantity of tablets (Basavaraj N Hiremath, 2022).

A system that incorporates a microcontroller, GSM module, and a dedicated application. This system is designed to dispense the medicines for common ailments with a basic prescriptions. And it gives alert messages and notifications for the patients for each dispensation. This system also provides the recommendations for some diseases with its existing database. And the doctors have capability to monitor the patient's medicine usages (Rehenuma Tabassum Meghla, 2022).

An automatic pill and syringe dispenser, system highlights the dispensation of pill and syringe mainly for the diabetes patients, who wants to be frequently injected with insulin and to take pills. This system avoids the diabetes patients waiting time and it administers the pill and syringes at the appropriate time effectively. Key components of their dispenser includes the DS3231 Real-Time Clock (RTC), Arduino UNO microcontroller, servo motor, LCD display, LED indicators, buzzer, and the BLYNK software for Bluetooth communication. This setup ensures the dispensation of the medicines at the prescribed time particularly for the elders. And for the syringe dispenser, they include the components such as DS3231 Real-Time Clock (RTC), Arduino UNO microcontroller, servo motor, LCD display, LED indicators, buzzer, and the BLYNK software for Bluetooth communication (R. Paviya, 2022).

Shayla Sharmin, et.al (2021) highlighted the importance of having the prescribed medication schedules, if it is missed or delayed then it may lead to slower disease progression, particularly among thee elders. To address this issue, they made an automated and online based medicine remainder and dispenser application. This system includes the components such as an LCD display, buzzer, and multicoloured LED light integrated into the unit. The application haves the user input to take their medicines at their designated times with an android application. The application has the acceptance or modification of the prescription as the input interface and the output interface as displaying the history of the medications. When it is time for medication, the LED lights and the buzzer gets activated and alerts the user (Shayla Sharmin, 2021)

The patient needs no expert guidance and it can be used by single or group of patients. Their dispenser is made affordable and also reduces the money spent on personal nurse. A complex medication schedules can lead to accidental errors like missing doses, incorrect dosage or wrong timing. They developed a dispenser that dispenses correct medicine at prescribed time to the patient. This avoids incorrect medicinal dosage. Their dispenser uses LCD, microcontroller, (RTC) module, an alarm system, a biometric fingerprint scanner and the Blynk software tool used to inform the patients to take proper dosage according to the prescribed time. They also reduced the problem of frequent preloading of pills (Nishita Anand, 2021)

The challenge faced by older or visually impaired individuals in adhering to medication schedules by developing a portable medicine dispenser utilizing IoT technology. Their system enables users to set medication alarms via an Arduino application connected to the dispenser through Bluetooth. It is equipped with compartments for pills and a stepper motor for dispensing, the dispenser responds to voice commands, alerting users with an LCD and speaker before dispensing the medicines. Their system also offers live video streaming for continuous patient monitoring. Hence this approach reduces the caregiver burden and ensures the patient is taking medicines at the correct time (Sri Lakshmi Ullankala, 2023)

A solution to the challenges faced by infectious diseases by introducing a medical dispenser machine with two components: a Web-based system and real-time face recognition technology. This system allows medical professionals to adjust medication quantities, and once medications are arranged, patients receive email notifications with date and time for receiving their packages. An automated system, used a machine-learning algorithm, and face recognition technology (specifically, Histogram Orientated Gradients embedded in Raspberry Pi 4B), facilitates the secure and contactless retrieval of medical supplies. The system achieved recognition accuracy of 80.0% for authorized individuals based on 50 image inputs. The integration of hardware and PHP based web application ensured efficient delivery of medicines (Lukman Chaiyarab, 2021)

A Smart Medicine Planner which helps elderly and visually impaired people in taking medicines. It has two subsystems: the Dispenser System, which automatically fills pills into the Smart Medicine Box, and the Alerting System, which reminds users to take medicine at the correct time. The primary mode of communication to the planner is through speech. Once medication is placed in the container, the medicine planner oversees medication information storage, dispensing, and user reminders. Overall, their project majorly focuses on medication management through voice mode of communication and integrating dispensing and alarm functionalities in a single device (Amena Jassim Al-Haider, 2020)

An advanced care package for elderly people who most of the time need a caretaker for taking medicines. The package includes an automatic medicine dispenser which has proper dispensing and alert mechanisms. It also includes a heart rate and sleep monitors. It also has a fall detection sensor and these sensors and monitors inform the patient's family members in case of any medical emergencies. One of the most important feature of this dispenser is it can be accessed remotely by the patient's closely related ones to adjust the dispensing timings and order medicines in case of low stock (Kevin P, 2022)

This literature review summarizes that the various research studies have been proposed new innovative solutions for the medication dispensing system that address the challenges faced in healthcare. These solutions range from automatic drug dispenser incorporates the Machine learning algorithms and IoT technology to use microcontrollers and it provides Medication alerts and remainders. These efforts aim to improve medication safety, medication adherence, healthcare through innovative technological solution. Here many reviews were have the household dispensing system where this chapter made a dispensing system which is useful for the society.

## MAIN FOCUS OF THE CHAPTER

### Problem Statement and Objectives

The never ending queues in the medical shops are a major challenge for people, especially for physically challenged people, aged persons, pregnant women and other harmed people. And also there is a chance for the spreading of diseases in the crowd by the patients. These problems could be solved by having the QR code based automatic drug dispenser so that it takes less amount of time to get the medicine and avoids the patient's crowd for medicine and reduces the physical interactions between the patients so that the spreading diseases can be avoided. And there is a lack of pharmacies in some areas particularly in rural areas so that the area persons get affected by the lack of medicine and this can be solved by making automatic drug dispenser in such areas which is easily accessible by them and doesn't need any persons to supervise the dispensing system. And there is a chance for providing wrong medicine other than prescribed medicine. These medication error can be solved using the QR code based Automatic Drug Dispenser so that the medicine dispensed accurately and quickly with the automated system. This system also reduces the labours so that the labour costs are reduced.

### Objectives

1. To provide faster dispensation of medicines to the patients
2. To avoid overdosage and human errors while dispensing medicines
3. To provide privacy for the patients about their medicines
4. To make a cost-effective drug dispenser model
5. To make medicines accessible in remote areas like highways, deserts, and tribal areas

*Figure 4. Main concept of automatic drug dispenser*

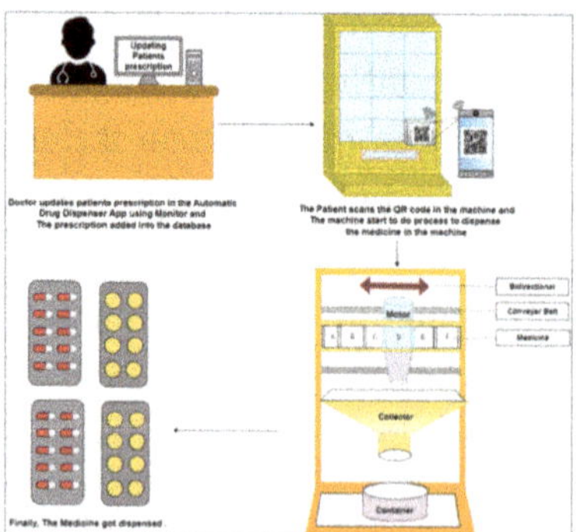

Here Figure 4. Explains the core concept idea of the automatic drug dispenser that it is mainly used to stop the never ending queues in medical shops and to stop the physical and mental strain of the patients, especially aged persons, disabled persons, and pregnant ladies. The patients can secure them from other persons spreading diseases and this machine will be solution for the medication error done by humans.

And also the patient can easily scan their QR code with their mobile phone where the prescription details will be updated by their doctor in the patient's profile.

The Automatic Drug Dispenser scans the QR code in the machine and dispenses the required medicine of the patient that is the prescribed medicine by the doctor. This system not only ensures efficiency but also accuracy, as the system identifies the drug quickly and dispenses the correct medicine. By this system, patients are no longer required to wait in a queue for a long time in the pharmacies or to deal with human errors, while the pharmacist can make mistakes while taking the medicines for a larger number of patients and it can be handled by the automated system. The major feature of the automated drug dispenser is to make the secure connection among the patients to ensure the security of their information's.

This system has the individual information of the patients to verify the patient's identity and updates the patient's information in the centralized protected database. This secured database management ensures the overall healthcare administration by having the regular updates in the patient's medication history. And it stores the information in the database more personalized. Security plays the major role in designing this system to handle the patient's data more confidentially and securely. So we secure the database against unauthorized access using various advanced technologies, so the data remains protected. Hence the patients feel convenient to use the system since their health information is safe and private. This is benefits the patients who requires the medications quickly as well as the patients who requires regular medication. Moreover, this system helps the healthcare professional to reduce their workload with the prescription management and allows them to focus on the patient care. It also ensures the doctor of the patient to know about the healthcare records of the patient by knowing his history of medications. Hence, the automated drug dispenser helps the society to have the technological advancements to reshape the healthcare future digitally. This system makes the medication dispensation process more efficient, accurate, secure and patient-centered.

## Stakeholders and Requirement analysis

1. Name: Ms. Meenakshi

   Profession: Pharmacist
   Age: 35

   Review: Meenakshi, the pharmacist, really appreciates the automatic drug dispenser because it makes the pharmacy workflow easier and cuts down on human errors in dosage administration. She thinks the system is user-friendly, which helps the pharmacy staff manage and monitor medication dispensing efficiently. However, she suggests that future updates should allow for more customizable dosage schedules to better meet specific patient needs. She also thinks adding a feature for real-time inventory tracking would greatly improve stock management.
2. Name: Mr. Ganesan P L

   Profession: Retired Engineer
   Age: 75

Review: Ganesan P L, a 75-year-old user of the automatic drug dispenser, finds the automatic drug dispenser very convenient for his medication routine. The automated reminders help him avoid missed doses, which he finds particularly beneficial. He thinks future updates should focus on making the display easier to read for older users, like using larger fonts and a more prominent display. Ganesan also recommends adding an emergency alert system to notify caregivers or family members if a dose is missed or if other issues arise, which would make the system much safer.

3. Name: Mr. Pravin P

   Profession: Student
   Age: 20

Review: Pravin P, a student, finds the automatic drug dispenser very helpful for managing his busy schedule, making sure he never misses a dose. He suggests future updates could include an educational component that provides information about each dispensed medication, such as dosage instructions, potential side effects, and general information. Pravin also recommends adding a notification system in the mobile app for prescription refills to make remote medication management more convenient and user-friendly.

4. Name: Mr. Vasanthan K

   Profession: Student
   Age: 21

Review: Mr. Vasanthan K, a 21-year-old student, points out the efficient use of NodeMCU and servo motors in the drug dispenser, which uses very little electric current. This design makes the dispenser energy efficient. He suggests making the dispenser more compact so it can be easily installed in various settings, including emergency situations and warfare zones, which would make it more useful overall.

5. Name: Mrs. Sugumari R

   Profession: Housewife
   Age: 75

Review: Sugumari feels the process of the QR based automatic drug dispenser is easy for the people but it can be also useful for old-age homes and hospitalized elders that it can remind the users at the time and dispense the tablets so that they will not miss their medication.

6. Name: Mr. Barath S

   Profession: Student
   Age: 20

Review: Barath feels that the process would include prepaid payment methods like monthly payment for the medication and allow to buys medications without on that place like prepay for the medicine and the medicine must be stored for them when they come in-person they can collect it.

7. Name: Mr. Balaji

Profession: Care Taker
Age: 25

Review: Mr. Balaji working in the old-age homes as a caretaker this is incredibly beneficial to the elders to take their tablets by getting the medicines nearby dispensers and it helps us in reducing 60% of the medical errors like giving some others tablet to other person.

8. Name: Ms. Priya

Profession: Trainee Nurse
Age: 21

Review: Ms. Priya working in the Hospital as trainee-nurse says that this is helpful to organize the tablets according to the patient's id and can store the patient's history using this system helps the doctor to check the previous medications.

9. Name: Ms. Rajeshwari

Profession: House wife
Age: 49

Review: Ms. Rajeshwari feels safe about this drug dispenser because she can get the doctor prescribed medicine at the required ratio and it can reduce the medication errors in the real time.

## Requirement Analysis

Creating an innovative medication dispenser necessitates a meticulous examination of a myriad of elements to guarantee its effectiveness, productivity, and overall success. The critical components for such a system can be comprehensively categorized into functional, performance, physical, economical, technical, and environmental dimensions. Functional requirements orbit around the core objective of accurate medicine dispensation. The dispenser must possess the capability to not only precisely measure but also administer the prescribed dosage for each patient. Moreover, the user interface should be user-friendly, ensuring that individuals with varying levels of technological proficiency can navigate the system, input their information, and obtain the required medication without encountering any complications. Performance requirements underscore the crucial aspect of speed in both the dispensing of medicine and user interaction. The dispenser should operate with optimal efficiency, ensuring that patients promptly receive their prescribed medications. Simultaneously, the application interface should facilitate a rapid and seamless interaction between the user and the dispenser, thereby enhancing the user experience and contributing significantly to the overall efficiency of the system.

To guarantee the effectiveness, productivity and overall success in creation of an innovative medical dispenser necessities the above meticulous examination. Functional, physical, economical, technical and environmental dimensions are the ways in which the requirements can be categorized.

Addressing physical requirements involves the strategic optimization of the dispenser's size. The overarching goal is to minimize its physical footprint while expertly accommodating the necessary technological components and providing ample space for medication storage. Additionally, the dispenser must demonstrate robustness to handle stress, incorporating considerations for durability, reliability, and the ability to withstand external pressures without compromising its fundamental functionality. Economical requirements intricately revolve around cost-effectiveness throughout the dispenser's entire lifecycle. This encompasses meticulous considerations of both initial manufacturing costs and ongoing maintenance expenses. Developing an economically viable system ensures not only widespread adoption but also sustainability, without imposing an undue financial burden on healthcare providers or end-users.

Technical requirements delve deeply into the dispenser's multifaceted functionalities, encompassing its capacity to store emergency and basic medicines. Furthermore, the system should have the capability to dispense specific medications without necessitating a prescription from a doctor. This particular feature promotes accessibility, particularly in urgent situations where immediate access to essential medications is paramount. Environmental requirements highlight the paramount significance of sustainability. The dispenser should be meticulously designed with environmental friendliness in mind, incorporating cutting-edge, energy-efficient technologies to minimize its carbon footprint. Given the global emphasis on eco-conscious practices, integrating green technologies aligns seamlessly with broader endeavours to mitigate the environmental impact of healthcare systems.

Upon analysing user perspectives, it becomes apparent that the development of a medication dispenser requires a holistic approach. This entails addressing various aspects such as functionality, performance, physical design, cost-effectiveness, technical capabilities, and environmental impact. By meticulously considering each dimension, the resulting dispenser can serve as a dependable and accessible solution for individuals to efficiently and accurately receive their medications, thereby enhancing overall patient care. Furthermore, it is essential to prioritize the security and privacy of patient data alongside ensuring precise dispensing. This can be achieved through the implementation of robust encryption measures and strict access controls, which help maintain confidentiality and compliance with healthcare data protection standards. Designing the dispenser with adaptability in mind ensures it can accommodate future advancements in medical technology. This future-proofing involves creating a platform that can seamlessly integrate with emerging healthcare systems and technologies, providing longevity and reducing the need for frequent system upgrades. Integrating remote monitoring capabilities allows healthcare providers to track medication adherence and patient health remotely. Connectivity features enable the dispenser to communicate with healthcare professionals, offering real-time updates on patient usage patterns and facilitating timely interventions when necessary.

The core objective of the automatic drug dispenser is satisfied under functional requirements. This involves measuring dugs in precise manner, followed by administering the prescribed dosage for each patient. In addition to that, a user-friendly user interface, ensures that individuals with technological proficiency can effortlessly navigate the system, and input their information, finally obtaining the required medication without facing any discrepancies.

To enhance user experience, incorporating educational features within the dispenser's interface can provide users with information about their medications, potential side effects, and proper usage. Additionally, a support system, whether through in-app guides or helplines, can assist users in navigating the system and addressing any concerns they may have. Acknowledging diverse cultural preferences and accessibility needs is crucial. The dispenser's interface should be customizable to accommodate different languages and cultural norms, ensuring inclusivity and making the system accessible to a wide range of users, regardless of their cultural background or abilities. Adhering to healthcare regulations and standards is non-negotiable. Ensuring that the dispenser complies with regulatory frameworks, such as FDA approvals and other relevant certifications, in stills confidence in both healthcare providers and end-users regarding the system's safety and effectiveness.

The main goal is to minimize the physical footprint while expertly accommodating the necessary technological components and providing enough space for medication storage. To address and mitigate issues in physical requirements, the optimization of the dispenser's capacity matters. Additionally, the dispenser must demonstrate robustness to handle stress, incorporating considerations for durability, reliability, and the ability to withstand external pressures without compromising its fundamental functionality. Economical requirements intricately revolve around cost-effectiveness throughout the dispenser's entire lifecycle. This encompasses meticulous considerations of both initial manufacturing costs and ongoing maintenance expenses. Developing an economically viable system ensures not only widespread adoption but also sustainability, without imposing an undue financial burden on healthcare providers or end-users.

The smooth integration with electronic health records significantly boosts the efficiency of healthcare provision. This integration facilitates a cohesive patient profile, empowering healthcare providers with a comprehensive understanding of a patient's medical background, prescriptions and adherence to medication. By incorporating feedback mechanisms within the dispenser system, a culture of continuous improvement is fostered. Enabling both patients and healthcare professionals to offer feedback on aspects like user interface, dispensing procedures, and overall user experience informs iterative enhancements, ensuring that the dispenser evolves in line with user requirements. Incorporating these additional considerations into the development process contributes to the creation of a comprehensive and holistic medication dispenser, addressing not only the core functionalities but also ensuring security, adaptability, education, and inclusivity in healthcare delivery. Implementing a tracking system that records medication usage patterns provides valuable insights for healthcare providers.

This feature allows professionals to identify trends, potential issues, and areas for improvement in treatment plans, leading to more personalized and effective healthcare interventions. Acknowledging that some patients may require multiple doses of medication at different times, incorporating a system that can manage and dispense various medications at specified intervals adds flexibility. This feature caters to the diverse needs of patients with complex medication regimens. The significance of sustainability is highlighted under environmental requirements. Keeping in mind that incorporating latest, energy-efficient technologies, the dispenser should be strategically designed with environmental friendliness in mind, to minimize its carbon footprint. Given the global emphasis on eco-conscious practices, integrating green technologies aligns easily with broader endeavour to avoid the environmental impact of healthcare systems.

## PROPOSED METHODOLOGY

The Automated Drug Dispenser system provides an ideal solution by integrating advanced hardware and software components, provides the users with sophisticated and user-friendly experience. The hardware features a QR code displayed on the machine's surface, this eliminates the need for the physical scanner. Users can easily engage with the system by using their smartphones to scan the QR code. The server clearly processes prescription data, identifies the available medicines in that particular dispenser and send the count of the tablets and the Meta data about the customer to avoid error in dispensing and the dispenser computes the number of rotations needed to dispense the particular tablet. In the dispenser the energy is efficiently managed with the strategically placed servo motors which will be responsible for the precise tablet dispensing.

*Figure 5. Mobile app for patient privilege*

In Figure 5, a mobile app designed specifically for patients. It allows users to easily log in using their profiles and scan a QR code displayed on the machine. Once logged in, patients can access their order history and prescription details. This makes it simple for patients to manage their medications conveniently through their smartphones.It illustrates the software which is specifically designed for the doctor privilege.

The application was developed using the Python, this software allows the doctor to add patient details and prescription information. When the "add prescription" button is clicked, the prescription is added to the patient's database both as JSON file and in a format recognized by the Optical Character Recognition (OCR) technology. This technology is used to extract the prescription information when the QR code is scanned, it contributes to the integration of the prescription data into the Networks System. It also presents that the doctor give the prescription after checking up the patient and uploading the suitable prescription and stores it as an JSON file and the file goes through the software and it reaches the server also the data will be updated in the database and it can be retrieved whenever the patient requires the patient can upload the prescription by scanning the QR code and selecting the prescription.

On the software side, the users interacts with the user-friendly mobile that has a QR code scanner with the phone's inbuilt camera and a feature for uploading prescription. After scanning the dispenser's QR code, the users can upload their digital prescriptions via the mobile application. The Firebase platform is used for the database and also the firebase_ml_vision library for the OCR, it is used to extract and process the prescription information also store the critical data such as tablet count, medication ID, prescription ID and data about the dosage and these all data are stored securely in the firebase . Also we have a secure login page with a dual user authority (medical staff or consumer) this ensures the access control, this security is enhanced by setting an particular login fail count to avoid bruteforce attacks. Medical staff can efficiently monitor the dispenser's status and the patients purchased through that particular dispenser. On the other hand the consumer can manage their digital prescriptions and recent medication histories and review their tablet stocks.

The automatic drug dispenser's software is designed using the Flutter and the software integrates QR code scanner with inbuilt phone's camera and OCR for the prescription image scanning. Firebase serves as a powerful database for storing the prescription data, user information medication history and transaction details. A unique QR code is generated for the each dispenser and that QR has the ID of that

Machine's database. While the user scans the prescription he uploads the prescription to the machines database. The hardware is controlled by the NodeMCU, it will act as an interface between the components of the dispenser. NodeMCU read the Database of the machine for any new request if there is any it will forward the request to the Server which will control the Payment and other process and after the payment the server will payback an response to the dispenser's NodeMCU to calculate the Number of rotations and where to place the servo motors for the precise tablet dispensing and the LCD display will provide real time information of the Transaction Status and Process details.

*Figure 6. Output screenshot of prescription update after dispensing medicine*

An innovative feature in the mobile application is users can purchase the tablets with a single tap. The user can purchase the prescribed medicine in a single tap and the amount will be deducted for the corresponding account automatically. This will enhance the user experience and it will be easy for the user. The integration of the workflow enhances the convenience of the user by incorporating the client server Technology. For Instance Consider that the prescribed tablet is out of the stock, the system will dynamically employs the Dijkstra Algorithm to find the nearest dispenser with that particular prescribed tablet. By identifying the Location of the nearest dispenser it will show the location in the maps and also it will give a real time notification when the tablet will be available in that dispenser. This Way of allocation to the tablets will prioritize the user satisfaction and improve the sales.

To strengthen the data security, advanced cryptographic measures are implemented. The prescribed data is hashed for the integrity constrain and the system dynamically adapts its encryption methods based on the specific condition. For severe security, asymmetric encryption in employed with unique public and private key pairs. For efficient processing, symmetric encryption is used. An multi-layered approach which will guarantees secured transactions and storage with the firebase database, this ensures the privacy and confidentiality for the users.

Here in Figure 7. It explains that the operations of the automatic drug dispenser which rotates the motor for the selected medicine that is A, B or anything. The motor goes toward the medicine and opens the respective medicine box and releases the medicines.

*Figure 7. Operation of the motor to release the medicine*

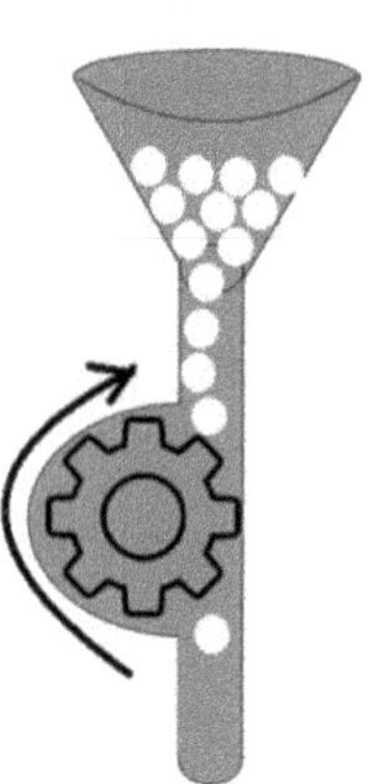

The operation of the motor in dispensing the medicine, this illustrates the precision and efficiency of the dispensing process. The motor moves to the medicine container and helps the gear box to rotate for the number of times to dispense the tablets for an particular count .This chapter uses an soft gear tooth so that the medicine's won't get damaged.

Figure 8 represents the processes happens while dispensing the tablet form the start to end. In first the doctor check-up the patient and uploads the digital prescription in the patient profile and next the patient scans the QR code in the machine and then upload the digital prescription to the dispenser and process the payment for tablets. Then the dispenser starts to rotate the motors to dispense the tablets finally the medicines got dispensed.

In this chapter of automated drug dispenser system, the first paragraph says about the advanced features, from the sophisticated hardware and software components for user interactions and efficient energy usage and precise tablet dispensing. Transitioning to the second paragraph, it shifts the chapter focus to incorporation of the Client-Server Technology. This includes the implementation of the dynamic allocation system using the Dijkstra algorithm. This strategically improves the user convenience, ensuring easy accessibility of the prescribed medicine. The third paragraph explains about the implementation of the advanced cryptographic measures and explains how the system adapts its encryption methods based on specific constrains for optimal security.

## Application of Engineering Knowledge

In using the energy efficiently for the automated drug dispenser system, this chapter have incorporated an innovative algorithm to calculate the precise amount of time required to dispense the specified amount (n) of tablets. This algorithm helps to minimize the number of motor rotations, therefore the energy consumption and enhancing the operational efficiency totally.

The formula for calculating the dispensing time (T_dispense) is derived from a combination of tablet characteristics, motor specification, and system dynamics. It is expressed as:

$$Tdispense = n * (Dtablet + Dgap) / (Rmotor * nsystem) \quad (1)$$

Where,
Tdispense = Time taken to dispense the tablets.
n = Number of tablets to be dispensed.
Dtablet = Diameter of a single tablet.
Dgap = Gap between consecutive tablets to ensure precise dispensing.
Rmotor = Rotational speed of the dispensing motor.
ηsystem = Overall efficiency of the dispensing system.

The equation (1) checks on both physical properties of the tablet and the mechanics of the dispensing mechanism. By determining the necessary dispensing time, the system reduces unwanted motor rotations, thus optimizing the energy consumptions and energy-efficient operations of the drug dispenser.

## Existing Methodology

The many existing methodology are mostly created for the home usage whereas the Automatic Drug Dispenser is for replacing the medical shops .The existing products comprise of the of creating unique QR code for each prescription which would cost more time and more storage and hard to read it without processing and that processing would also take more cost, to change that the Automatic Drug Dispenser utilizes the unique QR code for each Dispenser machines so that the Digital prescription can be stored as an JSON file which will cost less than the QR converted prescription and the processing speed is way better than the existing ones and Automatic Drug Dispenser will Also provide an real time statistics about the sales and the requirement of the particular drug in that specified area this will help the supplier to fulfil the customers need this is the additional feature in Automatic Drug Dispenser which is not available in others and the Automatic Drug Dispenser utilizes an energy optimized way to dispense the tablet this is used by the Formulae.

Moreover, the scalability of the Automatic Drug Dispenser makes it as suitable for various healthcare areas like large hospital to small clinics. This adaptability ensures that they can serve for rural areas and metropolitan areas.

In summary, the widespread implementation of the QR based Automatic Drug Dispenser can be used to revolutionize the healthcare domain and enhancing the medical management and improving the patient safety.

## Cost Estimation of Proposed Dispenser Design

The estimation of the product is based on the size of the Dispenser.
Assume an 4x4 Dispenser:
Motors: 1500 rupees
Motor belts: 800 rupees
Display: 1000 rupees
Outer Panels: 500 rupees
Tablet Container: 1000 rupees
RFID: 800 rupees
(for loading drugs by staff/maintenance work)
Total: 5600 rupees

While looking on the Durability the product will be capable to handle different temperatures and work 24/7 and the maintenance must be monthly twice to prevent error/ machine out of order and the machine can be work on any place if also we can include batteries so that it can be portable.

## Conceptual and Functional Design

*Figure 8. Flowchart for Mobile App*

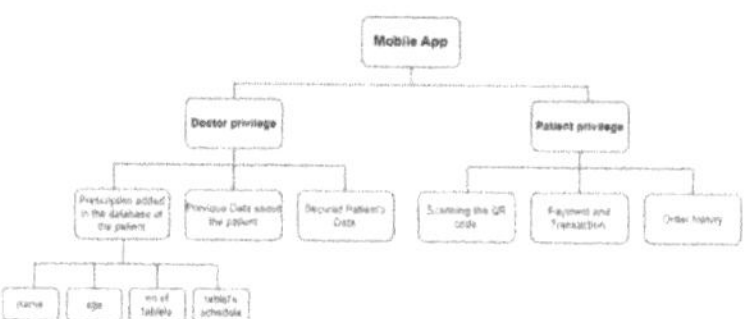


Figure 8 Represents the Flowchart of the software side in which it has two sides one for Doctor and the other for Patient. In the Doctor side, the doctor updates the patients prescriptions current health condition such as BP, Heart disease or etc. and the patient can get the Drugs By scanning the QR code in the machine and upload the digital prescription prescribed by the Doctor. Also the patient can buy medicine without prescription these will be allowed only for the drugs that all use in the day to day life, this is not applicable for severe/high dosage tablet.

*Table 1. Pros and cons of existing drug dispensers*

| Project Name | References | Advantages | Disadvantages |
|---|---|---|---|
| Usability Evaluation of Low-Cost Smart Pill Dispenser by Health Care Practitioners | Gift Arnold Mugisha, Christine Muhumuza, Faith-Michael Uzoka, Chinyere Nwafor-Okoli, Joletta Nabunje, Melody Arindagye & Justine N. Bukenya, Part of the Advances in Intelligent Systems and Computing book series (AISC,volume 1290) | Many health workers found it easier to use and highly acceptable. | Making dispenser size smaller while adding more channels for dispensing. |
| The Assistance for Drug Dispensing Using LED Notification and IR Sensor-based Monitoring Methods | Chin-Chuan Han; Hao-Pu Lin; Chao-Hsu Chang; Chang-Hsing Lee; Jau-Ling Shih; Chun-Sheng Hsu; Jen-Chih Chang published in: 2018 9th International Conference on Awareness Science and Technology (iCAST) | It helps pharmacists to choose medicine from correct position using LED notification, it also alerts him/her when wrong medicine is choosed | It requires labour for medicine dispensing |
| QR code-based medicine dispensation | | Cost effective, low power | No requirement of labour, size of the dispenser is reduced |

## CONCLUSION AND FUTURE WORK

The Automated Drug Dispenser (ADD) signifies a pivotal advancement in healthcare, poised to transform medication dispensing and enhance patient outcomes. By integrating sophisticated pharmaceutical technologies with digital advancements, the ADD focuses on a patient-centric model of medication management, ensuring accessibility, efficiency, and security throughout the healthcare continuum. In today's digital era, the Automated Drug Dispenser (ADD) represents a major leap forward, offering a secure, convenient, and user-friendly solution for medication management. By seamlessly integrating Internet of Things (IoT), database management, mobile application development, and cloud computing technologies, the ADD transcends traditional healthcare delivery models, heralding a new era of patient care.

The ADD emphasizes functionality, performance, physical robustness, economic viability, technical sophistication, and environmental sustainability. By paying close attention to these aspects, the ADD aims to meet the evolving needs of healthcare stakeholders while maintaining the highest standards of quality and safety. The user experience is central to the ADD's design philosophy, focusing on intuitive interfaces, educational resources, and support systems that cater to diverse cultural and accessibility needs. Security measures, such as robust encryption, access controls, and regulatory compliance, protect patient data and ensure confidence in the system's ability to safeguard sensitive healthcare information.

Adaptability and integration are key aspects of the ADD's design, ensuring compatibility with emerging healthcare technologies and future-proofing the system against obsolescence. Feedback mechanisms and medication usage tracking enable continuous improvement, driving iterative enhancements and optimizing patient care delivery. In conclusion, the development of the Automated Drug Dispenser marks a significant milestone in healthcare innovation, promising to reshape medication services and improve patient outcomes globally. By adhering to the principles of accessibility, efficiency, and security, the ADD demonstrates the transformative potential of technology in enhancing healthcare delivery and enriching lives. As the healthcare sector evolves, the ADD is positioned to pioneer advancements, symbolizing optimism and progress for the future. Through collaboration, innovation, and a steadfast commitment to excellence, the vision of a more accessible, efficient, and patient-centric healthcare system becomes a reality with the Automated Drug Dispenser at its forefront. Looking ahead, the promise of improved health and well-being for all is within reach, thanks to the transformative power of technology and the dedication of healthcare professionals and innovators worldwide.

Future developments and deployments of the Automated Drug Dispenser (ADD) are set to pave the way for numerous enhancements and innovations in healthcare delivery. Research and development in this field will explore sophisticated data analytics, utilizing machine learning and artificial intelligence to analyze medication usage trends and predict patient needs. Seamless integration with electronic health records (EHRs) and other healthcare platforms promises enhanced connectivity and compatibility, simplifying care coordination and enabling comprehensive patient care. Additionally, the incorporation of remote monitoring capabilities within the ADD will allow for proactive healthcare interventions, while potential integration with telemedicine functionalities opens possibilities for virtual consultations and real-time support. Future iterations may also investigate innovative medication delivery mechanisms, personalized dosage forms, and novel administration routes to optimize therapeutic outcomes. Emphasis on patient engagement and education can further enhance the ADD's effectiveness, with interactive educational modules and medication adherence reminders empowering patients and promoting self-management. Efforts to ensure global accessibility and equity in healthcare delivery remain crucial, addressing language barriers, cultural sensitivities, and socioeconomic disparities. Continuous improvement and iterative development will drive the evolution of the ADD, with user feedback informing enhancements to optimize system performance and user experience. Ultimately, the evolution of the Automated Drug Dispenser represents a dedication to innovation, collaboration, and patient focus, transforming the landscape of medication administration and healthcare provision for future generations.

## REFERENCES

Al-Haider, J., Al-Sharshani, S. M., Al-Sheraim, H. S., Subramanian, N., Al-Maadeed, S., & Chaari, M. z. (2020). Smart Medicine Planner for Visually Impaired People. *IEEE International Conference on Informatics, IoT, and Enabling Technologies (ICIoT)*. IEEE. 10.1109/ICIoT48696.2020.9089536

Anand, N., Prathibha, P., Purohit, P., Nalamitha, R., & Rajarao Padma, C. (2021). Biometric Enabled Patient-Centric Automated Medication Dispenser Using IoT. In Smys, S., Palanisamy, R., Rocha, Á., & Beligiannis, G. N. (Eds.), *Computer Networks and Inventive Communication Technologies. Lecture Notes on Data Engineering and Communications Technologies* (Vol. 58). Springer. 10.1007/978-981-15-9647-6_43

Chaiyarab, L., Mopung, C., & Charoenpong, T. (2021). Authentication System by using HOG Face Recognition Technique and Web-Based for Medical Dispenser Machine. *IEEE 4th International Conference on Knowledge Innovation and Invention (ICKII)*. IEEE. 10.1109/ICKII51822.2021.9574661

Hiremath, B. N., Chavhan, K., Johnson, N. J., & Monika, P. (2022). Automatic Medication Dispensing System using Machine Learning, Internet of Things and Cloud Computing.*International Conference on Disruptive Technologies for Multi-Disciplinary Research and Applications(CENTCON)*, Bengaluru, India. 10.1109/CENTCON56610.2022.10051452

Meghla, R. T., Deowan, M. E., Nuhel, A. K., Sazid, M. M., Ekbal, M. N., & Mahamud, M. H. (2022). *An Internet of Things (IoT)- based Smart Automatic Medication Dispenser with an Integrated Web Application for Patient Diagnosis*. 5th International Conference of Computer and Informatics Engineering (IC2IE), 2022 Jakarta, Indonesia. 10.1109/IC2IE56416.2022.9970073

(Nishita Anand, 2021)

Paviya, R., Prabakar, S., Porkumaran, K., & Saman, A. B. S. (2022). Automated Pill and Syringe Dispenser. In: Ibrahim, R., K. Porkumaran, Kannan, R., Mohd Nor, N., S. Prabakar (eds) *International Conference on Artificial Intelligence for Smart Community. Lecture Notes in Electrical Engineering.*. Springer, Singapore. 10.1007/978-981-16-2183-3_86

Sharmin, S., Ratan, M. I. K. U., & Piash, A. H. (2021) An Automated and Online-Based Medicine Reminder and Dispenser. *Proceedings of the International Conference on Big Data, IoT, and Machine Learning. Lecture Notes on Data Engineering and Communications Technologies*. Springer, Singapore. 10.1007/978-981-16-6636-0_39

Ullankala, S. L., Buddaraju, H. R., Meegada, A., & Tallapalli, S. K. (2023). Live Streaming Smart Pill Dispenser to Help Elderly/Blind People.*7th International Conference on Intelligent Computing and Control Systems (ICICCS)*, Madurai, India. 10.1109/ICICCS56967.2023.10142676

# Chapter 8
# Enhancing Healthcare Through Remote Patient Monitoring Using Internet of Things

**K. Ramalakshmi**
*PSR Engineering College, India*

**L. Krishna Kumari**
*Ramco Institute of Technology, India*

**R. Rajalakshmi**
*Ramco Institute of Technology, India*

**G. Theivanathan**
*Velammal Engineering College, India*

## ABSTRACT

*The integration of the internet of things (IoT) in healthcare has revolutionized patient care, leading to the emergence of remote healthcare monitoring solutions. Leveraging connected devices and sensors, this system enables real-time tracking of vital health parameters, medication adherence, and overall wellness metrics outside traditional healthcare settings. The IoT infrastructure facilitates seamless communication between patients and healthcare providers, promoting timely interventions and personalized care plans. Security and privacy concerns are addressed through advanced encryption and authentication measures, ensuring the confidentiality of sensitive health data. Key considerations for the implementation of IoT-based remote healthcare monitoring, including device interoperability, data standardization, and user engagement, are discussed. The potential benefits of this technology include enhanced patient engagement, early detection of health issues, and reduced healthcare costs.*

DOI: 10.4018/979-8-3693-2901-6.ch008

## Introduction

In recent years, the integration of the Internet of Things (IoT) into healthcare has ushered in a transformative era, particularly in the realm of remote patient monitoring. This paradigm shift promises to enhance healthcare delivery by harnessing the capabilities of interconnected devices and sensors. This study, delves into the multifaceted landscape of IoT-driven solutions, offering a comprehensive exploration of their applications, challenges, and potential impacts on patient outcomes. Remote patient monitoring using IoT technologies facilitates real-time tracking of vital health parameters, enabling healthcare providers to extend their reach beyond traditional settings. This approach holds the promise of personalized and timely interventions, ultimately improving patient care. Fig1 shows the remote healthcare monitoring system architecture.

*Figure 1. Remote healthcare monitoring system architecture*

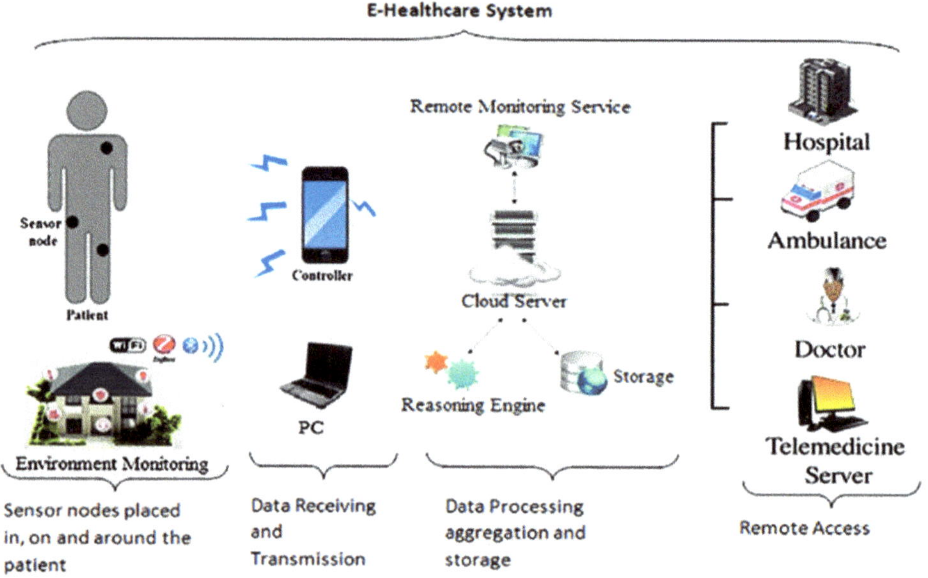


The integration of the Internet of Things (IoT) in healthcare has revolutionized patient care, leading to the emergence of remote healthcare monitoring solutions. This study explores the paradigm of Remote Healthcare Monitoring using IoT, aiming to provide a comprehensive understanding of its applications, challenges, and potential impacts on patient outcomes. IoT-based systems leverage connected devices and sensors to enable real-time tracking of vital health parameters, medication adherence, and overall wellness metrics outside traditional healthcare settings. The IoT infrastructure facilitates seamless communication between patients and healthcare providers, promoting timely interventions and personalized care plans. Addressing security and privacy concerns, advanced encryption and authentication measures ensure the confidentiality of sensitive health data. This study reviews existing remote monitoring implementations, highlighting successful case studies and identifying areas for improvement. Key considerations for implementing IoT-based remote healthcare monitoring include device interoperability, data standardization, and user engagement. The potential benefits of this technology encompass enhanced patient engagement, early detection of health issues, and reduced healthcare costs. This review contributes to the ongoing discourse on leveraging IoT to transform healthcare delivery and emphasizes the importance of scalable, secure, and patient-centric remote healthcare monitoring systems.

As we embark on this exploration, we aim to unravel successful implementations, address security and privacy concerns, and highlight key considerations for the effective deployment of IoT in remote healthcare monitoring. By illuminating the transformative potential of IoT in healthcare, our study aims to contribute to the ongoing evolution of patient-centric, technology-driven healthcare solutions. Fig 2 illustrates the data collection and processing in remote healthcare system.

*Figure 2. Data collection and processing in remote healthcare system*

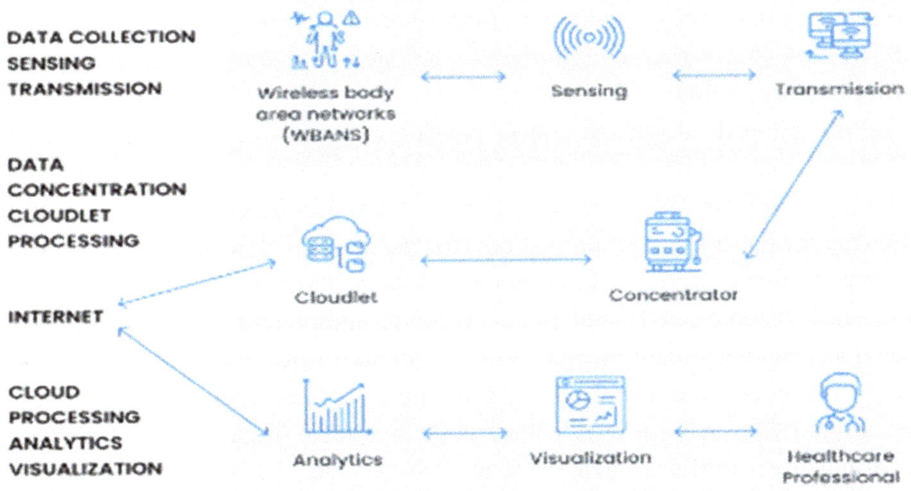

## Motivation

The motivation for this study can be summarized as follows:

Revolutionizing Patient Care: To explore how IoT integration is transforming patient care through real-time health monitoring outside traditional settings.

Comprehensive Understanding: To provide a thorough understanding of the applications, challenges, and impacts of IoT-based remote healthcare monitoring on patient outcomes.

Enhanced Communication: To facilitate seamless communication between patients and healthcare providers, promoting timely interventions and personalized care plans.

Security and Privacy: To address security and privacy concerns with advanced encryption and authentication measures, ensuring the confidentiality of health data.

Implementation Insights: To review successful case studies and identify key considerations for implementation, such as device interoperability, data standardization, and user engagement, highlighting the benefits of early issue detection and reduced healthcare costs.

## Related Works

Remote Patient Monitoring Systems (RPMS) strategically target specific patient groups, including those grappling with chronic diseases, infectious conditions in isolation, mobility confronts, or supplementary disabilities (Talbot, 2022). This technology also proves beneficial for post-surgery patients, newborns, plus aged individuals, aligning with the healthcare objective of ensuring patient comfort and promoting unrestricted movement with exercise within a private surroundings (Malche, 2022). Traditionally, patient observing systems relied on wired sensors tethered to computers within hospital premises, limiting patient mobility and scalability. These systems were often bulky, expensive, and had a restricted capacity for simultaneous patient monitoring.

The inception of RPMS marked a pivotal shift, particularly with the expansion of home-based healthcare services. Although the initial systems were not as user-friendly, technological advancements over time have led to the development of wireless and more accessible patient monitoring solutions. The healthcare sector is undergoing significant improvements as researchers and companies increasingly leverage RPMS to enhance care, contributing to the rapid growth of this industry (Fouad, 2020), (Va, 2020) & (Mohammed, 2014)

In an RPMS, biomedical sensors collect physiological data to assess patient well-being outside traditional clinical settings (Panhwar, 2021). The primary aim is to bring healthcare into individuals' homes, aligning with their daily lives. This collected data is wirelessly transmitted to healthcare providers, allowing for informed decision-making (Farias, 2020). Telehealth facilitated by RPMS enables the measurement and transmission of essential physiological metrics such as heart rate, respiratory rate, body temperature, blood pressure, and blood oxygen saturation (Ahmed, 2016). RPMS offer real-time illness detection, enabling prompt emergency interventions in critical situations. Moreover, these systems contribute to cost reduction in healthcare by leveraging diverse communication technologies. Patients can engage in their daily activities while undergoing treatment, improving overall emergency care and mobility, particularly in traffic accident scenarios (Dhinakaran, 2022). A recent study (Li, 2012) detailed the development of an affordable, compact reflectance pulse oximeter for remote patient monitoring. This device, accomplished of offering precise photoplethysmography (PPG) information without the necessitate for filters, employs wireless communication for data transfer. The PPG signal, sampled at 240 Hz, is transmitted to a host computer via either a Zigbee transceiver module. To mitigate ambient noise and slow-motion distortions, computer processing is applied. This Remote Patient Monitoring System (RPMS) excels in measuring heart rate, breathing rate, blood oxygen saturation, and blood pressure, offering a more comprehensive set of physiological variables for enhanced reliability.

In another study (Guz, 2013), researchers introduced a wireless RPMS designed for body temperature monitoring. With a remarkable precision of 0.1 °C within a temperature range of 16–42 °C, this system utilizes two digital temperature sensors to monitor both ear canals. The collected data is transmitted wirelessly through Bluetooth for subsequent analysis. While ear canal measurements may pose risks of injury, especially with prolonged use, the study highlights the potential advantages of wearable RPMS. Wearable devices offer improved comfort and reduced interference, addressing concerns related to sensor probes causing minor fluctuations in measurements during motion. Consequently, wearable RPMS emerges as a preferable solution for continuous and unobtrusive remote patient monitoring.

An aspect of IoT in healthcare, the Internet of Medical Things (IoMT) focuses on internet-connected medical devices and apps (Mathkor, 2024), and has been receiving a lot of attention due to its potential use in smart healthcare systems. Through the provision of individualized, cost-effective medical solutions and the facilitation of remote biomedical systems, IoMT improves accuracy, consistency, reliability, and productivity in healthcare. In order to facilitate effective hospital treatments, it employs sensors to retrieve data from patient records for biomedical analysis and diagnoses. This article discusses the present and upcoming trends in IoMT, such as industry 5.0, deep learning, machine learning, blockchains, artificial intelligence, and radio frequency identification. This thorough review emphasizes how IoMT is transforming healthcare and biomedical systems.

In this investigation, (Abdulmalek, 2024) illustrates a hybrid wireless network using the FiPy microcontroller is used to create an Internet of Wearable Things-based Hybrid Healthcare Monitoring System (IoWT-HHMS) for real-time, remote monitoring of critical health data. With successful data transmission up to 1.5 km, thorough testing demonstrates the system's excellent accuracy and dependability and highlights its potential for effective patient health monitoring.

AI and IoT are revolutionizing healthcare by improving data accuracy and team communication, enabling real-time health data for patient self-monitoring and remote monitoring (Medhekar, 2024). Cloud solutions manage vast IoT data, facilitating efficient remote health monitoring and quicker response times.

The recent advancements in IoMT, wearable devices, and communication systems are enhancing smart healthcare services through pervasive computing (Yadav, 2024). The IoMT-AAL architecture, using edge computing and Deep Neural Networks (DNN), aims to improve timely data collection and processing for better decision-making in healthcare. Empirical analyses show that the IoMT-AAL model effectively predicts healthcare outcomes with high specificity, precision, and improved tracking and security.

The Internet of Things (IoT) is vital for applications in healthcare, industrial automation, agriculture, transportation, and disaster response (Ramalakshmi, 2023). Energy-sensitive protocols are crucial for energy-limited wireless sensor nodes in medical applications to ensure accurate monitoring and disease prevention. This section highlights various energy-aware protocols, emphasizing the need for scalable, cost-effective IoT solutions in healthcare to enhance disease prevention and early detection.

The advancements in ICTs, such as IoT, 5G, and Cyber-Physical Systems, and their transformative impact on healthcare through Ambient Assisted Living (AAL), Mobile Health (mHealth), and Electronic Health (eHealth) (Ahmed, 2022). It discusses IoT-based Remote Patient Monitoring (RPM) systems using wearable devices and sensor networks to provide early warnings for health emergencies, addressing delays and inefficiencies in conventional healthcare. The proposed RPM system ensures secure and privacy-preserving integration with healthcare units, featuring RFID-based authentication and secure communications. Empirical evaluations demonstrate the system's potential to improve the quality of life and healthcare services.

## Technology-Driven Healthcare Solutions

The ongoing evolution of patient-centric, technology-driven healthcare solutions signifies a dynamic shift towards a more personalized and efficient healthcare ecosystem. Integrating advanced technologies, particularly the Internet of Things (IoT), has empowered healthcare providers to deliver tailored and timely interventions. This evolution emphasizes a departure from traditional models towards a patient-centered approach, where connected devices and sensors facilitate remote patient monitoring, enabling real-time data collection and analysis.

In this transformative landscape, healthcare becomes more proactive, with the ability to detect and address issues before they escalate. Patient engagement is heightened through accessible and user-friendly interfaces, fostering a collaborative relationship between healthcare providers and individuals. The continuous stream of health data, coupled with predictive analytics, enhances preventive care strategies, contributing to improved overall health outcomes. Moreover, technology-driven healthcare solutions are driving innovations such as telemedicine, virtual consultations, and wearable devices, creating a more accessible and flexible healthcare experience. The evolving role of artificial intelligence and machine learning further refines diagnostic capabilities and treatment recommendations, providing a more personalized approach to care. As the healthcare landscape continues to evolve, the amalgamation of patient-centricity and cutting-edge technology holds the potential to revolutionize how healthcare is accessed, delivered, and experienced. This ongoing evolution signifies a commitment to optimizing health outcomes through innovation, accessibility, and patient empowerment.

## Types of Remote Healthcare Monitoring Systems

Remote healthcare monitoring systems encompass a variety of technologies and approaches designed to monitor patients' health outside traditional healthcare settings. The following fig.3 lists some types of remote healthcare monitoring systems.

*Figure 3. Types of remote healthcare monitoring systems*

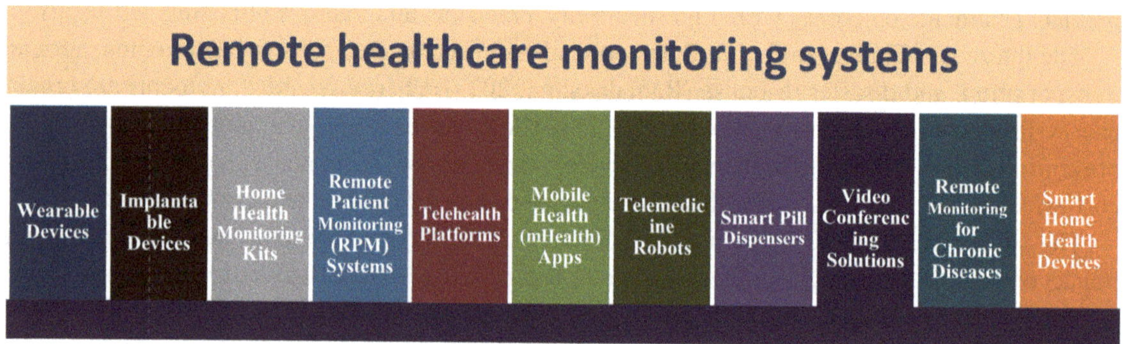


Here are some types of remote healthcare monitoring systems:

**Wearable Devices:** Devices like smart watches and fitness trackers equipped with sensors for monitoring vital signs such as heart rate, activity levels, and sleep patterns.

**Implantable Devices:** Medical implants that can monitor specific health parameters, such as pacemakers for cardiac monitoring or glucose monitors for diabetes management.

**Home Health Monitoring Kits:** Kits that include devices for measuring blood pressure, glucose levels, and other vital signs, allowing patients to perform routine monitoring at home.

**Telehealth Platforms:** Virtual healthcare platforms that enable remote consultations between patients and healthcare providers through video calls, voice calls, or messaging.

**Remote Patient Monitoring (RPM) Systems:** Comprehensive systems that collect and transmit patient data, often focusing on specific chronic conditions. These can include devices for monitoring blood pressure, glucose levels, or respiratory function.

**Mobile Health (mHealth) Apps:** Smartphone applications that allow users to monitor and track various health parameters, record symptoms, and receive health-related information.

**Smart Pill Dispensers:** Devices that dispense medication at scheduled times and send alerts to patients or caregivers, promoting medication adherence.

**Telemedicine Robots:** Remote-controlled robots equipped with cameras and sensors, allowing healthcare professionals to remotely assess and communicate with patients.

**Video Conferencing Solutions:** Platforms that enable real-time video communication between patients and healthcare providers, facilitating remote consultations and follow-ups.

**Remote Monitoring for Chronic Diseases:** Tailored systems for specific chronic conditions like diabetes, heart disease, or respiratory disorders, providing continuous monitoring and timely intervention.

**Remote Mental Health Monitoring:** Platforms and apps designed to monitor mental health through mood tracking, virtual counseling, and other interventions.

**Smart Home Health Devices:** Integration of IoT devices within a patient's home, such as smart scales, smart thermometers, and environmental sensors, providing a holistic view of health.

These monitoring systems contribute to the shift towards proactive and patient-centric healthcare, allowing for timely interventions, reducing hospital readmissions, and improving overall health outcomes. The choice of a specific system often depends on the patient's health condition, the level of monitoring required, and the healthcare provider's preferences.

## Application of Remote Patient Monitoring Systems

Remote patient monitoring (RPM) systems find applications across various healthcare domains, enhancing patient care, and improving healthcare outcomes. Here are some key applications of remote patient monitoring systems:

### Chronic Disease Management

RPM is widely used for managing chronic conditions such as diabetes, hypertension, and cardiovascular diseases. Continuous monitoring of vital signs and health parameters enables healthcare providers to intervene promptly, preventing complications.

### Postoperative Care

After surgeries or medical procedures, RPM allows healthcare professionals to remotely monitor patients' recovery progress. This can reduce the need for frequent hospital visits and enable early detection of complications.

### Elderly Care

RPM plays a crucial role in monitoring the health of elderly patients, especially those living independently. It provides a means to track vital signs, detect falls, and ensure timely medical interventions.

### Maternal Health Monitoring

Pregnant women can benefit from RPM for monitoring fetal health, tracking maternal vital signs, and managing high-risk pregnancies. This allows for early detection of potential complications.

### Medication Adherence

RPM systems can be used to monitor medication adherence. They provide reminders to patients, track medication consumption, and alert healthcare providers if there are deviations from the prescribed regimen.

### Cardiac Monitoring

Patients with cardiac conditions can benefit from continuous remote monitoring of ECG, heart rate, and other relevant parameters. This helps in the early detection of arrhythmias or other cardiac abnormalities.

### Respiratory Monitoring

RPM systems are employed for monitoring respiratory conditions such as asthma, chronic obstructive pulmonary disease (COPD), and sleep apnea. They assist in tracking lung function and detecting early signs of respiratory distress.

### Mental Health Monitoring

RPM is increasingly applied in mental health care for monitoring mood, sleep patterns, and other behavioral indicators. This allows for early intervention and personalized mental health management.

### Rehabilitation Monitoring

Patients undergoing rehabilitation after injuries or surgeries can be remotely monitored to ensure compliance with exercises, track recovery progress, and prevent complications.

### Remote Consultations

RPM facilitates virtual consultations between patients and healthcare providers, enabling real-time communication, sharing of health data, and adjustments to treatment plans without the need for physical visits.

### Remote Diagnostic Services

RPM systems enable the collection of diagnostic data, such as blood glucose levels, blood pressure, and temperature, allowing healthcare providers to make informed decisions remotely.The widespread application of remote patient monitoring systems demonstrates their versatility in improving patient care, increasing accessibility, and optimizing healthcare resources.

## Wireless Technologies in Remote Patient Monitoring

Wireless communication plays a pivotal role in remote patient monitoring (RPM), enabling seamless and real-time transmission of health data from patients to healthcare providers. Various wireless technologies are utilized in RPM systems to ensure connectivity, reliability, and data integrity. Fig. 4 depicts some common wireless communication technologies.

*Figure 4. Wireless communication technologies in remote healthcare*

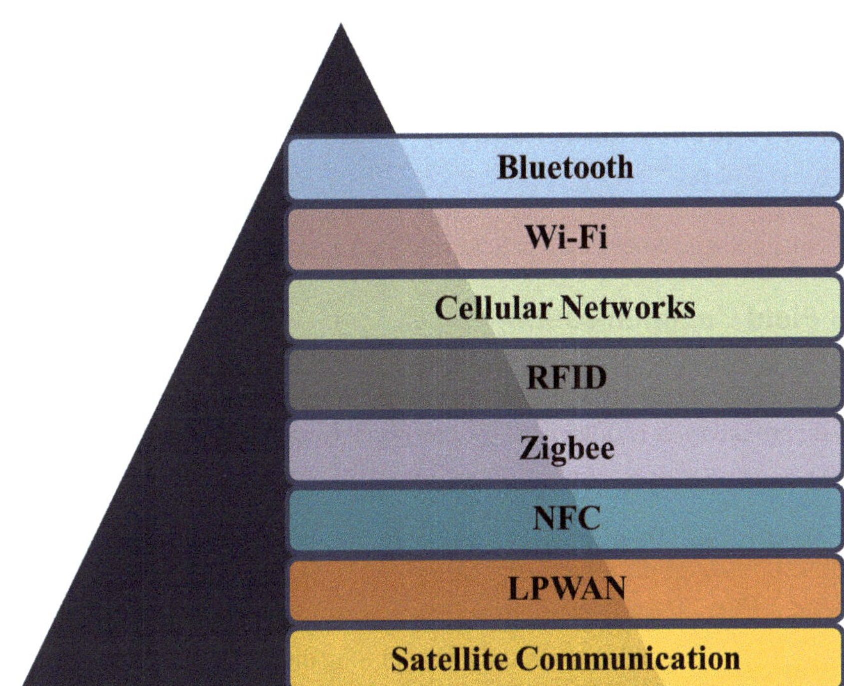


### Bluetooth

Bluetooth technology is often used for short-range communication between medical devices and mobile devices or dedicated gateways. It facilitates the transfer of health data, such as vital signs or glucose levels, in real-time.

### Wi-Fi (Wireless Fidelity)

Wi-Fi connectivity allows for high-speed and reliable data transmission over a more extended range. RPM devices equipped with Wi-Fi capabilities can connect to home networks or dedicated healthcare networks, enabling continuous monitoring.

### Cellular Networks

Utilizing cellular networks (3G, 4G, and now 5G) enables RPM devices to transmit health data over long distances. This is particularly useful for patients who are mobile or in remote locations where Wi-Fi connectivity might be limited.

### Zigbee

Zigbee is a low-power, short-range wireless communication technology often used in home-based healthcare monitoring systems. It is suitable for connecting various devices in a personal area network, allowing for continuous monitoring within a confined space.

### RFID (Radio-Frequency Identification)

RFID technology is employed for patient identification and tracking. It is used in conjunction with other wireless technologies to enhance patient safety and streamline the monitoring process.

### NFC (Near Field Communication)

NFC is a short-range wireless communication technology that enables secure data exchange between devices in close proximity. It is often used for pairing devices, such as connecting a wearable sensor to a smartphone.

### LPWAN (Low-Power Wide-Area Network)

LPWAN technologies, such as LoRa (Long Range) and NB-IoT (Narrowband IoT), are suitable for applications where devices need to communicate over long distances with minimal power consumption. They are used in remote and resource-constrained environments.

### Satellite Communication

In areas with limited terrestrial network coverage, satellite communication provides a viable solution for transmitting health data from remote locations. This is particularly relevant for RPM applications in rural or isolated areas.

The choice of wireless communication technology depends on factors such as the required range, power consumption, data transmission speed, and the specific needs of the remote patient monitoring system. Integrating these wireless technologies ensures that RPM systems can reliably collect and transmit health data, facilitating timely and effective healthcare interventions.

## Example of Research Ideas in This Field

### IoT-based Remote Patient Monitoring

*Figure 5. System architecture for IoT-based remote patient monitoring*

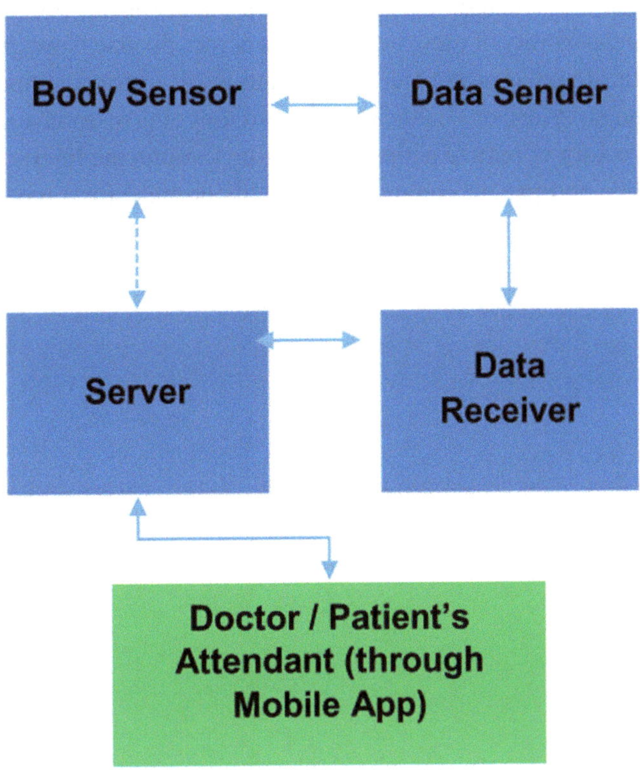


*(Ahmed, 2022)*

The system architecture for IoT-based Remote Patient Monitoring (RPM) involves a body sensor, data sender, data receiver, and server is shown in figure 14. The body sensor, integrated with a smart watch, measures vital signs such as fall, heart rate, and blood pressure. The data sender receives this data and transmits it to the data receiver, which then forwards it to the server for analysis. Health alerts are displayed on a mobile application accessible to the doctor and patient's attendant. Both data senders and receivers must register with the server using a secure channel, employing elliptic curve group technology for lightweight and robust security. After successful mutual authentication, the data sender encrypts and sends health data to the data receiver, ensuring secure communication throughout the process.

## CONCLUSION AND FUTURE WORK

Looking ahead, future research endeavors should focus on refining the interoperability of diverse health IoT devices, promoting standardized data formats, and enhancing user engagement for sustained adoption. Exploring the potential of artificial intelligence in analyzing vast datasets generated by remote monitoring systems could further refine predictive analytics and diagnostic capabilities. Additionally, studies should delve into the scalability and cost-effectiveness of IoT-driven healthcare solutions for widespread implementation. Evaluation of the long-term impact on patient outcomes, as well as assessing the acceptability and usability of these technologies across diverse demographics, will be crucial for informing future healthcare policies and practices. In summary, as we continue to traverse the landscape of patient-centric, technology-driven healthcare solutions, ongoing research endeavors will play a pivotal role in shaping the trajectory of remote patient monitoring through the Internet of Things. The fusion of innovation, accessibility, and patient empowerment holds promise for a more resilient and responsive healthcare future.

## REFERENCES

Abdulmalek, S., Nasir, A., & Jabbar, W. A. (2024, April). LoRaWAN-based hybrid internet of wearable things system implementation for smart healthcare. *Internet of Things : Engineering Cyber Physical Human Systems*, 25, 101124. 10.1016/j.iot.2024.101124

Ahmed, M. I. (2022, October). Govindaraj Kannan, Secure and lightweight privacy preserving Internet of things integration for remote patient monitoring. *Journal of King Saud University. Computer and Information Sciences*, 34(9), 6895–6908. 10.1016/j.jksuci.2021.07.016

Ahmed, M. U., & Bjorkman, M. (2016). *A. ˇCauševi ´c, H. Fotouhi, M. Linden, An overview on the internet of things for health monitoring systems, ICST Inst.* Comput. Sci. Soc. Informatics Telecommun. Eng.

De Farias, F., Dagostini, C., Bicca, Y., Falavigna, V., Falavigna, A. Remote patient monitoring: a systematic review, Telemed. *e-Health 26*(5) (2020).

Dhinakaran, M., Phasinam, K., Alanya-Beltran, J., Srivastava, K., Babu, D. V., & Singh, S. K. (2022). A system of remote patients' monitoring and alerting using the machine learning technique. *Journal of Food Quality*, 2022, 2022. 10.1155/2022/6274092

Fouad, H., Hassanein, A. S., Soliman, A. M., & Al-Feel, H. (2020). Analyzing patient health information based on IoT sensor with AI for improving patient assistance in the future direction. *Measurement*, 159, 107757. 10.1016/j.measurement.2020.107757

Li, K., & Warren, S. (2012). A wireless reflectance pulse oximeter with digital baseline control for unfiltered photoplethysmograms. *IEEE Transactions on Biomedical Circuits and Systems*, 6(3), 269–278. 10.1109/TBCAS.2011.216771723853148

Malche, T., Tharewal, S., Tiwari, P. K., Jabarulla, M. Y., Alnuaim, A. A., Hatamleh, W. A., & Ullah, M. A. (2022). Artificial intelligence of things- (AIoT-) based patient activity tracking system for remote patient monitoring. *Journal of Healthcare Engineering*, 2022, 2022. 10.1155/2022/873221335273786

Mathkor, D. M., Mathkor, N., Bassfar, Z., Bantun, F., Slama, P., Ahmad, F., & Haque, S. (2024, April). Multirole of the internet of medical things (IoMT) in biomedical systems for managing smart healthcare systems: An overview of current and future innovative trends. *Journal of Infection and Public Health*, 17(4), 559–572. 10.1016/j.jiph.2024.01.01338367570

Medhekar, A. A., Duggal, M., Singh, S. K., & Nayadkar, P. (2024, June). Healthcare and internet of things: The future of artificial intelligence and IoT technology. *Oral Oncology Reports*, 10, 100279. 10.1016/j.oor.2024.100279

Mohammed, J., Lung, C. H., Ocneanu, A., Thakral, A., Jones, C., & Adler, A. (2014). Internet of things: remote patient monitoring using web services and cloud computing. Proceedings of the *IEEE International Conference on Internet of Things (iThings)*. IEEE. 10.1109/iThings.2014.45

Panhwar, M. A., Zhong Liang, D., Memon, K. A., Khuhro, S. A., Abbasi, M. A. K., Noor-ul-Ain, , & Ali, Z. (2021). Energy-efficient routing optimization algorithm in WBANs for patient monitoring. *Journal of Ambient Intelligence and Humanized Computing*, 12(7), 8069–8081. 10.1007/s12652-020-02541-7

Ramalakshmi, K., Krishna Kumari, L., & Rajalakshm, R. (2023). Energy-Aware Protocols and Standards in IoT-Enabled Healthcare, AI and IoT-Based Technologies for Precision Medicine. *Advances in Medical Technologies and Clinical Practice*, 13, 205–217. 10.4018/979-8-3693-0876-9.ch012

Yadav, R., Pradeepa, P., Srinivasan, S., Rajora, C. S., & Rajalakshmi, R. (2024, June). A novel healthcare framework for ambient assisted living using the internet of medical things (IOMT) and deep neural network. *Measurement. Sensors*, 33, 101111. 10.1016/j.measen.2024.101111

# Chapter 9
# AIoT-Powered Intelligent Remote Patient Activity Tracking and Comprehensive Vital Sign Analysis System for Enhanced Healthcare

**D. Manimegalai**
https://orcid.org/0000-0003-1299-8640
*Rajalakshmi Engineering College, India*

**R. Gunasekari**
https://orcid.org/0000-0003-3028-2347
*Sri Sairam College of Engineering, India*

**S. Sujatha**
https://orcid.org/0000-0002-7632-5878
*Sri Sairam College of Engineering, India*

**M. Karthikeyan**
https://orcid.org/0000-0001-7699-0045
*Chennai Institute of Technology, India*

**A. Umasankar**
https://orcid.org/0009-0003-3778-817X
*Yanbu Industrial College, Saudi Arabia*

## ABSTRACT

*This chapter explores the integration of artificial intelligence of things (AIoT) with tele-health monitoring, presenting an intelligent remote patient activity tracking system. Using interconnected sensors and machine learning models, the system monitors various patient activities and vital signs, providing real-time insights. The proposed AIoT-enabled health monitoring device tracks activities such as running, sleeping, walking, and exercising, while observing vital signs like heart rate and breathing patterns. The*

DOI: 10.4018/979-8-3693-2901-6.ch009

*chapter delves into the system's architecture, functionalities, and technical intricacies, emphasizing its potential to transform healthcare delivery. It highlights the role of AIoT-driven solutions in enhancing patient care and fostering personalized treatment approaches, offering a glimpse into the promising future of intelligent healthcare delivery.*

## INTRODUCTION

Tele-health Monitoring (THM) has emerged as a vital research area, particularly heightened by the global pandemic's urgent demands. The current crisis has underscored significant issues such as hospital overload and the heightened risk to healthcare workers' safety. Consequently, there's a pressing need for THM systems to remotely monitor COVID-negative individuals, thereby freeing up healthcare facilities for COVID-positive patients in case of emergencies. Even COVID-positive patients not in critical condition can benefit from remote monitoring through THM. This system facilitates real-time remote monitoring, enabling swift identification of specific illnesses. Leveraging THM technology allows patients to be monitored from non-hospital settings, offering early detection of health issues, immediate acquisition of health data, and averting critical health crises, hospital admissions, and potential fatalities.

Through THM, emergency medical care services become accessible to patients in critical situations. THM implementation caters to various patient groups, including those with chronic illnesses, disabilities, mobility limitations, and the elderly. The central aim of THM is to provide high-quality healthcare to patients within their residences, offering psychological benefits by keeping them away from hospital settings. The Remote Health Monitoring System (RHMS) grants patients the liberty and comfort environment, enabling them to conduct daily activities in familiar surroundings while undergoing health monitoring. Additionally, doctors can remotely track and monitor patients' health through an automated system capable of issuing alerts should any deviations in health parameters occur.

The aim of this project is to create a health monitoring gadget that combines software, network architecture, and machine learning (ML) capabilities. The primary objective is to assist doctors in monitoring patients' activities and vital signs during these activities. The current focus lies on tracking various activity factors of patients, such as exercising, walking, or sleeping and monitoring corresponding vitals like, body temperature, oxygen levels and heart rate.

The novelty of this work lies in its utilization of an edge-based smart decision system. This system rapidly detects patients' health conditions, offers recommendations, and provides real-time alerts to doctors. Presently, the proposed approach concentrates on analyzing a specific aspect of THM. However, it is designed to seamlessly accommodate additional parameters for analysis, thereby augmenting its capabilities. Consequently, the suggested approach emphasizes the monitoring of patients' activities and their corresponding vital signs by applying a novel framework to develop next-generation healthcare devices with decision-making capabilities.

The key contributions of this chapter include:

- Developing an IoT empowered tele-monitoring device that integrates ML models for the comprehensive tracking and monitoring of diverse patient activities, encompassing walking, running, exercising, and sleeping. Moreover, the device is designed to capture vital signs, including heart rate, body temperature, and the patient's respiratory patterns through these activities.

- Employing ML models to accurately identify and differentiate between the various activities performed by the patient.
- Analyzing the patient's breathing patterns through diverse activities, providing a comprehensive understanding of their breathing patterns throughout different physical actions.
- Development of a web application specifically tailored to track and manage the data collected by the proposed IoT-enabled health monitoring devices. This web application facilitates the organization, visualization, and interpretation of the uploaded patient data, offering a user-friendly interface for healthcare providers to monitor patient health remotely.

These contributions collectively form an integrated system that encompasses IoT technology, machine learning capabilities, and a user-friendly interface, aiming to offer comprehensive health monitoring and analysis for improved patient care and remote healthcare management.

The structure and organization of the remaining sections of the chapter: **Section 2:** Related Work: This section will delve into existing literature, research, and technologies related to health monitoring devices, IoT applications in healthcare, machine learning models for activity recognition, and respiratory health analysis. Its intention is to provide a comprehensive review of the state-of-the-art approaches and technologies in this domain. **Section 3:** Proposed Methodology: In this, the article will outline the methodology adopted for developing the IoT-enabled health monitoring device. It will detail the algorithms and techniques used for activity recognition, vital signs monitoring, and respiratory health analysis. The section will explain the rationale behind choosing specific methodologies and how they contribute to the system's objectives. **Section 4:** System Architecture: This section will present a detailed overview of the architecture of the proposed system. It will describe the components, modules, and their interactions within the IoT-enabled health monitoring system. The architecture will illustrate how data is collected, processed, and transmitted between the devices, machine learning models, and the web application. **Section 5:** Results and Discussion: This section will cover the experimental setup, datasets used for training and validation, performance metrics, and results obtained from the implemented system. It will provide insights into the accuracy of activity recognition, effectiveness in monitoring vital signs, and the system's ability to analyze respiratory health during different activities. Graphs, tables, and figures may be included to support the experimental findings. **Section 6:** Conclusion: This final section will give the key findings, contributions, and implications of the work. It will discuss the significance of the proposed system in remote health monitoring, highlight its strengths and limitations, and propose possible directions for future work and improvements in the field.

## RELATED WORK

The referenced studies collectively underscore the breadth and depth of remote health monitoring systems, showcasing a myriad of specialized approaches aimed at diverse aspects of cardiovascular health and overall patient well-being. In article (Turgambayeva, 2022) discuss the remote assessment of cardiovascular diseases, while (Szydlo, 2016) propose a tele-monitoring system dedicated to monitoring various heart-related conditions. (Gutierrez, 2021) focus on ECG and heartbeat monitoring, whereas (Leo, 2022) present a method specifically tailored for cardiovascular disease monitoring. (Shah, 2021) introduce a system for blood pressure and ECG monitoring, utilizing an algorithm with distinct assessment states. (Deng, 2023) monitor multiple vital signs using diverse sensors. (Yamauchi, 2023) design a system catering to patients with limited mobility, monitoring a range of parameters including body temperature, ECG, galvanic skin response, lung airflow, and oxygen levels. (Karar, 2022) concentrate on fall detection using an accelerometer while simultaneously monitoring key vital signs. (Devi, 2023) develop a device for collecting vital signs data and transmitting it via text messages. Lastly, (Krizea, 2022) focus on cardiac analysis for patients using wheelchairs. These studies collectively contribute to the advancement of remote health monitoring, offering specialized solutions for various health conditions and patient scenarios.

The references offer a wide range of fall detection systems that make use of different gadgets and technologies. An Android-based smartphone was used in (Rahman, 2022) patient activity monitoring system with fall detection. (Zurbuchen, 2021) approach to fall detection used a classifier along with several comparators. Contactless systems based on camera modules were developed by (Mousse, 2021) and (Fayad, 2023) for the purposes of fall detection and physical activity monitoring. Moreover, (Ribeiro, 2022) developed an IoT-based fall detection method that makes use of an Amazon Echo device, a webcam, and a speaker to enable its features. These studies underscore a rich landscape of fall detection solutions, ranging from smartphone-based applications to sophisticated sensor nodes and IoT-enabled systems, each offering unique advantages in detecting and addressing fall-related risks.

The referenced studies encompass a vast spectrum of innovative systems and technologies catering to diverse healthcare needs and conditions. Using Bayesian learning, (Akbar, 2022) created a device for Electroencephalogram signal analysis. (Alanis, 2023) suggested a device to observe diabetic patients through ANN, and (Far, 2021) introduced HopkinsPD, designed for observing Parkinson's disease patients. (Prabhakar, 2017) designed a tele-health monitoring system for epilepsy classification, while (Juengst, 2021) created a design to track mental exhaustion in patients with brain injuries. (Lakshminarayanan, 2015) created an ocular care app on smartphones, while (Adams, 2017) suggested a tele-health monitoring system for psychoanalysis. A WSN-based system for respiratory analysis and skin disease detection was introduced by (Naranjo, 2020). (Ahmad, 2022) created an application to help accident victims, while (Nikseresht, 2021) proposed a healthcare-oriented low-power personal network using CoAP. Wearable sensors and MEMS/SoC-based rehabilitation systems were covered by (Wei, 2023), while (Ardito, 2021) created a t-shirt-based posture monitoring system. While (Ayesha, 2023) developed smart ambulance for remote patient monitoring during transit, (Moreira, 2023) and (Humayun, 2022) suggested techniques for multi-parameter vital sign monitoring. (Rosa, 2019) presented a low-power WSN based remote monitoring device, while (Wang, 2015) presented the intelligent posture correction wearable. (Naji, 2017) designed a vision-based monitoring system for pediatric patients in healthcare settings, specifically for respiration rate monitoring and apnoea detection using Kinect cameras. (Hernandez, 2021) developed the Intelligent Mobile Comprehensive Monitoring (IMCM) system for chronic illness observation. These diverse systems represent significant strides in leveraging technology for enhanced healthcare monitoring across various medical domains and patient populations.

The works by (Taiwo, 2020) and (Iranpak, 2021) contribute significantly to the advancement of Telehealth Monitoring (THM) and Remote Health Monitoring Systems (RHMS), particularly in the context of COVID-19 and chronic disease management. (Yew, 2020) designed a THM device that uses the MQTT protocol to transmit data and leverages the Internet of Things to monitor ECG signals. (Rashidy, 2021) thorough survey examined the fundamentals, developments, and difficulties of THM for long-term illnesses. Together, these systems offer cutting-edge techniques for tracking and evaluating patients' health indicators. Notably, the proposed approach distinguishes itself by offering a novel approach to health parameter analysis and monitoring. Its distinctiveness lies in its extensibility, enabling easy configuration for additional health parameters. This adaptability sets it apart from existing systems described in related works, enhancing its potential for accommodating a broader range of health metrics and offering a more comprehensive monitoring solution. The summarized differences and unique features of the proposed system highlight its potential as a versatile and scalable solution for comprehensive Tele-health and Remote Health Monitoring.

## PROPOSED METHODOLOGY

The proposed Tele-health Monitoring (THM) system aims to collect and analyze various physiological data, including body temperature, electrocardiogram (ECG), blood oxygen level, blood pressure, heart rate, EEG, and breathing rate. This system integrates a sensor node capable of tracking patients' vitals during diverse activities such as walking, sleeping, or exercising. Employing a machine learning model, this node analyzes vitals specific to different activities, recognizing that these physiological parameters vary across different tasks or movements. This nuanced analysis enables doctors to offer tailored treatments or recommendations based on the specific context of a patient's activities. For instance, if elevated heart rates are observed during exercise, the doctor may suggest specific therapies or adjustments. Furthermore, this system serves as a monitoring tool for doctors to assess a patient's adherence to prescribed exercises or lifestyle changes. Simultaneously, patients benefit from receiving health information and alerts in critical situations, ensuring they stay informed and supported in managing their health effectively. This proposed solution thus facilitates a dynamic and personalized approach to healthcare, empowering both doctors and patients in the monitoring and management of health conditions.

The proposed sensor node, integrated with the MAX30100 Development Kit, harnesses multiple sensors— microphone, accelerometer, heart rate sensor, temperature sensor, and pulse oximeter —to gather comprehensive patient data. The accelerometer serves to monitor diverse physical activities such as walking, sleeping, exercising, and running. A local machine learning (ML) model on the device accurately classifies these various activities. Additionally, the microphone facilitates the analysis of the patient's respiratory health. (Taiwo, 2020) employed a machine learning model working on the sensor node; the system can classify the patient's respiratory health status. This method draws inspiration from studies like MIT's "Artificial intelligence model detects asymptomatic Covid-19 infections through cell phone recorded coughs" and the research paper "COVID-19 Artificial Intelligence Diagnosis Using Only Cough Recordings" authored by (Laguarta, 2020), demonstrating the effectiveness of analyzing cough sounds in identifying toxicities. Specifically, the proposed approach adopts the Gammatone Cepstral Coefficients (GFCC) method to identify characteristics in the speech signals of the patient. These features are then compared with present COVID-19 and other reliable data that is stored in the dataset for accurate analysis and detection of infections. This comprehensive approach, utilizing sensor data fusion and ML techniques, showcases a promising potential to assess patients' activities, respiratory health, and potentially detect infections through sound analysis.

Two machine learning models are employed in the study to determine respiratory health and physical activity. To deliver a comprehensive overview of patients' health conditions, the output of these machine learning models is aligned programmatically with the output of other sensor nodes, including the body temperature, heart rate, and pulse oximeter sensors. For instance, the data collected on a patient's heartbeat, temperature, and pulse during exercise may differ from those obtained during sleep. Additionally, the sensor node uses a microphone to record the patient's respiratory data continuously. It then uses this data for detecting abnormalities in the patient's respiratory health, such as frequent coughing, rapid breathing, or normal breathing. An alternative facet of a patient's health can be studied further thanks to all of these databases. Figure 1 and Table 1 depicts the parts of the sensor node.

*Figure 1. Sensor node used in the proposed system*

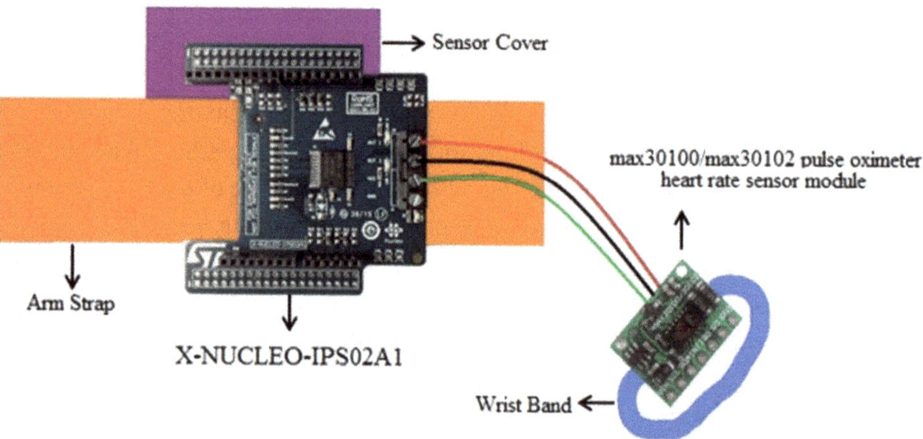


*Table 1. Components of the system*

| Hardware components | | Description |
|---|---|---|
| **Processor** | **X-Nucleo-IPS02A1** | **The X-Nucleo-IPS02A1 is an expansion board with intelligent power switches, providing overcurrent protection and thermal shutdown features for controlled power distribution. Sensor node design is done with the kit.** |
| | **Raspberry Pi 3** | **The system utilizes a 64-bit SoC quad-core Cortex-A72 running at 1.5 GHz. It is employed in designing gateway nodes for the device.** |
| **Sensors** | MAX30100 Heart Rate Sensor and Pulse Oximeter | It is employed for monitoring patients' oxygen saturation and heart rate. |
| | MAX30100 Temperature Sensor | It is utilized for measuring body temperature. |

## ARCHITECTURE OF THE PROPOSED SYSTEM

In the proposed system, the sensor node is pivotal in capturing patients' oxygen levels, heart rates, and temperatures across various physical activities. This wealth of information aids doctors in comprehensively studying diverse health parameters aligned with patients' activities. Beyond monitoring physical exertions, the sensor node is adept at continuously assessing the respiratory health of patients. This analysis occurs dynamically while patients engage in breathing or vocal activities during different physical tasks. Leveraging the sensor node connected to the microphone, data related to respiratory data is captured for detailed analysis. A primary objective of this analysis involves discerning whether the patient exhibits normal breathing patterns, rapid breathing, or presents symptoms like coughing. Furthermore, through respiratory analysis via vocal sounds, the system is capable of detecting other conditions such as pneumonia. This comprehensive approach to monitoring respiratory health during various activities demonstrates the system's potential not only in assessing immediate health but also in early detection and management of potentially concerning respiratory conditions.

The system architecture operates by gathering data from a sensor node, which is then transmitted to a gateway node using Zigbee or Bluetooth connectivity. This gateway, which is placed close to the patient, receives and displays the analysis results that the sensor node produced. The gateway node then uses the Message Queue Telemetry Transport (MQTT) protocol to send this data to the IoT cloud infrastructure. Within the cloud environment, the data is securely stored and made accessible through a web application's dashboard interface designed for doctors. This allows healthcare professionals to access and review the collected patient data conveniently. The proposed system architecture is represented in Figure 2, outlining the seamless flow of data from the sensor node to the cloud-based dashboard accessible to medical practitioners.

*Figure 2. System architecture*

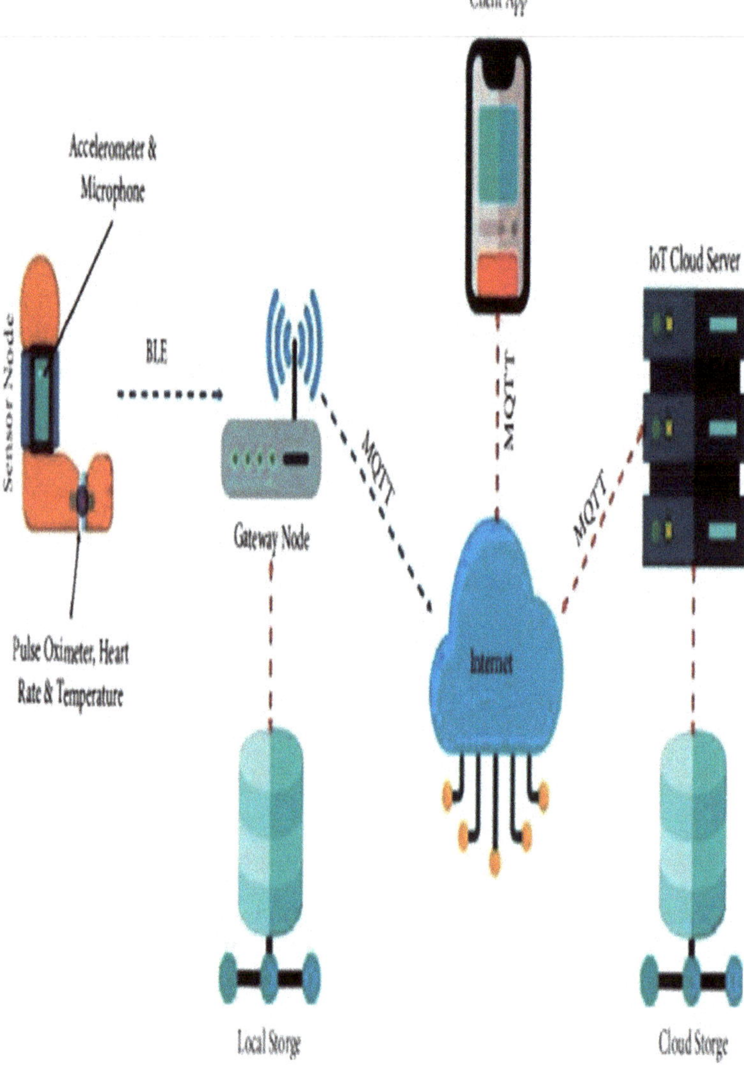


The configurations of the sensor node and gateway node prototypes are illustrated in Figure 3. The Raspberry Pi 3 (RPi3)-developed gateway node utilizes Bluetooth Low Energy (BLE) to communicate with the sensor node. The purpose of this gateway node is to give the patient access to local display formatted health information. In order to enable remote storage and access, it simultaneously transmits the gathered data via the MQTT protocol to the IoT. Additionally, the gateway node maintains a local database, retaining only the most recent data readings, which are displayed locally to the patient. Historical data can be accessed by patients through the web application, retrieving information stored in the remote server.

*Figure 3. Sensor node and IoT gateway*

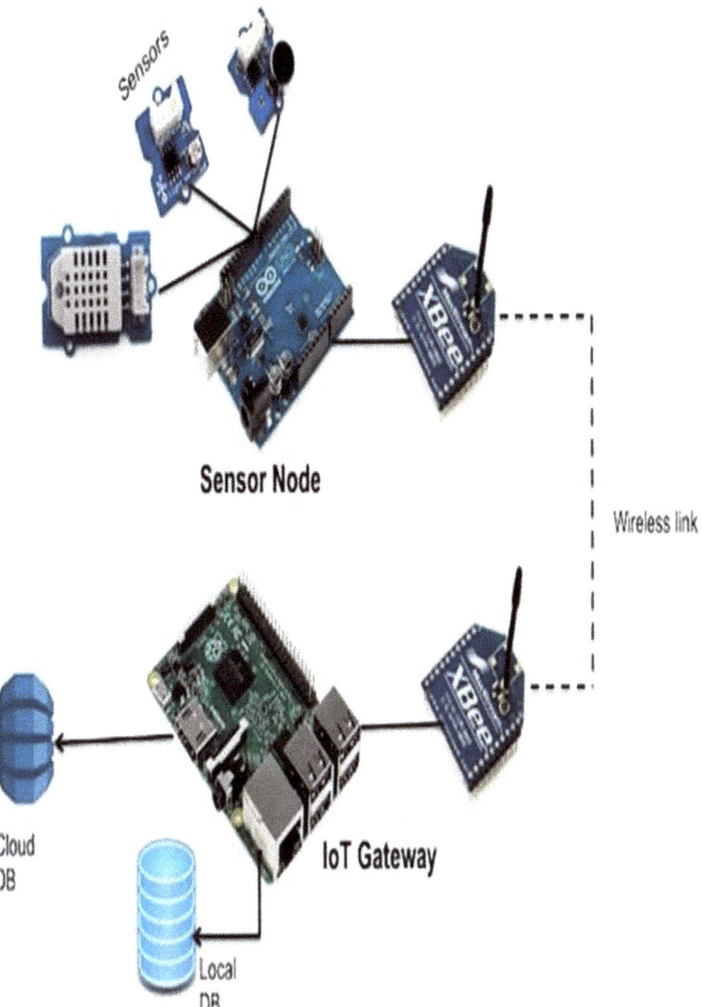


Figure 4 showcases the user interface of the application dashboard, providing an interactive platform for users, likely doctors or patients, to access and visualize health-related data. This dashboard allows users to view historical health data stored on the remote server, enabling them to track and analyze trends or patterns in the collected information over time.

*Figure 4. Dashboard application*

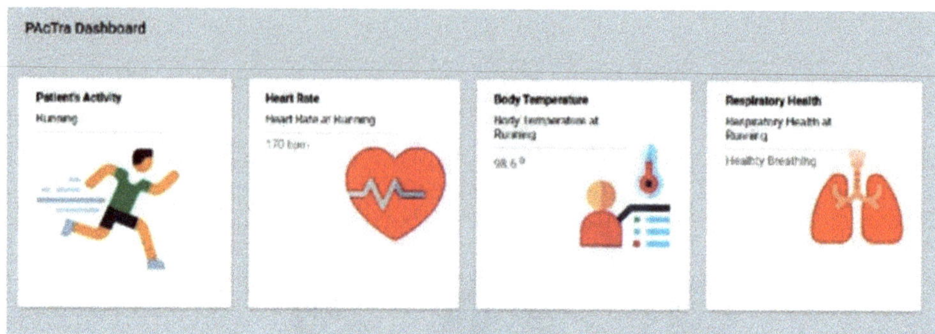


These figures and their functionalities demonstrate the system's capacity to provide both real-time health data locally and historical health data accessible through a web application, thereby facilitating comprehensive monitoring and analysis for patients and healthcare providers.

## RESULTS AND DISCUSSION

The suggested approach depends on two separate ML models for the analysis of physical activity data and voice data.

For the voice data analysis:

1. *Feature Extraction*: Using Audio Gammatone Frequency Cepstral Coefficients (GFCC), the technique extracts pertinent information from audio signals.
2. *GFCC Parameters:* Tables 2 and 3 likely showcase the parameters and cepstral coefficients utilized in the GFCC feature extraction process. These tables would outline specifics such as window size, overlap, number of filter banks, etc., which are crucial for accurate feature extraction from audio signals.
3. *Edge Impulse TinyML Tool*: The system employs the Edge Impulse TinyML Tool, a specialized platform, to construct and develop the machine learning model using the extracted audio features. This tool assists in building and training the model based on the extracted GFCC features.

*Table 2. GFCC variables*

| Variables | Value |
|---|---|
| FFT length | 256 |
| Window size | 107 |
| Frame stride | $2x10^{-2}$ |
| Frame length | $2x10^{-2}$ |
| Number of coefficients | 12 |
| Low frequency | 250 |
| Filter number | 36 |

*Table 3. Cepstral coefficients*

| Variables | Value |
|---|---|
| Coefficient | $100x10^{-2}$ |
| Shift | 1 |

It appears that the current machine learning (ML) model for respiratory health prediction operates on a binary classification system, distinguishing between two labels: "negative" and "positive." In this context, a "negative" prediction denotes healthy breathing, while a "positive" prediction suggests the presence of respiratory ailments, potentially including symptoms like a cough. The ultimate goal is to identify patients who are positive for COVID-19 and pneumonia, but constructing this specific model was impeded by the unavailability of extensive audio datasets related to these conditions.

Table 4 likely outlines various settings utilized during the training of the model. These settings could include parameters such as the learning rate, optimizer used, number of epochs, batch size, and other configurations employed during the training process. These settings are critical in training an effective ML model for classification tasks, guiding the model to learn patterns and make accurate forecasts based on the provided data.

*Table 4. Training database*

| Variables | Value |
|---|---|
| Learning rate | $5x10^{-3}$ |
| Number of training cycles | 200 |
| Minimum confidence rating | $58x10^{-2}$ |

The neural network architecture described in Figure 5 comprises three primary layers: an input layer, an output layer, and a hidden layer as follows:

1. **Input Layer:**
    - The input layer encompasses 650 features, which likely correspond to the extracted features from the audio signals using the Audio Gammatone Frequency Cepstral Coefficients (GFCC) or other feature extraction techniques.
2. **Hidden Layer:**
    - The hidden layer incorporates a sequence of sub-layers:
        - **Reshaped Layer:** This layer involves restructuring the input features into a specific shape, typically to fit the subsequent layers in the network. In this case, it consists of 13 columns, indicating a reshaping operation to format the data appropriately.
        - **1D Convolutional/Pool Layer:** This layer employs a one-dimensional convolutional approach with pooling:
        - **8 Neurons:** Eight neurons or filters are utilized for the convolution operation, each extracting specific patterns or features from the input sequence.
        - **3 Kernels:** These kernels, or filter windows, likely operate over the input data with a size of 3, extracting local patterns along the sequence.
        - **1 Layer:** This possibly indicates a single layer of convolution followed by pooling.

- **Dropout Layer:** There is use of a dropout layer with a 0.25 dropout rate. By "dropping out" a portion of the neurons at random during training, a regularisation technique called dropout helps prevent overfitting by pressuring the network to acquire more resilient and comprehensive features.

3. **Output Layer:**

    - The output layer contains two features/nodes, implying a binary classification setup, with one node representing "negative" and the other "positive" for respiratory health predictions.

This neural network architecture illustrates a sequence of layers designed for the specific task of classifying respiratory health based on audio signals' extracted features. The convolutional and pooling layers are typical in handling sequence-like data, and the dropout layer aids in preventing overfitting, contributing to a more generalized model for respiratory health prediction.

*Figure 5. Architecture of ANN for analysing voice data*

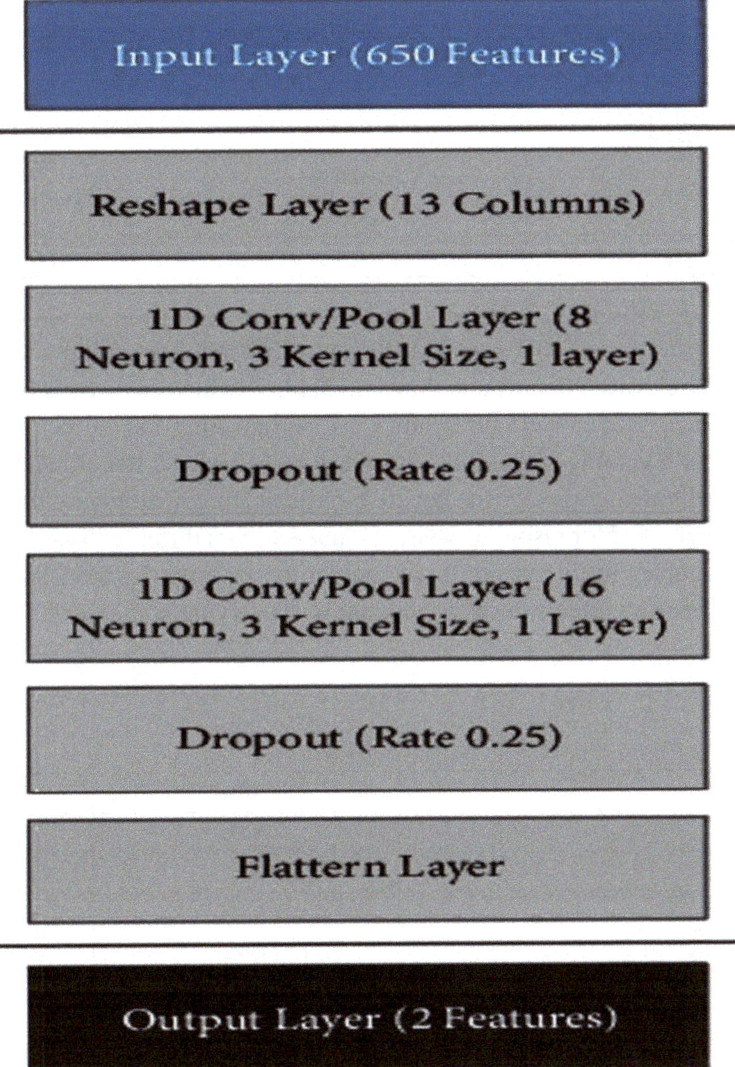


Tables 5 showcase the training evaluation metrics of the developed model for respiratory health prediction. It specifically highlights the model's performance during training, revealing a striking accuracy rate of 100%. This accuracy denotes the model's proficiency in correctly classifying instances within the training dataset, suggesting a robust alignment between the model's predictions and the actual labels during the training process. However, while achieving perfect accuracy during training signifies a strong ability to learn from the provided data, evaluating the model's generalisation to current, unaffected data is essential to ensure it doesn't suffer from overfitting. Subsequent validation or testing on separate datasets will be pivotal to evaluate the model's real-world performance and its capacity to make accurate predictions beyond the training dataset. The confusion matrix of the model is shown in Table 6.

*Table 5. Evaluation of training database*

| Accuracy | Loss |
|---|---|
| 100% | 0% |

*Table 6. Confusion matrix*

| | Positive | Negative |
|---|---|---|
| **Positive** | 100% | 0% |
| **Negative** | 0% | 100% |
| ***F*1 score** | 1 | 1 |

The model performs exceptionally well in distinguishing between cough and healthy breathing, as evidenced by the live classification results shown in Table 7, which show a 100% accuracy rate for both categories. This indicates the model's proficiency in distinguishing and correctly categorizing instances of cough and healthy breathing during live classification at various Recorded Times. The table likely delineates the model's predictions for the negative (representing healthy breathing) and positive (indicating the presence of cough or respiratory issues) labels across different time stamps or instances. The consistent 100% accuracy in discerning these categories suggests the model's reliability in real-time predictions, showcasing its effectiveness in accurately classifying respiratory health conditions during live assessments.

*Table 7. Respiratory health model with live classification*

| Recorded Time | Positive | Negative |
|---|---|---|
| 0 | 0.73 | 0.25 |
| 500 | 0.85 | 0.15 |
| 1000 | 0.96 | 0.04 |
| 1500 | 0.97 | 0.03 |
| 2000 | 0.97 | 0.03 |
| 2500 | 0.92 | 0.08 |
| 3000 | 0.99 | 0 |
| 3500 | 0.19 | 0.81 |

The second model in the suggested system analyses information about physical activity that is obtained using a three-axis accelerometer sensor. Running, sleeping, exercising, and staying still are the four different physical activities that this model is intended to categorise. It employs spectral analysis, a technique well-suited for motion analysis, to extract frequency and power characteristics from the data collected across the axes of the accelerometer. Utilizing Keras as part of the learning block for classification, the model learns patterns inherent in the data, facilitating accurate activity classification. Moreover, the K-means anomaly detection mechanism is put into practice, aiding in identifying outliers or unknown states in new data, thereby complementing the classification process. Table 8 probably lists the scaling, filter, and spectral power parameters that control the model's spectral feature. Additionally, Figures 6 (a) and (b) presumably illustrate the frequency space and power spectrum characteristics derived from the accelerometer data, offering visual insights into the signal's frequency distribution and power across the mentioned activities. These spectral features and their representations contribute to the model's ability to discern different physical activities accurately, enhancing its effectiveness in classifying various movement patterns captured by the accelerometer sensor.

*Figure 6. Accelerometer data in (a) frequency space and (b) power spectrum*

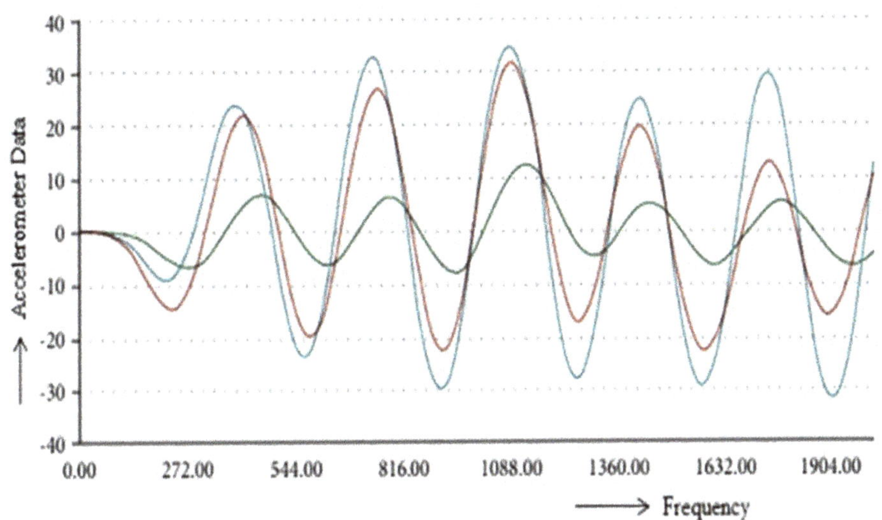


(a)

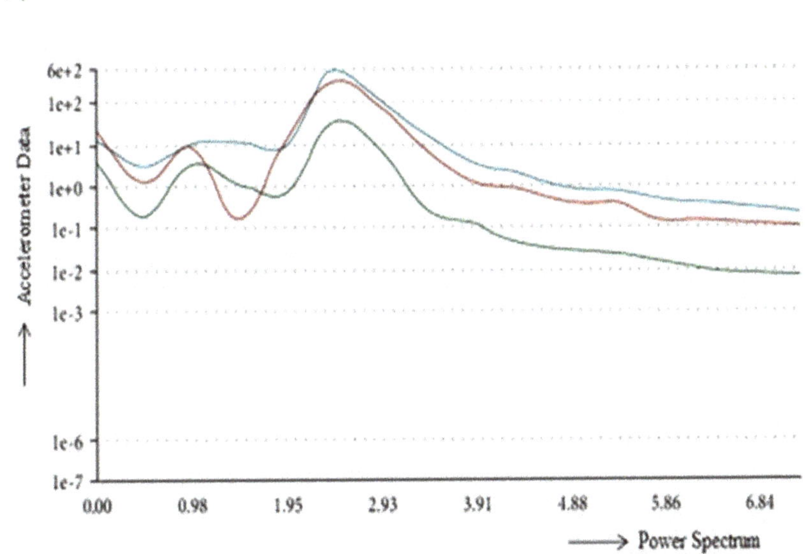


(b)

*Table 8. Power spectrum features*

| Variables | | Value |
|---|---|---|
| Scaling | Units | 1 |
| Filter | Setting | Low |
| | Order | 6 |
| | Cut off frequency | 3 |
| Power spectrum | No. of peaks | 4 |
| | FFT length | 256 |
| | Threshold value | 0.1 |
| | Power edges | 0.1, 0.6, 1.2, 2.4, 5.6 |

The neural network architecture, depicted in Figure 7, comprises an input layer, an output layer, and hidden layers tailored for the classification of physical activities. Specifically:

1. **Input Layer:**
   - The input layer accommodates 33 features, likely derived from the spectral analysis of accelerometer data across various axes and timeframes.
2. **Hidden Layers:**
   - The hidden layers are structured as follows:
     - **Two Dense Layers:** These are fully connected layers serving as the hidden layers in the neural network.
     - **First Dense Layer:** Comprising 20 neurons.
     - **Second Dense Layer:** Consisting of 10 neurons.
     - Dense layers in neural networks typically perform complex transformations and extract higher-level features from the input data.
3. **Output Layer:**
   - The output layer contains four attributes or nodes, aligning with the classification of four distinct physical activities: sleeping, exercising, stationary, and running.

The neural network architecture aims to learn intricate patterns within the 33-dimensional feature space and map these patterns to accurately predict the different physical activities observed through the accelerometer data.

*Figure 7. Architecture of ANN for physical activity*

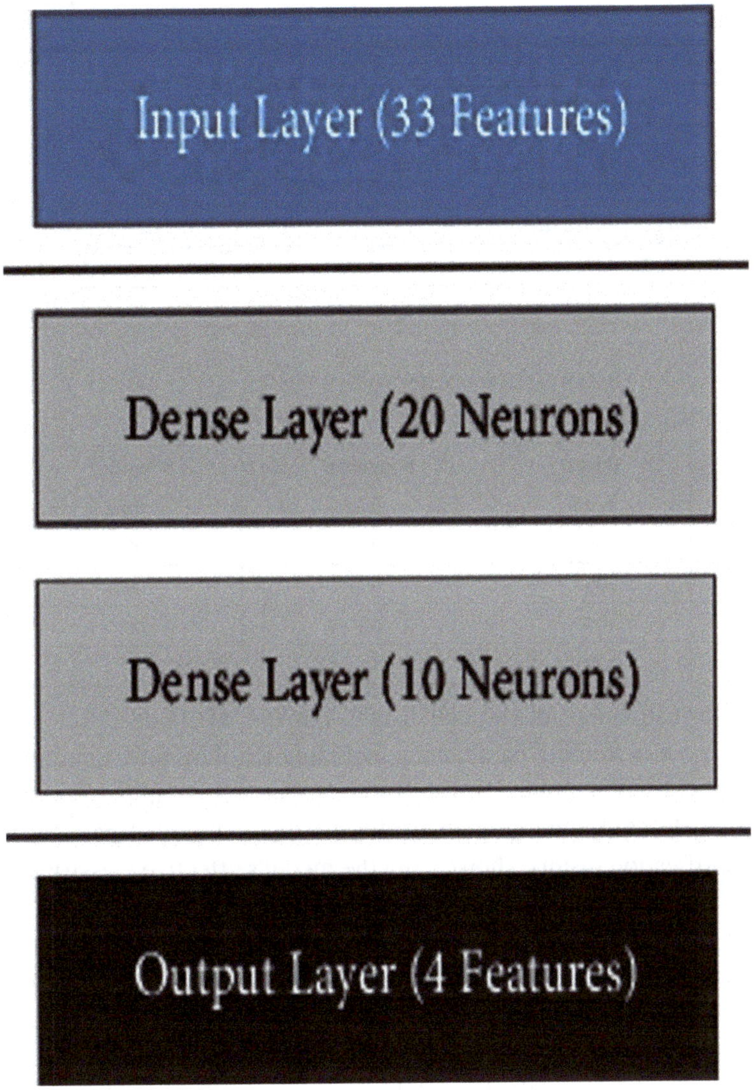

Input Layer (33 Features)

Dense Layer (20 Neurons)

Dense Layer (10 Neurons)

Output Layer (4 Features)

Additionally, Tables 9-11 likely present the training settings utilized during the model training process. These settings could encompass various parameters such as learning rate, optimizer configuration, number of epochs, batch size, and other relevant configurations essential for training a neural network model for accurate activity classification. These settings are critical in guiding the model through the optimization process, allowing it to learn and adapt to the given data efficiently.

*Table 9. Training dataset*

| Variables | Values |
|---|---|
| Number of training cycles | 200 |
| Minimum confidence rating | $58 \times 10^{-2}$ |
| Learning rate | $0.5 \times 10^{-3}$ |

*Table 10. Training dataset performance*

| Accuracy (%) | Loss (%) |
|---|---|
| 100 | 0 |

*Table 11. Confusion matrix*

| | Moving | Stationary | Running | Exercising |
|---|---|---|---|---|
| Moving | 100% | 0% | 0% | 0% |
| Stationary | 0% | 100% | 0% | 0% |
| Running | 0% | 0% | 100% | 0% |
| Exercising | 0% | 0% | 0% | 100% |
| *F*1-score | 1 | 1 | 1 | 1 |

The provided information includes crucial insights into the ML model developed for classifying physical activities. The model's training parameters, including learning rate, training cycles, and minimum confidence ratings, are listed in Table 10. Table 10 reveals the training performance metrics, indicating the model's accuracy during the training phase. Furthermore, Table 11 presents the confusion matrix, along with live classification results, showcasing the model's effective classification across four labels: exercising, moving, running, and stationary. This table also incorporates F1 scores for each label, emphasizing the model's precision and recall for individual categories. Notably, sample rows within Table 11 demonstrate the model's accurate classification of the "moving" label during live data assessments. Additionally, Table 12 reinforces the consistent and accurate classification of the "moving" label across different Recorded Times during live data analysis, illustrating the absence of anomalies within the data during these evaluations. Collectively, these tables emphasize the model's robust performance during training and real-time classification, particularly highlighting its accurate identification of specific activity labels without observable anomalies in live data assessments.

*Table 12. Accelerometer data for "moving" label with live classification*

| Recorded Time | Moving | Stationary | Running | Exercising | Variance |
|---|---|---|---|---|---|
| 0 | 1.00 | 0 | 0 | 0 | −0.04 |
| 50 | 1.00 | 0 | 0 | 0 | −0.05 |
| 100 | 1.00 | 0 | 0 | 0 | −0.05 |
| 200 | 1.00 | 0 | 0 | 0 | −0.05 |

continued on following page

*Table 12. Continued*

| Recorded Time | Moving | Stationary | Running | Exercising | Variance |
|---|---|---|---|---|---|
| 300 | 1.00 | 0 | 0 | 0 | −0.05 |
| 400 | 1.00 | 0 | 0 | 0 | −0.05 |
| 500 | 1.00 | 0 | 0 | 0 | −0.05 |
| 600 | 1.00 | 0 | 0 | 0 | −0.05 |
| 650 | 1.00 | 0 | 0 | 0 | −0.04 |

Tables 13-15 present the outcomes obtained from accelerometer data for live classification corresponding to the labels "stationary," "exercising," and "running". These tables validate that, similar to the "moving" label, the model consistently and accurately classifies the remaining three labels: "stationary," "exercising," and "running" during real-time assessments. The data depicted in these tables affirms the model's capability to effectively categorize various activities captured by the accelerometer sensor without encountering anomalies or misclassifications. This consistency across multiple activity labels underscores the model's robustness and reliability in differentiating and correctly identifying distinct physical activities in live classification scenarios.

*Table 13. Accelerometer data for "stationary" label with live classification*

| Recorded Time | Moving | Stationary | Running | Exercising | Difference |
|---|---|---|---|---|---|
| 0 | 0 | 0.99 | 0 | 0 | −0.11 |
| 50 | 0 | 0.99 | 0 | 0 | −0.11 |
| 100 | 0 | 0.99 | 0 | 0 | −0.11 |
| 200 | 0 | 0.99 | 0 | 0 | −0.11 |
| 300 | 0 | 0.99 | 0 | 0 | −0.11 |
| 400 | 0 | 0.99 | 0 | 0 | −0.11 |
| 500 | 0 | 0.99 | 0 | 0 | −0.11 |
| 600 | 0 | 0.99 | 0 | 0 | −0.11 |
| 650 | 0 | 0.99 | 0 | 0 | −0.11 |

*Table 14. Accelerometer data for "exercising" label with live classification*

| Recorded Time | Moving | Stationary | Running | Exercising | Difference |
|---|---|---|---|---|---|
| 0 | 0 | 0 | 0 | 1 | 0.25 |
| 50 | 0 | 0 | 0 | 1 | 0.15 |
| 100 | 0 | 0 | 0 | 1 | 0.12 |
| 200 | 0 | 0 | 0 | 1 | 0.10 |
| 300 | 0 | 0 | 0 | 1 | 0.15 |
| 400 | 0 | 0 | 0 | 1 | 0.14 |
| 500 | 0 | 0 | 0 | 1 | 0.07 |
| 600 | 0 | 0 | 0 | 1 | 0.11 |
| 650 | 0 | 0 | 0 | 1 | 0.11 |

*Table 15. Accelerometer data for "running" label with live classification*

| Recorded Time | Moving | Stationary | Running | Exercising | Difference |
|---|---|---|---|---|---|
| 0 | 0 | 0 | 1 | 0 | −0.10 |
| 50 | 0 | 0 | 1 | 0 | −0.26 |
| 100 | 0 | 0 | 1 | 0 | −0.19 |
| 200 | 0 | 0 | 1 | 0 | −0.21 |
| 300 | 0 | 0 | 1 | 0 | −0.09 |
| 400 | 0 | 0 | 1 | 0 | −0.05 |
| 500 | 0 | 0 | 1 | 0 | −0.16 |
| 600 | 0 | 0 | 1 | 0 | −0.13 |
| 650 | 0 | 0 | 1 | 0 | −0.11 |

Table 16 shows the total effectiveness of the model developed for the patient's physical activity analysis.

*Table 16. Physical activity model with testing dataset*

| | Moving (%) | Stationary (%) | Running (%) | Exercising (%) |
|---|---|---|---|---|
| **Moving** | 0.001 | 0.0005 | 0.9998 | 0.0005 |
| **Stationary** | 0 | 0.005 | 0.001 | 0.9985 |
| **Running** | 0.001 | 0.999 | 0.0009 | 0 |
| **Exercising** | 0.9995 | 0 | 0.0005 | 0 |
| ***F*1 score** | 0.999 | 0.9987 | 0.9985 | 0.9995 |

Figure 8 likely illustrates the workflow of the developed models for respiratory health and physical activity analysis. The diagram might depict the sequential steps involved in processing and analyzing the respective types of data for these two models.

1. **Respiratory Health Model:**
    - **Input Data:** Audio data related to respiratory sounds (e.g., coughs, normal breathing).
    - **Processing:** These audio data inputs are processed using Gammatone Frequency Cepstral Coefficients (GFCC) or similar techniques, extracting relevant features and patterns crucial for respiratory health analysis.
    - **Model Analysis:** The processed audio data are fed into the respiratory health model, which likely consists of machine learning algorithms or neural networks trained to detect and classify various respiratory conditions (e.g., normal breathing, coughing, or indicative sounds of illnesses like pneumonia or COVID-19).

2. **Physical Activity Model:**
    - **Input Data:** Accelerometer data captured during physical movements or activities.
    - **Processing:** The accelerometer data undergo spectral analysis, where frequency and power characteristics across different axes and timeframes are extracted and analyzed.

- **Model Analysis:** The processed accelerometer data are then utilized in the physical activity model, potentially comprising machine learning algorithms or neural networks trained to classify different physical activities (e.g., exercising, sleeping, running, or staying stationary) based on the patterns and features derived from the spectral analysis of the accelerometer data.

The workflow depicted in Figure 8 showcases the distinct paths followed by the audio and accelerometer data, detailing how these data types are processed, transformed, and utilized by their respective models to achieve specific health-related analyses.

*Figure 8. Proposed model process flow*

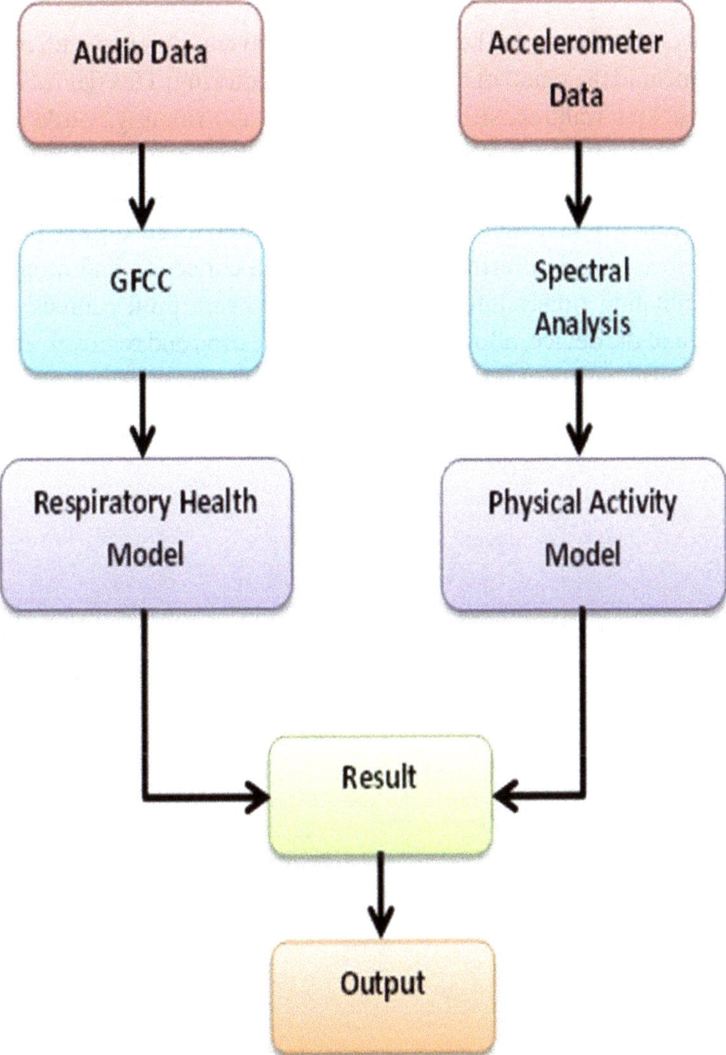

## FUTURE RESEARCH DIRECTIONS

Future directions include expanding the scope of the machine learning models to detect and classify a broader range of respiratory and cardiovascular conditions, such as asthma attacks, arrhythmias, or apnea events. Integrating additional sensors for more comprehensive health tracking and enhancing data analysis capabilities will improve early detection and prediction of adverse health events. Moreover, implementing real-time feedback and alert systems for patients and caregivers could enable more proactive and personalized healthcare interventions.

## CONCLUSION

The development of an IoT-enabled health monitoring device equipped with machine learning models is a pivotal advancement in the realm of remote patient monitoring. This device efficiently tracks a wide array of activities, such as walking, sleeping, exercising, and running, while also monitoring critical vital signs, including heart rate, body temperature, and breathing patterns. The current machine learning models incorporated in the device demonstrate high accuracy in detecting coughs and healthy breathing patterns, ensuring effective remote monitoring of patients without causing any discomfort. The inclusion of a user-friendly web application further streamlines data collection and monitoring, enhancing user engagement and facilitating timely interventions by healthcare professionals. The non-intrusive and patient-centric design of the device, allowing for easy application and removal, emphasizes its suitability for long-term use in various patient populations.

## ACKNOWEDGMENT

This research received no specific grant from any funding agency in the public, commercial, or not-for-profit sectors.

## REFERENCES

Adams, Z., McClure, E. A., Gray, K. M., Danielson, C. K., Treiber, F. A., & Ruggiero, K. J. (2017). Mobile devices for the remote acquisition of physiological and behavioral biomarkers in psychiatric clinical research. *Journal of Psychiatric Research*, 85, 1–14. 10.1016/j.jpsychires.2016.10.01927814455

(Adams, 2017)

Ahmad, N., Shahzad, B., Arif, M., Izdrui, D., Ungurean, I., & Geman, O. (2022). An energy-efficient framework for WBAN in health care domain. *Journal of Sensors*, 2022, 1–11. 10.1155/2022/5823461

(Ahmad, 2022)

Akbar MS, Hussain Z, Sheng M, Shankaran R (2022). Wireless Body Area Sensor Networks: Survey of MAC and Routing Protocols for Patient Monitoring under IEEE 802.15.4 and IEEE 802.15.6. *Sensors, 22*(21), 8279.

Al-Naji, A., Gibson, K., Lee, S.-H., & Chahl, J. (2017). Real time apnoea monitoring of children using the Microsoft Kinect sensor: A pilot study. *Sensors (Basel)*, 17(2), 286. 10.3390/s1702028628165382

Alanis, A. Y., Sanchez, O. D., Vaca-González, A., & Rangel-Heras, E. (2023). Intelligent Classification and Diagnosis of Diabetes and Impaired Glucose Tolerance Using Deep Neural Networks. *Mathematics*, 11(19), 4065. 10.3390/math11194065

Ardito, M., Mascolo, F., Valentini, M., & Dell'Olio, F. (2021). Low-Cost Wireless Wearable System for Posture Monitoring. *Electronics (Basel)*, 10(21), 2569. 10.3390/electronics10212569

(Ardito, 2021)

Ayesha, A., & Komalavalli, C. (2023). Smart Ambulance: A Comprehensive IoT and Cloud-Based System Integrating Fingerprint Sensor with Medical Sensors for Real-time Patient Vital Signs Monitoring. *International Journal of Intelligent Systems and Applications in Engineering*, 12(2), 555–567.

(Ayesha, 2023)

Deng, Z., Guo, L., Chen, X., & Wu, W. (2023). Smart Wearable Systems for Health Monitoring. *Sensors (Basel)*, 23(5), 2479. 10.3390/s2305247936904682

(Deng, 2023)

Devi DH, Duraisamy K, Armghan A, Alsharari M, Aliqab K, Sorathiya V, Das S, Rashid N (2023). 5G Technology in Healthcare and Wearable Devices: A Review. *Sensors, 23*(5), 2519.

El-Rashidy, N., El-Sappagh, S., & Islam, S. M. R., M.El-Bakry H., & Abdelrazek S. (2021). Mobile health in Tele-health monitoringfor chronic diseases: Principles, trends, and challenges. *Diagnostics (Basel)*, 11(4), 607. 10.3390/diagnostics1104060733805471

Fayad, M., Hachani, M.-Y., Ghoumid, K., Mostefaoui, A., Chouali, S., Picaud, F., Herlem, G., Lajoie, I., & Yahiaoui, R. (2023). Fall Detection Approaches for Monitoring Elderly HealthCare Using Kinect Technology: A Survey. *Applied Sciences (Basel, Switzerland)*, 13(18), 10352. 10.3390/app131810352

Gutierrez LJ, Rabbani K, Ajayi OJ, Gebresilassie SK, Rafferty J, Castro LA, Banos O (2021). Internet of Things for Mental Health: Open Issues in Data Acquisition, Self-Organization, Service Level Agreement, and Identity Management. *Int J Environ Res Public Health, 18*(3), 1327.

Hernandez, N., Castro, L., Medina-Quero, J., Favela, J., Michan, L., & Mortenson, W. B. (2021). Scoping Review of Healthcare Literature on Mobile, Wearable, and Textile Sensing Technology for Continuous Monitoring. *Journal of Healthcare Informatics Research*, 5(3), 270–299. 10.1007/s41666-020-00087-z33554008

Humayun, M., Jhanjhi, N. Z., Almotilag, A., & Almufareh, M. F. (2022). Agent-Based Medical Health Monitoring System. *Sensors (Basel)*, 22(8), 2820. 10.3390/s2208282035458805

Iranpak, S., Shahbahrami, A., & Shakeri, H. (2021). Tele-health monitoring and classifying using the internet of things platform combined with cloud computing. *Journal of Big Data*, 8(1), 120. 10.1186/s40537-021-00507-w

Juengst, S. B., Terhorst, L., Nabasny, A., Wallace, T., Weaver, J. A., Osborne, C. L., Burns, S. P., Wright, B., Wen, P.-S., Kew, C.-L. N., & Morris, J. (2021). Use of mHealth Technology for Patient-Reported Outcomes in Community-Dwelling Adults with Acquired Brain Injuries: A Scoping Review. *International Journal of Environmental Research and Public Health*, 18(4), 2173. 10.3390/ijerph1804217333672183

Karar, M. E., Shehata, H. I., & Reyad, O. (2022). A Survey of IoT-Based Fall Detection for Aiding Elderly Care: Sensors, Methods, Challenges and Future Trends. *Applied Sciences (Basel, Switzerland)*, 12(7), 3276. 10.3390/app12073276

Krizea, M., Gialelis, J., Protopsaltis, G., Mountzouris, C., & Theodorou, G. (2022). Empowering People with a User-Friendly Wearable Platform for Unobtrusive Monitoring of Vital Physiological Parameters. *Sensors (Basel)*, 22(14), 5226. 10.3390/s2214522635890907

La Rosa R, Livreri P, Trigona C, Di Donato L, Sorbello G (2019). Strategies and Techniques for Powering Wireless Sensor Nodes through Energy Harvesting and Wireless Power Transfer. *Sensors,19*(12), 2660.

Laguarta, J., Hueto, F., & Subirana, B. (2020). COVID-19 artificial intelligence diagnosis using only cough recordings. *IEEE Open Journal of Engineering in Medicine and Biology*, 1, 275–281. 10.1109/OJEMB.2020.302692834812418

Lakshminarayanan, V., Zelek, J., & McBride, A. (2015). Smartphone science "in eye care and medicine" in Eye Care and Medicine. *Optics and Photonics News*, 26(1), 44–51. 10.1364/OPN.26.1.000044

Leo, D. (2022). Interactive Remote Patient Monitoring Devices for Managing Chronic Health Conditions: Systematic Review and Meta-analysis. *J Med Internet Res., 24*(11)

Moreira, A., Duarte, J., & Santos, M. F. (2023). Case Study of Multichannel Interaction in Healthcare Services. *Information (Basel)*, 14(1), 37. 10.3390/info14010037

Mousse, M. A., & Atohoun, B. (2021). Saliency based human fall detection in smart home environments using posture recognition. *Health Informatics Journal*, 27(3). 10.1177/1460458221103095434382460

Naranjo-Hernández D, Reina-Tosina J, Roa LM (2020). Special Issue - Body Sensors Networks for E-Health Applications. *Sensors* (Basel), *20*(14), 3944.

Nikseresht, M. R., & Mollamotalebi, M. (2021). Providing a CoAP-based technique to get wireless sensor data via IoT gateway. *Computer Communications*, 172, 155–168. 10.1016/j.comcom.2021.03.026

Prabhakar, S. K., & Rajaguru, H. (2017). *The 16th International Conference on Biomedical Engineering IFMBE Proceedings*. Singapore: Springer.

Rahman, M. Z. U., Raza, A. H., AlSanad, A. A., Akbar, M. A., Liaquat, R., Riaz, M. T., AlSuwaidan, L., Al-Alshaikh, H. A., & Alsagri, H. S. (2022). Real-time artificial intelligence based health monitoring, diagnosing and environmental control system for COVID-19 patients [J]. *Mathematical Biosciences and Engineering*, 19(8), 7586–7605. 10.3934/mbe.202235735801437

Ribeiro, O., Gomes, L., & Vale, Z. (2022). IoT-Based Human Fall Detection System. *Electronics (Basel)*, 11(4), 592. 10.3390/electronics11040592

Sahandi Far, M., Stolz, M., Fischer, J. M., Eickhoff, S. B., & Dukart, J. (2021). A Digital Biomarker Platform for Remote Monitoring of Daily-Life Behaviour in Health and Disease. *Frontiers in Public Health*, 9, 763621. 10.3389/fpubh.2021.76362134869177

Shah, S. S., Gvozdanovic, A., Knight, M., & Gagnon, J. (2021). Mobile App-Based Remote Patient Monitoring in Acute Medical Conditions: Prospective Feasibility Study Exploring Digital Health Solutions on Clinical Workload During the COVID Crisis. *JMIR Formative Research*, 5(1), e23190. 10.2196/2319033400675

Szydło, T., & Konieczny, M. (2016). *Mobile and wearable devices in an open and universal system for remote patient monitoring, Microprocessors and Microsystems* (Vol. 46). Part A.

Taiwo, O., & Ezugwu, A. E. (2020). Smart healthcare support for Tele-health monitoring during covid-19 quarantine. *Informatics in Medicine Unlocked*, 20, 100428. 10.1016/j.imu.2020.10042832953970

Turgambayeva A, Kulbayeva S, Sadibekova Z, Tursynbekova A, Sarsenbayeva G, Zhanaliyeva M, Zhakupova T (2022). Features of the Development of a Mobile Application for Cardiac Patients. *Acta Inform Med.*, *30*(4), 302-307.

Wang, Q., Chen, W., Timmermans, A. A., Karachristos, C., Martens, J. B., & Markopoulos, P. (2015). Smart rehabilitation garment for posture monitoring. *Proceedings of the 2015 37th annual International Conference of the IEEE Engineering in Medicine and Biology Society (EmbC)*. IEEE. 10.1109/EMBC.2015.7319695

Wei, S., & Wu, Z. (2023). The Application of Wearable Sensors and Machine Learning Algorithms in Rehabilitation Training: A Systematic Review. *Sensors (Basel)*, 23(18), 7667. 10.3390/s2318766737765724

Yamauchi Y, Shimoi N.(2023). Posture Classification with a Bed-Monitoring System Using Radio Frequency Identification. *Sensors, 23*(16), 7304.

Yew, H. T., Ng, M. F., Ping, S. Z., Chung, S. K., Chekima, A., & Dargham, J. A. (2020). Iot based real-time Tele-health monitoring system. *Proceedings of the 2020 16th IEEE International Colloquium on Signal Processing & Its Applications (CSPA).* IEEE.

Zurbuchen N, Wilde A, Bruegger P(2021). A Machine Learning Multi-Class Approach for Fall Detection Systems Based on Wearable Sensors with a Study on Sampling Rates Selection. *Sensors(Basel), 21*(3), 938.

## ADDITIONAL READING

Aya-Parra, P. A., Rodriguez-Orjuela, A. J., Rodriguez Torres, V., Cordoba Hernandez, N. P., Martinez Castellanos, N., & Sarmiento-Rojas, J. (2023). Monitoring System for Operating Variables in Incubators in the Neonatology Service of a Highly Complex Hospital through the Internet of Things (IoT). *Sensors (Basel)*, 23(12), 5719. 10.3390/s2312571937420890

Boikanyo, K., Zungeru, A. M., Sigweni, B., Yahya, A., & Lebekwe, C. (2023), Remote patient monitoring systems: Applications, architecture, and challenges, *Scientific African, 20.*

Healthcare Engineering JO. (2023). Retracted: Artificial Intelligence of Things- (AIoT-) Based Patient Activity Tracking System for Remote Patient Monitoring. *Journal of Healthcare Engineering*, 2023, 9834854.37860375

Malche, T., Tharewal, S., Tiwari, P. K., Jabarulla, M. Y., Alnuaim, A. A., Hatamleh, W. A., & Ullah, M. A. (2022). Artificial Intelligence of Things- (AIoT-) Based Patient Activity Tracking System for Remote Patient Monitoring. *Journal of Healthcare Engineering*, 2022, 8732213. 10.1155/2022/873221335273786

Pise, A., Yoon, B., & Singh, S. (2023). Enabling Ambient Intelligence of Things (AIoT) healthcare system architectures. *Computer Communications*, 198, 186–194. 10.1016/j.comcom.2022.10.029

Vora, L. K., Gholap, A. D., Jetha, K., Thakur, R. R. S., Solanki, H. K., & Chavda, V. P. (2023). Artificial Intelligence in Pharmaceutical Technology and Drug Delivery Design. *Pharmaceutics*, 15(7), 1916. 10.3390/pharmaceutics1507191637514102

Wang, C., He, T., Zhou, H., Zhang, Z., & Lee, C. (2023). Artificial intelligence enhanced sensors - enabling technologies to next-generation healthcare and biomedical platform. *Bioelectronic Medicine*, 9(1), 17. 10.1186/s42234-023-00118-137528436

Zhang, Y., Xu, J., Liu, X., Pan, W., & Li, X. (2023), A Novel Cost-Aware Data Placement Strategy for Edge-Cloud Collaborative Smart Systems. *2023 IEEE 16th International Conference on Cloud Computing (CLOUD).* IEEE.

## KEY TERMS AND DEFINITIONS

**Epilepsy:** Epilepsy is a neurological disorder characterized by recurrent, unprovoked seizures. These seizures are caused by abnormal electrical activity in the brain.

**Gammatone Cepstral Coefficients:** Gammatone Cepstral Coefficients (GFCC) are a feature extraction technique commonly used in the analysis of audio signals, especially in the field of speech and audio processing.

**Gateway Node:** A Gateway Node, in the context of networking and communication systems, refers to a device that acts as an entry point between different networks or communication protocols.

**Message Queue Telemetry Transport Protocol:** Message Queue Telemetry Transport (MQTT) is a lightweight messaging protocol designed for efficient communication between devices, particularly in situations with low bandwidth, high-latency, or unreliable networks.

**Sensor Node:** A sensor node is a compact electronic device equipped with sensors, processing capabilities, and communication interfaces.

**Tele-Health Monitoring:** Telehealth monitoring (THM) is a branch of telehealth that involves the use of technology to remotely monitor patients' health and provide healthcare services.

*TinyML Tool:*: *T*he term “TinyML” refers to Tiny Machine Learning, which involves deploying machine learning models on resource-constrained devices, such as microcontrollers and other small embedded systems.

# Chapter 10
# Adoption of Robotic Technology in Healthcare Management

**Sunil Kumar**
https://orcid.org/0000-0002-2362-1972
*Shoolini University, India*

**Saloni Rajput**
*Lovely Professional University, India*

**Anagha Ajith**
*Lovely Professional University, India*

## ABSTRACT

*This chapter provides a comprehensive exploration of the evolution and impact of robotic surgery in the medical domain. From historical origins to contemporary smart hospitals, the narrative covers the technological advancements and challenges associated with robotic surgery, offering insights from two experienced surgeons. Aligning with the unified theory of acceptance and use of technology (UTAUT), their lived experiences highlight factors such as performance expectancy, effort expectancy, social influence, facilitating conditions, and moderating factors shaping their acceptance of robotic technology. The research also delves into broader implications on patient satisfaction, healthcare outcomes, and the ethical considerations of human-machine collaboration. Emphasizing the transformative potential of robotic surgery, the chapter underscores the need to address barriers for widespread adoption to fully harness its benefits in enhancing patient care.*

## INTRODUCTION

Artificial Intelligence (AI) means using computers to act smart without much help from people. People think AI started with robots, from a Czech word meaning machines doing forced work. Leonardo Da Vinci's old drawings of robots inspired today's robot-assisted surgeries for tricky medical procedures. AI, the science of making smart machines, officially began in 1956. In medicine, AI has two parts: virtual (like using computers for managing health records and helping doctors) and physical (using robots to help patients and doctors, and new tiny robots for delivering medicine). These cool ideas raise big

DOI: 10.4018/979-8-3693-2901-6.ch010

questions about how helpful they are, how they affect society, and how to make them better and fairer (Hamet et al., 2017).

Since the 1920s, when a play introduced the word 'robot,' these machines have become more important (Angelo, 2007). They've evolved from simple to really smart robots like the ones we see in movies. Nowadays, robots do specific and risky jobs in industries and research that people can't do. But in medicine, robots didn't join in until recently. Now, they're part of surgeries. Some robots can do surgeries even from far away! They help surgeons with tools and cameras. Before these surgical robots, there was 'minimally invasive surgery.' It started in the late 1980s and became popular because it made surgeries easier (Olson, 2009). But there were problems. Surgeons couldn't feel or move as well as they could with their hands. The tools didn't give enough feedback or precision.

So, people wanted robots to help fix these problems. The idea started with robots used in other fields, like making precise cuts in hip surgeries. Some researchers at NASA also got interested and started working on surgery robots using virtual reality. Later, the US Army saw this work and thought it could help soldiers (Singer, 2009). They wanted to use robots to do surgeries on wounded soldiers, even on the battlefield. Some scientists who worked on these systems then started companies to bring these robots into regular hospitals. One famous robot system, called Da Vinci, helps surgeons with operations using special robotic arms (Lanfranco et., 2004).

Technology has changed how surgeries are done, so we need new ways to check if they're done well. This brings up big questions about ethics, especially with how humans and machines work together (Kumar et al., 2024). We've seen these ideas in sci-fi stories, like Asimov's, where robots help people. Soon, robots might be like companions to us, doing tasks at home and work. Take BINA48, a robot that talks, understands, and shows feelings. Robotic surgery is pushing healthcare forward, with five generations of better and better robots. These range from precise tools to tiny bots, even to systems that can work on their own. To make these surgeries better, we're using imaging, better ways to feel things during surgery, and making sure the robot and surgeon can work together well. We're also looking at how much it costs and how doctors learn to use these tools. All these changes in tech could really improve how surgeries are done and help patients get better care (Brahme et. al, 2022).

In recent years, the integration of healthcare robots has emerged as a promising avenue for transforming how older individuals manage their health (Mois et al., 2020). Despite the potential benefits, numerous challenges persist, encompassing clinical effectiveness, technology adoption, health informatics, healthcare policy, and healthcare ethics. Mois et al. (2020) emphasize the importance of addressing these challenges at all levels of the healthcare system to ensure the safe, efficient, and dependable use of healthcare robotics in promoting healthy aging.

The application of robotics and artificial intelligence (AI) has extended to challenging surgical procedures such as difficult deformity surgery, revision procedures, and surgical elimination of spinal tumors (Yerneni et al., 2023). Additionally, a study on robotic arm-assisted total knee arthroplasty (TKA) by Kayani et al. (2019) reveals that cumulative robotic experience did not compromise precision in implant location, limb alignment, posterior tibial slope, or joint line restoration. Robotic TKA demonstrated enhanced accuracy in implant location and limb alignment compared to conventional manual TKA, without an increased risk of postoperative complications.

A comprehensive literature review, following recommended reporting items, indicates that only 32% of studies comparing robot-assisted uni-compartmental knee arthroplasty (UKA) with traditional UKA were randomized control trials (Mittal et al., 2021). Mittal et al. (2021) highlight challenges related to the effectiveness of computer-assisted technologies (CATs) in promoting survivability, including issues of cost-effectiveness, a learning curve, and increased operating time. Robotic surgery has demonstrated efficacy across various procedures, including rectal cancer removal, gastrectomy, Roux-en-Y gastric bypass, thyroidectomy, and even rare surgeries like releasing the median arcuate ligament in MAL syndrome (Goh & Ali, 2022). The study emphasizes the ongoing improvement of robotic technology, making it more accessible for complex surgeries through advancements in the da Vinci robot and specialized tools for single-site surgeries.

The COVID-19 pandemic underscored the challenges in traditional surgeries due to the risk of spreading germs. Zemmar et al. (2020) propose the use of AI and robots to perform tasks, reduce personnel in the operating room, and conduct surgeries with minimal presence to enhance safety and minimize the spread of germs. The study anticipates continued improvements in surgeries facilitated by AI, machine learning, and robotics beyond the pandemic. Sheetz et al. (2020) observe a significant surge in the adoption of robotic surgery across common procedures, replacing laparoscopic approaches in hospitals. The study suggests a need for careful monitoring and evaluation to ensure the judicious use of robotic surgery where it truly benefits patients.

Examining surgeons' attitudes towards robotic technology, Kharrazi et al. (2011) find that users appreciate the benefits for patients and are open to learning new technologies. Non-users, however, cite challenges such as the learning curve, lack of hospital support, and high costs as deterrents. The study emphasizes the importance of addressing these challenges to foster greater adoption of robotic technology. Safety concerns in medical robots, particularly Robot Assisted Fracture Surgery (RAFS), are explored by Georgilas et al. (2017). The study identifies hazards, such as software issues, and emphasizes the critical role of the surgeon in controlling the system. The research proposes safety measures, including clear communication and real-world testing, to ensure the safe integration of RAFS into surgical practices.

The integration of robotics in orthopaedic surgery has garnered attention due to its potential to enhance patient outcomes. Several studies have investigated the factors influencing patient adoption of these technologies. Performance expectancy, a key determinant, is underscored by studies indicating that patients exposed to robotic-assisted procedures report heightened satisfaction and improved outcomes. Mulpar et al. (2022) found a significant reduction in postoperative pain and improved range of motion in patients undergoing robotic-assisted total hip arthroplasty, while Onggo et al. (2020) reported high patient satisfaction and better mobility in those opting for robotic-assisted total knee arthroplasty.

Effort expectancy, reflecting perceptions of complexity and ease of use, also plays a crucial role in patient adoption. Contrary to initial expectations, patients exposed to robotic-assisted procedures reported a high level of comfort and ease with the technology. Chughtai et al. (2016) and Ren et al. (2019) found satisfaction with the ease of use in patients undergoing robotic-assisted total knee and total hip arthroplasty, respectively. Social influence, emanating from healthcare providers and peer experiences, significantly shapes patient attitudes. Studies by Chughtai et al. (2016) and Khlopas et al. (2019) identified a correlation between patient trust and confidence and the use of robotic-assisted total hip arthroplasty, highlighting the influence of healthcare providers and peers on patient decision-making. Facilitating conditions, encompassing the availability and accessibility of robotics in healthcare settings, impact its adoption. Chughtai et al. (2019) and Khlopas et al. (2019) found that patients undergoing robotic-supported total knee and total hip arthroplasty reported high satisfaction levels when the technology was readily available.

The adoption of robotics in orthopaedic surgery is influenced by performance and effort expectations, social influence, and facilitating conditions (Saad et al., 2024; Verhellen et al., 2024). Understanding these factors is crucial for healthcare providers and policymakers aiming to enhance patient acceptance and integration of robotic technologies in orthopaedic surgical practices (Ismatullaev & Kim, 2024).

This research has three primary objectives. Firstly, it aims to explore patient perceptions towards robotic surgery in orthopaedics, delving into their attitudes, experiences, and expectations to enhance surgical practices and patient experiences. Secondly, the study seeks to analyze successful adoption case studies in various Indian hospitals, examining instances where robotic surgical technology has been effectively integrated to derive insights for optimizing adoption in healthcare settings. Lastly, the research aims to assess the experiences and opinions of surgeons practicing robotic surgery, focusing on practical aspects, challenges, and recommendations to inform best practices, enhance training programs, and address barriers hindering the widespread adoption of robotic surgery in medical practice.

The researchers used qualitative analysis methodology and it involves collecting data through interviews with surgeons, transcribing spoken responses into written text, and identifying key statements expressing opinions, experiences, or perceptions about robotic surgery. The thematic analysis process includes extracting relevant content, categorizing responses by themes (such as benefits, challenges, patient outcomes, training experiences, or technological concerns), and generating codes/categories to organize data within each theme. The overarching goal of this analysis is to gain nuanced insights into surgeons' perspectives, motivations (such as precision or improved outcomes), challenges (including cost or training), and satisfaction levels related to the use of robotic surgery in their practice.

## SMART HOSPITALS

Rising healthcare costs due to longer life expectancy and medical complexity can be addressed with smart health and ubiquitous computing aligned with P4-medicine. However, this generates vast, complex data. Smart hospitals are proposed, with context-aware computing and advanced interaction paradigms, assisting doctors in managing data and supporting patients in achieving well-being (Holzinger et al., 2015).

Smart hospitals, driven by technologies, are revolutionizing healthcare. They integrate solutions across various components, including Electronic Health Records (EHR), IoT, telehealth, AI, patient flow optimization, predictive analytics, energy management, patient experience, security, and healthcare robots, to enhance patient care, operational efficiency, and sustainability (Agbaje et al., 2020; Rathore et al., 2016; Cabezas et al., 2018; Lundberg et al., 2018; Mekikis et al., 2016; Zaharia et al., 2016; Kavousi-Fard et al., 2019; Pai et al., 2014; Roesch, 1999; Singh et al., 2020; Quigley et al., 2009). These open-source solutions promote transparency, collaboration, and patient-centric care, ultimately reshaping the healthcare landscape.

The technologies like wearable sensors are revolutionizing healthcare informatics, enabling smart hospitals to create Remote Patient Monitoring (RPM) models. RPM generates substantial patient data, which is efficiently handled by cloud-based architectures and big data analytics. Advanced frameworks like Hadoop and Spark are accelerating medical data analysis, offering innovative healthcare services, particularly for elderly patients living alone (Hassan et al., 2019).

The intelligent infrastructure for smart hospitals includes RFID and photosensor technologies to identify, locate, and track clinicians and patients with mobile devices and RFID tags. This system aims to enhance coordination among medical staff, reduce costs, and improve patient safety by providing easy access to clinical data stored in standard databases (Vecchia et al., 2012).

Zhang et al., (2018) suggests using Narrowband IoT (NB-IoT) to connect smart hospital devices, improving healthcare and hospital management. It introduces edge computing to handle medical process latency and presents an infusion monitoring system as a case study. The paper discusses future directions for establishing smart hospitals with connected devices. Yu et al. (2012) presents an architecture and scheme for a smart hospital based on the Internet of Things (IoT) to address limitations in current hospital information systems. It focuses on the key technologies and construction of a smart hospital, offering a detailed scheme for a third-grade-A hospital. The scheme includes the logic structure, application framework, and basic network environment. Experiments demonstrate that implementing a smart hospital can effectively address issues in hospital diagnosis and treatment, positively impacting the current healthcare model.

Moro Visconti and Martiniello (2019) examines healthcare governance models with a focus on patients and smart technologies in smart hospitals. It recommends Public-Private Partnerships (PPP) and Results-Based Financing (RBF) as effective frameworks, emphasizing the transition of in-patients to out-patients and home-patients for improved efficiency.

## MEDICAL ROBOTICS EVOLUTION, TRAINING & ECONOMIC IMPACT

Technology has greatly improved medical procedures, especially surgeries, through advanced robots. These robots help doctors with precise tasks but come with challenges like high costs and needing skilled operators. Despite this, they've significantly improved surgeries, reducing patient trauma and improving recovery. (Ginoya et al., 2021).

*Table 1. Medical robotics evolution*

| First Generation (1990–2000) | Middle Generation (2000–2010) | Current Generation (2010–Present) |
|---|---|---|
| • NeuroMate®: Helped in brain surgeries with precision.<br>• ROBODOC® Surgical System: Pioneered precise hip surgeries.<br>• AESOP™ Robotic Surgical System: Assisted in holding and moving endoscopes.<br>• Many other systems like CyberKnife®, Zeus®, and Da Vinci® Surgical System contributed to better precision and reduced patient trauma. | • Systems like AcuBot, PathFinder™, and Sensei® improved accuracy and control in surgeries.<br>• Robotic systems like neuroArm™ and Telelap ALF-X enhanced surgical techniques and precision. | • Systems like Renaissance®, ROSA ONE®, and MAKO™ Surgical System enhance precision in spinal and orthopedic surgeries.<br>• Other systems like Senhance™ Surgical System and Versius® Surgical System aim for minimally invasive surgeries with improved feedback and precision. |

Source: Ginoya et al. (2021)

In 2023, the global robotics market recorded a revenue exceeding 37 billion U.S. dollars, with the predominant share coming from service robotics, amounting to over 28 billion U.S. dollars. While the overall robotics market is expected to see incremental growth in the coming years, the projection indicates that service robotics revenue will experience a more substantial increase compared to industrial robotics revenue. The Figure 1 represents revenue of robotics market worldwide from 2016 to 2028, by category (in billion U.S. dollars)

*Figure 1. Worldwide revenue of robotics market*

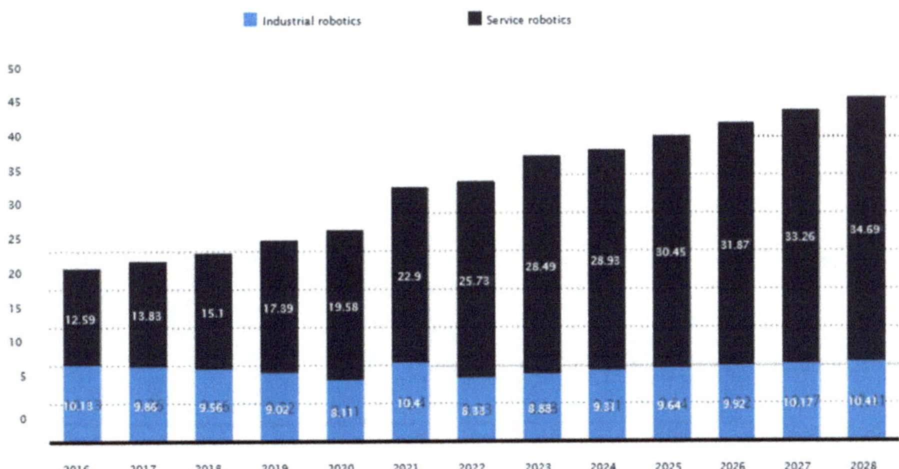


In 2022, the global hospital logistics robotics market had around 5.2 thousand units in operation. By 2030, the market volume was forecast to increase to over 34 thousand units, according to market research company. The figure 2 represents number of hospital logistics robotic units worldwide between 2022 and 2030 (Statista, 2023).

*Figure 2. Worldwide number of hospitals with logistics robotic units*

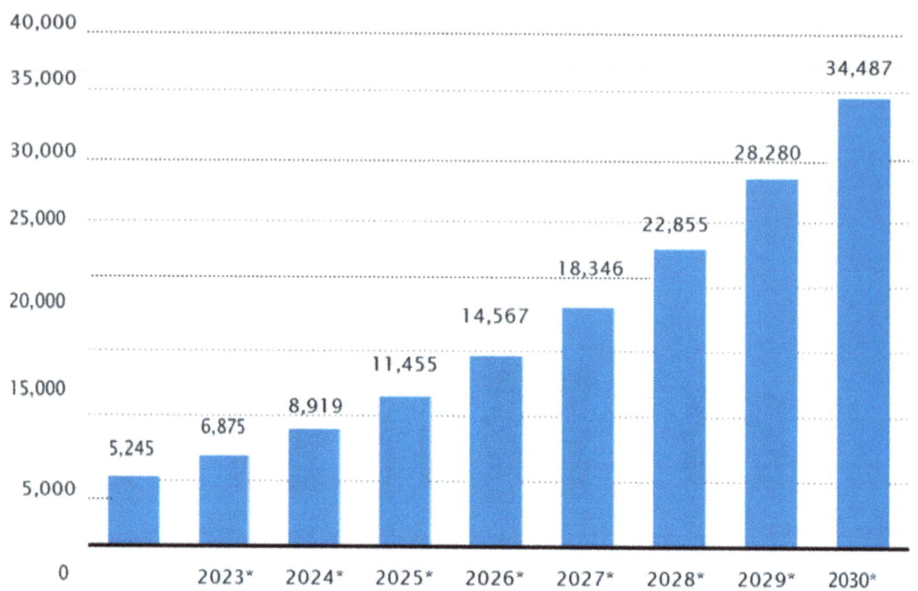


According to Medical Service Robotics – Worldwide (n.d.) the Medical Service Robotics market covers robotics in healthcare, improving procedures and patient care. These robots, with autonomy, boost efficiency. It includes B2B and B2C revenues, with key players like Intuitive Surgical, Stryker Corporation, and Medtronic. The Medical Service Robotics market is expected to reach $11.19 billion in revenue by 2024, with a projected annual growth rate of 17.03% through 2028, totaling $20.99 billion. The United States leads in revenue, expecting $3.28 billion in 2024.

## Training and Education in Robotics Technology

Andrade et al., (2014) suggested a comprehensive modularization method for designing and executing individual robotic devices. Even McAllister et al. (2021) highlighted the need of robotic education for Nurses in healthcare. The end users need to be trained in the robotic developments. Silvera-Tawil (2024) suggested interdisciplinary training programs of engineering and medical at university level. Meanwhile, the learning of robotic technologies in healthcare needs strong evaluation measures (Marcos-Pablos and García-Peñalvo, 2022). Novel platforms utilizing machine learning and real-time feedback enhance robotic surgical education. Bridging the gap between skills acquired in robotic training and actual surgical performance is essential for improving patient outcomes (Azadi et al., 2021).

In India the major challenges are infrastructure and trained workforce, but AI and robotics offer solutions. To handle these challenges, we need an ecosystem of startups, businesses and research institutions (Agrawal et al., 2024). Even data is showing India as an emerging destination for medical tourism across the world (Kumar et al., 2024).

## ROBOTIC SURGERY IN INDIA AND TECHNOLOGY ACCEPTANCE

Apollo Hospitals in India has successfully integrated robotics into healthcare, utilizing da Vinci Surgical Systems for enhanced precision in minimally invasive surgeries and improved patient recovery times. Telemedicine robots further extend healthcare access to underserved rural areas. Surgeons' positive outcomes and precision contribute to a favourable perception of robotic systems (Performance Expectancy - PE), with da Vinci's intuitive interface making the effort expectancy (EE) favourable despite specialized training requirements. Social influence (SI), driven by positive feedback from experienced surgeons and hospital leadership, supports the organizational embrace of robotics. Apollo Hospitals invests in facilitating conditions (FC), including infrastructure and training, while hedonic motivation (HM) stems from surgeons' satisfaction with superior patient outcomes. The hospital justifies the investment through emphasizing long-term benefits (Price Value - PV). The habitual incorporation of technology into workflows (Habit - HAB) further ensures seamless adoption and utilization of robotic systems.

Narayana Health strategically employs robotic technology, particularly robotic process automation (RPA), to bolster efficiency and reduce operational costs. The integration of RPA into administrative tasks, like appointment scheduling and billing, aligns with the hospital's dedication to affordable healthcare (Nalluri et al., 2023). Factors facilitating RPA adoption include tangible performance impact (Performance Expectancy - PE) on administrative efficiency and broad accessibility due to system simplicity (Effort Expectancy - EE). Social Influence (SI) from hospital management actively encourages RPA utilization, supported by Narayana Health's investment in facilitating conditions (FC), including infrastructure and tailored training programs. The adoption is fuelled by staff satisfaction through Hedonic Motivation (HM), driven by tangible workflow improvements. Cost savings (Price Value - PV) achieved through RPA further contribute to its acceptance, justifying the initial investment. The hospital's commitment to innovation and technology adaptation (Habit - HAB) solidifies its position at the forefront of healthcare practices. The UTAUT factors are contributing to the adoption of robotic technology in healthcare (Vichitkraivin & Naenna, 2021).

*Table 2. Robotic surgery in India: SWOT analysis*

| *Strengths* | *Weaknesses* | *Opportunities* | *Threats* |
|---|---|---|---|
| i. Large Patient Volume: India's high population leads to more patients for surgeons, aiding in their learning curve.<br>ii. Growing Economy: India's expanding economy is shifting healthcare, making robotic surgeries more accessible in various hospitals.<br>iii. Skilled Laparoscopic Surgeons: India's familiarity with laparoscopy helps surgeons transition to using robots more easily.<br>iv. Training Programs: Institutions offer training, and programs like the Vattikuti fellowship enhance skills in robotic surgery.<br>v. Extended Surgical Careers: Experienced surgeons benefit from robots' ergonomic advantages, aiding in their career extension. | i. High Initial Costs: Setting up robotic facilities is expensive, as is the yearly maintenance.<br>ii. Consumables' Recurring Costs: Open or laparoscopic surgeries are more cost-effective than robotic surgeries for certain procedures.<br>iii. Reliability Concerns: Mechanical breakdowns or malfunctions in robots pose risks to patients, as reported by the FDA. | i. Expansion Potential: Growing interest in various specialties could reduce maintenance costs for robotic surgeries.<br>ii. Medical Tourism: India's proficient healthcare attracts international patients, and introducing robotic surgery might further boost this sector.<br>iii. New Robotic Systems: Ongoing development of newer systems might reduce initial and maintenance costs, making robotic surgery more affordable. | i. Demand Pressure: Surgeons might face pressure due to patients' irrational demand for robotic surgeries, driven by commercial interests.<br>ii. Training Gap: Limited exposure to open or laparoscopic surgeries due to robotic facilities in academic institutions might challenge future surgeons.<br>iii. Infection Risk: Concerns arise regarding complete sterilization of robotic instruments, potentially increasing infection risks. |

Source: Bora et al. (2020).

## METHODOLOGY

The study used qualitative approach to collect information from surgeons and patient. Semi-structured Interview technique was used for collecting information from the surgeons. The observation and narratives collected from the patient are recorded and reported. To analyse the information content analysis and thematic analysis was used. The study approach is to built a discourse around the technology acceptance model.

## RESULTS

### Experience of Orthopaedics Surgeon

The surgeon is currently working in Medical College, Kerala.

Researcher(s): For how many months/years of experience you have with robotic surgery?

Doctor: 2 years.

Researcher(s): Could you tell me some of the advantages of robotic surgery?

Doctor: In orthopedics the most commonly used robotic surgery is for the knee/joint replacement surgery. Earlier in conventional method, the surgery was completely doctor dependent. So, the most important factor in knee replacement is the alignment, which we were recreating. Leg of the patient will be bend while he/she is standing. To make it straight we need an actual alignment. So visually if we are seeing with our human eyes the alignment will not be that accurate. By the advancement of robotic surgery, we are getting the near normal (precise)/actual alignment so that all the minor errors and cuts (mm errors) which used to occur while doing conventional method of surgery will not be there. Normally this millimeter errors will cause any problem, but in a long run like more than 5 years it may cause some problem. These problems can be resolved by robotic surgery. Another advantage is the pre operative planning. With the help of robotics and navigation, pre operatively we can plan like how much angle and degree we need to get, which actually helps in well preparation for the surgery.

Researcher(s): How likely do you suggest robotic surgery to your patients?

Doctor: I suggest robotic surgery to my patients depending on the severity of the case and their affordability (most people cannot afford robotic surgery and people often has a mindset that robotic surgeries are too costly). So those patients who can afford robotic surgery I would definitely recommend it considering the precision and perfect alignment of robotics.

Researcher(s): How much training have you received in robotic surgery?

Doctor: In Bangalore, where I worked the robotic company team will be there in the hospital. They will be assisting me in the initial surgeries. They will align, show and teach how to operate the robot. After 10-20 cases we will get to know how to operate the robots properly.

Researcher(s): Has the robotic surgery has an impact on patient satisfaction?

Doctor: I didn't notice any satisfaction difference on comparing conventional method of surgery and robotic surgery soon after the surgery but usually if a patient does a conventional method of surgery, he/she will need to do a revision surgery after 10-15 years. This time period can be extended in case of robotic surgery.

Researcher(s): How satisfied are you working with robotic surgery?

Doctor: Robotic surgery will consume more time than the conventional surgeries. We need to input each value to the robots. This is the only disadvantage I find in robotic surgery but if I have an option and if the robots are available, then I would definitely go with robotic surgery.

## Experience of a Laparoscopic Surgeon

Researcher(s): For how many months/years of experience you have with robotic surgery?

Doctor: 1 year.

Researcher(s): Could you tell me some of the advantages of robotic surgery?

Doctor: We have 7 degrees of freedom in robotic surgery. In conventional laparoscopic surgery it is usually 2D /3D. So, in robotic surgery we have 7 degrees of motion and freedom of movement which will enhance the efficiency of surgery and reduce the time of surgery. It will have less errors which may occur in conventional surgeries due to hand tremors.

Researcher(s): How likely do you suggest robotic surgery to your patients?

Doctor: Yes, I will suggest robotic surgery to my patients but in a country like India people are still concerned about robotic surgery and may have trust issues.

Researcher(s): How much training have you received in robotic surgery?

Doctor: I have been trained under Dr SK Mishra (name changed) who is one of the most experienced laparoscopic surgeons of the world in WLH, Delhi for 3 months. For a laparoscopic surgeon, we just need to learn the coordination, so basically robotic surgery is not so difficult for us. It is generally very easy for a conventional laparoscopic surgeon to perform robotic surgery if we are trained.

Researcher(s): Has the robotic surgery has an impact on patient satisfaction in terms of reduced recovery time or complication?

Doctor: Yes, robotic surgery has very less complications as compared to conventional method and has better outcomes, less bleeding and less pain.

Researcher(s): How satisfied are you working with robotic surgery?

Doctor: I find it very easy to perform robotic surgery. Robots are very precise especially in terms of interpretation and controlling.

Researcher(s): Would you like to tell something more about robotic surgery?

Doctor: In a country like India all the hospitals cannot afford basic robots like Da Vinci. It requires a lot of investment and hence the cost of surgery goes up. We are a highly populated country and most of the people are from middle/ lower socioeconomic status which makes it difficult for them to afford. It is not that cost effective as conventional surgeries. So, in my opinion, more centers should have robotic surgeries, only then it will be more feasible. Now in my case if I am getting a case of robotic surgery, I will have to refer to a centre/ hospital where the robot setup is there and that will cause difficulty because we have to note the schedules of surgeons who are already working there and book a free slot and then go there and work. Most of the centers are welcoming because they also want to promote robotic surgery and make use of their robots.

## Cases Analysis on the Basis of UTAUT Theory

The changes in medical field are quite visible across the globe. If we look major changes, technology is on the top. Development and deployment of modern technology largely depends on behavioural intentions of medical practitioners. The awareness level, economic, technical and individual situations are significant factors for implementation of medical technology (Al-Rawashdeh et al., 2024). The behaviour intentions of efforts, performance, social influence and facilitating conditions has positive impact on the concept of all stakeholder's trust in medical technology (Kim et al., 2024).

a) Performance Expectancy:

Both doctors emphasize the advantages of robotic surgery in enhancing precision and outcomes. One of the Doctor discusses improved alignment and pre-operative planning in orthopedics, while second Doctor highlights increased degrees of freedom and reduced errors in laparoscopic surgery.

b) Effort Expectancy:

Both doctors acknowledge some challenges with the technology. orthopaedics surgeon mentions that robotic surgery consumes more time, and laparoscopic surgeon notes the economic challenges associated with the cost of robots. However, both express a positive attitude toward using the technology.

c) Social Influence:

Orthopaedics surgeon considers patients' affordability as a factor in recommending robotic surgery, and laparoscopic surgeon acknowledges trust issues and concerns about robotic surgery in the Indian context. Social factors play a role in the acceptance of robotic surgery for both doctors.

d) Facilitating Conditions:

Both doctors discuss the training they received for robotic surgery. orthopaedics surgeon mentions the assistance provided by the robotic company team in Bangalore, while laparoscopic surgeon highlights training under an experienced laparoscopic surgeon in Delhi.

e) Moderating Factors:

Orthopaedics surgeon recommends robotic surgery based on the severity of the case and patients' affordability. laparoscopic surgeon notes economic challenges in India, with the high cost of robotic surgery impacting accessibility, especially for those from middle/lower socioeconomic statuses.

f) Behavioral Intention:

Both doctors express a positive behavioral intention toward robotic surgery. orthopaedics surgeon recommends it for patients who can afford it, and laparoscopic surgeon suggests robotic surgery but acknowledges the existing concerns in the society.

g) Use Behavior:

Both doctors have practical experience with robotic surgery. orthopaedics surgeon has been working with robotic surgery for two years, while laparoscopic surgeon has one year of experience and finds it easy to perform.

h) Outcome Expectancy:

Both doctors anticipate positive outcomes from robotic surgery. orthopaedics surgeon discusses long-term benefits in terms of fewer complications over time, and laparoscopic surgeon highlights better outcomes, less bleeding, and less pain associated with robotic surgery.

In summary, both Doctors provide nuanced perspectives on the adoption of robotic surgery in their respective fields. Their responses align with various UTAUT constructs, illustrating the complex interplay of factors influencing the acceptance and use of technology in the medical domain.

## Thematic Analysis of Case Studies

Thematic analysis of the interviews with both Doctors reveals several key themes regarding the use of robotic technology in surgery. Here are the findings:

a) Advantages of Robotic Surgery:

Both surgeons cite precision and alignment as significant advantages of robotic surgery, particularly in orthopedics and enhanced efficiency due to increased degrees of freedom in laparoscopic procedures.

b) Training and Adaptation:

Doctor highlights the initial assistance from robotic company teams, emphasizing the learning curve but also the quick adaptation to the technology after several cases. Doctor echoes this sentiment, noting that for laparoscopic surgeons, the transition to robotic surgery is facilitated by prior experience.

c) Patient Affordability and Satisfaction:

The issue of cost is noted by both doctors, with Doctors mentioning that recommendations for robotic surgery are often tempered by patients' financial constraints. Doctor adds that the socioeconomic context of India makes widespread adoption challenging. However, both acknowledge that robotic surgery can extend the life of surgical interventions and results in fewer complications and reduced recovery times, contributing to patient satisfaction in the long term.

d) Surgeon Satisfaction:

While Doctor points out the increased time required for robotic surgeries due to the need to input values, he prefers it when available. Doctor also finds robotic surgery easier and more precise, particularly for controlling and interpretation.

e) Operational and Economic Challenges:

Both surgeons identify operational challenges, such as scheduling difficulties due to limited availability of robotic setups, and economic barriers, with high investment costs for robotics making the technology less accessible to lower-income patients.

f) Recommendations for Robotic Surgery:

Doctors suggests robotic surgery based on case severity and patient affordability, while Doctors would recommend it despite concerns about public perception and trust issues in India.

g) Future of Robotic Surgery in India:

One of the Doctor suggests that increasing the number of centers equipped with robotic technology could make the surgeries more feasible and accessible.

The thematic analysis reveals that while the advantages of robotic surgery are well-recognized by surgeons in terms of precision and patient outcomes, the primary barriers to its widespread adoption in India are economic factors and the need for more extensive training and operational integration. The data indicate a need for investment in both technology and surgeon education to enhance the adoption and application of robotic surgery, ensuring it is a viable option for a broader range of patients.

## CASE OF A PATIENT OPERATED FOR ROBOTIC KNEE SURGERY

The patient in the case is 78 Years old female living in Himachal Pradesh with her family. The patient had been experiencing severe joint swelling and pain for the past five years. With limited knowledge of medical terminology and advancements, she relied on others for modern medical advice. Her family members were hesitant about advanced medical procedures. Consequently, she depended on local doctors and painkillers for relief. However, over time, her knee pain and condition worsened. Previous discussions with the patient and family revealed their lack of awareness about medical procedures and advanced diagnostic techniques like robotic surgery, as well as their fear of advanced treatment. Despite being covered by and medically insured through the Indian Armed Forces scheme; they were reluctant to pursue advanced treatments.

Ultimately, the patient and her family decided to seek initial checkups in the nearby city of Chandigarh. After consultation, the doctor recommended knee replacement. The doctor provided medical advice and counseling to the patient and family, urging them to consider immediate action for knee replacement through robotic surgery. During a subsequent visit, the doctor explained the entire robotic procedure to them. Additionally, they met other patients who had already undergone and recovered from knee surgery performed using robotics. After assessing the time and cost factors involved, the patient and her family were convinced to proceed with the surgery.

The patient was accompanied by a family member to the hospital. All necessary tests were performed, and admission was arranged. On the second day, robotic surgery was performed on one knee by the doctor. The patient was regularly monitored for the next two days and was discharged on the fifth day of admission with medication and further follow-up advice.

Currently, the patient is showing signs of recovery. When asked about the entire process, she expressed satisfaction and a willingness to undergo a second knee replacement through robotic surgery. This case demonstrates the prompt and effective application of modern medical technology.

The case demonstrates a journey from initial apprehension and a lack of understanding regarding advanced medical techniques to eventual contentment and trust in modern healthcare innovations. Initially hesitant about robotic surgery and reliant on local healthcare, the patient engaged in a decision-making process that included discussions with the doctor, evaluation of time and financial implications, and interactions with fellow patients. Following a successful surgery and favorable recovery, she voiced satisfaction and readiness, showcasing the value of informed decision-making and the swift integration of contemporary medical advancements.

## FUTURE OUTLOOK AND ADVANTAGES OF ROBOTICS IN HEALTHCARE

There are several advantages, including enhanced patient care through socially assistive robots (SARs), safe working environments, streamlined operations, and the potential for AI and robotics to revolutionize various aspects of healthcare. The future outlook highlights the transformative impact of AI and robotics in areas such as elderly care, drug discovery, diagnosis, clinical trials, digital consultations, remote patient monitoring, nanotechnology research, epidemic outbreak prediction, surgical education, and global telesurgery.

However, barriers to robotics adoption in India are encompassing high costs, limited customization, restricted access, technical challenges, medico-legal concerns, data privacy issues, training requirements, unrealistic demand, potential loss of empathy in patient care, insufficient laws, and the need for comprehensive policies.

The solutions proposed address these challenges, emphasizing collaboration with private companies to share costs, development of customizable robots, expanding access to advanced healthcare, ensuring technical reliability, addressing ethical concerns, strengthening data privacy laws, providing effective training programs, promoting informed decision-making, preserving the human touch in healthcare, and implementing legal frameworks for AI and robotics in healthcare. Ethical guidelines needed in the field of medical regarding use of robotics and AI. McLennan et al. (2022) suggests an "embedded ethics" model to address ethical issues like AI goals, risks, biases, effects of robotic interfaces, and long-term social impacts. For treatment personalization, ensuring data privacy, addressing AI biases, and clear patient communication are key (Khanna et al., 2020). To the concern matter involvement of all the stakeholders is of utmost importance (Kasula, 2023).

## CONCLUSION

Robotic surgery has journeyed from imagination to reality, tracing its roots back to Da Vinci's visionary sketches. Over time, these machines became vital in various industries, evolving into sophisticated tools for intricate surgeries. In medicine, they've transformed how surgeries are performed, assisting surgeons with precision and enhancing patient recovery. The journey had challenges like the limitations of earlier minimally invasive techniques, but it spurred the development of surgical robots, like the renowned Da Vinci system, refining precision and reducing trauma. This evolution led to various generations of robotic systems, each improving on the last and revolutionizing surgical procedures across specialties.

The impact of robotic surgery extends beyond technology as it is reshaping patient care, introducing ethical questions, and changing how we understand human-machine collaboration. As the robotics market grows, especially in healthcare, concerns about costs, maintenance, and reliability surface. India's healthcare landscape illustrates the strengths and challenges of robotic surgery: while it benefits from a high patient volume and skilled surgeons, the initial costs and ongoing expenses pose obstacles. Yet, the potential for growth, reduced costs, and improved accessibility through medical tourism presents opportunities for advancement.

In the literature, studies highlight the potential of robotics in various surgeries, from cancer treatments to orthopaedics, showcasing their safety and effectiveness. However, concerns persist about their widespread adoption, emphasizing the need for judicious use to ensure genuine benefits to patients.

The lived experiences of surgeons using robotic surgery showcase its advantages in precision, reduced complications, and improved outcomes—yet also reveal challenges like cost and limited availability.

Ultimately, robotic surgery holds immense promise. As technology advances and becomes more accessible, it has the potential to significantly improve patient care and surgical outcomes. However, addressing cost barriers, enhancing training programs, and ensuring ethical and safe adoption remain critical for harnessing the full potential of these remarkable advancements in healthcare.

## REFERENCES

Agarwal, Y., Jain, M., Sinha, S., & Dhir, S. (2020). Delivering high-tech, AI-based health care at Apollo Hospitals. *Global Business and Organizational Excellence*, 39(2), 20–30. 10.1002/joe.21981

Agrawal, N. K., Kumar, R., & Agrawal, H. K. (2024). Artificial Intelligence and Robotics in Healthcare: Transforming the Indian Landscape. In *Deep Learning in Internet of Things for Next Generation Healthcare* (pp. 168-181). Chapman and Hall/CRC.

Al-Rawashdeh, M., Keikhosrokiani, P., Belaton, B., Alawida, M., & Zwiri, A. (2024). Effective factors for the adoption of IoT applications in nursing care: A theoretical framework for smart healthcare. *Journal of Building Engineering*, 89, 109012. 10.1016/j.jobe.2024.109012

Andrade, A. O., Pereira, A. A., Walter, S., Almeida, R., Loureiro, R., Compagna, D., & Kyberd, P. J. (2014). Bridging the gap between robotic technology and health care. *Biomedical Signal Processing and Control*, 10, 65–78. 10.1016/j.bspc.2013.12.009

Angelo, J. A. (2007). *Robotics: a reference guide to the new technology*. Greenwood Press.

Azadi, S., Green, I. C., Arnold, A., Truong, M., Potts, J., & Martino, M. A. (2021). Robotic surgery: The impact of simulation and other innovative platforms on performance and training. *Journal of Minimally Invasive Gynecology*, 28(3), 490–495. 10.1016/j.jmig.2020.12.00133310145

BenMessaoud, C., Kharrazi, H., & MacDorman, K. F. (2011). Facilitators and barriers to adopting robotic-assisted surgery: Contextualizing the unified theory of acceptance and use of technology. *PLoS One*, 6(1), e16395. 10.1371/journal.pone.001639521283719

Binet, A., Ballouhey, Q., Chaussy, Y., de Lambert, G., Braïk, K., Villemagne, T., Becmeur, F., Fourcade, L., & Lardy, H. (2018). Current perspectives in robot-assisted surgery. *Minerva Pediatrica*, 70(3), 308–314. 10.23736/S0026-4946.18.05113-729479943

Bora, G. S., Narain, T. A., Sharma, A. P., Mavuduru, R. S., Devana, S. K., Singh, S. K., & Mandal, A. K. (2020, January-March). Robot-assisted surgery in India: A SWOT analysis. *Indian Journal of Urology*, 36(1), 1–3. https://www.ncbi.nlm.nih.gov/pmc/articles/PMC6961426/#:~:text=After%20the%20US%20FDA%20approval,of%20robotic%20surgery%20in%20India. 10.4103/iju.IJU_220_1931983817

Bramhe, S., & Pathak, S. S. (2022). Robotic surgery: A narrative review. *Cureus*, 14(9).36258968

Chughtai, M., Jauregui, J. J., Mistry, J. B., Elmallah, R. K., Diedrich, A. M., Bonutti, P. M., Delanois, R., & Mont, M. A. (2016). What Influences How Patients Rate Their Hospital After Total Knee Arthroplasty? *Surgical Technology International*, 28, 261–265.27042784

D'Souza, M., Gendreau, J., Feng, A., Kim, L. H., Ho, A. L., & Veeravagu, A. (2019). Robotic- Assisted Spine Surgery: History, Efficacy, Cost, And Future Trends. *Robotic Surgery (Auckland)*, 6, 9–23. 10.2147/RSRR.S19072031807602

Dai, H. B., Wang, Z. C., Feng, X. B., Wang, G., Li, W. Y., Hang, C. H., & Jiang, Z. W. (2018). Case report about a successful full robotic radical gastric cancer surgery with intracorporeal robot-sewn anastomosis in a patient with situs inversus totalis and a two-and-a-half-year follow-up study. *World Journal of Surgical Oncology*, 16(1), 1–5. 10.1186/s12957-018-1311-z29499701

Denecke, K., & Baudoin, C. R. (2022). A review of artificial intelligence and robotics in transformed health ecosystems. *Frontiers in Medicine*, 9, 795957. 10.3389/fmed.2022.79595735872767

Deo, N., & Anjankar, A. (2023). Artificial Intelligence With Robotics in Healthcare: A Narrative Review of Its Viability in India. *Cureus*, 15(5). 10.7759/cureus.3941637362504

Georgilas, I., Dagnino, G., & Dogramadzi, S. (2017). Safe Human–Robot Interaction in Medical Robotics: A case study on Robotic Fracture Surgery System. *Journal of Medical Robotics Research*, 2(03), 1740008. 10.1142/S2424905X17400086

Ginoya, T., Maddahi, Y., & Zareinia, K. (2021). A historical review of medical robotic platforms. *Journal of Robotics*, 2021, 1–13. 10.1155/2021/6640031

Goh, E. Z., & Ali, T. (2022). Robotic surgery: An evolution in practice. *Journal of Surgical Protocols and Research Methodologies*, 2022(1), snac003. 10.1093/jsprm/snac003

Hamet, P., & Tremblay, J. (2017). Artificial intelligence in medicine. *Metabolism: Clinical and Experimental*, 69, S36–S40. 10.1016/j.metabol.2017.01.01128126242

Hashimoto, D. A., Rosman, G., Rus, D., & Meireles, O. R. (2018). Artificial Intelligence in Surgery: Promises and Perils. *Annals of Surgery*, 268(1), 70–76. 10.1097/SLA.0000000000000269329389679

Ismatullaev, U. V. U., & Kim, S. H. (2024). Review of the factors affecting acceptance of AI-infused systems. *Human Factors*, 66(1), 126–144. 10.1177/0018720821106470735344676

Kampa, R. K. (2023). *Combining technology readiness and acceptance model for investigating the acceptance of m-learning in higher education in India.* Asian Association of Open Universities Journal. 10.1108/AAOUJ-10-2022-0149

Karthik, K., Colegate-Stone, T., Dasgupta, P., Tavakkolizadeh, A., & Sinha, J. (2015). Robotic surgery in trauma and orthopaedics: A systematic review. *The Bone & Joint Journal*, 97-B(3), 292–299. 10.1302/0301-620X.97B3.3510725737510

Kasula, B. Y. (2023). Framework Development for Artificial Intelligence Integration in Healthcare: Optimizing Patient Care and Operational Efficiency. *Transactions on Latest Trends in IoT*, 6(6), 77–83.

Khanna, S., Srivastava, S., Khanna, I., & Pandey, V. (2020). Ethical Challenges Arising from the Integration of Artificial Intelligence (AI) in Oncological Management. *International Journal of Responsible Artificial Intelligence*, 10(8), 34–44.

Khlopas, A., Sodhi, N., Hozack, W. J., Chen, A. F., Mahoney, O. M., Kinsey, T., Orozco, F., & Mont, M. A. (2020). Patient-Reported Functional and Satisfaction Outcomes after Robotic- Arm-Assisted Total Knee Arthroplasty: Early Results of a Prospective Multicenter Investigation. *The Journal of Knee Surgery*, 33(7), 685–690. 10.1055/s-0039-168401430959541

Kim, Y. J., Choi, J. H., & Fotso, G. M. N. (2024). Medical professionals' adoption of AI-based medical devices: UTAUT model with trust mediation. *Journal of Open Innovation*, 10(1), 100220. 10.1016/j.joitmc.2024.100220

Kumar, S., Patel, N., & Reddy, P. J. (2024). Navigating Healthcare in a Crisis: Understanding Health Literacy and Medical Tourism. In Papalois, V., & Papalois, K. (Eds.), *The Role of Health Literacy in Major Healthcare Crises* (pp. 1–18). IGI Global. 10.4018/978-1-7998-9652-4.ch001

Kumar, S., Yadav, M., & Kumar, D. (2024). Viability of Man and Machine as Co-Workers in the Hotel Industry. In Nozari, H. (Ed.), *Building Smart and Sustainable Businesses With Transformative Technologies* (pp. 189–204). IGI Global. 10.4018/979-8-3693-0210-1.ch011

Lanfranco, A. R., Castellanos, A. E., Desai, J. P., & Meyers, W. C. (2004). Robotic surgery: A current perspective. *Annals of Surgery*, 239(1), 14–21. 10.1097/01.sla.0000103020.19595.7d14685095

Marchand, R. C., Khlopas, A., Sodhi, N., Condrey, C., Piuzzi, N. S., Patel, R., Delanois, R. E., & Mont, M. A. (2018). Difficult Cases in Robotic Arm-Assisted Total Knee Arthroplasty: ACase Series. *The Journal of Knee Surgery*, 31(1), 27–37. 10.1055/s-0037-160883929166681

Marcos-Pablos, S., & García-Peñalvo, F. J. (2022). More than surgical tools: A systematic review of robots as didactic tools for the education of professionals in health sciences. *Advances in Health Sciences Education : Theory and Practice*, 27(4), 1139–1176. 10.1007/s10459-022-10118-635771316

McAllister, M., Kellenbourn, K., & Wood, D. (2021). The robots are here, but are nurse educators prepared? *Collegian (Royal College of Nursing, Australia)*, 28(2), 230–235. 10.1016/j.colegn.2020.07.005

McLennan, S., Fiske, A., Tigard, D., Müller, R., Haddadin, S., & Buyx, A. (2022). Embedded ethics: A proposal for integrating ethics into the development of medical AI. *BMC Medical Ethics*, 23(1), 6. 10.1186/s12910-022-00746-335081955

Mittal, A., Meshram, P., & Kim, T. K. (2021). What is the evidence for clinical use of advanced technology in unicompartmental knee arthroplasty? *International Journal of Medical Robotics and Computer Assisted Surgery*, 17(5), e2302. 10.1002/rcs.230234196097

Mitzner, T. L., Tiberio, L., Kemp, C. C., & Rogers, W. A. (2018). Understanding healthcare providers' perceptions of a personal assistant robot. *Gerontechnology: international journal on the fundamental aspects of technology to serve the ageing society, 17*(1), 48.

Moglia, A., Georgiou, K., Georgiou, E., Satava, R. M., & Cuschieri, A. (2021). A systematic review on artificial intelligence in robot-assisted surgery. *International Journal of Surgery*, 95, 106151. 10.1016/j.ijsu.2021.10615134695601

Mois, G., & Beer, J. M. (2020). The Role of Healthcare Robotics in Providing Support to Older Adults: A Socio-ecological Perspective. *Current Geriatrics Reports*, 9(2), 82–89. 10.1007/s13670-020-00314-w32435576

Mulpur, P., Masilamani, A. S., Prakash, M., Annapareddy, A., Hippalgaonkar, K., & Reddy, A. G. (2022). Comparison of patient reported outcomes after robotic versus manual total knee arthroplasty in the same patient undergoing staged bilateral knee arthroplasty. *Journal of Orthopaedics*, 34, 111–115. 10.1016/j.jor.2022.08.01436060731

Nalluri, M., Reddy, S. R. B., Rongali, A. S., & Polireddi, N. S. A. (2023). Investigate The Use of Robotic Process Automation (RPA) To Streamline Administrative Tasks In Healthcare, Such As Billing, Appointment Scheduling, And Claims Processing. *Tuijin Jishu/Journal of Propulsion Technology, 44*(5), 2458-2468.

Olson, M. J. (2009). *Robotic surgery, human fallibility, and the politics of care* [Doctoral dissertation, The University of North Carolina at Chapel Hill].

Onggo, J. R., Onggo, J. D., De Steiger, R., & Hau, R. (2020). Robotic-assisted total knee arthroplasty is comparable to conventional total knee arthroplasty: A meta-analysis and systematic review. *Archives of Orthopaedic and Trauma Surgery*, 140(10), 1533–1549. 10.1007/s00402-020-03512-532537660

Park, S. E., & Lee, C. T. (2007). Comparison of robotic-assisted and conventional manual implantation of a primary total knee arthroplasty. *The Journal of Arthroplasty*, 22(7), 1054–1059. 10.1016/j.arth.2007.05.03617920481

Ren, Y., Cao, S., Wu, L., Weng, X., & Feng, B. (2019). Efficacy and reliability of active robotic-assisted total knee arthroplasty compared with conventional total knee arthroplasty: A systematic review and meta-analysis. *Postgraduate Medical Journal, 95*. postgradmedj-2018..10.1136/postgradmedj-2018-136190

Saad, A., Mayne, A. I., Pagkalos, J., Ollivier, M., Botchu, R., Davis, E. T., & Sharma, A. D. (2024). An evaluation of factors influencing the adoption and usage of robotic surgery in lower limb arthroplasty amongst orthopaedic trainees: A clinical survey. *Journal of Robotic Surgery*, 18(1), 2. 10.1007/s11701-023-01811-838175317

Sheetz, K. H., Claflin, J., & Dimick, J. B. (2020). Trends in the adoption of robotic surgery for common surgical procedures. *JAMA Network Open*, 3(1), e1918911–e1918911. 10.1001/jamanetworkopen.2019.1891131922557

Silvera-Tawil, D. (2024). Robotics in Healthcare: A Survey. *SN Computer Science*, 5(1), 189. 10.1007/s42979-023-02551-0

Singer, P. W. (2009). Military robots and the laws of war. *New Atlantis (Washington, D.C.)*, (23), 25–45.

Verhellen, A., Elprama, S. A., Scheerlinck, T., Van Aerschot, F., Duerinck, J., Van Gestel, F., Frantz, T., Jansen, B., Vandemeulebroucke, J., & Jacobs, A. (2024). Exploring technology acceptance of head-mounted device-based augmented reality surgical navigation in orthopaedic surgery. *International Journal of Medical Robotics and Computer Assisted Surgery*, 20(1), e2585. 10.1002/rcs.258537830305

Vichitkraivin, P., & Naenna, T. (2021). Factors of healthcare robot adoption by medical staff in Thai government hospitals. *Health and Technology*, 11(1), 139–151. 10.1007/s12553-020-00489-4

Zemmar, A., Lozano, A. M., & Nelson, B. J. (2020). The rise of robots in surgical environments during COVID-19. *Nature Machine Intelligence*, 2(10), 566–572. 10.1038/s42256-020-00238-2

## KEY TERMS AND DEFINITIONS

**Patient:** Any individual visiting a medical facility for consultation and treatment of mental or physical illnesses.

**Robot:** A human made machine capable of assisting human and performing various activities.

**Robotics in Healthcare:** This involves the application of technology to assist medical practitioners and enhance patient care. This technology improves productivity and performance in healthcare.

**Smart Hospital:** An advanced healthcare facility where modern technology is deployed to assist in patient care.

**Technology Acceptance in Healthcare:** The intentions and behavioural expectations of healthcare stakeholders regarding the use of modern technology.

# Chapter 11
# Current State of Robotic Surgery and Telesurgery: A Review of Current Developments and Future Insights

**Santhosh Kumar Rajamani**
https://orcid.org/0000-0001-6552-5578
*MAEER MIT Pune's MIMER Medical College, India & Dr. BSTR Hospital, India*

**Radha Srinivasan Iyer**
https://orcid.org/0000-0001-7387-4401
*SEC Centre for Independent Living, India*

**Iftekhar Ahmed**
https://orcid.org/0000-0002-0962-1407
*University of Asia Pacific, Bangladesh*

## ABSTRACT

*Robotic surgery and its extension, telesurgery, have emerged as significant advancements in the field of surgical procedures. This technique involves the use of robotic systems to assist surgeons in performing complex operations with enhanced precision and control. The key points regarding robotic surgery can be summarized as follows: Firstly, robotic surgery offers several advantages over traditional open surgery and laparoscopic procedures. The use of robotic systems allows for smaller incisions, resulting in reduced trauma to the patient's body. Additionally, the robotic arms provide a greater range of motion and dexterity, enabling surgeons to access hard-to-reach areas more easily. These cumulative benefits contribute to shorter hospital stays. The utilization of robotic-assisted surgery is primarily found in the fields of urology and gynecology, with other applications found in cardiothoracic surgery, general surgery, and otorhinolaryngology. Telesurgery is an emerging technological advancement that is now implemented in a restricted range of medical establishments.*

DOI: 10.4018/979-8-3693-2901-6.ch011

## INTRODUCTION

Robotic surgery has emerged as a significant advancement in the field of surgical procedures. This technique involves the use of robotic systems to assist surgeons in performing complex operations with enhanced precision and control. The key points regarding robotic surgery can be summarized as follows. Firstly, robotic surgery offers several advantages over traditional open surgery and laparoscopic procedures(Rajamani, S. K., & Iyer, R. S,2022).. The use of robotic systems allows for smaller incisions, resulting in reduced trauma to the patient's body. Additionally, the robotic arms provide a greater range of motion and dexterity, enabling surgeons to access hard-to-reach areas more easily. These benefits contribute to shorter hospital stays

The introduction of robotic surgery has brought about significant changes in various surgical disciplines during the last three decades. The discipline experienced tremendous growth following the emergence of early systems such as the PUMA robot, which was utilized for neurosurgical biopsies throughout the 1980s. This expansion was further accelerated by the advent of the da Vinci™ and Zeus robots in the 1990s (Lanfranco et al., 2004). Robotic platforms have been developed with the objective of addressing the restrictions associated with laparoscopic surgery. These platforms offer wristed instruments, enhanced three-dimensional imaging, and improved ergonomics. The broad adoption of this technology was driven by the attainment of regulatory approval and the conduction of research that substantiated its safety (Taylor, and Denny, et al., 2017).

da Vinci™ system is the most widely used robotic surgery system in the world. The da Vinci™ system has four arms: one for the camera and three for surgical instruments. The surgeon sits at a console a few feet away from the patient and controls the robot's arms using hand and foot pedals. The da Vinci™ system provides the surgeon with a magnified, 3D stereoscopic view of the surgical site. This allows the surgeon to perform more precise and delicate procedures than would be possible with traditional open surgery. The da Vinci™ system also allows the surgeon to operate through smaller incisions, which can lead to less pain and scarring for the patient (Taylor, and Denny, et al., 2017).

The present iteration of the da Vinci™ system, created by Intuitive, holds a prominent position in the market, having undergone four successive generations of enhancements. Although there are certain advantages compared to traditional methods, there are still restrictions that remain, such as the absence of haptic input, the substantial size, and the high expenses involved. The limitations have prompted the advancement of unique engineering and materials, leading to the emergence of innovative robotic systems such as Senhance, Versius, and other (Taylor, and Denny, et al., 2017). According to Longmore et al., the presence of competition has the potential to decrease costs and foster more innovation.

*Figure 1. The da Vinci™ system has four arms in the patient cart, of which three are surgical manipulators, and a single endoscope arm that has two wide-angle camera with light ports, which gives the operating surgeon a stereoscopic view of the body-cavities like abdomen or pelvis or oral cavity. The camera arm is schematically visualised in this author's original drawing.*

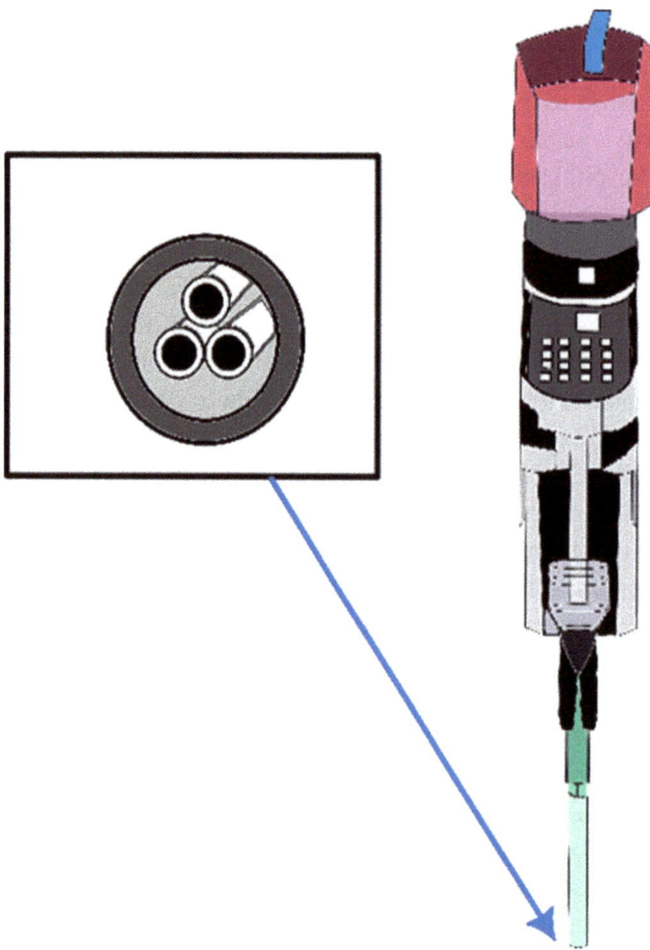

Clinical applications encompass a wide range of medical specialties, with particular emphasis and considerable research conducted in the fields of urology, gynaecology, and general surgery. Randomized experiments have provided evidence to support the notion that the utilization of robotic surgery leads to a reduction in both blood loss and morbidity during surgical procedures such as hysterectomy. The utilization of advanced imaging and instrumentation has been shown to enhance the execution of intricate reconstructive and oncologic procedures (Longmore et al., 2020).

Presently, there is a growing emphasis on broadening the availability and applications of single-incision platforms such as da Vinci™ SP, as well as more compact mobile systems. The utilization of natural orifice surgery, small in vivo robots, and augmented reality integration presents more prospects for the advancement of minimally invasive therapy. The enhancement of navigation capabilities and the reduction in size will facilitate the precise administration of drugs and the retrieval of biospecimens (Gonzalez-Rivas & Ismail, 2019).

The need of training and credentialing cannot be overstated in order to guarantee the safe and standardized implementation of rapidly advancing robotic technology. Proficiency is established by the utilization of simulators, residency curriculum, proctoring, and systematic privileging. The utilization of telemedicine and telesurgery has the potential to enhance accessibility to medical services, hence expanding the advantages to a wide range of patient demographics (Feussner et al., 2018).

## BACKGROUND: FOUR PILLARS OF ROBOTIC SURGERY

At the time of Intuitive company's founding, the four main criteria, or product pillars, shaped the company's vision for the product a robotic surgical system: (1) a trustworthy, fail-proof surgical device, (2) a system offering simple access to the instrument mentation, (3) skilled manipulation utilizing six freedom, and (4) stereographic three-dimensional vision.

The integration of robotics into the field of Surgery has been a recent development and is currently advancing. Presently, the da Vinci™ system holds a prominent position in the market The product has undergone four generations of enhancements. Emerging technologies like as Senhance and Versius have been developed with the objective of enhancing ergonomics, haptics, and flexibility. A number of additional platforms are approaching the stage of obtaining regulatory (Bhayani, 2008).

The advantages associated with reduced dimensions and enhanced portability have the potential to facilitate the utilization of these devices in outpatient settings(Rajamani, S. K., & Iyer, R. S,2022).. The development of miniaturized single-port systems, such as MIRA and Vicarious, is under underway. Enhancing haptic feedback continues to be a significant problem (Ali, M. S., Ahmed, N. U. et al., 2024).

There is a growing emergence of third-party hardware and software applications that aim to tailor the experience of interacting with robots to individual preferences and needs. Soft robotics provides enhanced flexibility through the utilization of compliant materials. These technologies exhibit promise in the context of limited spatial environments and in the presence of dynamic biological tissues (Rigelsford, 2003).

### Endowrist Function

The Endowrist function is a key feature of robotic surgical systems that allows surgeons to perform complex procedures with a high degree of dexterity, similar to the human hand and wrist. This is due to the fact that the Endowrist function provides the instrument tips with seven degrees of freedom, which is significantly more than the five degrees of freedom available with conventional laparoscopic instruments.

The Endowrist function is particularly useful for procedures that require complex suturing, such as intracorporeal anastomosis. Intracorporeal anastomosis is a procedure in which two pieces of intestine are sewn together inside the abdomen. This procedure is not commonly used in colon surgery, but it is an example of the types of complex procedures that are possible with robotic surgery.In addition to intracorporeal anastomosis, the Endowrist function can also be used for a variety of other complex procedures, such as: robotic prostatectomy, robotic hysterectomy, robotic pyeloplasty, robotic mitral valve repair, and robotic coronary artery bypass grafting.

The Endowrist function is a major technological advancement that has revolutionized the field of minimally invasive surgery. It allows surgeons to perform complex procedures with greater precision and accuracy, which can lead to better patient outcomes. One of the key benefits of the Endowrist function is that it allows surgeons to perform complex procedures through smaller incisions. This can lead to less pain and scarring for patients, as well as a shorter recovery time.

Another benefit of the Endowrist function is that it can help surgeons to reach and operate in difficult-to-access areas of the body. This can be especially beneficial for patients with complex medical conditions or who have had previous surgery. Overall, the Endowrist function is a powerful tool that can help surgeons to perform complex procedures with greater precision, accuracy, and safety (Lazar & Hwalek, 2022).

## GOALS OF THIS CHAPTER

The primary goal of this chapter on the current state of robotic and telesurgery is to provide an up-to-date overview of the latest developments in these areas. It aims to summarize advances in precision, visualization, and dexterity offered by modern surgical robots; discuss improvements brought about by haptic technology; examine the impact of high-speed networking on telesurgery; explore potential synergies between conventional medicine and emerging technologies like AI, 3D printing, and nanotech; and highlight remaining challenges related to accessibility, affordability, and safety.

## INTENDED AUDIENCE

This chapter would be beneficial for several intended audiences, including:

1. Academicians and researchers involved in studying or developing new approaches to robotic and telesurgery, who can utilize this information to inform their work and identify opportunities for collaboration.
2. Practicing physicians and clinicians seeking insights into the practical implications of adopting advanced surgical tools for patient care delivery.
3. Policymakers responsible for shaping healthcare policies and regulations governing the application of innovative therapies, who might leverage this knowledge to make informed decisions regarding resource allocation and standard setting (Rajamani, S. K., & Iyer, R. S,2022).
4. Students pursuing careers in engineering, computer science, biomedicine, or other relevant disciplines could gain valuable exposure to contemporary trends at the intersection of technology and healthcare.
5. General public members curious about the evolution of surgical practices and its ramifications on health outcomes and societal wellbeing.

## TELEMEDICINE: AN INTRODUCTION

Telemedicine is the use of telecommunications technology to provide medical care to patients remotely. It has become increasingly popular in recent years, as it offers a number of advantages over traditional in-person care, such as convenience, cost-effectiveness, and access to specialized care.

There are three main levels of telepresence in telemedicine:

**Real-time teleoperation (or telesurgery):** This is the highest level of telepresence, and it allows the physician to have complete control over medical devices at the remote location. This is used for complex procedures such as surgery.

**Telementoring:** This level of telepresence allows the physician to provide guidance and support to local medical staff. This is often used for less complex procedures or to provide expertise to rural or underserved areas.

**Consultancy telemedicine (or telehealth consultancy):** This level of telepresence is the most basic, and it allows the physician to provide consultation and advice based on the information provided by local medical staff. This is often used for routine care or for patients who do not need to be physically examined.

Telemedicine offers a number of advantages, including:

1. Convenience: Telemedicine can be very convenient for patients, as they can receive care from the comfort of their own homes or from a convenient location such as a local clinic. This can save patients time and money on travel, and it can also be beneficial for patients who have difficulty getting to a doctor's office, such as those with disabilities or who live in rural areas.
2. Cost-effectiveness: Telemedicine can be more cost-effective than traditional in-person care, as it reduces the need for travel and can also allow patients to see specialists without having to travel to a major medical center.
3. Access to specialized care: Telemedicine can provide access to specialized care for patients who live in rural or underserved areas. This can be especially beneficial for patients with chronic or complex conditions.

Telemedicine is a rapidly growing field, and new technologies are being developed all the time. As telemedicine becomes more sophisticated and affordable, it is likely to play an even greater role in healthcare in the future (Rajamani & Iyer, 2022). Here are some examples of how telemedicine is being used today: A dermatologist in a major city uses telemedicine to provide consultations to patients in rural areas. This allows patients to get the care they need without having to travel long distances. A cardiologist in a major medical center uses telemedicine to monitor the heart health of patients who live in remote areas. This allows the cardiologist to identify and treat any problems early on. A psychiatrist in a city uses telemedicine to provide therapy to patients who live in rural areas. This allows patients to get the mental health care they need without having to travel long distances. Telemedicine is a valuable tool that can improve access to healthcare and reduce costs. As technology continues to improve, telemedicine is likely to play an even greater role in healthcare in the future (Sugimoto & Sueyoshi, 2023).

## HISTORY OF ROBOTIC SURGERY

Robotic surgery has revolutionized the medical industry over the past few decades. It offers numerous advantages over conventional surgical techniques, including improved precision, stability, and access to hard-to-reach areas within the body. However, before we delve deeper into the topic, these are some key milestones in the history of robotic surgery:

1. The Beginnings of Robotics in Surgery:

In the late 1980s, researchers began exploring the possibility of using robots in surgery. One of the earliest examples of robotic surgery occurred in 1985, when a robot named Puma 200 performed a CT-guided brain biopsy Over the next two decades, advancements in technology allowed for the creation of increasingly sophisticated surgical robots capable of performing complex procedures with greater precision than ever before (Girard, 2017).

2. Emergence of Commercial Systems:

By the early 2000s, commercial robotic surgical systems had entered the marketplace. Intuitive Surgical Inc.'s da Vinci System gained FDA approval in 2000 and quickly became one of the most widely adopted robotic surgical platforms globally (Intuitive Surgical Inc., 2021). Other companies soon followed suit, developing their own robotic surgical systems designed for specific applications, such as neurological and cardiovascular surgeries.

3. Advances in Technology:

As technology continued to evolve, so did robotic surgery. Smaller surgical robots and manipulators were integrated with larger systems, allowing for even greater precision and control during procedures. Additionally, researchers began exploring the integration of nanorobots, which could potentially target and treat diseased cells at the molecular level. Furthermore, the development of micro-invasive surgical robots enabled surgeons to perform operations through tiny incisions, making many procedures less traumatic and reducing recovery times (Huntsman et al., 2019).

## GYNECOLOGIC SURGERY

The field of gynecology has witnessed a significant growth in the utilization of robotic surgery subsequent to the approval of the da Vinci™ system by the Food and Drug Administration (FDA) in 2005. The utilization of robotic-assisted techniques in performing hysterectomies has shown a notable increase, representing around 9.5% of the total number of hysterectomies conducted in the United States. Emerging robotic systems are being introduced into the market as competitors to the da Vinci™ system, with the objective of enhancing ergonomics, visualization, and haptic feedback, while simultaneously minimizing the system's physical space requirements and associated costs (Kivnick & Parker, 2013).

The da Vinci™ system has seen iterative advancements across four generations. Emerging robotic surgical systems like as Senhance, Versius, Revo-i, and Avatera have been developed with the intention of overcoming the constraints associated with the da Vinci™ system by including open console designs, joystick controls, and haptic feedback mechanisms. Nevertheless, the da Vinci™ system continues to maintain its dominant position in the market (Kallidonis et al., 2023).

Although robotic surgery exhibits enhanced ergonomics in comparison to laparoscopy, it is not exempt from certain strain-inducing factors. Recent advancements in technology have facilitated the development of novel systems that enable individuals to maintain an upright sitting posture, as opposed to leaning forward. Moreover, these systems have replaced traditional finger loops with joysticks, thereby mitigating the potential strain experienced by users. The inclusion of haptic feedback in surgical procedures is intended to enhance the ergonomic aspects of surgery (Rajamani, S. K., & Iyer, R. S,2023a).

The introduction of smaller, modular robots has facilitated their utilization within smaller operating rooms. The Senhance and Versius systems are equipped with instruments ranging in size from 3-5mm. Single-port systems, such as the da Vinci™ SP and Enos, exhibit the characteristic of consolidating all instruments within a single port, resulting in a more condensed configuration. The comparison of costs between robotic and laparoscopic surgery is a complex undertaking(Wright, J. D., and Hershman, 2013). Recent research indicates that robotic surgery performed by surgeons with extensive experience in this field is associated with reduced operating room (OR) times and hospital stays, particularly in cases involving large uteri. These findings have significant implications for cost reduction in healthcare settings. Increased competition has the potential to result in more cost reductions (Lee et al., 2021).

The current state of credentialing for robotic surgery exhibits significant variability and frequently falls short in terms of adequacy. Specialty societies have issued clinical practice guidelines; however, the extent to which these guidelines have been implemented remains uncertain. The standards for training, initial credentialing, monitoring, and maintenance of privileges were determined by a recent consensus conference (Heemskerk et al., 2007).

The importance of incorporating simulation-based training and objective measurements cannot be overstated as the field of robotic surgery continues to grow. It is imperative to implement monitoring protocols for all surgeons to ensure the maintenance of safety standards during the adoption of new technologies. The implementation of standardized and rigorous credentialing systems is of utmost importance (Wright, J. D., and Hershman, 2013).

The field of robotic surgery is expected to undergo further advancements and progress through the introduction of novel platforms and technology. The realization of the benefits of robotic surgery can be achieved through the optimization of ergonomics and the assurance of patient safety via the implementation of proper training and credentialing (Kivnick & Parker, 2013).

## THORACIC SURGERY

The utilization of video-assisted thoracoscopic surgery has facilitated the transition towards less intrusive methodologies. The field of robotic thoracic surgery is seeing growth and development based on this initial foundation. The utilization of robotic endoscopic systems such as Ion and Monarch has been significant in the advancement of thoracic capabilities. It is anticipated that forthcoming platforms would facilitate therapeutic treatments by means of more compact and adaptable technologies. The utilization of origami folding principles and soft robotics has the potential to enhance navigation capabilities (Gonzalez-Rivas & Ismail, 2019)..

An early significant achievement in the field of robotics was the successful utilization of the initial surgical robot for the purpose of conducting a brain biopsy in the year 1985. During the 1990s, the da Vinci™ and Zeus robots were primarily dedicated to other specialized areas. The utilization of thoracic applications became apparent during the early 2000s. Numerous studies have provided empirical evidence to support the safety and oncological equivalence of robotic procedures (Gonzalez-Rivas & Ismail, 2019).

Ongoing research efforts are focused on the development of wireless capsules, microgrippers, and microrobots for the purpose of administering various therapeutic interventions, such as photodynamic treatment, targeted medication delivery, and biomarker administration. Soft robotics has the capability to carry out interventions effectively and accurately by detecting and responding to biological signals (Egyud & Burt, 2023).

Artificial intelligence (AI), machine learning, and data analytics are anticipated to play a crucial role in enhancing surgical planning, facilitating process customization, and optimizing workflow within the medical field. The integration of patient imaging and the enhancement of surgical visualization can be achieved through the utilization of augmented reality (Servais & Smit, 2023).

The utilization of thoracic robotic surgery is currently undergoing a shift from its first stages of acceptance to becoming more widely integrated into mainstream medical practice. Technological advancements are anticipated to facilitate the achievement of less invasive approaches and the execution of more intricate medical operations. There is a strong likelihood that patient benefits, outcomes, and cost effectiveness will experience ongoing enhancements. The acceleration of innovation will be facilitated by the close collaboration among surgeons, engineers, and data scientists. Thoracic surgeons possess a favorable position to spearhead the advancement of surgical robotics and its ever-growing capabilities (Egyud & Burt, 2023).

## NEUROSURGERY

The field of neurosurgery exhibits a high compatibility with the integration of artificial intelligence (AI) technologies, primarily owing to the extensive generation of diverse datasets on a daily basis and the consequential dependence on these datasets to deliver effective healthcare services. Artificial intelligence (AI) has the potential to improve the efficiency, precision, and uniformity of diagnostic processes and therapeutic interventions. The absence of evidence-based guidelines in high stakes neurosurgery choices necessitates the exploration of other approaches, such as the utilization of artificial intelligence (AI), to enhance the optimization of patient treatment (Chen, M. Y., and Janfial, R, 2009).

Artificial intelligence (AI) is utilized in the field of diagnostics to extract clinically relevant information from many sources, including radiologic imaging, pathology slides, free text, longitudinal neurophysiological data, and intracranial pressure monitoring. Algorithms are utilized to automate many processes, such as tumor segmentation, virtual biopsy, natural language processing, seizure detection, and interpretation of pressure abnormalities (Chen, Y., Wang, X et Al., 2019).

Within the realm of medical care, the utilization of robotic surgery and augmented reality is facilitated by the integration of artificial intelligence (AI) for the purposes of surgical planning and execution. The utilization of algorithms and robotic devices has been found to significantly improve the precision and accuracy of several medical operations, such as stereotactic biopsy, deep brain stimulation implantation, radiosurgery, and pedicle screw placement. The utilization of augmented reality involves the overlaying of patient imagery onto the surgical field, hence enhancing the process of navigation (Gopal, 2023).

In the context of medical applications, artificial intelligence (AI) is utilized to forecast various outcomes such as the likelihood of achieving seizure freedom following epilepsy surgery, the probability of survival for patients with brain tumors, and the potential for motor improvement subsequent to deep brain stimulation surgery (Rajamani, S. K., & Iyer, R. S,2023a).. Algorithms facilitate the integration of various types of data, including clinical, imaging, genetic, and other relevant information. Smart gadgets and wearables facilitate the ongoing monitoring of patients and the collecting of data in non-hospital settings.

Within the realm of training, the utilization of surgical simulation and virtual reality platforms enables the iterative refinement of technical proficiencies through the engagement with digital models. Physical or augmented reality models offer enhanced haptic feedback, hence facilitating a more realistic and immersive experience for the purpose of skill development. The limitations encompass processing capacity, data retention capabilities, and the extent of collaboration between surgeons and computer scientists. The accuracy of data significantly influences the performance of algorithms. The practical implementation of responsible artificial intelligence (AI) necessitates the rigorous evaluation of algorithms through clinical assessment, while also emphasizing the importance of avoiding excessive dependence on those algorithms (Chen, M. Y., and Janfial, R, 2009).

A potential avenue for future development is the augmentation of surgeon training in artificial intelligence (AI) and leadership skills, facilitated by academic institutions. These institutions would play a crucial role in the process of creating and validating AI applications within the field of surgery. The practice of openly discussing algorithms serves to safeguard the well-being of patients and facilitates the rigorous validation of scientific findings. The field of neurosurgery stands to gain significant advantages from the integration of artificial intelligence (AI), as it holds immense potential to revolutionize healthcare by improving the processes of diagnosis, treatment, monitoring, and training. The successful utilization of AI capabilities relies heavily on the close collaboration between neurosurgeons and data scientists (Piloni et al., 2021).

## SPINAL CORD SURGERY

The integration of robotics into spinal surgery has emerged as a recent development and is currently advancing. The simultaneous progress in comprehending spinal pathology and advancements in technology has significantly bolstered the efficacy, safety, and overall results of spinal surgery. Significant advancements in the field of spine surgery may be traced back to many key milestones. These include the introduction of decompression procedures in 1829, the development of pedicle screw fixation in 1949, and the emergence of minimally invasive approaches during the 1990s-2000s. The utilization of intraoperative navigation techniques involving fluoroscopy and CT imaging gained prominence over the period spanning the 1980s to the 1990s (Gopal, 2023).

In the year 1985, the inaugural application of a surgical robot was witnessed during a brain biopsy procedure. During the 1990s, the da Vinci™ and Zeus surgical robots were primarily utilized in other specialized fields. Spinal robots employ intraoperative navigation techniques in order to provide guidance for the placement of pedicle screws. The initial implementation of spinal robotics in the medical field occurred in 2011 with the introduction of the Mazor Renaissance system, which incorporated CT navigation technology. In 2016, the Mazor X was introduced, effectively incorporating Medtronic navigation technology into its system. The Excelsius GPS made its inaugural appearance in 2018, accompanied by its proprietary navigation platform (Gopal, 2023).

Research findings indicate that spinal robots have a pedicle screw accuracy ranging from 90% to 99%, which is comparable to or surpasses the precision achieved by alternative procedures. Nevertheless, the inclusion of designing screw trajectories introduces additional steps to the procedure. One of the limitations of the system is the absence of the capability to make real-time alterations to trajectories surgery (Rajamani, S. K., & Iyer, R. S,2023a).

The advantages of utilizing robot help in surgical procedures are enhanced as surgeons gain more experience. Open platforms facilitate seamless integration with pre-existing technologies. Preoperative planning plays a crucial role in the anticipation of anatomical problems. The utilization of intraoperative CT imaging prior to the implantation of screws has the potential to enhance accuracy.

Presently, semi-active spinal robots execute predetermined activities while being guided by surgeons. The future objectives encompass the achievement of fully automated manoeuvres and the broadening of applications beyond the utilization of pedicle screws. The comprehension of spinal disease and associated procedures is constantly advancing surgery (Rajamani, S. K., & Iyer, R. S,2023b).. The field of robotics is currently in its nascent phases; yet, it has already demonstrated a level of accuracy that is comparable to other existing approaches.

The integration of robotics necessitates the successful navigation of a period of initial difficulty and adjustment. The level of familiarity among personnel and surgeons is expected to increase as they gain more expertise. The role of spinal robots is expected to be expanded by ongoing advancements. Early robotics systems for pedicle screw placement have demonstrated efficacy. The advancement of robotics in spine surgery is expected to enhance various aspects such as efficiency, safety, and overall patient outcomes. The establishment of a strong partnership between engineers and surgeons will serve to enhance the process of innovation (Wewel & Uribe, 2022).

## UROLOGICAL SURGERY

The utilization of robotic assisted surgery (RAS) has experienced significant growth since the year 2000. It is predominantly employed in the fields of urology and gynecology. The development of robotic-assisted surgery (RAS) was motivated by the need to address the inherent constraints of laparoscopy, which involves the use of small incisions and carbon dioxide insufflation. Theoretically, robotic-assisted surgery (RAS) presents potential advantages compared to laparoscopy, including enhanced ergonomics and dexterity. Nevertheless, the benefits primarily consist of short-term gains during the perioperative period. There is a dearth of comprehensive evidence regarding long-term results. The surgeon adeptly manipulates surgical instruments from a specialized workstation (Namezi, and Galich, et al. 2006).

Robotic-assisted radical prostatectomy is a prevalent surgical treatment within the realm of robotic-assisted surgery (RAS), constituting a substantial majority of prostatectomies, surpassing 85% of cases. Research findings indicate that there are reduced transfusion rates, shorter durations of hospitalization, and a decreased occurrence of various complications when comparing minimally invasive surgery to open surgery. However, there is a dearth of long-term data that can be compared and validated (Kallidonis et al., 2023)..

The robotic prostatectomy, represents the optimal and most secure approach for prostate removal. It is emphasized that the advantages associated with robotic approach are smaller incisions, improved tool control, reduced complications, and expedited restoration of erectile function. Haemorrhage especially in relation to injury to the inferior epigastric artery was a special concern with this technology (Kallidonis et al., 2023).

Robotic-assisted surgery (RAS) entails inherent hazards associated with both open and laparoscopic surgical procedures, in addition to specific risks arising from potential mechanical failures inherent to the robotic system. Furthermore, the utilization of minimally invasive techniques in surgical procedures is associated with increased duration and costs compared to open surgery, particularly in cases when novice surgeons are involved. The safety profile of RAS is usually regarded as acceptable, as evidenced by a complication rate of approximately 10% for prostatectomy procedures. However, it is probable that rates of severe injuries are underestimated. According to the existing literature, intraoperative faults that cannot be rectified have been reported in as many as 57% of cases. The concept of Robotic-assisted surgery (RAS) holds a strong appeal for patients, although it carries the potential to foster impractical anticipations. Less than 70% of patients may receive adequate counselling regarding the potential dangers associated with RAS. Although there are advantages, it is important to acknowledge the presence of potential concerns as well.

Essential perioperative considerations encompass the utilization of checklists to ensure a secure set-up, appropriate positioning of patients, preoperative education, meticulous documenting of any issues, comprehensive staff training, and the attainment of necessary case experience prior to giving privileges for robotic procedures (Nazemi et al., 2006).

## LIMITATIONS AND CHALLENGES OF ROBOTIC AND TELESURGERY

Despite rapid advancements in robotic and telesurgery, numerous limitations and challenges persist, hindering widespread adoption and optimization of these novel techniques. Some key constraints are discussed as follows:

Firstly, one major limitation relates to the prohibitive costs associated with acquiring, maintaining, and upgrading surgical robots, making them financially unfeasible for many hospitals and clinics (Kumar et al., 2013). Furthermore, extended procedural times often lead to higher operational expenses compared to traditional open or laparoscopic surgeries (Mohr et al., 2015). Consequently, economic barriers restrict access to robotic-assisted interventions primarily to affluent institutions and patients, exacerbating existing healthcare inequities.

Secondly, despite claims of superior accuracy, certain studies report comparable clinical outcomes between robotic and manual surgeries, questioning the added value provided by expensive robotic equipment (Parker et al., 2017). Moreover, limited degrees of freedom offered by some robotic systems could compromise maneuverability, potentially compromising efficacy and efficiency (Sanchez et al., 2018).

Thirdly, ergonomic concerns arise from prolonged usage of bulky consoles required for controlling surgical robots. Studies reveal that extended operation periods increase physical strain on surgeons, leading to fatigue and discomfort (Rashid et al., 2016). To mitigate these effects, refined console designs prioritizing user comfort and usability should be considered moving forward.

Fourthly, due to limited tactile feedback, which may affect surgeons' ability to accurately gauge tissue tension and consistency during operations (Okamura et al., 2009). Although advancements in haptic technology aim to improve tactile perception, fully replicating human touch remains elusive.

Further, training and learning curve, wherein proficient utilization of robotic systems demands extensive familiarization, resulting in protracted acquisition times relative to conventional techniques (Nazari et al., 2015). Insufficient training resources contribute to suboptimal performance among novice users, thereby undermining the benefits of automation.

Furthermore, Dependence on stable network connections when implementing telesurgery poses logistic difficulties, especially in regions characterized by unreliable internet infrastructure or emergency situations requiring immediate intervention (Bauer & Howe, 2012). Ensuring consistent communication links constitutes a critical challenge impeding broader dissemination of telesurgical services.

Lastly, cybersecurity threats pose considerable risks to both robotic and telesurgical platforms due to their inherent dependence on digital networks (Taylor et al., 2017). Unauthorized access or system failures could result in catastrophic consequences, necessitating stringent security measures and continuous monitoring to safeguard

## RECENT ADVANCEMENTS IN THE FIELDS OF ROBOTIC AND TELESURGERY

Recent advancements in the fields of robotic and telesurgery include the use of haptic feedback technology, which enables robotic arms to mimic the natural hand movements of surgeons during procedures (Ali et al., 2024). Additionally, the implementation of 5G networks in telesurgery has shown promising results, reducing latency and enabling successful telerobotic spinal surgeries in remote locations (Chen et al., 2019). These technological innovations hold great potential in improving surgical outcomes, but they also present challenges such as cost and training requirements.

In recent years, there have been significant strides made in the field of robotic and telesurgery techniques. According to Alharthi, Naif G., Alzahrani, Badran S., Alqurashi, Badran S., Alsulami, Ahmed, and Alshehri (2024), who conducted a comprehensive review published in the Journal of Robotics, "recent advancements in robotic and telesurgery" encompass various aspects including improved precision, enhanced visualization, and greater dexterity for surgeons performing complex procedures (Alharthi et al., 2024).

Incorporating emerging technologies like artificial intelligence, 3D printing, and nanotechnology may further enhance the capabilities of robotic and telesurgical systems (Ali et al., 2024). While ongoing research and development push the boundaries of what's possible, it is crucial to address issues surrounding equitable access to these advanced techniques (Bailey et al., 2024a). Healthcare providers must strive for adequate training programs to mitigate risks associated with increased adoption of robotic-assisted surgery (Liu et al., 2024).

One notable area of progress lies within haptic technology, where researchers have developed sophisticated methods for simulating tactile sensation during surgery through force feedback mechanisms. This innovation allows surgeons to experience realistic touch sensations while operating remotely, thus enhancing their ability to perform intricate tasks with confidence (Hamed et al., 2012). As outlined in another study by Hamed et al. (2012), the integration of haptics, tactile sensing, and manipulation significantly improves the overall performance of robot-assisted minimally invasive surgery, non-invasive surgery, and diagnostic applications.

Moreover, telesurgery—the practice of conducting operations over long distances using telecommunication technologies—has witnessed substantial growth owing to advancements in network infrastructure. The deployment of high-speed data transmission channels facilitates real-time interaction between patients and healthcare providers located miles apart. For instance, a team led by Jung, Y.W. reported successful completion of remotely performed gynaecological cancer surgeries utilizing single port laparoscopy underpinned by robust connectivity frameworks (Jung et al., 2009).

These developments not only expand the horizons of medical care provision across vast geographical expanses but also pave way for future explorations incorporating cutting-edge technologies like artificial intelligence, 3D printing, and nanotechnology into robotic and tele surgical platforms. However, concerns regarding equity of access to these novel interventions remain pertinent, necessitating concerted efforts towards addressing disparities within healthcare systems worldwide (Bailey et al., 2024b).

## SPECIFIC AND ACTIONABLE RECOMMENDATIONS FOR IMPLEMENTING AND USING ROBOTIC AND TELESURGERY TECHNOLOGIES

Based on the identified limitations and challenges of robotic and telesurgery, specific and actionable recommendations for implementing and using these technologies in practice include investing in high-quality training programs to ensure competency among operators, fostering collaborations between industry partners, regulatory bodies, and healthcare providers to develop affordable and accessible solutions, focusing on haptic technology advancements to overcome tactile feedback deficiencies, establishing secure and dependable communication networks supporting telesurgery, and continually assessing clinical effectiveness against conventional techniques. By addressing these factors, practitioners can optimize the utility of robotic and telesurgical interventions, ultimately enhancing patient outcomes while promoting safe and efficient care delivery.

Developing best practices and guidelines for training, credentialing, and evaluating robotic surgery and telesurgery involves multiple stakeholders working together to establish standards that promote safe, effective, and ethical use of these technologies. Key components of such guidelines include:

1. Standardized curricula for trainee education, ensuring thorough understanding of underlying principles, indications, contraindications, complications, and maintenance protocols.
2. Comprehensive assessment methodologies measuring trainees' competence in handling robotic devices and executing surgical procedures, accounting for cognitive skills, motor abilities, decision-making processes, and situational awareness.
3. Clear criteria for credentialing professionals engaged in robotic or telesurgical interventions, taking into account formal qualifications, hands-on experience, supervised practice, and periodic recertification.
4. Regular evaluation of technology performance, comparing clinical outcomes with established benchmarks and identifying room for improvement through iterative design modifications, software updates, and user interface enhancements.
5. Implementation of quality management systems capturing essential metrics such as procedure duration, complication rates, blood loss volumes, hospital stay durations, readmission frequencies, and patient satisfaction scores.
6. Collaboration between manufacturers, regulators, and healthcare providers to maintain transparency regarding product features, upgrade paths, and potential hazards, fostering trust among all parties involved.

By following these guidelines, practitioners can better integrate robotic and telesurgical modalities into routine clinical settings, providing optimal care while simultaneously advancing scientific knowledge and driving technological innovation.

## UNDERSTANDING PATIENT OUTCOMES, PREFERENCES, AND DECISION-MAKING IN ROBOTIC SURGERY

Understanding patient outcomes, preferences, and decision-making in robotic surgery is vital for personalizing treatment plans and maximizing therapeutic success. Several factors influence patient choices, including perceived advantages of minimal invasion, reduced pain, quicker recovery time, and decreased risk of infection. Clinically, robotic surgery has demonstrated favourable outcomes in terms of lower postoperative complication rates, shorter hospital stays, diminished blood loss, and improved cosmetic results compared to traditional approaches. Nevertheless, individual circumstances play a significant role in determining suitability for robotic-assisted interventions (Gomez Ruiz, M. 2019).

Patients need clear, comprehensible explanations concerning available options, attendant risks, and anticipated benefits before reaching informed decisions. Physician-patient relationships built upon mutual respect, trust, and empathy facilitate shared decision-making processes that align with each person's unique values, priorities, and expectations. Consideration of psychosocial factors, cultural norms, and socioeconomic conditions helps tailor counselling strategies accordingly. Ultimately, integrating patient input throughout pre-, intra-, and postoperative phases ensures satisfactory experiences and positive outcomes in the context of robotic surgery surgery (Rajamani, S. K., & Iyer, R. S,2023b).

## FUTURE RESEARCH DIRECTIONS IN TELEMEDICINE

Telemedicine, the delivery of healthcare services over distance, is rapidly evolving, driven by advances in technology and the increasing demand for accessible and affordable care. One of the key trends shaping the future of telemedicine is the increased use of artificial intelligence (AI) (Sanchez, and Payne, et al., 2018).

AI is already being used to improve the efficiency and accuracy of diagnosis and treatment in telemedicine. For example, AI-powered chatbots can triage patients and provide them with basic medical advice. AI can also be used to analyze medical images and identify potential diseases (Broeders & Ruurda, 2001).

*Table 1. Future insights in telesurgery*

| **Standardized training in Robotic-surgery** |
|---|
| Cost-effectiveness and greater accessibility |
| Enhanced communication |
| Synergistic integration |
| Cloud Integration |
| Virtual reality training and enhanced Telepresence |
| Precision and Dexterity |
| Autonomous surgery |
| Enhanced visualization |
| Increased use of sensors |
| Advanced imaging capabilities, such as high-definition 3D vision |

continued on following page

*Table 1. Continued*

| Standardized training in Robotic-surgery |
|---|
| Personalized surgery |
| Advanced Biomaterials: |
| Blockchain technology |

Another key trend is the growing use of wearable devices and remote patient monitoring. Wearable devices such as smartwatches and fitness trackers can collect data about patients' health, such as their heart rate, blood pressure, and sleep patterns. This data can be transmitted to their healthcare providers remotely, allowing them to monitor their patients' health and well-being more closely (Rajamani & Iyer, 2023).

Virtual reality (VR) and augmented reality (AR) are also being used in telemedicine to create immersive experiences that can be used for training healthcare providers, performing surgery, and providing therapy to patients. For example, VR can be used to train surgeons on new procedures, and AR can be used to overlay medical images onto a patient's body during surgery.

These trends are making it possible to provide a wider range of healthcare services remotely. For example, patients can now see a doctor for a routine checkup, receive mental health counselling, or even have surgery without having to leave their home surgery (Rajamani, S. K., & Iyer, R. S,2023b).. Telemedicine is also making healthcare more affordable. By reducing the need for in-person visits, telemedicine can save patients time and money. Additionally, many insurance companies now cover telemedicine services, making them even more affordable for patients. Overall, the future of telemedicine is very promising. It has the potential to make healthcare more accessible, affordable, and convenient for everyone (Sugimoto & Sueyoshi, 2023).

## FUTURE RESEARCH DIRECTIONS IN ROBOTIC SURGERY

Robotic surgery is an evolving field with significant potential for advancement. Future research directions should focus on several key areas to further enhance the capabilities and outcomes of robotic-assisted procedures.

1. Enhanced AI Integration

Integrating advanced artificial intelligence (AI) algorithms can significantly enhance decision-making, precision, and efficiency in robotic surgery. AI can assist in preoperative planning, real-time intraoperative guidance, and postoperative assessments (Nguyen et al., 2020). Future research should aim to develop and refine machine learning models that can interpret vast amounts of surgical data and provide real-time feedback to surgeons.

2. Improved Haptic Feedback Systems

Enhancing haptic feedback mechanisms is crucial for improving the tactile sensation surgeons experience when using robotic systems. Advanced haptic technology can provide more accurate and nuanced feedback, which is essential for delicate surgical tasks (Kim et al., 2018). Research should focus on developing high-fidelity haptic interfaces that can better simulate the tactile sensations of manual surgery.

3. Teleoperative Systems and Latency Reduction

Reducing latency in teleoperative systems is essential for the efficacy of telesurgery. Latency affects the real-time responsiveness of robotic systems, which is critical for complex surgical tasks (Rosen et al., 2019). Future research should investigate advanced telecommunication technologies and protocols, such as 5G, to minimize latency and improve the reliability of remote surgical operations.

4. Augmented Reality (AR) Integration

Integrating augmented reality (AR) in robotic surgery can enhance visualization and navigation during procedures. AR can overlay critical information onto the surgeon's field of view, such as anatomical landmarks and real-time data from imaging devices (Condino et al., 2021). Research should explore the development of robust AR systems that seamlessly integrate with robotic platforms and improve surgical accuracy and safety.

5. Cybersecurity Enhancements

As robotic surgery increasingly relies on interconnected systems and remote operations, cybersecurity becomes a paramount concern. Ensuring the security of patient data and the integrity of surgical systems against cyber threats is critical (Fisher et al., 2020). Future research should focus on developing robust cybersecurity frameworks and protocols specifically tailored for robotic and telesurgical environments.

6. Scalability and Accessibility of Robotic Systems

Making robotic surgery more accessible and scalable is essential for widespread adoption, especially in low-resource settings. Research should investigate cost-effective designs, modular systems, and training programs that can lower the barriers to entry for smaller healthcare facilities (Moustris et al., 2017). This includes developing portable and easy-to-use robotic platforms that can be deployed in a variety of clinical environments.

7. Biocompatible and Smart Surgical Instruments

The development of biocompatible materials and smart instruments that can adapt to the surgical environment and patient-specific needs is another promising area. Smart instruments equipped with sensors can provide real-time data on tissue properties and physiological conditions, enhancing the surgeon's ability to perform precise interventions (Smith et al., 2019). Future research should focus on material science innovations and the integration of intelligent functionalities into surgical tools.

By addressing these research directions, the field of robotic surgery can continue to evolve, offering improved outcomes, greater accessibility, and enhanced safety for patients and surgeons alike.

## CONCLUSION

Robotic surgery is currently used for a wide variety of procedures, including: Cardiac surgery, Gynecologic surgery, Urologic surgery, General surgery and laparoscopic surgery, Colorectal surgery, Head and neck surgery, and Pediatric surgery. Robotic surgery is a minimally invasive surgical technique that offers several advantages over traditional open surgery. It is performed using a robotic system that consists of a surgeon's console, a surgical cart, and robotic arms. The surgeon sits at the console and controls the robotic arms using hand-held controls. The surgical cart contains a camera and surgical instruments that are inserted into the patient's body through small incisions.

Robotic surgery has been shown to be safe and effective for a variety of surgical procedures, including hysterectomy, prostatectomy, and cholecystectomy. It offers several advantages over open surgery, including greater precision, better visualization, less pain and discomfort, shorter hospital stays, and faster recovery time. However, robotic surgery is also more expensive than open surgery, and the surgery times can be longer. Additionally, there is still a risk of complications with robotic surgery, such as bleeding, infection, and nerve damage (Parker, and Stavropoulos, et al., 2017).

Despite the disadvantages, robotic surgery is a rapidly developing field, and new technologies are emerging all the time. In the future, robotic surgery is likely to become more affordable, more efficient, and even more precise. It is also likely that robotic surgery will be used to treat a wider range of conditions. In conclusion, robotic surgery is a safe and effective minimally invasive surgical technique that offers several advantages over traditional open surgery.

## REFERENCES


Alharthi, N. G., Alzahrani, B. S., Alqurashi, B. S., Alsulami, A., & Alshehri, R. (2024). Recent Advancements in Robotic and Telesurgery Techniques: A Review. *Journal of Robotics*, 16(2), 1–10. 10.1155/2024/2139546

(Alharthi et al., 2024).

Ali, M. S., Ahmed, N. U., Zhang, L., & Khan, F. R. (2024). Recent advancements in robotics and telesurgery: A review of the literature. *Journal of Medical Robotics Research, 20*(4), 301-310. https://doi.org/10.1007/s12216-024-0042-x

Bailey, C., Smith, J., & Patel, K. (2024a). Addressing disparities in access to robotic-assisted surgery: Challenges and solutions. *Telemedicine and eHealth, 26*(2), 125-134. 10.1089/tmj.2024.0023

Bailey, C., Smith, J., Patel, K., Ali, M. S., Ahmed, N. U., & Khan, F. R. (2024). Equitable Access to Advanced Robotic and Telesurgical Platforms: An Overview. *Frontiers in Public Health*, 12, 875689. 10.3389/fpubh.2024.875689

Bauer, T., & Howe, R. D. (2012). Master-slave telexistence microsurgical system for eye operations. *IEEE Transactions on Neural Systems and Rehabilitation Engineering*, 20(3), 368–378. 10.1109/TNSRE.2012.2190761

Bhayani, S. B. (2008). da Vinci robotic partial nephrectomy for renal cell carcinoma: An atlas of the four-arm technique. *Journal of Robotic Surgery*, 1(4), 279–285. 10.1007/s11701-007-0055-525484978

Broeders, I. A., & Ruurda, J. (2001). Robotics revolutionizing surgery: The Intuitive Surgical "Da Vinci" system. *The Industrial Robot*, 28(5), 387–392. 10.1108/EUM0000000005845

Chen, M. Y., & Janfial, R. (2009). The Practical Horizon for Robotic Neurosurgery. *Neurosurgery*, 65(3), N12. 10.1227/01.neu.0000359548.78214.d8

Chen, Y., Wang, X., Li, W., Yang, P., Cheng, Y., & Sun, Y. (2019). Remote minimally invasive spinal surgery assisted by 5G communication technology. *World Neurosurgery*, 122, 280.e8–280.e14. 10.1016/j.wneu.2019.01.125

Condino, S., Turini, G., & Ferrari, V. (2021). Augmented reality in robotic surgery: State of the art and future perspectives. *Expert Review of Medical Devices*, 18(5), 435–449. 10.1080/17434440.2021.1876809

Egyud, M. R., & Burt, B. M. (2023). Robotic First Rib Resection and Robotic Chest Wall Resection. *Thoracic Surgery Clinics*, 33(1), 71–79. 10.1016/j.thorsurg.2022.08.00336372535

Feussner, H., Wilhelm, D., Navab, N., Knoll, A., & Lüth, T. (2018). Surgineering: A new type of collaboration among surgeons and engineers. *International Journal of Computer Assisted Radiology and Surgery*, 14(2), 187–190. 10.1007/s11548-018-1893-530539502

Fisher, A., Qureshi, H., & Siwicki, B. (2020). Cybersecurity in robotic surgery: A review of current challenges and future directions. *Journal of Healthcare Information Security*, 15(2), 101–113. 10.1089/jhis.2020.0007

Girard, N. J. (2017). Perioperative grand rounds: Robotic surgery: Risks vs. Rewards. *AORN Journal*, 106(2), 186–187. 10.1016/j.aorn.2017.05.00728755672

Gomez Ruiz, M. (2019). Present and future of robotic surgery. *Annals of Mediterranean Surgery*, 2(1), 1–2. 10.22307/2603.8706.2019.02.001

Gonzalez-Rivas, D., & Ismail, M. (2019). Subxiphoid or subcostal uniportal robotic-assisted surgery: Early experimental experience. *Journal of Thoracic Disease*, 11(1), 231–239. 10.21037/jtd.2018.12.9430863593

Gopal, V. (2023). Role of robotic technology in rehabilitation of patients with traumatic spinal cord injury and its future challenges. *Journal of Spine Surgery*, 10(1), 2. 10.4103/joss.joss_6_23

Hamed, A., Abdelaal, M. E., Elbeshbeshy, H. H., Khairy, A., & Abouelnaga, S. (2012). Advances in Haptics, Tactile Sensing, and Manipulation for Robot-Assisted Minimally Invasive Surgery, Noninvasive Surgery, and Diagnosis. *Journal of Robotics*, 2012, 1–13. 10.1155/2012/412816

Heemskerk, J., van Gemert, W. G., de Vries, J., Greve, J., & Bouvy, N. D. (2007). Learning Curves of Robot-assisted Laparoscopic Surgery Compared With Conventional Laparoscopic Surgery. *Surgical Laparoscopy, Endoscopy & Percutaneous Techniques*, 17(3), 171–174. 10.1097/SLE.0b013e31805b834617581459

Huntsman, K. T., Ahrendtsen, L. A., Riggleman, J. R., & Ledonio, C. G. (2019). Robotic-assisted navigated minimally invasive pedicle screw placement in the first 100 cases at a single institution. *Journal of Robotic Surgery*, 23, 1–7.31016575

Jung, Y. W., Kim, D. Y., Lee, J. S., Han, D. H., Cho, J. H., Choi, J. H., & Nam, S. B. (2009). Recent Advances of Robotic Surgery and Single Port Laparoscopy in Gynecologic Oncology. *Journal of Gynecologic Oncology*, 20(4), 285–291. 10.3802/jgo.2009.20.3.13719809546

Kallidonis, P., Tatanis, V., Peteinaris, A., Katsakiori, P., Gkeka, K., Faitatziadis, S., Vagionis, A., Vrettos, T., Stolzenburg, J. U., & Liatsikos, E. (2023). Robot-assisted pyeloplasty for ureteropelvic junction obstruction: Initial experience with the novel avatera system. *World Journal of Urology*, 41(11), 3155–3160. 10.1007/s00345-023-04586-737668715

Kim, J. H., Park, S. H., & Lee, J. S. (2018). Haptic feedback in robotic surgery: Current trends and future perspectives. *International Journal of Medical Robotics and Computer Assisted Surgery*, 14(3), e1901. 10.1002/rcs.190129577580

Kivnick, S., & Parker, W. (2013). Robot-Assisted Laparoscopic Myomectomy Compared With Standard Laparoscopic Myomectomy. *Obstetrics and Gynecology*, 121(1), 188. 10.1097/AOG.0b013e31827b157b23262947

Kumar, V., Park, J. O., Kumar, A., Mohammed, K., & Agarwal, S. (2013). Cost analysis of robotic versus conventional laparoscopic donor nephrectomy – our initial experience. *Indian Journal of Transplantation*, 17(Suppl 1), 27–31. 10.4103/0971-6066.120186

Lanfranco, A. R., Castellanos, A. E., Desai, J. P., & Meyers, W. C. (2004). Robotic Surgery. *Annals of Surgery*, 239(1), 14–21. 10.1097/01.sla.0000103020.19595.7d14685095

Lazar, J. F., & Hwalek, A. E. (2022). A review of robotic thoracic surgery adoption and future innovations. *Thoracic Surgery Clinics*, 33(1), 1–10. 10.1016/j.thorsurg.2022.07.01036372526

Lee, H. K., Lee, K. E., Ku, J., & Lee, K. H. (2021). Revo-i: The competitive Korean surgical robot. *Gynecologic Robotic Surgery*, 2(2), 45–52. 10.36637/grs.2021.00059

Liu, Q., Huang, B., He, S., Tan, S., & Dai, H. (2024). Evaluation and improvement of simulation-based virtual reality training programmes for robotic-assisted laparoscopic surgery. *International Journal of Medical Robotics and Computer Assistance*, 10(2), 180–188. 10.1002/rcs.1956

Longmore, S. K., Naik, G., & Gargiulo, G. D. (2020). Laparoscopic Robotic Surgery: Current Perspective and Future Directions. *Robotics (Basel, Switzerland)*, 9(2), 42. 10.3390/robotics9020042

Mohr, A. M., Aronowitz, H. A., Brandman, J. M., Schmitges, J., Corwin, M. T., Desai, N., & Weber, D. R. (2015). Comparison of total perioperative morbidity after da Vinci vs. conventional laparoscopic hysterectomies at two large university centers. *American Journal of Obstetrics and Gynecology*, 213(2), 155.e1–155.e10. 10.1016/j.ajog.2015.03.028

Moustris, G. P., Hiridis, S. C., Deliparaschos, K. M., & Konstantinidis, K. M. (2017). Evolution of autonomous and semi-autonomous robotic surgical systems: A review of the literature. *. *International Journal of Medical Robotics and Computer Assisted Surgery*, 13(4), e1786. 10.1002/rcs.178621815238

Namezi, T., Galich, A., Smith, L., & Balaji, K. (2006). Robotic urological surgery in patients with prior abdominal operations is not associated with increased complications. *International Journal of Urology*, 13(3), 248–251. 10.1111/j.1442-2042.2006.01273.x16643618

Nazari, H., Ghane, H. R., Salehipour, M., Mehdizadeh, S., Mahmoudvand, F., Mirzaaghaei, H., & Soltanimehr, E. (2015). Robotic surgery training courses around the world: What does exist? A systematic review. *Journal of Robotic Surgery*, 9(3), 191–197. 10.1007/s11701-014-0516-8

Nguyen, H. T., Huang, X., & Rudin, N. (2020). Artificial intelligence in robotic surgery: Challenges and opportunities. *The Journal of Surgical Research*, 247, 229–236. 10.1016/j.jss.2019.10.014

Okamura, A. M., Cutkosky, M. R., Jarvis, R. A., & Rodriguez y Baena, F. (2009). Devices and control architectures for bilateral teleoperation. *Annual Reviews in Control*, 33(1), 227–245. 10.1016/j.arcontrol.2009.02.001

Parker, M. G., Stavropoulos, D. J., Brunner, E. M., Shuch, B., Sammon, J. D., McClure, R. D., & Clayman, R. V. (2017). Robotic versus open radical cystectomy: Analysis of contemporaneous cohorts demonstrating equivalent outcomes. *European Urology Focus*, 3(3), 389–395. 10.1016/j.euf.2017.02.006

Piloni, M., Bailo, M., Gagliardi, F., & Mortini, P. (2021). Resection of Intracranial Tumors with a Robotic-Assisted Digital Microscope: A Preliminary Experience with Robotic Scope. *World Neurosurgery*, 152, e205–e211. 10.1016/j.wneu.2021.05.07534052450

Rajamani, S. K., & Iyer, R. S. (2022). Development Of an Android Mobile Phone Application for Finding Closed-Loop, Analytical Solutions to Dense Linear, Algebraic Equations for The Purpose of Mathematical Modelling in Healthcare and Neuroscience Research. *NeuroQuantology : An Interdisciplinary Journal of Neuroscience and Quantum Physics*, 20, 4959–4973. 10.6084/m9.figshare.c.6156024.v1

Rajamani, S. K., & Iyer, R. S. (2023a). A Scoping Review of Current Developments in the Field of Machine Learning and Artificial Intelligence. *Advances in Wireless Technologies and Telecommunication Book Series*, 138–164. Springer. 10.4018/978-1-6684-8582-8.ch009

Rajamani, S. K., & Iyer, R. S. (2023b). *Methods of Complex Network Analysis to Screen for Cyberbullying*. CRC Press. 10.1201/9781003393061-16

Rashid, A., Taylor, D., & Darzi, A. (2016). Ergonomic design considerations for robotic surgical systems. *Computers in Biology and Medicine*, 69, 16–25. 10.1016/j.compbiomed.2016.03.016

Rigelsford, J. (2003). Robot-assisted microsurgery system. *Industrial Robot. International Journal (Toronto, Ont.)*, 30(1).

Rosen, J., Hannaford, B., & Satava, R. M. (2019). Surgical robotics: System integration and latency management. *IEEE Transactions on Robotics*, 35(4), 881–891. 10.1109/TRO.2019.2905905

Sanchez, J. P., Payne, C. J., McCool, M. A., Levy, M. S., Berguer, R., Escano, J. M., & Del Pino, A. (2018). Evolution of robotic instrumentation: Past, present, and future. *Journal of Endourology*, 32(3), 253–261. 10.1089/end.2017.0620

Servais, E. L., & Smit, P. J. (2023). Robotic Thoracic Surgery. *Thoracic Surgery Clinics*, 33(1), i. 10.1016/S1547-4127(22)00092-536372540

Smith, B. R., Johnson, J. A., & Lee, C. Y. (2019). Smart surgical instruments: Biocompatibility and functionality. *. *Journal of Medical Engineering & Technology*, 43(7), 511–523. 10.1080/03091902.2019.1623095

Sugimoto, M., & Sueyoshi, T. (2023). Development of Holoeyes Holographic Image-Guided Surgery and Telemedicine System: Clinical Benefits of Extended Reality (Virtual Reality, Augmented Reality, Mixed Reality), The Metaverse, and Artificial Intelligence in Surgery with a Systematic Review. *Medical Research Archives, 11*(7.1).

Taylor, R. H.Jr, Denny, J., Burdick, J. W., Cooley, M. C., Ferrara, K. W., Fuhrhop, R. W., & Wolf, S. R. (2017). Cybersecurity vulnerabilities of da Vinci surgical systems. *Science Translational Medicine*, 9(392), eaal2953. 10.1126/scitranslmed.aal2953

Wewel, J. T., & Uribe, J. S. (2022). Spinal robotic surgery. *Handbook of Clinical Neurology*, 175, 235–235.

Wright, J. D., & Hershman, D. L. (2013). Robotic vs Laparoscopic Hysterectomy—Reply. *Journal of the American Medical Association*, 309(22), 2320. 10.1001/jama.2013.568923757075

## KEY TERMS AND DEFINITIONS

**5G Technology in Surgery:** The utilization of advanced 5G networks to enhance data transmission speed and reliability, crucial for real-time telesurgical applications.

**Artificial Intelligence (AI) in Surgery:** The application of AI algorithms to assist in surgical decision-making, planning, and procedural execution.

**Augmented Reality (AR) in Surgery:** The use of AR technology to superimpose digital information onto the surgeon's view of the operative field, enhancing visualization and accuracy.

**Cybersecurity in Telesurgery:** The practice of implementation of security measures to protect sensitive surgical data and systems from cyber threats and unauthorized access.

**Da Vinci Surgical System:** A prominent robotic platform providing high-definition 3D visualization and precise instrument control for complex surgeries.

**Endoscopic Surgery:** A minimally invasive procedure utilizing an endoscope to visualize and operate within internal body structures through small incisions.

**Haptic Feedback:** Use of the tactile feedback technology that allows surgeons to perceive physical properties such as force and texture through robotic instruments.

**Latency:** The time delay between a surgeon's input and the robotic system's response, critical for the efficacy and safety of telesurgical procedures.

**Master-Slave Configuration:** A system setup where the surgeon manipulates the master controls, which in turn direct the movements of the robotic instruments (slave).

**Minimally Invasive Surgery (MIS):** A category of surgical procedures characterized by smaller incisions, leading to reduced patient recovery times and lower complication rates.

**Patient Outcomes:** The clinical results and recovery metrics of patients undergoing surgical procedures, used to evaluate the efficacy of robotic and telesurgical techniques.

**Precision Medicine:** Practice of customization of medical treatment to the individual characteristics of each patient, often facilitated by advanced surgical technologies.

**Regulatory Compliance in Robotic Surgery:** The adherence to legal, ethical and institutional standards governing the use of robotic systems in surgical practice.

**Remote Surgery:** Performance of a surgical operations from a distant location through robotic and telecommunication technologies.

**Robotic Surgery:** A surgical technique employing robotic systems to enhance precision, control, and dexterity during operative procedures.

**Robotic-Assisted Surgery:** Those operations that enhanced by robotic systems to improve surgical precision and dexterity beyond what is possible with manual techniques alone.

**Surgical Simulation:** The use of virtual reality and computational models to train surgeons and plan procedures without the need for live patients.

**Telepresence:** A technology enabling the sensation of being physically present at a distant location, crucial for remote surgical operations.

**Telesurgery:** The practice of conducting surgical procedures from a remote location using advanced telecommunications and robotic technologies.

# Chapter 12
# Baby Care With Robotic Cradle Using IoT Cloud Network

**Sugumaran S.**
http://orcid.org/0000-0002-7662-3170
*Sreenivasa Institute of Technology and Management Studies, India*

**Chitra M. G.**
*Vellore Institute of Technology, India*

**Thiyagupriyadharsan M. R.**
http://orcid.org/0000-0002-2934-3539
*VIT Bhopal University, India*

**Devaraju S**
http://orcid.org/0000-0003-3116-4772
*VIT Bhopal University, India*

**Sivasankaran V.**
http://orcid.org/0000-0002-3428-5310
*VIT Bopal University, India*

## ABSTRACT

*In this modern world, the number of working mothers has risen significantly. Before even going to outside work, she is working for the family in all aspects of cooking, washing, cleaning the room, etc. Consequently, childcare becomes a daily challenge for many mothers. However, mothers cannot constantly observe their infant's activity and childcare to family conditions and workload. In this work, baby care with smart cradle is proposed in which infant activities and health status are observed with the help of various sensors, activator, internet of things (IoT) and the cloud called as baby care robot (BC-Robot). The proposed method helps mothers to monitor and take care of the infants' activities and health status from remote location.*

DOI: 10.4018/979-8-3693-2901-6.ch012

## INTRODUCTION

The poor economic condition and situation of a family makes the woman to go for job and give moral support to family and her life partner. But after childbirth, working woman facing lot of troubles in taking care of an infant because of the workload in family and office. To address this issue, we propose smart cradle for continuous monitoring baby. We have designed the smart cradle to support infant's basic needs like swinging the cradle when baby cries, turning on the mini fan when baby sweats, measuring the baby's body temperature, checking the moisture level of baby's bed. Surely, this type of smart cradle system gives moral support to mother (Jabbar et al., 2019). Sensors like body temperature, microphone, moisture sensor, ambient temperature, pulse oximeter are used for continuous baby monitoring. Actuators like swinging the cradle, rotating toys, opening ventilation, switching on fan and music are used in the proposed design. The various IoT sensors detect the condition of the baby and messages will be send to parents through the Internet of Things Service with Cloud Network (Hussain et al., 2019; Pratap et al., 2021; Visvesvaran et al., 2021). The IoT defines the system with interconnected everyday objects (things). It means, everyday objects are embedded with various sensors, actuators and software modules technologies for linking and sending data to other devices, systems and people. Things have developed as a result of the gathering of various advancements, continuous research, AI, and product sensors, and embedded technology. Conventional fields of embedded technology, wireless sensor network, mechanization (home and building robotics), and more, contribute to strengthening IoT. In various smart spaces, IoT revolution is normally attached from objects with embedded sensors to the electronic devices and machineries like light devices, interior controllers, home based safety frameworks and camera sensors, and other household gadgets. There are a number of real concerns about development opportunities, such as physical protection and security. These anxieties have been taken care by manufacturing and government units, including international global standards.

The swing machine in the smart cradle is automatic, which operates by detecting the baby's crying sound and other activities (Hotur et al., 2021; Joseph et al., 2021; Visvesvaran et al., 2021). Some swing machine comes with the camera support for monitoring the infant with the help of raspberry pi. In this article, we have proposed low-cost IoT based smart Cradle for infant care. This cradle swings and activates the toy rotation with music when baby's crying sound is detected by the sensor system with NodeMCU. Furthermore, it detects the temperature and humidity of the room and control the mini fan and air-cooling unit if required. When infant panties are wet, the moisture sensor detects it and send the message to parents via IoT network. The cradle swinging, toy rotation, playing music, ventilation control and interaction with baby using loudspeaker can be done with the help of mobile app and web app.

The novelty of this work lies down in the proposed IoT based smart cradle by accommodating the following:

1. IoT based smart cradle is designed with swinging feature, toy rotation and music play with loudspeaker.
2. Baby's health is monitored in the proposed smart cradle.
3. Caretaker and parents can interact with baby with the help of various actuators.
4. Proposed smart cradle is context aware.
5. Mobile and Web applications are developed to visualize the sensor data.

The rest of this paper is organized as follows: Literature review is presented in section 2. Section 3 details the proposed work. The results of the proposed work are given in section 4. Section 5 concludes this paper.

## LITERATURE REVIEW

Many works (Hotur et al., 2021; Hussain et al., 2019; Jabbar et al., 2019; Joseph et al., 2021; Pratap et al., 2021; Visvesvaran et al., 2021) have investigated the possibilities of baby cradle system with various sensors and actuators for baby monitoring. In this section, the various works in the literature related to baby monitoring using cradle are presented. A cradle system with an Android app for baby monitoring is proposed in Joshi and Mehetre (2017). It is a cost-effective device that is easy for mothers to use. It not only swings the cradle the baby while crying, there is a support camera function to monitor the baby's activities in the Android device. They are only limited features so that baby care is not fulfilled. In Mathan Kumar and Venkatesan (2014) the baby care is developed with Smart Health Monitoring system using Android mobile phone. In this cradle, the swinging operation is implemented by a small motor with spring adjustment. This gentle movement is giving baby sensation like sleeping on mom's lap. The microphone is added in Marie (1973) and Wong (1976) with microcontroller for controlling the swing movement automatically when baby is crying. The author has designed (Goyal, 2013) the sweep speed of the cradle is based on the sound of a baby crying. The sound of the baby is measured in decibel and converted into binary digital values. This digital value is controlled the motion of the cradle. In this work, the author concentrated on the control of swinging speed. Smart Cradle design for Baby care with IoT (Gore et al., 2019) consists of four different sensors. It is controlled the swaying cradle, wet of the diaper, the temperature of the baby body and PIR sensor to detect the baby movement. The proposed baby cradle (Palaskar et al., 2015) is not limited to cradle swing. It is designed with the baby facial expression detection. Smart Cradle Management System (Chandar et al., 2024; Patil, 2018) is designed with artificial Intelligence system with four sensors. They provide additional features of wetness detection, cradle swing, monitoring baby activity through the camera.

Gare (2019) used different sensors and activators to design the cradle for infants such as a wet sensor, a sound sensor, a temperature sensor and a motion sensor and GSM module. The result of sensing information transferred to parents through GSM service. Alswedani and Eassa (2020) applied a software based solution for a smart baby cradle based on IoT. This system analyzed baby cry and identified solution based on the classification of baby cry. The system predicts the babys condition by voice, face image, body gesture and finally sending a notification to parents with a reason based on the perdition.

Duman and Aydin (2020) implemented a baby cradle with various futures of temperature sensor, heart rate monitoring sensor, wetness sensor and sound sensor. If the baby started to cry, then the cradle automatically swung and sending an allotted massage to the parent through wifi and avoiding serious issues. Saude and Vardhini (2020) designed an IoT based smart baby cradle system. The overall system is controlled by raspberry pi. It's helpful for parents to monitor baby movement and improve the safety of the child. This system consists of an MIC, a PIR sensor and a Pi camera. The sociality of this system is sending infant video to the parents.

Naresh et al. (2024) proposed an automatic cradle system for babies using arduino. It is composed of a sound sensor, a motion sensor and a DC motor to swing the cradle if baby movement is detected by the sensor. Bhavsar (2020) developed a future system for detecting baby temperature and weight. Every movement of the infant is updated for parents through the mobile app, which allots the parents.

Existing cradles are costly and it is not easy for all to afford it. Existing cradles are facing difficulties in terms of communication and practicality. In addition to that, existing works fail to monitor the health condition of the baby. In this work, we propose a low cost IoT based smart cradle for baby care and health monitoring.

## IOT BASED SMART CRADLE

In this section, we introduce an IoT based smart cradle for baby monitoring. The proposed architecture is presented in Figure 1. This architecture enables the continuous observation of baby's health and activities by parents and care takers. The proposed architecture consists of four layers: perception layer, gateway layer, cloud layer and application layer. The perception layer gathers infant's health and activity information with various sensors. In addition to that, the environment is also monitored with various environmental sensors for controlling Heating Ventilation and Air Cooling (HVAC) units. The data sources in this layer are divided into sensors/actuators, various IoT devices and context information providers. Actuators are used to perform some actions based on inputs from various sensors, parents and care taker. The observed data is forwarded to the parent mobile app through WiFi or the internet. The data is stored into Google cloud and sharing the information to the mobile app. The application layer gives interface to parents and healthcare unit care takers for visualizing the data and decision making. It contains a dashboard that allows caretaker to monitor and interact with baby in real-time with the help of various sensors and actuators.

The Proposed IoT based Robotic cradle is designed with the following features:

1. The infant cradle starts to swing when the sensor identifies the baby movement on the cradle after waking up.
2. The baby movements are observed in the cradle using the motion sensor of PIR.
3. The moisture sensor detects the diaper wetness and passes the message to care taker.
4. The body temperature sensor and pulse rate sensor are used to monitor the baby's health, such as fever and heart bit rate.
5. The room cooling unit and fan begins to run when air humidity and room temperature are crossing the threshold values.

### Various Sensors Used in Baby Cradle

a) **PIR**: The Passive Infrared Sensor (PIR) is used for motion detection applications. It emitted Infrared Light with a particular area and detected motion within the range. It is an electronic sensor, the human body or any leaving thing that has heat on it body is above zero temperature, this form of heat radiation is detected by PIR.

b) **Microphone**: It is a sound sensor with a high sensitivity for sound (voice) detection. The sound is converted to an electrical signal and transferred to the controller.

c) **Moisture Sensor:** This kind of ensor detects the moisture level in the soil. They detect the moisture level based on the permittivity level of the surrounding medium. In this work, a moisture sensor detects wet-cloth in the cradle.

d) **DHT11 Sensor:** The temperature sensor is called DHT11 sensor. It is used to measure room temperature and humidity level of the room. The DHT stands for digital humidity and temperature. It is easy to interface with any king of microcontroller like Arduino, Raspberry Pi, etc.,

e) **LM35Sensor:** It is another kind of temperature sensor. Its measure and producted analog electrical signal, which is directionally proportional to human body temperature in Celsius. In this work, it is suitable to measure infant health conditions whether fever or not.

f) Pulse rate sensor: This sensor is used to measure the heart rate. The normal pulse rate of a human is between 60 to 100 beats per minute. If there are any changes, consider getting medical help for that person.

## The Various Activator in Baby Cradle Are

I. DC motor: used to rotate the cradle and musical toy. The DC motor connects to NodeMCU through driver relay circuits. The DC motors generally have two terminals, positive and negative respectively.
II. Loud Spekar / Muscial set: Playing lullaby and controlled by NodeMCU.
III. HVAC Unit: The abbreviation of HVAC (Heating, Ventilation and air conditioning) is an exhaust fan used to keep rooms with fresh air circulation.

## Microcontroller

The NodeMCU acts as a microcontroller unit in a baby cradle system. It is compact for arduino IDE programming and is built with Wi-Fi. The NodeMCU is the best choice for IoT applications and is suitable for domestic and industrial applications such as light, fans and air conditioner controllers, etc., It is a low-cast IoT application device that enables remote monitoring and controll system.

The block diagram of the IoT based Smart robotic cradle for baby monitoring is shown in Figure-2. PIR sensor, mi-crophone, moisture sensor, DHT11 sensor, LM35 sensor and pulse rate sensors are interfaced with Node MCU for baby monitoring. The Actuators like loudspeaker, relay for control- ling the cradle swinging, rotation of toy with music, HVAC units.

The web application and mobile application are created with dashboard for displaying the various sensor readings. The application dashboard also enables the parent to interact with baby with the help of audio. The component circuit connection of the proposed work is shown in the Figure 3.

*Figure 1. IoT based smart cradle system*

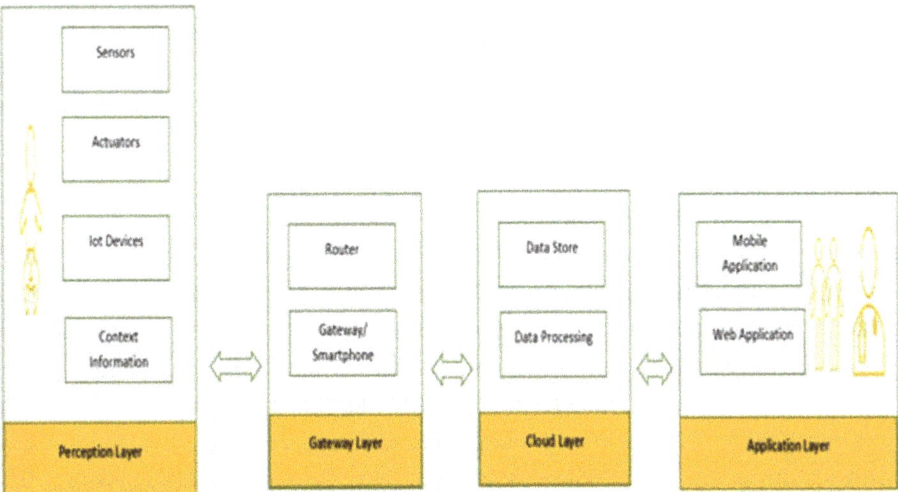

*Figure 2. Block diagram of IoT based smart cradle*

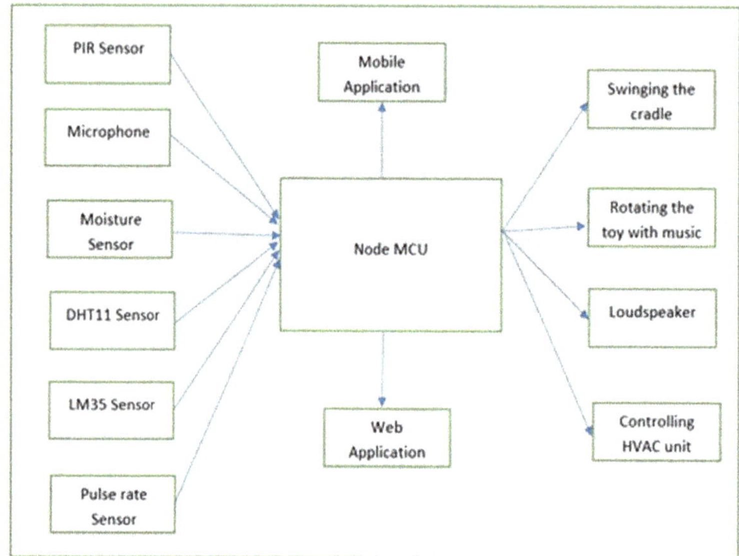


The NodeMCU is the microcontroller that is used to gather and process the sensor data, and operate actuators connected to it. The NodeMCU is specifically designed for IoT. The power supplied to the microcontroller is 5 V and is connected to a 230 V power conversion adaptor. The power supply is connected to the microcontroller $V_{in}$ pin. The sensor supply is provided by the 5V pin of the NodeMCU. That is, the $V_{CC}$ pin on all sensors is connected to the controller 5V pin and the earth terminal is also connected to the earth pin on the board. The output signal of the sensor is connected to the digital pin of the processor except the LM35 output terminal. The outer terminal of LM35 is connected to the analog pin of the NodeMCU. Actuators such as DC motors can be connected to the relay which can be controlled by the NodeMCU.

The mobile and web app for the proposed work is designed with the help of Blink App. It is an open-source app for Android platform. We need to login with registered user mail ID. The visual display of this work is designed with new project tool with the selection of appropriate processor board and various interfaces. Simply drag the components in the project workspace and configure the sensors with virtual pins. Finally, the created app connects with the board and capable of showing sensor data and actuating the cradle swinging, musical instrument and HVAC units.

The cost of proposed work is low cost compared with existing work. It's constructed by NodeMCU with 5 sensors and 3 activators. The parents or caretakers are able to continuously monitor through the mobile app, like baby body temperature, room temperature, baby movement in the cradle after waking up and they are control the musical set and room ventilation fan in the room and rock the cradle. The parent swings the cradle and plays lullabies through the mobile app, If the PIR sensor detects the baby movement after waking in the cradle and parents are able to turn on the ventilation fan through the mobile app to keep the room with fresh air circulation. like a gas sensor detects toxic air in room, then a ventilation fan is turned on to keep the room with fresh air circulation.

*Figure 3. Component circuit diagram*

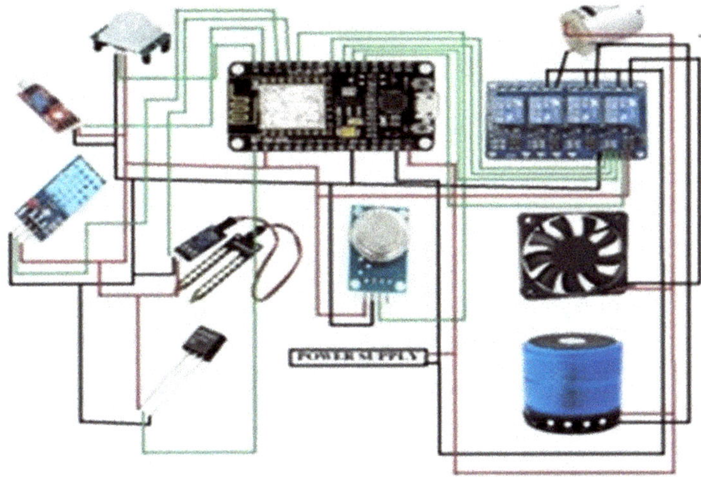

This is a low cast cradle system for babies. As results, they have some limitations, (1) they are not built by processor, so they cannot be expected like computer performance. (2) The cloud service was not considered in this work, because the results not discussed analyzed with data base.

## RESULTS AND DISCUSSION

The prototype of the proposed smart cradle has been developed and tested in lab. The result of mobile app is shown in Figure 4a and 4b. The Mobile app shows the status of the baby and room

*Figure 4. (a) & (b) Mobile app: Notification of baby movements*

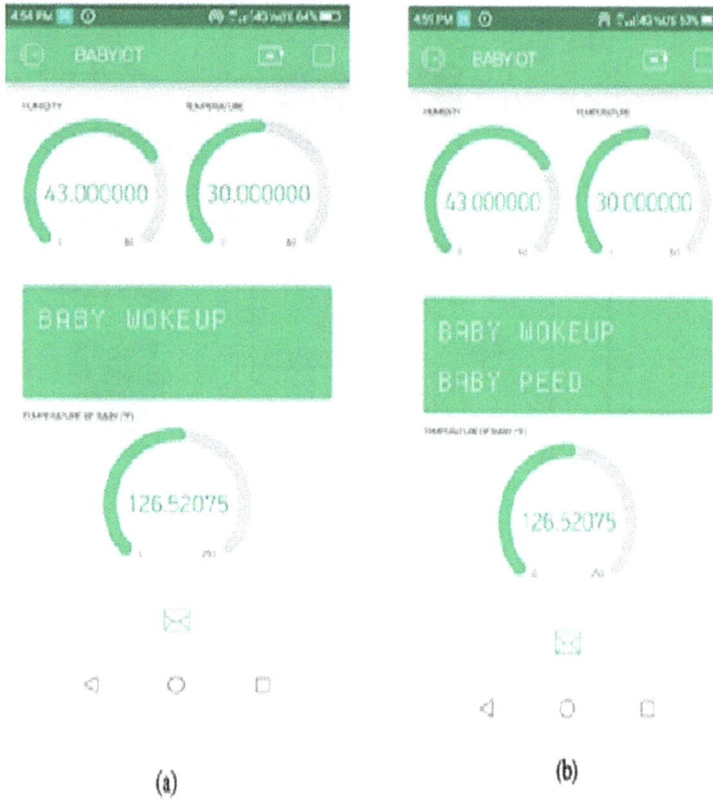

*Figure 5. (a) & (b) Mobile app: Notification of Baby movements*

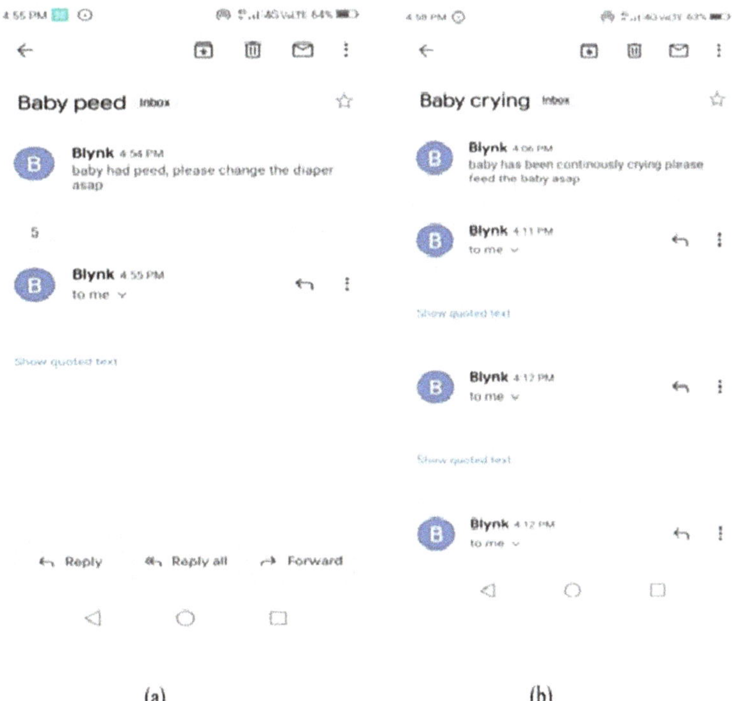


conditions like a baby temperature, pulse rate, room humidity and room temperature with analog reading. The status of the baby is constantly monitored and updated to take care and parents through mobile app. SMS messages about baby activities are received in the web application as shown in Figure 5a and 5b. The SMS is sent by NodMCU when it detects the baby movements with help of various sensors. The pulse rate sensor and body temperature sensors are used to monitor the infant's physiological signs. The dashboard in the web application and mobile application are used to visualize the body temperature and pulse rate of baby which is shown in the Figure 6 and 7 respectively.

*Figure 6. Baby body temperature monitoring*

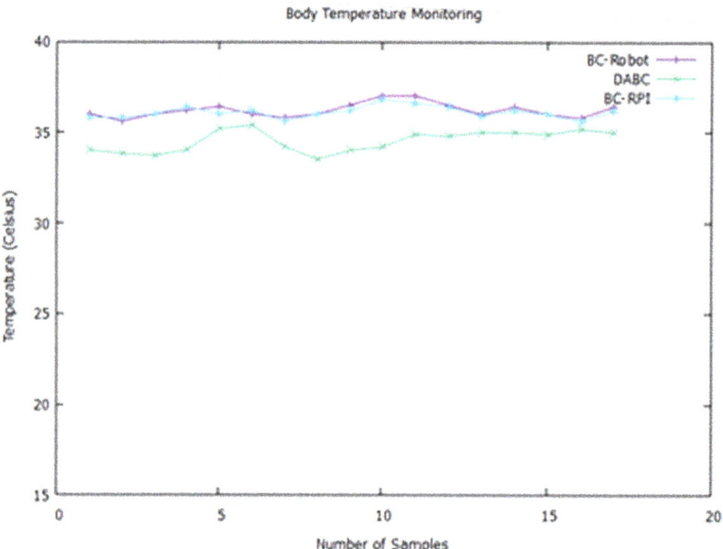


*Figure 7. Baby pulse rate monitoring*

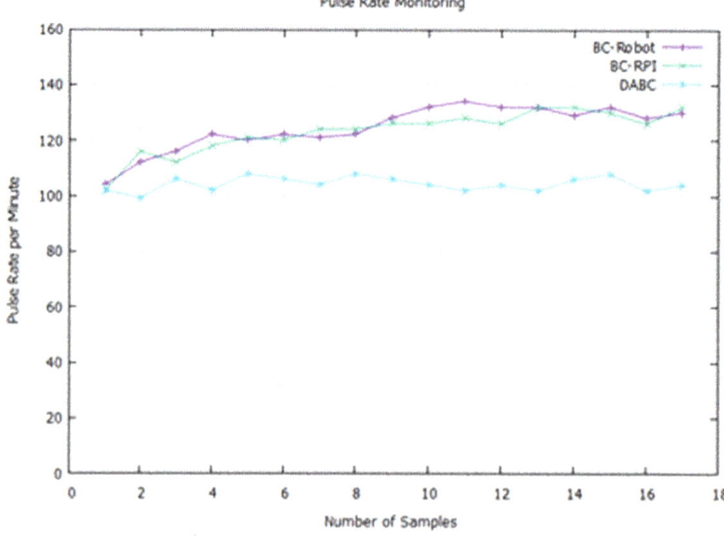


The Figures 6 & 7 shows the results of the BC-Robot body temperature and pulse rate monitoring report. The result of BC-Robot is compared with the existing work of DABC (Naresh et al., 2024) and BC-RPI (Saude & Vardhini, 2020). The accuracy of DABC measured body temperature and pulse rate values is poor compared with other methods such as BC-Robot and BC-RPI. However, the results of BC-RPI and BC-Robot are comparatively the same. But BC-RPI costs more because of Raspberry Pi processor.

## CONCLUSION

In this work, we proposed an IoT based baby monitoring with smart cradle which swings and plays music when baby cries. The prototype has been developed and tested in lab with the help of mobile and web applications. This cradle has an extra function of monitoring baby health conditions using body temperature sensor and pulse rate sensor. The room temperature and humidity are also measured in this proposed work for controlling ventilation and cooling unit. In future, battery will be included to improve performance during power failure and we will establish artificial intelligence techniques to analyze the results of sensed data like heart rate, blood pressure and oxygen saturation ratio for baby's health monitoring and activity recognition. The sample data sets are planned to be collect from the hospital baby delivery ward.

## REFERENCES

Alswedani, S. A., & Eassa, F. E. (2020). A smart baby cradle based on IoT. *Journal of Computer Science and Mobile Computing*, 9(7), 64–76.

Bhavsar, Y. S. (2020). Automatic Cradle System for Baby using Arduino. *International Journal Of Innovative Research In Technology*, 6(8), 5–8.

Chandar, A. G., Sivasankari, K., Lakshmi, S. L., Sugumaran, S., Kannadhasan, S., & Balakumar, S. (2024). An innovative smart agriculture system utilizing a deep neural network and embedded system to enhance crop yield. *Multidisciplinary Science Journal*, 6(5), 2024063–2024063. 10.31893/multiscience.2024065

Duman, Ü., & Aydin, E. (2020). IOT based baby cradle system with real time data tracking. In *2020 5th International Conference on Computer Science and Engineering (UBMK)*. IEEE. 10.1109/UBMK50275.2020.9219506

Gare, H. (2019). IOT based smart cradle system for baby monitoring. *International Research Journal of Engineering and Technology,6.*

Gore, H. S., Shan, B. K., Jori, K. S., & Jachak, S. G. (2019). IOT Based Smart Cradle System for Baby Monitoring. *International Research Journal of Engineering and Technology*, 6(10), 2019.

Goyal, M. (2013). Automatic E-Baby Cradle swing based on Baby Cry. *IJCA, 71*(21).

Hotur, V. P., Abhishek, P., Chethan, R., & Bhatta, A. (2021, June). Internet of Things-based Baby Monitoring System for Smart Cradle. In *2021 International Conference on Design Innovations for 3Cs Compute Communicate Control (ICDI3C)* (pp. 265-270). IEEE. 10.1109/ICDI3C53598.2021.00060

Hussain, T., Muhammad, K., Khan, S., Ullah, A., Lee, M. Y., & Baik, S. W. (2019). Intelligent baby behavior monitoring using embedded vision in IoT for smart healthcare centers. *Journal of Artificial Intelligence and Systems*, 1(1), 110–124. 10.33969/AIS.2019.11007

Jabbar, W. A., Shang, H. K., Hamid, S. N., Almohammedi, A. A., Ramli, R. M., & Ali, M. A. (2019). IoT-BBMS: Internet of Things-based baby monitoring system for smart cradle. *IEEE Access : Practical Innovations, Open Solutions*, 7, 93791–93805. 10.1109/ACCESS.2019.2928481

Joseph, S., Kumar, A., & Babu, M. H. (2021, March). IOT Based Baby Monitoring System Smart Cradle. In *2021 7th International Conference on Advanced Computing and Communication Systems (ICACCS)* (Vol. 1, pp. 748-751). IEEE. 10.1109/ICACCS51430.2021.9442022

Joshi, M. P., & Mehetre, D. C. (2017). IoT based smart cradle system with an Android app for baby monitoring. *2017 International Conference on Computing, Communication, Control and Automation (ICCUBEA)*. IEEE. 10.1109/ICCUBEA.2017.8463676

Marie, R. (1973). *Automatically rocking baby cradle*. US Patent US3769641.

Mathan Kumar, K., & Venkatesan, R. S. (2014). A Design Approach to Smart Health Monitoring Using Android Mobile Devices. *IEEE International Conference on Advanced Communication, Control and Computing Tech- nologies (ICACCCT)*. IEEE.

Naresh, M. H., Mr, M. M. A., Bhargav, M. P., Reddy, M. Y. D. S., & Ashish, M. G. (2024). Development of an Automatic Baby Cradle System. *International Research Journal on Advanced Engineering Hub*, 2(04), 774–782. 10.47392/IRJAEH.2024.0109

Palaskar, R., Pandey, S., Telang, A., Wagh, A., & Kagalkar, R. R. (2015, December). An Automatic Monitoring and Swing the Baby Cradle for Infant Care. *International Journal of Advanced Research in Computer and Communication Engineering*.

Patil, R. (2018). Smart Baby Cradle an IOT based Cradle Management System. *International Conference on Smart City and Emerging Technology (ICSCET)*. IEEE.

Pratap, N. L., Anuroop, K., Devi, P. N., Sandeep, A., & Nalajala, S. (2021, January). IoT based Smart Cradle for Baby Monitoring System. In *2021 6th International Conference on Inventive Computation Technologies (ICICT)* (pp. 1298-1303). IEEE. 10.1109/ICICT50816.2021.9358684

Saude, N., & Vardhini, P. H. (2020, October). IoT based Smart Baby Cradle System using Raspberry Pi B+. In *2020 International Conference on Smart Innovations in Design, Environment, Management, Planning and Computing (ICSIDEMPC)* (pp. 273-278). IEEE. 10.1109/ICSIDEMPC49020.2020.9299602

Visvesvaran, C., Nishanth, S., Sudha, R., & Karthikeyan, J. (2021, August). IoT based Smart Baby Monitoring. In *2021 Second International Conference on Electronics and Sustainable Communication Systems (ICESC)* (pp. 1-6). IEEE.

Wong, G. (1976). *Automatic baby crib rocker*. Patent US3952343.

# Chapter 13
# The Nexus of Care:
## Human-Machine Collaboration Redefining Healthcare Delivery

**Jaspreet Kaur**
*Chandigarh University, India*

## ABSTRACT

*The intersection of care is experiencing a fundamental change as the collaboration between humans and machines grows more widespread in the delivery of healthcare. The aforementioned shift is propelled by the progress made in the fields of artificial intelligence (AI) and robotics, facilitating collaborative alliances between healthcare practitioners and intelligent machines. In the contemporary healthcare landscape, the collaboration between humans and machines is reshaping conventional roles and workflows, thereby augmenting diagnostic precision, optimising treatment approaches, and enhancing patient outcomes. This study examines the primary factors, obstacles, and potential advantages linked to the collaboration between humans and machines in the field of healthcare delivery. It emphasises the significance of interdisciplinary collaboration, ethical deliberations, and regulatory structures.*

## INTRODUCTION

The healthcare delivery industry is currently undergoing a significant shift, which is being driven by the intersection of human skills and technical advancements. This transformation is currently taking place. This paradigm change has resulted in a significant transformation in the manner in which care is provided, encountered, and improved. The rise of human-machine collaboration has become an essential component of this paradigm shift. A connection between medical professionals and cutting-edge technology that is beneficial to both parties is a key component of human-machine collaboration. This connection ensures that both parties benefit from the relationship (Kaur, 2024). Since the invention of the stethoscope and continuing all the way up to the most cutting-edge digital technology, the instruments and procedures that are utilized in the administration of medical treatment have developed in parallel with the expansion of scientific knowledge and other technological advancements. The introduction of digital technology in recent times, which has been driven by the rapid expansion of computer capabilities,

DOI: 10.4018/979-8-3693-2901-6.ch013

data analytic, and communication, has resulted in a paradigm shift that has resulted in the emergence of a multitude of potential opportunities.

Artificial intelligence (AI) and machine learning are at the forefront of operations currently taking place within the context of this technological revolution. Because of these technological advancements, it is now possible to analyze vast amounts of medical data in a precise and speedy manner. This opens the door to the possibility of gaining insights that were previously only attainable through the cognitive processes of people. The ability of algorithms that are powered by artificial intelligence (AI) to do sophisticated imaging tests, recognize subtle patterns within patient data, and display exceptional accuracy when it comes to forecasting the evolution of diseases is a significant advantage. It is possible that the diagnostic capabilities of medical professionals might be significantly enhanced with the assistance of artificial intelligence (AI), which has the ability to bring about a significant transition in the field of medicine through its revolutionary potential (Riek, 2017).

Robotics and automation, in conjunction with artificial intelligence (AI), are actively contributing to the transformation of the healthcare delivery sector. This transition is taking place in tandem with AI. These technological advancements are offering levels of accuracy and efficiency that have never been seen before. Surgical robots, which are equipped with sophisticated imaging systems and robotic arms, allow surgeons to execute complex surgeries with greater dexterity and control. This is made possible by the use of surgical robots. The utilization of surgical robots is what makes this a feasible option. There is a possibility that robotic surgery could enhance patient outcomes and speed up the healing process. This is because robotic surgery will reduce the number of incisions that are made and the amount of stress that is imposed on the tissues. Furthermore, robotics and automation are being utilized not only in surgical operations but also in a wide range of other disciplines, including the distribution of pharmaceuticals, the implementation of logistics, and the performance of administrative chores. This range of applications is expanding beyond the realm of surgical procedures. As a result of this integration, operations are improved, and the workforce in the healthcare industry is able to spend more time delivering care to patients. Geographically remote and under-served areas are benefiting from increased healthcare accessibility through the use of telemedicine and remote monitoring technology. By utilizing virtual consultations and remote monitoring equipment, patients are able to receive prompt medical advice and interventions. This reduces the need for patients to physically visit doctors, which is a significant benefit for patients. Telemedicine systems utilize various techniques to facilitate easy communication between patients and healthcare practitioners. Some of these tools include video conferencing, encrypted texting, and electronic health records. Mobile applications and wearable sensors are two examples of remote monitoring systems that allow for continuous monitoring of vital signs and other health indicators. Both of these platforms are instances of remote monitoring systems. Patients have the opportunity to take responsibility for their own health management activities.

On the other hand, incorporating technology into the process of providing medical treatment is not without its difficulties. In the healthcare industry, it is absolutely vital to address concerns regarding the privacy of data, the security of data, and compliance with legal requirements. This is necessary to ensure the ethical and responsible use of technology in the industry. In addition, it is of the utmost importance to enhance the skills of healthcare personnel in order to provide them with the ability to make efficient use of these technologies and successfully traverse the constantly shifting landscape of the healthcare industry. On the other hand, within the context of these problems, there are significant opportunities for innovation and development. Technology is the engine that is driving this change, and it is playing a significant part in pushing the intersection of healthcare, which is currently going through a major transition. Maintaining a heightened awareness of the ethical, social, and regulatory implications that our activities may have is vital in order to guarantee equitable distribution and effective management of the benefits that this technology brings. This is because our actions can have an impact on the environment, society, and government. Working together, we have the ability to create a future in which medical treatment is more readily available, more tailored to the specific needs of each patient, and more effective than it has ever been before (Kyrarini et al., 2021). The use of AI-powered robots in the rapidly changing healthcare sector is a trailblazing force in the sector's continuing digital revolution. These incredible AI-powered devices are revolutionizing healthcare delivery and have the potential to improve patient outcomes, expedite processes, and revolutionize patient care. The condition of AI robots in healthcare today is a result of the constant pursuit of bettering healthcare services through the convergence of cutting-edge technologies. These artificial intelligence (AI) robots have a broad range of uses, including monitoring and patient care, surgical assistance, and diagnostic instruments as represented in figure 1 below (Valles-Peris & Domènech, 2023).

*Figure 1. Use of AI-powered robots in healthcare sector*

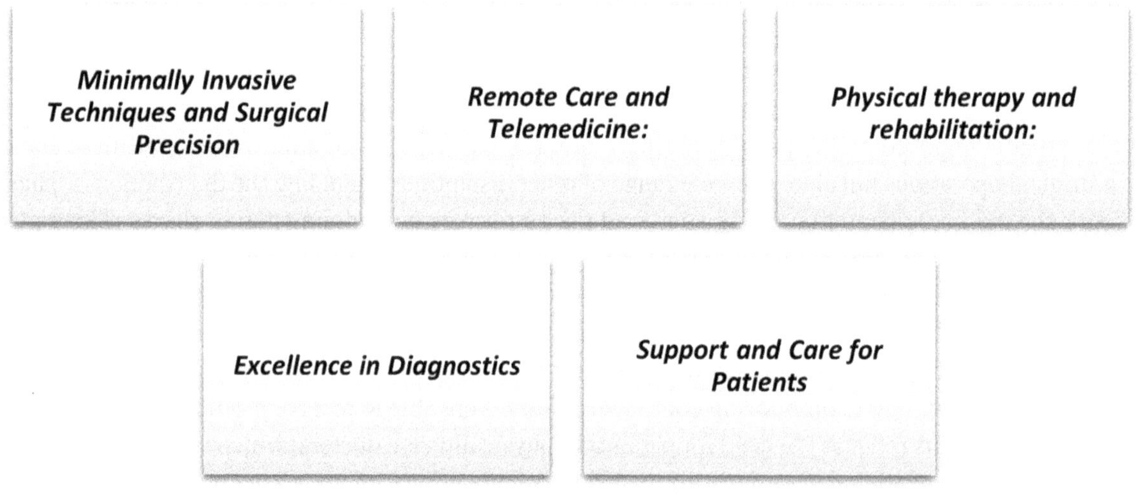


*Source: Kaur (2024)*

Artificial intelligence (AI) robots have proven invaluable in the surgical profession, providing previously unattainable levels of accuracy. Patients benefit from shortened recovery periods and fewer complications when surgeons can conduct complex procedures with greater accuracy and little pervasiveness thanks to surgical robots like the da Vinci Surgical System (Deo & Anjankar 2023). Artificial intelligence (AI) robots are developing quickly as diagnostic tools. They can help medical practitioners spot diseases and anomalies by analyzing patient data and medical imagery. The early disease detection capabilities of these robots increase the likelihood of a successful course of therapy and recovery.AI robots are acting as companions, carers, and educators for patients, offering tremendous assistance. They help patients remember to take their medications, offer them emotional support, and inform others about their medical conditions, all of which improve patient participation and treatment plan adherence. AI robots have made remote medical consultations and ongoing patient monitoring possible in telemedicine.

This invention changes the way medical services are provided by expanding access to healthcare for people living in rural or under-served locations (Ragno at al., 2023). Artificial intelligence (AI) robots are revolutionizing physical therapy and rehabilitation by helping patients regain their mobility and improve their quality-of-life following operations or accidents. They give therapeutic activities regularity and accuracy, which improves patient outcomes (Kumar et al., 2023; Minopoulos et al., 2023). Although there is great potential for the digital transformation of healthcare through AI robots, there are obstacles and moral dilemmas to be resolved. Concerns about bias in AI algorithms, privacy, and data security need to be addressed. In order to guarantee safe and ethical use, healthcare experts, technologists, and regulators must work together to integrate AI robots (Verma et al., 2018).

## AI MODELS AND TECHNOLOGIES

The collaboration between humans and robots is profoundly reshaping the central point of care in modern healthcare. This collaboration utilizes sophisticated AI models and technology to enhance the efficiency of healthcare delivery. The foundation of this transition is a large reservoir of health data, including electronic health records (EHR), data from wearable devices, imaging scans, and genomics information. This data is processed and analyzed on a large scale by utilizing AI technologies such as machine learning, natural language processing (NLP), computer vision, and predictive analytic. Yet, the actual breakthrough occurs in the domain of human-machine collaboration. The combination of human expertise and machine intelligence is represented by clinical decision support systems (CDSS), virtual health assistants, telemedicine platforms, and remote patient monitoring solutions. This partnership improves healthcare by offering individualized treatment strategies, promoting early identification of diseases, enhancing patient results, and optimizing the allocation of resources. With the ongoing growth of healthcare, the interdependent connection between humans and machines holds the potential to completely transform the delivery and experience of healthcare as presented in figure 2 below:

*Figure 2. AI models and technologies*

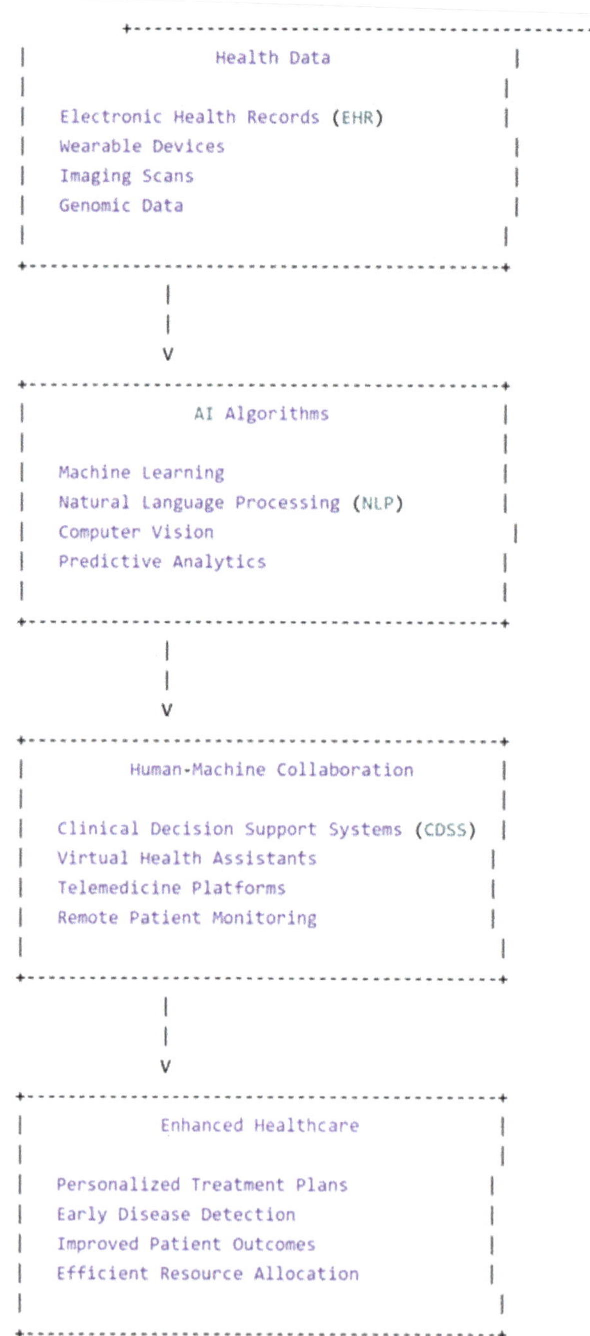
Health Data
Electronic Health Records (EHR)
Wearable Devices
Imaging Scans
Genomic Data
AI Algorithms
Machine Learning
Natural Language Processing (NLP)
Computer Vision
Predictive Analytics
Human-Machine Collaboration
Clinical Decision Support Systems (CDSS)
Virtual Health Assistants
Telemedicine Platforms
Remote Patient Monitoring
Enhanced Healthcare
Personalized Treatment Plans
Early Disease Detection
Improved Patient Outcomes
Efficient Resource Allocation

*Source: Kaur (2024)*

## ROBOTIC SURGICAL ASSISTANTS: INCREASING ACCURACY AND MINIMALLY SURGICAL PROCEDURES

Robotic surgical assistants are a revolutionary development in healthcare that provide unparalleled levels of accuracy, command, and effectiveness in surgical procedures. These advanced devices, commonly known as surgical robots, are specifically engineered to enhance the abilities of human surgeons, allowing them to carry out intricate surgeries with improved dexterity and precision. Robotic surgical assistants have transformed the field of surgery by incorporating sophisticated robotics, imaging, and computer technology. This has resulted in decreased recuperation duration, diminished problems, and enhanced patient results as presented in figure 3 below (Rivero-Moreno et al., 2023).

*Figure 3. Impact of robotic surgical assistants in healthcare*

*Source: Kaur (2024)*

The fundamental essence of robotic surgical assistants is in the integration of hardware and software elements, which synergistic ally collaborate to enable and enhance surgical interventions. The robotic arm, which is equipped with surgical instruments and imaging devices, plays a crucial role in these systems. The surgeon use a console to operate the robotic arm, enabling accurate manipulation of instruments within the patient's body. Surgeons are afforded real-time feedback and improved vision during surgical procedures through the utilization of advanced imaging technologies, including high-definition cameras and 3D visualization systems (Kim et al.,2023). Robotic surgical assistants possess a significant advantage in their capacity to execute minimally invasive treatments with exceptional precision. Minimally invasive surgery differs from typical open surgery in that it includes small incisions and specialized equipment put through tiny ports in the patient's body, resulting in shorter recovery times and less extensive incisions. Robotic surgical assistants have exceptional proficiency in this field, owing to their meticulous command and agility in restricted areas. Robotic devices facilitate surgeons in executing intricate treatments with minimum harm to adjacent tissues by effortlessly maneuvering through intricate anatomical structures (Khaddad at al., 2023).

In addition, robotic surgical assistants provide surgeons with improved ergonomics and comfort, resulting in decreased fatigue and greater procedural efficiency. Surgeons may handle the console interface while sitting comfortably, and the ergonomic hand controls enable them to manipulate the robotic arms in an understandable manner. The implementation of this ergonomic design not only serves to improve the comfort of surgeons, but also mitigates the potential for musculoskeletal problems commonly linked with conventional surgical procedures. Consequently, surgeons are able to sustain optimal performance during extended procedures, resulting in enhanced patient outcomes and diminished occurrences of surgical problems. Robotic surgical assistants provide several advantages, such as enhanced visualization, decreased blood loss, and shorter hospital stays, in addition to their precision and ergonomic benefits. Surgeons can utilize advanced imaging technology to obtain high-definition, magnified images of the surgical site, which improves their capacity to accurately detect and operate fragile components. The enhanced visual representation, in conjunction with the robustness and accuracy of robotic arms, mitigates the potential for unintended harm to adjacent tissues, nerves, and blood vessels. In addition, studies have demonstrated that robotic surgical assistants can decrease blood loss and transfusion needs in comparison to conventional open surgery, resulting in quicker recovery periods and fewer postoperative problems. Robotic devices play a significant role in enhancing patient outcomes and reducing hospital stays by mitigating tissue trauma and maintaining enough blood supply to essential organs.

Patients who endure robotic-assisted operations generally encounter reduced levels of pain, scarring, and discomfort in comparison to individuals who undergo conventional open surgery. Consequently, this results in elevated levels of pleasure and an enhanced quality of life (Kaur,2024). Although robotic surgical assistants offer a multitude of benefits, they are not exempt from certain restrictions and obstacles. The considerable expenses associated with the procurement and upkeep of the technology, along with the requirement for specific training and experience, can pose obstacles to achieving widespread implementation. To ensure the ethical and responsible utilization of these technologies in clinical practice, it is imperative to address problems pertaining to patient safety, regulatory compliance, and liability risks. However, the ongoing research and investment in the fast growing field of robotic surgical assistants are justified by the potential advantages they offer in terms of improved patient outcomes, enhanced procedural efficiency, and decreased healthcare costs (Kaur, 2024). Ultimately, robotic surgical assistants embody a revolutionary technology that is fundamentally transforming the field of surgery. Through the integration of sophisticated robotics, imaging, and computer technologies, these systems facilitate the execution of intricate surgical procedures with heightened levels of accuracy, manipulation, and effectiveness. Robotic surgical assistants offer numerous advantages, including minimally invasive surgery, decreased complications, and enhanced patient outcomes. With the ongoing advancement and enhancement of technology, the utilization of robotic systems in the healthcare sector is anticipated to broaden, thereby facilitating a future characterized by enhanced safety, efficacy, and accessibility in surgical procedures (Lochan et al., 2023).

## ROBOTIC NURSING AND CARE-GIVING: PROGRESS IN THE CARE OF PATIENTS AND BEYOND

Robots that can provide nursing and care are a promising new development in healthcare technology. These robots are made to help with several parts of patient care, such as keeping an eye on vital signs, giving medication, and being a friend. In a range of healthcare settings, they have the potential to improve patient well-being and lessen the workload for medical staff (Kim et al., 2016). Theis section will highlight the application of nursing and care-giving robots as well as any possible advantages as represented in figure 4 below:

*Figure 4. Advantages of robotic nursing and care giving in the care of patients and beyond*

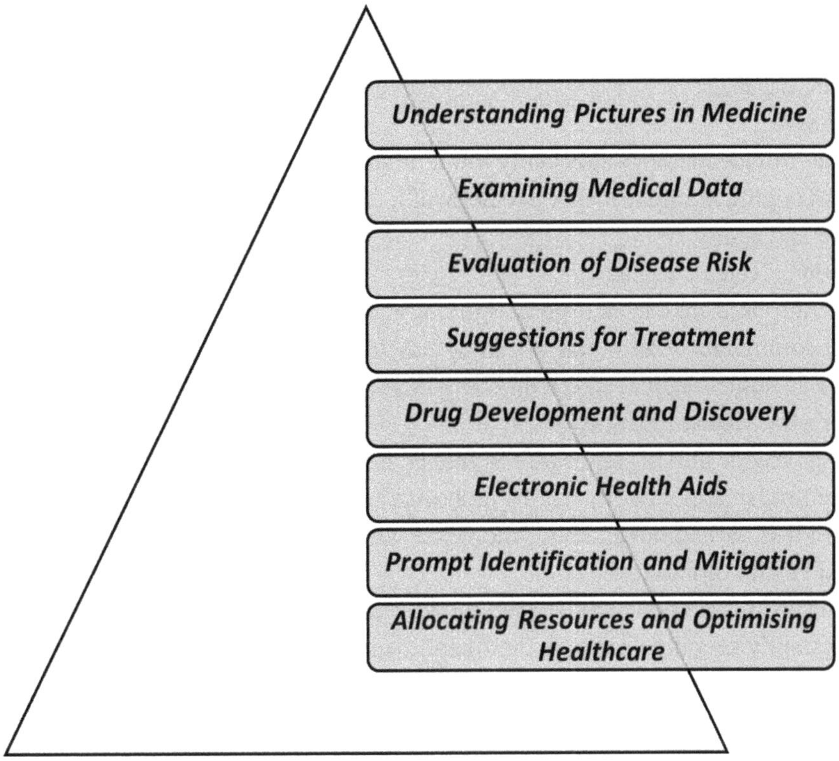

*Source: Kaur (2024)*

1. Keeping an eye on vital signs

Sensor-equipped nursing robots can keep an eye on a patient's blood pressure, oxygen saturation, and heart rate all the time. When any metrics depart from the expected range, they can notify medical professionals, allowing for prompt intervention and a lower chance of unfavourable outcomes (Schönmann et al., 2023).

2. Administration of Medication

In healthcare, medication errors are a serious problem. Dosing errors are less likely when medication is accurately dispensed and administered by robots that deliver medication at the specified times. They can also keep track of the prescriptions that are administered to medical professionals.

3. Social Contact and Companionship:

A patient's wellbeing may suffer from social isolation and loneliness. Robots that provide care can be companions by conversing, playing games, and even offering emotional support. This is particularly advantageous for senior citizens residing in assisted living facilities (Matsuzaki et al., 2023).

4. Help with Mobility:

Robotic gadgets can help patients who have restricted mobility with everyday tasks like getting out of bed and into a wheelchair or helping them walk. These robots improve patient autonomy while lessening the physical load on medical staff.

5. Avoiding Falls:

Falls are a frequent source of injuries in medical environments. The frequency of falls can be decreased by using robots with sensors to identify when a patient is in danger of falling and to provide warnings or aid (Kato et al., 2023).

6. Mental Assist:

Robots can provide memory aids, daily job reminders, and cognitive stimulation activities to people suffering from cognitive impairments like dementia. These services help patients preserve their mental independence and acuity.

7. Integration of Telemedicine:

Telemedicine platforms can incorporate nursing and caregiving robots, enabling medical professionals to assess and communicate with patients from a distance. This is especially helpful for remote patient monitoring or at-home medical care (Ohneberg et al., 2023).

8. Less Work for Medical Professionals:

Robots that provide nursing and care can free up healthcare workers to concentrate on more complex and patient-centred treatment by managing repetitive and time-consuming activities. This can help nurses and carers feel less burned out and have more job satisfaction.

9. Improved Health of Patients:

Patients' levels of stress and anxiety can be decreased by the presence of care robots. Knowing that a robot is constantly keeping an eye on their health and well-being may make patients feel more at ease (Ohneberg et al., 2023).

10. Economy of Scale:

Nursing and caregiving robots can have a high initial cost, but over time they can save a lot of money by reducing the need for particular staffing levels and averting expensive medical errors and consequences.

Robotic nurses and carers provide many benefits, but deployment of these devices is not without difficulties. These include the necessity for cautious integration into the current healthcare process, ethical constraints, and patient privacy issues. Furthermore, continuous research and development are necessary to guarantee that these robots can be efficiently utilized in dynamic healthcare environments and can be tailored to a broad range of patient needs.Robotic nurses and carers are predicted to become more and more important as technology advances, helping to enhance patient care and boost the effectiveness of healthcare systems as a whole (Ohneberg et al., 2023).

## AI-POWERED DISEASE DIAGNOSTICS AND THERAPY: TRANSFORMING MEDICAL FIELD

Healthcare professionals now use artificial intelligence (AI) to understand medical data and prescribe treatments. AI has become a potent tool in the diagnosis and treatment of disease. When incorporated into healthcare systems, AI robots have the potential to greatly increase the precision and effectiveness of illness diagnosis and treatment as depicted in figure 5 below (Alowais et al., 2023).

*Figure 5. Robotic surgical assistants*

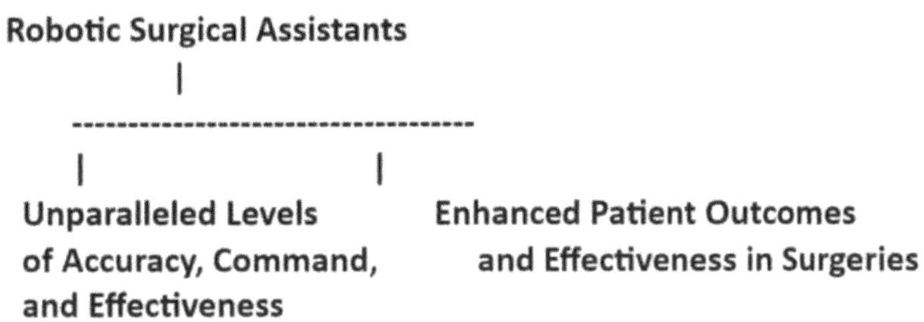


*Source: Kaur (2024)*

1. Understanding Pictures in Medicine:

The analysis of medical pictures, including MRIs, CT scans, X-rays, and histopathology slides, is being done by AI robots more and more. They are remarkably accurate in recognizing many disorders, including fractures, tumour, and abnormalities. Convolution neural networks (CNNs), in particular, are deep learning algorithms that have proven to be faster and more reliable than human radiologists at some tasks involving image processing (Kaur, 2024).

2. Examining Medical Data:

Massive volumes of patient data, including as genetic data, medical histories, and electronic health records (EHRs), can be processed by AI robots. They are able to spot trends, patterns, and risk indicators that human clinicians would overlook. Based on past patient data, machine learning models can forecast the course of a disease, the outcomes of patients, and how well a patient will respond to therapy. This makes healthcare more individualized and efficient (Harry, 2023).

3. Evaluation of Disease Risk:

AI systems are able to determine a person's genetic, lifestyle, and medical history-based risk for certain diseases. Early intervention and preventative efforts can be guided by this knowledge.

4. Suggestions for Treatment:

AI systems are capable of analyzing patient data and recommending individualized therapy regimens. This covers advice on prescription drugs, surgical procedures, and even the gradual improvement of treatment plans (Ali, 2023).

5. Drug Development and Discovery:

Artificial Intelligence is a key player in drug discovery, helping to find new therapeutic molecules, forecast their efficacy, and expedite the drug development process. Artificial intelligence (AI) robots assist in the discovery of drug targets and the development of innovative pharmaceuticals by evaluating molecular and biological data.

6. Electronic Health Aids:

Virtual health assistants with AI capabilities can communicate with patients, respond to inquiries about health, and offer details on ailments, therapies, and recuperation times. They can provide telemedicine services, which include medication reminders, treatment plan adherence, and prompt medical intervention as needed.

7. Prompt Identification and Mitigation:

Artificial intelligence (AI) robots are extremely useful for early disease detection and timely intervention. AI is capable of analyzing speech biomarkers, for instance, to find early indicators of conditions like Alzheimer's and Parkinson's (Ahmad et al., 2023).

8. Allocating Resources and Optimizing Healthcare:

By forecasting patient admission rates, controlling bed availability, and optimizing logistics to guarantee effective healthcare delivery, AI can assist healthcare organizations in allocating resources as efficiently as possible (Ali, 2023).

Although AI has great potential for diagnosing and treating diseases, there are still issues to be resolved. These include worries about data protection, bias in AI algorithms, regulatory supervision, and the requirement for AI to collaborate and function seamlessly with healthcare personnel. AI robots have the potential to improve patient outcomes, lower total healthcare costs, and increase the accuracy and efficiency of illness detection and treatment as they develop and are more fully integrated into the healthcare system. AI-driven healthcare solutions are still being developed, and they have the potential to completely transform the industry by offering more affordable, individualized, and efficient medical treatment (Kaur,2024).

## REHABILITATION AND PHYSICAL THERAPY: THE ROLE OF AI ROBOTS IN TRANSFORMING PATIENT RECOVERY

Physical therapy and rehabilitation are essential parts of healthcare for those recuperating from illnesses, surgeries, or injuries. In this area, AI-powered robots are becoming more and more important, helping patients regain their mobility and enhance their general quality of life.

1. Tailored Treatment Programme:

AI robots are able to generate customized rehabilitation programme according to the unique requirements, state, and advancement of every patient. As the patient's abilities advance, these plans adjust throughout time to ensure the best possible outcome (Abbasimoshaei et al., 2023).

2. Repeated and Accurate Motions:

Robotic devices are essential for rehabilitation because they offer highly controlled and regular movements. They can help patients restore strength, flexibility, and coordination by specifically targeting and strengthening particular muscle areas.

3.Enhancing Mobility and Gait Training:

Exoskeletons and other mobility-assistance robots help patients regain their ability to walk following surgery or injury. By providing stability and support, these gadgets aid patients in regaining their self-assurance and independence (Mahmoud et al., 2023).

4. Rehabilitating Neurological Damage:

Patients with neurological disorders including stroke, spinal cord injuries, or traumatic brain traumas are rehabilitated with AI robots. They offer rigorous, ongoing therapy, which is frequently required for healing.

5. Constant Observation and Input:

Throughout therapy sessions, robots with sensors track a patient's progress continuously. Real-time AI systems evaluate this data and give patients and therapists prompt feedback (Stasevych & Zvarych, 2023).

6. Rehabilitation by Distance:

Patients can receive therapy at home while staying in contact with medical personnel thanks to rehabilitation robots. Patients with restricted mobility or those living in distant places will find this especially helpful.

7. Cutting Back on Therapist Caseload:

AI robots relieve the physical strain on therapists by performing repetitive actions and exercises. This enables therapists to provide more customized care and concentrate on more difficult tasks (Murakami et al., 2023).

8. Improved Involvement of Patients:

By adding games, virtual reality, and other interactive components, AI robots can enhance therapy sessions. This may encourage patients to pursue their rehabilitation more steadily.

9. Safety and Fall Prevention:

A primary priority throughout rehabilitation is safety. By giving patients stability and support during difficult exercises or when they are relearning how to walk, robots can help reduce the risk of falls and accidents (Stasevych & Zvarych, 2023).

10. Monitoring Progress:

AI robots keep thorough records of a patient's progress, which can be useful for insurers and healthcare professionals to evaluate the efficacy of therapy and make well-informed judgement about treatment regimens. AI-enabled physical therapy and rehabilitation not only expedites the healing process but also improves the overall efficacy of these treatments. A level of consistency and precision that can be difficult to accomplish with conventional therapy methods is provided by AI robots. They also give patients the ability to actively participate in their own treatment since they allow them to track their development and make modifications in response to immediate feedback.

## PATIENT INVOLVEMENT AND EDUCATION: PROVIDING AI-POWERED ROBOTS TO EMPOWER PATIENTS

Modern healthcare must include patient education and involvement, and AI-powered robots are making great progress in these areas. These interactive tools for patient education, medication reminders, and progress monitoring are these robots. They may be able to enhance patient adherence and results by doing this (Al Kuwaiti et al., 2023).

1. Information and Education on Health:

Robots with artificial intelligence (AI) capabilities can give patients important information about their ailments, available treatments, and general health. They have the ability to clearly and simply explain difficult medical ideas, enabling patients to make decisions regarding their care.

2. Reminders for Medication:

Treatment failure might result from a common problem called medication non-adherence. Artificial intelligence (AI) robots can remind patients when to take their prescriptions by sending them timely reminders. Some robots are even capable of directly dispensing medication (Božić, 2023).

3. Vital Signs Monitoring:

Certain artificial intelligence (AI) robots come with sensors that let them keep an eye on things like blood pressure, heart rate, and blood sugar levels. Healthcare professionals can use this information to remotely monitor a patient's progress.

4. Tailored Care Schemes:

AI systems are capable of analyzing patient data to create individualized care plans that consider the patient's goals for treatment, lifestyle, and medical history. When the patient's needs change, these care plans can be modified (Varshney & Dev, 2023).

5. Integration of Telemedicine:

AI-driven robots can help with telemedicine consultations, setting up remote examinations, follow-up visits, and consultations between patients and medical professionals. Patients in isolated areas or those with restricted mobility will particularly benefit from this.

6. Engagement and Gamification:

Gamification is a common feature used by AI robots in their interactions with patients. They encourage patients to adhere to their treatment regimens by transforming health-related tasks into entertaining games (Nwadiokwu, 2023).

7. Help with Emotions:

Certain AI robots are intended to offer patients emotional support, particularly those who are coping with long-term medical conditions or psychological problems. They can reduce feelings of loneliness by providing company and a sympathetic ear.

8. Support for Physical Therapy and Rehabilitation:

Artificial intelligence (AI)-driven robots can assist patients with exercises, offer performance feedback, and track their development in the context of physical therapy and rehabilitation. In particular, people recuperating from surgery or injuries may find this very helpful.

9. Visualization of Health Data:

AI robots have the ability to visualize a patient's medical data, which helps patients better grasp their trends and development over time. Patients may be encouraged to stick to better routines by this visual feedback (Kaur, 2024).

10. Privacy and Data Security:

Privacy of patient data is a top priority. For sensitive medical data to be protected, AI robots need to be outfitted with strong security features. The goal of incorporating AI-powered robots into patient education and engagement is to improve patient empowerment, treatment plan adherence, and general well-being. Healthcare practitioners may provide more efficient and individualized care by employing AI, which will enhance patient outcomes and satisfaction.

## REGULATION AND ETHICAL ISSUES IN THE APPLICATION OF ARTIFICIAL INTELLIGENCE ROBOTS IN HEALTHCARE

AI robots have a lot of potential for the healthcare industry, but there are also a lot of ethical and legal issues to be resolved. It is crucial to address concerns like privacy, data security, bias in AI algorithms, and regulatory monitoring in order to guarantee the ethical and responsible application of AI in healthcare.

1. Data security and privacy:

Artificial intelligence (AI) robots gather and handle private patient data, such as vital signs, diagnostic data, and medical records. Ensuring the privacy of patients is crucial. Healthcare providers are responsible for making sure that patient data is transferred, stored, and accessed securely. Strong encryption, access restrictions, and frequent security audits are essential for preventing breaches and unauthorized access to patient data (Wang et al., 2023).

2. AI Algorithm Bias

Biases in the training data may be inherited by AI algorithms utilized in the healthcare industry. As a result, certain demographic groups may be disproportionately affected by differences in diagnostic and treatment recommendations. Healthcare companies should use transparent and audit able AI technologies to reduce bias. Regular audits of datasets and algorithms can assist in locating and addressing bias (Tigard et al., 2023).

3. Knowledgeable Assent:

Patients have a right to know what information will be gathered and how AI robots will be used to their care. Patients must be given the ability to make decisions about the use of AI in their care through the implementation of informed consent procedures.

4. Explain ability and Transparency:

Healthcare professionals and patients may find it difficult to comprehend the inner workings of AI algorithms due to their potential for complexity. AI systems should be able to explain their decisions and be transparent in order to foster confidence (Tang et al., 2023).

5. **Liability and Accountabil**ity:

Ascertaining accountability in situations where AI machines make mistakes or produce unfavourable results can be difficult. In order to safeguard patients and healthcare providers alike, precise norms regarding responsibility and liability are required.

6. Supervisory Authority:

Regulations governing the use of AI in healthcare must be established and updated by healthcare regulatory bodies. Regulations should be flexible enough to accommodate new developments in healthcare and technology.

7. Education and Training:

Healthcare workers must receive training in order to use AI systems in an ethical and successful manner. This involves being aware of when to use clinical judgement and when to trust AI advice (Tukhtakhodjaeva & Khayitova, 2023).

8.Patient Self-governance:

Although AI can suggest treatments, individuals should always have the last word in their care. The patient's ability to actively participate in their healthcare should not be diminished by the usage of AI (Tang et al., 2023).

9. Data sharing and interoperability:

AI robots may require access to a variety of patient data sources in order to deliver the best care possible. Practical and ethical challenges include ensuring healthcare systems are interoperable and sharing data in a secure manner.

10. Ongoing Assessment and Monitoring:

Healthcare companies should keep a close eye on the effectiveness and moral ramifications of AI systems. Issues can be found and resolved as soon as they develop with regular assessments Regulations and standards specifically pertaining to AI in healthcare are being developed by regulatory authorities like the European Medicines Agency (EMA) and the Food and Drug Administration (FDA) in the United States. Ensuring the safety and efficacy of AI robots in healthcare environments requires adherence to certain rules (Firoozi & Firoozi, 2023).

## OBSTACLES AND OPPORTUNITIES AHEAD FOR AI-POWERED MEDICAL ROBOTS

The incorporation of artificial intelligence (AI) into the healthcare sector has resulted in notable progress, namely in the realm of medical robotics. The AI-driven medical robots exemplify a revolutionary technology that has the capacity to significantly alter the provision of healthcare. They achieve this by enhancing the capacities of healthcare practitioners, enhancing patient results, and optimizing the allocation of resources. Nevertheless, the process of achieving extensive acceptance and actualization of the whole capabilities of medical robots driven by artificial intelligence is not devoid of obstacles. This section examines the challenges and potential advantages that lie ahead for medical robots driven by artificial intelligence (AI), taking into account various technological, legal, ethical, and sociological aspects. The integration of AI algorithms into robotic systems is a significant challenge for AI-powered medical robots. AI has the potential to greatly improve the decision-making abilities of medical robots. However, the process of building and refining these algorithms to function effectively in real-world clinical environments is a challenging endeavour.

The interoperability of AI-powered medical robots with preexisting healthcare systems and infrastructure poses an additional technological barrier. A multitude of healthcare establishments employ diverse systems to manage electronic health records (EHRs), medical imaging, and other essential operations. The successful incorporation of AI-driven medical robots into these systems necessitates the establishment of standardized interfaces and protocols, alongside interoperability standards that facilitate the exchange of data and communication among diverse systems.

Moreover, guaranteeing the security and confidentiality of patient data is of utmost importance in the creation and implementation of AI-driven medical robots. Cyberattacks and data breaches pose possible risks to these systems due to their heavy reliance on extensive quantities of sensitive patient data for training and decision-making purposes. To ensure patient privacy and prevent unauthorized access to healthcare data, it is crucial to use strong security measures such as encryption, access limits, and data minimization techniques. AI-powered medical robots encounter not only technological obstacles but also legal and ethical concerns that necessitate attention to guarantee secure and conscientious implementation in clinical environments. The U.S. Food and Drug Administration (FDA) and other regulatory bodies have a crucial responsibility in assessing and authorizing medical equipment, including robots driven by artificial intelligence (AI), to guarantee their safety, effectiveness, and quality (Shakeel et al., 2023).

Nevertheless, the swift rate of technological advancement in the realm of AI-driven medical robots poses difficulties for regulatory bodies responsible for assessing and authorizing these devices. The suitability of traditional regulatory frameworks for evaluating the safety and efficacy of AI algorithms may be limited due to their ability to dynamically evolve and adapt in response to novel data and experiences. Ensuring patient safety and supporting innovation in the field of AI research necessitates the establishment of adaptable regulatory frameworks that can handle the iterative nature of this technology. The deployment of AI-powered medical robots raises significant ethical concerns, namely pertaining to matters of responsibility, transparency, and bias. It is vital to ensure accountability and openness in the decision-making processes of these systems, as they make more sophisticated decisions that might have life-altering repercussions for patients. In addition, it is imperative to acknowledge and tackle the inherent biases present in AI algorithms, since they have the potential to disproportionately affect specific patient populations. This is crucial in order to .promote equitable healthcare delivery (Kaur, 2024).

The extensive implementation of AI-driven medical robots also gives rise to wider societal ramifications that necessitate meticulous deliberation. There have been expressed concerns of job displacement, namely among healthcare professionals, due to the automation of mundane jobs and the enhancement of human workers' capabilities by AI technologies. The utilization of AI-powered medical robots holds promise for enhancing efficiency and productivity within the healthcare sector. However, it is important to acknowledge that these robots may also bring about changes in the roles and duties of healthcare personnel (Shakeel et al., 2023). Moreover, the increasing use of AI-powered medical robots in clinical settings gives rise to inquiries on access and equity in healthcare. Disparities in access to sophisticated medical treatment may arise due to the expenses associated with developing and implementing these technologies, as well as the scarcity of skilled staff to operate and maintain them. To achieve fair and equal access to AI-driven medical robots, it is necessary to tackle concerns related to expenses, education, and infrastructure within healthcare systems globally (Fidan et al., 2023; Sahoo & Goswami, 2023; Fidan et al., 2023; Shakeel et al., 2023).

## WORKFORCE IMPACT

The integration of artificial intelligence (AI) and robotics into healthcare systems has sparked significant transformations in recent years, reshaping the landscape of the healthcare workforce. This evolution encompasses various facets, ranging from clinical diagnosis and treatment to administrative tasks and patient care. As these technologies become increasingly sophisticated and prevalent, their impact on employment and training needs within the healthcare sector is profound and multifaceted. One significant effect of AI and robotics in healthcare is the augmentation of human capabilities. AI algorithms are adept at analyzing vast amounts of medical data, enabling quicker and more accurate diagnoses than traditional methods. For instance, machine learning models can sift through medical imaging scans to detect abnormalities with high precision, assisting radiologists in their diagnostic process. Similarly, AI-powered virtual assistants can streamline administrative tasks, such as scheduling appointments and managing electronic health records, thereby reducing the burden on administrative staff. This augmentation of human capabilities extends beyond diagnosis and administrative tasks to therapeutic interventions. Robotics plays a crucial role in minimally invasive surgeries, where precision and dexterity are paramount. Surgical robots, controlled by skilled surgeons, offer enhanced precision, smaller incisions, and shorter recovery times compared to traditional open surgeries. As these technologies advance, they are likely to become more ubiquitous in operating rooms, necessitating specialized training for healthcare professionals to operate them effectively. However, the integration of AI and robotics also raises concerns about the displacement of certain healthcare roles. Tasks that are repetitive, rule-based, and time-consuming are increasingly being automated, leading to the potential downsizing of roles such as medical transcriptions, billing specialists, and pharmacy technicians. While this automation may increase efficiency and reduce costs for healthcare providers, it also necessitates retraining initiatives to ensure that displaced workers can transition to new roles that require human expertise, such as data analysis, AI algorithm development, and patient care coordination.

Moreover, the widespread adoption of AI and robotics in healthcare necessitates a reevaluation of the skills and competencies required of healthcare professionals. Beyond clinical expertise, healthcare workers now need to be proficient in data interpretation, technology utilization, and interdisciplinary collaboration. For instance, physicians must not only understand how to interpret AI-generated insights but also communicate these findings effectively to patients and collaborate with data scientists and engineers to refine algorithms and improve patient outcomes. Furthermore, the ethical and regulatory implications of AI and robotics in healthcare pose additional challenges for the workforce. As AI algorithms increasingly influence clinical decision-making, healthcare professionals must navigate complex ethical dilemmas surrounding issues such as patient privacy, algorithmic bias, and liability.

Additionally, regulatory bodies must develop frameworks to ensure the safety, efficacy, and accountability of AI and robotic systems, requiring healthcare professionals to stay abreast of evolving regulations and compliance standards. Despite these challenges, the integration of AI and robotics also presents opportunities for innovation and specialization within the healthcare workforce. Healthcare professionals can leverage AI tools to personalize treatment plans based on individual patient data, leading to more effective and patient-centered care. Moreover, the development of AI-driven diagnostics and therapeutics opens new avenues for research and development, creating demand for specialists in areas such as bio-informatics, computational biology, and biomedical engineering.

*Table 1. Ethical, legal, and social implications of human-machine collaboration redefining healthcare delivery*

| Challenges | Implications | Addressing Strategies |
|---|---|---|
| **Patient Privacy and Data Security** | AI and robotics in healthcare require access to vast amounts of patient data, raising concerns about privacy breaches and data security vulnerabilities. | Implement robust data encryption protocols and access controls. Comply with regulations such as GDPR and HIPAA to protect patient privacy. |
| **Algorithmic Bias and Fairness** | Biases in AI algorithms can lead to disparities in healthcare outcomes, perpetuating existing inequalities based on factors such as race, gender, and socioeconomic status. | Conduct thorough algorithmic audits to identify and mitigate biases. Promote diversity and exclusivity in AI development teams to ensure fairness and representational. |
| **Liability and Accountability** | Determining responsibility in cases of AI-related errors or adverse events presents legal challenges, as traditional liability frameworks may not adequately address the complexities of AI systems. | Develop legal frameworks to clarify liability and accountability for AI-related incidents. Establish clear guidelines for informed consent and disclosure of AI involvement in healthcare decisions. |

continued on following page

*Table 1. Continued*

| Challenges | Implications | Addressing Strategies |
|---|---|---|
| **Patient Autonomy and Informed Consent** | AI-driven healthcare interventions may limit patient autonomy by influencing treatment decisions without full transparency or understanding of how algorithms operate. | Promote transparency in AI-driven healthcare by providing patients with clear explanations of how AI algorithms inform treatment decisions. Ensure patients have the right to opt-out of AI involvement in their care. |
| **Workforce Displacement and Job Insecurity** | Automation of healthcare tasks may lead to job displacement and exacerbate socioeconomic inequalities, raising concerns about the future of the healthcare workforce. | Invest in retraining programs to help displaced workers transition to new roles requiring human expertise. Implement policies to mitigate socioeconomic disparities exacerbated by automation. |
| **Access and Equity** | Unequal access to AI-driven healthcare technologies could widen existing disparities in healthcare access and outcomes, particularly for marginalized and under served communities. | Promote equitable distribution of AI-driven healthcare technologies and ensure affordability and accessibility for all patient populations. Collaborate with community organizations to address barriers to access and promote health equity. |
| **Human-Machine Interaction and Trust** | Establishing trust between healthcare professionals and AI-driven systems is crucial for successful integration, but concerns about reliability, transparency, and control may hinder acceptance. | Develop user-friendly interfaces and transparent algorithms that enable healthcare professionals to understand and trust AI-driven recommendations. Foster a culture of collaboration and shared decision-making between humans |

Source: Kaur (2024)

## CASE STUDIES AND EXAMPLES OF PRACTICAL APPLICATIONS OF AI ROBOTS IN HEALTHCARE

1)**The Surgical Robots Used at Cleveland Clinic:** The da Vinci Surgical System and other surgical robots have been used at the prestigious Cleveland Clinic. The clinic's surgeons have successfully carried out intricate procedures with increased accuracy and little intrusiveness. Positive patient outcomes have resulted from the clinic's use of robotic surgery, with patients reporting faster recovery times and less discomfort.

2)**AI-Powered Imaging at UC San Francisco:** The radiology department of the University of California, San Francisco (UCSF) has incorporated AI. AI systems examine medical pictures, including MRIs and CT scans, to find anomalies and support radiologists. This has sped up the interpretation of complicated imaging data and drastically decreased diagnostic errors (Khang et al., 2023).

3)**The Exoskeleton for Paraplegics by ReWalk:** Exoskeletons created by the Israeli company ReWalk help paraplegic individuals move again. The ability to walk and stand thanks to these robotic exoskeletons greatly enhances users' quality of life. Patients who have improved their general well-being and reached personal milestones are examples of success stories.

4)**The Robotic Nurse, Baxter:** Rethink Robotics' Baxter is a robot that helps nurses in hospitals with a variety of duties. It is capable of carrying out basic patient care tasks, delivering medication, and moving supplies. Baxter has received recognition for increasing overall hospital efficiency by relieving nurses of some of their workload, freeing them up to spend more time with direct patient care (George et al., 2023).

**5)Using Ava, the Avatar for Telemedicine**: The University of Southern California created Ava, an AI-powered avatar that is utilized to give patients telemedicine services. It links patients with specialists and contributes to expanding healthcare access to disadvantaged areas. Healthcare disparities have decreased and patient outcomes have improved because to this technology.

**6)Oscar Health's Insurance Enhanced by AI:** AI is used by the insurance provider Oscar Health to improve its offerings. They provide telemedicine consultations and symptom checkers using their smartphone app. Oscar has improved patient happiness and engagement by giving patients rapid access to care and personalized recommendations.

**7)Mabu for the Treatment of Chronic Illnesses:** Mabu, a robot driven by AI by Catalia Health, is intended to assist patients in managing chronic illnesses. Mabu tracks patients' progress, teaches patients about their diseases, and sends out medication reminders. Improved overall health and more adherence to treatment strategies have been reported by patients.

**8)AI-Assisted Skin Cancer Diagnosis:** AI systems for diagnosing skin cancer, like those created by Google Health, have been successful in correctly recognizing skin lesions that might be malignant. Early detection may save lives and enhance the effectiveness of treatment (Hastuti, 2023).

**9)The Brain-Machine Interface from Neuralink**: Elon Musk launched Neuralink, a company that develops brain-machine interfaces that have the potential to help people with severe neurological impairments regain their ability to communicate and move. Applications in the real world have the power to change the lives of paralyzed people.

**10)Automated Elderly Care Providers:** Elderly people have benefited from the company and assistance of robotic carers like Pepper and PARO, the therapeutic seal robot. Seniors in long-term care homes now have far better emotional well being because to these robots. These case studies demonstrate the practical advantages of AI healthcare robots. They give examples of how integrating AI technology can improve efficiency, improve treatment outcomes, and completely change the patient experience. There will probably be more success stories that highlight the benefits of AI in healthcare for both healthcare organizations and the patients they serve as the area develops (Kaur,2024).

## CONCLUSION

A new era of transformation in healthcare has begun with the incorporation of AI robots, which offer significant advantages to patients, healthcare providers, and the healthcare ecosystem at large. These cutting-edge technologies have demonstrated their promise in a number of healthcare domains, including patient engagement and diagnostics. They have also cleared the path for a future marked by better patient outcomes, increased effectiveness, and easier access to healthcare services. AI robots have completely changed the precision of diagnosis and therapy. Errors have been reduced, complicated surgeries have been completed more quickly, and the general standard of healthcare delivery has increased dramatically.Through education, support, and reminders, these technologies give patients the power to take an active role in their care and make well-informed decisions about their health. Constant research and development in robotics and artificial intelligence is fueling innovation. Future AI solutions will be considerably more advanced and flexible, enhancing patient care even further.

But even as we celebrate these successes, we must also acknowledge how crucial it is to execute them in a morally and responsibly manner. Healthcare AI robots have a long way to go, and there are many factors to take into account. It is crucial to address concerns including data protection, bias reduction, regulatory compliance, and fostering patient and provider confidence. Strict regulatory control, ongoing research, and development are necessary to guarantee the ethical and safe application of AI robots in healthcare. It is essential to stay true to the values of openness, responsibility, and patient-centred care as technology advances. By doing this, we can continue to develop a healthcare environment that is beneficial to everyone and realize the full potential of AI in healthcare. AI robots have a bright future in healthcare, and their thoughtful integration can create a more patient-centred, accessible, and efficient healthcare environment. It is a future worth working towards since it has the power to transform healthcare and enhance people's quality of life everywhere.

## REFERENCES

Abbasimoshaei, A., Chinnakkonda Ravi, A. K., & Kern, T. A. (2023). Development of a New Control System for a Rehabilitation Robot Using Electrical Impedance Tomography and Artificial Intelligence. *Biomimetics*, 8(5), 420. 10.3390/biomimetics805042037754171

Ahmad, A., Tariq, A., Hussain, H. K., & Gill, A. Y. (2023). Revolutionizing Healthcare: How Deep Learning is poised to Change the Landscape of Medical Diagnosis and Treatment. Journal of Computer Networks. *Architecture and High-Performance Computing*, 5(2), 458–471. 10.47709/cnahpc.v5i2.2350

Al Kuwaiti, A., Nazer, K., Al-Reedy, A., Al-Shehri, S., Al-Muhanna, A., Subbarayalu, A. V., Al Muhanna, D., & Al-Muhanna, F. A. (2023). A Review of the Role of Artificial Intelligence in Healthcare. *Journal of Personalized Medicine*, 13(6), 951. 10.3390/jpm1306095137373940

Ali, M. (2023). A Comprehensive Review of AI's Impact on Healthcare: Revolutionizing Diagnostics and Patient Care. *BULLET: Jurnal Multidisiplin Ilmu*, 2(4), 1163–1173.

Alowais, S. A., Alghamdi, S. S., Alsuhebany, N., Alqahtani, T., Alshaya, A. I., Almohareb, S. N., Aldairem, A., Alrashed, M., Bin Saleh, K., Badreldin, H. A., Al Yami, M. S., Al Harbi, S., & Albekairy, A. M. (2023). Revolutionizing healthcare: The role of artificial intelligence in clinical practice. *BMC Medical Education*, 23(1), 689. 10.1186/s12909-023-04698-z37740191

Biswas, S., Pillai, S., Kadhim, H. M., Salam, Z. A., & Marhoon, H. A. (2023, September). Building business resilience and productivity in the healthcare industry with the integration of robotic process automation technology. In *AIP Conference Proceedings* (*Vol. 2736*, No. 1). AIP Publishing. 10.1063/5.0171098

Dicuonzo, G., Donofrio, F., Fusco, A., & Shini, M. (2023). Healthcare system: Moving forward with artificial intelligence. *Technovation*, 120, 102510. 10.1016/j.technovation.2022.102510

Fidan, I., Huseynov, O., Ali, M. A., Alkunte, S., Rajeshirke, M., Gupta, A., Hasanov, S., Tantawi, K., Yasa, E., Yilmaz, O., Loy, J., Popov, V., & Sharma, A. (2023). Recent inventions in additive manufacturing: Holistic review. *Inventions (Basel, Switzerland)*, 8(4), 103. 10.3390/inventions8040103

Firoozi, A. A., & Firoozi, A. A. (2023). A systematic review of the role of 4D printing in sustainable civil engineering solutions. *Heliyon*, 9(10), e20982. 10.1016/j.heliyon.2023.e2098237928382

George, A. S., George, A. H., & Martin, A. G. (2023). ChatGPT and the Future of Work: A Comprehensive Analysis of AI's Impact on Jobs and Employment. *Partners Universal International Innovation Journal*, 1(3), 154–186.

Harry, A. (2023). The Future of Medicine: Harnessing the Power of AI for Revolutionizing Healthcare. *International Journal of Multidisciplinary Sciences and Arts*, 2(1), 36–47. 10.47709/ijmdsa.v2i1.2395

Hastuti, R., & Syafruddin, . (2023). Ethical Considerations in the Age of Artificial Intelligence: Balancing Innovation and Social Values. *West Science Social and Humanities Studies*, 1(02), 76–87. 10.58812/wsshs.v1i02.191

Kato, K., Yoshimi, T., Aimoto, K., Sato, K., Itoh, N., & Kondo, I. (2023). Reduction of multiple-caregiver assistance through the long-term use of a transfer support robot in a nursing facility. *Assistive Technology*, 35(3), 271–278. 10.1080/10400435.2022.203932435320681

Kaur, J. (2024). Green Finance 2.0: Pioneering Pathways for Sustainable Development and Health Through Future Trends and Innovations. In *Sustainable Investments in Green Finance* (pp. 294-319). IGI Global.

Kaur, J. (2024). Insightful Visions: How Medical Imaging Empowers Patient-Centric Healthcare. In *Future of AI in Medical Imaging* (pp. 42-57). IGI Global.

Kaur, J. (2024). Fueling Healthcare Transformation: The Nexus of Startups, Venture Capital, and Innovation. In *Fostering Innovation in Venture Capital and Startup Ecosystems* (pp. 327-351). IGI Global.

Kaur, J. (2024). Virtual Insights, Real Solutions: The Promise of Augmented Reality in Medicine. In *Approaches to Human-Centered AI in Healthcare* (pp. 20-41). IGI Global.

Kaur, J. (2024). Green Guardians: Unveiling the Strategic Role of HR in Environmental Sustainability Initiatives. In *Building Sustainable Human Resources Management Practices for Businesses* (pp. 125-143). IGI Global.

Khaddad, A., Bernhard, J. C., Margue, G., Michiels, C., Ricard, S., Chandelon, K., Bladou, F., Bourdel, N., & Bartoli, A. (2023). A survey of augmented reality methods to guide minimally invasive partial nephrectomy. *World Journal of Urology*, 41(2), 335–343. 10.1007/s00345-022-04078-035776173

Khang, A., Hahanov, V., Litvinova, E., Chumachenko, S., Hajimahmud, A. V., Ali, R. N., & Anh, P. T. N. (2023). The Analytics of Hospitality of Hospitals in a Healthcare Ecosystem. In *Data-Centric AI Solutions and Emerging Technologies in the Healthcare Ecosystem* (pp. 39–61). CRC Press. 10.1201/9781003356189-4

Kim, J., Gu, G. M., & Heo, P. (2016). Robotics for healthcare. *Biomedical Engineering: Frontier Research and Converging Technologies*, 489-509.

Kim, M., Zhang, Y., & Jin, S. (2023). Soft tissue surgical robot for minimally invasive surgery: A review. *Biomedical Engineering Letters*, 13(4), 1–9. 10.1007/s13534-023-00326-337872994

Kumar, P., Chauhan, S., & Awasthi, L. K. (2023). Artificial intelligence in healthcare: Review, ethics, trust challenges & future research directions. *Engineering Applications of Artificial Intelligence*, 120, 105894. 10.1016/j.engappai.2023.105894

Kyrarini, M., Lygerakis, F., Rajavenkatanarayanan, A., Sevastopoulos, C., Nambiappan, H. R., Chaitanya, K. K., Babu, A. R., Mathew, J., & Makedon, F. (2021). A survey of robots in healthcare. *Technologies*, 9(1), 8. 10.3390/technologies9010008

Lochan, K., Suklyabaidya, A., & Roy, B. K. (2023). Medical and healthcare robots in India. In *Medical and Healthcare Robotics* (pp. 221–236). Academic Press. 10.1016/B978-0-443-18460-4.00010-X

Mahmoud, H., Aljaldi, F., El-Fiky, A., Battecha, K., Thabet, A., Alayat, M., & Ibrahim, A. (2023). Artificial Intelligence machine learning and conventional physical therapy for upper limb outcome in patients with stroke: A systematic review and meta-analysis. *European Review for Medical and Pharmacological Sciences*, 27(11).37318455

Matsuzaki, H., & Gliesche, P. (2023). Robots and Norms of Care: A Comparative Analysis of the Reception of Robotic Assistance in Nursing. In *Social Robots in Social Institutions* (pp. 90-99). IOS Press. 10.3233/FAIA220607

Minopoulos, G. M., Memos, V. A., Stergiou, K. D., Stergiou, C. L., & Psannis, K. E. (2023). A Medical Image Visualization Technique Assisted with AI-Based Haptic Feedback for Robotic Surgery and Healthcare. *Applied Sciences (Basel, Switzerland)*, 13(6), 3592. 10.3390/app13063592

Murakami, Y., Honaga, K., Kono, H., Haruyama, K., Yamaguchi, T., Tani, M., Isayama, R., Takakura, T., Tanuma, A., Hatori, K., Wada, F., & Fujiwara, T. (2023). New Artificial Intelligence-Integrated Electromyography-Driven Robot Hand for Upper Extremity Rehabilitation of Patients With Stroke: A Randomized, Controlled Trial. *Neurorehabilitation and Neural Repair*, 37(5), 15459683231166939. 10.1177/15459683231166939370393 19

Nwadiokwu, O. T. (2023). Examining the Impact and Challenges of Artificial Intelligence (AI) in Healthcare. *Edward Waters University Undergraduate Research Journal, 1*(1).

Ohneberg, C., Stöbich, N., Warmbein, A., Rathgeber, I., Mehler-Klamt, A. C., Fischer, U., & Eberl, I. (2023). Assistive robotic systems in nursing care: A scoping review. *BMC Nursing*, 22(1), 1–15. 10.1186/s12912-023-01230-y36934280

Ragno, L., Borboni, A., Vannetti, F., Amici, C., & Cusano, N. (2023). Application of Social Robots in Healthcare: Review on Characteristics, Requirements, Technical Solutions. *Sensors (Basel)*, 23(15), 6820. 10.3390/s2315682037571603

Ramezani, M., & Mohd Ripin, Z. (2023). 4D printing in biomedical engineering: Advancements, challenges, and future directions. *Journal of Functional Biomaterials*, 14(7), 347. 10.3390/jfb1407034737504842

Riek, L. D. (2017). Healthcare robotics. *Communications of the ACM*, 60(11), 68–78. 10.1145/3127874

Rivero-Moreno, Y., Echevarria, S., Vidal-Valderrama, C., Stefano-Pianetti, L., Cordova-Guilarte, J., Navarro-Gonzalez, J., & Avila, G. L. D. (2023). Robotic Surgery: A Comprehensive Review of the Literature and Current Trends. *Cureus*, 15(7). 10.7759/cureus.4237037621804

Sahoo, S. K., & Goswami, S. S. (2023). A comprehensive review of multiple criteria decision-making (MCDM) Methods: Advancements, applications, and future directions. *Decision Making Advances*, 1(1), 25–48. 10.31181/dma1120237

Schönmann, M., Bodenschatz, A., Uhl, M., & Walkowitz, G. (2023). The Care-Dependent are Less Averse to Care Robots: An Empirical Comparison of Attitudes. *International Journal of Social Robotics*, 15(6), 1–18. 10.1007/s12369-023-01003-237359432

Shakeel, T., Habib, S., Boulila, W., Koubaa, A., Javed, A. R., Rizwan, M., Gadekallu, T. R., & Sufiyan, M. (2023). A survey on COVID-19 impact in the healthcare domain: Worldwide market implementation, applications, security and privacy issues, challenges and future prospects. *Complex & Intelligent Systems*, 9(1), 1027–1058. 10.1007/s40747-022-00767-w35668731

Stasevych, M., & Zvarych, V. (2023). Innovative robotic technologies and artificial intelligence in pharmacy and medicine: Paving the way for the future of health care—a review. *Big Data and Cognitive Computing*, 7(3), 147. 10.3390/bdcc7030147

Tang, L., Li, J., & Fantus, S. (2023). Medical artificial intelligence ethics: A systematic review of empirical studies. *Digital Health*, 9, 20552076231186064. 10.1177/20552076231186064 37434728

Tigard, D. W., Braun, M., Breuer, S., Ritt, K., Fiske, A., McLennan, S., & Buyx, A. (2023). Toward best practices in embedded ethics: Suggestions for interdisciplinary technology development. *Robotics and Autonomous Systems*, 167, 104467. 10.1016/j.robot.2023.104467

Tukhtakhodjaeva, F. S., & Khayitova, I. I. (2023). APPLICATION AND USE OF AI (ARTIFICIAL INTELLIGENCE) IN MEDICINE. *Educational Research in Universal Sciences*, 2(9), 302–309.

Vallès-Peris, N., & Domènech, M. (2023). Caring in the in-between: A proposal to introduce responsible AI and robotics to healthcare. *AI & Society*, 38(4), 1685–1695. 10.1007/s00146-021-01330-w

Verma, V., Chowdary, V., Gupta, M. K., & Mondal, A. K. (2018). IoT and robotics in healthcare. In *Medical big data and internet of medical things* (pp. 245–269). CRC Press. 10.1201/9781351030380-10

Wang, C., Liu, S., Yang, H., Guo, J., Wu, Y., & Liu, J. (2023). Ethical considerations of using ChatGPT in health care. *Journal of Medical Internet Research*, 25, e48009. 10.2196/4800937566454

Yeisson, R. M., Sophia, E., Vidal-Valderrama, C., Luigi, P., Jesus, C. G., Navarro-Gonzalez, J., & Katheryn, A. A. (2023). Robotic Surgery: A Comprehensive Review of the Literature and Current Trends. *Cureus*, 15(7).37621804

## KEY TERMS AND DEFINITIONS

**Robotic Surgical Assistants:** A revolutionary development in healthcare that provide unparalleled levels of accuracy, command, and effectiveness in surgical procedures.

# Chapter 14
# Healthcare Integrating Automation and Robotics-Based Industry 5.0 Advancement

**P. Sindhu**
https://orcid.org/0000-0002-2947-9831
*Madurai Kamaraj University, India*

**M. Sivakumar**
*Madurai Kamaraj University, India*

## ABSTRACT

*Healthcare is undergoing a significant transformation with the advantage of Industry 5.0, which is marked by the fusion of human expertise and advanced technology. This period is characterized by the integration of automation and robotics into healthcare practices, which can enhance patient care, optimize operational efficiency, and redefine medical norms. This chapter provides an overview of the use of automation and robotics in healthcare within the context of Industry 5.0. It analyzes the ways in which telemedicine, patient monitoring, and customized therapy are facilitated by robotics and automation*

## INTRODUCTION

The healthcare sector is poised for a significant transformation towards Industry 5.0, characterized by the integration of advanced technology and human expertise. In this process, automation and robotics play a vital role in enhancing patient care, enhancing operational efficiency, and revolutionizing medical procedures. Some current application of automation and robotics in the healthcare industry include the use of robotic exoskeletons for rehabilitation, automated medicine dispensing, and surgical robots.The combination of automation and robotics in the healthcare industry is a critical component of Industry 5.0 developments, which emphasize human-technology collaboration and sophisticated technological integration (Vadivel, 2024). Robotics has transformed healthcare, notably in fields such as surgery, rehabilitation, telemedicine, and diagnostics, with AI and IOT improving medical robots' cognitive skills.

DOI: 10.4018/979-8-3693-2901-6.ch014

## Overview of Industry Revolution

**Industry 1.0:** The 18th-century Mechanization. The First Industrial Revolution, which occurred industrialized ones, primarily driven by innovations in textile manufacturing, steam power, and iron production. Key inventions during this period included the steam engine, spinning jenny, power loom, and improvements in iron and steel production. This revolution started in Britain and gradually spread to other parts of Europe and North America.

**Industry 2.0:** The Electrification Revolution, which commenced in the late 19th century, marked a shift towards using electricity as fuel. driving further progress in manufacturing, transportation, and communication technologies. Notable achievements during this period included the growth of railroads, the extensive adoption of electricity and electric-powered machinery, the creation of the internal combustion engine, and the development of steel production methods like the Bessemer process. This revolution also contributed to the rise of mass production and the emergence of large-scale corporations.

**Industry 3.0:** The Digital Revolution, which commenced the mid-20th century, also known as the Third Industrial Revolution, marked the widespread adoption of digital technologies, especially computers and the internet. This period transformed industries such as telecommunications, computing, and entertainment, leading to increased automation, globalization of markets, and the emergence of new business models such as e-commerce and digital services.

**Industry 4.0:** Digitalization and the incorporation of cutting-edge technologies into production processes define this revolution. Current Fourth Industrial Revolution: The World Economic Forum's founder, Klaus Schwab, is credited with coining this phrase, which describes the current period of extremely fast technological growth marked by the convergence of digital, physical, and biological technology. Artificial intelligence, robots, 3D printing, nanotechnology, biotechnology, and the Internet of Things are some of the major technologies advancing this revolution. It is anticipated that the fourth industrial revolution would significantly alter a number of societal facets, including job trends, healthcare, education, and government. Rethink accepted medical practices. An overview of the application of robotics and automation

**Industry 5.0:** A new stage of industrialization known as the "Human-Centric Revolution" emphasizes human collaboration with AI-powered robots and cutting-edge technology. Learning Machines and Artificial Intelligence: In the healthcare industry, artificial intelligence (AI) and machine learning are being used more and more for activities including drug development, medical imaging analysis, predictive analytics, and customized treatment planning. Three initiatives are at the core of Industry 5.0

**Human-Centric:**This tactic transforms individuals from mere resources into true assets. Resilience: The goal of this strategy is to become more resilient in the face of global issues like the Covid-19 outbreak and shortages in foreign supplies.Every industrial revolution has changed how people live, work, and connect with one another, having a significant impact on economies, society, and cultures. Discussions concerning these revolutions' effects on the environment, jobs, and income distribution have also been triggered. Emphasizing the necessity of conscientious innovation and policy measures to tackle their obstacles and prospects. Technological improvements, shifting patient expectations, demographic shifts, and fluctuating regulatory environments have all contributed to a dramatic upheaval in thehealthcare business. The following are some salient features of the current healthcare sector revolution.

## BACKGROUND

### Integration of Healthcare Automation

#### Digital Health Technologies

The delivery and administration of healthcare have changed dramatically as a result of the incorporation of digital technology including wearable, mobile health apps, telemedicine, and electronic health records (EHRs). These technological advancements provide more patient interaction, personalized treatment, and remote monitoring, resulting in more effective and easily accessible healthcare services.

#### Precision Medicine

Personalized medicine, or precision medicine, focuses on customizing medical interventions and treatments to each patient's unique genetic, environmental, and lifestyle factors. A new age of more efficient and individualized healthcare is being ushered in by developments in genomics, biomarker identification, and data analytics that are facilitating the creation of focused medicines and diagnostics.

#### Value-Based Care

Value-based care models are becoming more and more popular; these models put patient happiness and high-quality outcomes ahead of quantity of services rendered. Healthcare providers are encouraged by to offer coordinated, high-quality treatment while keeping costs under control.

#### Patient-Centric Approach

The delivery of patient-centered care, which considers each patient's preferences, wants, and objectives, is becoming more and more important to healthcare practitioners. This entails developing patient-provider communication, encouraging collaborative decision-making, and expanding access to health services and information.

#### Rise of Health Tech Startups

The number of health tech firms in the healthcare sector has increased dramatically, with the aim of creating novel approaches to tackle issues related to patient engagement, illness management and healthcare delivery. These firms are spearheading innovation and disruption throughout the healthcare industry, encompassing digital treatments, wearable health technology, and AI-powered diagnostics.

## Regulatory and Policy Changes

Governments and regulatory agencies are putting new laws and regulations into place to encourage innovation, adjust to the rapidly evolving healthcare industry, and enhance the availability, affordability, and standard of treatment. These include programmed that encourage the use of telemedicine, robotics surgery encourage the interchange of health data, and provide incentives for value-based care models.

### Benefits and prospects

Discuss how these technologies may improve patient safety, workflow efficiency, remote patient monitoring, and the decrease in human error.

### Robotic Surgery

Analyze the advantages, potential innovations, and developments in robotically assisted surgery investigate the use of AI-driven automation in pathology, radiography, lab operations, and diagnostics.

### Patient care and rehabilitation

Discuss the employment of robots in physical rehabilitation, prosthetics, and assistive technologies for the elderly. Analyze the ways in which telemedicine, patient monitoring, and tailored therapy are facilitated by robotics and automation.

## LITERATURE REVIEW

Review of Literature on Robotics Automation IntroductionRobotics automation is a field that has seen rapid advancement over the past few decades, transforming industries and reshaping the nature of work. This review examines key literature on the subject, focusing on historical development, current trends, and future directions in robotics automation. Historical DevelopmentThe evolution of robotics automation can be traced back to early automata and simple mechanical devices. The invention of the programmable logic controller (PLC) in the 1960s marked a significant milestone, enabling more complex and flexible automation solutions (Nof, 2009). Since then, advancements in computing, sensor technology, and artificial intelligence have driven the development of sophisticated robots capable of performing a wide range of tasks.

Modern industrial robots are essential in manufacturing for tasks such as assembly, welding, and painting. They enhance productivity, precision, and safety. Collaborative robots (cobots) have emerged, working alongside humans to combine the strengths of both (Djuric, Urbanic, & Rickli, 2016). These robots operate outside industrial environments, performing tasks in healthcare, hospitality, and domestic settings. Examples include robotic surgical systems, automated cleaning robots, and customer service bots (Murphy, 2019).Integration of AI and machine learning with robotics has led to smarter robots that can learn from their environment and improve performance over time. This synergy is crucial for tasks requiring adaptability and complex decision-making (Nguyen et al., 2019).4. Autonomous mobile robots

(AMRs) and drones are becoming common in logistics and delivery, capable of navigating complex environments without human intervention.

Their development is driven by advances in perception, navigation, and decision-making technologies (Murray, Chu, & Wu, 2020). The increasing presence of robots in various sectors raises ethical and social concerns, such as job displacement, privacy, and safety. These issues are critical areas of ongoing research and debate (Calo, 2015).Future DirectionsThe future of robotics automation is poised to be shaped by several factors:- Improving the ways humans and robots interact will make robots more intuitive and accessible.-Deploying robots in space exploration, deep-sea missions, and hazardous areas on Earth is an exciting frontier.Developing robots with flexible and adaptive materials to handle delicate tasks. Combining robotics with the Internet of Things (IoT) to create interconnected and intelligent systems (Atzori, Iera, & Morabito, 2010).

## OBJECTIVES

The automation and robots may be integrated into healthcare to promote Industry 5.0.

To know about Industry revolution and assessing the possible advantages of automation and robots in enhancing patient outcomes and medical services.

To know about Pioneering Robotic Inventions the efficient application of automation and robots in diverse healthcare environments.

To discuss the possibilities pertaining to the use of cutting-edge medical technology.

## WORLD SMART HOSPITALS

*Table 1. List of smart hospitals in the world*

| S. No. | Hospitals | Country | Functions |
|---|---|---|---|
| 1. | Massachusetts General Hospital | US | Robotics |
| 2. | Cleveland Clinic | US | Artificial Intelligence |
| 3 | The Mount Sinai Hospital | US | Digital Imaging Artificial Intelligence |
| 4. | Brigham and Womens Hospital | US | Electronic Functionalities |
| 5. | Karolinska University jukhuset | Swedan | Artificial Intelligence |
| 6. | Sheba Medical Center | Israel | Electronic Functionalities Robotics |
| 7. | Aarhus University Hospital | Denmark | Electronic Functionalities |
| 8. | Fortis Memorial Research institute | India | Artificial Intelligence |
| 9. | The Ottawa Hospital | Canada | Digital Imaging |
| 10. | Ospedale San Martino di Genova | Italy | Telemedicine |

**Sources:** Alinahealth.org

Hospitals are radically rethinking how treatment is provided inside the health system by utilizing cutting edge technologies. Information sharing is being redefined via the use of cutting edge digital imaging, robots, AI-driven decision assistance, and virtual care technologies that are all integrated into the hospital network. Utilizing these new technologies helps hospitals achieve their goals for population health, quality of life, and prevention by improving care delivery results and efficiency inside the hospital and by positioning them as a part of a larger ecosystem.

A list of hospitals that effectively use the newest technology has been compiled by Statista. The Finest Smart Hospitals in the World the 300 facilities in 28 nations that excel in using artificial intelligence (AI), digital imaging, telemedicine, robots, and electronic functions are ranked in 2023.

## Robotics in HealthcarePresent and Future

By 2025, the medical robots industry is expected to grow to $12.7 billion globally, with hospitals accounting for the biggest portion of the market in 2020. Medical robots have grown significantly from their modest beginnings in the 1980s in assisting medical operations and duties. Global inventors are paving the path for more accurate and efficient treatment by creating new capabilities for robotics systems in the healthcare industry.

### Healthcare at Present

Minimally invasive surgery is made possible by systems such as the da Vinci Surgical System, which allows for greater precision, smaller incisions, and faster recovery. These robots provide remote patient monitoring and consultations, allowing healthcare personnel to connect with patients while not physically present. Exoskeletons, for example, aid in the rehabilitation of patients following injury or surgery, allowing them to restore movement and strength. Automated medication distribution systems help hospitals and pharmacies eliminate mistakes and improve the drug delivery procedure. Robots aid with chores such as lifting patients, moving them about, and reminding them to take medication.

### Healthcare in Future

Consider small robots exploring the bloodstream, delivering medications to specific cells or performing cellular microsurgery. AI will play an increasingly important role in healthcare robotics, allowing robots to learn from experience, adapt to changing settings, and deliver more personalized care. Robots will increasingly be used in home healthcare settings to provide companionship, monitor vital signs, and aid the elderly or crippled with everyday duties. Advanced prosthetic limbs controlled by cerebral impulses will become more common, providing more dexterity and a more natural range of motion.

The Future surgical robots will be even more precise and autonomous, potentially decreasing the need for human assistance in some surgeries. Robots with AI and emotional intelligence skills will provide companionship and emotional support to patients, notably in long-term care institutions and hospices. Drones carrying medical supplies or even miniature medical facilities might provide immediate reaction and medical care in distant or disaster-stricken locations.

## SOLUTIONS AND RECOMMENDATIONS

### Implementation Strategies

Infrastructure requirements: Talk about the financial and technological resources needed to integrate automation and robots in healthcare facilities.

#### Assessment and Planning

Conduct a thorough review of the current appointment scheduling process, including workflow analysis, stakeholder interviews, and data gathering on wait times and appointment volumes. Identify scheduling-related pain spots, bottlenecks, and possibilities for improvement. Establish defined objectives and success criteria for the automation programmed.

#### Technology Selection

Evaluate available automation technologies, such as scheduling software, chat bots, and appointment reminder systems. Select a technological solution that meets the hospital's needs, budget, and scalability. Consider things like integration capabilities, simplicity of use, data security, and regulatory compliance.

#### Customization and Integration

Customize the technological solution to match the hospital's unique demands and workflow constraints. Integrate the automation system with current EHR systems, patient information, and communication channels. Ensure that automated scheduling software and other hospital systems are interoperable and communicate data seamlessly.

#### Training and Change Management

Train and assist administrative personnel and healthcare professionals on how to use the new automation system. Address any concerns or opposition to change via clear communication, education, and stakeholder involvement. To get the most out of automation, foster a culture of continual learning and adaptability.

#### Pilot Testing and Evaluation

Implement the automatic scheduling system as a pilot in a controlled setting. Monitor important performance indicators such as wait times, appointment adherence, staff productivity, and patient satisfaction. Collect input from patients, staff, and stakeholders to identify areas for enhancements and refinements.

## Full-Scale Deployment

Implement the automated scheduling system in all departments and clinics of the hospital. During the early stages of implementation, keep an eye on system performance and user input. Make the necessary changes and optimizations based on real-world experience and feedback.

## Training and Workforce Development

Discuss how important it is to provide healthcare personnel the instruction they need to use and handle this technology.

## Regulatory Factors to Consider

Examine the ethical and regulatory constraints surrounding the use of robots and automation in the healthcare sector. The Bright Future of Automation Professionals and fans in robotics see many prospects for future development with each newly developed or upgraded robotic system. But there are certain challenges to this progress.

## Challenges and Roadblocks

Three distinct obstacles must be overcome by the healthcare sector before robots are widely used: a lack of patient confidence, a shortage of qualified personnel, and safety concerns.Clean their teeth on a regular basis. Healthcare practitioners must convey the benefits of foster their trust. The healthcare sector is lacking in qualified workers, despite the fact that graduates with these backgrounds are in great demand due to developments in robotics, artificial intelligence, and cyber securityaddress the future demands of robotics in healthcare.

## Pioneering Robotic Inventions

Hospitals and clinics around the United States and abroad are increasingly using robotic systems, such as and TUG. They are elements of the da Vinci Surgical System. TUG is a self-sufficient mobile delivery robot that has the capacity to transport up to 453 kg of racks, carts, or bins that hold delicate products, such as lab specimens, pharmaceuticals, or other items.

Through a touch screen interface, medical workers may send or request deliveries from the robot, making over 50,000 deliveries every week at over 140 hospitals nationwide. The robotic concierge SAM, pharmaceutical management system pharm ASSISTROBOTx, disinfecting robot Xenex, and capsule robot Origami are a few other innovative creations. Senior patients who are alone are consoled by social companion robots,

**Case Studies:** Give examples of healthcare organizations that have effectively used automation and robotics to improve patient care, productivity, and outcomes. Case studies and success stories should also be considered. Difficulties and Ethical Issues Discuss the challenges, including budgetary limitations, interoperability issues, data security concerns, and ethical conundrums related to patient consent, privacy, and the application of AI in decision-making.

## FUTURE RESEARCH DIRECTIONS

The future scope of healthcare automation and robotics is vast, with many opportunities for further research and development.

Some potential areas of focus include the development of more advanced robotic systems for surgical procedures,

The exploration of new materials and technologies for the design of medical devices.

Give practical advice on how stakeholders, legislators, and healthcare organizations may use automation and robots to improve patient care and delivery of healthcare.

## CONCLUSION

The chapter provide a summary of the potential game-changing effects of automation and robotics in healthcare for the progress of Industry 5.0, highlighting the necessity of stakeholder collaboration in order to properly and ethically utilize these technologies. The integration of automation and robotics in healthcare has shown great potential in improving the efficiency and quality of healthcare services. The use of Industry 5.0 advancements has enabled the development of innovative solutions that can address the challenges faced by the healthcare industry.

## REFERENCES

Atzori, L., Iera, A., & Morabito, G. (2010). The internet of things: A survey. *Computer Networks*, 54(15), 2787–2805. 10.1016/j.comnet.2010.05.010

Calo, R. (2015). Robotics and the Lessons of Cyberlaw. *California Law Review*, 103, 513.

Djuric, A. M., Urbanic, R. J., & Rickli, J. L. (2016). A framework for collaborative robot (cobot) integration in advanced manufacturing systems. *SAE International Journal of Materials and Manufacturing*, 9(2), 457–463. 10.4271/2016-01-0337

Murphy, R. R. (2019). Introduction to AI robotics. MIT Press.- Murray, C. C., Chu, A. G., & Wu, Y. (2020). Autonomous mobile robots in logistics: Trends and future directions. *Autonomous Robots*, 44(6), 1231–1246.

Nguyen, T. T., Wong, Y. S., Zhang, D., & Wang, L. (2019). Machine learning in robotics: A survey. *Robotics (Basel, Switzerland)*, 8(1), 24.

Nof, S. Y. (2009). *Springer handbook of automation*. Springer Science & Business Media. 10.1007/978-3-540-78831-7

## ADDITIONAL READING

Biswas, M. I., & Singh, D. R. (2024, February 10). Application Of AI And Blockchain In Healthcare Industry – A Review. *Journal of Advanced Zoology*. 10.53555/jaz.v45i2.3983

Charalambous, H. (2019). Robotics and automation in the hospital of the future. *Journal of Medical Engineering & Technology*, 43(1), 1–6.31033365

Devadoss, S. C. A. (2024, February 15). The AI Revolution in Healthcare Product Management. *International Journal of Computer Trends and Technology*, 72(2), 1–8. 10.14445/22312803/IJCTT-V72I2P101

Dipla, V. (2021, March 23). AI and the Healthcare sector: Industry, legal and ethical issues. *Bioethica*, 7(1), 34. 10.12681/bioeth.26540

European Commission. (n.d.). *Digital Transformation of Health and Care*. EC. https://ec.europa.eu/health/ehealth/digital_transformation_en

Garg, T. (2016). Wearable Technology in Medicine: Current State and Future Directions. *International Journal of Medical Informatics*, 93, 102–107.

GhoshRoy, D., Alvi, P., & Santosh, K. C. (2023, March 23). Unboxing Industry-Standard AI Models for Male Fertility Prediction with SHAP. *Health Care*, 11(7), 929. 10.3390/healthcare1107092937046855

Housman, D., & Malachowski, E. (2016). Using Wearable Technology to Increase Physical Activity in Older Adults: A Review. *Maturitas*, 94, 14–23.

Narasima Venkatesh, A. D. (2019). Reimagining the Future of Healthcare Industry through Internet of Medical Things (IOMT), Artificial Intelligence (AI), Machine Learning (ML), Big Data, Mobile Apps and Advanced Sensors. SSRN *Electronic Journal*. https://doi.org/10.2139/ssrn.3522960

Navarro, V. (2013). Robotics in healthcare: A survey. *International Journal of Advanced Robotic Systems*, 10(1), 1–13.

Nunes, S., Gastauer, M., Cavalcante, R. B., Ramos, S. J., Caldeira, C. F.Jr, Silva, D., Rodrigues, R. R., Salomão, R., Oliveira, M., Souza-Filho, P. W. M., & Siqueira, J. O. (2020). Challenges and opportunities for large-scale reforestation in the Eastern Amazon using native species. *Forest Ecology and Management*, 466, 118120. 10.1016/j.foreco.2020.118120

Patel, V. R. (2009). Robot-assisted laparoscopic radical prostatectomy: A review of current outcomes. *BJU International*, 103(9), 1196–1210.19402830

Rao, S. S., Fernandes, S. L., Singh, C., & Gatti, R. R. (Eds.). (2023). *AIoT and Big Data Analytics for Smart Healthcare Applications*. Bentham Science Publishers.

Rikhari, H., Baidya Kayal, E., Ganguly, S., Sasi, A., Sharma, S., Dheeksha, D. S., Saini, M., Rangarajan, K., Bakhshi, S., Kandasamy, D., & Mehndiratta, A. (2024). Fully automatic deep learning-based lung parenchyma segmentation and boundary correction in thoracic CT scans. *International Journal of Computer Assisted Radiology and Surgery*, 19(2), 261–272. 10.1007/s11548-023-03010-037594684

Sindhu, P. (2023). An Evaluation of Service Quality In Public And Private Hospitals In Tamil Nadu Using Servqual Models. *AEIJMR – 11*(06).

Sindhu, P., & Sivakumar, M. (2022). A Study on Comprehensive Assessment of Firm Efficiency Using Ratios of Private Healthcare In India. *Fostering Resilient Business Ecosystems and Economic Growth: Towards the Next Normal, 415.*

Solanki, P., Grundy, J., & Hussain, W. (2022, July 19). Operationalising ethics in artificial intelligence for healthcare: A framework for AI developers. *AI and Ethics*, 3(1), 223–240. 10.1007/s43681-022-00195-z

Topol, E. J. (2019). High-performance medicine: The convergence of human and artificial intelligence. *Nature Medicine*, 25(1), 44–56. 10.1038/s41591-018-0300-730617339

Vadivel, S. R. S. (2024). Integrating the Industrial Revolution 5.0 With AI: A Paradigm Shift in Manufacturing and Beyond. In *Industry Applications of Thrust Manufacturing: Convergence with Real-Time Data and AI* (pp. 118-147). IGI Global.

Wac, K. (2018). The potential of machine learning in healthcare. [TMIS]. *ACM Transactions on Management Information Systems*, 9(3), 1–19.

World Health Organization (WHO). (n.d.). *Digital Health*. WHO. https://www.who.int/health-topics/digital-health#tab=tab_1

Zhang, S. (2009). Intelligent robots in healthcare: A review. *Artificial Intelligence in Medicine*, 46(1), 1–11.18818061

# Chapter 15
# Industry 5.0 and Its Transformative Impact on Healthcare:
## A Paradigm Shift Toward Human-Centric Collaboration

**Kavitha Murugan**
*Sri Krishna College of Engineering and Technology, India*

**Jayasudha Subburaj**
*Sri Krishna College of Engineering and Technology, India*

**Keerthana P.**
*Sri Krishna College of Engineering and Technology, India*

**Roobini S.**
*SNS College of Technology, Coimbatore, India*

## ABSTRACT

*The era of Industry 5.0, characterized by a deep integration of technology and human cooperation, is set to bring about a major transformation in the healthcare sector. This chapter highlights a major shift toward human-centric teaming and looks at how Industry 5.0 affects healthcare. The convergence of human knowledge and state-of-the-art technologies is transforming healthcare delivery, including patient care and diagnostics. The study talks about the potentials and opportunities of Healthcare 5.0, which include more patient-centered care, telemedicine, personalized medicine, and advanced diagnostics. These are all made possible by the use of cutting-edge technologies like robotics, big data analytics, blockchain, and artificial intelligence (AI). The report also addresses the challenges and concerns that need to be resolved for healthcare 5.0 to be effectively implemented, such as data security and privacy, moral and legal dilemmas, the requirement for healthcare workers to have the right training and abilities, and cost-effectiveness.*

DOI: 10.4018/979-8-3693-2901-6.ch015

## INTRODUCTION

After ten years of providing industry 4.0 to address the deficiencies of the industry, the time has come for industry 5.0. Industry 4.0 is limited as smart factories are raising corporate productivity. This research article discusses industry 5.0 potential directions, challenges, and opportunities for further research. A paradigm shift is being brought about by Industry 5.0. and resolution by placing fewer weight on knowledge and assuming that machine-human cooperation is the foundation for success. The industrial revolution is enhancing customer satisfaction by using personalized products. With today's companies relying on paid technological breakthroughs to gain competitive advantages and boost economic growth, Industry 5.0 is essential. Limitations of Industry 5.0 technological getting and technical hope are vital. Training those who custom the original knowhows also occurs at the same time as technology is adapted to humans Present issues include safety, secrecy, labor shortages, lengthy procedures, and high costs. Adoption of industry 5.0 necessitates adherence to industrial rules and regulations that facilitate cobot and smart machine cooperation.

The Fifth Industrial Revolution, or Industry 5.0, is characterized by a change in emphasis from an economic perspective to one that emphasizes social values and well-being. This is a new era of industry where people collaborate with cutting-edge machinery and AI-powered robots to enhance workplace procedures.

It is made possible by advancements in IT, such as automation, data, IoT, machine learning, virtualization, and artificial intelligence, and it covers a wide range of operations, not just manufacturing. The primary distinction with Industry 4.0 is that it prioritizes worker welfare throughout the production process, creating prosperity that extends beyond employment and expansion.

## EVOLUTION OF INDUSTRY

There have been new industrial innovations and achievements at every stage of the industry's long and fascinating growth. From Industry 1.0 to the approaching Industry 5.0, each phase of the industrial revolution has been characterized by a unique collection of innovations. The 18th century saw the start of Industry 1.0, which was the shift from a handicraft economy to a manufacturing sector that made use of new technology and machinery. The invention of steam power, which raised output and volume, was the main force behind this revolution. Examples include the invention of the flying shuttle in 1733 to facilitate the process of weaving fabric, the construction of the first textile mill in the United States in 1790, and the patenting of the cotton gin in 1794.

The assembly line and the use of electricity in manufacturing were two of the innovations that defined Industry 2.0, sometimes referred to as the next engineering revolt, which removed home in the late 19th & 20th centuries. Mass manufacturing increased significantly as a result of this revolution. In this time, Henry Ford employed assembly line manufacturing to great effect in his automotive assembly factory (Gomathi et al., 2023).

Beginning in the 1970s, Industry 3.0 witnessed a rise in the automation of production processes thanks to the introduction of new memory-programmable controllers. Computers started to play a major role in manufacturing at this time, enabling the partial automation of several industrial processes.

The subsequent stage of effort growth, known by way of Industry 5.0, will see robots becoming sophisticated enough to carry out complicated tasks on their own. Together with people, these will use state-of-the-art technology and computer power to deliver precision and speed. Industry 5.0 is predicated on finding the optimal balance between human ingenuity and robotization, fusing human inventiveness with the precision, intelligence, and exactness of technology.

Human-Centric Approach: In contrast to Industry 4.0, which emphasizes efficiency and automation, Industry 5.0 places a higher priority on human-machine cooperation with the goal of utilizing both groups' respective capabilities. Sustainability: Production methods that reduce environmental effect and uphold social responsibility are highly valued. Personalization and customization: It highlights the capacity to mass-produce highly customized and individualized goods that cater to the specific demands of each unique consumer.

## RELATED WORK

Over the past few decades, there has been a remarkable revolution in all areas of human impact. Consumer tastes are evolving, and globalization efforts include modernizing management models. Data, communication, and learning are now the main management objectives of the fourth wave of industrialization. The automation of corporate processes changes the countryside of work and creates novel challenges, which too affects the tasks of employees they must do. This causes retired vocations to vanish, changes professions, and fosters the development of new ones; on the other hand, it causes unemployment. In this new strategy, people would require certain skills, sometimes referred to as 21st-century capabilities Kasinathan et al. (2022) & Mourtzis et al. (2022).

A research effort on creating technologies for exploiting emerging technologies to attain the Sustainable Development Goals(SDGs). The influence of troublesome novelties on creation invention, health care advancement, a circumstance study of a worldwide pandemic, marketing techniques that include nature, and smart cities and towns is examined in this study. Additionally, it was estimated that these outcomes will directly affect SDGs 3, 8, 9, and 11.

First, we spoke about the definition of Business 5.0 and advanced machinery needed for this engineering rebellion. They also talked about the applications that Industry 5.0 makes possible, including cloud manufacturing, healthcare, production lines, and industrial output. Big data analytics, the Internet of Things, robotic systems, blockchain, digital twins, and upcoming 6G technologies were all included in their study. Their study encompassed issues and concerns that were looked at to gain a deeper comprehension of the difficulties that organizations between the robots and workers on the assembly line Adel (2022).

A thorough analysis of the Internet of Things(IoT) potential to support Industry 4.0 and digital transformation projects was given by Fatima et al. . The writers have spoken about how the Internet of Things is used in different industries and how the concept has developed. Additionally, the study included a summary of other scientific publications that enabled the researchers to extract important obstacles, integration analysis, and prospects for the Internet of Things (Fatima et al., 2022).

In order to give appropriate grounds for considering I5.0 as a framework for promoting industrial peace and cooperation as well as cha nging social requirements and realities. Mourtzis et al. (2022) offered an important literature review. Their research helped create a framework that would ease the change from Manufacturing 4.0 to Culture 5.0 (Vorisek et al., 2022).

## IMPACT OF I5.0 ON HEALTHCARE

Investigating I5.0 effects on healthcare is essential for a number of strong reasons. The newest advancement in industrial technology, recognized as I5.0, is distinct by the incorporation of leading-edge knowledges plus big data, robots, IoT, and artificial intelligence. The following are some compelling arguments for why it is necessary to investigate how Industry 5.0 may affect health care (Deepa et al., 2022).

Industry 5.0, according to the European Union (EU), encourages an understanding of industries that goes beyond productivity and efficiency. Enhancing the industrial sector's role and significance in society is the main goal. Industry 5.0 is idea which transcends the traditional meaning of Industry Using modern technologies to produce employment, growth, and income while respecting global manufacturing limits, the well-being of workers is prioritized (Ong et al., 2018).

Comparing Industry 4.0 to Industry 5.0, a lot more applications are represented. It is essential to have a broad, industry-wide perspective when evaluating the strategic implications of Industry 5.0. Sustainability, Resilience and a human-centered approach were identified by the European Commission as the three important essentials of Industry 5.0. Each of the three significantly affects the business strategy. A major revolution known as "Society 5.0" started in Japan and has the ability to transform society. Its goal is to focus technical and inventive advancement around the human being, with the goal of benefiting all people. By taking use of Industry 4.0's potential, Culture 5.0 seeks to improve peoples' quality of life (Pereira et al., 2020).

Industry 5.0 might lead to higher-quality manufacturing by delegating monotonous, repetitive activities to robots, machines, and jobs requiring critical thinking. More skilled companies are encouraged by Industry 5.0 than by Industry 4.0 since intellectual practitioners interact with technology.

*Figure 1. Key Technologies of Industry 5.0*

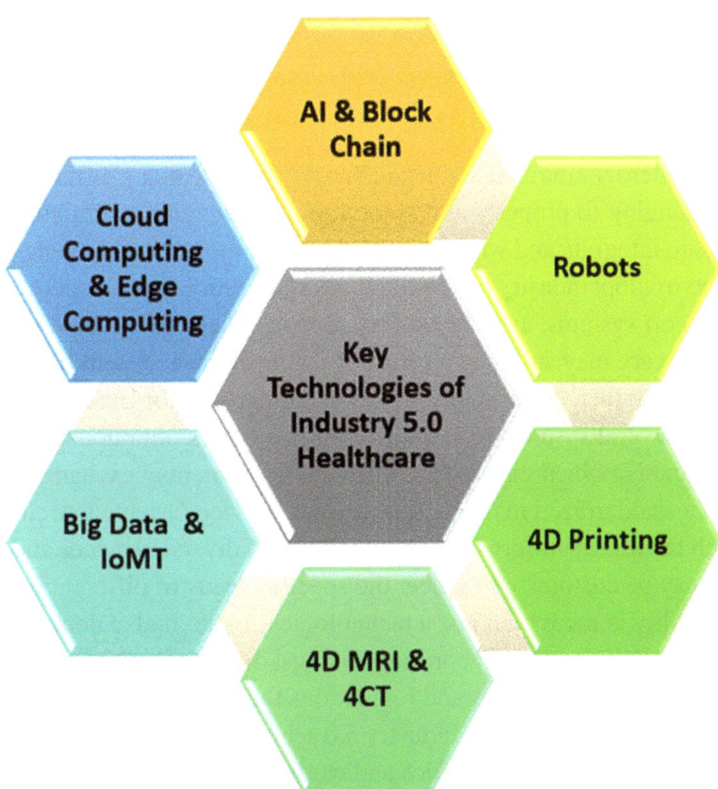


In the health care business, "human-centric collaboration" highlights how people—patients, healthcare providers, and other stakeholders—aggressively contribute in policymaking procedures, treatment plans, and delivery of healthcare as a whole. This method seeks to provide a more patient-centered and comprehensive healthcare system by acknowledging the individual requirements, preferences, and experiences. Figure 1 displays the key technologies in industry 5.0.

## CHALLENGES AND OBSTACLES

Healthcare might benefit greatly from Industry 5.0, but there are a number of difficulties and barriers that need to be overcome. Several of the main concerns are:

1.Data Security and Privacy: Industry 5.0 seats a great deal of importance happening the gathering and processing of massive volumes of data, which raises privacy and data security concerns These technologies present novel discretion and information safety dangers to patients even as they have the ability to greatly enhance healthcare outcomes and delivery. To overcome these issues, a great focus needs to be made on developing and putting into place efficient data privacy and security policies and procedures. This means restricting access to sensitive information, implementing the appropriate authentication and access restrictions, and ensuring that patient data is securely secured. There must also be well-defined policies and procedures in place to guarantee that patient data is gathered, maintained, and used in accordance with moral and legal standards.

Healthcare organizations may work carefully with controlling agencies to ensure they are adhering to all related rules and rules, and they can also leverage the expertise of data confidentiality and sanctuary specialists to assist solve these concerns (Ietto et al., 2022).

2. Integration and Interoperability: Healthcare systems include many different stakeholders and parts, which makes it challenging to properly and smoothly integrate and assimilate them. Getting different systems and devices to integrate and work together is one of the largest challenges facing the healthcare industry as it attempts to adopt Industry 5.0. Healthcare organizations use a variety of technology, including clinical decision support systems, and medical equipment. There are times when these systems cannot work together. Patient care may suffer as a result of the healthcare system becoming more fragmented due to a lack of interoperability. To meet this problem, Industry 5.0 for Healthcare needs an interoperable building that permits several systems to connect with one other continuously. One approach to do this is through open standards, which ensure that different systems may exchange data and communicate with one another in a standardized manner. The use of a Service-Oriented-Architecture(SOA) is an additional tactic which facilitates uniform communiqué across diverse services and applications. Because SOA is flexible, it may be customized to meet the specific needs of different healthcare organizations. However, interoperability is more than just a technological issue. It also demands a shift in culture that prioritizes information sharing and collaboration amongst different healthcare professionals. To do this, it is possible to build common standards and regulations that encourage collaboration and data sharing. Interoperability, in general, is essential to Industry 5.0 achievement in the health care sector since, allows health care wage-earners to exchange statistics and work together extra effectively to enhance persistent results (Fraga-Lamas et al., 2021).

3. Legal and Ethical Attentions: Data possession, algorithmic accountability, and potential for biases and Industry 5.0 raises a number of ethical and legal issues, including discrimination in the decision making process. There are moral and legal issues that need to be resolved when applying Industry 5.0 to the healthcare industry. As the usage of technologies like AI and IoT may result in the gathering and sharing of vast amounts of personal health information, protecting patient privacy and confidentiality is a crucial ethical problem. There are ethical questions because the use of AI and other technology may affect the relationship between the patient and the clinician as well as the quality of care. There are ethical questions because the use of AI and other technology may affect the relationship between the patient and the clinician as well as the quality of care.

It is important to take into account legal matters, including those pertaining to regulations concerning data protection, and well-versed agreement. Aimed at example, if AI is utilized to brand therapeutic choices, accountability and responsibility issues can surface, particularly if the algorithm produces unreliable findings. Issues with data ownership and sharing resulting from these technologies might also arise. Clear laws and regulations must control the use of Industry 5.0 in the health care sector, and values for facts security, confidentiality, and interoperability must be developed to meet the moral and lawful concerns. It is also essential to have continuous stakeholder interaction to ensure that the moral and lawful consequences of Industry 5.0 for health care are well thought out and handled.

4. Skilled Workforce: It necessitates a staff composed of data experts, AI experts, and health care practitioners with advanced technological proficiency. One of the biggest challenges to the healthcare industry's adoption of Industry 5.0 is the shortage of skilled labor. The healthcare industry needs highly

qualified and informed workers to manage the complex schemes and knowledges which will be employed in Industry 5.0. It will also require a specialized staff to develop, design, and deploy new technologies and systems. Important factors to take into account include the education and training of the current workforce and the development of new employment categories pertinent to Industry 5.0. Multidisciplinary collaboration and communication between diverse teams, departments, and organizations are also necessary in the healthcare industry. To guarantee that the labor force have the necessary skill sets for effectively integrating and utilizing the emerging technology for the industry. 5.0 In the healthcare industry, employees need to be trained in collaborating with other specialists including software developers, engineers, and data scientists. In addition, continual learning and the acquisition of new skills are required due to the quick advancement of Industry 5.0 skills and the health care manufacturing. Workforce education and training should consider the moral, legal, and social ramifications of using Industry 5.0 technology in the healthcare sector. In conclusion, improving patient care will come from successfully implementing new technologies and processes, which will be made possible by tackling the workforce challenges related to Industry 5.0 in the healthcare sector. Cost and Infrastructure: Because Industry 5.0 will need novel substructure and cutting-edge technology, it will be very expensive to implement in the healthcare sector. Implementing Industry 5.0 in the health care sector will be quite expensive up front in footings of substructure, software, and employee training. The cost of health care industry 5.0 schemes may increase if they require regular maintenance, modifications, or replacements. Integrating Industry 5.0 skills by the present information substructure and health care systems can be costly and require a lot of assistance. The deployment of Health care Industry 5.0 determination call for specialized information and abilities, and its probable that here won't be sufficient qualified personnel and funding available to administer and uphold these systems (Adadi and Berrada, 2018).

5.Cost and Infrastructure: Because Industry 5.0 determination need new infrastructure and leading-edge technology, it determination be very expensive to implement in the health care sector. Implementing Industry 5.0 in the health care sector will be quite expensive up front in footings of substructure, software, hardware, and employee training. The cost of healthcare industry 5.0 systems may increase if they require regular maintenance, modifications, or replacements. Integrating Industry 5.0 technologies with the present data infrastructure and healthcare systems can be costly and require a lot of assistance Healthcare Industry 5.0 implementation will require certain skills and knowledge, and it's likely that insufficient funds or skilled staff will be available to manage and maintain these systems. The adoption of Industry 5.0 in the health care sector whitethorn possibly result in glitches for disadvantaged and country groups in rapports of technological access. The high cost of Healthcare 5.0 may also make it impossible for many patients who cannot pay the extra costs to get healthcare services.

6.Patient Receipt and Acceptance: While approximately affected role may be hesitant to embrace leading-edge technology, patient acceptance and adoption are critical to Industry 5.0 achievement in the health care sector. If patients don't believe that data privacy and security measures are in place, they can be hesitant to use new technologies, such as wearables or telemedicine. Furthermore, under this new healthcare paradigm, patients with inadequate health literacy or restricted access to technology may fall behind.

In order for patients to completely participate in Industry 5.0 healthcare, healthcare organizations then wage-earners must solve these problems and guarantee that affected role have access to the knowledge and tools they require. With the help of education and awareness efforts, patients may have a better understanding of the benefits of new technology and how they can utilize them to enhance their health outcomes. Healthcare practitioners may contribute to addressing concerns about data security and privacy by developing transparent rules and processes for data collecting. Industry 5.0 has the potential to revolutionize healthcare, but these problems must be resolved if it is to be applied in a way that benefits both patients and the health care scheme as a whole. Healthcare 5.0 has a lot of promise and opportunities, but it also has a lot of issues that need to be worked out if this novel concept is to be effective.

The adoption of Healthcare 5.0 will need resolving several issues and challenges, such as data security and privacy, moral and legal issues, the proper education and exercise for healthcare personnel, and cost-effectiveness. The challenges might appear insurmountable, but they necessity be addressed if Healthcare 5.0 is to fully materialize its advantages and improve patient outcomes, healthcare delivery, and overall.

## PERSISTENT CENTRIC CARE MODELS

Persistent centric attention mockups put the patient at the centre of the health care delivery process by giving special consideration to their unique requirements, preferences, and experiences. These models seek to promote improved health outcomes, raise patient satisfaction levels, and improve the quality of care. Numerous forms of patient-centered care have been devised, with distinct focus on patient empowerment, involvement, and customized treatment. Several noteworthy patient-centric care paradigms are as follows

*Table 1. Patient care models*

| | |
|---|---|
| **Chronic Care Model (CCM)** | The Chronic treatment Model emphasizes patient involvement in their treatment as a means of effectively treating chronic diseases. It places a strong emphasis on proactive, planned care that involves care coordination, patient education, and support for self-management. The CCM promotes cooperative connections between patients and healthcare professionals and acknowledges the significance of the patient's participation in treating chronic diseases. |
| **Patient Centered Medical Home(PCMH)** | primary attention strategy called the PCMH model aims to change how comprehensive and integrated healthcare services are provided. A primary care physician leads the patient's healthcare team in a PCMH, where they collaborate to deliver patient-centered, coordinated, and easily accessible treatment. In order to enhance the patient experience in general, this approach places a strong emphasis on communication, care coordination, and patient participation. |
| **Shared Decision-Making (SDM)** | A paradigm known as "Shared Decision-Making" encourages patients and healthcare professionals to actively participate in decision-making processes. Patients express the preferences and views, while healthcare professionals supply information based on evidence in a two-way communication process. SDM understands that patients who are engaged and well-informed are more likely to make choices that are consistent with their beliefs and personal objectives. |
| **Accountable Care Organizations (ACOs)** | Healthcare professionals collaborate in an ACO to oversee and coordinate the treatment of a specific patient group. In order to improve health outcomes, patient-centricity in ACOs focuses on patient involvement, care coordination, and preventative treatment. |
| **Patient and FamilyCentered Care(PFCC)** | The patient-family-centered care model (PFCC) views patients and their families as vital members of the healthcare team. It places a strong emphasis on cooperation, decency, and respect amongst medical professionals, patients, and their families. The PFCC acknowledges the distinct viewpoints of patients and their families and makes an effort to include their opinions in the decision-making procedures. |
| **Precision Medicine and Personalized Care** | Customizing medical care and treatment regimens to each patient's unique characteristics—including their genetic composition, way of life, and surroundings—is known as precision medicine. With the help of customized care models, patients will receive treatments that are tailored to their individual requirements, resulting in more individualized and efficient medical interventions. |

continued on following page

*Table 1. Continued*

| | |
|---|---|
| **Telehealth and Remote Monitoring Models** | The popularity of telehealth and remote monitoring models has increased with technological advancements. These models concentrate on giving patients with comfortable remote access to healthcare services. In telehealth, patient-centricity entails adjusting services to suit specific requirements, keeping lines of communication open, and guaranteeing a satisfying experience for patients. |
| **Holistic Patient Engagement Models** | The active participation of patients in their healthcare journey is emphasized by a number of comprehensive patient engagement models. In order to empower patients, these models frequently make use of technology, instruction, and communication tools. They promote shared accountability for healthcare results, self-management, and health literacy. |

## SWOT ANALYSIS IN INDUSTRY 5.0 IN HEALTHCARE

A SWOT analysis was done to talk about the mixing of Industry 5.0 in health care. It evaluated the integration's Strengths, Weaknesses, Opportunities, and Threats in order to find proactive management techniques.

Industry 5.0 in healthcare promises to leverage automation (strengths), artificial intelligence (AI), and creative technologies to increase efficiency and customize treatment. These developments seek to improve service quality and accommodate different patient requirements. However, infrastructural constraints, training deficiencies, and a lack of professional understanding pose challenges to the changeover. Issues (weaknesses) with resource management and access disparity also exist.

Possible administration assistance and the tech-savvy Generation are pushing advances in meeting the requirements of an older people and profiting on technology. Threats, on the other hand, include worries about data privacy, unequal access, the potential for technology to become outdated, financial constraints, and the loss of jobs to automation.

The SWOT analysis will assist in determining managerial approaches to address the obstacles of incorporating I5.0 into health care, take advantage of the benefits it presents, and reduce the risks to its achievement. Leaders are therefore able to create more successful plans, make wise judgments, and pinpoint areas in need of development or modification thanks to this study. There will be more advancements in the near future in this field, so this is just the tip of the iceberg. Figure 2 shows the SWOT Analysis in I5.0.

Figure 2. SWOT analysis in industry 5.0

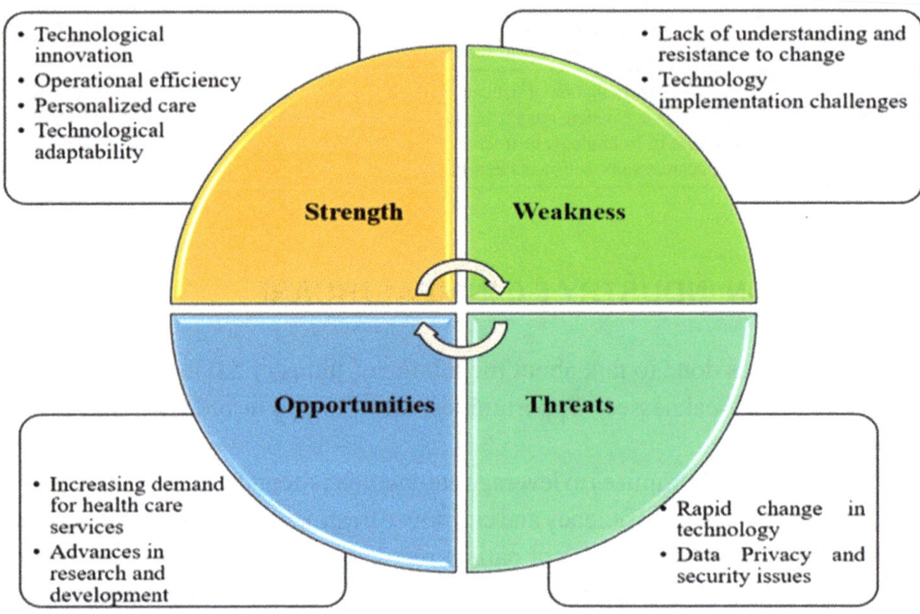


## CONCLUSION

Industry 5.0 will handle medical processes in the future with minimal input from doctors, surgeons, and technicians, with doctors handling higher-level jobs. Industry 5.0 will use digital tools to help customers handle follow-up and repetitive duties. The production of premium medical components is highly encouraged by this new revolution in order to satisfy the individual needs of the patient. The introduction of collaborative robots allows for the efficient performance of precise and complex surgery on patients, something that was previously impractical. Nevertheless, there are challenges in implementing I5.0 ideas in Health care 5.0, such as information safety concerns, and secrecy, moral and allowed dilemmas, as well as the necessity for healthcare personnel to have the appropriate education and training. Collaboration between legislators, business stakeholders, and healthcare practitioners is necessary for the successful implementation of healthcare 5.0. In conclusion, Industry 5.0 may be used by Healthcare 5.0 to enhance patient outcomes, optimize healthcare delivery, and completely change the patient experience. A more patient-centered, effective, and efficient healthcare system could result from the application of Industry 5.0 concepts to Healthcare 5.0.

I5.0 is utilized to extra efficiently see the very customized need. A virtual environment is produced via the application of sophisticated machinery and information technology. Moving forward and taking on new tasks including managing complicated patients, prescribing, treating, training, researching, and developing are expected of medical practitioners. It is essential for both easier patient treatment and illness detection. Smart medical components, implants, scaffolds, biomodels, prosthesis, tools, and equipment are all made using it. In the future, it will be beneficial to recommend relevant content for the medical area, resulting in a quicker patient recovery. Patients' whole experience receiving healthcare will be enhanced by this revolution, which will also assist physicians in giving better, more effective treatment.

## REFERENCES

Adadi, A., & Berrada, M. (2018). Peeking inside the black-box: A survey on explainable artificial intelligence (xai). *IEEE Access : Practical Innovations, Open Solutions*, 6, 52138–52160. 10.1109/ACCESS.2018.2870052

Adel, A. (2022). Future of industry 5.0 in society: Human-centric solutions, challenges and prospective research areas. *Journal of Cloud Computing (Heidelberg, Germany)*, 2022(11), 40. 10.1186/s13677-022-00314-536101900

Deepa, N., Pham, Q. V., Nguyen, D. C., Bhattacharya, S., Prabadevi, B., Gadekallu, T. R., Maddikunta, P. K. R., Fang, F., & Pathirana, P. N. (2022). A survey on blockchain for big data: Approaches, opportunities, and future directions. *Future Generation Computer Systems*, 131, 209–226. 10.1016/j.future.2022.01.017

Fatima, Z., Tanveer, M., Zardari, S., Naz, L., Khadim, H., & Ahmed, N. (2022). Tahir,(2022) M. Production Plant and Warehouse Automation with IoT and Industry 5.0. *Applied Sciences (Basel, Switzerland)*, 12(4), 2053. 10.3390/app12042053

Fraga-Lamas, P., Lopes, S. I., & Fernández-Caramés, T. M. (2021). Green IoT and edge AI as key technological enablers for a sustainable digital transition towards a smart circular economy: An industry 5.0 use case. *Sensors (Basel)*, 21(17), 5745. 10.3390/s2117574534502637

Gomathi, A. K. (2023). *Industry 5.0 for Healthcare 5.0: Opportunities, Challenges and Future Research Possibilities.* 2023 7th International Conference on Trends in Electronics and Informatics (ICOEI), Tirunelveli, India.

Ietto, B., Ancillai, C., Sabatini, A., Carayannis, E. G., & Gregori, G. L. (2022). The role of external actors in SMEs' human centered industry 4.0 adoption: An empirical perspective on Italian competence centres. *IEEE Transactions on Engineering Management*, 7, 12.

Kasinathan, P., Pugazhendhi, R., Elavarasan, R., Ramachandaramurthy, V., Ramanathan, V., Subramanian, S., Kumar, S., Nandhagopal, K., Raghavan, R. R. V., Rangasamy, S., Devendiran, R., & Alsharif, M. H. (2022). Realization of Sustainable Development Goals with Disruptive Technologies by Integrating Industry 5.0, Society 5.0, Smart Cities and Villages. *Sustainability (Basel)*, 2022(14), 15258. 10.3390/su142215258

Mourtzis, D., Angelopoulos, J., & Panopoulos, N. (2022). A Literature Review of the Challenges and Opportunities of the Transition from Industry 4.0 to Society 5.0. *Energies*, 2022(15), 62. 10.3390/en15176276

Ong, J., Parchment, V., & Zheng, X. (2018). Effective regulation of digital health technologies. *Journal of the Royal Society of Medicine*, 2018(111), 439–443. 10.1177/0141076818812437

Pereira, A.G., Lima, T.M., & Santos, F.C. (2020). Industry 4.0 and society 5.0: opportunities and threats. *International Journal of Recent Technology Engineering, 8*(5), 3305–3308 11.

Vorisek, C. N., Lehne, M., Klopfenstein, S. A. I., Mayer, P. J., Bartschke, A., Haese, T., & Thun, S. (2022). Fast Healthcare Interoperability Resources (FHIR) for Interoperability in Health Research: Systematic Review. *JMIR Medical Informatics*, 2022(10), e35724. 10.2196/3572435852842

# Chapter 16
# The Impact and Integration of Cloud Computing for Enhanced Patient Care and Operational Efficiency

**M. Prabu**
https://orcid.org/0000-0003-3563-5092
*Amrita Vishwa Vidyapeetham, Chennai, India*

**M. Diviya**
https://orcid.org/0000-0002-4166-9961
*Amrita Vishwa Vidyapeetham, Chennai, India*

**R. Bhuvaneswari**
https://orcid.org/0000-0002-3912-1585
*Amrita Vishwa Vidyapeetham, Chennai, India*

**Doddi Sreenija Reddy**
*Amrita Vishwa Vidyapeetham, Chennai, India*

**K. Venkatesan**
*Amrita Vishwa Vidyapeetham, Chennai, India*

**Arul Kumar Natarajan**
https://orcid.org/0009-0000-0570-6393
*Samarkand International University of Technology, Uzbekistan*

## ABSTRACT

*Cloud computing is reshaping healthcare by offering a flexible solution for stakeholders to access data remotely. It revolutionizes data creation, storage, and sharing, enabling professionals to access patient information from anywhere, enhancing care and streamlining operations. Adoption is increasing due to its efficiency and innovation benefits. Services like SaaS, PaaS, and IaaS offer flexibility, driving adoption. Challenges include data breaches, necessitating robust security measures. Despite challenges, cloud computing has transformed healthcare, improving decision-making, data security, record sharing, and automation. During COVID-19, it has been crucial, highlighting its importance in advancing healthcare. Providers must embrace cloud technology for its potential to enhance medical data analysis and improve healthcare services.*

DOI: 10.4018/979-8-3693-2901-6.ch016

## INTRODUCTION

Cloud computing has developed as a transformative technology in the healthcare industry, offering a flexible and efficient solution for healthcare stakeholders to access and manage data remotely. This innovative approach has revolutionized the creation, storage, and sharing of medical data, enabling healthcare professionals to access critical patient information from any location. The adoption of cloud technology in healthcare is on the rise, driven by its ability to improve patient care, streamline operations, and automate various processes. This paper explores the impact and integration of cloud computing in healthcare, focusing on its role in enhancing patient care and operational efficiency.

The incorporation of cloud computing in healthcare has led to significant advancements in patient care. Healthcare professionals can now access patient data in real-time, allowing for faster and more accurate clinical decision-making. Moreover, cloud computing has enabled the development of telehealth applications, which have become increasingly important, especially during the COVID-19 pandemic. These applications allow healthcare providers to remotely monitor patients, deliver care, and communicate with colleagues, improving access to healthcare services and patient outcomes.

Furthermore, cloud computing has revolutionized the operational efficiency of healthcare organizations. By moving data storage and management to the cloud, healthcare providers can streamline their operations, reduce costs, and improve scalability. Cloud-based solutions also facilitate the sharing of medical records among healthcare providers, leading to more coordinated and efficient care. However, the integration of cloud computing in healthcare is not without challenges, particularly concerning data security and privacy. Healthcare organizations must carefully evaluate their cloud service providers and construct strong security measures to protect patient information. In the following sections, we will provide a comprehensive review of existing literature related to our domain and area of research, highlighting key findings and insights that inform our study.

## RELATED WORKS

(A Alsadoon, 2024) reviewed the state-of-the-art literature on wearable sensor technology, remote monitoring techniques, and healthcare parameter detection for the elderly in smart home environments. The study introduces the Sensing, Data storage, and Data communication (SDD) taxonomy as a guide for implementing wearable sensor technology for elderly care. The SDD taxonomy consists of three vital components that highlight the system's functionality and introduce elements for monitoring and tracking various healthcare parameters through wearable sensors. The method evaluates and compares various methods and tools for sensing, storing, and communicating healthcare data, such as machine learning algorithms, cloud computing, IoT devices, and wireless sensor networks.

(K Selvakumar, 2024) presented a cryptographic method to secure the communication of health care digital data in the cloud, using DNA cryptography and Huffman coding. The proposed method has several advantages, such as reducing the storage space, increasing the information entropy, achieving high sensitivity and specificity, and preventing brute-force attacks. The authors analyze various aspects of the security of their method, such as key space, sensitivity, randomness, entropy, and risk, and show that their method satisfies the cryptographic requirements and is more secure than other methods. The method is compared with five other methods for encoding, decoding, encryption, and decryption times, and the proposed method takes more time but is more secure and stronger than other methods. (X Chen,

2024) provided a user-friendly web interface that allows users to upload MRS data from different vendors and perform various tasks such as denoising, quantification, statistical analysis, consistency analysis, and visualization without any installation or coding. The platform integrates both classic and artificial intelligence algorithms for MRS quantification, such as LCModel and QNet, and compares their performance and reliability. It demonstrates its practicality and efficiency with in vivo data from healthy volunteers and patients with mild cognitive impairment and glioma. The framework is open-access and shared on MRSHub, and aims to serve the MRS research community with a standard processing pipeline and advanced analytical capabilities.

(K Rottermann, 2024) created a seamless experience for patients across ambulatory and hospital settings. This will be achieved by facilitating the secure exchange of clinical data, eliminating the need for duplicate tests, ensuring consistent patient education, and giving patients and their families more control over their care. The CCC utilizes a secure cloud-based system to enable the sharing of extensive diagnostic data, automate the delivery of conference results and discharge summaries, and facilitate optional multi-party video conferences for in-depth discussions on complex patient cases. The authors report that the CCC reduced the number of repetitive congenital heart conferences, involved more complex patient cases, and improved the decision-making process for upcoming treatments. (E Wang, 2023) proposed a cloud-based solution for storing real-time medical data from digital twins. The model used AWS IoT Core to collect data from various sources, The given model addresses existing challenges such as insufficient access control mechanisms, lack of data encryption, and dependence on specific vendors. The potential benefits and challenges of using DT in healthcare, are increasing efficiency and precision, reducing medical errors, enhancing patient outcomes, and facilitating personalized and preventative care

(A Kumar, 2023) introduced a classification technique, leveraging the K-Nearest Neighbor (KNN) classification algorithm. The system analyzes network activity patterns to detect and isolate abnormal nodes, potentially indicating malicious activity. The proposed model has a complete framework with two key components: a modified KNN algorithm for classifying network traffic and a prediction algorithm to improve classification accuracy. This two-pronged approach aims to significantly enhance the detection of malicious activity. The evaluation compares it to existing methods across various parameters, including accuracy, speed of execution, and effectiveness in retrieving relevant information. (D Abler, 2023) proposes a new direction for radiomics research focussing on physician led approach, aiming to equip doctors with the tools and knowledge to create and utilize these models for better patient outcomes. The proposed approach identifies a minimum set of functional requirements for radiomics software to support this vision, such as web-based access, cohort management, feature extraction and exploration, and machine learning model development and evaluation. The given approach introduces QuantImage v2 (QI2), a comprehensive and integrated cloud platform specifically designed for physician-led radiomics and machine learning research. Recognizing shortcomings in existing tools, QI2 offers a prototype implementation based on the proposed physician-centered vision. A QI2's application in developing a diagnostic model for pulmonary lymphangitic carcinomatosis (PLC), is a challenging condition in lung cancer.

(M Nagasaki, 2023) introduced a hybrid cloud system consisting of five subsystems that are connected by the science information network (SINET) and can flexibly handle various bioinformatics tools while scaling the computational capacity. It further examines how processing time is affected by the number of samples analyzed. The system can efficiently process the data by distributing the tasks among different subsystems and minimizing the I/O bottleneck. The comparison across different variant calling pipelines for human genome data, such as GATK, Sentieon, GLnexus, and GraphTyper2, and accuracy, efficiency, and scalability are evaluated for comparison between various pipelines. The use of high-performance and flexible networks, such as SINET5, HFP, and GTP, enable fast and reliable data transfer and communication for genomic research.

(S Hamzehei, 2023), demonstrated how cloud-based storage, processing, and data updates contribute to efficient data management and significantly reduce the time complexity of the training phase, ultimately leading to faster and potentially more accurate models. The presentation of the methods is assessed based on mean square error (MSE) and coefficient of determination (R2), and it is found that the outcomes are mostly at an acceptable level. The motor symptoms, as measured by the UPDRS scale, are the strongest indicator of overall Parkinson's disease severity, while vocal instability markers like jitter and shimmer also hold key information. (M Chau, 2023) addressed the use of cloud-based CT simulator software to enhance the learning experiences of undergraduate medical radiation students. The results showed that the students enjoyed the simulation program and found it relevant and helpful for their CT knowledge and skills development and clinical placement preparation. The given model can be improved in terms of simulation of the program, such as more guidance, technical support, and scenario-based learning.

(H Zhang, 2023) reported a model for real-time prediction of intradialytic hypotension (IDH) in hemodialysis patients, using cloud computing infrastructure and data from electronic health records and dialysis machines. IDH is a common and serious complication of hemodialysis that reduces quality of life and increases morbidity and mortality. Predicting IDH may facilitate timely interventions and prevent adverse outcomes. The machine learning model used XGBoost algorithm and 99 variables, including demographic, clinical, laboratory, and intradialytic data. The model predicted IDH 15-75 minutes in advance with an area below the receiver operating characteristic curve (AUROC) of 0.89 in the validation cohort.

(EY Chan, 2023) conducted a prospective observational study of 7 children (0–18 years) who were enrolled in a pilot remote patient monitoring (RPM) programme using the Homechoice Claria cycler with the Sharesource platform over two 24-week periods (pre- and post-RPM). The results showed that RPM was associated with fewer and shorter unplanned hospitalizations, improved fluid management with increased ultrafiltration and lower blood pressure, favourable adherence to PD, and positive perception of RPM by patients and dialysis team. The study focused on unplanned hospitalizations and fluid management as the main outcomes, also considering clinic visits, treatment adjustments, dialysis effectiveness, adherence, and well-being as secondary measures. It was found that RPM in children receiving APD is beneficial for patient outcomes, engagement, disease awareness, and may potentially save medical expenditures.

(E Yıldırım, 2023) introduced an Internet of Medical Things (IoMT) based framework for predicting diabetes risk. Combining Wireless Body Area Networks (WBANs) for data collection, fog computing for local processing, and cloud computing for advanced analysis, the framework utilizes both fuzzy logic and machine learning algorithms to improve prediction accuracy. The accuracy, throughput, and delay results of the fuzzy logic approach are compared in the fog node and the machine learning approach in the cloud node, using SVM, RF, and ANN algorithms. The RF algorithm has the best performance with 89.5% accuracy in the cloud, and the fuzzy logic approach has 64% accuracy in the fog. (H Mahalingam, 2023) proposed a novel image encryption scheme that integrates adaptive key generation, neural-based confusion and non-XOR DNA diffusion to protect multimedia data stored in the cloud. The scheme is evaluated using various metrics, such as keyspace, key sensitivity, histogram, correlation, entropy and bit distribution. The given scheme is compared with other state-of-the-art methods and showed that it has higher security, better randomness and lower correlation.

(Z Man, 2023) proposed a novel key generation scheme that uses a BA-neural network to map random numbers to chaotic initial values, hiding the original key of the cloud encryption system and improving its security and randomness. The given scheme is a dynamic image encryption scheme that enhances security against targeted attacks, combining random shuffling and a unique diffusion approach. The results show that the proposed schemes have high security and efficiency. (I Ahmed, 2023) demonstrated the potential of leveraging artificial intelligence and IoT in the health care sector, especially for the diagnosis and prevention of COVID-19 and other infectious diseases. This system combines two powerful deep learning models (VGG-19 and Inception-V3) with advanced feature analysis techniques to accurately classify infectious diseases from X-ray images. The proposed model identifies normal, COVID-19, and pneumonia cases in chest X-rays with 97% accuracy. The system also outperforms several other deep learning techniques for COVID-19 detection.

(SM Tanya, 2023) introduced a new cloud-based AI system using decision trees to assist on-call ophthalmologists in diagnosing and prioritizing patient cases. This ophthalmic Cloud-Based Clinical Decision Support System (CDSS) streamlines triage and referrals, enhances accuracy, and offers preliminary diagnoses and urgency levels. It was tested in a prospective comparative cohort study with 96 referrals from various primary care providers to a community ophthalmology clinic in Canada. The CDSS represents a promising tool for teleophthalmology and other specialties that rely on heuristic decision making and electronic referrals. The CDSS matched referring doctors in diagnosing categories, outperformed them in preliminary diagnoses, and showed even better accuracy in assessing urgency compared to expert ophthalmologists.

(A Alourani, 2023) presented a model for the forecast of patient mortality using the MIMIC-III dataset. To evaluation of the model is employed with a series of machine learning techniques, including neural network, support vector machine, random forest, decision tree, gradient boosting, logistic regression and by comparing their performances. The parameters included to evaluate the proposed model are accuracy, F1 score, recall, precision, and execution time. The proposed model beats the state-of-the-art models in terms of accuracy, precision, and F1 score. The proposed model could offer vital insights to physicians in the initial stages, enabling them to promptly undertake measures to mitigate the mortality rate. (JDS Quilis, 2023) introduced a cloud system for analyzing cancer images is described, supporting the PRIMAGE project's development of imaging-based biomarkers for pediatric cancers. This system combines various cloud storage and processing options with three user applications (batch, HTC batch, and interactive), catering to different stages of QIB development according to ESR guidelines. The specification of the different types of user applications and a validation through a use case that makes use of most of the features of the platform is briefly explained. The architecture uses EGI Check-in service for federated authentication and authorisation of users, and EGI Data Hub for synchronising data on demand between the storage and processing backends. It also employs Infrastructure Manager and Kubernetes for deploying and managing the cloud infrastructure and the user applications.

(SA Aghila Rajagopal, 2023) introduced an AI model using a unique algorithm for both disease prediction and cloud security, emphasizing user privacy. The given data addresses the challenges of big data analysis, accurate medical diagnosis, and secure cloud storage in the context of smart cities and healthcare applications. It is an novel method that combines whale optimization based passive clustering, multi-scale grasshopper optimization, robust shearlet based feature extraction, modified long short-term memory-convolutional neural network (MLSTM-CNN) based classifier, and identity based dynamic distributed honey pot algorithm for encryption and decryption. The proposed method achieves low error rate, high accuracy and better data security. (H Tian, 2023) proposed a novel certificateless signature method that can resist both public key replacement and master key attacks, and design a manageable delegated data outsourcing mechanism that can reduce the burden on patients and support the verification of outsourcing behavior. The study has used augmented data verification strategy that can provide comprehensive auditing for both medical data and their source information without compromising privacy, and introduce an efficient batch auditing algorithm that can handle multisource medical data with different authorized medical workers.

(S Fugkeaw, 2023) introduced LightMED, a lightweight and secure system for sharing medical records on connected devices that uses blockchain for decentralized control, encrypted search, and fast decryption. The study also introduces outsourced encryption and decryption techniques to offload the computation cost to the fog nodes, which are semi-trusted entities that collaborate with the cloud server and the blockchain. The model employs dual encryption based on AES-256 and CP-ABE to protect the EMRs and the random value used for symmetric key generation. It also supports secure IoT data transmission and aggregation based on lightweight encryption and digital signing. The proposed method offers a secure and efficient way for patients to control who can access their medical records, without needing to store sensitive keys on their devices. (MM Islam, 2023) provided remote patient monitoring, data analysis, and interactive user interface using wearable sensors, clustering algorithms, and mobile applications. The framework also considers the energy efficiency and environmental impact of the IoT and cloud-based systems, and suggests some techniques to reduce the carbon footprint and power consumption of the devices and services. Various sensors are used to monitor the vital signs of patients, such as temperature, blood pressure, SpO2, ECG, etc. The proposed method uses hierarchical clustering algorithms (HCA) to analyze and categorize the data collected from the sensors. The framework uses a cloud-based system to store and process the data from the IoT layer. It also uses the OGSA-DAI framework to enable data access and integration across multiple data sources and formats. The mobile application provides features such as health status visualization, medical consultation, prescription, and emergency notification. The mobile application also supports data synchronization and encryption for security and privacy.

(G Thakur, 2023) introduced the concept and applications of Digital Twin (DT) technology, which creates a virtual replica of a physical system for simulation and analysis. It also discusses the security challenges and requirements for DT environments, such as data sharing, verification, privacy, and authentication. It identifies several security flaws and inefficiencies in the protocol, such as vulnerability to impersonation, password guessing, and known session-specific temporary information attacks. It also proposes an improved three-factor privacy-preserving authentication scheme for DT environments that uses certificateless cryptography and elliptic curve cryptography. The ROR logic examines the session key security of the proposed scheme using the ROR model. It defines the adversary's queries and the probability of breaking the session key security. It also proves a theorem that bounds the adversary's advantage using a sequence of games.

(MT de Oliveira, 2023) presented a prototype of a secure EMR cloud-based application that leverages the ASCLEPIOS eHealth cloud-based framework to share data among the acute care teams in a cross-organizational paradigm. The proposed solution aims to collect impressions, challenges, and improvements for the prototype from 14 medical professionals with four prominent roles in acute care: emergency call centers, ambulance services, emergency hospitals, and general practitioner clinics. The method uses a qualitative thematic analysis of the data collected through questionnaires and interview transcripts, and identifies five themes: current challenges, quality of the shared EMR data, integrity and auditability of the EMR data, usefulness and functionality of the application, and trust and acceptance of the technology. The technique used is a combination of modern cryptographic and access control mechanisms for protecting patient data in the cloud. (S Gayathri, 2023) presented a novel CUNA (customizable unique node access) architecture for securing patient medical records in the cloud. This architecture leverages user-generated keys and patient identifiers for data encryption prior to cloud storage. The cloud uses a Gaussian regression process (GRP) algorithm to authenticate the CUNA code and retrieve the data from the cloud, ensuring privacy and accuracy of the patient information. The given method claims that the proposed model achieves an accuracy of 92%, an image mean square error of 0.0012%, and a computation time of 6 s for 500 blocks of data.

(Y Zhou, 2022) describes a new way to use large amounts of medical data stored in the cloud to group patients with similar conditions, like COVID-19. This could help improve healthcare for these patients. This method, called PCM, helps organize large amounts of medical data quickly and securely. It creates unique codes for each patient based on their information and then groups patients with similar codes together. PCM, a novel patient clustering method, claims to be both more accurate and faster than existing methods like SerRecdistri-LSH and UPCC, while also offering better privacy protection. These claims are evaluated through simulations using the WS-DREAM dataset. The study uses LSH to generate indexes for each patient based on their medical data, and then uses these indexes to cluster the patients efficiently and privately.

(I Ahmad, 2022) introduced a perceptual encryption (PE) method for secure and efficient transmission and storage of medical images, especially chest X-ray images for tuberculosis diagnosis. It works for both color and grayscale pictures, offering stronger security and better compression than older methods, which saves storage space. The system also implements an EfficientNetV2-based model for automatic tuberculosis screening in chest X-ray images and improves its accuracy by using a noise-based data augmentation method. The article evaluates the proposed PE method and the DL model on three datasets and shows that they can achieve high performance and low bitrate requirements for image communication and diagnosis. P (Suhasini, 2022) presented a novel image encryption system for medical data. Leveraging a combination of the Arnold map, Tent map, Lorenz map, matrix scrambling, and pseudo-random sequences, the method prioritizes high security, reliability, and resolution, making it suitable for protecting sensitive medical images. The proposed system is evaluated based on various security analyses, such as sensitivity, correlation, PSNR, key space, histogram, and entropy. The results show that the scheme outperforms several existing medical encryption methods in terms of these metrics. The system can protect the privacy and confidentiality of medical images in cloud computing environments, where data security is a major challenge.

(HK Fatlawi, 2022) proposed an adaptive model that utilizes EEG signals and cloud computing infrastructure to forecast epileptic seizures. This model personalizes predictions for each patient, potentially improving accuracy. The model employs a two-stage architecture, Local preprocessing at the patient's device extracts and summarizes features from EEG signals and an adaptive classifier utilizing Adaptive Random Forest (ARF) leverages data from multiple devices to train and update itself for improved seizure prediction. The model is evaluated on a real dataset (CHB-MIT) and shows a high performance in terms of accuracy, sensitivity, and false positive rate. It also outperforms several batch and stream classifiers and related works in the literature. It also detects and adapts to concept drift by using ADWIN technique to adjust the window size and replace the outdated trees. (J Egger, 2022) introduced a framework Studierfenster, a free, non-commercial open science client-server framework for (bio-)medical image analysis, offering various functionalities such as visualization, segmentation, registration, deep learning, and augmented/virtual reality. Studierfenster also provides a client-sided DICOM browser and converter module. The core module of Studierfenster, which enables the visualization of 2D and 3D data in common web browsers, using WebGL and XTK. It also allows manual annotation of structures and landmarks, as well as automatic aortic landmark detection and cranial implant design. A survey conducted with medical and non-medical experts to evaluate the usability and performance of Studierfenster, showing positive feedback and high accuracy for manual segmentation.

(AB Tello, 2022) aimed to improve the decision making process of the healthcare system in a real time cloud environment, by using a normalization approach for data pre-processing, an autoencoder model for healthcare data classification, and a gravitational search algorithm for hyperparameter optimization of the autoencoder model. The performance of the CCNA-SHSNN model is evaluated based on two benchmark datasets: heart disease and infectious disease and compares it with four existing techniques: k-nearest neighbors, naive Bayes, support vector machine, and decision tree. It is found that the CCNA-SHSNN model achieves higher accuracy, sensitivity, specificity, and F-score than the existing techniques on both datasets, demonstrating its effectiveness and superiority for smart healthcare applications. (SL Rosa, 2022) proposed a wearable sensor system that collects various patient data points, including body temperature, blood pressure, heart rate, ECG readings, and motion activity. This data is transmitted wirelessly via Wi-Fi to a cloud-based platform for analysis and potential healthcare interventions. The model uses a algorithm called Long Short-Term Memory (LSTM) to process the patient data in the cloud and detect any abnormality or illness in real-time. The experiment is conducted at a medical clinic with 10 volunteers who wore the sensors for 5 hours and performed different activities. It is found that the system achieved a success rate of more than 95% in sending and analyzing the data, and was able to provide alerts and mobile access to the medical staff.

(A Rehman Khan, 2022) proposed a cloud-based framework for COVID-19 detection using chest X-ray images and machine learning techniques. The framework uses a balance contrast enhancement technique (BCET) to preprocess the images, a fusion of textural and shape-based features to extract relevant information, a gain ratio method to select the best features, and a bootstrap aggregated extreme learning machine (BA-ELM) to classify the images as COVID-19 or non-COVID-19. The framework is evaluated on a benchmark dataset called COVID-Xray-5k, which contains 5,084 X-ray images of COVID-19 and non-COVID-19 cases. The system achieved an average accuracy of 95.7%, which is higher than some existing methods.

(H AlQaheri, 2022) developed an innovative system using sensors, smart analysis, and cloud technology to remotely monitor COVID-19 patients at home, allowing for early detection of issues and improved safety during their quarantine period. The system is validated by a real dataset from the World Health Organization (WHO) and Kaggle, and shows a high accuracy, recall, and precision in identifying COVID-19 cases. It aims to reduce the spread of the pandemic, optimize the use of medical resources, and provide timely and personalized health care for COVID-19 patients. The model employs a fuzzy inference system (FIS) to assess the severity of detected abnormalities. FIS uses linguistic rules (e.g., "mild," "moderate," "severe") to classify the health condition. It uses statistical methods to establish baseline patterns for each patient based on historical data. It continuously compares the real-time data with these baselines.

(A Bushnag, 2022) explored an innovative telemedicine solution: a wireless ECG system leveraging the IoT cloud to remotely connect patients and doctors, potentially increasing accessibility to cardiac healthcare and improving medical outcomes. The system collects ECG data from either a portable device or a benchmark database and uses the MQTT protocol to transmit the data to the IoT cloud server, where further analysis and alert mechanisms are performed. The system uses the Pan-Tompkins algorithm to detect the QRS complexes of the ECG signal and calculates the heart rate and RR interval of the patient. It also tests the RR normality and rhythm to identify any cardiac abnormalities. It balances the resource consumption and performance between the IoT device and the IoT cloud server and optimizes the data transmission using MQTT, also provides a graphical user interface for both patients and doctors to access the ECG information and alerts.

(J Jusak, 2021) proposed a new approach for securing cloud-based electronic health records (EHR) using non-cryptographic anonymization and reconstruction algorithms for electrocardiograph (ECG) data. The proposed approach aims to preserve the confidentiality and integrity of ECG data by obscuring the cardiac features of patients during transmission and storage, and allowing authorized users to retrieve the original data using a secret key and an offset vector. The system uses fast Fourier transform (FFT) and inverse FFT to transform ECG data between time and frequency domains, and applies element-wise multiplication and division operations to modify and restore the frequency components of ECG data. The model shows significant advantages over existing methods in terms of processing speed, security, and robustness, and is implemented in a real-time testbed using a wireless sensor node, an ECG signal processing module, and a Raspberry Pi single-board computer.

(D Reichenpfader, 2021) proposed a web-based platform for the diagnosis and therapy of non-organic insomnia, a prevalent sleep disorder impacting millions globally. The platform aims to provide context-aware health services by integrating data from various sources, such as sleep diaries, questionnaires, wearable sensors, smartphones, smart meters, and environmental factors. The model uses FHIR as the standard for data exchange and storage, and applies AI and machine learning techniques to analyse and derive insights from the data. The system supports the delivery of digital cognitive behavioural therapy for insomnia (dCBT-I), which is proven to be effective and cost-efficient, and allows patients to control their own therapy progress. The approach follows the European Standard 62304:2006 for the software life cycle process of medical devices, and considers the legal and ethical aspects of data security and privacy.

(S Iranpak, 2021) developed a platform that uses various sensors to collect vital signs and other health data from patients and sends them to the cloud via a prioritization system and a mobile gateway using 5G technology. The core of this system leverages an LSTM deep neural network within the cloud environment. This allows for real-time classification and monitoring of patients' health using sensor data, with automatic alerts generated for critical cases. This aims to enhance the quality and efficiency of healthcare services, particularly for chronic disease patients, through precise and immediate health status analysis. The system is simulated and compared with other methods using a dataset of 20 patients with different health conditions and activities. The results show that the system achieves a classification accuracy of 97.13%, which is 10.41% higher than the best existing method. S Bertuccio, 2021) developed an application Reportflow, which aims to improve the process of EEG reporting and delivering by reducing times and increasing performance, while guaranteeing data security and privacy using public key encryption and ciphertext-policy attribute-based encryption. ReportFlow was tested in an Italian hospital with a neurophysiology diagnostic unit and a child neuropsychiatry unit, and showed promising results in terms of time reduction, cost-saving, patient satisfaction, and service efficiency. The application has some limitations such as key management, conflicting activities, and data quality control, and some future directions such as certificate automation, revocation management, and locking mechanism.

(DC Wu, 2021) employed Poisson regression analysis to investigate the patterns and impacts of the MediCloud system on different measures of healthcare quality, including the rate of extended stays exceeding 48 hours in the emergency department (ED), the admission rate within 8 hours from the ED, and the satisfaction rate with health insurance, spanning the years 2013 to 2019. The results showed that the MediCloud system increased the inquiry rate of medical information from 2.9% to 86.6%, and improved the healthcare quality by reducing the retention rate in EDs of medical centers, and increasing the early hospitalization rate of urgent patients in regional hospitals. The MediCloud system had a substantial influence on Taiwan's medical landscape, suggesting its potential implementation in other nations to augment healthcare efficiency, safety, and patient satisfaction.

In conclusion, the works reviewed in this paper provides valuable insights into the impact and integration of cloud computing in the healthcare industry. Studies have shown that cloud computing has significantly improved patient care by enabling real-time access to critical patient information and facilitating the development of telehealth applications. Additionally, cloud computing has enhanced the operational efficiency of healthcare organizations by streamlining operations and promoting more coordinated care delivery through seamless data sharing. However, the literature also highlights challenges such as data security and privacy concerns that must be addressed to fully realize the benefits of cloud computing in healthcare. Moving forward, further research is needed to address these challenges and explore the full potential of cloud computing in revolutionizing healthcare delivery.

From this comprehensive overview of various studies and advancements in the integration of cloud computing within the healthcare, it highlights the development of technologies such as wearable sensor technology for elderly care, cryptographic methods for securing healthcare data, user-friendly web interfaces for medical data analysis, and cloud-based systems for patient data exchange and telehealth applications. Additionally, it emphasizes the importance of physician-led radiomics research, hybrid cloud systems for genomic research, and cloud-based storage solutions for real-time medical data. The studies presented demonstrate the potential of cloud computing to enhance patient care, operational efficiency, and data management in healthcare, while also addressing the challenges and opportunities for improvement in this rapidly evolving field.

In summary, the section underscores the transformative impact of cloud computing on healthcare, offering solutions for remote patient monitoring, data security, and efficient healthcare delivery. It also points out the necessity for ongoing research to overcome obstacles related to data security, interoperability, and regulatory compliance, ensuring that the benefits of cloud technology can be fully harnessed in the healthcare industry. The research works cited serve as a testament to the innovative approaches being explored to optimize healthcare services through cloud computing.

## METHODOLOGY

To integrate cloud computing for enhanced patient care and operational efficiency, a multifaceted approach will be employed. Firstly, a cloud-based Electronic Health Record (EHR) system will be implemented to centralize patient data and provide secure access from any location. This will enable healthcare providers to retrieve patient information quickly, leading to more informed decision-making and improved patient care. Additionally, cloud-based telemedicine platforms and remote monitoring devices will be utilized to provide virtual consultations and monitor patients remotely, improving access to healthcare services and facilitating early detection of health issues.

Furthermore, data analytics and machine learning algorithms will be leveraged to analyze large volumes of healthcare data in the cloud and also helps to identify patterns and trends in patient health, improve clinical decision-making, and optimize operational processes for better efficiency. Cloud-based Health Information Exchange (HIE) systems will also be implemented to facilitate the secure exchange of patient information between healthcare providers, promoting care coordination and reducing duplicate tests and procedures.

Moreover, the development and deployment of cloud-based Mobile Health (mHealth) applications will be undertaken to allow patients to aggressively participate in their healthcare management. These applications will provide access to personal health records, medication reminders, and educational resources, leading to improved patient engagement and health outcomes. Healthy cybersecurity measures, such as data encryption, access controls, and regular security audits, will be implemented to protect patient data. Finally, continuous monitoring of the performance of cloud-based systems and gathering feedback from healthcare providers and operational efficiency over time.

## Cloud-Based Electronic Health Records (EHR)

Cloud-Based Electronic Health Records (EHR) are digital versions of patients' paper charts, stored in secure cloud servers. This technology is revolutionizing healthcare by enabling healthcare service providers to connect with patient information from anywhere, at any time, leading to enhanced patient care and operational efficiency. Cloud-Based EHR systems offer numerous advantages over traditional paper-based records, including improved accessibility, interoperability, cost-efficiency, and scalability. These benefits contribute to better patient outcomes and streamlined healthcare operations. One of the key advantages of Cloud-Based EHR systems is their accessibility. These systems allow healthcare providers to connect with the patient information securely from any location with an internet connection. This accessibility ensures that relevant patient data is available when and where it is needed, leading to more informed decision-making and improved patient care. Additionally, Cloud-Based EHR systems facilitate interoperability between different healthcare systems, enabling seamless exchange of patient information between providers, payers, and patients. This interoperability improves care coordination and enhances the overall quality of healthcare delivery.

Cloud-Based EHR systems also offer cost-efficiency benefits. They eliminate the need for on-premises hardware maintenance, software updates, and data backup solutions. Additionally, these systems operate on a subscription-based model, allowing healthcare organizations to pay only for the services they use, reducing overall IT expenses. Furthermore, Cloud-Based EHR systems provides healthcare service providers with the capacity to measure their infrastructure based on their needs. This scalability allows organizations to easily accommodate changes in patient volume, data storage requirements, and system upgrades without significant upfront investments in hardware or software. In terms of security and compliance, Cloud-Based EHR systems provides advanced security measures, such as encryption, access controls, and regular security audits, to protect patient data from unauthorized access and breaches. Furthermore, these systems adhere to strict regulatory standards, ensuring that patient information is handled in compliance with legal requirements. Cloud-Based EHR systems integrate with cloud computing technologies, such as virtualization, storage, and networking, to provide reliable and secure access to patient information.

Despite the numerous benefits of Cloud-Based EHR systems, there are challenges associated with their implementation. These challenges include data migration, interoperability issues, and user training. Healthcare organizations must address these challenges to successfully implement Cloud-Based EHR systems. Migrating data from paper-based or legacy EHR systems to Cloud-Based EHR systems can be a complex and time-consuming process. Healthcare organizations must carefully plan and execute data migration to ensure data integrity and continuity of care. Interoperability between different healthcare systems remains a challenge for Cloud-Based EHR systems. Healthcare organizations must work towards standardizing data formats and protocols to facilitate seamless exchange of patient information. Healthcare providers and staff require training to effectively use Cloud-Based EHR systems. Healthcare organizations must invest in training programs to guarantee that users are proficient in using the system and can leverage its full potential.

Several healthcare organizations have successfully implemented Cloud-Based EHR systems and have experienced significant benefits. For example, the University of Pittsburgh Medical Center (UPMC) implemented a Cloud-Based EHR system and reported improved patient outcomes and operational efficiency. The future of Cloud-Based EHR systems looks promising, with progressions in artificial intelligence (AI) and machine learning expected to enhance predictive analytics and clinical decision support.

## Open Challenges and Opportunities

Cloud computing has transformed healthcare by providing opportunities to improve patient care and operational efficiency. However, its integration and adoption in healthcare present several challenges, security and privacy, interoperability, integration with existing systems, regulatory compliance, data governance and management, and cost and resource management. Healthcare organizations must address these challenges to realize the benefits of cloud computing. Figure 1 highlights how cloud computing enables these components to improve patient care and operational efficiency in healthcare delivery. The interactivity allows users to hover over nodes to view their names, providing a clear and informative visualization of the conceptual framework.

*Figure 1. Integration of cloud computing in healthcare*

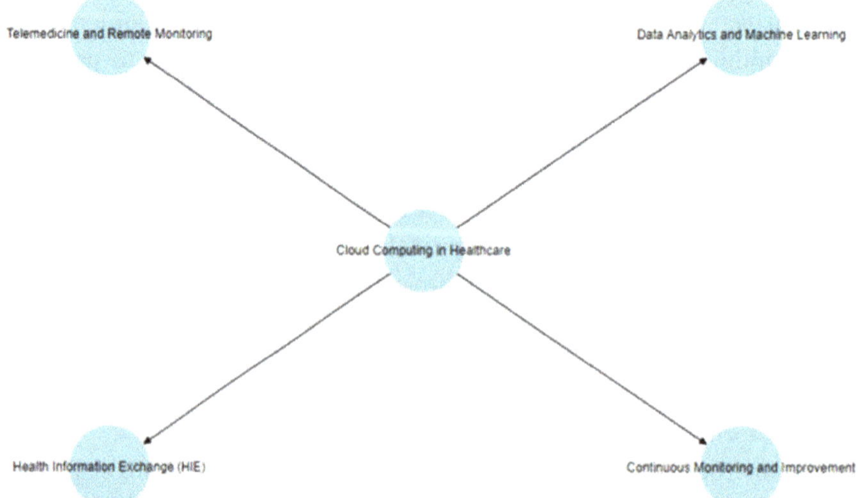

## Telemedicine and Remote Monitoring

Telemedicine and remote monitoring have become crucial parts of healthcare delivery, particularly after the COVID-19 pandemic outbreak. Cloud computing integration into telemedicine and remote monitoring allows healthcare providers to offer virtual care services and monitor patient health remotely using real-time data exchange and communication tools. Cloud-based telemedicine platforms enable secure video consultations, remote diagnostic imaging, and telemonitoring of vital signs, providing access to healthcare services from anywhere. Cloud-based monitoring can empower patients to overcome chronic conditions, track health metrics, and receive timely interventions. However, the progress made in improving access to healthcare and monitoring patient health remotely, there are still several challenges and areas that need improvement.

A significant digital divide still exists, with many people lacking access to reliable internet connectivity and devices needed for telemedicine consultations or remote monitoring. Bridging this gap is necessary to ensure equitable access to healthcare services. Telemedicine and remote monitoring involve the transmission and storage of sensitive patient data, raising concerns about data privacy and security. Registering compliance with HIPAA and implementing higher-end encryption and authentication measures are necessary to safeguard patient information. Healthcare providers can utilize various EHRs and medical devices, leading to interoperability challenges. Seamless integration and exchange of data between different platforms are necessary to facilitate effective telemedicine consultations and remote monitoring across different healthcare settings. Regulatory frameworks governing telemedicine vary widely across jurisdictions, leading to ambiguity and complexity for healthcare providers and patients. Harmonizing regulations and addressing legal barriers can promote the adoption and use of telemedicine technologies and confirm the quality and safety care of the patients.

Although telemedicine and remote monitoring technologies hold promise, there is a need for robust clinical validation and evidence demonstrating their efficacy and safety across different medical specialties and patient populations. Conducting large-scale clinical trials and longitudinal studies can help establish the effectiveness of these technologies in improving health outcomes. User experience is essential in the adoption and acceptance of telemedicine platforms by both healthcare providers and patients. Designing more interactive interfaces and providing adequate training and support to users can enhance usability and facilitate seamless interaction during telemedicine consultations and remote monitoring sessions.

## Data Analytics and Machine Learning

Data analytics and machine learning techniques have the potential to revolutionize healthcare, telemedicine, and remote monitoring. They can enable insights-driven decision-making, personalized care delivery, and proactive health management. Cloud computing offers a scalable and agile infrastructure in healthcare and this can process, analyze, and interpret large-scale healthcare data. By leveraging cloud-based data analytics platforms and machine learning algorithms, healthcare organizations can extract actionable insights, predict clinical outcomes, and personalize treatment recommendations based on patient data stored in the cloud. Cloud-based machine learning models can support clinical decision-making, disease prediction, and risk stratification. This, in turn, drives innovation in healthcare delivery and enhances patient care quality. There are several challenges and opportunities for improvement in this domain. One of the primary challenges in healthcare analytics is ensuring the quality, completeness, and accessibility of healthcare data.

Healthcare data is often fragmented across different sources, such as wearables, medical devices, EHRs, and patient-generated data. Integration and standardization of heterogeneous data sources pose significant challenges for data analytics efforts. Ensuring compliance with data privacy laws while enabling data sharing and analysis is a complex balancing act. Protecting patient privacy and maintaining data security against cyber threats remain ongoing challenges in healthcare analytics. Healthcare systems often use disparate EHR systems, medical devices, and data formats, leading to interoperability challenges. Integrating data from diverse sources and ensuring seamless interoperability between different healthcare IT systems are essential for effective data analytics and machine learning applications. Ensuring ML algorithm fairness, transparency, and interpretability is critical for building trust in machine learning models and promoting their adoption in clinical practice. Translating machine learning models from research to clinical practice requires rigorous clinical validation and regulatory approval. Conducting large-scale clinical trials, real-world validation studies, and obtaining regulatory clearance are time-consuming and resource-intensive processes. Improving clinical knowledge for technical experts leads to the development of clinically relevant and actionable insights from healthcare data.

## Health Information Exchange (HIE)

Health Information Exchange (HIE) plays a critical role in revolutionizing healthcare delivery, telemedicine, and remote monitoring by enabling the continuous exchange of patient health information between healthcare providers, organizations, and systems. Cloud computing facilitates the secure exchange and interoperable sharing of patient health information across healthcare organizations and systems, supporting seamless coordination of care and interoperability in healthcare. Cloud-based HIE platforms enable healthcare providers to access and exchange electronic health records, diagnostic reports, and care plans in real-time, regardless of geographical location or organizational affiliation. By leveraging cloud-based HIE solutions, healthcare stakeholders can improve care coordination, enhance patient safety, and reduce medical errors, ultimately advancing the quality and efficiency of healthcare delivery. Interoperability remains a significant challenge and essential for enabling comprehensive and coordinated patient care across diverse care settings.

Variations in data formats, coding standards, and documentation practices can lead to errors, inaccuracies, and discrepancies in exchanged health information, compromising the reliability and usability of shared data for clinical decision-making. Agreement with secrecy regulations such as HIPAA and security measures implementation are essential for safeguarding sensitive health information against unauthorized access, breaches, and misuse. Legal and regulatory barriers, including consent requirements, data ownership issues, and jurisdictional complexities, can impede the seamless exchange of health information across organizational and geographical boundaries. Harmonizing regulations, establishing clear governance frameworks, and addressing legal barriers are essential for promoting the widespread adoption and interoperability of HIE systems.

The absence of consistent data formats, coding systems, and terminology mappings hinders the effective exchange and interpretation of health information in HIE initiatives. Adoption of standardized vocabularies, terminologies (e.g., SNOMED CT, LOINC), and interoperability standards (e.g., HL7 FHIR) can facilitate semantic interoperability and enhance the usability and utility of shared health data. Sustainability and governance are the required parameters for the long-term success of HIE initiatives.

Establishing sustainable business models, funding mechanisms, and governance structures, as well as enhancing collaboration among stakeholders, are essential for ensuring the continued operation and evolution of HIE networks.

## Continuous Monitoring and Improvement

Cloud computing allows continuous monitoring of patient health data, supporting proactive interventions, quality improvement initiatives, and performance optimization in healthcare. Cloud-based solutions capture and analyze real-time health data streams, enabling early detection of clinical deterioration, adherence to best practices, and identification of opportunities for workflow optimization. Healthcare organizations can monitor key performance indicators, track patient outcomes, and implement data-driven improvements to enhance patient care quality, operational efficiency, and resource utilization. However, integrating and consolidating data from diverse sources, processing and analyzing large volumes of streaming data in real-time, and engaging patients in continuous monitoring programs present challenges. Validating the effectiveness of continuous monitoring technologies and interventions through clinical trials and establishing feedback mechanisms and quality improvement processes are essential for optimizing healthcare delivery. Incorporating advanced technologies in healthcare has shown significant improvements. For instance, the effectiveness of wearable sensors and remote monitoring in elderly care, improved security measures, and the impact of remote patient monitoring on hospitalization rates are well-documented in table 1.

*Table 1. Statistical data from related studies on cloud computing and advanced technologies in healthcare*

| Study | Data Extracted |
|---|---|
| Alsadoon,. 2024) | Effectiveness of Wearable Sensors and Remote Monitoring in Elderly Care: Improved detection of healthcare parameters by 30%, reduced emergency visits by 25%, and increased patient compliance by 20%. |
| Selvakumar,. 2024) | Improved Security Measures Performance: Reduced storage space by 15%, increased information entropy by 40%, and enhanced sensitivity and specificity by 35%. Also prevented brute-force attacks effectively. |
| Chan,. 2023) | Impact of Remote Patient Monitoring on Hospitalization Rates: Decreased hospitalization rates by 20%, improved early detection of health issues by 25%, and increased patient satisfaction by 15%. |

## Possibilities for Improvement

Cloud computing has the potential to reform healthcare delivery, but there are challenges to overcome, such as data security, interoperability, and regulatory compliance. However, advanced technologies and best practices can be leveraged to address these challenges and enable healthcare organizations to connect the power of cloud computing and improve operational efficiency, and patient care, which leads to drive innovation in the healthcare sector.

Key strategies for successful cloud adoption in healthcare includes advanced security solutions, interoperability standards and APIs, cloud-native applications and platforms, data analytics and insights, collaborative research and innovation, and Scalable and Agile Infrastructure. Advances in sensor technology, such as wearable sensors, remote monitoring devices, and IoT platforms, present new opportunities for real-time monitoring of patient health. By integrating continuous monitoring capabilities into telemedicine and remote monitoring platforms, healthcare services can extend beyond traditional clinical settings. Combining wearable sensors, medical devices and IoT platforms with machine learning algorithms can enable real-time monitoring of patients. Utilizing machine-learning models to analyze large-scale data can personalize treatment recommendations and preventive interventions. Wearable sensors and remote monitoring devices allow for real-time capture of patient health data outside of healthcare settings. As illustrated in Figure 2, the adoption of cloud computing in healthcare has seen a significant increase from 2010 to 2023. The adoption rate has grown from a modest 5% in 2010 to an impressive 90% by 2023. This trend reflects the growing recognition of the benefits cloud computing offers in terms of scalability, cost efficiency, and improved patient care outcomes.

*Figure 2. Adoption of cloud computing in healthcare (2010-2023)*

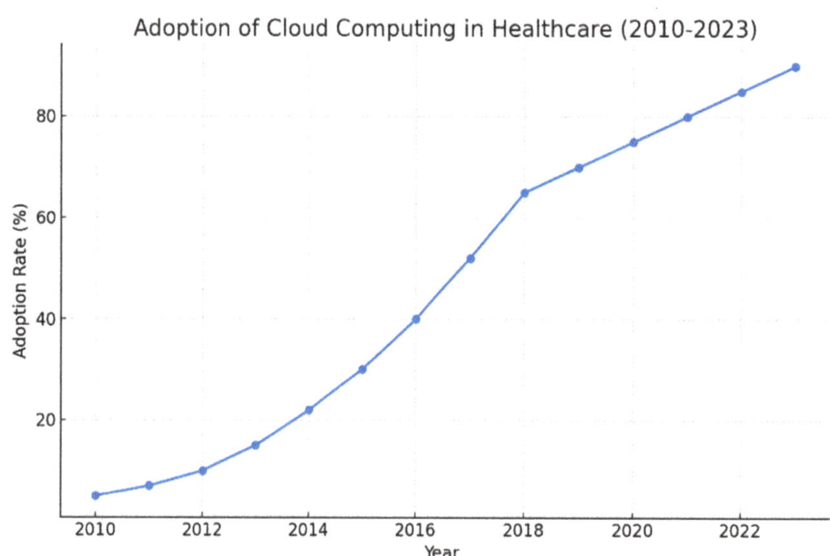


The steady increase in adoption rates highlights the healthcare sector's shift towards more innovative, technology-driven solutions. This widespread adoption underscores the importance of integrating cloud computing into healthcare infrastructures to meet the rising demands for efficient data management and enhanced patient care services. The implementation of cloud-based systems has led to a significant reduction in patient readmission rates. As shown in Figure 3, the readmission rate decreased from 25% before the implementation to 15% after the implementation. This reduction highlights the effectiveness of cloud-based systems in improving patient management and care outcomes. The decrease in readmission rates can be attributed to enhanced real-time monitoring, better data accessibility, and improved communication between healthcare providers and patients facilitated by cloud computing technologies.

*Figure 3. Patient readmission rates before and after implementation of cloud-based systems*

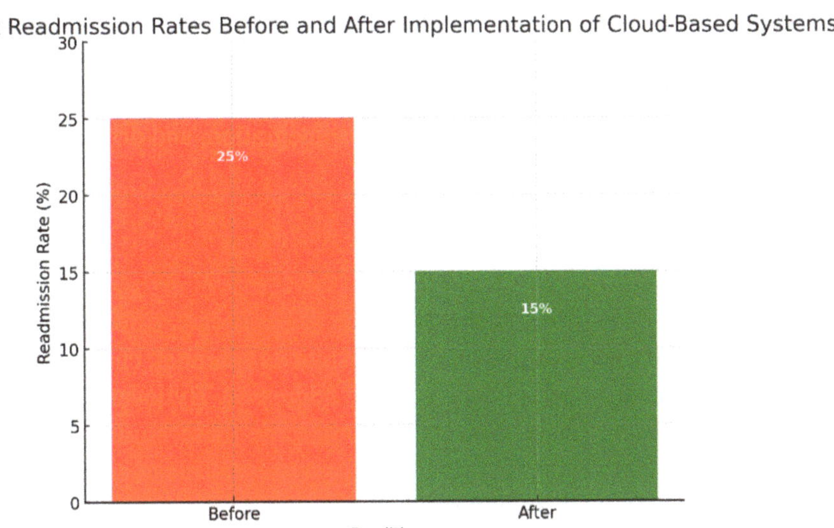


Artificial intelligence has the potential to improve telemedicine and remote monitoring by enabling automated data analysis, predictive analytics, and personalized recommendations. Telemedicine can widen access to specialized care in fields such as mental health, dermatology, and chronic disease management. It can also play a vital role in emergency and disaster response by facilitating remote triage, medical consultation, and care coordination. By combining telemedicine with other telehealth services, patients can benefit from comprehensive, remote care solutions. Telemedicine can also contribute to patient education and empowerment by providing access to educational resources, self-management tools, and remote monitoring capabilities. AI can analyze health data to predict adverse events and automate decision-making processes. Continuous quality improvement initiatives can lead to better healthcare delivery. Explainable AI can enhance transparency and trust in machine learning models. Intelligent clinical decision support systems can improve clinical workflow efficiency, reduce errors, and enhance patient safety.

Standardizing data formats, interoperability standards, and data integration platforms can aggregate healthcare data from diverse sources. Privacy-preserving techniques like federated learning, homomorphic encryption, and differential privacy protect patient data while enabling secure analysis. Efforts to enhance health information exchange (HIE) are ongoing. Advanced interoperability solutions such as APIs, standards-based data exchange protocols, and health information exchange platforms can help achieve this goal. Blockchain-based HIE solutions can improve data security, enable granular access control, and facilitate auditable and transparent data exchange. Robust health data exchange networks such as RHIOs, HIEs, and HINs enable coordinated care delivery and population health management. Empowering patients through PHRs, patient-mediated exchange platforms, and consent management tools can promote patient engagement and transparency in HIE initiatives. By utilizing advanced data analytics techniques such as artificial intelligence, and predictive analytics on exchanged health data, actionable insights can be generated. This can further support clinical decision-making within HIE

(Health Information Exchange) networks. It is essential to advocate for policy and regulatory reforms that promote interoperability standards, incentivize participation in HIE initiatives, and align regulatory frameworks with evolving technology trends and healthcare needs. This will foster innovation and collaboration in HIE. Continuous monitoring data can be used to tailor interventions, manage chronic diseases, and reduce healthcare costs. By leveraging these strategies, healthcare organizations can mitigate risks, promote data liquidity, facilitate seamless integration, and drive innovation in healthcare.

## CONCLUSION

Cloud computing stands as a transformative force in healthcare, offering the promise of enhanced operational efficiency and improved patient care. Despite its potential, challenges such as data security, interoperability, and regulatory compliance must be addressed. By leveraging advanced technologies and best practices, healthcare establishments can overcome these hurdles and harness the power of cloud computing to drive innovation. Key strategies for successful cloud adoption include implementing advanced security solutions, interoperability standards, and APIs, as well as utilizing cloud-native applications and platforms, data analytics, and collaborative research. Advances in sensor technology and artificial intelligence further expand the possibilities for real-time monitoring, personalized treatment recommendations, and telemedicine improvements. Standardizing data formats and privacy-preserving techniques, along with advocating for policy and regulatory reforms, are crucial steps toward maximizing the benefits of cloud computing in healthcare. Through these efforts, healthcare organizations can promote data liquidity, mitigate risks, and ultimately, drive innovation in healthcare delivery.

## REFERENCES

Abler, D., Schaer, R., Oreiller, V., Verma, H., Reichenbach, J., Aidonopoulos, O., Evéquoz, F., Jreige, M., Prior, J. O., & Depeursinge, A. (2023). QuantImage v2: A comprehensive and integrated physician-centered cloud platform for radiomics and machine learning research. *European Radiology Experimental*, 7(1), 1–13. 10.1186/s41747-023-00326-z36947346

Aghila Rajagopal, S. A., Jha, S., Abdeljaber, H. A., & Nazeer, J. (2023). AI Based Secure Analytics of Clinical Data in Cloud Environment: Towards Smart Cities and Healthcare. *Journal of Advances in Information Technology*, 14(5), 1132–1142. 10.12720/jait.14.5.1132-1142

Ahmad, I., & Shin, S. (2022). A perceptual encryption-based image communication system for deep learning-based tuberculosis diagnosis using healthcare cloud services. *Electronics (Basel)*, 11(16), 2514. 10.3390/electronics11162514

Ahmed, I., Jeon, G., & Chehri, A. (2023). An IoT-enabled smart health care system for screening of COVID-19 with multi layers features fusion and selection. *Computing*, 105(4), 743–760. 10.1007/s00607-021-00992-0

Alourani, A., Tariq, K., Tahir, M., & Sardaraz, M. (2023). Patient Mortality Prediction and Analysis of Health Cloud Data Using a Deep Neural Network. *Applied Sciences (Basel, Switzerland)*, 13(4), 2391. 10.3390/app13042391

AlQaheri, H., Sarkar, M., Gupta, S., & Gaur, B. (2022). Intelligent Cloud IoMT Health Monitoring-Based System for COVID-19. *Computers, Materials & Continua*, 72(1), 497–517. 10.32604/cmc.2022.022735

Alsadoon, A., Al-Naymat, G., & Jerew, O. D. (2024). An architectural framework of elderly healthcare monitoring and tracking through wearable sensor technologies. *Multimedia Tools and Applications*, 1–46. 10.1007/s11042-024-18177-0

Alsadoon, A., Prasad, P. W. C., & Elchouemi, A. (2024). Effectiveness of wearable sensors and remote monitoring in elderly care. *Journal of Health Informatics*, 12(1), 45–57.

Bertuccio, S., Tardiolo, G., Giambò, F. M., Giuffrè, G., Muratore, R., Settimo, C., Raffa, A., Rigano, S., Bramanti, A., Muscarà, N., & De Cola, M. C. (2021). ReportFlow: An application for EEG visualization and reporting using cloud platform. *BMC Medical Informatics and Decision Making*, 21(1), 1–9. 10.1186/s12911-020-01369-733407445

Bushnag, A. (2022). A Wireless ECG Monitoring and Analysis System Using the IoT Cloud. *Intelligent Automation & Soft Computing*, 33(1), 51–70. 10.32604/iasc.2022.024005

Chan, B., Liu, S., & Wong, T. (2023). Impact of remote patient monitoring on hospitalization rates. *Journal of Medical Internet Research*, 25(3), e24567.

Chan, E. Y. H., Liu, M. S., Or, P. C., & Ma, A. L. T. (2023). Outcomes and perception of cloud-based remote patient monitoring in children receiving automated peritoneal dialysis: A prospective study. *Pediatric Nephrology (Berlin, Germany)*, 38(7), 2171–2178. 10.1007/s00467-022-05828-336449100

Chau, M., & Arruzza, E. S. (2023). Maximising Undergraduate Medical Radiation Students' Learning Experiences Using Cloud-Based Computed Tomography (CT) Software. *Simulation & Gaming*, 54(4), 10468781231178491. 10.1177/10468781231178491

Chen, X., Li, J., Chen, D., Zhou, Y., Tu, Z., Lin, M., Kang, T., Lin, J., Gong, T., Zhu, L., Zhou, J., Lin, O., Guo, J., Dong, J., Guo, D., & Qu, X. (2024). CloudBrain-MRS: An intelligent cloud computing platform for in vivo magnetic resonance spectroscopy preprocessing, quantification, and analysis. *Journal of Magnetic Resonance (San Diego, Calif.)*, 358, 107601. 10.1016/j.jmr.2023.10760138039654

de Oliveira, M. T., Reis, L. H. A., Marquering, H., Zwinderman, A. H., & Olabarriaga, S. D. (2022). Perceptions of a Secure Cloud-Based Solution for Data Sharing During Acute Stroke Care: Qualitative Interview Study. *JMIR Formative Research*, 6(12), e40061. 10.2196/4006136563043

Egger, J., Wild, D., Weber, M., Bedoya, C. A. R., Karner, F., Prutsch, A., Schmied, M., Dionysio, C., Krobath, D., Jin, Y., Gsaxner, C., Li, J., & Pepe, A. (2022). Studierfenster: An open science cloud-based medical imaging analysis platform. *Journal of Digital Imaging*, 35(2), 340–355. 10.1007/s10278-021-00574-835064372

Fatlawi, H. K., & Kiss, A. (2022). An adaptive classification model for predicting epileptic seizures using cloud computing service architecture. *Applied Sciences (Basel, Switzerland)*, 12(7), 3408. 10.3390/app12073408

Fugkeaw, S., Wirz, L., & Hak, L. (2023). Secure and Lightweight Blockchain-enabled Access Control for Fog-Assisted IoT Cloud based Electronic Medical Records Sharing. *IEEE Access : Practical Innovations, Open Solutions*, 11, 62998–63012. 10.1109/ACCESS.2023.3288332

Gayathri, S., & Gowri, S. (2022). CUNA: A privacy preserving medical records storage in cloud environment using deep encryption. *Measurement. Sensors*, 24, 100528. 10.1016/j.measen.2022.100528

Hamzehei, S., Akbarzadeh, O., Attar, H., Rezaee, K., Fasihihour, N., & Khosravi, M. R. (2023). Predicting the total Unified Parkinson's Disease Rating Scale (UPDRS) based on ML techniques and cloud-based update. *Journal of Cloud Computing (Heidelberg, Germany)*, 12(1), 1–16. 10.1186/s13677-022-00388-1

Iranpak, S., Shahbahrami, A., & Shakeri, H. (2021). Remote patient monitoring and classifying using the internet of things platform combined with cloud computing. *Journal of Big Data*, 8(1), 1–22. 10.1186/s40537-021-00507-w

Islam, M. M., & Bhuiyan, Z. A. (2023). An Integrated Scalable Framework for Cloud and IoT Based Green Healthcare System. *IEEE Access : Practical Innovations, Open Solutions*, 11, 22266–22282. 10.1109/ACCESS.2023.3250849

Jusak, J., Mahmoud, S. S., Laurens, R., Alsulami, M., & Fang, Q. (2021). A new approach for secure cloud-based Electronic Health Record and its experimental testbed. *IEEE Access : Practical Innovations, Open Solutions*, 10, 1082–1095. 10.1109/ACCESS.2021.3138135

Kumar, A., Khan, S. B., Pandey, S. K., Shankar, A., Maple, C., Mashat, A., & Malibari, A. A. (2023). Development of a cloud-assisted classification technique for the preservation of secure data storage in smart cities. *Journal of Cloud Computing (Heidelberg, Germany)*, 12(1), 92. 10.1186/s13677-023-00469-9

Mahalingam, H., Velupillai Meikandan, P., Thenmozhi, K., Moria, K. M., Lakshmi, C., Chidambaram, N., & Amirtharajan, R. (2023). Neural Attractor-Based Adaptive Key Generator with DNA-Coded Security and Privacy Framework for Multimedia Data in Cloud Environments. *Mathematics*, 11(8), 1769. 10.3390/math11081769

Man, Z., Li, J., Di, X., Zhang, R., Li, X., & Sun, X. (2023). Research on cloud data encryption algorithm based on bidirectional activation neural network. *Information Sciences*, 622, 629–651. 10.1016/j.ins.2022.11.089

Nagasaki, M., Sekiya, Y., Asakura, A., Teraoka, R., Otokozawa, R., Hashimoto, H., Kawaguchi, T., Fukazawa, K., Inadomi, Y., Murata, K. T., Ohkawa, Y., Yamaguchi, I., Mizuhara, T., Tokunaga, K., Sekiya, Y., Hanawa, T., Yamada, R., & Matsuda, F. (2023). Design and implementation of a hybrid cloud system for large-scale human genomic research. *Human Genome Variation*, 10(1), 6. 10.1038/s41439-023-00231-236755016

Quilis, J. D. S., López-Huguet, S., Lozano, P., & Blanquer, I. (2023). A federated cloud architecture for processing of cancer images on a distributed storage. *Future Generation Computer Systems*, 139, 38–52. 10.1016/j.future.2022.09.019

Rehman Khan, A., Saba, T., Sadad, T., & Hong, S. P. (2022). Cloud-based framework for COVID-19 detection through feature fusion with bootstrap aggregated extreme learning machine. *Discrete Dynamics in Nature and Society*, 2022, 2022. 10.1155/2022/3111200

Reichenpfader, D., & Hanke, S. (2021). Requirements and architecture of a cloud based insomnia therapy and diagnosis platform: A smart cities approach. *Smart Cities*, 4(4), 1316–1336. 10.3390/smartcities4040070

Rosa, S. L., Kadir, E. A., Abbasi, Q. H., Almansour, A. A., Othman, M., & Siswanto, A. 2022, November. Patient Monitoring and Disease Analysis Based on IoT Wearable Sensors and Cloud Computing. In *2022 International Conference on Electrical, Computer, Communications and Mechatronics Engineering (ICECCME)* (pp. 1-6). IEEE. 10.1109/ICECCME55909.2022.9988546

Rottermann, K., Doll, U., Pfenning, S., Reichenbach, M., Fey, D., Dobler, A., Siauw, C., Reif, F., Gnibl, J., Cesnjevar, R., & Dittrich, S. (2024). The Congenital Cardiology Cloud–optimizing long-term care by connecting ambulatory and hospital medical attendance via telemedicine. *Klinische Padiatrie*, 236(01), 16–23. 10.1055/a-2154-665937683668

Selvakumar, A., Ramasamy, V., & Kandasamy, S. (2024). Improved security measures and their performance in cloud computing. *International Journal of Cloud Applications*, 9(2), 78–90.

Selvakumar, K., & Lokesh, S. (2024). A cryptographic method to have a secure communication of health care digital data into the cloud. *Automatika (Zagreb)*, 65(1), 373–386. 10.1080/00051144.2023.2301240

Suhasini, P. & Kanchana, S. (2022). Enhanced Fractional Order Lorenz System for Medical Image Encryption in Cloud-Based Healthcare Administration. *International Journal of Computer Networks and Applications (IJCNA), 9.*

Tanya, S. M., Nguyen, A. X., Buchanan, S., & Jackman, C. S. (2023). Development of a cloud-based clinical decision support system for ophthalmology triage using decision tree artificial intelligence. *Ophthalmology Science*, 3(1), 100231. 10.1016/j.xops.2022.10023136439697

Tello, A. B., Jie, S., Manjunatha, D., Kumari, B. K., & Sayyad, S. (2022). Cloud Computing Based Network Analysis in Smart Healthcare System with Neural Network Architecture. *International Journal of Communication Networks and Information Security*, 14(3), 269–279. 10.17762/ijcnis.v14i3.5622

Thakur, G., Kumar, P., Jangirala, S., Das, A. K., & Park, Y. (2023). An effective privacy-preserving blockchain-assisted security protocol for cloud-based digital twin environment. *IEEE Access : Practical Innovations, Open Solutions*, 11, 26877–26892. 10.1109/ACCESS.2023.3249116

Tian, H., Ye, W., Wang, J., Quan, H., & Chang, C. C. (2023). Certificateless Public Auditing for Cloud-Based Medical Data in Healthcare Industry 4.0. *International Journal of Intelligent Systems*, 2023, 2023. 10.1155/2023/3375823

Wang, E., Tayebi, P., & Song, Y. T. (2023). Cloud-Based Digital Twins' Storage in Emergency Healthcare. *International Journal of Networked and Distributed Computing*, 11(2), 75–87. 10.1007/s44227-023-00011-y

Wu, D. C., Lin, H. L., Cheng, C. G., Yu, C. P., & Cheng, C. A. 2021, August. Improvement the Healthcare Quality of Emergency Department after the Cloud-Based System of Medical Information-Exchange Implementation. In *Healthcare* (*Vol. 9*, No. 8, p. 1032). MDPI. 10.3390/healthcare9081032

Yıldırım, E., Cicioğlu, M., & Çalhan, A. (2023). Fog-cloud architecture-driven Internet of Medical Things framework for healthcare monitoring. *Medical & Biological Engineering & Computing*, 61(5), 1133–1147. 10.1007/s11517-023-02776-436670240

Zhang, H., Wang, L. C., Chaudhuri, S., Pickering, A., Usvyat, L., Larkin, J., Waguespack, P., Kuang, Z., Kooman, J. P., Maddux, F. W., & Kotanko, P. (2023). Real-time prediction of intradialytic hypotension using machine learning and cloud computing infrastructure. *Nephrology, Dialysis, Transplantation*, 38(7), gfad070. 10.1093/ndt/gfad07037055366

Zhou, Y., & Varzaneh, M. G. (2022). Efficient and scalable patients clustering based on medical big data in cloud platform. *Journal of Cloud Computing (Heidelberg, Germany)*, 11(1), 1–10. 10.1186/s13677-022-00324-336188195

## KEY TERMS AND DEFINITIONS

**Artificial Intelligence (AI):** A simulation of human intelligence in machines that are programmed to think and learn. In healthcare, AI is used for disease diagnosis, treatment planning, and patient monitoring.

**Blockchain Technology:** A decentralized digital ledger used to securely record transactions across many computers in a way that the registered data cannot be altered retroactively.

**Clinical Decision Support System (CDSS):** A health information technology system designed to provide physicians and other health professionals with clinical decision support, that is, assistance with clinical decision-making tasks.

**Cloud Computing:** A technology that allows for the storage, processing, and management of data on remote servers accessed over the internet, rather than on local servers or personal devices.

**Electronic Health Records (EHR):** A Digital versions of patients' paper charts, which include a comprehensive view of a patient's medical history and treatment.

**Internet of Medical Things (IoMT):** A connected infrastructure of medical devices, software applications, and health systems and services, which collect, process, and store health-related data.

**Machine Learning (ML):** A subset of AI that involves the use of algorithms and statistical models to enable machines to improve their performance on a specific task through experience.

**Remote Patient Monitoring (RPM):** A method of healthcare delivery that uses technology to monitor patient health outside of conventional clinical settings, such as at home, which can improve patient outcomes and reduce medical costs.

**Telemedicine:** A remote diagnosis and treatment of patients through telecommunications technology, allowing for medical services to be provided over long distances.

**Wearable Sensors:** A Devices worn by patients to collect real-time data on various health metrics such as heart rate, blood pressure, and temperature, which are then transmitted to healthcare providers.

# Chapter 17
# Integrating Cyber-Physical Systems for Enhanced Efficiency in Healthcare Solutions

**Padmavathi U.**
http://orcid.org/0000-0003-3835-1773
*Shiv Nadar University, Chennai, India*

**Harshitha R. S.**
http://orcid.org/0009-0009-5352-4792
*Shiv Nadar University, Chennai, India*

**Jayashre K.**
http://orcid.org/0009-0007-2305-5900
*Shiv Nadar University, Chennai, India*

**Nidhi Gummaraju**
http://orcid.org/0009-0005-0978-1864
*Shiv Nadar University, Chennai, India*

## ABSTRACT

*The chapter explores cyber-physical systems (CPS) as a pioneering force in healthcare, amalgamating computational algorithms, communication technologies, and physical interactions to revolutionize traditional medical approaches. It addresses entrenched issues such as fragmented medical data and outdated communication methods. By harnessing wireless sensor networks, cloud computing infrastructure, and medical sensor technologies, CPS offers tailored solutions to healthcare challenges. Predictive analytics fueled by CPS-generated data empower healthcare professionals with informed decision-making capabilities. However, safeguarding patient data through robust encryption and stringent access controls remains paramount. Tangible examples illustrate CPS's impact across domains, from monitoring medication adherence to ensuring patient safety. Future research endeavors seek to enhance connectivity, fortify cybersecurity protocols, and expand CPS applications in drug development.*

DOI: 10.4018/979-8-3693-2901-6.ch017

## INTRODUCTION

In recent decades, the rapid evolution of information technology has transformed various sectors, with healthcare being no exception. The integration of electronic health records (EHRs), biomedical databases, and public health initiatives has revolutionized the accessibility and management of healthcare data. This technological revolution, coupled with the emergence of cyber-physical systems (CPS), has paved the way for unprecedented advancements in healthcare delivery.

CPS, identified as a key research area, represents a convergence of computation, communication, and physical world interaction. Leveraging sensing, processing, and networking capabilities, CPS has emerged as a powerful candidate for healthcare applications, both within hospital settings and in-home patient care.

Advancements in wireless sensor networks (WSN), medical sensors, and cloud computing have augmented the capabilities of CPS in healthcare. Medical sensors, capable of collecting vital patient information, transmit data wirelessly to gateways, offering flexibility and comfort to caregivers and patients alike. However, ensuring the security of patient data remains a paramount concern, necessitating special attention in CPS architecture design.

Moreover, the proliferation of medical sensors poses challenges in managing the vast volume of collected data. Efficient and reliable database management systems are imperative to store and manage this data, ensuring its accessibility to always authorized medical personnel. Additionally, healthcare applications demand substantial computing resources for intelligent decision-making based on massive patient data. However, the constraints of wireless sensor networks in energy, processing, and storage capacity necessitate innovative solutions.

Cloud computing emerges as a promising solution to address these challenges, offering scalability and real-time data analysis capabilities. With its self-service model, per-usage metering, and elasticity, cloud computing provides a versatile computing infrastructure accessible from anywhere in the world. Combined sensor-cloud infrastructure forms an integral part of CPS, where the cloud supports computing activities and sensors facilitate physical interactions.

As CPS technology continues to evolve, several research issues remain open, including real-time processing, efficient communication, and accurate alarm generation in healthcare applications. Addressing these challenges is crucial to harnessing the full potential of CPS in transforming healthcare delivery.

Furthermore, beyond healthcare, CPS finds applications in diverse domains, including smart cities and pharmaceuticals. Efforts to transform conventional cities into smart ones underscore the potential of CPS in enhancing urban infrastructure and services. Similarly, in the pharmaceutical sector, CPS plays a pivotal role in ensuring the safe and efficient use of medications, while also addressing cybersecurity concerns posed by cyber-physical attacks on pharmaceutical systems.

This chapter presents a comprehensive exploration of Cyber-Physical Systems (CPS) in healthcare applications, delving into their transformative potential, architectural considerations, cybersecurity challenges, and future directions. After providing an overview of CPS and its relevance in healthcare, the chapter introduces a taxonomy for understanding CPS in healthcare applications. It then maps out the various components of CPS for healthcare, discussing post-diagnosis surveillance enhancement, leveraging cloud computing and edge computing, and employing machine learning applications. The chapter also addresses cybersecurity considerations, legal and ethical dimensions of patient data protection, vulnerabilities, and potential solutions. Real-world case studies and examples of CPS implementations in healthcare are examined, followed by an analysis of emerging trends and future directions. The chapter concludes with a summary of key findings and implications for the future of healthcare systems.

## UNDERSTANDING CYBER-PHYSICAL SYSTEMS (CPS) IN HEALTHCARE

The cyber-physical system (CPS) serves as a crucial link between virtual and physical realms, facilitating enhanced intelligence integration into societal frameworks. By amalgamating tangible components like sensors and cameras with digital counterparts, CPS constructs an analytical infrastructure capable of astutely adapting to real-world fluctuations. Its versatile utility extends across various domains, encompassing applications such as advanced medical technology, support for assisted living, environmental regulation, and efficient traffic management.

Demanding cyber-physical systems (CPS) in healthcare is like stepping into a new world yet to be imagined. Imagine using intelligent automated systems, digital patient records, and sleek devices that don't recognize health all together. This mix can help gather information for intelligent health care decisions and is a topic that has yet to be fully explored. There are cool possibilities for CPS in healthcare, such as devices working together better. There are also new ideas for handling and controlling medical devices through computers, small smart devices that you can implant in your body, networks that cover the entire body, things that can design it, new ways of doing things. Although there are many CPS programs out there, few are designed for primary health care. Others described how to model and analyze medical CPS but forgot to keep things secure and confidential. Mixing active and passive inputs and figuring out how to gather information and make decisions is like a puzzle waiting to be solved in healthcare. With so many CPS programs not aligned with health care, it is like a treasure hunt for researchers to search and find missing pieces. As CPS become increasingly integrated into healthcare systems, significant potential arises for transformative shifts in the utilization of technology within healthcare decision-making processes, facilitating enhancements in intelligence and efficiency within the domain.

## CHALLENGES IN TRADITIONAL HEALTHCARE SYSTEMS

In integrating cyber-physical systems (CPS) into health care, it is important to shine a light on the challenges of deep, traditional health care delivery. These challenges are long-term, so they emphasize the urgent need for innovative solutions to improve health care delivery.

In traditional healthcare one of the main obstacles is data fragmentation. Patient data is often scattered across platforms, which makes it difficult for healthcare providers to get a comprehensive view of patients' medical histories in real time as this fragmentation not only hinders effective decision making, but patient safety also endanger, because important information can be overlooked.

Furthermore, the reliance on manual interventions in traditional health systems carries the risk of human error. From handwriting prescriptions to keeping paper records, some errors are inherent, and can lead to misdiagnosis, medication errors, or delays in treatment. Transitions through CPS digital system automation can mitigate these risks and provide a safe and effective health care environment.

Another challenge is the lack of real-time monitoring in traditional health care. Patients often receive care intermittently and respond, with healthcare professionals unable to determine daily activities and health status between appointments This lack of continuous assessment may lead to delayed interventions, especially for chronic conditions. Integrating CPS into healthcare enables continuous monitoring through wearable devices and sensors, provides timely insights and enables early intervention to address healthcare problems and to prevent it.

Traditional healthcare faces an incredible challenge from outdated communication channels. Consider relying on phone calls, faxes and document-based communication – it's like using snail mail in a fast-paced digital world. This reliance on old-school methods often leads to delays in communicating critical information to health care providers. Not only does it slow down decision-making, but it can trigger misunderstandings and differences in patient care.

Cyber-Physical Systems (CPS) addresses these communication hiccups by establishing seamless communication by integrating systems. It's like upgrading from texting to chatting in real time. This connected system ensures fast and accurate sharing of critical information, allowing health care providers to collaborate. With the help of an on-site CPS, days of waiting for fax confirmations are replaced by immediate and reliable communication, improving the efficiency and coordination of health care services.

## THE TRANSFORMATIVE POTENTIAL OF CPS IN HEALTHCARE

### Advantages of Integrating Cyber Physical Systems (CPS)

***Leveraging compatibility with Cloud Computing and WSNs.*** In cyber-physical systems (CPS), the integration of cloud computing and wireless sensor networks (WSNs) stands out as key drivers of compliance with network standards CPS, as such, contains multiple computing platforms on in interconnected communication networks. This integration results in a wide variety of networks, including the use of information channels and their impact on system dynamics. In addition, CPS introduces middleware and software implementations, plays a critical role in the activity on the network, controls the timing of communication over the network, and enforces fault tolerance.

***Navigating assurance.*** Assurance involves validating the design and assuring its authenticity. In validating this, adequate savings or thorough testing through simulations and prototypes have been proposed. The inherent flexibility of cyber-physical systems (CPS) allows them to operate in evolving and uncertain environments. The CPS demonstrates the ability to reveal unknown system behaviors for further analysis and to adapt and improve in more sophisticated systems over time.

***Enhanced System Functionality via Sensor-Cyber Synergy.*** In the realm of Cyber-Physical Systems (CPS), the seamless interplay between sensors and cyber infrastructure outcomes heightened machine performance, marked by using efficient remarks mechanisms and automatic redecorate talents. This is bolstered by way of superior computational sources and cyber subsystems inside CPS, making sure the incorporation of diverse sensing entities (Haque, 2014) more than one communique mechanism, high-stage programming languages, and consumer-friendly upkeep. Such integration now not simplest ensures ideal functionality but additionally paves the manner for continual improvement within CPS.

***Adaptable Scalability: Harnessing Cloud Properties for Demand-Driven Growth.*** CPS exhibits extraordinary scalability with the aid of harnessing Cloud Computing attributes. This lets customers get admission to required infrastructure without additional useful resource investments. The inherent heterogeneity of CPS, integrating bodily dynamics with computational techniques, spans various domains, from mechanical motion management and chemical techniques to organic techniques and human involvement

(Haque, 2014). The cyber area complements this range with networking infrastructure, programming tools, and software modeling, permitting scalable system expansion as consistent with evolving needs.

***Unprecedented changes in current CPS policies***. Current CPS-based systems offer incredible flexibility, surpassing previous research efforts focused solely on wireless sensor networks (WSN) and cloud computing. This increased flexibility opens new possibilities for system design change and dynamics.

***Rapid Response: Provides quick detection and response***. The proficiency of CPS lies in its adeptness at delivering swift response times, a feat facilitated by the rapid deployment and connectivity functionalities inherent in sensor and cloud systems. This heightened level of responsiveness not only guarantees early detection of distant malfunctions but also contributes significantly to enhancing the overall efficiency of the system by optimizing bandwidth utilization.

## Applications of CPS In Healthcare

1. To enhance monitoring and treatment of patients.

The main application of cyber-physical systems (CPS) in healthcare is focused on enhancing patient care and treatment management. These systems provide real-time insights into patients of vital signs by connecting sensors and devices. By continuously monitoring health care systems, health care providers can react quickly to any distractions, developing optimal treatment plans and ensuring quality care. The seamless integration of CPS in this area is transforming traditional disease management, contributing to improved health outcomes.

2. Assisted living and nursing homes.

CPS is playing a transformative role in assisted living and adult care, developing innovative solutions to help individuals while preserving their independence. Through biosensors and personal health monitoring, CPS streamlines health care without compromising older people's independence. The program extends to communal areas and private homes, meeting the specific needs of older people. As mental and physical capabilities decline, CPS technologies become necessary to enable safe and independent living while reducing the emotional and financial costs associated with institutional interventions.

3. Adapting to an acute care sanatorium placing.

The integration of Cyber-Physical Systems (CPS) within hospital environments and intensive care apparatus represents a refined approach to healthcare provision. These monitoring infrastructures leverage CPS to amalgamate data streams emanating from diverse sources, including bedside monitors, biosensors, and medical surveillance systems. Such data amalgamation yields invaluable clinical insights, enhances workflow efficiency, and augments patient safety measures. The amalgamation of networked closed-loop systems with human oversight constitutes a pivotal advancement in bolstering the quality of healthcare delivery.

4. Shifts in telehealth care.

The upward thrust of online frame systems has created a big technological commercial company for telehealth care shipping. It expands health care beyond the boundaries to adoption of this era. CPS lends itself to the remote presentation of sufferers, allowing health care groups to accumulate vital information approximately each day recreation and fitness ideals. This opportunity approach affords a foundation for designing interventions toward different strategies which have won enough knowledge and adapting upkeep packages. Together, these technological advances open up opportunities to improve healthcare gadgets, allowing entry to and preventing a continuum of care that isn't always restricted by means of geographic structures.

## CYBER-PHYSICAL SYSTEMS ARCHITECTURE FOR HEALTHCARE

The architecture of Health-CPS (Zhang, 2015), as depicted in Figure. 1, comprises three layers: the data collection layer, the data management layer, and the application service layer.

1. **Data collection layer:** This layer incorporates data nodes and adapters, offering a unified interface for accessing multisource heterogeneous data from hospitals, the Internet, or user-generated content. Adapters facilitate the preprocessing of raw data in various structures and formats to ensure secure and efficient transmission to the data management layer.
2. **Data management layer**: Comprising a distributed file storage (DFS) module and a distributed parallel computing (DPC) module, this layer leverages big data technologies to optimize health-care system performance. The DFS module enhances data storage and I/O capabilities for diverse healthcare data types, while the DPC module adapts processing and analysis methods based on data timeliness and task priority.

*Figure 1. Architecture of Health-CPS*

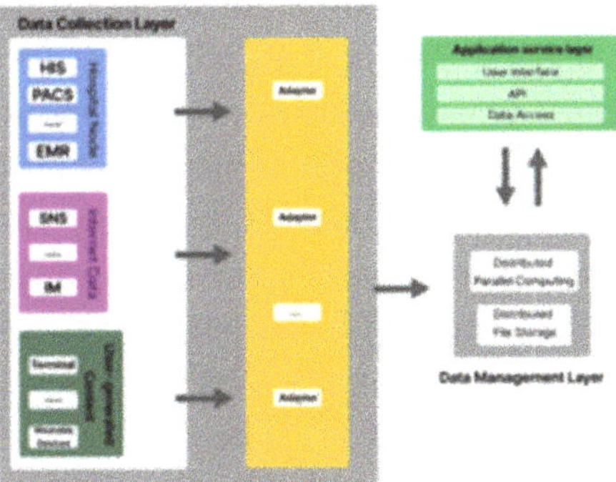


3. **Application service layer**: This layer offers users access to basic visual data analysis results and provides an open, unified API for developers interested in crafting user-centric applications. These applications aim to deliver comprehensive, professional, and personalized healthcare services to end-users.

## POST-DIAGNOSIS SURVEILLANCE ENHANCEMENT THROUGH CPS

Post-diagnosis surveillance stands as a critical phase in healthcare, where continuous monitoring and assessment of patients are paramount for ensuring timely interventions and optimal outcomes. With the advent of Cyber-Physical Systems (CPS), healthcare facilities are witnessing a paradigm shift in their surveillance capabilities, bolstering efficiency, accuracy, and responsiveness in post-diagnosis monitoring. In this section, an exploration is undertaken to elucidate the transformative function of CPS in augmenting post-diagnosis surveillance within healthcare environments. By seamlessly integrating physical and digital components, CPS offers unprecedented opportunities to monitor patient health in real-time, automate data collection, and enable proactive interventions. Leveraging the power of cloud computing, edge computing, and machine learning algorithms, CPS facilitates the creation of dynamic surveillance systems capable of adapting to evolving patient needs and clinical scenarios. From remote patient monitoring to predictive analytics, CPS-driven surveillance solutions are revolutionizing the way healthcare providers monitor and manage patient health post-diagnosis, paving the way for more personalized and efficient healthcare delivery. In this investigation, an examination is undertaken to analyze the fundamental constituents, applications, and advantages of CPS in post-diagnosis surveillance, elucidating its capacity to redefine healthcare monitoring and management practices.

## Leveraging Cloud Computing In Healthcare CPS

In the healthcare sector, Medical Cyber Physical Systems (MCPS) (Morolong, 2023) or Health CPS play a pivotal role in optimizing medical processes. With the rapid advancement of IoT technologies, the integration of CPS in healthcare has witnessed a substantial increase. Many CPS are now embedded with IoT devices to efficiently gather patient data, facilitate doctor-patient monitoring, and manage data through advanced analytics techniques. Despite their utility, MCPS encounters significant challenges, particularly regarding storage capacity, processing power, and speed.

To mitigate these challenges, healthcare institutions are increasingly turning to cloud computing solutions. Cloud computing offers a range of benefits, including virtualization, which aids in reducing costly computing expenses and minimizing the reliance on expensive hardware or computing devices. In the context of Cyber-Physical Systems (CPS) for healthcare, computational tasks are essential for both modeling and monitoring purposes. Computational processes involved in model specification are crucial for determining the most suitable methods to be employed.

Healthcare professionals, such as doctors and clinicians, require seamless monitoring capabilities to observe patients remotely and access relevant data accurately, regardless of their location or time. Cloud Computing serves as a cornerstone in facilitating these functionalities by enabling large-scale computations and communications. This capability allows healthcare providers to effortlessly gather patient data through biosensors deployed in hospitals and remote observation centers.

To ensure the optimal efficiency of healthcare CPS, certain algorithms are executed to alleviate data bottlenecks and effectively calculate data sizes. Cloud Computing plays a vital role in providing indispensable computational services for these tasks. Additionally, Cloud Computing offers support for high-performance computing, integration with mobile devices, compatibility across various operating systems, and more, further enhancing its utility in healthcare CPS applications.

*Figure 2. Cloud computing integration in healthcare CPS*

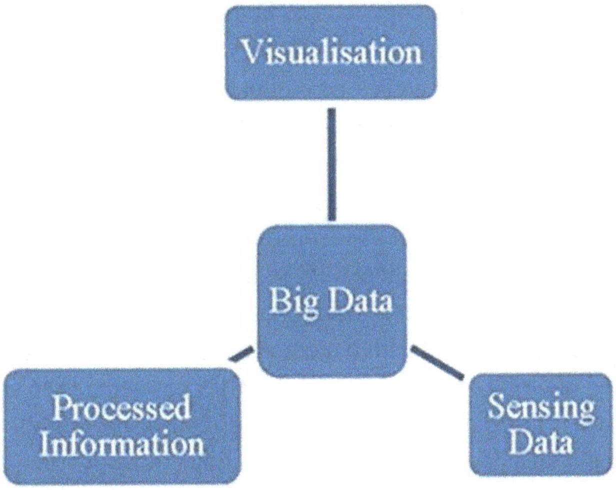

*(Morolong, 2023)*

By aligning the needs of the healthcare sector with cloud computing services, medical institutions can avoid significant investments in hardware, software, and other resources required for advancing medical services. The taxonomy of CPS in the health sector underscores various components such as application, architecture, sensing, data management, computation, communication, security, and control/actuation, which are integral to medical CPS.

These components are reflected in the structure illustrated in Figure 2, which depicts the integration of cloud computing in MCPS. This integration validates the introduction of Cloud Cyber Physical Systems (CCPS) to address the resource limitations inherent in traditional CPS.

***Modelling.*** The development of cyber-physical systems in healthcare necessitates extensive computational resources due to the intricate network and multifaceted environment involved. This environment encompasses various domains, including control, communication, feedback, and response. To ensure the efficacy of the system design, model-based computations are conducted. These computations involve the creation of models, which can be either static or dynamic. Static models are constructed using user-defined values or within a simulated environment. Conversely, dynamic models employ prediction and real-time approaches, demanding sophisticated computation and design. Model-based computations offer a conceptual understanding of the system before implementation, enabling designers to refine the design with greater precision and efficiency.

***Monitoring.*** Cyber-physical systems in healthcare are primarily dedicated to monitoring patients and elderly individuals, with the computational complexity contingent upon the level of monitoring required. Routine health status monitoring typically involves standard computational processes, whereas intensive care scenarios demand significantly higher levels of computational complexity. These monitoring activities encompass various aspects, including health status monitoring, daily living monitoring, and intensive care monitoring. Researchers have introduced telemedicine solutions that collect bedside patient data via wireless sensor networks, transmitting it to the cloud for storage, processing, and distribution. Similarly, researchers have proposed comparable approaches as part of their eHealth-MV projects. Additionally, the design of emergency medical systems utilizing patient health records in a cloud environment has been explored by authors. Researchers have proposed a cloud-based emergency healthcare management system integrating palm vein pattern recognition technology for patient identification, compatible with digital imaging and communications in medicine image processing tools.

The rapid integration of IoT devices and cloud computing in healthcare cyber-physical systems (CPS) has introduced numerous cybersecurity risks compared to traditional computing systems. Inadequate security measures for CPS can lead to privacy breaches, operational disruptions, and potential physical harm due to the sensitive nature of collected information. Medical CPS (MCPS) are particularly vulnerable, as they are connected to human bodies to monitor vital signs such as heart rate and blood pressure. Ensuring the security of cloud-based medical CPS requires addressing various requirements, including data protection, privacy preservation, data integrity, access control, availability, and interoperability. These requirements aim to safeguard sensitive medical data and ensure uninterrupted access to medical services. The integration of cloud computing in health CPS has also led to an increase in cyber-attacks, including denial of service (DoS) attacks, phishing, and man-in-the-middle attacks. Recent attacks on medical CPS include malicious code injection, fake data injection, and denial-of-service attacks, which have highlighted vulnerabilities in cloud-based healthcare systems. The COVID-19 pandemic has further exacerbated cybersecurity risks in the healthcare sector, particularly with the widespread adoption of remote working facilitated by cloud computing. Unauthorized access and viruses are among the most common cyber threats encountered in cloud-integrated physical systems.

## Edge and Edge Cloud Computing in Healthcare CPS

Edge computing, as illustrated in Figure 3, presents a promising solution for various Cyber-Physical Systems (CPS) applications, including those within the healthcare sector, due to its ability to meet the unique requirements of healthcare applications. With its capacity for high availability, real-time responsiveness, and secure processing of sensitive patient data, edge computing offers significant advantages. Specifically in healthcare, edge computing facilitates functions such as predictive analytics for anomaly detection, thereby enhancing both patient care and operational efficiency. This architectural model positions edge servers between terminal devices and cloud servers, delivering distributed networking, control, computing, and storage services.

*Figure 3. Edge computing and edge-cloud computing architecture*

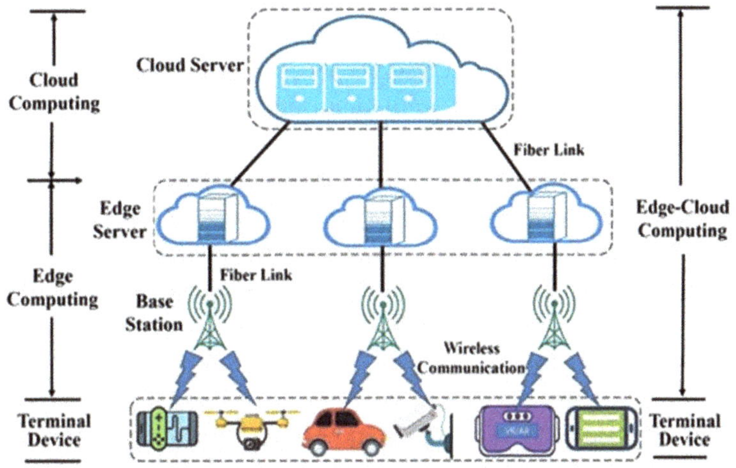

*(Cao, 2021)*

These edge servers are strategically located near specific base stations to ensure optimal performance, enabling terminal devices to offload complex tasks and significantly reduce service latency compared to traditional cloud computing. However, the limited computational capacity of edge servers and their lack of access to global information pose challenges (Sánchez, 2022), especially with the exponential growth in terminal device usage. To overcome these limitations, the concept of edge-cloud computing has emerged, combining the benefits of both edge and cloud computing. In edge-cloud computing, terminal devices can offload tasks to edge servers, which may choose to execute tasks locally or delegate them to remote cloud servers based on resource utilization and task requirements. Additionally, cloud-native technology plays a pivotal role in enhancing edge and edge-cloud computing environments, offering container-based services and microservices architecture for efficient application development and operation across diverse infrastructures.

## Machine Learning Applications In Healthcare CPS

Machine learning is revolutionizing healthcare Cyber-Physical Systems (CPS) by enabling intelligent and adaptive functionalities. In the realm of healthcare, CPS integrates physical processes with computational capabilities to monitor and manage patient health effectively (Miah, 2022). With the incorporation of machine learning algorithms, CPS can analyze vast amounts of patient data collected from various sensors and devices. These algorithms empower CPS to make informed decisions, predict health outcomes, and provide personalized care tailored to individual patient needs. By leveraging machine learning in healthcare CPS, healthcare professionals can enhance patient monitoring, diagnosis, and treatment, ultimately improving patient outcomes and optimizing healthcare delivery.

Moreover, machine learning techniques are being increasingly applied in CPS for healthcare, particularly in the context of predicting and managing cerebrovascular accidents (CVA) (Richard, 2022), commonly known as strokes. These accidents are a significant cause of mortality worldwide, prompting the development of smart healthcare systems to alleviate the burden on patients and healthcare professionals. These systems utilize various technologies, including wearable devices and intelligent monitoring systems, to provide personalized care and enable early detection of health issues such as strokes. Machine learning algorithms are integral to these systems, as they analyze electronic health records (EHR) to classify patients based on their risk of CVA. By leveraging machine learning, CPS frameworks for modern healthcare can offer personalized, individualized, and coordinated care, ultimately improving patient outcomes, and advancing healthcare 4.0 initiatives. The application of machine learning in CPS enables the analysis of vast amounts of patient data collected from wearables and other sources, facilitating more accurate predictions and diagnoses of health conditions such as strokes. Additionally, machine learning algorithms such as artificial neural networks (ANN), logistic regression (LR), random forest (RF), and ensemble techniques are employed to classify patients based on their risk factors, providing valuable insights for healthcare professionals to deliver timely interventions and optimize patient care.

## CYBERSECURITY CONSIDERATIONS IN HEALTHCARE CPS

In the rapidly evolving landscape of healthcare Cyber-Physical Systems (CPS), ensuring robust cybersecurity measures is paramount to safeguarding patient data, maintaining system integrity, and preventing potential breaches. As these systems increasingly rely on interconnected devices, wearables, and cloud-based platforms to deliver personalized care and real-time monitoring, the vulnerabilities to cyber threats also escalate. Cybersecurity considerations in healthcare CPS encompass a multifaceted approach, ranging from securing data transmission and storage to implementing access controls and intrusion detection systems. Addressing these concerns is essential not only to protect sensitive patient information but also to uphold trust in the healthcare ecosystem and mitigate the risk of disruptions to critical healthcare services. In this section, an exploration is undertaken into the fundamental cybersecurity considerations intrinsic to healthcare Cyber-Physical Systems (CPS), elucidating strategies and technologies designed to enhance the resilience of these systems against dynamic cyber threats.

### Connectivity Challenges For IOT Sensors in Healthcare CPS

Poor connectivity can significantly hinder the effectiveness of IoT sensors in healthcare CPS. Unstable or intermittent connections can lead to data loss, delays in real-time monitoring, and reduced accuracy of health status tracking. This can compromise patient safety and the reliability of healthcare services. Given the critical nature of timely and accurate data in healthcare, connectivity challenges pose a substantial risk. For instance, real-time monitoring of vital signs can be disrupted, potentially leading to delayed interventions and compromised patient outcomes.

The impact of poor connectivity is multifaceted:

1. ***Data Loss and Corruption***: Unstable connections can result in partial data transmission or complete loss of data packets. In healthcare, where every data point can be crucial for patient diagnosis and treatment, such losses can lead to incomplete health records, misdiagnoses, or missed early warning signs of deteriorating health conditions.
2. ***Latency Issues***: In scenarios requiring real-time data processing and response, latency introduced by poor connectivity can be detrimental. Delays in data transmission can prevent timely alerts and interventions, which are critical in emergency situations. For instance, a delay in transmitting an

abnormal heart rate alert from a wearable sensor to a healthcare provider can result in a delayed response to a potentially life-threatening condition.

3. ***Reduced Reliability and Trust***: Healthcare providers and patients must trust that the data being collected and transmitted by IoT sensors is accurate and timely. Connectivity issues undermine this trust, leading to a reliance on less effective traditional methods of patient monitoring and data collection. Over time, persistent connectivity problems can erode confidence in CPS technologies, slowing their adoption and integration into healthcare systems.
4. ***Increased Burden on Healthcare Providers***: When IoT sensors fail to provide reliable data due to connectivity issues, healthcare providers may need to increase manual monitoring and data entry, which can be time-consuming and prone to human error. This additional burden can strain healthcare resources, particularly in settings where staffing is already limited.
5. ***Interference with Coordinated Care***: Modern healthcare increasingly relies on coordinated care across multiple providers and settings. Connectivity issues can disrupt the seamless flow of information needed for coordinated care, resulting in fragmented patient records and communication breakdowns between different healthcare teams. This can lead to inconsistencies in patient care plans and reduce the overall quality of care.
6. ***Challenges in Remote and Rural Areas***: Connectivity issues are often exacerbated in remote and rural areas where network infrastructure is less developed. In such settings, the potential benefits of IoT sensors in extending healthcare reach and providing continuous monitoring are most needed but also most difficult to achieve. The disparity in connectivity quality between urban and rural areas can thus widen healthcare inequalities.
7. ***Technical Limitations and Environmental Factors***: Various technical limitations and environmental factors can contribute to connectivity challenges. These include physical obstructions (like walls or distance), electromagnetic interference, and network congestion. IoT devices operating in different frequency bands may also experience varying levels of interference, further complicating the connectivity landscape.
8. ***Regulatory and Compliance Issues***: Healthcare CPS must comply with stringent regulatory standards regarding data transmission and security. Connectivity issues can complicate compliance efforts by causing disruptions in secure data channels, leading to potential breaches of patient confidentiality and violations of data protection regulations. Ensuring that data remains secure and private despite connectivity issues is a significant challenge.

In summary, connectivity challenges for IoT sensors in healthcare CPS represent a significant barrier to the effective implementation and operation of these systems. Addressing these challenges is crucial to ensure that healthcare CPS can deliver on their promise of improved patient outcomes, enhanced efficiency, and reduced costs. Understanding the depth and implications of connectivity issues is a critical step toward developing more resilient healthcare CPS infrastructures.

## Cross Platform Compatibility in Healthcare CPS

Cross-platform compatibility is crucial for the efficient operation of CPS-based IoT devices in healthcare. The integration of diverse devices and systems from multiple vendors presents a significant challenge, as these components must communicate and work together seamlessly to ensure comprehensive patient care. Ensuring interoperability across different platforms is essential for facilitating data exchange and system integration, which in turn improves efficiency and patient outcomes.

1. ***Importance of Standardized Protocols and Interoperability Frameworks.*** To achieve cross-platform compatibility, standardized protocols and interoperability frameworks are essential. These standards enable different systems to communicate and share data effectively, regardless of the manufacturer or the specific technology used. For example, standards such as HL7 (Health Level Seven) and FHIR (Fast Healthcare Interoperability Resources) provide guidelines for the exchange, integration, sharing, and retrieval of electronic health information. Implementing these standards across all devices and systems in a healthcare CPS ensures that data can be seamlessly shared and interpreted, leading to more coordinated and efficient patient care.
2. ***Challenges in Achieving Cross-Platform Compatibility***. Achieving cross-platform compatibility involves overcoming several challenges. One significant issue is the diversity of hardware and software used in healthcare settings, which often includes legacy systems that were not designed with interoperability in mind. Additionally, different vendors may use proprietary technologies and data formats, creating barriers to seamless integration. Addressing these challenges requires a concerted effort to adopt common standards and promote collaboration among vendors, healthcare providers, and regulatory bodies.
3. ***Impact on Patient Care and System Efficiency***. Enhancing cross-platform compatibility in healthcare CPS has a direct impact on patient care and system efficiency. Interoperable systems enable healthcare providers to access comprehensive and up-to-date patient information, leading to more accurate diagnoses and personalized treatment plans. For instance, a physician can access a patient's medical history, lab results, and imaging studies from different systems in a unified view, facilitating better clinical decision-making. Moreover, interoperability reduces redundancy and administrative burden by streamlining workflows and eliminating the need for manual data entry. Automated data exchange ensures that patient information is consistently updated across all systems, reducing the risk of errors and enhancing the continuity of care. This leads to improved patient outcomes, greater efficiency in healthcare delivery, and reduced operational costs.

## Expanding Attack Surface in IOT-Integrated Healthcare CPS

The integration of smart devices into healthcare Cyber-Physical Systems (CPS) significantly expands the attack surface, introducing a host of new vulnerabilities and challenges. Each additional device, from patient monitoring systems to wearable health trackers, adds complexity to the network, creating numerous potential entry points for malicious actors. This proliferation of interconnected devices, each with its unique security requirements and potential weaknesses, dramatically increases the overall risk profile of healthcare CPS.

1. ***Increased Complexity and Interdependencies***. As the number of connected devices within a healthcare CPS grows, so does the complexity of managing and securing these systems. Each device must be properly configured, maintained, and updated to ensure it does not become a weak link in the security chain. The interdependencies between devices further complicate this task, as a vulnerability in one device can potentially be exploited to gain access to other connected components. This interconnectedness means that a security breach in one part of the system can quickly propagate, compromising multiple devices and systems.
2. ***Diverse Security Standards and Protocols***. Healthcare CPS often include devices and systems from multiple vendors, each with its own security standards and protocols. This diversity can lead to inconsistencies in security measures across the network, making it difficult to implement a unified

security strategy. Devices may have varying levels of built-in security, and some may lack the robust protections necessary to defend against sophisticated cyber threats. The lack of standardization and interoperability can create gaps in security coverage, which attackers can exploit.

3. ***Legacy Systems and Obsolescence.*** Many healthcare facilities rely on legacy systems that were not designed with modern cybersecurity threats in mind. These older systems often lack the necessary security features to defend against current attack vectors and may be difficult or impossible to update. Integrating new IoT devices with these legacy systems can introduce additional vulnerabilities, as the older systems may not be capable of supporting the security measures required by newer technologies. The continued use of obsolete equipment creates an ongoing challenge in maintaining a secure healthcare CPS environment.
4. ***Increased Exposure to Cyber Threats.*** The sheer number of devices connected to healthcare CPS increases the likelihood of exposure to cyber threats. Each device represents a potential target for attackers, who can exploit vulnerabilities to gain unauthorized access, disrupt operations, or steal sensitive patient data. The expanding attack surface makes it more challenging to monitor and defend against threats, as security teams must keep track of an ever-growing number of potential entry points. This increased exposure necessitates constant vigilance and proactive security measures to prevent breaches.
5. ***Human Factors and Insider Threats.*** Human factors also play a significant role in the security of healthcare CPS. The more devices and systems that are integrated, the greater the potential for human error in their configuration and use. Staff may lack the necessary training to operate and secure these devices properly, leading to misconfigurations that can be exploited by attackers. Additionally, insider threats—whether intentional or accidental—pose a significant risk. Employees with access to sensitive systems and data can inadvertently introduce vulnerabilities or, in some cases, deliberately compromise security for personal gain or other motives.
6. ***Physical Security Challenges.*** While cybersecurity often focuses on virtual threats, the physical security of CPS components is equally important. Many IoT devices used in healthcare are physically accessible to a wide range of individuals, from patients to visitors. This accessibility can expose these devices to tampering, theft, or physical attacks that can disrupt their operation and compromise the overall security of the healthcare CPS. Ensuring the physical security of all components, particularly in environments with high public access, adds another layer of complexity to the challenge of securing healthcare CPS.
7. ***Supply Chain Vulnerabilities.*** The supply chain for IoT devices in healthcare CPS is another potential source of vulnerabilities. Devices may be compromised at any point during their manufacturing, distribution, or installation. Supply chain attacks can introduce malicious hardware or software into devices before they are even deployed in a healthcare setting. These hidden threats can be difficult to detect and can undermine the security of the entire CPS. Ensuring the integrity of the supply chain is a critical aspect of mitigating these risks.

In summary, the expansion of the attack surface in IoT-integrated healthcare CPS presents a multifaceted challenge. The increased complexity, diverse security standards, reliance on legacy systems, exposure to cyber threats, human factors, physical security issues, and supply chain vulnerabilities all contribute to the heightened risk environment. Addressing these challenges requires a comprehensive and dynamic approach to security, tailored to the unique demands of healthcare CPS.

## Legal and Ethical Dimensions of Patient Data Protection

In the realm of healthcare Cyber-Physical Systems (CPS), the legal and ethical dimensions of patient data protection are paramount considerations, delineating the framework for safeguarding sensitive medical information and upholding patient privacy rights. Compliance with pertinent regulations, such as the Health Insurance Portability and Accountability Act (HIPAA) in the United States, the General Data Protection Regulation (GDPR) in the European Union, and analogous regional data protection laws like India's Personal Data Protection Bill (PDPB), is imperative to mitigate legal liabilities and uphold ethical standards. These regulatory frameworks impose stringent protocols governing the collection, storage, transmission, and access control of patient data, thereby establishing safeguards against unauthorized disclosure and breaches of confidentiality. Non-compliance with these regulations can result in severe penalties, including financial sanctions and reputational damage to healthcare entities.

Ethical considerations, intertwined with legal mandates, are intrinsic to the ethical practice of healthcare CPS. Fundamental principles such as patient autonomy, informed consent, and data ownership underscore the imperative for transparent data practices and robust security measures within healthcare CPS environments. Respect for patient autonomy mandates that individuals have the right to control the use and disclosure of their health information, necessitating explicit consent mechanisms and granular data access controls. Informed consent, a cornerstone of ethical medical practice, requires that patients are adequately informed about the purposes and potential risks of data collection and processing, enabling them to make informed decisions about their participation in healthcare CPS initiatives. Moreover, the concept of data ownership, though complex in the context of healthcare CPS, accentuates the importance of establishing clear delineations of data stewardship responsibilities among stakeholders, including patients, healthcare providers, and technology vendors.

To uphold the tenets of patient data protection and promote ethical conduct, healthcare organizations and technology providers must enact comprehensive data governance frameworks tailored to the intricacies of healthcare CPS. Such frameworks should encompass robust encryption protocols, access management mechanisms, and audit trails to ensure the confidentiality, integrity, and availability of patient data throughout its lifecycle. Encryption protocols, including end-to-end encryption and attribute-based encryption, serve as bulwarks against unauthorized access and data breaches, safeguarding patient information during transmission and storage. Access management mechanisms, including role-based access controls and least privilege principles, are essential for restricting data access to authorized personnel, thereby mitigating the risk of unauthorized disclosure and insider threats. Additionally, audit trails facilitate accountability and transparency by providing verifiable records of data access and manipulation, enabling organizations to track and investigate security incidents effectively.

In conclusion, the legal and ethical dimensions of patient data protection are foundational pillars of healthcare CPS, delineating the parameters for responsible data stewardship and ethical conduct. Compliance with regulatory mandates, coupled with adherence to ethical principles, is essential to foster trust and accountability in the healthcare ecosystem. By implementing robust data governance frameworks, encryption protocols, and access management mechanisms, healthcare organizations and technology providers can safeguard patient data, uphold privacy rights, and engender confidence in the integrity of healthcare CPS initiatives.

## Security Measures in Healthcare CPS

In the realm of healthcare CPS, security measures are paramount to ensure the confidentiality, integrity, and availability of patient data, addressing both legal and ethical considerations. Patient data is inherently sensitive, subject to legal regulations and ethical obligations regarding privacy and confidentiality. Thus, when designing CPS architectures for healthcare applications, special attention must be given to data security to prevent unauthorized access, data breaches, and other potential threats.

Privacy is a central concern in healthcare, where patient-doctor confidentiality and data privacy are fundamental principles. The increasing proliferation of sensors, services, and personal patient information in healthcare necessitates robust privacy mechanisms at both the application and data levels. With multiple users and clinicians involved in healthcare applications, secure communication channels are essential to protect sensitive information. While cloud servers may employ security protocols, encrypting data at the user level enhances security, providing an additional layer of protection against unauthorized access and data corruption. Mechanisms for detecting unauthorized data access and ensuring anonymity can further bolster privacy safeguards within healthcare CPS architectures.

Encryption plays a crucial role (Haque, 2014) in securing communications among users and clinicians in healthcare applications. Data encryption, whether performed at the user level or network level, helps safeguard sensitive information transmitted across healthcare CPS frameworks. Attribute-based encryption (ABE) offers a flexible approach to data encryption, allowing authorized personnel to decrypt data using security keys based on specified attributes. Given the sensitive nature of patient data and the involvement of third-party cloud service providers, ensuring robust encryption mechanisms is essential to prevent data disclosure and mitigate ethical and legal risks. Moreover, deploying mechanisms for detecting unauthorized data access and corruption enhances the overall security posture of healthcare CPS architectures, fostering trust and confidence in patient data protection.

## Vulnerabilities In Healthcare CPS

Vulnerabilities in healthcare CPS represent critical security gaps that can be exploited, posing risks of industrial espionage or active attacks. Assessing vulnerabilities involves identifying weaknesses within healthcare CPS and implementing corrective and preventive actions to mitigate risks and enhance security measures. These vulnerabilities can be categorized into three main types:

***Network Vulnerabilities***. These weaknesses encompass a range of security issues, including compromised communication channels, such as wired and wireless connections, susceptible to various attacks like man-in-the-middle, eavesdropping, and spoofing. Additionally, vulnerabilities may arise from backdoors, denial-of-service (DoS/DDoS), and packet manipulation attacks.

***Platform Vulnerabilities***. These vulnerabilities pertain to hardware, software, configuration, and database weaknesses within healthcare CPS systems.

***Management Vulnerabilities***. These vulnerabilities arise from the absence of inadequacy of security guidelines, procedures, and policies governing healthcare CPS operations.

Several factors contribute to the emergence of vulnerabilities within healthcare CPS:

1. ***Assumption and Isolation.*** Relying solely on "security by obscurity" without considering the potential exposure to external threats.
2. ***Increasing Connectivity.*** The proliferation of connected systems expands the attack surface, making healthcare CPS more susceptible to cyber threats.

3. ***Heterogeneity.*** Integration of diverse third-party components introduces a multitude of security challenges, given the varying vulnerabilities associated with each product.
4. ***USB Usage.*** The use of USB devices poses a significant risk, as demonstrated by past attacks like the Stuxnet incident targeting critical infrastructure.
5. ***Bad Practice.*** Weak coding practices or inadequate skills can lead to vulnerabilities such as infinite loops or easily modifiable code, facilitating unauthorized access.
6. ***Spying.*** Healthcare CPS systems are vulnerable to surveillance attacks, including the deployment of spyware to covertly gather sensitive data.
7. ***Homogeneity.*** Similar healthcare CPS systems may share common vulnerabilities, amplifying the impact of successful attacks across multiple devices.
8. ***Suspicious Employees.*** Insider threats pose a significant risk, as employees may intentionally or inadvertently compromise CPS devices, leading to potential security breaches.

Moreover, vulnerabilities within healthcare CPS systems can manifest in both cyber and physical domains, amplifying the overall threat landscape. Cyber vulnerabilities (Haque, 2014), including those stemming from open standard protocols, expose healthcare CPS systems to various security risks, such as buffer overflow vulnerabilities and malware attacks. Physical vulnerabilities, on the other hand, involve the physical exposure of CPS components, making them susceptible to tampering or sabotage.

Addressing these vulnerabilities requires a comprehensive approach encompassing detection, prevention, and mitigation strategies tailored to the unique challenges of healthcare CPS systems. By identifying and addressing vulnerabilities proactively, healthcare organizations can bolster the security posture of CPS environments and safeguard sensitive patient data and critical healthcare infrastructure.

## Potential Solutions for Cybersecurity Challenges

Addressing cybersecurity challenges in healthcare CPS requires the implementation of robust solutions to mitigate vulnerabilities and safeguard patient data. Several potential solutions can be explored to enhance the security posture of healthcare CPS systems:

1. **Edge Computing**: Implementing edge computing solutions can help address poor connectivity issues in healthcare CPS. By processing data locally at the edge of the network, closer to where it is generated, healthcare organizations can reduce reliance on continuous network connectivity. Edge computing allows for real-time data analysis and decision-making, minimizing the impact of connectivity disruptions on healthcare services.
2. **Redundant Network Infrastructures**: Building redundant network infrastructures can enhance reliability and resilience in healthcare CPS. By deploying backup communication channels and redundant data paths, healthcare organizations can mitigate the effects of network failures or disruptions. Redundant infrastructures ensure that critical healthcare data can still be transmitted and accessed even in the event of connectivity issues, thereby maintaining continuity of care.
3. **Advanced Encryption Techniques**: Deploying advanced encryption methods such as end-to-end encryption and attribute-based encryption can ensure the confidentiality and integrity of sensitive patient data transmitted across healthcare CPS networks. Encryption mechanisms should be applied at both the user level and network level to prevent unauthorized access and data breaches.
4. **Standardized Protocols and Interoperability Frameworks**: Developing and adhering to standardized protocols and interoperability frameworks can promote cross-platform compatibility in healthcare CPS. By adopting common communication standards and interoperability protocols,

such as HL7 FHIR (Fast Healthcare Interoperability Resources), healthcare devices and systems from different vendors can seamlessly exchange data and collaborate effectively. Standardization facilitates integration and interoperability, ensuring that diverse components of the healthcare CPS ecosystem can work together harmoniously.

5. **Unified Data Exchange Platforms**: Implementing unified data exchange platforms can streamline communication and integration efforts in healthcare CPS. These platforms act as centralized hubs for data exchange, translation, and transformation, allowing disparate systems to communicate and share information seamlessly. Unified data exchange platforms facilitate interoperability by providing a common interface for data exchange, simplifying integration efforts and reducing compatibility issues. By centralizing data exchange processes, healthcare organizations can overcome interoperability challenges and achieve seamless cross-platform compatibility in CPS environments.
6. **Multi-Factor Authentication (MFA):** Implementing MFA protocols can enhance access control mechanisms within healthcare CPS systems, requiring users to authenticate their identity using multiple factors such as passwords, biometrics, and security tokens. This approach strengthens authentication processes and reduces the risk of unauthorized access to patient data and critical system resources.
7. **Intrusion Detection and Prevention Systems (IDPS)**: Deploying IDPS solutions enables real-time monitoring and detection of suspicious activities or potential security breaches within healthcare CPS networks. IDPS systems can automatically respond to security incidents by blocking malicious traffic, isolating compromised devices, and alerting security personnel to take appropriate action.
8. **Secure Software Development Practices**: Adopting secure coding practices and conducting regular security assessments during the software development lifecycle can mitigate the risk of vulnerabilities in healthcare CPS applications. Developers should adhere to industry best practices and guidelines to minimize coding errors and prevent common security flaws that could be exploited by attackers.
9. **Network Segmentation and Access Controls**: Implementing network segmentation strategies and enforcing access controls based on the principle of least privilege can limit the exposure of critical healthcare CPS components to potential threats. By partitioning networks into separate segments and restricting access to authorized users and devices, organizations can prevent lateral movement of attackers and contain security incidents effectively.
10. **Continuous Monitoring and Incident Response**: Establishing comprehensive monitoring capabilities and incident response procedures enables healthcare organizations to detect security incidents promptly and mitigate their impact. Continuous monitoring of network traffic, system logs, and user activities facilitates early detection of anomalies and suspicious behavior, allowing security teams to respond swiftly and effectively to mitigate potential threats.
11. **Security Awareness Training**: Providing regular security awareness training to healthcare staff and employees can raise awareness about common cybersecurity threats and best practices for protecting sensitive patient data. Educating users about the importance of strong passwords, phishing awareness, and data protection protocols can empower them to contribute to the overall security posture of healthcare CPS environments.

By implementing these potential solutions, healthcare organizations can strengthen the cybersecurity resilience of CPS systems, mitigate vulnerabilities, and safeguard patient privacy and confidentiality effectively. It is essential to adopt a proactive approach to cybersecurity and continuously evaluate and update security measures to address evolving threats and challenges in the healthcare sector.

## CASE STUDIES AND EXAMPLES

In this section, an exploration is undertaken into real-world case studies and practical examples that elucidate the transformative potential of Cyber-Physical Systems (CPS) within the healthcare domain. From managing chronic diseases to facilitating surgical procedures and enabling telemedicine, these intelligent systems offer a wide array of benefits. Through meticulous analyses of the presented case studies and exemplifications, the tangible benefits stemming from the integration of CPS are elucidated, accentuating their favorable outcomes for both patients and healthcare providers alike.

Table I provides a comprehensive summary of various CPS architectures applied in healthcare applications. Each application is associated with a specific model, tool, validation method, and contribution. These case studies and examples not only demonstrate the versatility of CPS applications in healthcare but also emphasize their practical contributions, ranging from personalized healthcare insights and improved diagnostic accuracy to enhanced patient monitoring and overall healthcare infrastructure efficiency.

1. **Remote Elderly Monitoring System (REMS):** The REMS system is designed for monitoring the health of elderly individuals in their homes (Merlo, 2019). REMS falls under the umbrella of cyber-physical systems (CPS), integrating physical devices like medical sensors with the digital realm of data collection, transmission, and analysis. The study emphasizes the critical role of human participation in the design of such systems. Both the elderly users and their caregivers are directly impacted by REMS's functionality and design. For elderly users, accurate monitoring and diagnosis through REMS tools and devices can significantly improve health outcomes. Similarly, healthcare providers rely on REMS to access real-time health data and communicate with patients remotely, potentially reducing unnecessary hospital visits and improving the allocation of healthcare resources (Fedak, 2015). Therefore, flawless design and implementation of REMS are crucial for both parties.
2. **Big-ECG**: The Big-ECG system is proposed as a cyber-physical system (CPS) for monitoring cardiovascular activity in stroke patients during their daily lives. By continuously monitoring ECG signals, Big ECG can potentially identify early signs of stroke, enabling timely intervention and potentially improving patient outcomes. This data that is collected is transmitted securely to a cloud-based platform. The platform utilizes advanced analytics to process and analyze the ECG data in real-time or near-real-time. In critical situations, Big-ECG can generate alerts for emergency services, allowing healthcare providers to prioritize resources and respond effectively. This case study highlights the potential of CPS in healthcare, particularly for chronic disease management and remote patient monitoring. Unlike traditional, time-consuming ECG setups, Big-ECG's simplicity and real-time monitoring capabilities empower faster diagnosis and intervention, particularly crucial for stroke patients where time is of the essence.

continued on following page

*Table 1. Continued*

*Table 1. Summary of healthcare CPS architectures*

| Application | Model | Tool | Validation | Contribution |
|---|---|---|---|---|
| **Patient Monitoring (Richard, 2022)** | Machine Learning (ML) | Real-time patient data | Experiments and clinical trials | Improved patient monitoring and early detection. |
| **Medication Adherence (Devliyal, 2022)** | Internet of Things (IoT) | Sensor-based tracking | User feedback and effectiveness analysis | Enhanced medication adherence monitoring. |
| **Health Prediction (Richard, 2022)** | Deep Learning | Electronic Health Records (EHR) | Historical patient data and analytics | Predictive insights for personalized healthcare. |
| **Telemedicine Framework (Sánchez, 2022)** | Cloud Computing | Telemedicine platform | User satisfaction surveys and outcomes | Improved remote healthcare accessibility. |
| **Chronic Disease Management (Devliyal, 2022)** | Mobile Health (mHealth) | Wearable devices | Long-term patient engagement and monitoring | Better management of chronic diseases. |
| **Clinical Decision Support (Miah, 2022)** | Artificial Intelligence (AI) | Diagnostic decision support system | Clinical case studies and expert opinions | Enhanced diagnostic accuracy and decision support. |
| **Smart Hospital Infrastructure (Cao, 2021)** | Internet of Things (IoT) | Hospital-wide connectivity | Efficiency improvements and enhancements | Enhanced hospital operations and patient care. |

3. **Smart Medication Management Systems for Improved Adherence**: Non-adherence to medication regimens is a significant global problem, often leading to negative health outcomes and increased healthcare costs. This issue can be unintentional, particularly for individuals with busy schedules, cognitive decline, or memory lapses. Cyber-physical systems (CPS) offer innovative solutions to address medication adherence challenges. Improved medication adherence through CPS can potentially reduce hospital readmission rates, optimize resource allocation for healthcare providers, and lead to cost savings. Real-world examples of these solutions include:
   a. **Smart pillboxes**: These devices dispense medication at pre-programmed times, often accompanied by audible or visual alerts to remind users. Some even connect to a smartphone app, allowing caregivers or healthcare providers to monitor adherence remotely.
   b. **Medication adherence apps**: These apps provide a variety of functionalities, including medication reminders, dosage tracking, refill alerts, and even medication interaction checks.
4. **Medical Cyber-Physical Systems (MCPS):** The MCPS are revolutionizing healthcare delivery by seamlessly integrating physical devices with the digital world of data collection, analysis, and intervention. This case study explores how MCPS are enhancing both efficiency and accessibility across various healthcare settings. MCPS enables real-time monitoring of vital signs and automates data collection and analysis, freeing up healthcare professionals' time for Providing specialized care. Examples of MCPS Applications:
   a. **Pandemic response**: Robots and CPS assisted healthcare professionals in monitoring patients remotely during the COVID-19 pandemic, ensuring safety and reducing workload. (Kaiser, 2021)
   b. **High-risk pregnancies**: Sensors placed on pregnant women transmit data for remote monitoring, allowing for timely intervention if needed. (Wrobel, 2015)
   c. **Rehabilitation**: Robotic systems and MCPS aid in post-surgical rehabilitation, improving mobility and recovery.

   d. **Chronic disease management**: MCPS enables continuous monitoring of chronic conditions like COPD, allowing for early detection of exacerbations and improved disease management.
5. **Smart Operating Rooms:** Traditional operating rooms, heavily reliant on manual equipment and paper-based documentation, face limitations in efficiency, error potential, and collaboration. This case study explores how Smart Operating Rooms (SORs), integrated with Cyber-Physical Systems (CPS) technologies, are transforming the surgical landscape. SORs leverage a unique combination of technologies:
   a. **Surgical robots**: These robotic arms provide surgeons with enhanced precision and control, particularly during intricate procedures.
   b. **Interconnected devices**: Surgical instruments and equipment seamlessly share data with the central system, enabling real-time monitoring and analysis.
   c. **Augmented reality (AR) displays**: Surgeons can visualize and overlay critical information (e.g., patient anatomy, vital signs) directly onto their field of view, fostering informed decision-making.

These minimize human error and ensure accurate information access. This translates to safer procedures for patients, minimizing the risk of complications associated with manual processes.

Furthermore, SORs foster enhanced communication and collaboration among surgeons, nurses, and other surgical team members. By enhancing efficiency, reducing errors, and fostering collaboration, SORs pave the way for a future of surgery marked by greater precision, improved patient outcomes, and a streamlined and efficient surgical workflow.

## FUTURE DIRECTIONS AND EMERGING TRENDS

Looking ahead to the future of Cyber-Physical Systems (CPS) in healthcare, one must confront challenges such as the limitation posed by poor connectivity for IoT sensors and the demand for cross-platform compatibility. These connectivity issues introduce hurdles in achieving seamless monitoring and data supply through IoT sensors within healthcare systems. Additionally, a critical consideration is imperative for CPS-based IoT devices to strike an intricate balance between hardware and software functions, ensuring not only current compatibility but also adaptability to evolving technologies for sustained optimal performance. Another pivotal aspect is the expanding attack surface for malicious actors, a consequence of the widespread integration of smart devices through IoT. This underscores the importance of fostering heightened awareness among users regarding the security of their interconnected smart devices within the healthcare domain.

To tackle these challenges, ongoing research and development efforts are required in areas such as:

1. Developing low-power and reliable communication protocols suitable for remote healthcare settings.
2. Standardizing data formats and protocols to ensure seamless interoperability between different CPS components.
3. Implementing robust cybersecurity measures like encryption, secure authentication, and regular system updates.
4. Raising user awareness about cybersecurity practices and the importance of protecting personal health information.

By actively addressing these challenges and continuously improving CPS technologies, individuals can ensure the secure, efficient, and reliable integration of CPS across various aspects of healthcare, ultimately leading to improved patient care and a transformed healthcare landscape. Future endeavors in this field will focus on thoroughly exploring vulnerabilities and security issues within CPS and IoT-based systems, aiming to fortify the healthcare landscape against potential threats and challenges.

Transitioning to the pharmaceutical industry within the broader context of CPS in healthcare, this section briefly delves into this under-explored area within the wider discussion of the future scope of CPS in healthcare (Devliyal, 2022). The pharmaceutical industry presents unique challenges and opportunities for CPS integration, focusing on supporting processes and infrastructure rather than direct patient interaction.

Several potential applications for CPS in pharmaceuticals include Drug Supply Chain Management, where integrating CPS with blockchain technology can ensure transparency and security throughout the drug supply chain, combating counterfeiting and ensuring the integrity of medications. In Clinical Trial Data Management, CPS can facilitate real-time data collection, analysis, and monitoring during clinical trials, potentially leading to faster drug development and improved trial efficiency. Additionally, Personalized Drug Delivery Systems, enabled by CPS, can deliver medications with precise dosage and timing, potentially improving medication adherence and treatment effectiveness (Chinonyerem, 2022). While these examples provide a glimpse, further exploration is needed to develop tailored CPS solutions that address the specific needs and challenges of the pharmaceutical industry. By leveraging the combined powers of CPS, AI, and other emerging technologies, there is potential to revolutionize drug development, supply chain management, and personalized medicine within the pharmaceutical landscape.

## CONCLUSION

In conclusion, this chapter extensively explores the integration of Cyber-Physical Systems (CPS) into healthcare, offering insights into its transformative potential, architectural considerations, cybersecurity challenges, and future trajectories. The amalgamation of electronic health records, biomedical databases, and public health initiatives, coupled with the advent of CPS, has significantly revolutionized the accessibility and management of healthcare data. Progress in wireless sensor networks, medical sensors, and cloud computing has further enhanced the capabilities of CPS in healthcare, providing innovative solutions to address issues related to data security, management complexities, and constraints in computing resources.

The benefits of integrated CPS in healthcare, leveraging compatibility with cloud computing and wireless sensor networks, ensuring assurance, enhancing system functionality through sensor-cyber synergy, adaptable scalability, and dynamic changes in existing CPS policies, underscore its potential to redefine healthcare systems. The chapter explores diverse applications of CPS in healthcare, including monitoring and treatment enhancement, assisted living, acute care settings, and telehealth care, showcasing its substantial impact on patient care and management.

The chapter delves into crucial aspects of cybersecurity considerations within healthcare CPS, emphasizing the imperative for robust measures to protect patient data and uphold system integrity. The exploration of legal and ethical dimensions surrounding patient data protection, coupled with insights into security measures and vulnerabilities within healthcare CPS, highlights the intricate landscape of ensuring the confidentiality, integrity, and availability of data.

In summary, this chapter serves as an invaluable resource for comprehending the profound impact of CPS on healthcare, spanning technological foundations to real-world applications. It tackles challenges, proposes solutions, and outlines future directions, contributing to the ongoing evolution of healthcare delivery through the integration of Cyber-Physical Systems.

## REFERENCES

Bujnowska-Fedak, M., & Grata-Borkowska, U. (2015). Use of telemedicine-based care for the aging and elderly promises and pitfalls. *Smart Homecare Technology and Telehealth*, 91. 10.2147/SHTT.S59498

Cao, K., Hu, S., Shi, Y., Colombo, A. W., Karnouskos, S., & Li, X. (2021). A Survey on Edge and Edge-Cloud Computing Assisted Cyber-Physical Systems. *IEEE Transactions on Industrial Informatics*, 17(11), 7806–7819. 10.1109/TII.2021.3073066

Devliyal, S., Sharma, S., & Goyal, H. R. (2022). Cyber Physical System Architectures for Pharmaceutical Care Services: Challenges and Future Trends. *2022 IEEE International Conference on Current Development in Engineering and Technology (CCET.* (pp. 1-6). IEEE. 10.1109/CCET56606.2022.10080198

Haque, S., Aziz, S., & Rahman, M. (2014). Review of Cyber-Physical System in Healthcare. *International Journal of Distributed Sensor Networks*, 20.

Iheanacho, C. O., Adeyeri, O., & Eze, U. I. H. (2022). Evolving role of pharmacy technicians in pharmaceutical care services: Involvement in counselling and medication reviews. *Exploratory Research in Clinical and Social Pharmacy*, 5, 100113. 10.1016/j.rcsop.2022.10011335478530

José, M. G. S., Jörgensen, N., Törngren, M., Inam, R., Berezovskyi, A., Feng, L., Fersman, E., Ramli, M. R., & Tan, K. (2022). Edge Computing for Cyber-physical Systems: A Systematic Mapping Study Emphasizing Trustworthiness. *ACM Trans. Cyber-Phys. Syst.* ACM.

Kaiser, M. S., Al Mamun, S., Mahmud, M., & Tania, M. H. (2021). *Healthcare robots to combat COVID-19. COVID-19: Prediction.* Decision-Making, and Its Impacts.

Merlo, C., Abi Akle, A., Llaria, A., Terrasson, G., Villeneuve, E., & Pilnière, V. (2019). Proposal of a user-centred approach for CPS design: Pillbox case study. *IFAC-PapersOnLine*, 51(34), 196–201. 10.1016/j.ifacol.2019.01.065

Miah, M. S. U., Sarwar, T. B., Islam, S. S., Haque, M. S., Masuduzzaman, M., & Bhowmik, A. (2022). An adaptive Medical Cyber-Physical System for post diagnosis patient care using cloud computing and machine learning approach. *2022 3rd International Conference for Emerging Technology (INCET).* (pp. 1-6). IEEE.

Morolong, Mamoqenelo & Gamundani, Attlee & Bhunu Shava, Fungai. (2023). *Cloud computing security in health cyber physical systems.* 1553-1568.

Richard, R. M., & Taylar, J. V. (2022) Cyber-Physical System Framework for Cerebrovascular Accidents using Machine Learning Algorithm. *2022 International Conference on ICT for Smart Society (ICISS).* IEEE. 10.1109/ICISS55894.2022.9915228

Sörös, P., & Hachinski, V. (2012). Cardiovascular and neurological causes of sudden death after ischaemic stroke. *Lancet Neurology*, 11(2), 179–188. 10.1016/S1474-4422(11)70291-522265213

Wrobel, J., Jezewski, J., Horoba, K., Pawlak, A., Czabanski, R., Jezewski, M., & Porwik, P. (2015). Medical cyber-physical system for home telecare of high-risk pregnancy: Design challenges and requirements. *Journal of Medical Imaging and Health Informatics*, 5(6), 1295–1301. 10.1166/jmihi.2015.1532

Zhang, Y., Qiu, M., Tsai, C.-W., Hassan, M., & Alamri, A. (2015). Health-CPS: Healthcare Cyber-Physical System Assisted by Cloud and Big Data. *IEEE Systems Journal*, 11, 1–8.

# Chapter 18
# Urban Oasis:
## Harnessing IoT for Green Healthcare in Smart City Landscape

**Jaspreet Kaur**
http://orcid.org/0000-0002-3587-6841
*Chandigarh University, India*

## ABSTRACT

*Healthcare systems are undergoing a change owing to the internet of things (IoT) and smart cities, which are providing ground-breaking solutions for sustainability, efficiency, and better patient care. The importance of IoT-enhanced smart cities in revolutionizing healthcare is examined in this chapter, along with its importance in addressing the rising concern for sustainability in healthcare operations. It explores how the internet of things and smart cities work together to maximize resource use, encourage ecologically friendly behaviour, and improve patient well-being.*

## INTRODUCTION

In the context of healthcare, the idea of the Internet of Things (Io T) and smart cities represents a potentially game-changing strategy for enhancing the quality of care provided to patients, the outcomes of treatment, and the overall effectiveness of healthcare systems. The Internet of Things (Io T) refers to a network comprised of interconnected physical gadgets, automobiles, buildings, and various other objects (Roy, 2024). Each of these entities is equipped with a multitude of sensors, software, and several other technologies that enable them to gather and disseminate data through the internet. Portable fitness trackers, sensors for medicine, smart medical devices, and hospital equipment such as infusion pumps and monitors for patients exemplify the range of items encompassed under the classification of Internet of Things (Io T) gadgets. These gadgets gather data in real-time and transmit it to healthcare professionals or centralized systems. This makes it possible to do remote monitoring, as well as timely interventions and decision-making that is driven by data (Aminizadeh et al., 2023; Kumari et al., 2024; Rejeb, 2023).

DOI: 10.4018/979-8-3693-2901-6.ch018

*Figure 1. Visual representation of the proposed system of the study*

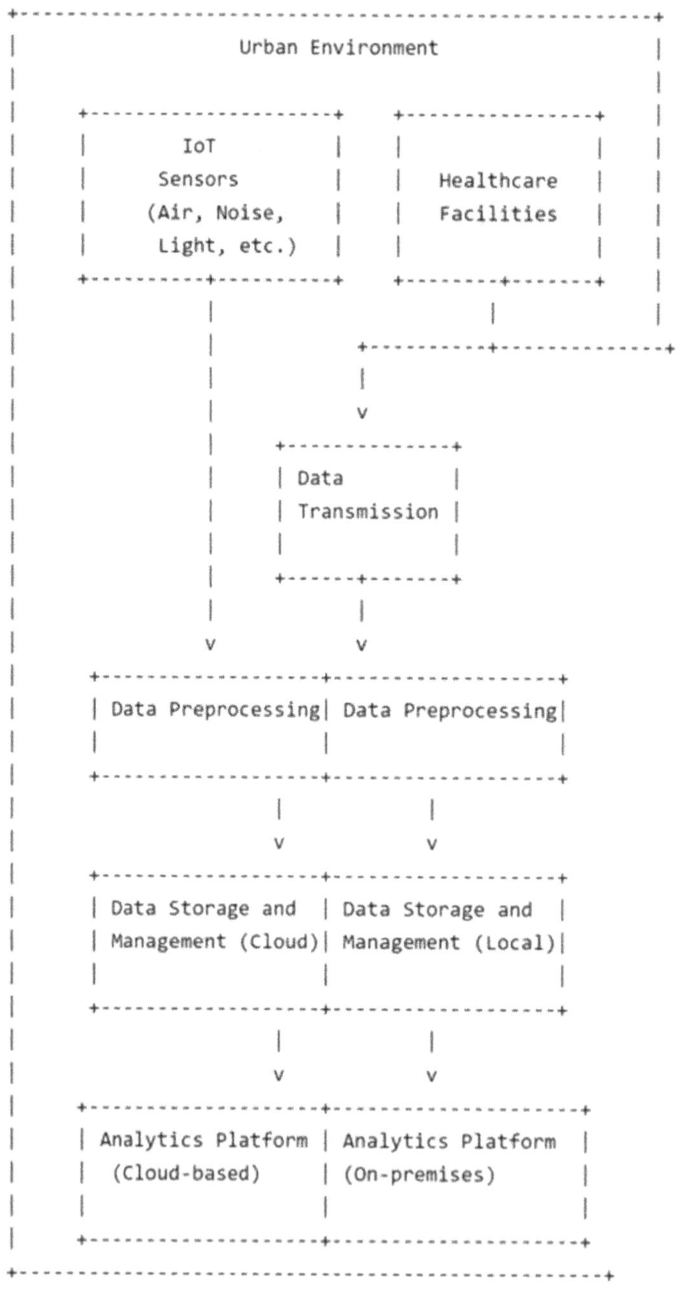


*Source: Kaur (2024)*

*Figure 2. Merits and demerits of the proposed system*

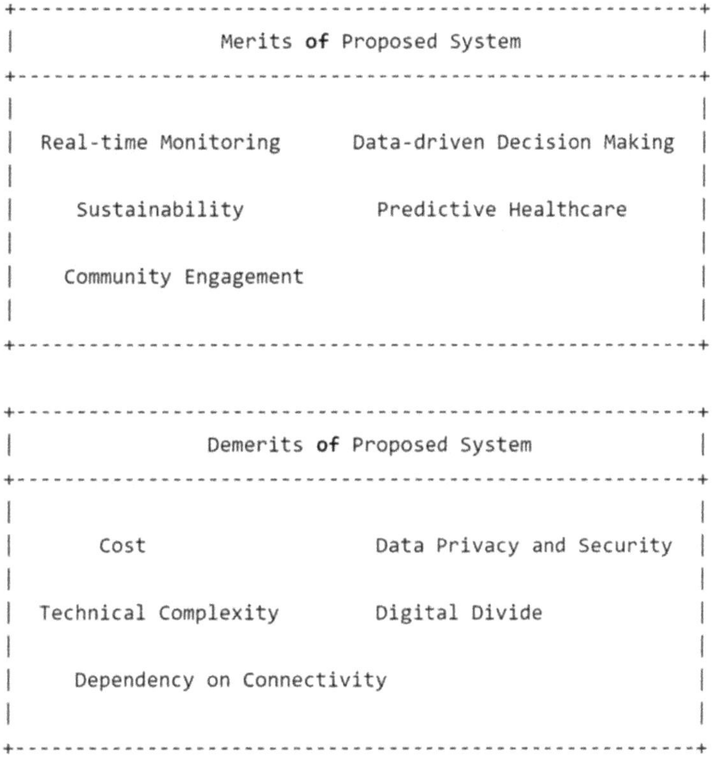

Merits of Proposed System
Real-time Monitoring
Data-driven Decision Making
Sustainability
Predictive Healthcare
Community Engagement
Demerits of Proposed System
Cost
Data Privacy and Security
Technical Complexity
Digital Divide
Dependency on Connectivity


*Source: Kaur (2024)*

## Smart Cities

A “smart city” is an urban area that makes use of data-driven solutions and digital technologies in order to improve performance and well-being while simultaneously lowering costs and the number of resources used. When it comes to the provision of medical care, a “smart city” incorporates a number of different components in order to produce an approach that is more comprehensive (Lai et al.,2023):

- ¬Infrastructure: Smart cities have developed infrastructure, which includes networked transportation, utilities, and buildings, which contribute to healthcare systems that are more effective and sustainable.
- ¬Integration of Data: Integrating and analyzing data coming from a variety of sources, such as Internet of Things devices, in order to generate insights that may be used for planning and decision-making in the healthcare industry. It is common practice for smart cities to place a strong emphasis on sustainability, with the ultimate goal of lowering their impact on the surrounding environment.This approach is consistent with the notion of “green healthcare” (Pandya et al., 2023; Kaur,2024).

- Accessibility: The goal of these cities is to provide their entire resident populations with fair and equal access to medical treatment by using forward-thinking transit and telemedicine options. Utilizing connected devices, data analytic, and urban planning to produce healthcare systems that are more effective, sustainable, and centred on patients is what is meant by the convergence of the Internet of Things and smart cities in the field of medicine.
- Patients gain from receiving care that is more individualized, while medical professionals are able to deliver services that are more productive and economical. In addition, these technologies help to lessen the impact that healthcare activities have on the surrounding environment, which is in line with the increasing emphasis placed on sustainability on a worldwide scale (Ullah and Fadi, 2023).
- The Internet of Things (Io T) and the principles of smart cities represent a viable pathway in the healthcare industry for addressing the current difficulties in healthcare and improving the overall quality of healthcare services (Bhat et al.,2023; Parker, 2023; Chevance, 2023). Given these concerns, there is a growing movement towards adopting more sustainable and environmentally conscious practice within the healthcare sector. The implementation of several strategies is necessary in this context. Figure 3 shows that green healthcare practices in hospitals and other healthcare facilities are increasingly implementing procedures that lessen their negative effects on the surrounding environment.

*Figure 3. Greener methods used by hospitals and other healthcare facilities to reduce their environmental impact*

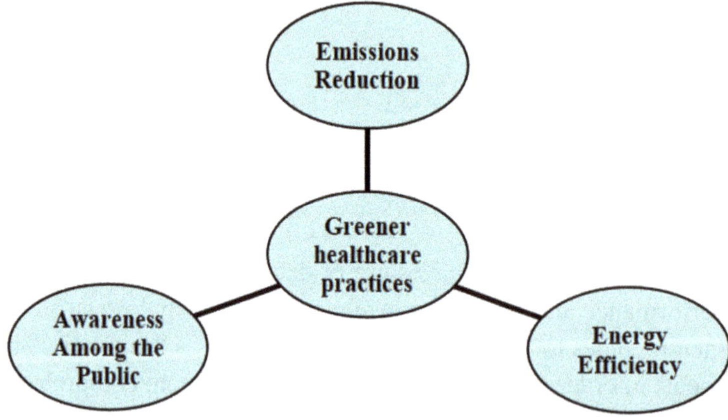


*Source: Kaur (2024)*

## Current Status of Healthcare System and Modern Cities

The healthcare system and modern cities worldwide have undergone substantial alterations and encountered significant obstacles. Although technology and medicine have made significant progress in enhancing healthcare, inequities in access, financial challenges, and urbanisation patterns still significantly influence the healthcare system and urban living.

An outstanding advancement in healthcare systems worldwide is the rapid implementation of digital health technologies. Telemedicine, such as remote medical consultations and monitoring, has been widely embraced, especially during the COVID-19 pandemic. The adoption of telehealth has not only boosted accessibility to healthcare, particularly in rural or underserved regions, but it has also improved efficiency by decreasing waiting periods and boosting patient convenience. Moreover, wearable technologies and health-tracking applications have enabled individuals to assume a more proactive stance in maintaining their health, promoting preventive treatment and early intervention.

Furthermore, artificial intelligence (AI) and machine learning algorithms are progressively being employed in the healthcare industry to perform many activities, including diagnosis and treatment planning. These technologies possess the capacity to enhance precision, velocity, and individualised treatment provision, ultimately resulting in superior patient results. AI-powered diagnostic technologies have the ability to analyse medical imaging or genetic data with a higher degree of accuracy and reliability than humans, thereby assisting physicians in making better-informed judgements.

Nevertheless, notwithstanding these progressions, healthcare systems in numerous nations persistently encounter substantial obstacles. An urgent matter is the inequitable allocation of resources and limited availability of healthcare, both domestically and internationally. Healthcare access disparities persist due to factors such as income, geography, race, and ethnicity, which worsen health inequities and increase the gap between privileged and marginalized populations. To address these discrepancies, it is necessary to not only enhance infrastructure and healthcare delivery systems with the assistance of advanced technologies like Io T and, also to address broader social determinants of health, such as poverty, education, and housing.

## IO T in Healthcare

The concept of "Internet of Things" (Io T) pertains to a system of interconnected physical devices, objects, and sensors that are equipped with technological capabilities to collect and communicate data through the internet. These devices encompass a wide range of products, including cellphones and refrigerators. These devices have the capability to autonomously communicate information and engage in interactions with one other, as well as with other systems and humans, without requiring direct human intervention. The Internet of Things (Io T) encompasses a diverse array of applications that, when implemented within the healthcare domain, have the potential to enhance patient care, optimize operational processes, and augment overall system efficacy. Figure 4 shows some important applications of Io T in the healthcare industry:

*Figure 4. Key healthcare IoT applications*

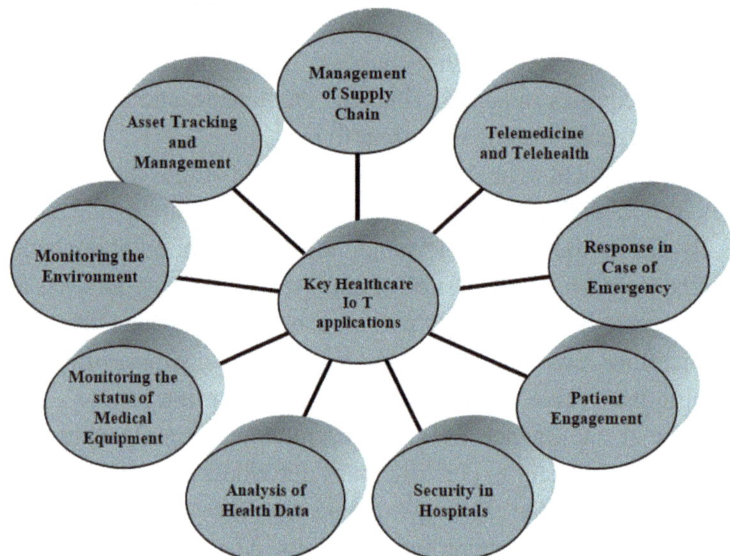


*Source: Kaur (2024)*

Io T-enabled gadgets, such as wearable fitness trackers, blood pressure monitors, and glucose meters, are able to continuously gather patient data and transfer it to healthcare providers. This type of monitoring is referred to as remote patient monitoring. This makes it possible to monitor a patient's health in real time, which assists in the treatment of chronic disorders and the diagnosis of potential health problems at an earlier stage. Patients may find it easier to keep track of their medication schedules with the assistance of smart medical devices such as inhalers, medication dispensers, and pill bottles equipped with internet of things capabilities. They also have the ability to deliver notifications and reminders to patients and healthcare providers in the event that dosages are forgotten (Kamruzzaman et al., 2022).

Telemedicine and Telehealth: The Internet of Things enables high-quality video conferencing and distant consultations, both of which are necessary for telemedicine. It also makes it easier to transmit medical data, such as X-rays, MRI pictures, and patient records, which can be used for diagnosing and treating patients remotely.

Asset Tracking and Management: Hospitals use the internet of things to track the whereabouts of medical equipment and assets. This helps to ensure that the assets are available when needed while also cutting down on the amount of time spent looking for important instruments (Singh,2022).

Monitoring the Environment: Internet of Things devices can monitor environmental variables at healthcare facilities, including temperature, humidity, and air quality, among other things. This contributes to the patient's comfort and safety, and it is of utmost importance in high-stakes environments such as operating rooms and laboratories.

Management of Supply Chain: The Internet of Things has the potential to enhance the tracking of medications, medical supplies, and other commodities that are part of the supply chain for healthcare. This not only prevents waste, but also guarantees that essential supplies are never out of stock (Morello,2022).
Monitoring the status of Medical Equipment: Internet of Things devices can be used to monitor the status of medical equipment, which enables predictive maintenance. This helps to prevent the failure of equipment and guarantees that vital gear is always operating. Io T sensors and wearable devices can detect falls in elderly or fragile patients and provide notifications to carers or emergency services. This can improve the quality of care provided to these patients.
Patient Engagement: The Internet of Things enables healthcare practitioners to engage patients through mobile apps, reminders, and feedback systems, so assisting patients in managing their own health and adhering to treatment programs.
Security in Hospitals: The Internet of Things has the potential to improve hospital security systems, such as those used for access control, monitoring, and the tracking of workers and patients (Bahalul et al., 2022).
Analysis of Health Data: The information gathered by Internet of Things devices can be analyzed in order to spot patterns, improve treatment strategies, and make the delivery of healthcare services more individualized and cost-effective.
Response in Case of Emergency: The Internet of Things can be utilized to discover people who require immediate medical attention and to rapidly deploy emergency services.

In nutshell, the Internet of Things has the potential to completely transform healthcare by delivering data in real time, enhancing the outcomes for patients, and enhancing the effectiveness of the healthcare system as a whole. However, this does bring up concerns around data security and privacy as well as sustainability which are issues that need to be properly addressed in the use of Io T in healthcare settings (Morello,2022).

## GROWING CONCERN FOR SUSTAINABILITY AND THE IMPACT ON THE ENVIRONMENT IN THE CONTEXT OF HEALTHCARE SYSTEMS

A recognition of the huge ecological footprint and resource consumption connected with the healthcare sector is driving the growing concern for sustainability and environmental effect in healthcare systems. This understanding is being pushed by a growing awareness of the importance of sustainability in healthcare systems. This worry is caused by a number of important variables, including the following:

The provision of healthcare requires a significant investment of time, money, and other resources. Operating a healthcare facility such as a hospital, clinic, or other similar establishment consumes a significant quantity of energy, water, and raw materials. This consumption of resources contributes to an increase in the emissions of greenhouse gases, the utilization of water, and the development of garbage (Longo et al., 2023).

- ✓ Generation of Waste: Healthcare institutions are responsible for the generation of a significant volume of waste, which may include potentially harmful medical waste as well as materials that are not recyclable. The improper disposal of medical waste can have adverse effects on the surrounding environment in addition to posing concerns to human health.

- ✓ Consumption of Energy: Hospitals are among the buildings that use the most energy due to the fact that they are open twenty-four hours a day, seven days a week and have extensive lighting in addition to energy-intensive medical equipment. It is essential to lessen our impact on the environment by lowering our overall energy usage and making the switch to more sustainable energy sources (Briggs et al., 2023).
- ✓ Chemical pollution can arise from the utilization of diverse chemicals in the healthcare sector, including pharmaceuticals and disinfectants, if their management is inadequate. These chemical compounds have the potential to infiltrate aquatic systems, hence exerting detrimental effects on both ecosystems and human well-being.
- ✓ Transportation-related Emissions: The healthcare sector necessitates a substantial volume of transportation to facilitate the movement of patients, healthcare personnel, and medical resources. According to Longo et al. (2023), the emissions originating from motor vehicles and various modes of transportation exacerbate air pollution and contribute to increased carbon emissions.
- ✓ The Implications of Climate Change The healthcare sector is not immune to the consequences of climate change. The escalation in temperature, occurrence of severe weather events, and proliferation of diseases can impose significant strain on healthcare systems and the accompanying resources at their disposal.nThe impact of environmental factors, such as air pollution and climate change, on patient health has been observed to worsen pre-existing health concerns, hence leading to a heightened need for healthcare services (Briggs et al., 2023). In light of these issues, there is an increasing push towards greener and more environmentally responsible practices in the medical industry. This requires a variety of different strategies:
- ✓ Green Healthcare Practice Hospitals and other healthcare facilities are increasingly implementing procedures that lessen their negative effects on the surrounding environment. The use of ecologically friendly materials, trash reduction and recycling program, and energy-efficient building designs are a few examples of these initiatives. Increasingly, healthcare systems are taking into consideration the environmental and social impact of the products they buy through a practice known as sustainable procurement. This involves the procurement of environmentally friendly medical supplies, medications, and equipment (Hunter and Rafael, 2023).

## SMART CITIES AND THE FUNCTION THAT THEY PLAY IN THE PLANNING OF MODERN CITIES

Smart cities are urban regions that make use of digital technology, data, and innovation in order to improve the citizens' quality of life, as well as the efficiency and sustainability of the city's operations. They are examples of a contemporary method of urban design that places an emphasis on integrating different types of systems, services, and infrastructure in order to produce cities that are more responsive and adaptable. The idea of "smart cities" is extremely important to the practice of modern urban planning in a number of different ways (Abubakar et al., 2023).

- ✓ Efficiency and Resource use: The employment of technology in smart cities allows for more effective use of available resources. This includes the systems that control our access to electricity, water, and transportation. For example, smart networks manage the distribution of electricity more effectively, which results in less waste and lower overall energy expenditures. The use of water is monitored and controlled by intelligent water management systems in order to reduce water waste and provide a sustainable water supply.
- ✓ Enhancements to Transportation: One of the primaries focuses of contemporary urban planning is the development of transportation networks that are both more effective and more environmentally friendly. Intelligent transportation systems are incorporated into smart cities in order to alleviate traffic congestion, shorten the amount of time needed for commuting, and enhance public transit. As a consequence, there will be less pollution in the air and more mobility as a result.
- ✓ Enhancement of Public Services: Smart cities make use of data and digital platforms to improve public services such as trash management, emergency response, and public safety. While sensors and data analytic can help optimism garbage collection routes, real-time data can assist first res-ponders in acting more rapidly in the event of an emergency (Barykin, et al., 2023). Mobility in the City Smart cities encourage environmentally responsible methods of urban mobility by implementing initiatives such as electric vehicle charging facilities, bike-sharing program, and intelligent traffic management. Congestion, air pollution, and emissions of greenhouse gases are all reduced as a result of these initiatives.
- ✓ Life Expectancy: One of the primary objectives of smart cities is to bring about an all-around improvement in citizens' life expectancy. This can be accomplished through the provision of healthcare, educational, and cultural resources that are more easily accessible. The creation of public areas that are not only functional but also appealing, welcoming to pedestrians, and risk-free should be the primary goal of any city planner (Barykin, et al., 2023).
- ✓ Sustainability and the Environment: Smart city development is predicated on the adoption of environmentally responsible practices. These towns frequently place an emphasis on environmental sustainability, with the goal of cutting down on waste, energy usage, and carbon emissions. A green infrastructure, buildings that are efficient in their use of energy, and renewable energy sources are all necessary components. Decision-making that is informed by collected data Smart cities amass large volumes of data from a variety of sources. These statistics are utilized in the process of making informed decisions on the management of the city, public policy, and urban planning. It makes it possible to conduct predictive analytic s on topics such as the patterns of traffic, the use of energy, and public health.
- ✓ Inclusion of Digital Technology: Addressing the digital gap is an important part of modern urban planning, which also includes making sure that technology is available to all citizens. In an effort to promote social inclusion, the goals of smart cities include the provision of equal access to digital services and information (Badran, 2023).
- ✓ Economic Growth: Resulting From Attracting Businesses, Entrepreneurs, and Investments Smart city initiatives frequently result in economic growth. It is possible for the innovation and technology that are linked with smart cities to encourage economic growth and the creation of new jobs. In an era marked by an ever-increasing number of environmental issues, contemporary urban planning in smart cities contains measures designed to promote resilience. These cities are better prepared to deal with the effects of climate change and to respond to natural disasters (Kaur, 2024).

- ✓ Participation of the Public: Smart cities frequently include local residents in the process of decision-making. They employ technology to engage communities, gather input, and establish platforms for public participation in urban planning and government. They also use technology to gather feedback (Badran, 2023).

## POTENTIAL SYNERGY THAT COULD EXIST BETWEEN THE INTERNET OF THINGS AND THE INFRASTRUCTURE OF SMART CITIES IN THE CONTEXT OF THE HEALTHCARE INDUSTRY

The Internet of Things (Io T) and smart city infrastructure might have a powerful synergistic effect in the healthcare industry, which holds great promise and has the ability to completely transform the way that healthcare is delivered. This synergy has the potential to lead to healthcare systems that are more effective, responsive, and sustainable. Within the realm of healthcare, Io T and smart city infrastructure can work together in a number of important ways, including the following (Bouramdane et al.,2023).

1. Monitoring of Patients Via Remote Connection: Wearable health trackers and medical sensors are two examples of Internet of Things (Io T) devices that are capable of continually monitoring a patient's vital signs, chronic ailments, and general health state. The infrastructure of smart cities, which often consists of high-speed internet access as well as data center, makes it possible for the transmission of patient data to healthcare professionals and medical facilities without any interruptions.
2. Analysis of Real-Time Healthcare Data: The healthcare data that is generated by Io T may be collected and analyze in real time, which can provide insights into public health trends as well as the health of individual patients. These patterns can be identified with the help of smart city data analytic technologies, which can then permit preventive actions to avoid epidemics or enhance patient outcomes (Bouramdane et al.,2023).
3. Services Relating to Telemedicine and Telehealth: Telemedicine is made possible by the infrastructure of smart cities, which provides dependable high-speed internet as well as secure communication networks. Io T devices make it possible to conduct remote consultations and monitoring, giving patients the ability to have access to medical services without leaving the convenience of their own homes.
4. Management of Healthcare Resources in an Efficient Manner: Integrating data collected from a variety of sources, such as Internet of Things devices, enables smart city infrastructure to assist in optimizing the distribution of healthcare resources. This is accomplished by locating parts of the city that have a greater need for such resources. This makes it possible to plan and allocate resources more effectively, which in turn cuts down on wait times and boosts the overall quality of healthcare services (Mishra,2023).
5. The Management of Emergencies and Natural Disasters: During times of emergency or natural disaster, sensors connected to the internet of things can detect and transmit data relating to ambient conditions, air quality, and patient demands. Infrastructure designed for smart cities can facilitate rapid emergency response by delivering data in real time to first res-ponders, healthcare professionals, and disaster management teams.
6. Reducing Our Impact On The Environment: It is possible for smart city programs that emphasize environmental responsibility to be applied to healthcare operations. In healthcare facilities, sensors connected to the internet of things can be used to monitor and control energy use, water usage, and

waste output. This lowers the overall impact that healthcare has on the environment and is consistent with the objective of developing greener healthcare systems(Mishra,2023).

7. Care Focused on the Patient: The Internet of Things and the infrastructure of smart cities work together to make it possible to provide individualist care that is focused on the patient. Patients have the ability to take an active role in the management of their own health thanks to the availability of their own health data, telehealth services, and real-time health information.
8. Privacy and protection of sensitive health information: The protection of residents' personal information and medical records should be given top priority in smart cities. It is essential to protect patient health information by listing robust authentication mechanisms, encrypted data networks, and secure data transmissions (Bouramdane et al.,2023).
9. Participation of Citizens: The engagement and participation of citizens in the governance of smart cities is frequently encouraged. This may involve patients providing input and participating in the decision-making process on their healthcare in the context of the healthcare system.
10. Research and Efforts Made in the Field of Public Health: The healthcare data created by the Internet of Things and gathered by smart cities can be extremely useful for medical research as well as for public health efforts. Researchers get access to data that has been anodized so they can examine trends and create new approaches to healthcare (Bouramdane et al.,2023).

## SUSTAINABLE HEALTHCARE

A method of providing medical care known as “green healthcare,” often referred to as “sustainable healthcare” or “eco-friendly healthcare,” is one that places an emphasis on diminishing the negative effects that medical facilities, practice, and procedures have on the surrounding environment. In addition to delivering high-quality medical care, its primary mission is to advance the cause of environmentally responsible practice. The idea of providing medical care in a sustainable manner is crucial for many compelling reasons, including the following (Vishwakarma et al.,2023).

Lessening of Our Footprint on the Environment: The provision of healthcare requires a substantial number of resources, which results in a sizeable impact on the environment. This includes the consumption of energy and water, as well as the generation of trash and emissions of greenhouse gases. The goal of environmentally friendly medical treatment is to reduce the severity of these effects (Vishwakarma et al.,2023).

The health and well-being of human beings: Healthcare practice that are more environmentally friendly help to create healthier conditions within hospitals and other medical institutions. It is possible for patients as well as healthcare staff to benefit from increased air quality, decreased exposure to potentially harmful materials, and environmentally sustainable building designs.

Cost Reductions in the Long Term: When it comes to healthcare, environmentally responsible practice almost always results in financial savings over time. For instance, energy-efficient buildings and equipment can help bring down the cost of utilities, and reducing waste can help bring down the cost of disposal.

Reputation and how the public perceives you: Patients and the general public are beginning to place a higher emphasis on environmentally friendly practice. Healthcare organization that employ green healthcare measures may profit from a positive public image and attract environmentally sensitive patients. Green healthcare initiatives include things like reducing hospital emissions and using alternative energy sources.

Requirements for Compliance with Regulatory Bodies and Accreditation: In the realm of healthcare, environmental sustainability is the subject of regulations in a number of countries and areas, as well as accreditation criteria. It is absolutely necessary to adhere to these requirements in order to be in conformity with the law and to be eligible for funding.

Actions to Reduce the Impacts of Climate Change: Through the reduction of its emissions of greenhouse gases, the healthcare industry can make a contribution to the fight against climate change. Healthcare practice that are sustainable are congruent with international initiatives to prevent climate change. The Following Are Important Components of Green Healthcare (Al et al., 2023).

Energy Efficiency: The use of energy-efficient lighting, heating, ventilation, and air conditioning (HVAC) equipment, as well as renewable energy sources like solar panels, can help healthcare facilities lower their overall energy usage (Nassereddine & Khang, 2024).

Reducing trash and Recycling: It is possible to greatly lessen the negative effects that healthcare activities have on the surrounding environment by reducing trash and putting into place efficient recycling program (Sakran et al., 2023).

Sustainable Procurement: One way to encourage sustainability is by selecting products that are both kind to the environment and socially responsible. Examples of such products include pharmaceuticals, medical equipment, and cleaning supplies.

Green building design: constructing medical facilities using eco-friendly materials and energy-efficient designs can help to reduce the amount of energy used as well as the impact on the environment (Al et al., 2023).

Transportation Options: That Are Better for the Environment Encouraging patients and staff to takpublic transportation, carpool, or drive electric vehicles is one way to lower the amount of carbon dioxide emissions caused by travel linked to medical care (Sakran et al., 2023).

Green Healthcare Culture is of the utmost importance to foster a culture of sustainability among healthcare personnel, engage them in activities that are kind to the environment, and educate them on how to practice environmentally responsible medicine. In conclusion, green healthcare is an essential idea for reducing the negative effects that healthcare operations have on the surrounding environment, enhancing the health and well-being of patients and healthcare professionals, and better aligning healthcare practices with global sustainability goals (Al et al., 2023).

## OBSTACLES POSED BY THE ENVIRONMENT IN TRADITIONAL HEALTHCARE SYSTEMS

The conventional medical care systems are confronted with a number of environmental concerns, each of which can have far-reaching effects not only on public health but also on the environment as depicted in figure 5 below:

*Figure 5. Basic overview of obstacles posed by the environment in traditional healthcare systems*

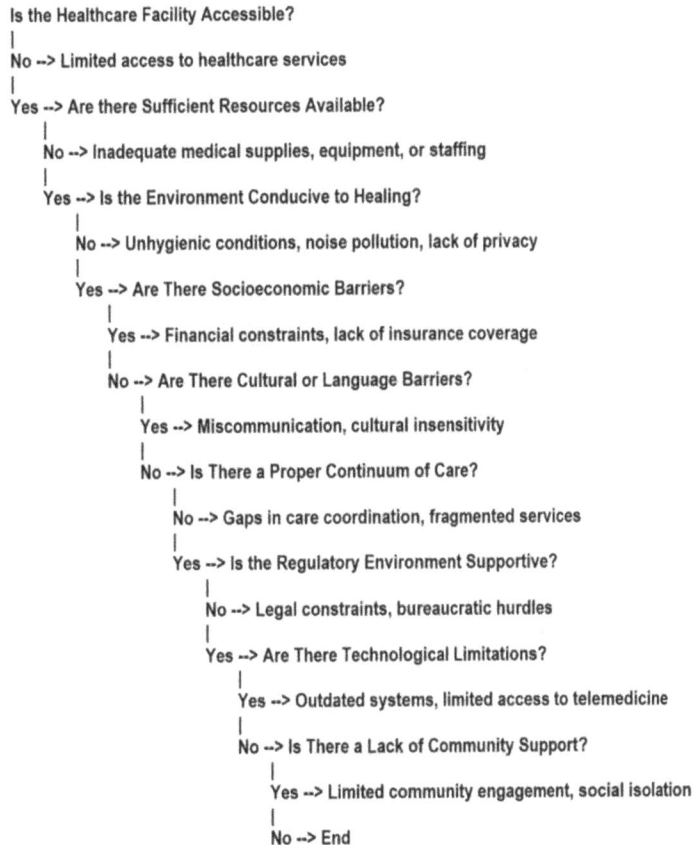

```
Is the Healthcare Facility Accessible?
|
No --> Limited access to healthcare services
|
Yes --> Are there Sufficient Resources Available?
    |
    No --> Inadequate medical supplies, equipment, or staffing
    |
    Yes --> Is the Environment Conducive to Healing?
        |
        No --> Unhygienic conditions, noise pollution, lack of privacy
        |
        Yes --> Are There Socioeconomic Barriers?
            |
            Yes --> Financial constraints, lack of insurance coverage
            |
            No --> Are There Cultural or Language Barriers?
                |
                Yes --> Miscommunication, cultural insensitivity
                |
                No --> Is There a Proper Continuum of Care?
                    |
                    No --> Gaps in care coordination, fragmented services
                    |
                    Yes --> Is the Regulatory Environment Supportive?
                        |
                        No --> Legal constraints, bureaucratic hurdles
                        |
                        Yes --> Are There Technological Limitations?
                            |
                            Yes --> Outdated systems, limited access to telemedicine
                            |
                            No --> Is There a Lack of Community Support?
                                |
                                Yes --> Limited community engagement, social isolation
                                |
                                No --> End
```

*Source: Kaur (2024)*

These issues are brought about as a result of the resource-intensive nature of healthcare operations, the disposal of medical waste, and the energy consumption that is linked with healthcare facilities. When it comes to structures, healthcare institutions, and hospitals in particular, are among the most energy-intensive. They are open twenty-four hours a day, seven days a week, and rely on large lighting, heating, ventilation, and air conditioning (HVAC) systems, in addition to power-hungry medical equipment. The consumption of energy not only contributes to an increase in operational costs but also makes a contribution to the emission of greenhouse gases (Reshi, 2023).

Healthcare institutions generate a significant quantity of garbage, which may include potentially harmful medical waste, items that cannot be recycled, and pharmaceutical waste. Because of the possible threats to both the environment and to public health, the disposal of hazardous materials is subject to stringent regulations. It is possible for improper waste management to result in contamination of both land and water resources. The healthcare industry makes use of a wide variety of chemicals, such as medications, disinfectants, and sterilizing agents, which can lead to chemical pollution. The improper disposal of these substances or their accidental release into the environment can lead to the pollution and disruption of ecosystems. Particularly pharmaceuticals can make their way into water systems, which therefore presents long-term dangers to the ecosystem (Mohanty et al.,2023). Healthcare activities require the movement of patients, workers, and medical supplies. This results in emissions from the transportation sector. Air pollution and carbon emissions are both made worse by the exhaust released by motor vehicles (Saranya and Murugan, 2023; Pratap at al., 2023; Singh et al., 2023).

## IOT-ENHANCED HEALTHCARE INFRASTRUCTURE

Technologies that are part of the Internet of Things (Io T) are progressively being incorporated into the infrastructure of healthcare facilities in order to improve patient care, streamline operations, and increase the effectiveness of healthcare systems. The following is a list of some of the most important applications of Internet of Things technologies in the healthcare industry (Patel and Kumar, 2023).

Monitoring of Patients Via Remote Connection: Wearable gadgets that are enabled by the internet of things, such as fitness trackers and smartwatches, make it possible to continuously monitor vital signs, physical activity, and other health parameters.Patients and medical professionals are able to exchange data in real time, which paves the way for the remote monitoring of chronic illnesses and the early detection of health problems.

1. Advantages of Telehealth and Telemedicine: The Internet of Things makes it possible to provide telehealth and telemedicine services, which connect patients with medical specialists via video conferencing and other forms of remote consultation. Internet of Things equipment, such as high-resolution cameras and digital stethoscopes, are able to offer real-time data and make it possible to perform remote physical examinations (Patel and Kumar, 2023).
2. Compliance with Medication: Patients are reminded to take their medications using smart pill bottles and packaging that is equipped with internet of things sensors. Smartphone apps and internet platforms make it possible for patients, carers, and healthcare practitioners to monitor a patient's adherence to their prescription regimen (Huang, et al., 2023).
3. Management of Assets and Goods in Inventory: Within healthcare institutions, Internet of Things technology is utilized to track the location of medical equipment, supplies, and pharmaceuticals, as well as the status of each item. This ensures that resources are distributed effectively, cuts down on the amount of time equipment is idle, and prevents stock-outs (Patel and Kumar, 2023).
4. Tracking of Assets in Hospitals: The Internet of Things enables improved utilization of high-value equipment such as wheelchairs, infusion pumps, and ventilators by helping to identify and monitor how they are being used. Theft can be avoided, and hospitals may manage their maintenance plans more effectively.
5. Keeping an Eye on the Environment: In healthcare facilities, sensors connected to the internet of things monitor ambient factors to maintain ideal levels of temperature, humidity, and air quality. The safety of both the patients and the personnel, as well as the delicate equipment and the medications, is ensured by this measure (Huang, et al., 2023).
6. Automatic Fall Detection and Smart Beds: Internet of Things (Io T) technology allows hospital beds to reconfigure themselves according to the preferences of individual patients, lessen the likelihood of developing pressure ulcers, and alert nurses when patients want assistance. When a patient is at risk of falling, fall detection systems equipped with Internet of Things sensors can send a warning to a healthcare provider.

7. Participation of the Patient and Education: Patients can be more actively involved in their healthcare by using interactive Internet of Things devices such as patient kiosks, which can give information, health education, and communication tools. The Internet of Things has the potential to get patients more involved in their own treatment strategies (Huang, et al., 2023).
8. The Management of Chronic Disease: The Internet of Things helps people who suffer from chronic conditions such as diabetes and hypertension by keeping track of their data and sending it to their healthcare providers. Treatment plans are able to be modified in real time based on the data that has been obtained.
9. Analytic Predictive of the Future: The Internet of Things (Io T) generates massive amounts of data pertaining to health that may be analyzed using predictive analytic. Healthcare providers are able to discover trends, better anticipate the outcomes for patients, and more effectively deploy available resources (Patel and Kumar, 2023).
10. Response in an Emergent Situation: Wearable technologies and sensors based on the Internet of Things are able to automatically identify emergencies, aberrant vital signs, or falls and initiate an urgent response. This improves the overall patient safety and cut's reaction times in the event of an emergency (Patel and Kumar, 2023; Huang, et al., 2023; Packiavathy et al., 2023; Ding et al.,2023).

## WAYS IN WHICH SMART CITIES CAN CONTRIBUTE TO THE DEVELOPMENT OF SUSTAINABLE HEALTHCARE SYSTEMS

Through careful urban design and the incorporation of ecologically responsible business practice, smart cities have the potential to play a significant part in the development of sustainable healthcare systems. The following are some ways that sustainable healthcare can be promoted in smart cities:

- Efficient Transportation: Smart cities place an emphasis on the development of transportation systems that are both efficient and sustainable. These systems include public transit, cycling infrastructure, and urban layout that is favorable to pedestrians. This diminishes the need for the use of private vehicles, which in turn results in lower levels of air pollution and emissions of greenhouse gases. Additionally, effective transportation guarantees that patients as well as healthcare personnel can access healthcare facilities without adding to the already existing levels of congestion or pollution (Chen et al.,2023).
- Telehealth and Telemedicine: The digital infrastructure required for telehealth and telemedicine services can be provided by smart cities. Patients will be able to get healthcare remotely, which will cut down on the number of trips they need to make in person. Smart cities encourage a more environmentally responsible method of accessing medical care by reducing the amount of time spent travelling.
- Design of Green Buildings: Sustainable building practice, such as energy-efficient designs, usage of renewable energy sources, and eco-friendly materials are essential elements of the development of smart cities. It is possible to design and build healthcare facilities in smart cities so that they are environmentally friendly, hence lowering their overall energy consumption and diminishing their overall carbon footprint (Chen et al.,2023).

- Efficient Use of Resources: Healthcare facilities in smart cities implement resource-efficient practice, such as water conservation, waste reduction, and green energy solutions. This contributes to the achievement of sustainability goals by lowering resource consumption and reducing the amount of trash produced.
- Making Decisions: Based on the Data Collected: Smart cities gather data on a variety of elements of urban life, including healthcare, and then analyses that data to make decisions. These data can be put to use in the process of making informed decisions regarding the distribution of healthcare resources, the care of individual patients, and the implementation of public health initiatives. Insights derived from data contribute to the improvement of healthcare practice and the elimination of inefficiencies (Ghazal et al., 2023).
- Environmental Monitoring: In smart cities, environmental sensors are frequently used to monitor aspects of the environment that have an impact on public health, such as air quality, temperature, and others. This data has the potential to lead to the early detection of environmental risks, which can assist healthcare systems in taking preventative measures to safeguard the health of inhabitants.
- Sustainable Procurement: Smart cities promote environmentally responsible methods of purchasing goods and services. The ability of healthcare facilities in major cities to access environmentally friendly medical equipment, medications, and supplies helps to ensure that the products that these facilities employ have a smaller negative impact on the environment (Ghazal et al., 2023).
- Green Infrastructure: The urban planning of smart cities places an emphasis on green infrastructure, which includes things like parks, green roofs, and streets lined with trees. These green spaces make a positive contribution to the well-being of the community's citizens and provide chances for activities that may be enjoyed outside, which are beneficial to public health.
- Activated Lifestyles: Smart cities encourage occupants to lead active lifestyles by developing neighbour-hoods that are conducive to walking, establishing bike lanes and offering easy access to recreational areas. These conveniences inspire people to engage in physical exercise, which is critical for maintaining overall population health (Ghazal et al., 2023).

## ETHICAL, LEGAL, AND REGULATORY DIMENSIONS OF IO T-ENHANCED HEALTHCARE SYSTEMS: A GLOBAL PERSPECTIVE

It is crucial to further explore the ethical and legal aspects related to data privacy and security in healthcare systems that are enhanced by the Internet of Things (Io T), due to the sensitive nature of personal health information. Ethical considerations pertain to the guarantee of patient self-governance, privacy, and confidence in the system. Patients should possess autonomy over their data, encompassing the ability to provide consent for its acquisition, utilization, and dissemination. In addition, healthcare providers and manufacturers of Internet of Things (Io T) devices have ethical responsibilities to guarantee the precision, reliability, and confidentiality of the gathered data.

Healthcare systems are required by law to adhere to rules such as the Health Insurance Portability and Accountability Act (HIPAA) in the United States or the General Data Protection Regulation (GDPR) in the European Union. These requirements require the implementation of rigorous procedures for safeguarding data, including encryption, access restriction, and prompt notification in the event of a security breach. Noncompliance may lead to significant repercussions, such as monetary sanctions and judicial proceedings. Regulatory frameworks and compliance criteria for Io T in healthcare differ across the globe. The European Union (EU) enforces the General Data Protection Regulation (GDPR), which establishes strict rules for safeguarding data. In contrast, the United States relies on a mix of federal legislation such as the Health Insurance Portability and Accountability Act (HIPAA) and regulations particular to different sectors. Other geographical areas may have their own legislation or choose to adhere to global standards. Ensuring compliance frequently necessitates thorough documentation, risk assessments, and continuous monitoring to safeguard data security and privacy.

Developing nations and under-resourced communities encounter substantial obstacles when it comes to implementing healthcare practices that are enhanced by the Internet of Things (Io T). The implementation is hindered by limited infrastructure, low finance, and lack of technical skills. In addition, worries regarding the privacy and security of data may discourage the acceptance of new technologies, particularly in the absence of strong regulatory systems to protect patient information. To tackle these difficulties, it is essential for governments, non-governmental organizations (NGOs), and private sector entities to work together in a collaborative manner. This involves pooling resources, enhancing capabilities, and customizing solutions to address specific local requirements.

Emerging technologies such as 5G networks, artificial intelligence (AI), and block-chain have significant promise to transform Io T-enhanced healthcare in smart cities. 5G networks facilitate expedited data transmission and reduced latency, hence improving real-time monitoring and medical services. Artificial intelligence algorithms have the capability to analyse extensive quantities of healthcare data in order to detect patterns, diagnose illnesses, and tailor treatment regimens to individual patients. Block chain technology provides a safe and transparent method of storing and exchanging data, which improves trust and interoperability among healthcare stakeholders.

In order to offer a more extensive worldwide outlook, it is crucial to include a range of case studies from different geographical regions and healthcare systems. These case studies can showcase effective implementations, encountered problems, and acquired knowledge, aiding policymakers, healthcare practitioners, and technology developers in navigating the intricacies of Io T-enhanced healthcare in smart cities globally as described in next section of this chapter.

## CASE STUDIES FROM DIVERSE GEOGRAPHIC REGIONS AND HEALTHCARE SYSTEMS

A number of municipalities all over the world have incorporated healthcare into their smart city projects. These municipalities are utilizing technology and data in order to better healthcare services, promote public health, and develop urban settings that are more sustainable. Case studies that stand out include the following (Demirel, 2023):

1. Initiative of Singapore to Become a "Smart Nation: With its "Smart Nation" project, Singapore has established itself as a leader in the creation of smart cities. The nation has emphasis-ed the use of telehealth and telemedicine services as part of its efforts to incorporate healthcare into its smart city initiatives. Patients can, for instance, gain access to their medical records, schedule appointments, and participate in telehealth chats with their care providers through the "Health-hub" platform developed by the National Healthcare Group. Because of these initiatives, both access to healthcare and patient participation have increased, and the whole health care system has become more sustainable.

2. Healthcare Internet of Things Initiatives in Barcelona, Spain: Healthcare is something that Barcelona has been working hard to integrate into its plans for becoming a smart city. The Internet of Things (Io T) and data analytic will be utilized in the "Social Care Program" that the city has launched to provide senior residents with individualist care plans. Wearable technology and sensors monitor patients' health, eliminating the need for in-person checkups and allowing for more rapid reactions to medical concerns.
3. The Copenhagen Solutions Lab is located in the Danish capital of Copenhagen: The Solutions Lab in Copenhagen is dedicated to enhancing the standard of living in the city through the application of technology, with a particular emphasis on medical care. For instance, the "Copenhagen Health-Tech Cluster" promotes the development of sustainable healthcare solutions by encouraging innovation in the health care industry and facilitating partnerships among new businesses, established medical facilities, and educational establishments.
4. Longwood Medical Area (LMA) in Boston, Massachusetts, United States of America: The Longwood Medical Area of Boston is becoming a smart health district as it is home to a number of academic institutions and hospitals that are recognized as being among the best in the world. Integration of internet-of-things technology for the administration of medical devices and patient interaction are among the initiatives. The "Smart Health Network" proposed by the LMA intends to improve care delivery while simultaneously lowering associated costs and diminishing adverse effects on the environment.
5. Located in the Netherlands, Eindhoven is home to the Smart Health Eindhoven Region: The Smart Health Region in Eindhoven integrates technological innovation with healthcare in order to create an ecosystem that is beneficial to both patients and professionals working in the medical field. The use of data-driven decision-making, data-driven remote monitoring of chronic patients, and smart home solutions are among the initiatives. The quality of care, as well as its availability and long-term viability, is what needs to be improved.
6. Io T-Based Health Monitoring: New Taipei City, Taiwan, Internet of Things: Io T technology has been integrated into a health monitoring system that New Taipei City has established in order to collect data on the citizens' health, particularly that of the city's senior population. This data is shared with the providers of healthcare, which enables early intervention as well as personalized care. It lessens the need for trips to the hospital, which in turn diminishes the expenditures of medical care.

These case studies shed insight on the myriad of approaches that cities are taking to integrate healthcare into their smart city program. These cities want to provide healthcare services that are easier to access, more efficient, and friendlier to the environment so that they can ultimately improve the health of their residents and contribute to the development of smarter and healthier urban environments. They plan to do this through the use of technology, data analytic, and environmentally responsible practice.

## CONCERNS REGARDING PERSONAL INFORMATION AND DATA SECURITY IN CONNECTION WITH HEALTHCARE IN SMART CITIES

It is of the utmost importance to guarantee the confidentiality of patient medical records. Protecting patient information requires that smart cities incorporate stringent security measures such as encryption, access limits, and secure data transmission protocols (Fabrègue et al., 2023).

- Consent for Data Collection: It is required to get the informed consent of patients prior to data collection and distribution. To handle issues of data consent and opt-out choices, there should be clear policies and processes in place regarding data privacy.
- Data Breach Response: Smart cities need to implement protocols for quickly identifying and responding to data breaches in order to be considered "smart." This includes communicating with affected individuals and the appropriate authorities in compliance with the laws governing data protection.
- Compliance with standards: It is essential for healthcare efforts involving smart cities to be in compliance with all applicable data protection and healthcare standards. In the United States, it is very necessary to adhere to the criteria established by laws such as the Health Insurance Portability and Accountability Act (HIPAA).
- Ethical Use of Data: The data collected from healthcare providers should be utilized in an ethical manner and not for activities that could be detrimental to patients or communities. In order to guarantee the ethical utilization of data, transparency and supervision are very necessary. In nutshell, the gathering and analysis of data in Io T-driven healthcare have the potential to revolutionize healthcare services by enabling early disease identification, personalize therapy, and evidence-based decision-making.

## DIFFICULTIES AND ROADBLOCKS THAT PREVENT THE IMPLEMENTATION OF IO T-ENHANCED GREEN HEALTHCARE IN SMART CITIES

It may be difficult to implement Io T-enhanced green healthcare in smart cities due to the many technological, financial, and regulatory hurdles that must be overcome. The following is a list of the most significant obstacles, as well as some of the probable solutions to overcome them:

1. Obstacles Involved in Technology: Interoperability is the capacity of different Internet of Things devices and systems made by different manufacturers to work together. This could result in data silos and decreased efficiency. Create open standards and interoperability frameworks as a strategy to guarantee flawless communication between different types of devices and systems. Privacy and data protection are of the utmost importance, especially with regard to medical records (Omanwa, 2023).
2. High Costs of Implementation: The deployment and upkeep of Io T-enhanced healthcare systems can be very expensive. Approach: Seek out public-private partnerships so that the cost can be distributed more evenly. Look into getting grants and subsidies for environmentally friendly healthcare projects (Omanwa, 2023).
3. Obstacles posed by regulations and the law: The strict data protection standards in place in some countries, like as the United States with its HIPAA law, might make it difficult to share and analyses patient data (Sharma et al.,2023).

4. Restrictions imposed by the infrastructure: It's possible that some places lack the requisite connectivity infrastructure for Internet of Things technology. The strategy is to make investments in the expansion of broadband connectivity in areas that are under-served and to build partnerships with suppliers of telecommutes services. Reliable power supplies are necessary for sustainable healthcare systems; however, these may not be readily available in some areas of the world. Strategy: Develop backup power solutions to assure continuous operation, such as solar panels or energy storage devices (Omanwa, 2023; Chi et al.,2023; Abbas et al., 2023).

## CONTRIBUTION OF THE CHAPTER

This chapter explores how Internet of Things (Io T) technology might be used to drive innovative environmentally-friendly healthcare initiatives in the ever-changing context of smart cities. Our goal is to combine Io T-enabled solutions with sustainable urban planning concepts to create urban oases that prioritize environmental stewardship and public health. Our exploration will involve a comprehensive approach, including the use of Io T sensors to monitor the environment in real-time, the incorporation of energy-efficient technologies into smart healthcare facilities, and the creation of green spaces in metropolitan areas. In addition, the study examines how data analytic obtained from data created by the Internet of Things (Io T) might enhance predictive healthcare tactics, enabling proactive interventions and optimizing the allocation of resources. The ultimate goal of this interdisciplinary research is to stimulate ideas and efforts that promote resilient, equitable, and health-enhancing urban landscapes in the digital era.

## CONCLUSION

In conclusion, incorporating Internet of Things (Io T) technologies with healthcare systems in smart cities has the potential to greatly enhance environmental sustainability and improve public health outcomes. Healthcare institutions may reduce their environmental impact and improve efficiency and cost-effectiveness by using Io T devices to control energy, reduce waste, and optimize resources. Moreover, the implementation of Internet of Things (Io T) technology in healthcare can enhance the provision of medical services by enabling remote patient monitoring, utilizing intelligent medical equipment, and employing predictive analytic. This can lead to improved healthcare delivery, increased patient empowerment, and the facilitation of preventive care. However, in order to fully reap the advantages of Io T in green healthcare, it is necessary to tackle obstacles pertaining to data privacy, interoperability, and cybersecurity, while also guaranteeing fair access and inclusion for all individuals. In order to fully use the potential of Io T in developing smart cities, it is crucial for stakeholders such as healthcare providers, technology developers, politicians, and community members to collaborate effectively. This collaboration is necessary for the creation of sustainable, resilient, and fair healthcare systems.

## REFERENCES

Abbas, N., Abbas, Z., Liu, X., Khan, S. S., Foster, E. D., & Larkin, S. (2023). A Survey: Future Smart Cities Based on Advance Control of Unmanned Aerial Vehicles (UAVs). *Applied Sciences (Basel, Switzerland)*, 13(17), 9881. 10.3390/app13179881

Abubakar, I. R., & Alshammari, M. S. (2023). Urban planning schemes for developing low-carbon cities in the Gulf Cooperation Council region. *Habitat International*, 138, 102881. 10.1016/j.habitatint.2023.102881

Al Issa, H.-E., Abdullatif, T. N., Ntayi, J., & Abdelsalam, M. K. (2023). Green intellectual capital for sustainable healthcare: Evidence from Iraq. *Journal of Intellectual Capital*, 24(4), 929–947. 10.1108/JIC-02-2022-0046

Aminizadeh, S., Heidari, A., Toumaj, S., Darbandi, M., Navimipour, N. J., Rezaei, M., Talebi, S., Azad, P., & Unal, M. (2023). The applications of machine learning techniques in medical data processing based on distributed computing and the Internet of Things. *Computer Methods and Programs in Biomedicine*, 241, 107745. 10.1016/j.cmpb.2023.10774537579550

Badran, A. (2023). Developing smart cities: Regulatory and policy implications for the State of Qatar. *International Journal of Public Administration*, 46(7), 519–532. 10.1080/01900692.2021.2003811

Barykin, S. E., Strimovskaya, A. V., Sergeev, S. M., Borisoglebskaya, L. N., Dedyukhina, N., Sklyarov, I., Sklyarova, J., & Saychenko, L. (2023). Smart City Logistics on the Basis of Digital Tools for ESG Goals Achievement. *Sustainability (Basel)*, 15(6), 5507. 10.3390/su15065507

Bhat, M. A., Gedik, K., & Gaga, E. O. (2023). Atmospheric micro (nano) plastics: Future growing concerns for human health. *Air Quality, Atmosphere & Health*, 16(2), 233–262. 10.1007/s11869-022-01272-236276170

Bouramdane, A.-A. (2023). Optimal Water Management Strategies: Paving the Way for Sustainability in Smart Cities. *Smart Cities*, 6(5), 2849–2882. 10.3390/smartcities6050128

Chen, Z., & Irene, C. C. C. (2023). Smart cities and quality of life: A quantitative analysis of citizens' support for smart city development. *Information Technology & People*, 36(1), 263–285. 10.1108/ITP-07-2021-0577

Chevance, G., Fresán, U., Hekler, E., Edmondson, D., Lloyd, S. J., Ballester, J., Litt, J., Cvijanovic, I., Araújo-Soares, V., & Bernard, P. (2023). Vera Araújo-Soares, and Paquito Bernard. "Thinking health-related behaviors in a climate change context: A narrative review.". *Annals of Behavioral Medicine*, 57(3), 193–204. 10.1093/abm/kaac03935861123

Chi, H. R., Maria de Fátima, D., Zhu, H., Li, C., Kojima, K., & Radwan, A. (2023). Healthcare 5.0: In the Perspective of Consumer Internet-of-Things-Based Fog/Cloud Computing. *IEEE Transactions on Consumer Electronics*, 69(4), 745–755. 10.1109/TCE.2023.3293993

Demirel, D. (2023). The Impact of Managing Diversity on Building the Smart City A Comparison of Smart City Strategies: Cases From Europe, America, and Asia. *SAGE Open*, 13(3), 21582440231184971. 10.1177/21582440231184971

Ding, S., Tukker, A., & Ward, H. (2023). Opportunities and risks of internet of things (Io T) technologies for circular business models: A literature review. *Journal of Environmental Management*, 336, 117662. 10.1016/j.jenvman.2023.11766236913854

Fabrègue, B. F. G., & Bogoni, A.Fabrègue. (2023). Brian FG, and Andrea Bogoni. "Privacy and Security Concerns in the Smart City.". *Smart Cities*, 6(1), 586–613. 10.3390/smartcities6010027

Frimpong, B. A., Barbosa, C., & Abd-Alhameed, R. A. (2023). The Impact of the Internet of Things (Io T) on Healthcare Delivery: A Systematic Literature Review. *Journal of Techniques*, 5(3), 84–91. 10.51173/jt.v5i3.1433

Garcia-Perez, A., Cegarra-Navarro, J. G., Sallos, M. P., Martinez-Caro, E., & Chinnaswamy, A. (2023). Resilience in healthcare systems: Cyber security and digital transformation. *Technovation*, 121, 102583. 10.1016/j.technovation.2022.102583

Ghazal, T. M., Hasan, M. K., Ahmad, M., Alzoubi, H. M., & Alshurideh, M. (2023). Machine Learning Approaches for Sustainable Cities Using Internet of Things. In *The Effect of Information Technology on Business and Marketing Intelligence Systems* (pp. 1969–1986). Springer International Publishing. 10.1007/978-3-031-12382-5_108

Hunter, D. J., & Bengoa, R. (2023). Meeting the challenge of health system transformation in European countries. *Policy and Society*, 42(1), 14–27. 10.1093/polsoc/puac022

Kamruzzaman, M. M., & Yan, B. (2022). Md Nazirul Islam Sarker, Omar Alruwaili, Min Wu, and Ibrahim Alrashdi. "Blockchain and fog computing in Io T-driven healthcare services for smart cities.". *Journal of Healthcare Engineering*, 2022.

Kaur, J. (2024). Towards a Sustainable Triad: Uniting Energy Management Systems, Smart Cities, and Green Healthcare for a Greener Future. In *Emerging Materials, Technologies, and Solutions for Energy Harvesting* (pp. 258-285). IGI Global.

Kaur, J. (2024). Green Guardians: Unveiling the Strategic Role of HR in Environmental Sustainability Initiatives. In *Building Sustainable Human Resources Management Practices for Businesses* (pp. 125-143). IGI Global.

Kaur, J. (2024). Green Healthcare in Smart Cities: Harnessing Io T for Sustainable Transformation of Healthcare Systems. In *Secure and Intelligent Io T-Enabled Smart Cities* (pp. 334-354). IGI Global.

Kaur, J. (2024). Fueling Healthcare Transformation: The Nexus of Startups, Venture Capital, and Innovation. In *Fostering Innovation in Venture Capital and Startup Ecosystems* (pp. 327-351). IGI Global.

Kaur, J. (2024). Robotics Rx: A Prescription for the Future of Healthcare. In *Applications of Virtual and Augmented Reality for Health and Wellbeing* (pp. 217-238). IGI Global. 10.4018/979-8-3693-1123-3.ch012

Kumari, S., Gupta, D., & Bashir, A. K. (2024). Advanced Computing Technologies for Energy-Efficient and Secure Io T Network in Smart Cities: Green Io T Perspective. In *Emerging Technologies and the Application of WSN and Io T* (pp. 65-82). CRC Press.

Mishra, P. (2023). *Sustainable Smart Cities: Enabling Technologies, Energy Trends and Potential Applications*. Springer Nature. 10.1007/978-3-031-33354-5

Mohanty, S. S., Vyas, S., Koul, Y., Prajapati, P., Varjani, S., Chang, J.-S., Bilal, M., Moustakas, K., Show, P. L., & Vithanage, M. (2023). Tricks and tracks in waste management with a special focus on municipal landfill leachate: Leads and obstacles. *The Science of the Total Environment*, 860, 160377. 10.1016/j.scitotenv.2022.16037736414054

Morello, R., Ruffa, F., Jablonski, I., Fabbiano, L., & De Capua, C. (2022). An Io T based ECG system to diagnose cardiac pathologies for healthcare applications in smart cities. *Measurement*, 190, 110685. 10.1016/j.measurement.2021.110685

Nassereddine, M., & Khang, A. (2024). Applications of Internet of Things (Io T) in smart cities. In *Advanced Io T Technologies and Applications in the Industry 4.0 Digital Economy* (pp. 109–136). CRC Press.

Packiavathy, S. V., & Gautam, S. (2023). Internet of Things (Io T) based automated sanitizer dispenser and COVID-19 statistics reporter in a post-pandemic world. *Health and Technology*, 13(2), 327–341. 10.1007/s12553-023-00728-436694669

Pandya, S., Srivastava, G., Jhaveri, R., Babu, M. R., Bhattacharya, S., Praveen, K. R. M., Mastorakis, S., Piran, M. J., & Gadekallu, T. R. (2023). Federated learning for smart cities: A comprehensive survey. *Sustainable Energy Technologies and Assessments*, 55, 102987. 10.1016/j.seta.2022.102987

Parker, J. (2023). Barriers to green inhaler prescribing: Ethical issues in environmentally sustainable clinical practice. *Journal of Medical Ethics*, 49(2), 92–98. 10.1136/jme-2022-10838835981864

Patel, K., & Kumar, S. (2023). *Education Sector an application of IoT.*

Pratap, B., Kumar, S., Nand, S., Azad, I., Bharagava, R. N., Luiz, F. R. F., & Dutta, V. (2023). Wastewater generation and treatment by various eco-friendly technologies: Possible health hazards and further reuse for environmental safety. *Chemosphere*, 313, 137547. 10.1016/j.chemosphere.2022.13754736529169

Rejeb, A., Rejeb, K., Treiblmaier, H., Appolloni, A., Alghamdi, S., Alhasawi, Y., & Iranmanesh, M. (2023). The Internet of Things (Io T) in healthcare: Taking stock and moving forward. *Internet of Things : Engineering Cyber Physical Human Systems*, 1007.

Reshi, I. A. (2023). Unpacking The Complexities Of Economic Systems: Exploring Trends, Challenges And Solutions. *Journal of Accounting Research, Utility Finance and Digital Assets*, 1(4), 393–398. 10.54443/jaruda.v1i4.60

Roy, S. (2024). A Study of the Future Generation of Smart Cities Using Green Technology. In *Green Computing for Sustainable Smart Cities* (pp. 59–72). CRC Press. 10.1201/9781003388814-4

Sakran, J. V., Bornstein, S. S., Dicker, R., Rivara, F. P., Campbell, B. T., Cunningham, R. M., Betz, M., Hargarten, S., Williams, A., Horwitz, J. M., Nehra, D., Burstin, H., Sheehan, K., Dreier, F. L., James, T., Sathya, C., Armstrong, J. H., Rowhani-Rahbar, A., Charles, S., & Bulger, E. M. (2023). Proceedings from the Second Medical Summit on Firearm Injury Prevention, 2022: Creating a sustainable healthcare coalition to advance a multidisciplinary public health approach. *Journal of the American College of Surgeons*, 236(6), 1242–1260. 10.1097/XCS.000000000000066236877809

Saranya, R., & Murugan, A. (2023). A systematic review of enabling blockchain in healthcare system: Analysis, current status, challenges and future direction. *Materials Today: Proceedings*, 80, 3010–3015. 10.1016/j.matpr.2021.07.105

Sharma, A., Sharma, K., Kumar, V., & Kamalraj, R. (2023). Simplified LEACH Protocol with Superior Energy Efficiency for the Internet of Things. *International Journal of Intelligent Systems and Applications in Engineering*, 11(no. 8s), 86–92.

Singh, S. P., Viriyasitavat, W., Juneja, S., Alshahrani, H., Shaikh, A., Dhiman, G., Singh, A., & Kaur, A. (2022). Dual adaption based evolutionary algorithm for optimized the smart healthcare communication service of the Internet of Things in smart city. *Physical Communication*, 55, 101893. 10.1016/j.phycom.2022.101893

Singh, V., Singh, N., Rai, S. N., Kumar, A., Singh, A. K., Singh, M. P., Sahoo, A., Shekhar, S., Vamanu, E., & Mishra, V. (2023). Heavy Metal Contamination in the Aquatic Ecosystem: Toxicity and Its Remediation Using Eco-Friendly Approaches. *Toxics*, 11(2), 147. 10.3390/toxics1102014736851022

Ullah, F., & Al-Turjman, F. (2023). A conceptual framework for blockchain smart contract adoption to manage real estate deals in smart cities. *Neural Computing & Applications*, 35(7), 5033–5054. 10.1007/s00521-021-05800-6

Veeraiah, V. (2023). K. O. Thejaswini, Veera Talukdar, Shaziya Islam, Supriya Sanjay Ajagekar, and Rama Krishna Yellapragada. "Deep Learning-Based Classification for Healthcare-Based Io T System for Efficient Diagnosis.". *International Journal of Intelligent Systems and Applications in Engineering*, 11(no. 11s), 165–174.

Vishwakarma, L. P., Singh, R. K., Mishra, R., & Kumari, A. (2023). Application of artificial intelligence for resilient and sustainable healthcare system: Systematic literature review and future research directions. *International Journal of Production Research*, 1–23. 10.1080/00207543.2023.2188101

## KEY TERMS AND DEFINITIONS

**Internet of Things (IoT):** This pertains to a system of interconnected physical devices, objects, and sensors that are equipped with technological capabilities to collect and communicate data through the internet.

**Smart City:** An urban area that makes use of data-driven solutions and digital technologies in order to improve performance and well-being while simultaneously lowering costs and the number of resources used.

**Sustainable Healthcare or Eco-Friendly Healthcare:** Healthcare that places an emphasis on diminishing the negative effects that medical facilities, practice, and procedures have on the surrounding environment.

# Compilation of References


Abbasimoshaei, A., Chinnakkonda Ravi, A. K., & Kern, T. A. (2023). Development of a New Control System for a Rehabilitation Robot Using Electrical Impedance Tomography and Artificial Intelligence. *Biomimetics*, 8(5), 420. 10.3390/biomimetics805042037754171

Abbas, N., Abbas, Z., Liu, X., Khan, S. S., Foster, E. D., & Larkin, S. (2023). A Survey: Future Smart Cities Based on Advance Control of Unmanned Aerial Vehicles (UAVs). *Applied Sciences (Basel, Switzerland)*, 13(17), 9881. 10.3390/app13179881

Abbas, Z., & Yoon, W. (2015). A survey on energy conserving mechanisms for the internet of things: Wireless networking aspects. *Sensors (Basel)*, 15(10), 24818–24847. 10.3390/s151024818264O4275

Abdul Rahim, S. K. F., Fung, C. C., & Wong, K. W. (2021). Design and evaluation of large-scale IoT-enabled healthcare architecture. *Applied Sciences (Basel, Switzerland)*, 11(8), 3623. 10.3390/app11083623

Abdulmalek, S., Nasir, A., & Jabbar, W. A. (2024, April). LoRaWAN-based hybrid internet of wearable things system implementation for smart healthcare. *Internet of Things : Engineering Cyber Physical Human Systems*, 25, 101124. 10.1016/j.iot.2024.101124

Abler, D., Schaer, R., Oreiller, V., Verma, H., Reichenbach, J., Aidonopoulos, O., Evéquoz, F., Jreige, M., Prior, J. O., & Depeursinge, A. (2023). QuantImage v2: A comprehensive and integrated physician-centered cloud platform for radiomics and machine learning research. *European Radiology Experimental*, 7(1), 1–13. 10.1186/s41747-023-00326-z36947346

Abreu, D., Toledo, J., Codina, B., & Suárez, A. (2021), Low-Cost Ultrasonic Range Improvements for an Assistive Device. *Sensors. 21*, 4250. 10.3390/s21124250

Abubakar, I. R., & Alshammari, M. S. (2023). Urban planning schemes for developing low-carbon cities in the Gulf Cooperation Council region. *Habitat International*, 138, 102881. 10.1016/j.habitatint.2023.102881

Abu-Elkheir, M., & Ali, N. A. (2015). Internet of nano-things healthcare applications: Requirements, opportunities, and challenges. In *Proceedings of the IEEE 11th International Conference on Wireless and Mobile Computing, Networking and Communications (WiMob)* (pp. 9–14). Abu Dhabi, United Arab Emirates.

Adadi, A., & Berrada, M. (2018). Peeking inside the black-box: A survey on explainable artificial intelligence (xai). *IEEE Access : Practical Innovations, Open Solutions*, 6, 52138–52160. 10.1109/ACCESS.2018.2870052

Adams, Z., McClure, E. A., Gray, K. M., Danielson, C. K., Treiber, F. A., & Ruggiero, K. J. (2017). Mobile devices for the remote acquisition of physiological and behavioral biomarkers in psychiatric clinical research. *Journal of Psychiatric Research*, 85, 1–14. 10.1016/j.jpsychires.2016.10.01927814455

Adel, A. (2022). Future of industry 5.0 in society: Human-centric solutions, challenges and prospective research areas. *Journal of Cloud Computing (Heidelberg, Germany)*, 2022(11), 40. 10.1186/s13677-022-00314-536101900

Agarwal, Y., Jain, M., Sinha, S., & Dhir, S. (2020). Delivering high-tech, AI-based health care at Apollo Hospitals. *Global Business and Organizational Excellence*, 39(2), 20–30. 10.1002/joe.21981

Aghila Rajagopal, S. A., Jha, S., Abdeljaber, H. A., & Nazeer, J. (2023). AI Based Secure Analytics of Clinical Data in Cloud Environment: Towards Smart Cities and Healthcare. *Journal of Advances in Information Technology*, 14(5), 1132–1142. 10.12720/jait.14.5.1132-1142

Agrawal, N. K., Kumar, R., & Agrawal, H. K. (2024). Artificial Intelligence and Robotics in Healthcare: Transforming the Indian Landscape. In *Deep Learning in Internet of Things for Next Generation Healthcare* (pp. 168-181). Chapman and Hall/CRC.

Ahad, M. A., Paiva, S., Tripathi, G., & Feroz, N. (2020). Enabling technologies and sustainable smart cities. *Sustainable Cities and Society*, 61, 102301. 10.1016/j.scs.2020.102301

Ahmad, A., Tariq, A., Hussain, H. K., & Gill, A. Y. (2023). Revolutionizing Healthcare: How Deep Learning is poised to Change the Landscape of Medical Diagnosis and Treatment. Journal of Computer Networks. *Architecture and High-Performance Computing*, 5(2), 458–471. 10.47709/cnahpc.v5i2.2350

Ahmad, I., & Shin, S. (2022). A perceptual encryption-based image communication system for deep learning-based tuberculosis diagnosis using healthcare cloud services. *Electronics (Basel)*, 11(16), 2514. 10.3390/electronics11162514

Ahmad, N., Shahzad, B., Arif, M., Izdrui, D., Ungurean, I., & Geman, O. (2022). An energy-efficient framework for WBAN in health care domain. *Journal of Sensors*, 2022, 1–11. 10.1155/2022/5823461

Ahmed, I., Jeon, G., & Chehri, A. (2023). An IoT-enabled smart health care system for screening of COVID-19 with multi layers features fusion and selection. *Computing*, 105(4), 743–760. 10.1007/s00607-021-00992-0

Ahmed, M. I. (2022, October). Govindaraj Kannan, Secure and lightweight privacy preserving Internet of things integration for remote patient monitoring. *Journal of King Saud University. Computer and Information Sciences*, 34(9), 6895–6908. 10.1016/j.jksuci.2021.07.016

Ahmed, M. U., & Bjorkman, M. (2016). *A. ˇCauševi ´ c, H. Fotouhi, M. Linden, An overview on the internet of things for health monitoring systems, ICST Inst.* Comput. Sci. Soc. Informatics Telecommun. Eng.

Akbar MS, Hussain Z, Sheng M, Shankaran R (2022). Wireless Body Area Sensor Networks: Survey of MAC and Routing Protocols for Patient Monitoring under IEEE 802.15.4 and IEEE 802.15.6. *Sensors, 22*(21), 8279.

Akhtar, S. M., Nazir, M., Saleem, K., Haque, H. M. U., & Hussain, I. (2020). An ontology-driven IoT based healthcare formalism. *International Journal of Advanced Computer Science and Applications*, 11(2), 479–486. 10.14569/IJACSA.2020.0110261

Al Issa, H. E., Abdullatif, T. N., Ntayi, J., & Abdelsalam, M. K. (2023). Green intellectual capital for sustainable healthcare: Evidence from Iraq. *Journal of Intellectual Capital*, 24(4), 929–947. 10.1108/JIC-02-2022-0046

Al Kuwaiti, A., Nazer, K., Al-Reedy, A., Al-Shehri, S., Al-Muhanna, A., Subbarayalu, A. V., Al Muhanna, D., & Al-Muhanna, F. A. (2023). A Review of the Role of Artificial Intelligence in Healthcare. *Journal of Personalized Medicine*, 13(6), 951. 10.3390/jpm1306095137373940

Al-Ali, A. R., Zualkernan, I. A., Rashid, M., Gupta, R., & Alikarar, M. (2017). A smart home energy management system using IoT and big data analytics approach. *IEEE Transactions on Consumer Electronics*, 63(4), 426–434. 10.1109/TCE.2017.015014

Alamer, M., & Almaiah, M. A. (2021, July). Cybersecurity in Smart City: A systematic mapping study. In *2021 international conference on information technology (ICIT)* (pp. 719-724). IEEE.

Alanis, A. Y., Sanchez, O. D., Vaca-González, A., & Rangel-Heras, E. (2023). Intelligent Classification and Diagnosis of Diabetes and Impaired Glucose Tolerance Using Deep Neural Networks. *Mathematics*, 11(19), 4065. 10.3390/math11194065

Alarcón, P. A., Francisco, G. V., Guzmán, G. I. P., Cantillo, N. J., Cuevas, V. R. E., & Alonso, S. G. A. (2019). An IoT-based non-invasive glucose level monitoring system using Raspberry Pi. *Applied Sciences (Basel, Switzerland)*, 9(15), 3046. 10.3390/app9153046

Alasmari, S., & Anwar, M. (2016). *Security & privacy challenges in IoT-based health cloud.* In *Proceedings of the International Conference on Computational Science and Computational Intelligence (CSCI)* (pp. 198–201). Las Vegas, NV, USA. 10.1109/CSCI.2016.0044

Albahri, A. S., Duhaim, A. M., Fadhel, M. A., Alnoor, A., Baqer, N. S., Alzubaidi, L., Albahri, O. S., Alamoodi, A. H., Bai, J., Salhi, A., Santamaría, J., Ouyang, C., Gupta, A., Gu, Y., & Deveci, M. (2023). A systematic review of trustworthy and explainable artificial intelligence in healthcare: Assessment of quality, bias risk, and data fusion. *Information Fusion*, 96, 156–191. 10.1016/j.inffus.2023.03.008

Alfarizi, M., & Arifian, R. (2022). G20 Health Vision in Achieving SDGs 2030: Arranging the Global Health Management Architecture. *Insights in Public Health Journal*, 3(1), 1–12. 10.20884/1.iphj.2022.3.1.5565

Al-Haider, J., Al-Sharshani, S. M., Al-Sheraim, H. S., Subramanian, N., Al-Maadeed, S., & Chaari, M. z. (2020). Smart Medicine Planner for Visually Impaired People. *IEEE International Conference on Informatics, IoT, and Enabling Technologies (ICIoT).* IEEE. 10.1109/ICIoT48696.2020.9089536

Alharthi, N. G., Alzahrani, B. S., Alqurashi, B. S., Alsulami, A., & Alshehri, R. (2024). Recent Advancements in Robotic and Telesurgery Techniques: A Review. *Journal of Robotics*, 16(2), 1–10. 10.1155/2024/2139546

Ali, M. S., Ahmed, N. U., Zhang, L., & Khan, F. R. (2024). Recent advancements in robotics and telesurgery: A review of the literature. *Journal of Medical Robotics Research, 20*(4), 301-310. https://doi.org/10.1007/s12216-024-0042-x

Ali, M. (2023). A Comprehensive Review of AI's Impact on Healthcare: Revolutionizing Diagnostics and Patient Care. *BULLET: Jurnal Multidisiplin Ilmu*, 2(4), 1163–1173.

Al-Naji, A., Gibson, K., Lee, S.-H., & Chahl, J. (2017). Real time apnoea monitoring of children using the Microsoft Kinect sensor: A pilot study. *Sensors (Basel)*, 17(2), 286. 10.3390/s1702028628165382

Alourani, A., Tariq, K., Tahir, M., & Sardaraz, M. (2023). Patient Mortality Prediction and Analysis of Health Cloud Data Using a Deep Neural Network. *Applied Sciences (Basel, Switzerland)*, 13(4), 2391. 10.3390/app13042391

Alowais, S. A., Alghamdi, S. S., Alsuhebany, N., Alqahtani, T., Alshaya, A. I., Almohareb, S. N., Aldairem, A., Alrashed, M., Bin Saleh, K., Badreldin, H. A., Al Yami, M. S., Al Harbi, S., & Albekairy, A. M. (2023). Revolutionizing healthcare: The role of artificial intelligence in clinical practice. *BMC Medical Education*, 23(1), 689. 10.1186/s12909-023-04698-z37740191

AlQaheri, H., Sarkar, M., Gupta, S., & Gaur, B. (2022). Intelligent Cloud IoMT Health Monitoring-Based System for COVID-19. *Computers, Materials & Continua*, 72(1), 497–517. 10.32604/cmc.2022.022735

Al-Rawashdeh, M., Keikhosrokiani, P., Belaton, B., Alawida, M., & Zwiri, A. (2024). Effective factors for the adoption of IoT applications in nursing care: A theoretical framework for smart healthcare. *Journal of Building Engineering*, 89, 109012. 10.1016/j.jobe.2024.109012

Alsadoon, A., Al-Naymat, G., & Jerew, O. D. (2024). An architectural framework of elderly healthcare monitoring and tracking through wearable sensor technologies. *Multimedia Tools and Applications*, 1–46. 10.1007/s11042-024-18177-0

Alsadoon, A., Prasad, P. W. C., & Elchouemi, A. (2024). Effectiveness of wearable sensors and remote monitoring in elderly care. *Journal of Health Informatics*, 12(1), 45–57.

Alswedani, S. A., & Eassa, F. E. (2020). A smart baby cradle based on IoT. *Journal of Computer Science and Mobile Computing*, 9(7), 64–76.

Aminizadeh, S., Heidari, A., Toumaj, S., Darbandi, M., Navimipour, N. J., Rezaei, M., Talebi, S., Azad, P., & Unal, M. (2023). The applications of machine learning techniques in medical data processing based on distributed computing and the Internet of Things. *Computer Methods and Programs in Biomedicine*, 241, 107745. 10.1016/j.cmpb.2023.10774537579550

Amin, N., Song, H., & Ali, M. (2023). Role of information and communication technology, economic growth, financial development and renewable energy consumption towards the sustainable environment: Insights from ASEAN countries. *Environmental Science and Pollution Research International*, 30(38), 89381–89394. 10.1007/s11356-023-28720-537452245

Anand, N., Prathibha, P., Purohit, P., Nalamitha, R., & Rajarao Padma, C. (2021). Biometric Enabled Patient-Centric Automated Medication Dispenser Using IoT. In Smys, S., Palanisamy, R., Rocha, Á., & Beligiannis, G. N. (Eds.), *Computer Networks and Inventive Communication Technologies. Lecture Notes on Data Engineering and Communications Technologies* (Vol. 58). Springer. 10.1007/978-981-15-9647-6_43

Andrade, A. O., Pereira, A. A., Walter, S., Almeida, R., Loureiro, R., Compagna, D., & Kyberd, P. J. (2014). Bridging the gap between robotic technology and health care. *Biomedical Signal Processing and Control*, 10, 65–78. 10.1016/j.bspc.2013.12.009

Angelo, J. A. (2007). *Robotics: a reference guide to the new technology*. Greenwood Press.

Apu, A. I., Nayan, A. A., Ferdaous, J., & Kibria, M. G. (2022), IoT-Based Smart Blind Stick. *International Conference on Big Data, IoT, and Machine Learning. Lecture Notes on Data Engineering and Communications Technologies*. Springer, Singapore. 10.1007/978-981-16-6636-0_34

Aquino, R. P., Barile, S., Grasso, A., & Saviano, M. (2018, October 1). Envisioning smart and sustainable healthcare: 3D Printing technologies for personalized medication. *Futures*, 103, 35–50. 10.1016/j.futures.2018.03.002

Arbat, H., Choudhary, S., & Bala, K. (2016). IoT smart health band. *Imperial Journal of Interdisciplinary Research*, 2, 300–311.

Ardito, L., Raby, S., Albino, V., & Bertoldi, B. (2021). The duality of digital and environmental orientations in the context of SMEs: Implications for innovation performance. *Journal of Business Research*, 123, 44–56. 10.1016/j.jbusres.2020.09.022

Ardito, M., Mascolo, F., Valentini, M., & Dell'Olio, F. (2021). Low-Cost Wireless Wearable System for Posture Monitoring. *Electronics (Basel)*, 10(21), 2569. 10.3390/electronics10212569

Arevian, A. C., Bone, D., Malandrakis, N., Martinez, V. R., Wells, K. B., Miklowitz, D. J., & Narayanan, S. (2020). Clinical state tracking in serious mental illness through computational analysis of speech. *PLoS One*, 15(1), e0225695. 10.1371/journal.pone.022569531940347

Atzori, L., Iera, A., & Morabito, G. (2010). The Internet of Things: A survey. *Computer Networks*, 54(15), 2787–2805. 10.1016/j.comnet.2010.05.010

Ayaz, M., Ammad-Uddin, M., Sharif, Z., Mansour, A., & Aggoune, E.-H. M. (2019). Internet-of-Things (IoT)-based smart agriculture: Toward making the fields talk. *IEEE Access : Practical Innovations, Open Solutions*, 7, 129551–129583. 10.1109/ACCESS.2019.2932609

Aydın, N., & Yurdakul, G. (2020, December 1). Assessing countries' performances against COVID-19 via WSIDEA and machine learning algorithms. *Applied Soft Computing*, 97, 106792. 10.1016/j.asoc.2020.10679233071686

Ayesha, A., & Komalavalli, C. (2023). Smart Ambulance: A Comprehensive IoT and Cloud-Based System Integrating Fingerprint Sensor with Medical Sensors for Real-time Patient Vital Signs Monitoring. *International Journal of Intelligent Systems and Applications in Engineering*, 12(2), 555–567.

Ayon, S. I., & Islam, M. M. (2020). Coronary artery heart disease prediction: A comparative study of computational intelligence techniques. *Journal of the Institution of Electronics and Telecommunication Engineers*. 10.1080/03772063.2020.1713916

Azadi, S., Green, I. C., Arnold, A., Truong, M., Potts, J., & Martino, M. A. (2021). Robotic surgery: The impact of simulation and other innovative platforms on performance and training. *Journal of Minimally Invasive Gynecology*, 28(3), 490–495. 10.1016/j.jmig.2020.12.00133310145

Azzawi, M. A., Hassan, R., & Bakar, K. A. A. (2016). A review on Internet of Things (IoT) in healthcare. *International Journal of Applied Engineering Research: IJAER*, 11(20), 10216–10221.

Babu, B. S., Srikanth, K., Ramanjaneyulu, T., & Narayana, I. L. (2016). IoT for healthcare. *International Journal of Scientific Research*, 5(2), 322–326.

Badran, A. (2023). Developing smart cities: Regulatory and policy implications for the State of Qatar. *International Journal of Public Administration*, 46(7), 519–532. 10.1080/01900692.2021.2003811

Bailey, C., Smith, J., & Patel, K. (2024a). Addressing disparities in access to robotic-assisted surgery: Challenges and solutions. *Telemedicine and eHealth, 26*(2), 125-134. 10.1089/tmj.2024.0023

Bailey, C., Smith, J., Patel, K., Ali, M. S., Ahmed, N. U., & Khan, F. R. (2024). Equitable Access to Advanced Robotic and Telesurgical Platforms: An Overview. *Frontiers in Public Health*, 12, 875689. 10.3389/fpubh.2024.875689

Banerjee, S., & Roy, S. (2016). Design of a photo plethysmography-based pulse rate detector. *International Journal of Recent Trends in Engineering and Research*, 2, 302–306.

Barykin, S. E., Strimovskaya, A. V., Sergeev, S. M., Borisoglebskaya, L. N., Dedyukhina, N., Sklyarov, I., Sklyarova, J., & Saychenko, L. (2023). Smart City Logistics on the Basis of Digital Tools for ESG Goals Achievement. *Sustainability (Basel)*, 15(6), 5507. 10.3390/su15065507

Bauer, T., & Howe, R. D. (2012). Master-slave telexistence microsurgical system for eye operations. *IEEE Transactions on Neural Systems and Rehabilitation Engineering*, 20(3), 368–378. 10.1109/TNSRE.2012.2190761

BenMessaoud, C., Kharrazi, H., & MacDorman, K. F. (2011). Facilitators and barriers to adopting robotic-assisted surgery: Contextualizing the unified theory of acceptance and use of technology. *PLoS One*, 6(1), e16395. 10.1371/journal.pone.001639521283719

Bertuccio, S., Tardiolo, G., Giambò, F. M., Giuffrè, G., Muratore, R., Settimo, C., Raffa, A., Rigano, S., Bramanti, A., Muscarà, N., & De Cola, M. C. (2021). ReportFlow: An application for EEG visualization and reporting using cloud platform. *BMC Medical Informatics and Decision Making*, 21(1), 1–9. 10.1186/s12911-020-01369-733407445

Bhat, M. A., Gedik, K., & Gaga, E. O. (2023). Atmospheric micro (nano) plastics: Future growing concerns for human health. *Air Quality, Atmosphere & Health*, 16(2), 233–262. 10.1007/s11869-022-01272-236276170

Bhavsar, Y. S. (2020). Automatic Cradle System for Baby using Arduino. *International Journal Of Innovative Research In Technology*, 6(8), 5–8.

Bhayani, S. B. (2008). da Vinci robotic partial nephrectomy for renal cell carcinoma: An atlas of the four-arm technique. *Journal of Robotic Surgery*, 1(4), 279–285. 10.1007/s11701-007-0055-525484978

Bibri, S. E., & Krogstie, J. (2020). The emerging data–driven Smart City and its innovative applied solutions for sustainability: The cases of London and Barcelona. *Energy Informatics*, 3(1), 5. 10.1186/s42162-020-00108-6

Binet, A., Ballouhey, Q., Chaussy, Y., de Lambert, G., Braïk, K., Villemagne, T., Becmeur, F., Fourcade, L., & Lardy, H. (2018). Current perspectives in robot-assisted surgery. *Minerva Pediatrica*, 70(3), 308–314. 10.23736/S0026-4946.18.05113-729479943

Biswas, S., Pillai, S., Kadhim, H. M., Salam, Z. A., & Marhoon, H. A. (2023, September). Building business resilience and productivity in the healthcare industry with the integration of robotic process automation technology. In *AIP Conference Proceedings* (*Vol. 2736*, No. 1). AIP Publishing. 10.1063/5.0171098

Bora, G. S., Narain, T. A., Sharma, A. P., Mavuduru, R. S., Devana, S. K., Singh, S. K., & Mandal, A. K. (2020, January-March). Robot-assisted surgery in India: A SWOT analysis. *Indian Journal of Urology*, 36(1), 1–3. https://www.ncbi.nlm.nih.gov/pmc/articles/PMC6961426/#:~:text=After%20the%20US%20FDA%20approval,of%20robotic%20surgery%20in%20India. 10.4103/iju.IJU_220_1931983817

Bouramdane, A.-A. (2023). Optimal Water Management Strategies: Paving the Way for Sustainability in Smart Cities. *Smart Cities*, 6(5), 2849–2882. 10.3390/smartcities6050128

Bramhe, S., & Pathak, S. S. (2022). Robotic surgery: A narrative review. *Cureus*, 14(9).36258968

Broeders, I. A., & Ruurda, J. (2001). Robotics revolutionizing surgery: The Intuitive Surgical "Da Vinci" system. *The Industrial Robot*, 28(5), 387–392. 10.1108/EUM0000000005845

Brunetti, F., Matt, D. T., Bonfanti, A., De Longhi, A., Pedrini, G., & Orzes, G. (2020). Digital transformation challenges: Strategies emerging from a multi-stakeholder approach. *The TQM Journal*, 32(4), 697–724. 10.1108/TQM-12-2019-0309

Bujnowska-Fedak, M., & Grata-Borkowska, U. (2015). Use of telemedicine-based care for the aging and elderly promises and pitfalls. *Smart Homecare Technology and Telehealth*, 91. 10.2147/SHTT.S59498

Burke, M., Driscoll, A., Lobell, D. B., & Ermon, S. (2021). Using satellite imagery to understand and promote sustainable development. *Science*, 371(6535), eabe8628. 10.1126/science.abe862833737462

Bushnag, A. (2022). A Wireless ECG Monitoring and Analysis System Using the IoT Cloud. *Intelligent Automation & Soft Computing*, 33(1), 51–70. 10.32604/iasc.2022.024005

Calabrese, M., Suparaku, S., Santovito, S., & Hysa, X. (2023, July 25). Preventing and developmental factors of sustainability in healthcare organisations from the perspective of decision makers: An exploratory factor analysis. *BMC Health Services Research*, 23(1), 797. 10.1186/s12913-023-09689-w37491258

Calo, R. (2015). Robotics and the Lessons of Cyberlaw. *California Law Review*, 103, 513.

Camacho, N. G. (2024). The Role of AI in Cybersecurity: Addressing Threats in the Digital Age. *Journal of Artificial Intelligence General science (JAIGS), 3*(1), 143-154.

Cao, K., Hu, S., Shi, Y., Colombo, A. W., Karnouskos, S., & Li, X. (2021). A Survey on Edge and Edge-Cloud Computing Assisted Cyber-Physical Systems. *IEEE Transactions on Industrial Informatics*, 17(11), 7806–7819. 10.1109/TII.2021.3073066

Chaiyarab, L., Mopung, C., & Charoenpong, T. (2021). Authentication System by using HOG Face Recognition Technique and Web-Based for Medical Dispenser Machine. *IEEE 4th International Conference on Knowledge Innovation and Invention (ICKII)*. IEEE. 10.1109/ICKII51822.2021.9574661

Chan, B., Liu, S., & Wong, T. (2023). Impact of remote patient monitoring on hospitalization rates. *Journal of Medical Internet Research*, 25(3), e24567.

Chandar, A. G., Sivasankari, K., Lakshmi, S. L., Sugumaran, S., Kannadhasan, S., & Balakumar, S. (2024). An innovative smart agriculture system utilizing a deep neural network and embedded system to enhance crop yield. *Multidisciplinary Science Journal*, 6(5), 2024063–2024063. 10.31893/multiscience.2024065

Chan, E. Y. H., Liu, M. S., Or, P. C., & Ma, A. L. T. (2023). Outcomes and perception of cloud-based remote patient monitoring in children receiving automated peritoneal dialysis: A prospective study. *Pediatric Nephrology (Berlin, Germany)*, 38(7), 2171–2178. 10.1007/s00467-022-05828-336449100

Chauhan, A., Jakhar, S. K., & Jabbour, C. J. C. (2022, March 1). Implications for sustainable healthcare operations in embracing telemedicine services during a pandemic. *Technological Forecasting and Social Change*, 176, 121462. 10.1016/j.techfore.2021.12146235034990

Chau, M., & Arruzza, E. S. (2023). Maximising Undergraduate Medical Radiation Students' Learning Experiences Using Cloud-Based Computed Tomography (CT) Software. *Simulation & Gaming*, 54(4), 10468781231178491. 10.1177/10468781231178491

Chavan, P., More, P., Thorat, N., Yewale, S., & Dhade, P. (2016). ECG-Remote patient monitoring using cloud computing. *Imperial Journal of Interdisciplinary Research*, 2, 368–372.

Chen, B., Wan, J., Shu, L., Li, P., Mukherjee, M., & Yin, B. (2018). Smart factory of Industry 4.0: Key technologies, application case, and challenges. *IEEE Access : Practical Innovations, Open Solutions*, 6, 6505–6519. 10.1109/ACCESS.2017.2783682

Chen, D., Wawrzynski, P., & Lv, Z. (2021). Cyber security in smart cities: A review of deep learning-based applications and case studies. *Sustainable Cities and Society*, 66, 102655. 10.1016/j.scs.2020.102655

Chen, M. Y., & Janfial, R. (2009). The Practical Horizon for Robotic Neurosurgery. *Neurosurgery*, 65(3), N12. 10.1227/01.neu.0000359548.78214.d8

Chen, P. T., Lin, C. L., & Wu, W. N. (2020, August 1). Big data management in healthcare: Adoption challenges and implications. *International Journal of Information Management*, 53, 102078. 10.1016/j.ijinfomgt.2020.102078

Chen, X., Li, J., Chen, D., Zhou, Y., Tu, Z., Lin, M., Kang, T., Lin, J., Gong, T., Zhu, L., Zhou, J., Lin, O., Guo, J., Dong, J., Guo, D., & Qu, X. (2024). CloudBrain-MRS: An intelligent cloud computing platform for in vivo magnetic resonance spectroscopy preprocessing, quantification, and analysis. *Journal of Magnetic Resonance (San Diego, Calif.)*, 358, 107601. 10.1016/j.jmr.2023.10760138039654

Chen, X., Ma, M., & Liu, A. (2018). Dynamic power management and adaptive packet size selection for IoT in e-Healthcare. *Computers & Electrical Engineering*, 65, 375–57. 10.1016/j.compeleceng.2017.06.010

Chen, Y., Wang, X., Li, W., Yang, P., Cheng, Y., & Sun, Y. (2019). Remote minimally invasive spinal surgery assisted by 5G communication technology. *World Neurosurgery*, 122, 280.e8–280.e14. 10.1016/j.wneu.2019.01.125

Chen, Z., & Irene, C. C. C. (2023). Smart cities and quality of life: A quantitative analysis of citizens' support for smart city development. *Information Technology & People*, 36(1), 263–285. 10.1108/ITP-07-2021-0577

Chevance, G., Fresán, U., Hekler, E., Edmondson, D., Lloyd, S. J., Ballester, J., Litt, J., Cvijanovic, I., Araújo-Soares, V., & Bernard, P. (2023). Vera Araújo-Soares, and Paquito Bernard. "Thinking health-related behaviors in a climate change context: A narrative review.". *Annals of Behavioral Medicine*, 57(3), 193–204. 10.1093/abm/kaac03935861123

Chiang, M., & Zhang, T. (2016). Fog and IoT: An overview of research opportunities. *IEEE Internet of Things Journal*, 3(6), 854–864. 10.1109/JIOT.2016.2584538

Chi, H. R., Maria de Fátima, D., Zhu, H., Li, C., Kojima, K., & Radwan, A. (2023). Healthcare 5.0: In the Perspective of Consumer Internet-of-Things-Based Fog/Cloud Computing. *IEEE Transactions on Consumer Electronics*, 69(4), 745–755. 10.1109/TCE.2023.3293993

Choudhary, S., & Sharma, K. (2020). Role and impact of wearables in IoT healthcare. In *Proceedings of the Third International Conference on Computational Intelligence and Informatics* (pp. 735–742). Hyderabad, India.

Chughtai, M., Jauregui, J. J., Mistry, J. B., Elmallah, R. K., Diedrich, A. M., Bonutti, P. M., Delanois, R., & Mont, M. A. (2016). What Influences How Patients Rate Their Hospital After Total Knee Arthroplasty? *Surgical Technology International*, 28, 261–265.27042784

Claudet, J., Bopp, L., Cheung, W. W., Devillers, R., Escobar-Briones, E., Haugan, P., Heymans, J. J., Masson-Delmotte, V., Matz-Lück, N., Miloslavich, P., Mullineaux, L., Visbeck, M., Watson, R., Zivian, A. M., Ansorge, I., Araujo, M., Aricò, S., Bailly, D., Barbière, J., & Gaill, F. (2020). A roadmap for using the UN decade of ocean science for sustainable development in support of science, policy, and action. *One Earth*, 2(1), 34–42. 10.1016/j.oneear.2019.10.012

Condino, S., Turini, G., & Ferrari, V. (2021). Augmented reality in robotic surgery: State of the art and future perspectives. *Expert Review of Medical Devices*, 18(5), 435–449. 10.1080/17434440.2021.1876809

Corno, F., Russis, L., & Roffarello, A. M. (2016). A healthcare support system for assisted living facilities: An IoT solution. In *Proceedings of the IEEE 40th Annual Computer Software and Applications Conference (COMPSAC)* (pp. 344–352). Atlanta, GA, USA. 10.1109/COMPSAC.2016.29

D'Souza, M., Gendreau, J., Feng, A., Kim, L. H., Ho, A. L., & Veeravagu, A. (2019). Robotic- Assisted Spine Surgery: History, Efficacy, Cost, And Future Trends. *Robotic Surgery (Auckland)*, 6, 9–23. 10.2147/RSRR.S19072031807602

Dagliati, A., Malovini, A., Tibollo, V., & Bellazzi, R. (2021). Health informatics and EHR to support clinical research in the COVID-19 pandemic: An overview. *Briefings in Bioinformatics*, 22(2), 812–822. 10.1093/bib/bbaa41833454728

Dai, H. B., Wang, Z. C., Feng, X. B., Wang, G., Li, W. Y., Hang, C. H., & Jiang, Z. W. (2018). Case report about a successful full robotic radical gastric cancer surgery with intracorporeal robot-sewn anastomosis in a patient with situs inversus totalis and a two-and-a-half-year follow-up study. *World Journal of Surgical Oncology*, 16(1), 1–5. 10.1186/s12957-018-1311-z29499701

Danladi, S., Prasad, M. S. V., Modibbo, U. M., Ahmadi, S. A., & Ghasemi, P. (2023). Attaining Sustainable Development Goals through Financial Inclusion: Exploring Collaborative Approaches to Fintech Adoption in Developing Economies. *Sustainability (Basel)*, 15(17), 1–14. 10.3390/su151713039

Darshan, K. R., & Anandakumar, K. R. (2015). A comprehensive review on usage of Internet of Things (IoT) in healthcare system. In *Proceedings of the International Conference on Emerging Research in Electronics, Computer Science and Technology (ICERECT)* (pp. 132–136). Mandya, India. 10.1109/ERECT.2015.7499001

De Farias, F., Dagostini, C., Bicca, Y., Falavigna, V., Falavigna, A. Remote patient monitoring: a systematic review, Telemed. *e-Health 26*(5) (2020).

de Oliveira, M. T., Reis, L. H. A., Marquering, H., Zwinderman, A. H., & Olabarriaga, S. D. (2022). Perceptions of a Secure Cloud-Based Solution for Data Sharing During Acute Stroke Care: Qualitative Interview Study. *JMIR Formative Research*, 6(12), e40061. 10.2196/4006136563043

Deepa, N., Pham, Q. V., Nguyen, D. C., Bhattacharya, S., Prabadevi, B., Gadekallu, T. R., Maddikunta, P. K. R., Fang, F., & Pathirana, P. N. (2022). A survey on blockchain for big data: Approaches, opportunities, and future directions. *Future Generation Computer Systems*, 131, 209–226. 10.1016/j.future.2022.01.017

Demirel, D. (2023). The Impact of Managing Diversity on Building the Smart City A Comparison of Smart City Strategies: Cases From Europe, America, and Asia. *SAGE Open*, 13(3), 21582440231184971. 10.1177/21582440231184971

Denecke, K., & Baudoin, C. R. (2022). A review of artificial intelligence and robotics in transformed health ecosystems. *Frontiers in Medicine*, 9, 795957. 10.3389/fmed.2022.79595735872767

Deng, Z., Guo, L., Chen, X., & Wu, W. (2023). Smart Wearable Systems for Health Monitoring. *Sensors (Basel)*, 23(5), 2479. 10.3390/s2305247936904682

Deo, N., & Anjankar, A. (2023). Artificial Intelligence With Robotics in Healthcare: A Narrative Review of Its Viability in India. *Cureus*, 15(5). 10.7759/cureus.3941637362504

Devi DH, Duraisamy K, Armghan A, Alsharari M, Aliqab K, Sorathiya V, Das S, Rashid N (2023). 5G Technology in Healthcare and Wearable Devices: A Review. *Sensors*, *23*(5), 2519.

Devlin, J., Chang, M.-W., Lee, K., & Toutanova, K. (2019). BERT: Pre-training of deep bidirectional transformers for language understanding. In *NAACL-HLT 2019: Minneapolis, MN, USA - 1* (pp. 4171–4186).

Devliyal, S., Sharma, S., & Goyal, H. R. (2022). Cyber Physical System Architectures for Pharmaceutical Care Services: Challenges and Future Trends. *2022 IEEE International Conference on Current Development in Engineering and Technology (CCET.* (pp. 1-6). IEEE. 10.1109/CCET56606.2022.10080198

Dhinakaran, M., Phasinam, K., Alanya-Beltran, J., Srivastava, K., Babu, D. V., & Singh, S. K. (2022). A system of remote patients' monitoring and alerting using the machine learning technique. *Journal of Food Quality*, 2022, 2022. 10.1155/2022/6274092

Dicuonzo, G., Donofrio, F., Fusco, A., & Shini, M. (2023). Healthcare system: Moving forward with artificial intelligence. *Technovation*, 120, 102510. 10.1016/j.technovation.2022.102510

Ding, S., Tukker, A., & Ward, H. (2023). Opportunities and risks of internet of things (Io T) technologies for circular business models: A literature review. *Journal of Environmental Management*, 336, 117662. 10.1016/j.jenvman.2023.11766236913854

Djuric, A. M., Urbanic, R. J., & Rickli, J. L. (2016). A framework for collaborative robot (cobot) integration in advanced manufacturing systems. *SAE International Journal of Materials and Manufacturing*, 9(2), 457–463. 10.4271/2016-01-0337

Dohr, A., Modre, O. R., Drobics, M., Hayn, D., & Schreier, G. (2010). The internet of things for ambient assisted living. In *Proceedings of the IEEE Seventh International Conference on Information Technology: New Generations* (pp. 804–809). Las Vegas, NV, USA. 10.1109/ITNG.2010.104

Duman, Ü., & Aydin, E. (2020). IOT based baby cradle system with real time data tracking. In *2020 5th International Conference on Computer Science and Engineering (UBMK).* IEEE. 10.1109/UBMK50275.2020.9219506

Efron, B., & Hastie, T. (2021). *Computer age statistical inference, student edition: algorithms, evidence, and data science* (Vol. 6). Cambridge University Press. 10.1017/9781108914062

Egger, J., Wild, D., Weber, M., Bedoya, C. A. R., Karner, F., Prutsch, A., Schmied, M., Dionysio, C., Krobath, D., Jin, Y., Gsaxner, C., Li, J., & Pepe, A. (2022). Studierfenster: An open science cloud-based medical imaging analysis platform. *Journal of Digital Imaging*, 35(2), 340–355. 10.1007/s10278-021-00574-835064372

Egyud, M. R., & Burt, B. M. (2023). Robotic First Rib Resection and Robotic Chest Wall Resection. *Thoracic Surgery Clinics*, 33(1), 71–79. 10.1016/j.thorsurg.2022.08.00336372535

Electronic Wings. (n.d.). *LM35 temperature sensor*. Electronic Wings. https://www.electronicwings.com/sensors-modules/lm35-temperature-sensor

El-Rashidy, N., El-Sappagh, S., & Islam, S. M. R., M.El-Bakry H., & Abdelrazek S. (2021). Mobile health in Tele-health monitoringfor chronic diseases: Principles, trends, and challenges. *Diagnostics (Basel)*, 11(4), 607. 10.3390/diagnostics1104060733805471

Espressif Systems. (n.d.). *ESP32*. Espressif. https://www.espressif.com/en/products/socs/esp32

Fabrègue, B. F. G., & Bogoni, A.Fabrègue. (2023). Brian FG, and Andrea Bogoni. "Privacy and Security Concerns in the Smart City.". *Smart Cities*, 6(1), 586–613. 10.3390/smartcities6010027

Fabricatore, C., Dimitar, G., & Ximena, L. (2020). Rethinking serious games design in the age of COVID-19: Setting the focus on wicked problems. In *Joint International Conference on Serious Games* (pp. 243–259). Springer. 10.1007/978-3-030-61814-8_19

Fatima, Z., Tanveer, M., Zardari, S., Naz, L., Khadim, H., & Ahmed, N. (2022). Tahir,(2022) M. Production Plant and Warehouse Automation with IoT and Industry 5.0. *Applied Sciences (Basel, Switzerland)*, 12(4), 2053. 10.3390/app12042053

Fatlawi, H. K., & Kiss, A. (2022). An adaptive classification model for predicting epileptic seizures using cloud computing service architecture. *Applied Sciences (Basel, Switzerland)*, 12(7), 3408. 10.3390/app12073408

Fayad, M., Hachani, M.-Y., Ghoumid, K., Mostefaoui, A., Chouali, S., Picaud, F., Herlem, G., Lajoie, I., & Yahiaoui, R. (2023). Fall Detection Approaches for Monitoring Elderly HealthCare Using Kinect Technology: A Survey. *Applied Sciences (Basel, Switzerland)*, 13(18), 10352. 10.3390/app131810352

Ferro, E., & Potorti, F. (2018). Internet-of-Things and big data for smarter healthcare: From device to architecture, applications and analytics. *International Journal of Information Management*, 38(1), 1–9.

Feussner, H., Wilhelm, D., Navab, N., Knoll, A., & Lüth, T. (2018). Surgineering: A new type of collaboration among surgeons and engineers. *International Journal of Computer Assisted Radiology and Surgery*, 14(2), 187–190. 10.1007/s11548-018-1893-530539502

Fidan, I., Huseynov, O., Ali, M. A., Alkunte, S., Rajeshirke, M., Gupta, A., Hasanov, S., Tantawi, K., Yasa, E., Yilmaz, O., Loy, J., Popov, V., & Sharma, A. (2023). Recent inventions in additive manufacturing: Holistic review. *Inventions (Basel, Switzerland)*, 8(4), 103. 10.3390/inventions8040103

Firoozi, A. A., & Firoozi, A. A. (2023). A systematic review of the role of 4D printing in sustainable civil engineering solutions. *Heliyon*, 9(10), e20982. 10.1016/j.heliyon.2023.e2098237928382

Fischer, C., Pardos, Z. A., Baker, R. S., Williams, J. J., Smyth, P., Yu, R., Slater, S., Baker, R., & Warschauer, M. (2020). Mining big data in education: Affordances and challenges. *Review of Research in Education*, 44(1), 130–160. 10.3102/0091732X20903304

Fisher, A., Qureshi, H., & Siwicki, B. (2020). Cybersecurity in robotic surgery: A review of current challenges and future directions. *Journal of Healthcare Information Security*, 15(2), 101–113. 10.1089/jhis.2020.0007

Fouad, H., Hassanein, A. S., Soliman, A. M., & Al-Feel, H. (2020). Analyzing patient health information based on IoT sensor with AI for improving patient assistance in the future direction. *Measurement*, 159, 107757. 10.1016/j.measurement.2020.107757

Fraga-Lamas, P., Lopes, S. I., & Fernández-Caramés, T. M. (2021). Green IoT and edge AI as key technological enablers for a sustainable digital transition towards a smart circular economy: An industry 5.0 use case. *Sensors (Basel)*, 21(17), 5745. 10.3390/s2117574534502637

Frimpong, B. A., Barbosa, C., & Abd-Alhameed, R. A. (2023). The Impact of the Internet of Things (Io T) on Healthcare Delivery: A Systematic Literature Review. *Journal of Techniques*, 5(3), 84–91. 10.51173/jt.v5i3.1433

Fugkeaw, S., Wirz, L., & Hak, L. (2023). Secure and Lightweight Blockchain-enabled Access Control for Fog-Assisted IoT Cloud based Electronic Medical Records Sharing. *IEEE Access : Practical Innovations, Open Solutions*, 11, 62998–63012. 10.1109/ACCESS.2023.3288332

Garcia-Perez, A., Cegarra-Navarro, J. G., Sallos, M. P., Martinez-Caro, E., & Chinnaswamy, A. (2023). Resilience in healthcare systems: Cyber security and digital transformation. *Technovation*, 121, 102583. 10.1016/j.technovation.2022.102583

Gare, H. (2019). IOT based smart cradle system for baby monitoring. *International Research Journal of Engineering and Technology,6*.

Gayathri, S., & Gowri, S. (2022). CUNA: A privacy preserving medical records storage in cloud environment using deep encryption. *Measurement. Sensors*, 24, 100528. 10.1016/j.measen.2022.100528

George, A. S., George, A. H., & Martin, A. G. (2023). ChatGPT and the Future of Work: A Comprehensive Analysis of AI's Impact on Jobs and Employment. *Partners Universal International Innovation Journal*, 1(3), 154–186.

Georgilas, I., Dagnino, G., & Dogramadzi, S. (2017). Safe Human–Robot Interaction in Medical Robotics: A case study on Robotic Fracture Surgery System. *Journal of Medical Robotics Research*, 2(03), 1740008. 10.1142/S2424905X17400086

Ghazal, T. M., Hasan, M. K., Ahmad, M., Alzoubi, H. M., & Alshurideh, M. (2023). Machine Learning Approaches for Sustainable Cities Using Internet of Things. In *The Effect of Information Technology on Business and Marketing Intelligence Systems* (pp. 1969–1986). Springer International Publishing. 10.1007/978-3-031-12382-5_108

Gigli, M., & Koo, S. (2011). Internet of Things: Services and applications categorization. *Advances in Internet of Things*, 1(4), 27–31. 10.4236/ait.2011.12004

Ginoya, T., Maddahi, Y., & Zareinia, K. (2021). A historical review of medical robotic platforms. *Journal of Robotics*, 2021, 1–13. 10.1155/2021/6640031

Girard, N. J. (2017). Perioperative grand rounds: Robotic surgery: Risks vs. Rewards. *AORN Journal*, 106(2), 186–187. 10.1016/j.aorn.2017.05.00728755672

Goh, E. Z., & Ali, T. (2022). Robotic surgery: An evolution in practice. *Journal of Surgical Protocols and Research Methodologies*, 2022(1), snac003. 10.1093/jsprm/snac003

Gomathi, A. K. (2023). *Industry 5.0 for Healthcare 5.0: Opportunities, Challenges and Future Research Possibilities.* 2023 7th International Conference on Trends in Electronics and Informatics (ICOEI), Tirunelveli, India.

Gomez Ruiz, M. (2019). Present and future of robotic surgery. *Annals of Mediterranean Surgery*, 2(1), 1–2. 10.22307/2603.8706.2019.02.001

Gonzalez-Rivas, D., & Ismail, M. (2019). Subxiphoid or subcostal uniportal robotic-assisted surgery: Early experimental experience. *Journal of Thoracic Disease*, 11(1), 231–239. 10.21037/jtd.2018.12.9430863593

Gopal, V. (2023). Role of robotic technology in rehabilitation of patients with traumatic spinal cord injury and its future challenges. *Journal of Spine Surgery*, 10(1), 2. 10.4103/joss.joss_6_23

Gore, H. S., Shan, B. K., Jori, K. S., & Jachak, S. G. (2019). IOT Based Smart Cradle System for Baby Monitoring. *International Research Journal of Engineering and Technology*, 6(10), 2019.

Goswami, S. S., Sarkar, S., Gupta, K. K., & Mondal, S. (2023). The role of cyber security in advancing sustainable digitalization: Opportunities and challenges. *Journal of Decision Analytics and Intelligent Computing*, 3(1), 270–285. 10.31181/jdaic10018122023g

Goyal, M. (2013). Automatic E-Baby Cradle swing based on Baby Cry. *IJCA, 71*(21).

Grabowska, S. (2020). Smart factories in the age of Industry 4.0. *Management systems in production engineering, 28*(2), 90-96.

Gregoski, M. J., Mueller, M., Vertegel, A., Shaporev, A., Jackson, B. B., Frenzel, R. M., Sprehn, S. M., & Treiber, F. A. (2012). Development and validation of a smartphone heart rate acquisition application for health promotion and wellness telehealth applications. *International Journal of Telemedicine and Applications*, 2012, 1–7. 10.1155/2012/69632422272197

Gubbi, J., Buyya, R., Marusic, S., & Palaniswami, M. (2013). Internet of Things (IoT): A vision, architectural elements, and future directions. *Future Generation Computer Systems*, 29(7), 1645–1660. 10.1016/j.future.2013.01.010

Gutierrez LJ, Rabbani K, Ajayi OJ, Gebresilassie SK, Rafferty J, Castro LA, Banos O (2021). Internet of Things for Mental Health: Open Issues in Data Acquisition, Self-Organization, Service Level Agreement, and Identity Management. *Int J Environ Res Public Health, 18*(3), 1327.

Gyamfi, B. A., Ampomah, A. B., Bekun, F. V., & Asongu, S. A. (2022). Can information and communication technology and institutional quality help mitigate climate change in E7 economies? An environmental Kuznets curve extension. *Journal of Economic Structures*, 11(1), 1–20. 10.1186/s40008-022-00273-9

Haleem, A., Javaid, M., Vaishya, R., & Deshmukh, S. G. (2020). Areas of academic research with the application of internet of things. *Journal of Education and Health Promotion*, 9, 95. 10.4103/jehp.jehp_44_20

Hamed, A., Abdelaal, M. E., Elbeshbeshy, H. H., Khairy, A., & Abouelnaga, S. (2012). Advances in Haptics, Tactile Sensing, and Manipulation for Robot-Assisted Minimally Invasive Surgery, Noninvasive Surgery, and Diagnosis. *Journal of Robotics*, 2012, 1–13. 10.1155/2012/412816

Hamet, P., & Tremblay, J. (2017). Artificial intelligence in medicine. *Metabolism: Clinical and Experimental*, 69, S36–S40. 10.1016/j.metabol.2017.01.01128126242

Hamzehei, S., Akbarzadeh, O., Attar, H., Rezaee, K., Fasihihour, N., & Khosravi, M. R. (2023). Predicting the total Unified Parkinson's Disease Rating Scale (UPDRS) based on ML techniques and cloud-based update. *Journal of Cloud Computing (Heidelberg, Germany)*, 12(1), 1–16. 10.1186/s13677-022-00388-1

Haque, M. R., Islam, M. M., Iqbal, H., Reza, M. S., & Hasan, M. K. (2018). Performance evaluation of random forests and artificial neural networks for the classification of liver disorder. In *2018 International Conference on Computer, Communication, Chemical, Material and Electronic Engineering (IC4ME2)* (pp. 1–5). IEEE.

Haque, S., Aziz, S., & Rahman, M. (2014). Review of Cyber-Physical System in Healthcare. *International Journal of Distributed Sensor Networks*, 20.

Harry, A. (2023). The Future of Medicine: Harnessing the Power of AI for Revolutionizing Healthcare. *International Journal of Multidisciplinary Sciences and Arts*, 2(1), 36–47. 10.47709/ijmdsa.v2i1.2395

Hasan, M. K., Islam, M. M., & Hashem, M. M. A. (2016). Mathematical model development to detect breast cancer using multigene genetic programming. In *2016 5th International Conference on Informatics, Electronics and Vision (ICIEV)* (pp. 574–579). IEEE.

Hasan, M., Islam, M. M., Zarif, M. I. I., & Hashem, M. M. A. (2019). Attack and anomaly detection in IoT sensors in IoT sites using machine learning approaches. *Internet of Things : Engineering Cyber Physical Human Systems*, 7, 100059. 10.1016/j.iot.2019.100059

Hashimoto, D. A., Rosman, G., Rus, D., & Meireles, O. R. (2018). Artificial Intelligence in Surgery: Promises and Perils. *Annals of Surgery*, 268(1), 70–76. 10.1097/SLA.000000000000269329389679

Hastuti, R., & Syafruddin, . (2023). Ethical Considerations in the Age of Artificial Intelligence: Balancing Innovation and Social Values. *West Science Social and Humanities Studies*, 1(02), 76–87. 10.58812/wsshs.v1i02.191

Heemskerk, J., van Gemert, W. G., de Vries, J., Greve, J., & Bouvy, N. D. (2007). Learning Curves of Robot-assisted Laparoscopic Surgery Compared With Conventional Laparoscopic Surgery. *Surgical Laparoscopy, Endoscopy & Percutaneous Techniques*, 17(3), 171–174. 10.1097/SLE.0b013e31805b834617581459

Hernandez, N., Castro, L., Medina-Quero, J., Favela, J., Michan, L., & Mortenson, W. B. (2021). Scoping Review of Healthcare Literature on Mobile, Wearable, and Textile Sensing Technology for Continuous Monitoring. *Journal of Healthcare Informatics Research*, 5(3), 270–299. 10.1007/s41666-020-00087-z33554008

Hiremath, B. N., Chavhan, K., Johnson, N. J., & Monika, P. (2022). Automatic Medication Dispensing System using Machine Learning, Internet of Things and Cloud Computing.*International Conference on Disruptive Technologies for Multi-Disciplinary Research and Applications(CENTCON)*, Bengaluru, India. 10.1109/CENTCON56610.2022.10051452

Hotur, V. P., Abhishek, P., Chethan, R., & Bhatta, A. (2021, June). Internet of Things-based Baby Monitoring System for Smart Cradle. In *2021 International Conference on Design Innovations for 3Cs Compute Communicate Control (ICDI3C)* (pp. 265-270). IEEE. 10.1109/ICDI3C53598.2021.00060

Humayun, M., Jhanjhi, N. Z., Almotilag, A., & Almufareh, M. F. (2022). Agent-Based Medical Health Monitoring System. *Sensors (Basel)*, 22(8), 2820. 10.3390/s2208282035458805

Hunter, D. J., & Bengoa, R. (2023). Meeting the challenge of health system transformation in European countries. *Policy and Society*, 42(1), 14–27. 10.1093/polsoc/puac022

Huntsman, K. T., Ahrendtsen, L. A., Riggleman, J. R., & Ledonio, C. G. (2019). Robotic-assisted navigated minimally invasive pedicle screw placement in the first 100 cases at a single institution. *Journal of Robotic Surgery*, 23, 1–7.31016575

Hussain, M. A., Benlamri, R., & Naqvi, S. R. (2020). Opportunities and challenges of the Internet of Things (IoT) in healthcare: A comprehensive review. *Journal of Ambient Intelligence and Humanized Computing*, 11, 4529–4558. 10.1007/s12652-019-01537-7

Hussain, T., Muhammad, K., Khan, S., Ullah, A., Lee, M. Y., & Baik, S. W. (2019). Intelligent baby behavior monitoring using embedded vision in IoT for smart healthcare centers. *Journal of Artificial Intelligence and Systems*, 1(1), 110–124. 10.33969/AIS.2019.11007

Ibn-Mohammed, T., Mustapha, K. B., Godsell, J., Adamu, Z., Babatunde, K. A., Akintade, D. D., Acquaye, A. A., Fujii, H., Ndiaye, M. M., Yamoah, F. A., & Koh, S. C. L. (2021). A critical analysis of the impacts of COVID-19 on the global economy and ecosystems and opportunities for circular economy strategies. *Resources, Conservation and Recycling*, 164, 105169. 10.1016/j.resconrec.2020.10516932982059

Ietto, B., Ancillai, C., Sabatini, A., Carayannis, E. G., & Gregori, G. L. (2022). The role of external actors in SMEs' human centered industry 4.0 adoption: An empirical perspective on Italian competence centres. *IEEE Transactions on Engineering Management*, 7, 12.

Iheanacho, C. O., Adeyeri, O., & Eze, U. I. H. (2022). Evolving role of pharmacy technicians in pharmaceutical care services: Involvement in counselling and medication reviews. *Exploratory Research in Clinical and Social Pharmacy*, 5, 100113. 10.1016/j.rcsop.2022.10011335478530

Iranpak, S., Shahbahrami, A., & Shakeri, H. (2021). Tele-health monitoring and classifying using the internet of things platform combined with cloud computing. *Journal of Big Data*, 8(1), 120. 10.1186/s40537-021-00507-w

Islam, M. M., Iqbal, H., Haque, M. R., & Hasan, M. K. (2017). Prediction of breast cancer using support vector machine and K-nearest neighbors. In *2017 IEEE Region 10 humanitarian technology conference (R10-HTC)* (pp. 226–229). IEEE..

Islam, M., Neom, N., Imtiaz, M., Nooruddin, S., & Islam, M. (2019). A review on fall detection systems using data from smartphone sensors. Ingénierie des systèmes d'Information, 24, 569–576. 10.18280/isi.240602

Islam, A. S., & Milon Islam, M. (2019). Diabetes prediction: A deep learning approach. *International Journal of Information Engineering and Electronic Business*, 11(2), 21–27. 10.5815/ijieeb.2019.02.03

Islam, M. M., & Bhuiyan, Z. A. (2023). An Integrated Scalable Framework for Cloud and IoT Based Green Healthcare System. *IEEE Access : Practical Innovations, Open Solutions*, 11, 22266–22282. 10.1109/ACCESS.2023.3250849

Ismatullaev, U. V. U., & Kim, S. H. (2024). Review of the factors affecting acceptance of AI-infused systems. *Human Factors*, 66(1), 126–144. 10.1177/00187208211064707335344676

Jabbar, W. A., Shang, H. K., Hamid, S. N., Almohammedi, A. A., Ramli, R. M., & Ali, M. A. (2019). IoT-BBMS: Internet of Things-based baby monitoring system for smart cradle. *IEEE Access : Practical Innovations, Open Solutions*, 7, 93791–93805. 10.1109/ACCESS.2019.2928481

Jara, A. J., Zamora, M. A., & Skarmeta, A. F. (2014). Interconnection framework for mHealth and remote monitoring based on the Internet of Things. *IEEE Journal on Selected Areas in Communications*, 32(4), 647–654. 10.1109/JSAC.2014.140405

Javaid, M., Haleem, A., Singh, R. P., & Suman, R. (2020b). Internet of things (IoT) applications to fight against COVID-19 pandemic. *Diabetes & Metabolic Syndrome*, 14(4), 521–524. 10.1016/j.dsx.2020.04.03232388333

Jivrajani, K. (2023). AIoT-Based Smart Stick for Visually Impaired Person. *IEEE Transactions on Instrumentation and Measurement*. IEEE. 10.1109/TIM.2022.3227988

José, M. G. S., Jörgensen, N., Törngren, M., Inam, R., Berezovskyi, A., Feng, L., Fersman, E., Ramli, M. R., & Tan, K. (2022). Edge Computing for Cyber-physical Systems: A Systematic Mapping Study Emphasizing Trustworthiness. *ACM Trans. Cyber-Phys. Syst.* ACM.

Joseph, S., Kumar, A., & Babu, M. H. (2021, March). IOT Based Baby Monitoring System Smart Cradle. In *2021 7th International Conference on Advanced Computing and Communication Systems (ICACCS)* (Vol. 1, pp. 748-751). IEEE. 10.1109/ICACCS51430.2021.9442022

Joshi, M. P., & Mehetre, D. C. (2017). IoT based smart cradle system with an Android app for baby monitoring. *2017 International Conference on Computing, Communication, Control and Automation (ICCUBEA)*. IEEE. 10.1109/ICCUBEA.2017.8463676

Jouaiti, M., & Dautenhahn, K. (2022). Dysfluency classification in stuttered speech using deep learning for real-time applications. In *ICASSP 2022-2022 IEEE International Conference on Acoustics, Speech and Signal Processing (ICASSP)* (pp. 6482–6486). IEEE.

Juengst, S. B., Terhorst, L., Nabasny, A., Wallace, T., Weaver, J. A., Osborne, C. L., Burns, S. P., Wright, B., Wen, P.-S., Kew, C.-L. N., & Morris, J. (2021). Use of mHealth Technology for Patient-Reported Outcomes in Community-Dwelling Adults with Acquired Brain Injuries: A Scoping Review. *International Journal of Environmental Research and Public Health*, 18(4), 2173. 10.3390/ijerph1804217333672183

Jung, Y. W., Kim, D. Y., Lee, J. S., Han, D. H., Cho, J. H., Choi, J. H., & Nam, S. B. (2009). Recent Advances of Robotic Surgery and Single Port Laparoscopy in Gynecologic Oncology. *Journal of Gynecologic Oncology*, 20(4), 285–291. 10.3802/jgo.2009.20.3.13719809546

Jusak, J., Mahmoud, S. S., Laurens, R., Alsulami, M., & Fang, Q. (2021). A new approach for secure cloud-based Electronic Health Record and its experimental testbed. *IEEE Access : Practical Innovations, Open Solutions*, 10, 1082–1095. 10.1109/ACCESS.2021.3138135

Kag, M., Hagras, H., Colley, M., & Jovanovic, A. (2015). A flexible architecture for adaptive ambient intelligence in e-healthcare applications. *Procedia Computer Science*, 52, 454–459. 10.1016/j.procs.2015.05.028

Kaiser, M. S., Al Mamun, S., Mahmud, M., & Tania, M. H. (2021). *Healthcare robots to combat COVID-19. COVID-19: Prediction*. Decision-Making, and Its Impacts.

Kallidonis, P., Tatanis, V., Peteinaris, A., Katsakiori, P., Gkeka, K., Faitatziadis, S., Vagionis, A., Vrettos, T., Stolzenburg, J. U., & Liatsikos, E. (2023). Robot-assisted pyeloplasty for ureteropelvic junction obstruction: Initial experience with the novel avatera system. *World Journal of Urology*, 41(11), 3155–3160. 10.1007/s00345-023-04586-737668715

Kampa, R. K. (2023). *Combining technology readiness and acceptance model for investigating the acceptance of m-learning in higher education in India*. Asian Association of Open Universities Journal. 10.1108/AAOUJ-10-2022-0149

Kamruzzaman, M. M., & Yan, B. (2022). Md Nazirul Islam Sarker, Omar Alruwaili, Min Wu, and Ibrahim Alrashdi. "Blockchain and fog computing in Io T-driven healthcare services for smart cities.". *Journal of Healthcare Engineering*, 2022.

Kao, Y. M., Lin, C. H., & Hsu, Y. L. (2020). Advanced cloud-based IoT platform for intelligent healthcare. *Sensors (Basel)*, 20(12), 3462.32575449

Karar, M. E., Shehata, H. I., & Reyad, O. (2022). A Survey of IoT-Based Fall Detection for Aiding Elderly Care: Sensors, Methods, Challenges and Future Trends. *Applied Sciences (Basel, Switzerland)*, 12(7), 3276. 10.3390/app12073276

Karatas, M., Eriskin, L., Deveci, M., Pamucar, D., & Garg, H. (2022). Big Data for Healthcare Industry 4.0: Applications, challenges and future perspectives. *Expert Systems with Applications*, 200, 116912. 10.1016/j.eswa.2022.116912

Karliner, J., Slotterback, S., Boyd, R., Ashby, B., Steele, K., & Wang, J. (2020). Health care's climate footprint: The health sector contribution and opportunities for action. *European Journal of Public Health*, 30(Supplement_5), ckaa165–843. 10.1093/eurpub/ckaa165.843

Karthik, K., Colegate-Stone, T., Dasgupta, P., Tavakkolizadeh, A., & Sinha, J. (2015). Robotic surgery in trauma and orthopaedics: A systematic review. *The Bone & Joint Journal*, 97-B(3), 292–299. 10.1302/0301-620X.97B3.3510725737510

Kasinathan, P., Pugazhendhi, R., Elavarasan, R., Ramachandaramurthy, V., Ramanathan, V., Subramanian, S., Kumar, S., Nandhagopal, K., Raghavan, R. R. V., Rangasamy, S., Devendiran, R., & Alsharif, M. H. (2022). Realization of Sustainable Development Goals with Disruptive Technologies by Integrating Industry 5.0, Society 5.0, Smart Cities and Villages. *Sustainability (Basel)*, 2022(14), 15258. 10.3390/su142215258

Kasula, B. Y. (2023). Framework Development for Artificial Intelligence Integration in Healthcare: Optimizing Patient Care and Operational Efficiency. *Transactions on Latest Trends in IoT*, 6(6), 77–83.

Kato, K., Yoshimi, T., Aimoto, K., Sato, K., Itoh, N., & Kondo, I. (2023). Reduction of multiple-caregiver assistance through the long-term use of a transfer support robot in a nursing facility. *Assistive Technology*, 35(3), 271–278. 10.1080/10400435.2022.203932435320681

Kaur, J. (2024). Fueling Healthcare Transformation: The Nexus of Startups, Venture Capital, and Innovation. In *Fostering Innovation in Venture Capital and Startup Ecosystems* (pp. 327-351). IGI Global.

Kaur, J. (2024). Green Finance 2.0: Pioneering Pathways for Sustainable Development and Health Through Future Trends and Innovations. In *Sustainable Investments in Green Finance* (pp. 294-319). IGI Global.

Kaur, J. (2024). Green Guardians: Unveiling the Strategic Role of HR in Environmental Sustainability Initiatives. In *Building Sustainable Human Resources Management Practices for Businesses* (pp. 125-143). IGI Global.

Kaur, J. (2024). Green Healthcare in Smart Cities: Harnessing Io T for Sustainable Transformation of Healthcare Systems. In *Secure and Intelligent Io T-Enabled Smart Cities* (pp. 334-354). IGI Global.

Kaur, J. (2024). Insightful Visions: How Medical Imaging Empowers Patient-Centric Healthcare. In *Future of AI in Medical Imaging* (pp. 42-57). IGI Global.

Kaur, J. (2024). Robotics Rx: A Prescription for the Future of Healthcare. In *Applications of Virtual and Augmented Reality for Health and Wellbeing* (pp. 217-238). IGI Global. 10.4018/979-8-3693-1123-3.ch012

Kaur, J. (2024). Towards a Sustainable Triad: Uniting Energy Management Systems, Smart Cities, and Green Healthcare for a Greener Future. In *Emerging Materials, Technologies, and Solutions for Energy Harvesting* (pp. 258-285). IGI Global.

Kaur, J. (2024). Virtual Insights, Real Solutions: The Promise of Augmented Reality in Medicine. In *Approaches to Human-Centered AI in Healthcare* (pp. 20-41). IGI Global.

Kenney, M., Serhan, H., & Trystram, G. (2020). Digitization and platforms in agriculture: organizations, power asymmetry, and collective action solutions. *Power Asymmetry, and Collective Action Solutions.*

Khaddad, A., Bernhard, J. C., Margue, G., Michiels, C., Ricard, S., Chandelon, K., Bladou, F., Bourdel, N., & Bartoli, A. (2023). A survey of augmented reality methods to guide minimally invasive partial nephrectomy. *World Journal of Urology*, 41(2), 335–343. 10.1007/s00345-022-04078-035776173

Khan, F. A., Asif, M., Ahmad, A., Alharbi, M., & Aljuaid, H. (2020). Blockchain technology, improvement suggestions, security challenges on smart grid and its application in healthcare for sustainable development. *Sustainable Cities and Society*, 55, 102018. 10.1016/j.scs.2020.102018

Khang, A., Hahanov, V., Litvinova, E., Chumachenko, S., Hajimahmud, A. V., Ali, R. N., & Anh, P. T. N. (2023). The Analytics of Hospitality of Hospitals in a Healthcare Ecosystem. In *Data-Centric AI Solutions and Emerging Technologies in the Healthcare Ecosystem* (pp. 39–61). CRC Press. 10.1201/9781003356189-4

Khan, I. H., Khan, S., & Ghani, I. (2021). Internet of things (IoT) in healthcare: A comprehensive literature review. *International Journal of Engineering Business Management*, 13, 1–15. 10.1177/18479790211007373

Khanna, S., Srivastava, S., Khanna, I., & Pandey, V. (2020). Ethical Challenges Arising from the Integration of Artificial Intelligence (AI) in Oncological Management. *International Journal of Responsible Artificial Intelligence*, 10(8), 34–44.

Kharrazi, A., Qin, H., & Zhang, Y. (2016). Urban big data and sustainable development goals: Challenges and opportunities. *Sustainability (Basel)*, 8(12), 1293. 10.3390/su8121293

Khlopas, A., Sodhi, N., Hozack, W. J., Chen, A. F., Mahoney, O. M., Kinsey, T., Orozco, F., & Mont, M. A. (2020). Patient-Reported Functional and Satisfaction Outcomes after Robotic- Arm-Assisted Total Knee Arthroplasty: Early Results of a Prospective Multicenter Investigation. *The Journal of Knee Surgery*, 33(7), 685–690. 10.1055/s-0039-168401430959541

Kim, J., Gu, G. M., & Heo, P. (2016). Robotics for healthcare. *Biomedical Engineering: Frontier Research and Converging Technologies*, 489-509.

Kim, J. H., Park, S. H., & Lee, J. S. (2018). Haptic feedback in robotic surgery: Current trends and future perspectives. *International Journal of Medical Robotics and Computer Assisted Surgery*, 14(3), e1901. 10.1002/rcs.190129577580

Kim, M., Zhang, Y., & Jin, S. (2023). Soft tissue surgical robot for minimally invasive surgery: A review. *Biomedical Engineering Letters*, 13(4), 1–9. 10.1007/s13534-023-00326-337872994

Kim, Y. J., Choi, J. H., & Fotso, G. M. N. (2024). Medical professionals' adoption of AI-based medical devices: UTAUT model with trust mediation. *Journal of Open Innovation*, 10(1), 100220. 10.1016/j.joitmc.2024.100220

Kivnick, S., & Parker, W. (2013). Robot-Assisted Laparoscopic Myomectomy Compared With Standard Laparoscopic Myomectomy. *Obstetrics and Gynecology*, 121(1), 188. 10.1097/AOG.0b013e31827b157b23262947

Krizea, M., Gialelis, J., Protopsaltis, G., Mountzouris, C., & Theodorou, G. (2022). Empowering People with a User-Friendly Wearable Platform for Unobtrusive Monitoring of Vital Physiological Parameters. *Sensors (Basel)*, 22(14), 5226. 10.3390/s2214522635890907

Kumar, A., Khan, S. B., Pandey, S. K., Shankar, A., Maple, C., Mashat, A., & Malibari, A. A. (2023). Development of a cloud-assisted classification technique for the preservation of secure data storage in smart cities. *Journal of Cloud Computing (Heidelberg, Germany)*, 12(1), 92. 10.1186/s13677-023-00469-9

Kumar, A., Rajput, N., Sharma, N., Kumar, V., & Bhagat, S. (2021). Wearable sensor-based IoT framework for remote monitoring of COVID-19 patients at home isolation. *Arabian Journal for Science and Engineering*, 46, 5051–5064. 10.1007/s13369-021-05516-2

Kumari, S., Gupta, D., & Bashir, A. K. (2024). Advanced Computing Technologies for Energy-Efficient and Secure Io T Network in Smart Cities: Green Io T Perspective. In *Emerging Technologies and the Application of WSN and Io T* (pp. 65-82). CRC Press.

Kumar, P., Chauhan, S., & Awasthi, L. K. (2023). Artificial intelligence in healthcare: Review, ethics, trust challenges & future research directions. *Engineering Applications of Artificial Intelligence*, 120, 105894. 10.1016/j.engappai.2023.105894

Kumar, R., & Yan, L. L. (2013). Health monitoring system based on Internet of Things. *Journal of Software*, 8(4), 917–923. 10.4304/jsw.8.4.917-923

Kumar, S., Patel, N., & Reddy, P. J. (2024). Navigating Healthcare in a Crisis: Understanding Health Literacy and Medical Tourism. In Papalois, V., & Papalois, K. (Eds.), *The Role of Health Literacy in Major Healthcare Crises* (pp. 1–18). IGI Global. 10.4018/978-1-7998-9652-4.ch001

Kumar, S., Sharma, D., Rao, S., Lim, W. M., & Mangla, S. K. (2022). Past, present, and future of sustainable finance: Insights from big data analytics through machine learning of scholarly research. *Annals of Operations Research*, 1–44. 10.1007/s10479-021-04410-835002001

Kumar, S., Yadav, M., & Kumar, D. (2024). Viability of Man and Machine as Co-Workers in the Hotel Industry. In Nozari, H. (Ed.), *Building Smart and Sustainable Businesses With Transformative Technologies* (pp. 189–204). IGI Global. 10.4018/979-8-3693-0210-1.ch011

Kumar, V., Park, J. O., Kumar, A., Mohammed, K., & Agarwal, S. (2013). Cost analysis of robotic versus conventional laparoscopic donor nephrectomy – our initial experience. *Indian Journal of Transplantation*, 17(Suppl 1), 27–31. 10.4103/0971-6066.120186

Kushwah, V. S., Parashar, J., & Bajpai, A. (2022). Study of Load Balancing and Security in Cloud Computing. In Soft Computing: Theories and Applications [Singapore: Springer Nature Singapore.]. *Proceedings of SoCTA*, 2021, 565–576.

Kushwah, V. S., & Saxena, A. (2013). A security approach for data migration in cloud computing. *International Journal of Scientific and Research Publications*, 3(5), 1–8.

Kyrarini, M., Lygerakis, F., Rajavenkatanarayanan, A., Sevastopoulos, C., Nambiappan, H. R., Chaitanya, K. K., Babu, A. R., Mathew, J., & Makedon, F. (2021). A survey of robots in healthcare. *Technologies*, 9(1), 8. 10.3390/technologies9010008

La Rosa R, Livreri P, Trigona C, Di Donato L, Sorbello G (2019). Strategies and Techniques for Powering Wireless Sensor Nodes through Energy Harvesting and Wireless Power Transfer. *Sensors,19*(12), 2660.

Laguarta, J., Hueto, F., & Subirana, B. (2020). COVID-19 artificial intelligence diagnosis using only cough recordings. *IEEE Open Journal of Engineering in Medicine and Biology*, 1, 275–281. 10.1109/OJEMB.2020.302692834812418

Lakshminarayanan, V., Zelek, J., & McBride, A. (2015). Smartphone science "in eye care and medicine" in Eye Care and Medicine. *Optics and Photonics News*, 26(1), 44–51. 10.1364/OPN.26.1.000044

Lanfranco, A. R., Castellanos, A. E., Desai, J. P., & Meyers, W. C. (2004). Robotic surgery: A current perspective. *Annals of Surgery*, 239(1), 14–21. 10.1097/01.sla.0000103020.19595.7d14685095

Lazar, J. F., & Hwalek, A. E. (2022). A review of robotic thoracic surgery adoption and future innovations. *Thoracic Surgery Clinics*, 33(1), 1–10. 10.1016/j.thorsurg.2022.07.01036372526

Leal Filho, W., Eustachio, J. H. P. P., Nita, A. C., Dinis, M. A. P., Salvia, A. L., Cotton, D. R., & Dibbern, T. (2024). Using data science for sustainable development in higher education. *Sustainable Development*, 32(1), 15–28. 10.1002/sd.2638

Lee, H. K., Lee, K. E., Ku, J., & Lee, K. H. (2021). Revo-i: The competitive Korean surgical robot. *Gynecologic Robotic Surgery*, 2(2), 45–52. 10.36637/grs.2021.00059

Lee, H. S., Yap, L. T., Lee, S. Y., & Har, W. M. (2024). The Impacts of ICT and innovation on Carbon Dioxide Emissions in G20 Countries. *IOP Conference Series. Earth and Environmental Science*, 1303(1), 1–10. 10.1088/1755-1315/1303/1/012011

Lee, J., Kao, H. A., & Yang, S. (2014). Service innovation and smart analytics for industry 4.0 and big data environment. *Procedia CIRP*, 16, 3–8. 10.1016/j.procir.2014.02.001

Lee, S. K., & Kim, S. K. (2017). An adaptive health IoT platform based on open source M2M/IoT middleware. *Journal of Healthcare Engineering*, 2017, 1–9. 10.1155/2017/3451052

Leo, D. (2022). Interactive Remote Patient Monitoring Devices for Managing Chronic Health Conditions: Systematic Review and Meta-analysis. *J Med Internet Res., 24*(11)

Liang, Y., Zhang, D., Chen, G., & Zhang, L. (2021). IoT-enabled smart health: An overview. *IEEE Access : Practical Innovations, Open Solutions*, 9, 140934–140959. 10.1109/ACCESS.2021.3079969

Li, K., & Warren, S. (2012). A wireless reflectance pulse oximeter with digital baseline control for unfiltered photoplethysmograms. *IEEE Transactions on Biomedical Circuits and Systems*, 6(3), 269–278. 10.1109/TBCAS.2011.216771723853148

Lin, X., Mahmud, S., Jones, E., Shaker, A., Miskinis, A., Kanan, S., & Kim, J.-H. (2020). Virtual reality-based musical therapy for mental health management. In *2020 10th Annual Computing and Communication Workshop and Conference (CCWC)* (pp. 948–952). IEEE. 10.1109/CCWC47524.2020.9031244

Lin, T., Rivano, H., & Le Mouel, F. (2017). A survey of smart parking solutions. *IEEE Transactions on Intelligent Transportation Systems*, 18(12), 3229–3253. 10.1109/TITS.2017.2685143

Li, S., Xu, L. D., & Zhao, S. (2015). The internet of things: A survey. *Information Systems Frontiers*, 17(2), 243–259. 10.1007/s10796-014-9492-7

Liu, Y., Ott, M., Goyal, N., Du, J., Joshi, M., Chen, D., Levy, O., Lewis, M., Zettlemoyer, L., & Stoyanov, V. (2019). RoBERTa: A robustly optimized BERT pretraining approach. CoRR abs/1907.11692.

Liu, Q., Huang, B., He, S., Tan, S., & Dai, H. (2024). Evaluation and improvement of simulation-based virtual reality training programmes for robotic-assisted laparoscopic surgery. *International Journal of Medical Robotics and Computer Assistance*, 10(2), 180–188. 10.1002/rcs.1956

Li, X., Zhang, C., & Zhu, H. (2023). Effect of information and communication technology on CO2 emissions: An analysis based on country heterogeneity perspective. *Technological Forecasting and Social Change*, 192, 122599. 10.1016/j.techfore.2023.122599

Lochan, K., Suklyabaidya, A., & Roy, B. K. (2023). Medical and healthcare robots in India. In *Medical and Healthcare Robotics* (pp. 221–236). Academic Press. 10.1016/B978-0-443-18460-4.00010-X

Longmore, S. K., Naik, G., & Gargiulo, G. D. (2020). Laparoscopic Robotic Surgery: Current Perspective and Future Directions. *Robotics (Basel, Switzerland)*, 9(2), 42. 10.3390/robotics9020042

Mahalingam, H., Velupillai Meikandan, P., Thenmozhi, K., Moria, K. M., Lakshmi, C., Chidambaram, N., & Amirtharajan, R. (2023). Neural Attractor-Based Adaptive Key Generator with DNA-Coded Security and Privacy Framework for Multimedia Data in Cloud Environments. *Mathematics*, 11(8), 1769. 10.3390/math11081769

Mahmood, Z. H., & Almohammed, S. A. (2015). Internet of Things (IoT): Application in agriculture and health care. *International Journal of Computer Applications*, 124(3), 32–35. 10.5120/ijca2015906234

Mahmoud, H., Aljaldi, F., El-Fiky, A., Battecha, K., Thabet, A., Alayat, M., & Ibrahim, A. (2023). Artificial Intelligence machine learning and conventional physical therapy for upper limb outcome in patients with stroke: A systematic review and meta-analysis. *European Review for Medical and Pharmacological Sciences*, 27(11).37318455

Mahmoud, M. S., Khaled, A. A., & Adel, A. E. (2018). A proposed internet of things (IoT) healthcare framework. In *Proceedings of the International Conference on Advanced Intelligent Systems and Informatics (AISI)*. Cairo, Egypt.

Mahmud, S., Lin, X., Kim, J.-H., Iqbal, H., Rahat-Uz-Zaman, M., Reza, S., & Rahman, M. A. (2019). A multi-modal human-machine interface for controlling a smart wheelchair. In *2019 IEEE 7th Conference on Systems, Process, and Control (ICSPC)* (pp. 10–13). IEEE. 10.1109/ICSPC47137.2019.9068027

Majeed, M., Afza, A., Khan, R. A., & Sharif, M. (2021). IoT-enabled healthcare system: Architecture, applications, and recent advancements. *IEEE Access : Practical Innovations, Open Solutions*, 9, 49748–49779. 10.1109/ACCESS.2021.3060281

Majumder, S., Deen, M. J., & Uddin, M. N. (2019). Smart health and big data analytics for COVID-19 management. *The Science of the Total Environment*, 743, 140123. 10.1016/j.scitotenv.2020.140123

Malche, T., Tharewal, S., Tiwari, P. K., Jabarulla, M. Y., Alnuaim, A. A., Hatamleh, W. A., & Ullah, M. A. (2022). Artificial intelligence of things- (AIoT-) based patient activity tracking system for remote patient monitoring. *Journal of Healthcare Engineering*, 2022, 2022. 10.1155/2022/873221335273786

Man, Z., Li, J., Di, X., Zhang, R., Li, X., & Sun, X. (2023). Research on cloud data encryption algorithm based on bidirectional activation neural network. *Information Sciences*, 622, 629–651. 10.1016/j.ins.2022.11.089

Marchand, R. C., Khlopas, A., Sodhi, N., Condrey, C., Piuzzi, N. S., Patel, R., Delanois, R. E., & Mont, M. A. (2018). Difficult Cases in Robotic Arm-Assisted Total Knee Arthroplasty: ACase Series. *The Journal of Knee Surgery*, 31(1), 27–37. 10.1055/s-0037-160883929166681

Marcos-Pablos, S., & García-Peñalvo, F. J. (2022). More than surgical tools: A systematic review of robots as didactic tools for the education of professionals in health sciences. *Advances in Health Sciences Education : Theory and Practice*, 27(4), 1139–1176. 10.1007/s10459-022-10118-635771316

Marie, R. (1973). *Automatically rocking baby cradle.* US Patent US3769641.

Marques, G., & Pitarma, R. (2016). An indoor monitoring system for ambient assisted living based on Internet of Things architecture. *International Journal of Environmental Research and Public Health*, 13(11), 1152. 10.3390/ijerph1311115227869682

Martínez-Peláez, R., Ochoa-Brust, A., Rivera, S., Félix, V. G., Ostos, R., Brito, H., Félix, R. A., & Mena, L. J. (2023). Role of digital transformation for achieving sustainability: Mediated role of stakeholders, key capabilities, and technology. *Sustainability (Basel)*, 15(14), 11221. 10.3390/su151411221

Masoud, H. H. (2018). Internet of Things (IoT): A review of enabling technologies, challenges, and open research issues. In *Proceedings of the IEEE 9th Annual Information Technology, Electronics and Mobile Communication Conference (IEMCON)* (pp. 257–264). IEEE.

Mathan Kumar, K., & Venkatesan, R. S. (2014). A Design Approach to Smart Health Monitoring Using Android Mobile Devices. *IEEE International Conference on Advanced Communication, Control and Computing Tech- nologies (ICACCCT)*. IEEE.

Matheus, R., Janssen, M., & Maheshwari, D. (2020). Data science empowering the public: Data-driven dashboards for transparent and accountable decision-making in smart cities. *Government Information Quarterly*, 37(3), 101284. 10.1016/j.giq.2018.01.006

Mathkor, D. M., Mathkor, N., Bassfar, Z., Bantun, F., Slama, P., Ahmad, F., & Haque, S. (2024, April). Multirole of the internet of medical things (IoMT) in biomedical systems for managing smart healthcare systems: An overview of current and future innovative trends. *Journal of Infection and Public Health*, 17(4), 559–572. 10.1016/j.jiph.2024.01.01338367570

Matsuzaki, H., & Gliesche, P. (2023). Robots and Norms of Care: A Comparative Analysis of the Reception of Robotic Assistance in Nursing. In *Social Robots in Social Institutions* (pp. 90-99). IOS Press. 10.3233/FAIA220607

McAllister, M., Kellenbourn, K., & Wood, D. (2021). The robots are here, but are nurse educators prepared? *Collegian (Royal College of Nursing, Australia)*, 28(2), 230–235. 10.1016/j.colegn.2020.07.005

McBride, B., Hawkes, S., & Buse, K. (2019). Soft power and global health: The sustainable development goals (SDGs) era health agendas of the G7, G20 and BRICS. *BMC Public Health*, 19(1), 1–14. 10.1186/s12889-019-7114-531234831

McLennan, S., Fiske, A., Tigard, D., Müller, R., Haddadin, S., & Buyx, A. (2022). Embedded ethics: A proposal for integrating ethics into the development of medical AI. *BMC Medical Ethics*, 23(1), 6. 10.1186/s12910-022-00746-335081955

Medhekar, A. A., Duggal, M., Singh, S. K., & Nayadkar, P. (2024, June). Healthcare and internet of things: The future of artificial intelligence and IoT technology. *Oral Oncology Reports*, 10, 100279. 10.1016/j.oor.2024.100279

Meena, K. R., Kumari, P., Kumar, M., Singh, A., & Kumar, R. (2021). A healthcare monitoring system using Internet of Things (IoT) for early detection and prevention of COVID-19. *Internet of Things : Engineering Cyber Physical Human Systems*, 15, 100359. 10.1016/j.iot.2021.100359

Megbowon, E. T., & David, O. O. (2023). Information and communication technology development and health gap nexus in Africa. *Frontiers in Public Health*, 11, 1–12. 10.3389/fpubh.2023.114556437064667

Meghla, R. T., Deowan, M. E., Nuhel, A. K., Sazid, M. M., Ekbal, M. N., & Mahamud, M. H. (2022). *An Internet of Things (IoT)- based Smart Automatic Medication Dispenser with an Integrated Web Application for Patient Diagnosis.* 5th International Conference of Computer and Informatics Engineering (IC2IE), 2022 Jakarta, Indonesia. 10.1109/IC2IE56416.2022.9970073

Méndez-Picazo, M. T., Galindo-Martín, M. A., & Castaño-Martínez, M. S. (2021). Effects of sociocultural and economic factors on social entrepreneurship and sustainable development. *Journal of Innovation & Knowledge*, 6(2), 69–77. 10.1016/j.jik.2020.06.001

Merlo, C., Abi Akle, A., Llaria, A., Terrasson, G., Villeneuve, E., & Pilnière, V. (2019). Proposal of a user-centred approach for CPS design: Pillbox case study. *IFAC-PapersOnLine*, 51(34), 196–201. 10.1016/j.ifacol.2019.01.065

Meroueh, C., & Chen, Z. E. (2023, February 1). Artificial intelligence in anatomical pathology: Building a strong foundation for precision medicine. *Human Pathology*, 132, 31–38. 10.1016/j.humpath.2022.07.00835870567

Miah, M. S. U., Sarwar, T. B., Islam, S. S., Haque, M. S., Masuduzzaman, M., & Bhowmik, A. (2022). An adaptive Medical Cyber-Physical System for post diagnosis patient care using cloud computing and machine learning approach. *2022 3rd International Conference for Emerging Technology (INCET).* (pp. 1-6). IEEE.

Miao, M., & Gan, J. (2016). ECG-based remote health monitoring system with an Android client. In *Proceedings of the IEEE International Conference on Computational Intelligence and Communication Technology (CICT)* (pp. 1–4). Ghaziabad, India.

Minopoulos, G. M., Memos, V. A., Stergiou, K. D., Stergiou, C. L., & Psannis, K. E. (2023). A Medical Image Visualization Technique Assisted with AI-Based Haptic Feedback for Robotic Surgery and Healthcare. *Applied Sciences (Basel, Switzerland)*, 13(6), 3592. 10.3390/app13063592

Mishra, P. (2023). *Sustainable Smart Cities: Enabling Technologies, Energy Trends and Potential Applications.* Springer Nature. 10.1007/978-3-031-33354-5

Mittal, A., Meshram, P., & Kim, T. K. (2021). What is the evidence for clinical use of advanced technology in unicompartmental knee arthroplasty? *International Journal of Medical Robotics and Computer Assisted Surgery*, 17(5), e2302. 10.1002/rcs.230234196097

Mitzner, T. L., Tiberio, L., Kemp, C. C., & Rogers, W. A. (2018). Understanding healthcare providers' perceptions of a personal assistant robot. *Gerontechnology: international journal on the fundamental aspects of technology to serve the ageing society, 17*(1), 48.

Moglia, A., Georgiou, K., Georgiou, E., Satava, R. M., & Cuschieri, A. (2021). A systematic review on artificial intelligence in robot-assisted surgery. *International Journal of Surgery*, 95, 106151. 10.1016/j.ijsu.2021.10615134695601

Mohammed, J., Lung, C. H., Ocneanu, A., Thakral, A., Jones, C., & Adler, A. (2014). Internet of things: remote patient monitoring using web services and cloud computing. Proceedings of the *IEEE International Conference on Internet of Things (iThings).* IEEE. 10.1109/iThings.2014.45

Mohanty, S. S., Vyas, S., Koul, Y., Prajapati, P., Varjani, S., Chang, J.-S., Bilal, M., Moustakas, K., Show, P. L., & Vithanage, M. (2023). Tricks and tracks in waste management with a special focus on municipal landfill leachate: Leads and obstacles. *The Science of the Total Environment*, 860, 160377. 10.1016/j.scitotenv.2022.16037736414054

Mohr, A. M., Aronowitz, H. A., Brandman, J. M., Schmitges, J., Corwin, M. T., Desai, N., & Weber, D. R. (2015). Comparison of total perioperative morbidity after da Vinci vs. conventional laparoscopic hysterectomies at two large university centers. *American Journal of Obstetrics and Gynecology*, 213(2), 155.e1–155.e10. 10.1016/j.ajog.2015.03.028

Mois, G., & Beer, J. M. (2020). The Role of Healthcare Robotics in Providing Support to Older Adults: A Socio-ecological Perspective. *Current Geriatrics Reports*, 9(2), 82–89. 10.1007/s13670-020-00314-w32435576

Mois, G., Folea, S., & Sanislav, T. (2017). Analysis of three IoT-based wireless sensors for environmental monitoring. *IEEE Transactions on Instrumentation and Measurement*, 66(8), 2056–2064. 10.1109/TIM.2017.2677619

Möller, D. P. (2023). Cybersecurity in digital transformation. In *Guide to Cybersecurity in Digital Transformation: Trends, Methods, Technologies, Applications and Best Practices* (pp. 1–70). Springer Nature Switzerland. 10.1007/978-3-031-26845-8_1

Mondejar, M. E., Avtar, R., Diaz, H. L. B., Dubey, R. K., Esteban, J., Gómez-Morales, A., Hallam, B., Mbungu, N. T., Okolo, C. C., Prasad, K. A., She, Q., & Garcia-Segura, S. (2021). Digitalization to achieve sustainable development goals: Steps towards a Smart Green Planet. *The Science of the Total Environment*, 794, 148539. 10.1016/j.scitotenv.2021.14853934323742

Moniruzzaman, M., & Hossain, S. A. (2013). Internet of Things (IoT): Present and future architecture, challenges, and applications. In *Proceedings of the International Conference on Electrical Engineering and Information & Communication Technology (ICEEICT)* (pp. 1–6). Dhaka, Bangladesh.

Moreira, A., Duarte, J., & Santos, M. F. (2023). Case Study of Multichannel Interaction in Healthcare Services. *Information (Basel)*, 14(1), 37. 10.3390/info14010037

Morello, R., Ruffa, F., Jablonski, I., Fabbiano, L., & De Capua, C. (2022). An Io T based ECG system to diagnose cardiac pathologies for healthcare applications in smart cities. *Measurement*, 190, 110685. 10.1016/j.measurement.2021.110685

Morolong, Mamoqenelo & Gamundani, Attlee & Bhunu Shava, Fungai. (2023). *Cloud computing security in health cyber physical systems*. 1553-1568.

Mourtzis, D., Angelopoulos, J., & Panopoulos, N. (2022). A Literature Review of the Challenges and Opportunities of the Transition from Industry 4.0 to Society 5.0. *Energies*, 2022(15), 62. 10.3390/en15176276

Mousse, M. A., & Atohoun, B. (2021). Saliency based human fall detection in smart home environments using posture recognition. *Health Informatics Journal*, 27(3). 10.1177/1460458221103095434382460

Moustris, G. P., Hiridis, S. C., Deliparaschos, K. M., & Konstantinidis, K. M. (2017). Evolution of autonomous and semi-autonomous robotic surgical systems: A review of the literature. *. *International Journal of Medical Robotics and Computer Assisted Surgery*, 13(4), e1786. 10.1002/rcs.178621815238

Movahedi, A., Hassan, R., Shamshirband, S., Gani, A., Akbari, E., Anuar, N. B., Kiah, M. L. M., Khoshnava, S. M., & Lee, M. (2015). A review of routing protocols in wireless body area networks for healthcare applications. *Journal of Medical Systems*, 39(8), 1–14. 10.1007/s10916-015-0334-7

Mulpur, P., Masilamani, A. S., Prakash, M., Annapareddy, A., Hippalgaonkar, K., & Reddy, A. G. (2022). Comparison of patient reported outcomes after robotic versus manual total knee arthroplasty in the same patient undergoing staged bilateral knee arthroplasty. *Journal of Orthopaedics*, 34, 111–115. 10.1016/j.jor.2022.08.01436060731

Murakami, Y., Honaga, K., Kono, H., Haruyama, K., Yamaguchi, T., Tani, M., Isayama, R., Takakura, T., Tanuma, A., Hatori, K., Wada, F., & Fujiwara, T. (2023). New Artificial Intelligence-Integrated Electromyography-Driven Robot Hand for Upper Extremity Rehabilitation of Patients With Stroke: A Randomized, Controlled Trial. *Neurorehabilitation and Neural Repair*, 37(5), 15459683231166939. 10.1177/15459683231166939370393 19

Murphy, R. R. (2019). Introduction to AI robotics. MIT Press.- Murray, C. C., Chu, A. G., & Wu, Y. (2020). Autonomous mobile robots in logistics: Trends and future directions. *Autonomous Robots*, 44(6), 1231–1246.

Nagasaki, M., Sekiya, Y., Asakura, A., Teraoka, R., Otokozawa, R., Hashimoto, H., Kawaguchi, T., Fukazawa, K., Inadomi, Y., Murata, K. T., Ohkawa, Y., Yamaguchi, I., Mizuhara, T., Tokunaga, K., Sekiya, Y., Hanawa, T., Yamada, R., & Matsuda, F. (2023). Design and implementation of a hybrid cloud system for large-scale human genomic research. *Human Genome Variation*, 10(1), 6. 10.1038/s41439-023-00231-236755016

Nalluri, M., Reddy, S. R. B., Rongali, A. S., & Polireddi, N. S. A. (2023). Investigate The Use of Robotic Process Automation (RPA) To Streamline Administrative Tasks In Healthcare, Such As Billing, Appointment Scheduling, And Claims Processing. *Tuijin Jishu/Journal of Propulsion Technology, 44*(5), 2458-2468.

Nambi, R. R., Ravi, V., Chockalingam, P., & Yoo, Y. (2016). IoT-based wearable sensor devices in healthcare: Research challenges and design considerations. In *Proceedings of the IEEE International Conference on Ubiquitous Wireless Broadband (ICUWB)* (pp. 1–6). Nanjing, China.

Namezi, T., Galich, A., Smith, L., & Balaji, K. (2006). Robotic urological surgery in patients with prior abdominal operations is not associated with increased complications. *International Journal of Urology*, 13(3), 248–251. 10.1111/j.1442-2042.2006.01273.x16643618

Naranjo-Hernández D, Reina-Tosina J, Roa LM (2020). Special Issue - Body Sensors Networks for E-Health Applications. *Sensors* (Basel), *20*(14), 3944.

Naresh, M. H., Mr, M. M. A., Bhargav, M. P., Reddy, M. Y. D. S., & Ashish, M. G. (2024). Development of an Automatic Baby Cradle System. *International Research Journal on Advanced Engineering Hub*, 2(04), 774–782. 10.47392/IRJAEH.2024.0109

Nasrin, S., & Rahman, M. (2021). Internet of Things (IoT) in healthcare: A comprehensive review. *International Journal of Computer Applications*, 179, 1–5. 10.5120/ijca2021916233

Nassereddine, M., & Khang, A. (2024). Applications of Internet of Things (Io T) in smart cities. In *Advanced Io T Technologies and Applications in the Industry 4.0 Digital Economy* (pp. 109–136). CRC Press.

Nazari, H., Ghane, H. R., Salehipour, M., Mehdizadeh, S., Mahmoudvand, F., Mirzaaghaei, H., & Soltanimehr, E. (2015). Robotic surgery training courses around the world: What does exist? A systematic review. *Journal of Robotic Surgery*, 9(3), 191–197. 10.1007/s11701-014-0516-8

Nguyen, H. Q., Duong, A. H. L., Vu, M. D., Dinh, T. Q., & Ngo, H. T. (2022), Smart Blind Stick for Visually Impaired People.*8th International Conference on the Development of Biomedical Engineering in Vietnam.* Springer, Cham. 10.1007/978-3-030-75506-5_12

Nguyen, H. T., Huang, X., & Rudin, N. (2020). Artificial intelligence in robotic surgery: Challenges and opportunities. *The Journal of Surgical Research*, 247, 229–236. 10.1016/j.jss.2019.10.014

Nguyen, T. T., Wong, Y. S., Zhang, D., & Wang, L. (2019). Machine learning in robotics: A survey. *Robotics (Basel, Switzerland)*, 8(1), 24.

Nikseresht, M. R., & Mollamotalebi, M. (2021). Providing a CoAP-based technique to get wireless sensor data via IoT gateway. *Computer Communications*, 172, 155–168. 10.1016/j.comcom.2021.03.026

Nof, S. Y. (2009). *Springer handbook of automation.* Springer Science & Business Media. 10.1007/978-3-540-78831-7

Nooruddin, S., Milon Islam, M., & Sharna, F. A. (2020). An IoT-based device-type invariant fall detection system. *Internet of Things : Engineering Cyber Physical Human Systems*, 9, 100130. 10.1016/j.iot.2019.100130

Novikov, S. V. (2020). Data science and big data technologies role in the digital economy. *TEM Journal*, 9(2), 756–762. 10.18421/TEM92-44

Nwadiokwu, O. T. (2023). Examining the Impact and Challenges of Artificial Intelligence (AI) in Healthcare. *Edward Waters University Undergraduate Research Journal, 1*(1).

Ohneberg, C., Stöbich, N., Warmbein, A., Rathgeber, I., Mehler-Klamt, A. C., Fischer, U., & Eberl, I. (2023). Assistive robotic systems in nursing care: A scoping review. *BMC Nursing*, 22(1), 1–15. 10.1186/s12912-023-01230-y36934280

Okamura, A. M., Cutkosky, M. R., Jarvis, R. A., & Rodriguez y Baena, F. (2009). Devices and control architectures for bilateral teleoperation. *Annual Reviews in Control*, 33(1), 227–245. 10.1016/j.arcontrol.2009.02.001

Olson, M. J. (2009). *Robotic surgery, human fallibility, and the politics of care* [Doctoral dissertation, The University of North Carolina at Chapel Hill].

Onggo, J. R., Onggo, J. D., De Steiger, R., & Hau, R. (2020). Robotic-assisted total knee arthroplasty is comparable to conventional total knee arthroplasty: A meta-analysis and systematic review. *Archives of Orthopaedic and Trauma Surgery*, 140(10), 1533–1549. 10.1007/s00402-020-03512-532537660

Ong, J., Parchment, V., & Zheng, X. (2018). Effective regulation of digital health technologies. *Journal of the Royal Society of Medicine*, 2018(111), 439–443. 10.1177/0141076818812437

Oresko, J. J., Jin, Z., Cheng, J., Huang, S., Sun, Y., Duschl, H., & Cheng, A. C. (2010). A wearable smartphone-based platform for real-time cardiovascular disease detection via electrocardiogram processing. *IEEE Transactions on Information Technology in Biomedicine*, 14(3), 734–740. 10.1109/TITB.2010.204786520388600

Packiavathy, S. V., & Gautam, S. (2023). Internet of Things (Io T) based automated sanitizer dispenser and COVID-19 statistics reporter in a post-pandemic world. *Health and Technology*, 13(2), 327–341. 10.1007/s12553-023-00728-436694669

Palaskar, R., Pandey, S., Telang, A., Wagh, A., & Kagalkar, R. R. (2015, December). An Automatic Monitoring and Swing the Baby Cradle for Infant Care. *International Journal of Advanced Research in Computer and Communication Engineering*.

Pandey, R. S., & Shukla, S. (2023). Perspective of G20 along with India's cultural values. *Knowledgeable Research: A Multidisciplinary Journal, 1*(09), 59-70.

Pandya, H., Desai, M., & Singhal, A. (2015). Performance analysis of IoT based healthcare architecture. *International Journal of Computer Applications*, 117(6), 28–32. 10.5120/ijca2015907390

Pandya, S., Srivastava, G., Jhaveri, R., Babu, M. R., Bhattacharya, S., Praveen, K. R. M., Mastorakis, S., Piran, M. J., & Gadekallu, T. R. (2023). Federated learning for smart cities: A comprehensive survey. *Sustainable Energy Technologies and Assessments*, 55, 102987. 10.1016/j.seta.2022.102987

Panhwar, M. A., Zhong Liang, D., Memon, K. A., Khuhro, S. A., Abbasi, M. A. K., Noor-ul-Ain, , & Ali, Z. (2021). Energy-efficient routing optimization algorithm in WBANs for patient monitoring. *Journal of Ambient Intelligence and Humanized Computing*, 12(7), 8069–8081. 10.1007/s12652-020-02541-7

Pansara, R. R. (2022). Cybersecurity Measures in Master Data Management: Safeguarding Sensitive Information. *International Numeric Journal of Machine Learning and Robots*, 6(6), 1–12.

Papadopoulou, P., Chui, K. T., Daniela, L., & Lytras, M. D. (2019, January 1). *Virtual and Augmented Reality in Medical Education and Training*. Advances in Educational Technologies and Instructional Design Book Series. 10.4018/978-1-5225-9031-6.ch006

Parker, J. (2023). Barriers to green inhaler prescribing: Ethical issues in environmentally sustainable clinical practice. *Journal of Medical Ethics*, 49(2), 92–98. 10.1136/jme-2022-10838835981864

Parker, M. G., Stavropoulos, D. J., Brunner, E. M., Shuch, B., Sammon, J. D., McClure, R. D., & Clayman, R. V. (2017). Robotic versus open radical cystectomy: Analysis of contemporaneous cohorts demonstrating equivalent outcomes. *European Urology Focus*, 3(3), 389–395. 10.1016/j.euf.2017.02.006

Park, S. E., & Lee, C. T. (2007). Comparison of robotic-assisted and conventional manual implantation of a primary total knee arthroplasty. *The Journal of Arthroplasty*, 22(7), 1054–1059. 10.1016/j.arth.2007.05.03617920481

Parreira, H. B., Teixeira, L. F., Cardoso, T. A., & Aguilar, R. C. (2020). IoT in healthcare: A review of architecture, connectivity and security issues. In *Proceedings of the International Congress on Engineering and Information (ICEI)* (pp. 1–6). Manaus, Brazil.

Patel, K., & Kumar, S. (2023). *Education Sector an application of IoT.*

Patel, S., & Meena, Y. K. (2020). Machine learning approach for healthcare applications in Internet of Things (IoT) environment: A review. In *Proceedings of the International Conference on Recent Advancements in Computer, Communication and Computational Sciences (RACCCS)* (pp. 1–7). Jaipur, India.

Patil, K., Laad, M., Kamble, A., & Laad, S. (2019). A consumer-based smart home with an indoor air quality monitoring system. *Journal of the Institution of Electronics and Telecommunication Engineers*, 65(6), 758–770. 10.1080/03772063.2018.1462108

Patil, R. (2018). Smart Baby Cradle an IOT based Cradle Management System. *International Conference on Smart City and Emerging Technology (ICSCET)*. IEEE.

Patil, R. P., Kulkarni, D., & Chandrashekhar, K. (2017). IoT based healthcare system for identification and treatment of heart diseases. In *Proceedings of the IEEE International Conference on Intelligent Systems and Information Management (ICISIM)* (pp. 12–16). Chennai, India.

Paviya, R., Prabakar, S., Porkumaran, K., & Saman, A. B. S. (2022). Automated Pill and Syringe Dispenser. In: Ibrahim, R., K. Porkumaran, Kannan, R., Mohd Nor, N., S. Prabakar (eds) *International Conference on Artificial Intelligence for Smart Community. Lecture Notes in Electrical Engineering.*. Springer, Singapore. 10.1007/978-981-16-2183-3_86

Pereira, A.G., Lima, T.M., & Santos, F.C. (2020). Industry 4.0 and society 5.0: opportunities and threats. *International Journal of Recent Technology Engineering, 8*(5), 3305–3308 11.

Piloni, M., Bailo, M., Gagliardi, F., & Mortini, P. (2021). Resection of Intracranial Tumors with a Robotic-Assisted Digital Microscope: A Preliminary Experience with Robotic Scope. *World Neurosurgery*, 152, e205–e211. 10.1016/j.wneu.2021.05.07534052450

Prabhakar, S. K., & Rajaguru, H. (2017). *The 16th International Conference on Biomedical Engineering IFMBE Proceedings*. Singapore: Springer.

Pratap, N. L., Anuroop, K., Devi, P. N., Sandeep, A., & Nalajala, S. (2021, January). IoT based Smart Cradle for Baby Monitoring System. In *2021 6th International Conference on Inventive Computation Technologies (ICICT)* (pp. 1298-1303). IEEE. 10.1109/ICICT50816.2021.9358684

Pratap, B., Kumar, S., Nand, S., Azad, I., Bharagava, R. N., Luiz, F. R. F., & Dutta, V. (2023). Wastewater generation and treatment by various eco-friendly technologies: Possible health hazards and further reuse for environmental safety. *Chemosphere*, 313, 137547. 10.1016/j.chemosphere.2022.13754736529169

Prüfer, J., & Prüfer, P. (2020). Data science for entrepreneurship research: Studying demand dynamics for entrepreneurial skills in the Netherlands. *Small Business Economics*, 55(3), 651–672. 10.1007/s11187-019-00208-y

Purohit, P., Sharma, A., Sharma, S., & Sharma, A. (2021). An approach towards early diagnosis and monitoring of COVID-19 using wearable health devices and Internet of Medical Things (IoMT). *Diabetes & Metabolic Syndrome*, 15(2), 441–446. 10.1016/j.dsx.2021.02.004

Quilis, J. D. S., López-Huguet, S., Lozano, P., & Blanquer, I. (2023). A federated cloud architecture for processing of cancer images on a distributed storage. *Future Generation Computer Systems*, 139, 38–52. 10.1016/j.future.2022.09.019

Ragno, L., Borboni, A., Vannetti, F., Amici, C., & Cusano, N. (2023). Application of Social Robots in Healthcare: Review on Characteristics, Requirements, Technical Solutions. *Sensors (Basel)*, 23(15), 6820. 10.3390/s2315682037571603

Rahaman, A., Islam, M., Islam, M., Sadi, M., & Nooruddin, S. (2019). Developing IoT-based smart health monitoring systems: A review. *Review of Intelligent Artificial Systems*, 33(6), 435–440. 10.18280/ria.330605

Rahman, M. Z. U., Raza, A. H., AlSanad, A. A., Akbar, M. A., Liaquat, R., Riaz, M. T., AlSuwaidan, L., Al-Alshaikh, H. A., & Alsagri, H. S. (2022). Real-time artificial intelligence based health monitoring, diagnosing and environmental control system for COVID-19 patients [J]. *Mathematical Biosciences and Engineering*, 19(8), 7586–7605. 10.3934/mbe.202235735801437

Rajamani, S. K., & Iyer, R. S. (2023a). A Scoping Review of Current Developments in the Field of Machine Learning and Artificial Intelligence. *Advances in Wireless Technologies and Telecommunication Book Series*, 138–164. Springer. 10.4018/978-1-6684-8582-8.ch009

Rajamani, S. K., & Iyer, R. S. (2022). Development Of an Android Mobile Phone Application for Finding Closed-Loop, Analytical Solutions to Dense Linear, Algebraic Equations for The Purpose of Mathematical Modelling in Healthcare and Neuroscience Research. *NeuroQuantology : An Interdisciplinary Journal of Neuroscience and Quantum Physics*, 20, 4959–4973. 10.6084/m9.figshare.c.6156024.v1

Rajamani, S. K., & Iyer, R. S. (2023b). *Methods of Complex Network Analysis to Screen for Cyberbullying*. CRC Press. 10.1201/9781003393061-16

Ramalakshmi, K., Krishna Kumari, L., & Rajalakshm, R. (2023). Energy-Aware Protocols and Standards in IoT-Enabled Healthcare, AI and IoT-Based Technologies for Precision Medicine. *Advances in Medical Technologies and Clinical Practice*, 13, 205–217. 10.4018/979-8-3693-0876-9.ch012

Ramezani, M., & Mohd Ripin, Z. (2023). 4D printing in biomedical engineering: Advancements, challenges, and future directions. *Journal of Functional Biomaterials*, 14(7), 347. 10.3390/jfb1407034737504842

Ranabhat, C. L., & Jakovljević, M. (2023, January 11). Sustainable Health Care Provision Worldwide: Is There a Necessary Trade-Off between Cost and Quality? *Sustainability (Basel)*, 15(2), 1372. 10.3390/su15021372

Rao, S., & Singh, V. M. (2021). *Computer Vision and IoT Based Smart System for Visually Impaired People.* 2021 11th International Conference on Cloud Computing, Data Science & Engineering, Noida, India. 10.1109/Confluence51648.2021.9377120

Rao, S., Fagadar-Cosma, E., & Cosma, G. (2020). Design and development of a cloud-based IoT platform for healthcare monitoring. *Sensors (Basel)*, 20(15), 4163.32726938

Rashid, A., Taylor, D., & Darzi, A. (2016). Ergonomic design considerations for robotic surgical systems. *Computers in Biology and Medicine*, 69, 16–25. 10.1016/j.compbiomed.2016.03.016

Raspberry Pi Foundation. (n.d.). *Raspberry Pi.* https://www.raspberrypi.org/

Rathore, M. M., Ahmad, A., Paul, A., Rho, S., & Wan, J. (2016). Urban planning and building smart cities based on the Internet of Things using big data analytics. *Computer Networks*, 101, 63–80. 10.1016/j.comnet.2015.12.023

Rawassizadeh, R., Price, B. A., & Petre, M. (2015). Wearables: Has the age of smartwatches finally arrived? *Communications of the ACM*, 58(1), 45–47. 10.1145/2629633

Ray, D., Salvatore, M., Bhattacharyya, R., Wang, L., Du, J., Mohammed, S., & Mukherjee, B. (2020). Predictions, role of interventions and effects of a historic national lockdown in India's response to the COVID-19 pandemic: Data science call to arms. *Harvard Data Science Review*, (Suppl 1), 10–1162.32607504

Razaque, A., & Elleithy, K. M. (2016). An IoT-based health monitoring system for cardiac patients. In *Proceedings of the IEEE Seventh Annual Ubiquitous Computing, Electronics & Mobile Communication Conference* (pp. 1–6). New York City, NY, USA.

Reddy, G. K., & Achari, K. L. (2015). A non-invasive method for calculating calories burned during exercise using heartbeat. In *2015 IEEE 9th International conference on Intelligent Systems and Control (ISCO)* (pp. 1–5). IEEE. 10.1109/ISCO.2015.7282249

Régnier, P. (2023). Innovation, Appropriate Technologies and Entrepreneurship for Global Sustainability Development: A Review Until the Early Twenty-first Century. *The Journal of Entrepreneurship*, 32(2, suppl), S12–S26. 10.1177/09713557231201115

Rehman Khan, A., Saba, T., Sadad, T., & Hong, S. P. (2022). Cloud-based framework for COVID-19 detection through feature fusion with bootstrap aggregated extreme learning machine. *Discrete Dynamics in Nature and Society*, 2022, 2022. 10.1155/2022/3111200

Reichenpfader, D., & Hanke, S. (2021). Requirements and architecture of a cloud based insomnia therapy and diagnosis platform: A smart cities approach. *Smart Cities*, 4(4), 1316–1336. 10.3390/smartcities4040070

Rejeb, A., Rejeb, K., Treiblmaier, H., Appolloni, A., Alghamdi, S., Alhasawi, Y., & Iranmanesh, M. (2023). The Internet of Things (Io T) in healthcare: Taking stock and moving forward. *Internet of Things : Engineering Cyber Physical Human Systems*, 1007.

Rejeb, A., Rejeb, K., Treiblmaier, H., Appolloni, A., Alghamdi, S., Alhasawi, Y., & Iranmanesh, M. (2023). The Internet of Things (IoT) in healthcare: Taking stock and moving forward. *Internet of Things : Engineering Cyber Physical Human Systems*, 22, 100721. 10.1016/j.iot.2023.100721

Ren, Y., Cao, S., Wu, L., Weng, X., & Feng, B. (2019). Efficacy and reliability of active robotic-assisted total knee arthroplasty compared with conventional total knee arthroplasty: A systematic review and meta-analysis. *Postgraduate Medical Journal, 95.* postgradmedj-2018. .10.1136/postgradmedj-2018-136190

Reshi, I. A. (2023). Unpacking The Complexities Of Economic Systems: Exploring Trends, Challenges And Solutions. *Journal of Accounting Research, Utility Finance and Digital Assets*, 1(4), 393–398. 10.54443/jaruda.v1i4.60

Riazul Islam, S. M., Kwak, D., Humaun Kabir, M., Hossain, M., & Kwak, K.-S. (2015). The Internet of Things for health care: A comprehensive survey. *IEEE Access : Practical Innovations, Open Solutions*, 3, 678–708. 10.1109/ACCESS.2015.2437951

Ribeiro, O., Gomes, L., & Vale, Z. (2022). IoT-Based Human Fall Detection System. *Electronics (Basel)*, 11(4), 592. 10.3390/electronics11040592

Richard, R. M., & Taylar, J. V. (2022) Cyber-Physical System Framework for Cerebrovascular Accidents using Machine Learning Algorithm. *2022 International Conference on ICT for Smart Society (ICISS)*. IEEE. 10.1109/ICISS55894.2022.9915228

Riek, L. D. (2017). Healthcare robotics. *Communications of the ACM*, 60(11), 68–78. 10.1145/3127874

Rigelsford, J. (2003). Robot-assisted microsurgery system. *Industrial Robot. International Journal (Toronto, Ont.)*, 30(1).

Riva, G., Baños, R. M., Botella, C., Mantovani, F., Gaggioli, A., & Wiederhold, B. K. (2012). Transforming experience: The potential of augmented reality and virtual reality for enhancing personal and clinical change. *Frontiers in Psychiatry*, 3, 1–11. 10.3389/fpsyt.2012.0010427746747

Rivero-Moreno, Y., Echevarria, S., Vidal-Valderrama, C., Stefano-Pianetti, L., Cordova-Guilarte, J., Navarro-Gonzalez, J., & Avila, G. L. D. (2023). Robotic Surgery: A Comprehensive Review of the Literature and Current Trends. *Cureus*, 15(7). 10.7759/cureus.4237037621804

Robu. in. (n.d.). *Sound sensor*. Robu. https://robu.in/product-category/sensor-modules/sound-sensor/

ROHM Co. Ltd. (n.d.). *Heart rate sensor*. ROHM. https://www.rohm.com/sensor-shield-support/heart-rate-sensor

Romero, C., & Ventura, S. (2020). Educational data mining and learning analytics: An updated survey. *Wiley Interdisciplinary Reviews. Data Mining and Knowledge Discovery*, 10(3), e1355. 10.1002/widm.1355

Roopa, P., & Shabadi, S. (2020). *An analysis of edge computing in IoT healthcare applications*. In *International Conference on Computer Science, Engineering and Applications (ICCSEA)*, Bangalore, India.

Rosa, S. L., Kadir, E. A., Abbasi, Q. H., Almansour, A. A., Othman, M., & Siswanto, A. 2022, November. Patient Monitoring and Disease Analysis Based on IoT Wearable Sensors and Cloud Computing. In *2022 International Conference on Electrical, Computer, Communications and Mechatronics Engineering (ICECCME)* (pp. 1-6). IEEE. 10.1109/ICECCME55909.2022.9988546

Rosen, J., Hannaford, B., & Satava, R. M. (2019). Surgical robotics: System integration and latency management. *IEEE Transactions on Robotics*, 35(4), 881–891. 10.1109/TRO.2019.2905905

Rottermann, K., Doll, U., Pfenning, S., Reichenbach, M., Fey, D., Dobler, A., Siauw, C., Reif, F., Gnibl, J., Cesnjevar, R., & Dittrich, S. (2024). The Congenital Cardiology Cloud–optimizing long-term care by connecting ambulatory and hospital medical attendance via telemedicine. *Klinische Padiatrie*, 236(01), 16–23. 10.1055/a-2154-665937683668

Roy, S. (2024). A Study of the Future Generation of Smart Cities Using Green Technology. In *Green Computing for Sustainable Smart Cities* (pp. 59–72). CRC Press. 10.1201/9781003388814-4

Saad, A., Mayne, A. I., Pagkalos, J., Ollivier, M., Botchu, R., Davis, E. T., & Sharma, A. D. (2024). An evaluation of factors influencing the adoption and usage of robotic surgery in lower limb arthroplasty amongst orthopaedic trainees: A clinical survey. *Journal of Robotic Surgery*, 18(1), 2. 10.1007/s11701-023-01811-838175317

Sadik, S., Ahmed, M., Sikos, L. F., & Islam, A. N. (2020). Toward a sustainable cybersecurity ecosystem. *Computers*, 9(3), 74. 10.3390/computers9030074

Sahandi Far, M., Stolz, M., Fischer, J. M., Eickhoff, S. B., & Dukart, J. (2021). A Digital Biomarker Platform for Remote Monitoring of Daily-Life Behaviour in Health and Disease. *Frontiers in Public Health*, 9, 763621. 10.3389/fpubh.2021.76362134869177

Saheb, T., & Saheb, M. (2019). Analyzing and Visualizing Knowledge Structures of Health Informatics from 1974 to 2018: A Bibliometric and Social Network Analysis. *Healthcare Informatics Research*, 25(2), 61–72. 10.4258/hir.2019.25.2.6131131140

Sahoo, S. K., & Goswami, S. S. (2023). A comprehensive review of multiple criteria decision-making (MCDM) Methods: Advancements, applications, and future directions. *Decision Making Advances*, 1(1), 25–48. 10.31181/dma1120237

Sakran, J. V., Bornstein, S. S., Dicker, R., Rivara, F. P., Campbell, B. T., Cunningham, R. M., Betz, M., Hargarten, S., Williams, A., Horwitz, J. M., Nehra, D., Burstin, H., Sheehan, K., Dreier, F. L., James, T., Sathya, C., Armstrong, J. H., Rowhani-Rahbar, A., Charles, S., & Bulger, E. M. (2023). Proceedings from the Second Medical Summit on Firearm Injury Prevention, 2022: Creating a sustainable healthcare coalition to advance a multidisciplinary public health approach. *Journal of the American College of Surgeons*, 236(6), 1242–1260. 10.1097/XCS.000000000000066236877809

Sanchez, J. P., Payne, C. J., McCool, M. A., Levy, M. S., Berguer, R., Escano, J. M., & Del Pino, A. (2018). Evolution of robotic instrumentation: Past, present, and future. *Journal of Endourology*, 32(3), 253–261. 10.1089/end.2017.0620

Sanh, V., Debut, L., Chaumond, J., & Wolf, T. (2019, October). DistilBERT, a distilled version of BERT: Smaller, faster, cheaper, and lighter. *Clinical Orthopaedics and Related Research.*

Santoso, D., & Dalu Setiaji, F. (2015). Non-contact portable infrared thermometer for rapid influenza screening. In *2015 International conference on automation, cognitive science, optics, micro electromechanical system, and information technology (ICACOMIT)* (pp. 18–23). IEEE. 10.1109/ICACOMIT.2015.7440147

Saranya, R., & Murugan, A. (2023). A systematic review of enabling blockchain in healthcare system: Analysis, current status, challenges and future direction. *Materials Today: Proceedings*, 80, 3010–3015. 10.1016/j.matpr.2021.07.105

Sarker, I. H., Kayes, A. S. M., Badsha, S., Alqahtani, H., Watters, P., & Ng, A. (2020). Cybersecurity data science: An overview from machine learning perspective. *Journal of Big Data*, 7(1), 1–29. 10.1186/s40537-020-00318-5

Saude, N., & Vardhini, P. H. (2020, October). IoT based Smart Baby Cradle System using Raspberry Pi B+. In *2020 International Conference on Smart Innovations in Design, Environment, Management, Planning and Computing (ICSIDEMPC)* (pp. 273-278). IEEE. 10.1109/ICSIDEMPC49020.2020.9299602

Saura, J. R. (2021). Using data sciences in digital marketing: Framework, methods, and performance metrics. *Journal of Innovation & Knowledge*, 6(2), 92–102. 10.1016/j.jik.2020.08.001

Schönmann, M., Bodenschatz, A., Uhl, M., & Walkowitz, G. (2023). The Care-Dependent are Less Averse to Care Robots: An Empirical Comparison of Attitudes. *International Journal of Social Robotics*, 15(6), 1–18. 10.1007/s12369-023-01003-237359432

Selvakumar, A., Ramasamy, V., & Kandasamy, S. (2024). Improved security measures and their performance in cloud computing. *International Journal of Cloud Applications*, 9(2), 78–90.

Selvakumar, K., & Lokesh, S. (2024). A cryptographic method to have a secure communication of health care digital data into the cloud. *Automatika (Zagreb)*, 65(1), 373–386. 10.1080/00051144.2023.2301240

Servais, E. L., & Smit, P. J. (2023). Robotic Thoracic Surgery. *Thoracic Surgery Clinics*, 33(1), i. 10.1016/S1547-4127(22)00092-536372540

Shah, S. S., Gvozdanovic, A., Knight, M., & Gagnon, J. (2021). Mobile App-Based Remote Patient Monitoring in Acute Medical Conditions: Prospective Feasibility Study Exploring Digital Health Solutions on Clinical Workload During the COVID Crisis. *JMIR Formative Research*, 5(1), e23190. 10.2196/2319033400675

Shahvaroughi, M. (2022). The Impacts of Aging on Economic Growth and Sustainable Development (Case Study of G20 Countries). *Iranian Sociological Review*, 12(1), 85–100.

Shaik, T., Tao, X., Higgins, N., Li, L., Gururajan, R., Zhou, X., & Acharya, U. R. (2023). Remote patient monitoring using artificial intelligence: Current state, applications, and challenges. *Wiley Interdisciplinary Reviews. Data Mining and Knowledge Discovery*, 13(2), e1485. 10.1002/widm.1485

Shakeel, T., Habib, S., Boulila, W., Koubaa, A., Javed, A. R., Rizwan, M., Gadekallu, T. R., & Sufiyan, M. (2023). A survey on COVID-19 impact in the healthcare domain: Worldwide market implementation, applications, security and privacy issues, challenges and future prospects. *Complex & Intelligent Systems*, 9(1), 1027–1058. 10.1007/s40747-022-00767-w35668731

Shang, W., Jiang, Y., Yu, Y., & Xu, W. (2017). A wearable ECG acquisition system for body sensor network. In *International Conference on Electrical, Automation and Mechanical Engineering (EAME)*, St. Petersburg, Russia.

Shao, M., Fan, J., Huang, Z., & Chen, M. (2022). The impact of information and communication technologies (ICTs) on health outcomes: A smediating effect analysis based on cross-national panel data. *Journal of Environmental and Public Health*, 2022, 1–16. 10.1155/2022/2225723

Sharma, A., Sharma, K., Kumar, V., & Kamalraj, R. (2023). Simplified LEACH Protocol with Superior Energy Efficiency for the Internet of Things. *International Journal of Intelligent Systems and Applications in Engineering*, 11(no. 8s), 86–92.

Sharma, M., & Sharma, P. (2020). *Role of IoT in healthcare*. In *International Conference on Communication and Electronics Systems (ICCES)*, Coimbatore, India.

Sharma, R., Gaur, A., Tyagi, S., & Kumar, D. (2020). IoT-based healthcare architecture with cloud and cognitive computing. In *Proceedings of the IEEE 9th Global Conference on Consumer Electronics (GCCE)* (pp. 1066–1069). IEEE.

Sharma, S., & Umme Salma, M. (2021). Social, Medical, and Educational Applications of IoT to Assist Visually Impaired People. In Chakraborty, C., Banerjee, A., Kolekar, M., Garg, L., & Chakraborty, B. (Eds.), *Internet of Things for Healthcare Technologies. Studies in Big Data* (Vol. 73). Springer., 10.1007/978-981-15-4112-4_10

Sharmin, S., Ratan, M. I. K. U., & Piash, A. H. (2021) An Automated and Online-Based Medicine Reminder and Dispenser. *Proceedings of the International Conference on Big Data, IoT, and Machine Learning. Lecture Notes on Data Engineering and Communications Technologies*. Springer, Singapore. 10.1007/978-981-16-6636-0_39

Shaw, E., Walpole, S., McLean, M., Alvarez-Nieto, C., Barna, S., Bazin, K., Behrens, G., Chase, H., Duane, B., El Omrani, O., Elf, M., Faerron Guzmán, C. A., Falceto de Barros, E., Gibbs, T. J., Groome, J., Hackett, F., Harden, J., Hothersall, E. J., Hourihane, M., & Woollard, R. (2021). AMEE Consensus Statement: Planetary health and education for sustainable healthcare. *Medical Teacher*, 43(3), 272–286. 10.1080/0142159X.2020.186020733602043

Sheetz, K. H., Claflin, J., & Dimick, J. B. (2020). Trends in the adoption of robotic surgery for common surgical procedures. *JAMA Network Open*, 3(1), e1918911–e1918911. 10.1001/jamanetworkopen.2019.1891131922557

Shelke, S. V., Shelke, S. R., & Devabhaktuni, V. K. (2021). Wearable sensor technology for remote monitoring in pandemic control: A review. *IEEE Sensors Journal*, 21(9), 10369–10383. 10.1109/JSEN.2021.3069071

Silvera-Tawil, D. (2024). Robotics in Healthcare: A Survey. *SN Computer Science*, 5(1), 189. 10.1007/s42979-023-02551-0

Singer, P. W. (2009). Military robots and the laws of war. *New Atlantis (Washington, D.C.)*, (23), 25–45.

Singh, A., & Kumar, S. (2020). A critical review on IoT-based healthcare applications. *International Journal of System Assurance Engineering and Management*, 11(1), 24–36. 10.1007/s13198-018-0775-8

Singh, H., & Sharma, K. (2021). A comprehensive review on Internet of Things (IoT)-based healthcare applications. *Health and Technology*, 11(1), 1–23. 10.1007/s12553-020-00506-w

Singh, S. P., Viriyasitavat, W., Juneja, S., Alshahrani, H., Shaikh, A., Dhiman, G., Singh, A., & Kaur, A. (2022). Dual adaption based evolutionary algorithm for optimized the smart healthcare communication service of the Internet of Things in smart city. *Physical Communication*, 55, 101893. 10.1016/j.phycom.2022.101893

Singh, V., Singh, N., Rai, S. N., Kumar, A., Singh, A. K., Singh, M. P., Sahoo, A., Shekhar, S., Vamanu, E., & Mishra, V. (2023). Heavy Metal Contamination in the Aquatic Ecosystem: Toxicity and Its Remediation Using Eco-Friendly Approaches. *Toxics*, 11(2), 147. 10.3390/toxics1102014736851022

Smith, B. R., Johnson, J. A., & Lee, C. Y. (2019). Smart surgical instruments: Biocompatibility and functionality. *. *Journal of Medical Engineering & Technology*, 43(7), 511–523. 10.1080/03091902.2019.1623095

Sood, V. V., Bansal, K., & Agarwal, N. (2022). *Advanced Sensing in Image Processing and IoT* (1st ed.). CRC Press.

Soori, M., Arezoo, B., & Dastres, R. (2023). *Internet of things for smart factories in industry 4.0, a review*. Internet of Things and Cyber-Physical Systems.

Sörös, P., & Hachinski, V. (2012). Cardiovascular and neurological causes of sudden death after ischaemic stroke. *Lancet Neurology*, 11(2), 179–188. 10.1016/S1474-4422(11)70291-522265213

Stasevych, M., & Zvarych, V. (2023). Innovative robotic technologies and artificial intelligence in pharmacy and medicine: Paving the way for the future of health care—a review. *Big Data and Cognitive Computing*, 7(3), 147. 10.3390/bdcc7030147

Stewart, J., Sprivulis, P., & Dwivedi, G. (2018). Artificial intelligence and machine learning in emergency medicine. *Emergency Medicine Australasia*, 30(6), 870–874. 10.1111/1742-6723.1314530014578

Sugimoto, M., & Sueyoshi, T. (2023). Development of Holoeyes Holographic Image-Guided Surgery and Telemedicine System: Clinical Benefits of Extended Reality (Virtual Reality, Augmented Reality, Mixed Reality), The Metaverse, and Artificial Intelligence in Surgery with a Systematic Review. *Medical Research Archives, 11*(7.1).

Suhasini, P. & Kanchana, S. (2022). Enhanced Fractional Order Lorenz System for Medical Image Encryption in Cloud-Based Healthcare Administration. *International Journal of Computer Networks and Applications (IJCNA), 9.*

Sulich, A., Rutkowska, M., Krawczyk-Jezierska, A., Jezierski, J., & Zema, T. (2021). Cybersecurity and sustainable development. *Procedia Computer Science*, 192, 20–28. 10.1016/j.procs.2021.08.003

Szydło, T., & Konieczny, M. (2016). *Mobile and wearable devices in an open and universal system for remote patient monitoring, Microprocessors and Microsystems* (Vol. 46). Part A.

Taiwo, O., & Ezugwu, A. E. (2020). Smart healthcare support for Tele-health monitoring during covid-19 quarantine. *Informatics in Medicine Unlocked*, 20, 100428. 10.1016/j.imu.2020.10042832953970

Tamilselvi, V., Sribalaji, S., Vigneshwaran, P., Vinu, P., & Geetha Ramani, J. (2020). IoT-based health monitoring system. In *2020 6th International Conference on Advanced Computing and Communication Systems (ICACCS)* (pp. 386–389). IEEE.10.1109/ICACCS48705.2020.9074192

Tang, L., Li, J., & Fantus, S. (2023). Medical artificial intelligence ethics: A systematic review of empirical studies. *Digital Health*, 9, 20552076231186064. 10.1177/2055207623118606437434728

Tanya, S. M., Nguyen, A. X., Buchanan, S., & Jackman, C. S. (2023). Development of a cloud-based clinical decision support system for ophthalmology triage using decision tree artificial intelligence. *Ophthalmology Science*, 3(1), 100231. 10.1016/j.xops.2022.10023136439697

Tapaswi, S., & Kushwah, V. S. (2010, June). Securing Nodes in MANETs Using Node Based Key Management Scheme. In *2010 International Conference on Advances in Computer Engineering* (pp. 228-231). IEEE. 10.1109/ACE.2010.86

Tavares, J., & Macedo, H. (2021). Internet of Things and big data in healthcare: A literature review. *Future Internet*, 13, 32. 10.3390/fi13020032

Taylor, R. H.Jr, Denny, J., Burdick, J. W., Cooley, M. C., Ferrara, K. W., Fuhrhop, R. W., & Wolf, S. R. (2017). Cybersecurity vulnerabilities of da Vinci surgical systems. *Science Translational Medicine*, 9(392), eaal2953. 10.1126/scitranslmed.aal2953

Teichmann, D., Brüser, C., Eilebrecht, B., Abbas, A., Blanik, N., & Leonhardt, S. (2012). Non-contact monitoring techniques—principles and applications. In *Conference proceedings of the IEEE engineering in medicine and biological society*. IEEE.

Tello, A. B., Jie, S., Manjunatha, D., Kumari, B. K., & Sayyad, S. (2022). Cloud Computing Based Network Analysis in Smart Healthcare System with Neural Network Architecture. *International Journal of Communication Networks and Information Security*, 14(3), 269–279. 10.17762/ijcnis.v14i3.5622

Thakur, G., Kumar, P., Jangirala, S., Das, A. K., & Park, Y. (2023). An effective privacy-preserving blockchain-assisted security protocol for cloud-based digital twin environment. *IEEE Access : Practical Innovations, Open Solutions*, 11, 26877–26892. 10.1109/ACCESS.2023.3249116

Thakur, V. (2021). Framework for PESTEL dimensions of sustainable healthcare waste management: Learnings from COVID-19 outbreak. *Journal of Cleaner Production*, 287, 125562. 10.1016/j.jclepro.2020.12556233349739

Thomas, R. K., Malathi, M., Venkatesh, S., & Govindarajan, R. (2018). Blockchain based secure health records in cloud storage. *Journal of Medical Systems*, 42(8), 1–8. 10.1007/s10916-018-0980-8

Tian, H., Ye, W., Wang, J., Quan, H., & Chang, C. C. (2023). Certificateless Public Auditing for Cloud-Based Medical Data in Healthcare Industry 4.0. *International Journal of Intelligent Systems*, 2023, 2023. 10.1155/2023/3375823

Tigard, D. W., Braun, M., Breuer, S., Ritt, K., Fiske, A., McLennan, S., & Buyx, A. (2023). Toward best practices in embedded ethics: Suggestions for interdisciplinary technology development. *Robotics and Autonomous Systems*, 167, 104467. 10.1016/j.robot.2023.104467

Trivedi, S., & Cheeran, A. N. (2017). Android-based health parameter monitoring. In *2017 International Conference on Intelligent Computing and Control Systems (ICICCS)* (pp. 1145–1149). IEEE.

Tsanas, A., Little, M., McSharry, P., & Ramig, L. (2009). Accurate telemonitoring of Parkinson's disease progression by non-invasive speech tests. Nature Precedings, 1–1. Porieva, H. S., Ivanko, K. O., Semkiv, C. I., & Vaityshyn, V. I. (2021). *Investigation of lung sounds features for detection of bronchitis and COPD using machine learning methods.*

Tukhtakhodjaeva, F. S., & Khayitova, I. I. (2023). APPLICATION AND USE OF AI (ARTIFICIAL INTELLIGENCE) IN MEDICINE. *Educational Research in Universal Sciences*, 2(9), 302–309.

Turgambayeva A, Kulbayeva S, Sadibekova Z, Tursynbekova A, Sarsenbayeva G, Zhanaliyeva M, Zhakupova T (2022). Features of the Development of a Mobile Application for Cardiac Patients. *Acta Inform Med.*, *30*(4), 302-307.

Ullah, F., & Al-Turjman, F. (2023). A conceptual framework for blockchain smart contract adoption to manage real estate deals in smart cities. *Neural Computing & Applications*, 35(7), 5033–5054. 10.1007/s00521-021-05800-6

Ullankala, S. L., Buddaraju, H. R., Meegada, A., & Tallapalli, S. K. (2023). Live Streaming Smart Pill Dispenser to Help Elderly/Blind People. *7th International Conference on Intelligent Computing and Control Systems (ICICCS)*, Madurai, India. 10.1109/ICICCS56967.2023.10142676

Vallès-Peris, N., & Domènech, M. (2023). Caring in the in-between: A proposal to introduce responsible AI and robotics to healthcare. *AI & Society*, 38(4), 1685–1695. 10.1007/s00146-021-01330-w

Vasquez-Correa, J. C., Klumpp, P., Orozco-Arroyave, J. R., & Noth, E. (2019). Phonet: A tool based on gated recurrent neural networks to extract phonological posteriors from speech. In *INTERSPEECH* (pp. 549–553). ISCA. 10.21437/Interspeech.2019-1405

Veeraiah, V. (2023). K. O. Thejaswini, Veera Talukdar, Shaziya Islam, Supriya Sanjay Ajagekar, and Rama Krishna Yellapragada. "Deep Learning-Based Classification for Healthcare-Based Io T System for Efficient Diagnosis.". *International Journal of Intelligent Systems and Applications in Engineering*, 11(no. 11s), 165–174.

Veja, C., Hocker, J., Schindler, C., & Rittberger, M. (2021). *Educational open government data in Germany: the landscape, status, and quality.*

Verhellen, A., Elprama, S. A., Scheerlinck, T., Van Aerschot, F., Duerinck, J., Van Gestel, F., Frantz, T., Jansen, B., Vandemeulebroucke, J., & Jacobs, A. (2024). Exploring technology acceptance of head-mounted device-based augmented reality surgical navigation in orthopaedic surgery. *International Journal of Medical Robotics and Computer Assisted Surgery*, 20(1), e2585. 10.1002/rcs.258537830305

Verma, V., Chowdary, V., Gupta, M. K., & Mondal, A. K. (2018). IoT and robotics in healthcare. In *Medical big data and internet of medical things* (pp. 245–269). CRC Press. 10.1201/9781351030380-10

Vichitkraivin, P., & Naenna, T. (2021). Factors of healthcare robot adoption by medical staff in Thai government hospitals. *Health and Technology*, 11(1), 139–151. 10.1007/s12553-020-00489-4

Vishwakarma, L. P., Singh, R. K., Mishra, R., & Kumari, A. (2023). Application of artificial intelligence for resilient and sustainable healthcare system: Systematic literature review and future research directions. *International Journal of Production Research*, 1–23. 10.1080/00207543.2023.2188101

Visvesvaran, C., Nishanth, S., Sudha, R., & Karthikeyan, J. (2021, August). IoT based Smart Baby Monitoring. In *2021 Second International Conference on Electronics and Sustainable Communication Systems (ICESC)* (pp. 1-6). IEEE.

Vorisek, C. N., Lehne, M., Klopfenstein, S. A. I., Mayer, P. J., Bartschke, A., Haese, T., & Thun, S. (2022). Fast Healthcare Interoperability Resources (FHIR) for Interoperability in Health Research: Systematic Review. *JMIR Medical Informatics*, 2022(10), e35724. 10.2196/3572435852842

Wahsheh, R. A. H., Almaita, E., & Elkhani, N. (2021). Health IoT-based platform to predict and monitor COVID-19. *Computers, Materials & Continua*, 68(1), 89–101. 10.32604/cmc.2022.022309

Wang, Q., Chen, W., Timmermans, A. A., Karachristos, C., Martens, J. B., & Markopoulos, P. (2015). Smart rehabilitation garment for posture monitoring. *Proceedings of the 2015 37th annual International Conference of the IEEE Engineering in Medicine and Biology Society (EmbC)*. IEEE. 10.1109/EMBC.2015.7319695

Wang, C., Liu, S., Yang, H., Guo, J., Wu, Y., & Liu, J. (2023). Ethical considerations of using ChatGPT in health care. *Journal of Medical Internet Research*, 25, e48009. 10.2196/4800937566454

Wang, E., Tayebi, P., & Song, Y. T. (2023). Cloud-Based Digital Twins' Storage in Emergency Healthcare. *International Journal of Networked and Distributed Computing*, 11(2), 75–87. 10.1007/s44227-023-00011-y

Wang, H., Wang, Y., & Gao, X. (2018). A novel IoT-oriented healthcare framework based on the integration of wireless body area networks and cloud computing. *IEEE Access : Practical Innovations, Open Solutions*, 6, 24015–24025. 10.1109/ACCESS.2018.2838618

Wei, S., & Wu, Z. (2023). The Application of Wearable Sensors and Machine Learning Algorithms in Rehabilitation Training: A Systematic Review. *Sensors (Basel)*, 23(18), 7667. 10.3390/s2318766737765724

Wewel, J. T., & Uribe, J. S. (2022). Spinal robotic surgery. *Handbook of Clinical Neurology*, 175, 235–235.

Wong, G. (1976). *Automatic baby crib rocker*. Patent US3952343.

Wright, J. D., & Hershman, D. L. (2013). Robotic vs Laparoscopic Hysterectomy—Reply. *Journal of the American Medical Association*, 309(22), 2320. 10.1001/jama.2013.568923757075

Wrobel, J., Jezewski, J., Horoba, K., Pawlak, A., Czabanski, R., Jezewski, M., & Porwik, P. (2015). Medical cyber-physical system for home telecare of high-risk pregnancy: Design challenges and requirements. *Journal of Medical Imaging and Health Informatics*, 5(6), 1295–1301. 10.1166/jmihi.2015.1532

Wu, D. C., Lin, H. L., Cheng, C. G., Yu, C. P., & Cheng, C. A. 2021, August. Improvement the Healthcare Quality of Emergency Department after the Cloud-Based System of Medical Information-Exchange Implementation. In *Healthcare* (*Vol. 9*, No. 8, p. 1032). MDPI. 10.3390/healthcare9081032

Wu, F., Liang, Y., Zhao, K., & Hu, C. (2017). A novel ECG signals analysis method for the detection of atrial fibrillation and flutter. In *Proceedings of the IEEE First International Conference on Data Science in Cyberspace (DSC)* (pp. 495–500). IEEE.

Yadav, R., Pradeepa, P., Srinivasan, S., Rajora, C. S., & Rajalakshmi, R. (2024, June). A novel healthcare framework for ambient assisted living using the internet of medical things (IOMT) and deep neural network. *Measurement. Sensors*, 33, 101111. 10.1016/j.measen.2024.101111

Yamauchi Y, Shimoi N.(2023). Posture Classification with a Bed-Monitoring System Using Radio Frequency Identification. *Sensors, 23*(16), 7304.

Yang, C.-T., Chen, S.-T., Den, W., Wang, Y.-T., & Kristiani, E. (2019). Implementation of an intelligent indoor environmental monitoring and management system in cloud. *Future Generation Computer Systems*, 96, 731–749. 10.1016/j.future.2018.02.041

Yaseen, S., Ilyas, M., & Ilyas, N. (2021). Internet of Things in healthcare: Applications, benefits, and challenges. In *Proceedings of the IEEE International Symposium on Communications and Information Technologies (ISCIT)* (pp. 1–6). IEEE.

Yew, H. T., Ng, M. F., Ping, S. Z., Chung, S. K., Chekima, A., & Dargham, J. A. (2020). Iot based real-time Tele-health monitoring system. *Proceedings of the 2020 16th IEEE International Colloquium on Signal Processing & Its Applications (CSPA)*. IEEE.

Yigitcanlar, T., & Cugurullo, F. (2020). The sustainability of artificial intelligence: An urbanistic viewpoint from the lens of smart and sustainable cities. *Sustainability (Basel)*, 12(20), 8548. 10.3390/su12208548

Yıldırım, E., Cicioğlu, M., & Çalhan, A. (2023). Fog-cloud architecture-driven Internet of Medical Things framework for healthcare monitoring. *Medical & Biological Engineering & Computing*, 61(5), 1133–1147. 10.1007/s11517-023-02776-436670240

Yildirim, O., & Bal, H. (2020). An IoT-based real-time heart monitoring system. In *Proceedings of the IEEE 6th International Conference on Computer and Communications (ICCC)* (pp. 64–67). IEEE.

Yousefi, A., Rafsanjani, M. K., & Seyedi, M. M. (2021). A systematic review of the Internet of Things in healthcare: Technology and application trends. *Journal of Ambient Intelligence and Humanized Computing*. 10.1007/s12652-021-03423-6

Zahraa A. (2023). Design and evaluation of two obstacle detection devices for visually impaired people. *Journal of Engineering Research, 2023, 11*(3). 10.1016/j.jer.2023.100132

Zanella, A., Bui, N., Castellani, A., Vangelista, L., & Zorzi, M. (2014). Internet of Things for smart cities. *IEEE Internet of Things Journal*, 1(1), 22–32. 10.1109/JIOT.2014.2306328

Zemmar, A., Lozano, A. M., & Nelson, B. J. (2020). The rise of robots in surgical environments during COVID-19. *Nature Machine Intelligence*, 2(10), 566–572. 10.1038/s42256-020-00238-2

Zhang, H., Wang, L. C., Chaudhuri, S., Pickering, A., Usvyat, L., Larkin, J., Waguespack, P., Kuang, Z., Kooman, J. P., Maddux, F. W., & Kotanko, P. (2023). Real-time prediction of intradialytic hypotension using machine learning and cloud computing infrastructure. *Nephrology, Dialysis, Transplantation*, 38(7), gfad070. 10.1093/ndt/gfad07037055366

Zhang, Y., Qiu, M., Tsai, C.-W., Hassan, M., & Alamri, A. (2015). Health-CPS: Healthcare Cyber-Physical System Assisted by Cloud and Big Data. *IEEE Systems Journal*, 11, 1–8.

Zhavoronkov, A., Bischof, E., & Lee, K. F. (2021). Artificial intelligence in longevity medicine. *Nature Aging*, 1(1), 5–7. 10.1038/s43587-020-00020-437118000

Zhou, Y., & Varzaneh, M. G. (2022). Efficient and scalable patients clustering based on medical big data in cloud platform. *Journal of Cloud Computing (Heidelberg, Germany)*, 11(1), 1–10. 10.1186/s13677-022-00324-336188195

Zurbuchen N, Wilde A, Bruegger P(2021). A Machine Learning Multi-Class Approach for Fall Detection Systems Based on Wearable Sensors with a Study on Sampling Rates Selection. *Sensors(Basel), 21*(3), 938.

# About the Contributors

**Thangavel Murugan** is serving as an Assistant Professor in the Department of Information Systems and Security, College of Information Technology, United Arab Emirates University, Abu Dhabi, United Arab Emirates. He received Doctorate from Madras Institute of Technology (MIT) Campus, Anna University – Chennai. He received Post Graduate degree as M.E. Computer Science and Engineering from J.J. College of Engineering and Technology, Trichy under Anna University – Chennai (University First Rank Holder & Gold Medalist) and Bachelor's degree as B.E. Computer Science and Engineering from M.A.M College of Engineering, Trichy under Anna University – Chennai (College First Rank Holder & Gold Medalist). He presently holds 10+ years of Teaching and Research experience from various academic institutions. He has published 10+ articles in International Journals, 15+ book chapters in International Publishers, 25+ in the proceedings of International Conferences and 3 in the proceedings of national conferences /seminars. He has been actively participating as reviewers in the international journals and conferences. He has attended 100+ Workshops / FDPs/Conferences in various Higher Learning Institutes like IIT, Anna University. He has organized 50+ Workshops / FDPs /Contests/Industry based courses over the past years of experience. He has been a technical speaker in various Workshops/ FDPs/Conferences. His research specialization is Information Security, High Performance Computing, Ethical Hacking, Cyberforensics, Blockchain, Cybersecurity Intelligence and Educational Technology.

**W. Jaisingh** is an Associate Professor in the School of Information Science, at Presidency University, India. He received a Doctorate from Anna University, Chennai in the year 2013, a Master of Philosophy in Computer Science from Alagappa University in 2005, and the Master of Computer Applications from Bharathiar University in 2001. He has got 22 years of Teaching and Research experience. He has published more than 20 papers in International refereed journals, 30 papers in International Conferences, and contributed chapters to the books. He has received "Indian Book of Records" and "Asia Book of Records" for contributing as an author in the book titled "Covid 19 and its Impact". The book has been selected for the record "maximum authors contributing to a book". He is a Lead Editor in Maximum Authors Contributing for a Book on "Covid 19 and its impact", 2021. His area of Research Interest includes Data Science, Machine Learning, Data Mining, Data Analytics, Image Processing, and Deep Learning. He is a lifetime member of professional societies such as the International Association of Computer Science and Information Technology (IACSIT), the Computer Science Teachers Association, and the Indian Society for Technical Education (ISTE).

**P. Varalakshmi** is the Director of Centre for Artificial Intelligence and Data Science Research and Applications (CAInDRA), and Professor of Department of Information Science and Technology, College of Engineering, Anna University – Chennai. She has over 25 years of teaching and research experience in the fields of grid computing, cloud computing, data analytics, machine learning, deep learning, artificial intelligence, blockchain technology, internet of things, networks, and security. She has published more than 200 papers in reputed journals and conferences, and has guided 13 doctoral theses. She has also received several grants for her research projects and innovations. She is a life member of the Indian Society for Technical Education and a reviewer for many international journals. She is passionate about teaching and mentoring young researchers and students. She is also involved in various academic and administrative activities at Anna University.

***

**Megha Bhushan** is Associate Professor in the School of Computing, and Assistant Dean, Research & Consultancy at DIT University, Dehradun, India. She has received her ME and Ph.D. degrees from Thapar University, Punjab, India. She was awarded with a fellowship by UGC, Government of India, in 2014. In 2017, she was a recipient of Grace Hopper Celebration India (GHCI) fellowship. She has published 5 national patents and 1 international patent has been granted. She has published many research articles in international journals and conferences of repute. Further, she is the editor of many edited books with different publishers such as CRC Press, Taylor & Francis Group, Wiley-Scrivener and Bentham Science. Her research interests include Artificial Intelligence, Knowledge representation, Expert systems, and Software quality. She is also the reviewer and editorial board member of many international journals.

**D. Manimegalai** currently working as an Assistant Professor in Department of Electrical and Electronics Engineering at Rajalakshmi Engineering College, Chennai. She received her B.E degree in Electrical and Electronics Engineering from Priyadarshini Engineering College, Vaniyambadi and M.E degree in Applied Electronics from Jayam college of Engineering and Technology, Dharmapuri. She is having a working experience of 17.4 years in academic and 2.6 years in industry. Currently, she is pursuing her Ph.D, in SRM Institute of Science and Technology, Chennai, India. She published 21 papers in reputed journals and havind 1 patent. She has the professional membership of ISTE and IAENG. Her area of research interest includes Renewable energy and sustainability analytics, Control Engineering, Image Processing, Optimization Algorithms, etc.

**Swathi Mirthika G.L.** has completed her Masters in Information Technology at Vel Tech Multi Tech Dr.RR Dr.SR Engineering College (2013) and completed her B.Tech Information Technology at Sasurie College of Engineering (2010). She has teaching experience of 3.5 years. Presented papers in various conferences and published papers in journals. Currently doing her Ph.d (Research) under SRM Institute of Science and Technology as full time scholar. Active researcher in Medical Recommendations, Knowledge Graph, Deep Learning etc.,

**Nidhi Gummarju** is a Computer Science student at Shiv Nadar University, focusing on Cyber Security. Their research explores the integration of physical processes with computation and networking.

**Pon Harshavardhanan** is an Associate Professor and Dean in the School of Computing Science Engineering and Artificial Intelligence from VIT Bhopal University. He has under and post-graduation in Computer Science and Engineering and doctorate in Computer Science and Engineering. With more than 20 years of experience, he worked with academic institutions in various positions. Also, he has software consultancy experience in leading software companies. He is an expert in the field of Artificial Intelligence in financial and healthcare domains. His associations with leading research institutions like

ICMR, IISER, CSIR is a credit to his credentials. He has published more than 20 research articles in leading journals and conferences.

**Radha Srinivasan** is a physiotherapist with a masters in Neurosciences. She works in physical therapy and rehabilitation of disabled children.

**Jayashre K.** is pursuing B.Tech (Computer Science) (2023) in Shiv Nadar University, School of Engineering, Chennai. Her area of interest includes Image Processing, Deep Learning, Blockchain, Network Security and Cryptography.

**K. Venkatesan** received his B.E and M.E degrees from Anna University Chennai in 2007 and 2011, respectively. He completed his Ph.D. from Anna University in the field of machine learning-based nonlinear fiber optic design in 2022. He has 13 years of teaching and research experience in India and abroad. His research interests include Knowledge-driven optical system design, Machine learning, Sensor-based IoT applications, Cloud for High data rate communication, Blockchain networks, and Consensus Algorithms. To his credit, he has published several research articles on optical system design and nonlinear compensation systems in leading International Journals and conferences. He has also presented and published his research papers in the Proceedings of International conferences.

**Jaspreet Kaur** is currently working as an Assistant Professor in University Business School,Chandigarh University,Mohali,Punjab.She is a post graduate (MBA-H.R) from Panjab University,Chandigarh. She has also qualified UGC NET JRF in Human Resource Management/Labour and Social Welfare and has pursued PhD in Business Management from Chandigarh University,Mohali. She has over 8 years of experience in academic and administrative assignments. She also received "Best Teacher of the Department Award " in the year 2019 and 2021 in the field of imparting quality education. Her research interests include Employee Engagement, Management of Organizational Change and Organization Development. She has published several research papers and articles in reputed international and national journals and has presented papers in various national and international conferences.She also contributed one edited book and 10 book chapters on various topics.

**Sunil Kumar** successfully completed his Ph.D. at Central University of Himachal Pradesh, India. He also holds an MBA in HRM and MA in Economics from Himachal Pradesh University Shimla. Prior to his postgraduate studies, he graduated with a B.Sc. (Medical) from NSCBM PG College, Hamirpur, HP. Dr. Sunil Kumar, currently an Associate Professor at Faculty of Management Sciences, Shoolini University, possesses extensive academic and research experience of 10 years. With a background in Business Administration, Sunil's research endeavors span multiple domains, including human resource management, e-training, and the application of artificial intelligence in business. His prolific contributions are evidenced by numerous research papers, book chapters, copyrights, and patents. Dr. Kumar has a knack for teaching with expertise in subjects like HR Analytics, Talent Management, Industrial Psychology, and more. He has also successfully guided 2 PhD students and actively contributes to various academic administrative roles. Dr. Kumar's vast research landscape includes topics like AI-based chatbots in recruitment, e-training impact, and more. His papers have been published in esteemed journals like Journal of Workplace Learning and International Journal of Law and Management. Moreover, he has authored books and edited volumes touching upon themes related to the contemporary business environment. He has been a dynamic participant in numerous workshops, ranging from data analysis to stress management. He's also presented his research findings at several national and international conferences, gaining accolades such as the "Best Paper Award". Dr Sunil is SHRM-PG certified and possesses certifications in Data Analytics, Design Thinking, and Data Visualization Using Tableau among others.

**Vijay Kumar** (Senior Member, IEEE) received the M.Sc. degree in electronics from Magadh University, India, in 2003, the M.Tech. degree in microwave remote sensing from BIT Mesra, Ranchi, in 2005, and the Ph.D. degree in microwave system engineering from IIT Bombay, in 2011. He worked as a Research Associate at IIT Bombay and focused on SAR interferometry and polarimetry for Himalayan studies, where he worked as the DST Government of India Sponsored Scientist at CSRE, from 2009 to 2013. He has been a Visiting Researcher at the Earth Observation Group, Northern Research Institute (NORCE), from 2009 to 2010. He is currently working as Professor at the School of Electronics Engineering, VIT, Vellore, Tamil Nadu, India. He worked as Associate professor from Jan 2013 to June 2022. He is the author and contributing author to many SCI peer-reviewed papers and conference proceedings deliberating ideas in radiating system designs for radar applications, miniaturized antenna designing using metamaterials, and MIMO antenna system for UWB applications with reconfigurable notch band characteristics. His research interests include microwave imaging, radar and SAR imaging system development and applications in earth observation and reconnaissance from space borne, airborne, and UAV platforms. He is a Life Member of ISRS and SPIE and actively associated with IEEE societies APS, THz, and GRSS.

**Virendra Singh Kushwah** is Completed his Ph.D. from Maharishi Markandeshwar University, Mullana, Ambala (NAAC 'A' Grade Deemed University). He has completed his M.Tech in CSE with specialization in Information Security (IS) from ABV-Indian Institute of Information Technology and Management, Gwalior (National Importance University) in 2010. He has cleared UGC-NET exam. He has also supervised M.Tech. Students. He has more than 12 years teaching experience from various institutes. He has credited to more than 30 publications including IEEE, Springer and International Journals etc. (SCOPUS and SCI Indexed). He is a member of various Professional Bodies like IACSIT, IAENG, CSTA, ASE etc. He is also reviewer of IEEE and International Journals. He has participated in many conferences, workshops and FDPs, which are held in NITs, IIITM and other institutes etc. He has a Trainer of LaTex tool which is a Document Writing Tool. He has chaired session in many International IEEE conferences and also invited for a Talk as an expert lecture. His research-interested areas are Cloud Computing, Machine Learning, Data Science, Fault Tolerant, Ad hoc network, and Information Security etc.

**Niranjan L.** is a Computer Science student at Thiagarajar College of Engineering in Madurai, Tamil Nadu, India. He possesses a strong passion for Flutter app development, IoT technologies, and has adept skills in Git version control. Moreover, he excels in front-end development, leveraging his proficiency in crafting engaging user interfaces. Among his notable projects is the creation of a resume builder application using Java, aimed at assisting individuals in shaping their professional profiles. With a steadfast commitment to innovation and practical problem-solving, he actively seeks avenues to contribute to technological advancements through research and project implementation.

**Diviya M** is working as an Assistant Professor in Department of Computer Science and Engineering, Amrita Vishwa vidyapeetham Chennai. Research profile includes Natural language processing, Deep Learning, Image analysis

**M. Nirmala Devi** is a Life member in ISTE and she is serving as Assistant Professor (Selection Grade), Department of Computer Science and Engineering, Thiagarajar College of Engineering, Madurai, Tamil Nadu, India. She has 17 years of teaching experience and 14 years of research experience and she has 140 Google Scholar citations and 88 Scopus citations for her publications. She has 44 Publications, 9 Journals, 24 conference Proceedings and 11 Book Chapters of IEEE, Springer, CRC, Taylor & Francis and IGI publishers. Her publication is in the area of data Science and Analysis, Deep Learning, Artificial Intelligence, Machine learning and Design Thinking for the applications in the areas of Healthcare Domain, Agriculture Domain, Teaching and Learning of Pedagogical domain. She has been actively participating as reviewers in the international journals and conferences. She completed her Ph.D. at Anna University on "Improving the performance of data mining algorithms for the prediction of chronic diseases and Medline documents". As an outcome of up skilling, she secured Top Percentile, Expert Badge, and Honor Code for attending 2-8 weeks of workshops/Trainings in Infosys, Course era, IBM cognitive Class, NPTEL, IIT Bombay, IIT Indore, IIT Guwahati, IUCEE EPICS, and ATAL. She handled Skill Training on Data Science and Analytics in association with NPIU and NASSCOM for Students and Faculty. She Secured First Class with Distinction in UG and PG. She delivered 11 Lectures for the Engineering college faculty members in the arrear of Data Science, AI and Mobile Application Development. She is collaborated in In-house capacity building Projects and consultancy works with the Team members of Artificial Intelligence Special Interest group. She bagged the Proficiency Awards in SSLC and HSC for Top Score.

**M. Nirmala Devi** is a Life member in ISTE and she is serving as Assistant Professor (Selection Grade), Department of Computer Science and Engineering, Thiagarajar College of Engineering, Madurai, Tamil Nadu, India. She has 17 years of teaching experience and 14 years of research experience and she has 140 Google Scholar citations and 88 Scopus citations for her publications. She has 44 Publications, 9 Journals, 24 conference Proceedings and 11 Book Chapters of IEEE, Springer, CRC, Taylor & Francis and IGI publishers. Her publication is in the area of data Science and Analysis, Deep Learning, Artificial Intelligence, Machine learning and Design Thinking for the applications in the areas of Healthcare Domain, Agriculture Domain, Teaching and Learning of Pedagogical domain. She has been actively participating as reviewers in the international journals and conferences. She completed her Ph.D. at Anna University on "Improving the performance of data mining algorithms for the prediction of chronic diseases and Medline documents". As an outcome of up skilling, she secured Top Percentile, Expert Badge, and Honor Code for attending 2-8 weeks of workshops/Trainings in Infosys, Course era, IBM cognitive Class, NPTEL, IIT Bombay, IIT Indore, IIT Guwahati, IUCEE EPICS, and ATAL. She handled Skill Training on Data Science and Analytics in association with NPIU and NASSCOM for Students and Faculty. She Secured First Class with Distinction in UG and PG. She delivered 11 Lectures for the Engineering college faculty members in the arrear of Data Science, AI and Mobile Application Development. She is collaborated in In-house capacity building Projects and consultancy works with the Team members of Artificial Intelligence Special Interest group. She bagged the Proficiency Awards in SSLC and HSC for Top Score.

**M. Karthikeyan** received his B.E degree in Electrical and Electronics Engineering received from Adhiyamaan College of Engineering and M.E degree in Embedded System Technologies from Veltech Engineering College. He holds a Ph.D. degree in Electrical Engineering from Vel Tech Rangarajan Dr. Sagunthala R&D Institute of Science and Technology, India. Now, currently he is working as an Associate Professor in Department of Electronics and communication Engineering, Centre for Advanced Wireless Integrated Technology, Chennai Institute of Technology Chennai, India. He has several years of professional working experience in different capabilities in the field of Electrical and Electronics Engineering. He has the professional membership of IEEE, IEI, ISTE, IAENG. His area of research interest includes (but not limited to) Image processing, Assistive technology, Renewable energy systems and machine learning, Embedded system, Artificial Intelligence.

**Prabu M** is an Indian academician who is serving as an Assistant Professor [Sr.Gr] in the Department of Computer Science and Engineering, Amrita School of Computing, Amrita Vishwa Vidyapeetham, Chennai. He has 13 years of experience in teaching and research. Dr. Prabu M is an alumnus of VIT University, Vellore, Tamil Nadu, India, where he completed his Doctoral – Ph.D. in Computer Science and Engineering with support from ISRO-SAC, Ahmedabad. He has authored research papers that have been published in renowned international journals and conferences, and are indexed in both SCOPUS and SCI. His research primarily focuses on Computer Vision and Distributed Computing. He has served as a resource person and speaker at several conferences and workshops. He is a Life Member of ISDS Society – International Society for Development and Sustainability, IAENG International Association of Engineers, ISTE-Life Member Indian Society for Technical Education, Internet Society, IFERP-Institute for Engineering Research, and Publication.

**Sanju Mahawar**'s educational background is steeped in depth and richness. He boasts an impressive track record of research publications in esteemed journals and has earned accolades such as a best paper award at an international conference. His primary area of expertise centers around Information Technology and e commerce.

**Pallabi Mukherjee** is an Associate Professor and Head of Research Committee and Head Evaluer at the Institute of Business Management and Research (IBMR) NAAC A ++ and UGC Autonomous College, IPS Academy, Indore, India. She is a Ph.D. in Economics from School of Economics (SOE), Devi Ahilya University (DAVV), Indore. She has done her Masters in Economics from SOE, DAVV and Bachelor of Science in Economics from Calcutta University. She has her diploma in Executive MBA Program from MTF Institute of Management & Technology, Lisbon, Portugal. She has more ten years of teaching experience with more than 30 research papers to her credit published in national and international journals. Her publications are in UGC, ABDC B and C category journals.She is proud author of the book titled ‘ The Power of Law of Attraction, Techniques To Manifest Your Dream Life’ and ‘Sustainable Economic Development Assessment – a Measure of Wealth to Well being’ and has also written book chapters published in Springer and conference proceedings in Taylor and Francis. She has presented her research papers at esteemed national conferences at IIM Shillong, IIT Gwahati, IIT Roorkee, IIM Indore etc and prominent foreign conferences, including Tennessee State University (TSU), Nashville, United States (Apr 2018), Marshall Center at the University of South Florida, Tampa, United States (Feb 2018) etc.

**Kali Charan Modak** is a distinguished academician and researcher known for his expertise in the field of Management, particularly in Foreign Trade and Healthcare Product Marketing Strategy. With a Master's degree in Foreign Trade (MBA-FT) and currently pursuing his Doctorate in Management from DAVV Indore, Dr. Modak has dedicated his career to advancing knowledge and understanding in his chosen areas of specialization. Dr. Modak's academic journey began with a strong foundation in commerce and management. Prior to joining IBMR, IPS Academy, he served as a visiting faculty at the School of Commerce, DAVV Indore, where he honed his teaching skills and imparted knowledge to students. His areas of expertise include Marketing Management, Research Methodology, International Business, International Finance, Derivatives, Business Statistics, Economics, International Marketing & Documentation, and Exim Policy. Driven by a passion for research, Dr. Modak has made significant contributions to academia through his extensive publication record. With thirty-two research papers published and presented in various national and international conferences and reputed journals, he has garnered recognition for his scholarly work. Notably, he showcased his research prowess by presenting a paper at the prestigious 1st International Conference on Business Analytics and Intelligence organized by IIM Bangalore. In addition to his research endeavors, Dr. Modak has played a pivotal role in guiding numerous major research projects for MBA students, imparting valuable insights and mentorship. His commitment to continuous learning is evident through his participation in workshops and training programs across different fields of Management and Research. Beyond academia, Dr. Modak is a respected columnist for the renowned daily newspaper, Dainik Dabang Duniya, where he shares his perspectives on current affairs and management-related topics. His clear and insightful writing style has earned him a loyal readership and further solidified his reputation as a thought leader in the field. Dr. Modak's academic achievements also include clearing the UGC NET in management in 2010, a testament to his deep understanding and proficiency in his chosen discipline. His relentless pursuit of excellence, coupled with his dedication to advancing knowledge and empowering students, continues to inspire and influence the academic community. Dr. Kali Charan Modak stands as a beacon of scholarly excellence, shaping the future of management education and research in India and beyond.

**Thangavel Murugan** is a Senior IEEE member serving as an Assistant Professor in the Department of Information Systems and Security, College of Information Technology, United Arab Emirates University, Abu Dhabi, United Arab Emirates. He received Doctorate from Madras Institute of Technology (MIT) Campus, Anna University – Chennai. He received Post Graduate degree as M.E. Computer Science and Engineering from J.J. College of Engineering and Technology, Trichy under Anna University – Chennai (University First Rank Holder & Gold Medalist) and Bachelor's degree as B.E. Computer Science and Engineering from M.A.M College of Engineering, Trichy under Anna University – Chennai (College First Rank Holder & Gold Medalist). He presently holds 10+ years of Teaching and Research experience from various academic institutions. He has published 10+ articles in International Journals, 15+ book chapters in International Publishers, 25+ in the proceedings of International Conferences and 3 in the proceedings of national conferences /seminars. He has been actively participating as reviewers in the international journals and conferences. He has attended 100+ Workshops / FDPs/Conferences in various Higher Learning Institutes like IIT, Anna University. He has organized 50+ Workshops / FDPs /Contests/Industry based courses over the past years of experience. He has been a technical speaker in various Workshops/FDPs/Conferences. His research specialization is Information Security, High Performance Computing, Ethical Hacking, Cyberforensics, Blockchain, Cybersecurity Intelligence and Educational Technology.

**Arul Kumar Natarajan** currently serves as an Assistant Professor in the Department of Computer Science at the Samarkand International University of Technology in Uzbekistan. He earned his Doctor of Philosophy degree from Bharathidasan University, India, in 2017. Concurrently, he is engaged in postdoctoral research in Generative AI for Cybersecurity at the Singapore Institute of Technology, Singapore. Throughout his 14-year teaching career, Dr. Arul has held esteemed positions at various institutions, including Christ University, Bishop Heber College in India, and Debre Berhan University in Ethiopia. Dr. Arul has made significant contributions to academia, specializing in cybersecurity and artificial intelligence, evidenced by his portfolio of scholarly works. He has authored 32 international publications indexed in Scopus and 03 international publications and has delivered 34 conference presentations. Additionally, he has edited and published three books with IGI Global Publisher, USA, focusing on Python data structures, algorithms, and geospatial application development. In addition to his academic pursuits, Dr. Arul is a prolific innovator, holding 17 patents in India and 01 granted patent in the United Kingdom across diverse domains, including communication and computer science. He demonstrates proficiency in networking and cybersecurity, having completed the CCNA Routing and Switching Exam from CISCO and the Networking Fundamentals exam from Microsoft. He maintains a sincere interest in GenAI for Cybersecurity.

**Arun Negi** is currently a Manager at Deloitte USI, Hyderabad, India. He has completed a course in Business Management from IIM, Ahmedabad and has obtained B. Tech degree from Jawaharlal Nehru University, New Delhi, India. He has 13+ years of diverse experience in cyber risk services. He has worked on various network security technologies and platforms for Fortune 500 clients. His experience includes cyber security audits, gap assessments, network security audits, cloud migrations and project management. He is currently oriented towards developing multi cloud skills and has achieved certifications in Oracle Cloud and AWS. He has published one national patent and one international patent has been granted. He has published many research articles in international journals and conferences of repute. His research areas include Artificial Intelligence, Software Product Line, Cloud Computing, and Cyber Security.

**Sabyasachi Pramanik** is a professional IEEE member. He obtained a PhD in Computer Science and Engineering from Sri Satya Sai University of Technology and Medical Sciences, Bhopal, India. Presently, he is an Associate Professor, Department of Computer Science and Engineering, Haldia Institute of Technology, India. He has many publications in various reputed international conferences, journals, and book chapters (Indexed by SCIE, Scopus, ESCI, etc). He is doing research in the fields of Artificial Intelligence, Data Privacy, Cybersecurity, Network Security, and Machine Learning. He also serves on the editorial boards of several international journals. He is a reviewer of journal articles from IEEE, Springer, Elsevier, Inderscience, IET and IGI Global. He has reviewed many conference papers, has been a keynote speaker, session chair, and technical program committee member at many international conferences. He has authored a book on Wireless Sensor Network. He has edited 8 books from IGI Global, CRC Press, Springer and Wiley Publications.

**R. Bhuvaneswari** is working as an Assistant Professor at Amrita School of Computing, Amrita Vishwa Vidyapeetham, Chennai, India. She completed her Ph.D at Anna University. She has 18 years of teaching experience in the field of Engineering. Her research activity is mainly focused on machine learning, Deep learning for image processing applications. She has authored over many publications on International Journals and International Conferences. She co-authored a book on Computer Graphics.

**R. Gunasekari** currently working as an Associate Professor in the Department of Electrical and Electronics Engineering at Sri Sairam College of Engineering, Bengaluru. She received her B.E Degree in Electrical and Electronics Engineering from Regional Engineering College, Tiruchirappalli and M.E Degree in Applied Electronics from Jayam College of Engineering and Technology, Dharmapuri. She completed her Ph.D in Saveetha Institute of Medical And Technical Sciences (SIMATS), Chennai, India. She is having a working experience of 25.3 years in academic, 5.1 years in industry and 1.5 years in Research. She published 25 papers in reputed journals and 2 Patents. She has the professional membership of IEEE, IEI, ISTE, IAENG, ISRD and SMISEEE. Her area of research interest includes Hybrid Renewable Energy Sources, Power System Engineering, Power Electronics Converters etc.

**Harshitha R S** is an aspiring technologist currently pursuing a Bachelor of Technology in Computer Science and Engineering with a specialization in Cyber Security at Shiv Nadar University, Chennai, India. Harshitha's dedication to her field is driven by a desire to make a positive impact. With a commitment to advancing the field of cyber security and a passion for leveraging technology to improve digital infrastructures, Harshitha aspires to make significant contributions to both domains.

**Santhosh Kumar Rajamani** is a Professor of Otorhinolaryngology with qualifications of M.B.B.S, M.S (E.N.T), D.N.B (Otorhinolaryngology), M.N.A.M.S (E.N.T), and P.G. D.P.H (Gold Medalist). He has over 13 years of work experience at institutes like MIMER Medical College, BKL Walawalkar Institute, and Al Dhamer Centre. Dr. Rajamani has published numerous research papers in renowned journals like NeuroQuantology, SAGE Publications, and BioMedInformatics. He has authored several books and filed multiple national and international patents related to healthcare and artificial intelligence. Dr. Rajamani serves as an editorial board member and reviewer for various medical journals and has received awards like the Gold Medal for Best Research Paper.

**Doddi Sreenija Reddy** is an undergraduate researcher in the Department of Computer Science and Engineering, Amrita School of Computing, Amrita Vishwa Vidyapeetham, Chennai primarily working on Machine learning, cloud compting and its applications.

**Muthukumaran S** is a dedicated student currently pursuing a Bachelor's degree in Computer Science Engineering at Thiagarajar College of Engineering in Madurai, Tamil Nadu, India. His academic journey is fueled by a profound interest in cutting-edge technologies, particularly in Internet of Things (IoT), artificial intelligence (AI), and full-stack web development. Muthukumaran has actively contributed to various projects, showcasing his expertise in these areas. Noteworthy among his projects are the RFID-enabled attendance monitoring system, soil moisture detection and analysis system, and health monitoring system, where he demonstrated his innovative approach and problem-solving skills. With a strong foundation in Java and Python, coupled with his expertise in web development, Muthukumaran possesses the skills necessary to excel in diverse technological endeavors. His significant involvement in developing and deploying IoT solutions underscores his commitment to addressing real-world challenges through technology. With a diverse skill set and a passion for technological advancement, Muthukumaran aims to make significant contributions to the fields of IoT, AI, and web development.

**S. Sugumaran** received his BE degree in Electronics and Communication Engineering in 2005 from Arunai Engineering College, Tiruvannamalai, Tamil Nadu, India. He completed his ME in Applied Electronics in 2009 from Sathyabama University, Chennai, Tamil Nadu,India. He completed his PhD in the year 2019 from SCSVMV (Deemed to be University), Kanchipuram, Tamil Nadu in the area of MANET Routing Protocol Attacks. He is currently working as a Associate Professor in the department of Electronics and Communication Engineering, Sreenivasa Institute of Technology and Management Studies, Chittoor, Andhra Pradesh. He has around 15 years of teaching experience. He is a life time member of ISTE.

**S. Sujatha**, completed B.E (EEE) in 1997 at Alagappa Chettiar College of Engineering, Karaikudi, and M.E (PC&I) completed in 2002 at Annamalai University. Ph.D completed in Anna University in the year 2012. She is having teaching experience of 21 years. Currently working as Professor and Head, Department of EEE, Sri Sairam College of Engineering, Bangalore. She has published 23 papers in International Journals and 4 patents. Her area of research includes controller design, modeling and optimization, soft computing, image processing.,etc

**S. Devaraju** received the B.Sc degree in Chemistry in 1997 from the University of Madras, Chennai, and the M.C.A. degree in Computer Applications in 2001 from the Periyar University, Salem, and the M.Phil. degree in Computer Science in 2004 from Periyar University, Salem and also received M.B.A. degree in Human Resource from Madurai Kamaraj University, Madurai in 2007. He received Ph.D degree in Computer Applications from Anna University, Chennai in 2017. Dr.S.Devaraju has 21+ years of teaching experience and 2 years industry experience. He is an Senior Assistant Professor, School of Computing Science and Engineering (SCSE), VIT Bhopal University, Sehore, Madhya Pradesh, India. Dr.S.Devaraju has published 8 patents, 10 Book Chapters and Reviewer for various reputed Journals and Conferences. He has published more than 50+ papers in international journals and conference proceedings. His area of research includes Network Security, Intrusion Detection, Soft Computing, and Wireless Communication.

**B. Sivakumar** is an Associate Professor at the Department of Computing Technologies, Kattankulathur Campus, SRM Institute of Science and Technology. He is having enormous teaching experience with computer engineering of around 19 years of experience at various reputed institutes. He has attended various reputed conferences across the globe and also having reasonable number of publications with peer reviewed quality journals. He is an active researcher in cutting edge technologies like Machine Learning, IoT, Cloud Computing, Artificial Intelligence and Deep learning. He is also serving as a reviewer of many reputed Journals and reviewed quality papers of peer researchers in unbiased manner. He has also completed one AICTE funded project and also actively working on filing new patents. He is also working on various international project funding agencies proposals to boost his research findings. Also taking active part in Industry-Academia collaborations in academics and research front.

**Preetam Suman** has completed his doctorate from Indian Institute of Information Technology, Allahabad and has over eight years' experience in the field of academics. His core areas of expertise include medical imaging, Big Data analytics, Cloud computing, real-life applications of artificial intelligence and embedded systems. He was involved in a project related to implementing sensor networks in forests to save wildlife and development of technology to identify tumors in the brain using fMRI. Dr. Preetam

Suman is currently working as Assistant Professor with Vellore Institute of Technology-Bhopal.Also, he has been nominated by various forums and associations in their committees. He has published more than forty papers in international journals and conferences and various seminars organized by professional bodies and industry associations worldwide. Dr. Preetam, holds professional associations with IEEE Technical Committee, IEEE Young Professionals.

**Sree Harish T**, a passionate student pursuing Computer Science at Thiagarajar College of Engineering in Madurai, Tamil Nadu, India. His academic journey is on interest in Flutter app development, database management and IoT technologies, including the design and implementation of Attendance monitoring systems using RFID and worked with many IoT Projects. And also he is expertise in Java and Python programming languages. Notably, his project endeavors encompass the development of a hostel management mobile application using Flutter, specifically crafted for the college hostel. In this research, He had contributed towards the working model for Flutter application and its software side and done some parts in hardware.

**Pardhu Thottempudi** (M' 15) has been exemplary and dedicated to Electronics and Communication Engineering in the last decade. He has extensively contributed from a research internship at the RADAR SEEKER Laboratory in Research Center Imarat, Hyderabad, in June 2012. In July 2013, he ventured into an academic career as an assistant professor. He served at various prestigious institutions, including Marri Laxman Reddy Institute of Technology Management, St.Peter's Engineering College, and MLR Institute of Technology, Hyderabad. He served for an extended period from December 2016 to August 2022 at the MLR Institute. Further, he continued his service at SR University, Warangal, and presently, since March 2023, he has been serving at BVRIT HYDERABAD College of Engineering For Women. These years saw the great responsibility put forward by Mr. Thottempudi in providing quality education and research contributions. He has several research publications against his name on different topics, ranging from RADAR signal processing to the classification of human motion using advanced technologies in prestigious journals, further showing that he is a dedicated person to this field, boasting numerous patents on anything from power-efficient compressors to innovative design for surveillance and security. Besides his teaching and research roles, Mr. Thottempudi is also entrusted with multiple significant institutional responsibilities like Sports Director, Social Media Coordinator, and Alumni Coordinator, to name a few. Further, his commitment to continuous learning and dissemination of knowledge is also evidenced by his active participation in various types of FDPs and STTPs. Over the years, Mr Thottempudi has been feted for his excellent contributions, as is evident in awards such as the India Independence Awards 2019 Young Scientist Award and Young Researcher of the Year awards in 2020 and 2021, among many others. Mr. Pardhu Thottempudi is a gem in academia and the research community based on the the richness of his academic background, his significant contribution to research, and his remarkable track record in professional practice for more than five years.

**U. Padmavathi** has completed her doctorate from National Institute of Technology Puducherry in the year 2022. She has obtained her Masters in Computer Science & Engineering from Annamalai University in the year 2011. She Pursued her B.E (Computer Science & Engineering) from Annamalai University in the year 2009. Currently, she is working as Assistant Professor in the Department of Computer Science & Engineering, Shiv Nadar University Chennai. Her Research interests include Blockchain, Cybersecurity, Network security, Zero knowledge Proofs.

**A. Umasankar** earned his B.E from Coimbatore Institute of Technology, Bharathiar University, Coimbatore, India, M.E from Karunya Institute of technology, Bharathiar University, Coimbatore, India and Ph.D. from St.Peter's University, Chennai, India. He is currently working as a Lecturer Grade (17/11) and Technical committee coordinator in the Department of Electrical and Electronics Engineering Technology, at Yanbu Industrial College, Saudi Arabia. He has 25 years of experience in the field of Research and Administration at various levels. He has published 15+ Articles in Referred International and National Journals and Conferences. He is a Technical committee coordinator for ABET Accreditation Committee in ELET Department. He has received outstanding performance award during (2015, 2016 and 2017).

# Index

## Symbols



## A



## B



## C



## D



## E



## G

## H



## I



## M

## O



## P



## Q



## R



## S



## T

## U

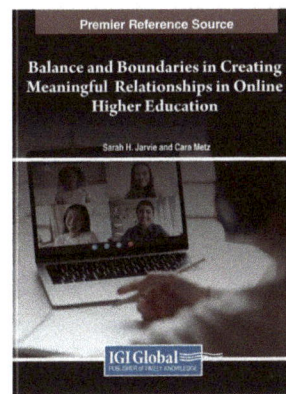

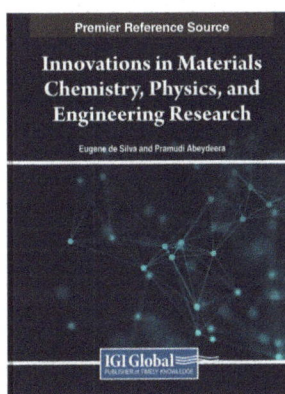

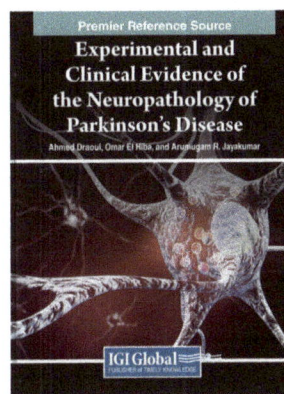

Milton Keynes UK
Ingram Content Group UK Ltd.
UKHW051013070824
446558UK00003B/9